Fodor's

SEE IT

LONDON

FODOR'S
TRAVEL PUBLICATIONS

NEW YORK • TORONTO
LONDON • SYDNEY • AUCKLAND

WWW.FODORS.COM

CONTENTS

KEY TO SYMBOLS

- Map reference
- Address
- Telephone number
- Opening times
- Admission prices
- Underground station
- Bus number
- Train station
- Ferry/boat
- Driving directions
- Tourist office
- Tours
- Guidebook
- Restaurant
- Cafe
- Bar
- Shop
- Number of rooms
- Air conditioning
- Swimming pool
- Gym
- Other useful information
- ▷ Cross reference
- ★ Walk/drive start point

225

146

179

UNDERSTANDING LONDON

Understanding London is an introduction to the city, its geography, economy, history and its people. Living London gets under the skin of London today, while The Story of London takes you through the city's past.

London is one of the world's most exciting and rewarding cities to visit. Two thousand years have left the capital of the United Kingdom with more than 19,000 buildings officially listed as having special architectural or historic interest. The city has grown largely unplanned, which makes for a piquant unpredictability as the scene and atmosphere change from one corner to the next. It has royal palaces and pageantry, stylish shops, theatres, music and art, and is also a dynamic financial and business hub. London is crowded and noisy and can be hard to get about in—and now and again it rains—but it is vigorously alive.

THE GEOGRAPHY

London lies in the southeast of England, some 64km (40 miles) inland from the North Sea. The rest of Britain has always complained that London and the southeast take up too much attention and too many resources. Greater London is an area of more than 1,550sq km (600sq miles), roughly oval in shape. Inside it is the smaller oval of inner London, covering about 260sq km (100sq miles), and at the heart of that are the two principal areas from the point of view of both Londoners and visitors—the West End and the City. Both lie on the north side of the River Thames, which winds its way through London from west to east before disappearing towards the North Sea.

WEST AND EAST

When Londoners speak of 'the City', they do not mean London as a whole. They mean the City of London itself, the area of just over 2.5sq km (1sq mile) where London's history began. The City is the financial district, crowded with office workers during the week but almost empty at weekends, with a resident population of only about 7,000. Its principal points of interest for visitors are the Tower of London, St. Paul's Cathedral, the Museum of London and the Barbican cultural complex, and there's some extraordinary post-modern architecture.

Lying to either side of the City are the West End, which was always upscale, and the East End, which was not. The East End is the world of the docks and working-class London, of cockneys and rhyming slang (▷ 9), and Jack the Ripper. It took a battering in World War II, and in the last 50 years the area has been substantially rebuilt.

The West End is posh, elegant London, the London of Buckingham Palace, Covent Garden and the National Gallery, Hyde Park, Piccadilly Circus and Trafalgar Square. It is where theatres cluster, along with most of the top shops and restaurants, nightclubs and hotels.

TWO IN ONE

London actually contains two cities, not one, and the West End is set in the second—the City of Westminster. Its nucleus is the area round Westminster Abbey, Big Ben, the Houses of Parliament and Whitehall, from which a quarter of the world's population was ruled in the days of the British Empire. Also in Westminster are Mayfair,

Left *The gleaming high-rises of Canary Wharf are a symbol of the revitalized Docklands*

St. James's and Soho, neighbourhoods with distinctive characters of their own.

Mayfair, lying east of Hyde Park, is the most expensive of all London districts to live, shop and eat in. It has the chic Bond Street dress shops, jewellers and art dealers, Park Lane and Berkeley Square, Savile Row, Claridge's, the Royal Academy and the Burlington Arcade. Immediately to the southeast, on the other side of Piccadilly, the St. James's area is known for gentlemen's clubs and gentlemen's tailoring, Fortnum and Mason, the Ritz Hotel and feeding the ducks in St. James's Park.

In contrast, Soho, east of Mayfair, is known for its sex shows, gay venues and a cosmopolitan mix of restaurants, as well as Liberty department store, Carnaby Street and Chinatown.

STYLE, ART AND INTELLECT

Southeast of Hyde Park, Belgravia is an aristocratic district with street after street of gleaming white neoclassical houses and a showcase of exclusive grandeur in Eaton Square. Knightsbridge, Kensington and Chelsea were country villages until London engulfed them. Today Knightsbridge is best known for Harrods and the chic shops in Sloane Avenue and Beauchamp Place, on the way to the museum district of South Kensington. Here you will find the Victoria & Albert Museum, the Natural History Museum and the Science Museum.

Kensington is expensive residential territory, known for the Royal Albert Hall, Kensington Gardens and Kensington Palace, where Diana, Princess of Wales lived. Lying along the river, the pretty streets of Chelsea make another quarter with an artistic and intellectual reputation, spiced with the upscale boutiques around Sloane Square and the King's Road.

To the northeast of Oxford Street, Bloomsbury has a high brow and arty reputation, partly because of the British Museum, London University and the Slade School of Art, an echo of the Bloomsbury Group of writers and artists, which formed around novelist Virginia Woolf and biographer Lytton Strachey before World War I.

To the east, Holborn (pronounced 'Hoe-b'n') has a quirky mixture of lawyers' offices in Lincoln's Inn and Gray's Inn, diamond dealers in Hatton Garden and Smithfield's meat market. Out to the northeast, Hoxton, which was, within living memory, one of London's worst slums, has turned into a trendy Brit Art area with galleries and the hippest London pop music scene.

SOUTH OF THE RIVER

The south bank of the Thames has been the poor relation of the north bank ever since Roman times, when the borough of Southwark (pronounced 'Suthuck') began to evolve at the wrong end of London Bridge. Today, however, it is home to the South Bank cultural complex, Tate Modern, the London Eye, the Globe Theatre and the Saatchi Gallery, not to mention the unspeakable horrors of the London Dungeon.

OUTER SUBURBS

Farther out from the heart of London, more country villages that were swallowed up by the remorselessly expanding city in the 19th century retain a distinctive character. In the west, Richmond has Georgian streets and a highly regarded theatre, Kew has the sumptuous botanical gardens and Wimbledon has the tennis championships.

To the north, on the range of hills called the Northern Heights, Hampstead is known for its village atmosphere and its concentration of high-minded intellectuals, supporting London's largest percentage of psychiatrists per head of population. Highgate, next door, has a Georgian high street and London's most evocative cemetery.

Away to the east, Greenwich is famous for the National Maritime Museum, the *Cutty Sark* and Greenwich Mean Time.

MAKING MONEY

A massive share of London's economy is taken up by the financial and business services sector, whose contribution to the city's gross domestic product is nearly 40 per cent—more than double the ratio in the United Kingdom as a whole. The City of London is one of the most successful financial centres in the world. It handles almost a third of the entire global foreign exchange market, nearly twice that of Wall Street. Manufacturing, by contrast, is no longer one of London's strengths. Before World War II, London's factories made beer and sweets, textiles and furniture, and soon moved on to electronics and pharmaceuticals, but there was a dramatic decline in the 1960s and 1970s as businesses found themselves new premises and a cheaper workforce elsewhere.

The same period saw the collapse of the London docks as, after 1960, ships and containers increased in size beyond their capabilities. The East India Dock was closed in 1967 and the others followed over the next 15 years. St. Katharine's Dock, near the Tower of London, was turned into a classy yacht marina and its warehouses were transformed into flats, shops and restaurants. Similar developments occurred farther down the river. From the 1980s the Isle of Dogs was redeveloped as a business and residential district, with the Canary Wharf tower, the London Arena, the Docklands Light Railway and some of the country's most striking post-modern architecture.

While manufacturing and the docks were in decline, London was profiting from an upsurge in the service sector, which brought a noticeable increase in the quantity of office accommodation in the capital. At the

LONDON'S DISTRICTS AT A GLANCE

Camden and Regent's Park In north London, home of the famous Madame Tussauds and the ZSL London Zoo.
Chelsea and Belgravia Upscale, leafy streets just north of the Thames with the King's Road and Sloane Square for shopping.
The City The original settlement, and now the financial heart of the capital, with the major attractions of the Tower of London, Tower Bridge and St. Paul's Cathedral.
Clerkenwell and Islington On the periphery of the City, heading northwards: traditional heartland of radical politics, now very trendy with expensive cafes and craftshops.
Docklands A happy blend of old and modern architecture—shops, offices and apartments—stretching downstream from the City.
Kensington Well-established and well-heeled swathe west of Hyde Park, focused on Kensington Palace and Kensington Gardens.
Knightsbridge High-profile shopping streets lying south of Hyde Park, with Harrods and Harvey Nichols leading the way.
Mayfair Relatively quiet, wealthy residential area east of Hyde Park, sandwiched between Oxford Street and Piccadilly.
Notting Hill and Holland Park Fashionable quarters associated with celebrities, northwest of Hyde Park: home of Portobello Road market and the Notting Hill Carnival.
Piccadilly and St. James's Elegant and expensive: right at the heart of the city, encompassing Green Park and St. James's, two royal parks, and Buckingham Palace.
Soho and Covent Garden Lively, very central areas north of Trafalgar Square, packed with individual shops, restaurants and nightlife.
South Bank Revamped riverside strip from Westminster to London Bridge, now dominated by the London Eye and Tate Modern.
South Kensington and Earl's Court Mansion houses and serious museums southwest of central London.
Westminster and Whitehall Seat of government, with key landmarks Westminster Abbey and the Houses of Parliament.

same time, the tourist industry boomed with the advent of cheap air travel and the city's 1960s reputation as 'swinging London'. Visitor numbers swelled from 1 million to 3 million a year between 1960 and 1965, and by 1977 had topped 8 million. The influx of visitors gave shops, restaurants and visitor attractions of all kinds a powerful boost. The number of visitors is now around 15 million a year, or five visitors for each inhabitant of inner London.

GETTING AROUND

London, like every heavily populated city in the world, has its problems. Litter is one of them; getting around is another. The average inner Londoner travels more than 6,500km (4,000 miles) a year inside the city—to get to work and back, on business, for shopping, to take the children to school, to go visiting—by some combination of car, taxi, motorcycle, bus, tube, bicycle or foot. The average inner Londoner walks about 400km (250 miles) a year altogether and cycles only about 50km (30 miles), while spending on transport fares is higher in London than in any other region of the United Kingdom. This is despite the fact that approximately half London's households own a car (10 per cent of London households have two or more cars). The speed of London's motorized traffic is notoriously slow; today's cars and buses move no faster than the horse-drawn traffic of the 1880s. The average daytime speed in central London is currently about 16kph (10mph), but the introduction of congestion charging in the city centre in 2003 is estimated to have cut the number of vehicles clogging the streets by nearly a quarter.

Below *Big Ben and the Houses of Parliament are illuminated at night*

Above *Tower Bridge also looks especially dramatic after dark*

RICH AND POOR

There has always been a gulf between London's rich and poor. The contrast was particularly glaring in Victorian days and the response was slum clearance. A start was made in the 1840s on demolishing the appalling St. Giles 'rookery' (⊳ 33) around the eastern end of Oxford Street. Today's theatre-lined Shaftesbury Avenue was carved through an area previously occupied by squalid slums in the 1870s and 1880s.

Although the divide is now less extreme, five of England's ten most deprived municipal areas are in London. Homelessness is a persistent problem and begging, in the street and the Underground, has re-emerged since the 1980s. Still, as big cities go, and provided you behave sensibly, London is not a dangerous place. So just relax and enjoy it!

POPULATION

The 2001 census produced population figures of 2.8 million for inner London and 4.4 million for outer London. The city has always drawn people from the rest of the country and the rest of the world, and today ethnic minorities account for 30 per cent of the population of inner London (in Greater London as a whole the figure is 25 per cent). The 1980s saw the downward trend in London's population—which had been above 8 million in 1951—beginning to reverse. The city stopped losing more people every year to emigration (mainly to the rest of the country) than it gained from immigration.

London's immigrants have all added to the city's vibrant mix, bringing their languages, traditions and food. As a result, there's a vast choice of ethnic establishments ranging from African crafts emporia to Arab bookshops, Austrian sausage parlours, Caribbean fishmongers, Chinese brocade galleries, Greek jewellers, Israeli crafts outlets, Lebanese butchers and Polish patisseries. Besides the main European, Indian, Chinese and Thai cuisines, you can find restaurants serving food from Brazil, Burma, Cuba, Egypt, Ethiopia, Jamaica, Japan, Mexico, Morocco, Peru, Poland, Russia, Scandinavia, Syria, Vietnam and elsewhere.

The great majority of Londoners speak English, but more than 300 languages from every corner of the globe may be heard on the street.

The majority of incomers to London are aged between 16 and 44. This helps to explain why London's death rate is 6 per cent lower than that of the country as a whole, while the birthrate is higher. The number of people above retirement age, on the other hand, is lower than outside. About 45 per cent of all London dwellings are apartments, compared with 25 per cent nationally.

MAIL ORDER

Greater London is divided up by postal areas, which can be confusing for outsiders. Since World War I, a combination of letters and numbers has been used, the letters indicating which part of the city the street is in: W standing for west, WC for west central, EC for east central, N for north, SW for southwest, and so on (except for NE and S, which are postcodes for other cities—Newcastle and Sheffield).

BETTER ADAM 'N' EVE IT

Cockney rhyming slang's origins are unknown, but some say it was developed to thwart the newly formed police force in the early 19th century. This was when expressions such as 'Would you Adam 'n' Eve [believe] it?' and 'Get up them apples and pears [stairs]' emerged among east Londoners. Some had a particularly sardonic note, as in 'trouble and strife' for wife or 'artful dodger' for lodger. The slang still peppers some Londoners' speech. Anyone lacking cash is 'borassic' (from boracic lint, rhyming with skint); a face is a 'boat' (from boat race) and a hat is a 'titfer' (from tit for tat). Lies are 'porkies' (from pork pies), taking a look is having a 'butcher's' (from butcher's hook) and 'Brahms and Liszt' means intoxicated. Celebrities can also end up as part of the vocabulary. American jockey Tod Sloane provided the expression 'on your Tod (own)', and a Gregory (Peck) is a cheque (check).

SOUTH BANK

The George Inn (▷ 91): Old 17th-century coaching inn with a lovely courtyard and traditional ales and menu.
Imperial War Museum (▷ 74): The country's most impressive military museum.
Ministry of Sound (▷ 87): Huge and famous club where you go to be seen.
Oxo Tower Restaurant (▷ 90): Tasty modern cuisine accompanied by amazing views over the Thames.
Southbank Centre (▷ 79): Top-flight concert halls and theatres in a sprawling complex on the river.
Tate Modern (▷ 80–81): Exceptional art collection housed in a palatial mansion.

FLEET STREET TO THE TOWER

The Bleeding Heart Tavern (▷ 124): Rustic tavern dating from the mid-18th century, serving good restaurant food.
The Eagle (▷ 124): One of London's first gastropubs, on the edge of Clerkenwell.
Moro (▷ 123): Busy Spanish-North African restaurant, with meals from a wood-fired oven.
Museum of London (▷ 103): Come here to discover the history of London.
The Peasant (▷ 124): Pub with Victorian interior, serving rustic-style food.
St. John (▷ 123): Traditional British food (for carnivores only) in Clerkenwell.
St. Paul's Cathedral (▷ 104–109): Sir Christopher Wren's masterpiece of baroque architecture, its great dome a city landmark.
Smiths of Smithfield (▷ 123): Organic food in a former warehouse near the City.
Tower of London (▷ 112–117): Nearly 1,000 years of Britain's royal history, and the Crown Jewels.

COVENT GARDEN TO BLOOMSBURY

Aldwych Theatre (▷ 156): The Royal Shakespeare Company's former base, with drama and dance.
The Bonnington in Bloomsbury (▷ 166): Smart, well-situated mid-range hotel in Bloomsbury.
British Museum (▷ 134–139): A vast array of antiquities from around the world.
Brown's Hotel (▷ 166): Very comfortable, traditional hotel in Mayfair.
Camden Lock Market (▷ 232): Sprawling market with trendy wares from all over the world.
Cittie of York (▷ 165): Sandwiches and simple dishes in one of London's oldest pubs.
Courtauld Gallery (▷ 150–151): A superb collection in the grand rooms of Somerset House.

Hakkasan (▷ 163): Exotic Chinese restaurant serving some of the best food of its kind in the city.
Hamleys (▷ 155): Britain's biggest toy shop.
Liberty (▷ 155): Classic clothing and expensive luxuries in a beautiful building.
Orrery (▷ 164): A Marylebone stalwart, serving fine French food.
Ronnie Scott's (▷ 158): Renowned jazz venue.
Sir John Soane's Museum (▷ 148–149): One man's taste: an unusual house packed with curiosities.
Theatre Royal Drury Lane (▷ 160): Venue of countless hit musicals in Covent Garden.

WESTMINSTER AND ST. JAMES'S

The Cinnamon Club (▷ 200): Traditional Indian cookery in the unlikely setting of a former library.
Fortnum and Mason (▷ 198): Famous food emporium.
The Halkin Hotel (▷ 203): Elegant, contemporary hotel with an excellent Thai restaurant.
National Gallery (▷ 182–187): European masterpieces from the 13th to the 19th centuries.
National Portrait Gallery (▷ 188–189): Pictures of royalty, the rich and the famous.
Nobu (▷ 201): Upscale restaurant serving exquisite but expensive modern Japanese cuisine.
Pigalle (▷ 199): Sophisticated 1940s-style club with an amazing atmosphere.
Westminster Abbey (▷ 194–195): London's largest surviving medieval church, packed with famous tombs.

HYDE PARK AND AROUND

Bibendum (▷ 238): Restaurant known for its wine, and housed in the fabulous art deco Michelin building.
Claridge's (▷ 243): Quintessentially British hotel, famous for its afternoon teas.
Harrods (▷ 233): Legendary department store selling practically everything you can think of.
Harvey Nichols (▷ 233): Ultra-chic department store with gorgeous window displays.
The Landmark London (▷ 244): One of the city's top hotels, providing every luxury.
Natural History Museum (▷ 220–221): Dinosaurs to lichens: millions of specimens from the natural world.
Portobello Road (▷ 234): Fascinating street market selling everything from antiques to vegetables.
Restaurant Gordon Ramsay (▷ 240): The mothership of the notorious chef's culinary empire offers classic dishes and impeccable service.
Royal Albert Hall (▷ 235): Venue for major classical and contemporary concerts, dance and the summer Proms.
Science Museum (▷ 222–223): Innovative hands-on museum that brings science to life.
Victoria & Albert Museum (▷ 224–228): A dazzling collection of decorative art.
Wallace Collection (▷ 229): Exceptional art collection housed in a palatial mansion.

Opposite *The Great Court of the British Museum*
Below *The Landmark London hotel*

TOP EXPERIENCES

Cross the river Stroll across the Millennium Bridge (▷ 77) or Westminster Bridge, preferably at sunset, for classic London river views.

Browse the markets Hunt for bargains and enjoy the atmosphere at a street market, such as Portobello Road (▷ 234) or Petticoat Lane (▷ 120).

Hop on a bus View the city from the top deck of a bus to get your bearings.

Go to Harrods Even if you don't want to buy anything, it's worth visiting this huge, luxurious store (▷ 233).

Shop at Covent Garden Find unusual items in the specialist shops in the area (▷ 142–143).

Ride on the London Eye The huge millennium wheel gives unrivalled views of London (▷ 75).

Take tea Skip lunch and go to Fortnum and Mason (▷ 198), or The Ritz (▷ 203), for a full afternoon tea.

Enjoy the parks and squares Take a picnic to one of the city's many green spaces.

See a live performance Whatever your taste, you'll find it in London. The choice of entertainment is huge.

Watch the Changing of the Guard Witness British tradition in action: daily ceremony outside Buckingham Palace (▷ 176).

Go on the river Take a boat trip on the Thames for a different perspective of the city (▷ 266–267).

Drink in a local Have a pint in a traditional London pub—many have changed little since Dickens's day.

Get out of town Leave the city centre for a day and visit at least one of the following: Greenwich, Hampstead Heath, Hampton Court, Kew Gardens (▷ 256–257, 258, 260–261, 268–269).

Wander off the beaten track Take a street map and explore areas such as Bloomsbury or the City on foot.

Lunch in style Try at least a couple of the city's superb restaurants: At lunchtime, prices are usually very reasonable.

Catch a traditional festival or event Look for the events, large and small, that take place year round (▷ 294–295).

Below left *Notting Hill Carnival is a riot of colour and exuberance*
Below right *A trip on the London Eye on a clear day affords fantastic views over the city*

LIVING LONDON

There's no simple way of defining a Londoner. The city has a population of about 7.5 million, swollen every day by a million commuters coming in to work by train, mainly from southeast England. More than 270 nationalities make up the fabric of the city itself, and ethnic minorities add up to roughly a quarter of all Londoners. Many have family roots in African countries and India, formerly parts of the British Empire. In the 1950s, a huge number of West Indians arrived. Within the city, the Thames provides another means of identification, dividing north London from south; some people never cross the river. Cockneys are east Londoners born 'within the sound of Bow Bells'—the bells of the church of St.-Mary-le-Bow, east of the City.

This is a city with a fascinating mix of tradition and change. You'll find the same types—the wealthy City worker, the lawyer in 18th-century wig and gown, the talkative London cabbie—but today they are men and women from a wide range of ethnic and social groups. The typical Londoner doesn't exist, and probably never did.

Clockwise from above *Soho by night is a bustling mix of locals and tourists looking for an entertaining evening out or simply enjoying the atmosphere; the familiar red London buses; singer, Lily Allen*

LONDONERS ALONE

One third of Londoners live alone. Many are single young people, with good jobs and money. They're at the forefront of a changing society with a 50 per cent divorce rate, serial marriages and freelance or part-time jobs. Many of them will not marry, or cohabit, until they are 30. Their income is 15 per cent higher than the rest of the country and this pushes up prices, especially for London property, where increases of 25 per cent a year have been common in recent years (though there are signs that the boom is slowing). These young people shop on the internet, eat out and network with their friends, who provide them with the stability once offered by the family group.

LONDON CABBIES
There are some 20,000 black cabs in London, and an average of 31,000 people looking for a ride each night, so cabbies have to move fast. Since 1851 budding cab drivers have had to take an exam, set up by the Public Carriage Office, to test them on the best routes round 25,000 streets. It's called the Knowledge, and it takes three years to prepare for. Scientists have found that parts of the brain used for navigation are actually larger in a cabbie—but this brainpower is now under threat. The PCO wants to computerize the exam, and some companies are actually introducing computerized navigation systems in their cabs. Unsurprisingly, cabbies don't like it. Computers can't tell if a route is traffic-jammed, they say—and how do they know where the best restaurants are?

RISING STAR
Local girl made good Lily Allen was born in Hammersmith to parents in the film and TV business, and made an early appearance in *The Comic Strip Presents* at the age of three. Her meteoric rise to fame in recent years, however, has been as a talented and quirky singer with such hits as *Smile* and *The Fear*. Writing her own songs of sharp social observations on the 21st century, Lily has won plaudits for her witty references to modern London life, delivered in an endearing mock Cockney accent. Her appearance in garish wigs and sporting of wildly imaginative make-up also attract attention and have made her quite an alternative fashion icon. When not performing, she cheers on her football team, Fulham.

BOLLYWOOD IS HERE
The Asian community in London is more than 200 years old and enjoys a thriving cultural and commercial life. There are well over 200 Indian millionaires living in London; Meena Pathak of Pathak Spices, for example, has created a hugely successful food brand. You can enjoy some of the best Indian food in the world at Veeraswamy's in Regent Street, the oldest of hundreds of Indian restaurants in the capital, or take your pick from the dozens of inexpensive Bangladeshi eateries along Brick Lane. Or why not see a film in Hindi, released direct from Bombay, in Upton Park. You can check out the saris and jewellery in major centres of the Asian community such as Southall or Tooting, which also offer a huge range of authentic restaurants and spice-filled groceries, catering to the locals.

SPEAKERS CORNER
Speakers Corner is at the northeast tip of Hyde Park, overlooking Marble Arch. Once the site of the Tyburn gallows (▷ 33), where public executions drew massive crowds, it's now a place devoted to free speech. Anyone can stand up, usually on a stepladder, and say anything they like—except, that is, about the Queen, as this is a royal park. Russian revolutionary Lenin (1870–1924) spoke here, as did novelist George Orwell (1903–50) and the Pankhurst family of suffragettes. Most speakers give vent to extreme views on religion, politics and diet at great and tedious length. Meanwhile the heckler plays an equally time-honoured part, shouting jokes or insults, which the best speakers answer back. In this modern age of e-mails and TV, Speakers Corner still provides that oldest form of communication, the shouting match.

London is the focal point of the three main English sports: football (soccer), rugby and cricket. Wembley Stadium traditionally hosts the Football Association (FA) Cup Final in May, the climax of the football year. The main ground for rugby, invented in 1823 by an English schoolboy tired of kicking the ball, is in the southwest suburb of Twickenham (▷ 259), and cricket has had its headquarters in St. John's Wood since the 1830s, when the Marylebone Cricket Club moved there (▷ 216). London will also host the Summer Olympic Games in 2012 (▷ 40).

Many Londoners take part in some form of physical activity, mainly walking, swimming or going to the gym. Some of this energy is expended on good causes. It is estimated that over £200 million has been raised by runners in the London Marathon since it began in 1980. It's the single biggest fund-raising event in the UK.

A favourite leisure pastime of Londoners is drinking. There are 5,000 pubs in the city, but they are no longer solely the domain of men and beer. Now you can buy wine, tea or coffee and often excellent food.

Clockwise from above *The England rugby team take on France at Twickenham; Marathon runners coming up to the finish line in The Mall; the new Wembley Stadium arch*

ARSENAL VS TOTTENHAM

The feud between these two great football teams began in 1913. Arsenal moved from southeast London to Highbury, near the north London home of Tottenham Hotspur (Spurs), White Hart Lane. Arsenal needed more fans, and soon the community was split. The teams are very different. Arsenal, under Arsene Wenger, are free-flowing and exciting, while Tottenham are also showing signs of a resurgence since Harry Redknapp took over as manager. One of their famous clashes was the 1991 Football Association Cup Semi-Final. The streets of north London were deserted. After a great match, Spurs won 3–1 and went on to win the Cup Final. Such passionate rivalries ensure the game's popularity across the country.

PUB CRAWL PROTOCOL

One of the best ways to get to know London and see a cross-section of the capital's population is to go on a pub crawl—an afternoon and/or evening spent visiting one pub after another. There's a pub on almost every corner, so areas such as Mayfair or Fleet Street can be studied at close quarters in an enjoyable way. It's not a bad idea to have only a half in each pub, to fit more in and still get home. Until 2003, Britain's licensing laws were a source of amazement and annoyance to visitors as they meant that pubs had to close at 11pm, but local authorities can now decide what time individual pubs and clubs shut their doors. Night owls and visitors certainly welcome the change, and most residents seem happy enough.

THE FIVE-DAY MARATHON

The British love to do mad or strange things to raise money for charity. More than 30,000 people take part in the London Marathon in April and most finish in a few hours, but in 2002 Lloyd Scott took more than five days. He was wearing an antique diving suit weighing 55kg (120lb). In 1987 he had been diagnosed with leukaemia. He beat the disease, and decided to raise money for research. He could walk only 400m (1,300ft) in his suit before stopping to recover his strength. It was all worth it: Scott raised more than £100,000. In 2006 he completed the marathon dressed in armour and in 2007 as Indiana Jones, bringing the total raised to more than £4 million.

A NEW STADIUM

Londoners have a special affection for Wembley Stadium. Its famous two white towers were part of the skyline since 1923. The great athletic, football and rugby events are played at Wembley, and the biggest rock stars in the world have played there. In 1996 a replacement stadium to hold 90,000 people—the world's most expensive, at £715 million—was announced. Then the problems started. The government gave £120 million, but banks refused to lend the rest, demanding to know who was in charge of the project—the government or the Football Association? When demolition of the old towers finally began they proved more stubborn than expected, and work was slow. However, the new stadium was opened in 2006, giving London a sporting and leisure landmark fit for the third millennium.

SALES MANIA

The January sales in London promise some great bargains after the Christmas spree, and Harrods (▷ 233) does it bigger and better than the rest. On the first day of the sale a high-profile film star draws up in a horse-drawn carriage, to the accompaniment of bagpipes, to open the doors which announces the start of the sale. Then, if they have any sense, they run, as it's not unknown for people to be trampled in the consumer frenzy. The daily average of 30,000 visitors swells to a scary 300,000, and staff sometimes have to shut the doors on a packed store. To be first in line shoppers arrive the previous day and sleep on the pavement. Seasoned bargain-hunters know the exact route to their chosen goods and make for them at top speed. With discounts of 50 or 60 per cent, who can blame them?

London's royal pageantry is unique. Members of the royal family, who have been through good times and bad, still star in a regular series of splendid parades and processions. Trooping the Colour in June and the State Opening of Parliament in November, for instance, feature hundreds of soldiers, golden carriages, music and the Queen dressed in diamonds. There are less showy traditions, too: At the New Year's Honours and the Birthday Honours in June, the Queen hands medals and awards to hundreds of people from all walks of life. Her official role as Head of State is reflected in meetings with the Prime Minister every Tuesday to discuss government business. As the head of a very public and expensive monarchy, she attracts both criticism and huge affection—as shown in the months of tours, parties and displays celebrating her Golden Jubilee (50 years on the throne) in 2002.

This heady combination of privilege and wealth has always intrigued and attracted visitors. Film stars and billionaires still like to be seen mingling with the royals, and the spectacle does its bit to pull in the 15 million tourists who spend about £7 billion every year.

Clockwise from above *Ladies Day at Ascot is a chance for the female visitors to sport their most outrageous headgear; London is peppered with Blue Plaques marking the residences of famous people; now in her 80s, the Queen would become the longest-reigning British monarch in 2015*

ROYAL MILESTONES

On 21 April 2006 the Queen turned 80, and, joined by Prince Philip, celebrated by enjoying a birthday walkabout among enthusiastic crowds in Windsor. On 20 November 2007 the Queen and Prince Philip celebrated their 60th wedding anniversary with a service held at Westminster Abbey on the previous day. The couple first met in 1939 when the then Princess Elizabeth was just 13 years old. The royal celebrations continued with a short trip to Malta, where the couple had lived from 1949 until 1951, away from the media spotlight. To complete the royal milestones, the Queen became the oldest reigning British monarch in history on 20 December 2007.

HOMES OF THE FAMOUS

Would Jimi Hendrix (1942–70) and George Frederick Handel (1685–1759) have got along, swapping notes on chords, tough crowds and the setting alight of instruments? Perhaps; they were neighbours, after all—albeit separated by 270 years, as well as a brick wall. Jimi stayed at No. 23 Brook Street in Mayfair from 1968 to 1969, entertaining, among others, the Beatles. George Frederick lived next door at No. 25 (▷ 212) for much of his life, making his name as a composer. Today this cosmic twist of fate is commemorated by a Blue Plaque, one of some 860 in London marking the homes of notable residents. Look hard enough and you'll spot one on virtually every corner, particularly in the Royal Borough of Kensington and Chelsea. The scheme, now looked after by English Heritage, has been extended across the country.

ROYAL WARRANTS

Keep your eyes open and you'll spot royal warrants everywhere in London. Companies and individuals appointed to provide goods and services to the royal family can display a royal coat of arms for five years. Royal warrants can be granted by the Queen, the Prince of Wales and the Duke of Edinburgh. To qualify, the business must have had the royal patron's custom for at least three years. The practice, which started in the 15th century, gives an interesting insight into the royal lifestyle. There is a royal mole controller and a chimney sweep. No fewer than six champagne houses have royal warrants, and several chocolatiers—Cadbury's for the staff, Prestat/Bendicks for the royals. This sporty family has providers of riding breeches and fishing tackle, four official gunmakers and a busy royal taxidermist.

THE SEASON HAMPER

Once upon a time Britain's social elite laid out rugs and picnics at the summer race meets and open-air operas that make up The Season. Today you're more likely to find corporate hospitality tents, but it's still worth making the effort to impress with the perfect picnic hamper. Smoked salmon for example, should be wild, not farmed; strawberries should be English rather than Spanish. Scots may prefer to include some specialities from north of the border, such as cullen skink soup or oatcakes. A small tub of Gentleman's Relish, an anchovy paste, adds a touch of class. There are simple rules for drinks: Cans must be avoided. Pimms, a sweet, deceptively alcoholic drink first created in the 1840s, is traditional, and chilled champagne is a must.

THE GREAT AND THE GOOD

In 2002 a portrait of the Queen by Lucian Freud—celebrated as Britain's greatest contemporary painter—was revealed. Although monarchists considered it unflattering, it testifies to the importance of the portrait in British history as a record of who's who. It's difficult to go around a stately home or an established art gallery without being watched by likenesses of the great and the good. The art of portraiture was given a boost by two factors: the fashion for genealogy among the aristocracy, and the Protestant Reformation, when artists sought an alternative market to religious imagery. The best place to see portraits is the National Portrait Gallery (▷ 188–189).

SIR
WINSTON
CHURCHILL
Lived in a house
on this site
1921-1924

London has some of the best theatre in the world. There are two government-subsidized companies—the Royal National Theatre and the Royal Shakespeare Company—and Shaftesbury Avenue forms the heart of commercial theatre in the West End. Movie stars such as Nicole Kidman and Kevin Spacey have come to soak up some of its prestige, Spacey taking up the role of artistic director of the Old Vic (▷ 87). BAFTA (British Academy of Film and Television Arts) has moved its awards ceremony to February, to avoid being overshadowed by the Oscars, and attracts many Hollywood stars. While they're here they have to face the toughest paparazzi in the world, as well as a voracious tabloid press.

Art and style are part of the London experience. The Tate Modern gallery (▷ 80–81), one of London's most exciting spaces, is so popular that it stays open until 10pm on Fridays and Saturdays. And the artists of the catwalk, London's fashion designers, are at the peak of their creativity, developing the city's quirky street fashion and producing radicals such as John Galliano, who heads Christian Dior, to revolutionize haute couture.

Clockwise from above The Rose (III) *by Cy Twombly on display at the Royal Academy of Arts; modern sculpture outside the British Museum; fashion designer Stella McCartney is the daughter of former Beatle Paul McCartney*

THE LOTTERY IN LONDON

Since it started in 1994 the National Lottery has raised hundreds of millions of pounds for big London institutions such as the Royal Opera House. But smaller amounts, which don't attract the headlines, are also distributed across the city to places such as Kentish Town's City Farm, a popular scheme for youngsters who might never have seen animals or the countryside. When the Lottery awarded the farm £47,000 for its drama and arts programme, it set up workshops for young asylum-seekers in the area to create their own stories and attend art classes. Debate about the Lottery continues to rage, but there's no denying that some of its contributions make a real difference.

ARCHITECTURAL SUPREMO

How far do you have to go to escape Sir Norman Foster's work? Not Bilbao, where the top British architect has redesigned much of the metro system. Not Berlin, where his renovation of the Reichstag won the Pritzker architecture prize. Nor Hong Kong, if you pass through Chek Lap Kok international airport, built on a man-made island. And certainly not London: Canary Wharf's transcendental tube station, the Great Court in the British Museum (▷ 134–139) and the Greater London Authority's new home, City Hall, are some of the most distinctive buildings in Britain, all designed by Foster and Partners. One of the most striking additions to London's skyline, 30 St. Mary Axe (aka the Gherkin), embodies environmentally friendly architecture with layers of 'light wells' inside and a largely self-ventilating structure.

RAGS TO RICHES

From London's East End to the fashion houses of Paris via Savile Row, the Alexander McQueen story crosses the capital and then the English Channel. McQueen was born in 1969, the son of an East End taxi driver, and left school at 16. More interested in couture than cab driving, he served his apprenticeship on Savile Row, before taking an MA at St. Martin's School of Art—other alumni include Stella McCartney and Matthew Williamson. After a celebrated final collection, fashion's *enfant terrible* left London for Paris, working for Givenchy and then Gucci. By 2001 the three-times British Designer of the Year had made his fortune and by the end of 2006 he had 21 boutiques across the globe; an online store was launched in 2008. His story has a tragic end, however: In 2010 McQueen committed suicide, at just 40 years of age.

THE PEOPLE'S ART

The Royal Academy Summer Exhibition is held between June and mid-August at the Royal Academy (▷ 146) in Piccadilly. First held in 1769, it is open to every artist in the country from the humblest amateur to the greatest professional. Anything can be submitted: drawings, prints, sculpture, traditional or abstract, and everything is viewed. The exhibition often has a theme which the artists use for inspiration—2009's was 'Making Space'. Around a thousand works are chosen to go on display, every one for sale. There was a time when artists queued all day with their submissions until an Academician shouted a very public acceptance or rejection. The selection process is more civilized these days, and for those whose work is accepted, there's always a chance of seeing their local landscape hanging next to a David Hockney.

THEATRE FOR ALL

Chickenshed is one of the largest theatre companies in the UK, and has a substantial theatre with a recording and dance studio in Southgate, north London. Jo Collins and Mary Ward founded it in 1974 with the simple aim of involving anyone with a love of theatre, including children. One of their most famous performances was *Anansi*, based on African tales, in which 1,000 London children took part. After seeing it, Diana, Princess of Wales became the company's patron, and when she died in 1997 Chickenshed recorded a tribute single, *I Am in Love With the World*, that reached No. 14 in the charts. Chickenshed projects have spread across the country, proving again that the simplest ideas are often the best. In 2007 Chickenshed went one stage further, extending projects across the globe.
www.chickenshed.org.uk

There are several layers of government in London. The British Parliament, made up of the House of Commons and the House of Lords, sits in the Houses of Parliament (▷ 179–180). Just up the road is Whitehall and the major offices of government, including the Prime Minister's official residence at No. 10 Downing Street. At the top of Whitehall, the Mall leads to Buckingham Palace, official home of the Queen, the constitutional Head of State.

Then comes the government of London itself—and this gets even more confusing. The City of London, known as 'the square mile', is its historic heart and financial centre, and still guards its medieval privileges. Since 1189 the Lord Mayor has been head of the fiercely independent Corporation of London, the first local authority in England. The modern city, encompassing its sprawl of suburbs, is known as Greater London and, in 2000, elected its first mayor, Ken Livingstone. He was ousted after two terms in 2008 by Boris Johnson. The Mayor and the Greater London Authority co-ordinate services such as transport across 32 London boroughs and have a budget of £4 billion.

Clockwise from above *The Houses of Parliament's Central Lobby; a row of highly desirable pastel-coloured houses off the King's Road, Chelsea; The House of Lords Chamber is much more richly decorated than the Commons Chamber*

POLITICIAN-AUTHORS

As if being part of the world's oldest parliamentary democracy didn't keep them busy enough, dozens of members of parliament (MPs) supplement their £60,000-plus salaries with second jobs. Many are directors of companies or highly paid consultants, some pulling in huge annual salaries. But the most intriguing moonlighters are the novelists. In the 1990s Tory MP Edwina Currie began writing racy novels in her spare time (eg *A Parliamentary Affair).* Fellow Tory Ann Widdecombe, known for her uncompromising views, was advanced £100,000 for two rather more restrained novels. Interestingly, one Labour MP's analysis in 2002 of MPs' voting records revealed that those who have second jobs turn up to 30 per cent fewer votes than those who don't.

HOUSE OF LORDS

Historically, the most reliable way of gaining a seat on the red leather benches of Parliament's upper chamber was to inherit it. But in 1999 the Labour government reforms threw all but 92 of the aristocrats out. So how do you get a life peerage today? You should be British: former owner of the *Daily Telegraph* Lord Black renounced his Canadian citizenship for the purpose. Senior figures in the military and the judiciary have an advantage, and Britain's 25 bishops are guaranteed a spot. Ex-politicians and business people aren't uncommon. And you needn't be old: Media mogul Lord Waheed Alli is in his 30s. You can even be nominated as one of 15 People's Peers—but with brain specialist Professor Susan Greenfield among them, they are hardly average, either.

WHO OWNS LONDON?

After the Queen and the Church, Gerald Grosvenor, 6th Duke of Westminster, is the greatest landowner in London. His ancestor, Mary Davies, married Sir Thomas Grosvenor in 1677. Mary owned 100ha (247 acres) of damp farmland. Today this is Mayfair and Belgravia, some of the most expensive land in the world. The Duke's rents and freeholds have created a fortune worth at least £5 billion. He owns more land elsewhere in the UK and in Canada, Australia and the USA. The present Duke lives simply, but his forebears spent on an imperial scale, splashing out on Old Masters and jewellery by Fabergé. The 4th Duke was a suitor of Paris fashion designer Coco Chanel, and, on finding that the mail was too slow for his liking, set up a private postal system just for her.

VOLATILE HOUSE PRICES

Sixty per cent of Londoners own their homes, but houses don't come cheap. London has among the highest property prices in the world. A small three-bedroom house in Chelsea will cost more than £1 million; a one-bedroom flat in an average area can easily top £200,000. Until 2007 prices were doubling every five years, but the recession had the inevitable effect of sending them back down—by 10 to 15 per cent—and the recovery is only just under way. For those who can afford it, even a small London property is still a great investment, but anyone earning less than £30,000 a year is in trouble. Teachers, nurses, firemen and policemen, all vital to the capital, are unable to afford their own homes, and mortgages have become even tougher to secure.

THE UK'S HIGHEST EARNERS

The incomes of the UK's richest one per cent are soaring ahead, despite the recent economic crisis, and most of the people earning more than £100,000 a year live in London or its hinterland. The posh west London district of Kensington and Chelsea has the highest concentration of high-earners in the country. The City of London, the financial district, is not far behind, and here many employees work for an incentive system that can lead to huge rewards. These districts are also where full-time gross weekly pay is highest—in Kensington and Chelsea it is in the vicinity of a cool £1,250. Seven of the ten best-paid workforces in the UK are in Greater London districts, as are the majority of the UK's millionaires.

URBAN WILDLIFE

Along with millions of people, London is home to a surprising amount of wildlife. Within 30km (20 miles) of St. Paul's, 2,000 species of flora and fauna thrive in parks, squares, churchyards, ponds and gardens. Flora includes the London plane tree and the pink-flowered saxifrage called London Pride. Fauna ranges from deer, foxes, badgers and rabbits to grey squirrels, the ubiquitous pigeons and stealthy armies of rats and mice. Voles do so well that the London Wildlife Trust has its own vole officer. The endangered stag beetle finds sanctuary in private gardens, and fish have returned to the once-polluted Thames.

Above left *An early-morning cycle ride in Kensington Gardens*
Above right *Trafalgar Square's ubiquitous pigeons flock around the National Gallery*

PIGEONS UNDER FIRE

The British have an odd relationship with the pigeon, and the Royal Pigeon Racing Association has around 46,000 members. Meanwhile, the famous pigeons of Trafalgar Square (▷ 190–191), all 30,000 of them, are on the wanted list. These 'rats with wings' carry disease and leave a mess behind them, in many people's opinion, so pigeons are on a diet—in the hope that they will go away. The general public is not allowed to feed them, and hawks go flapping overhead every so often to scare them off. These measures follow the phased eradication programme introduced by former mayor Ken Livingstone, which aims to reduce pigeon numbers.

PLANES VERSUS POLLUTION

As well as being beautiful, trees play a vital anti-pollution role. The Trees for London charity, which plants 10,000 of them a year, is campaigning for a million more by 2010 'to help London breathe'. A characteristic feature of the capital's streets and gardens, the London plane tree *(Platanus x hispanica)*, which periodically sheds its dirt-absorbing bark, is a hybrid of the oriental plane, introduced in 1562, and the western plane, which was imported from Virginia in 1636. The oldest surviving examples in garden squares are the huge ones in Berkeley Square (▷ 153), planted in 1789. William Wordsworth wrote a poem about the ancient plane tree at the corner of Cheapside and Wood Street in the City, which is still there.

FOXES ON THE RUN

Foxes like big cities because it is easy to find food. There are about 20,000 in London. Some people like foxes and encourage them into their gardens, but others are scared and dislike their piercing shrieks at night. The government officially recommends trapping the foxes and releasing them into the wild, which usually means they just come back, but one area of London has taken the drastic step of employing a hunter to kill the foxes. He traps the foxes and then shoots them. Animal rights activists oppose this and the man has to work anonymously. However, the major cause of fox death is less dramatic: Eighty per cent of them die before the age of two, squashed beneath the wheels of a car. Keep an eye out for them in leafier areas, especially at night.

THE STORY OF LONDON

THE BEGINNINGS OF LONDON

London is where it is because of a decision made by the Roman army commanders after their invasion of England in AD43. A site for a base was chosen on the north bank of the Thames at the highest point of the tide accessible to ships from the European Continent. A bridge was built across the river and quays along the bank, and the military base developed into a town, a busy commercial and administrative district that became the hub of the Roman road network and succeeded Colchester as the capital of Roman Britain. The civic heart was where Leadenhall Market (▷ 120) is now. Besides barracks, houses and shops, there were temples, public baths and an amphitheatre, and from around AD200 the whole town was surrounded by a wall.

After the Roman army withdrew from Britain, the Anglo-Saxons established their own town outside the wall on the west, in today's Aldwych area, but attacks by Vikings drove the inhabitants back inside the Roman wall in the 9th century. In the 11th century, King Edward the Confessor founded Westminster Abbey (▷ 194–195) a mile (1.6km) or so to the west, built a palace there and created a second London, the centre of the royal government, alongside the first.

Clockwise from above *Statue of warrior-queen Boadicea (Boudicca) on the Victoria Embankment; King Alfred the Great recaptured London from the Vikings in AD886; Roman head of the god Mithras (2nd to 3rd century) from the Temple of Mithras, now in the Museum of London*

THE PEOPLING OF ROMAN LONDON

All through its history London has grown by attracting settlers from elsewhere. The early population included many Celts from various parts of Britain, but London also imported people from all over the Roman Empire, from across the English Channel in Gaul (France)—such as Julius Classicianus, the first Londoner whose name is known—to Greece and the eastern Mediterranean. Soldiers, officials, doctors, shopkeepers, entertainers, craftsmen, clerks, cooks, slaves—some with their families—brought their gods and goddesses, languages, costumes, habits and traditions with them to create a cosmopolitan mix. Roman London probably resembled a frontier town in the Wild West—crowded, noisy, smelly and often dangerous.

BOADICEA'S REVOLT

Queen Boadicea (or Boudicca; the name means 'victory'), ruler of the Celtic Iceni people of East Anglia in AD60, was an ally of the Romans until enraged by their arrogance and mistreatment. After Roman soldiers had flogged her and raped her daughters, she led her tribespeople to sack Colchester and then descended on London in her war chariot, seeking vengeance. She plundered the fledgling town, burned it to the ground and slaughtered those inhabitants who had not fled the city. The Roman army quickly regrouped and defeated the Iceni in battle somewhere to the north, and Boadicea killed herself rather than be captured. London was quickly rebuilt, but archaeologists have found clear traces of extensive fire damage deep below the current ground level.

IN THE ARENA

One of the pleasures of life in Roman London was going to the amphitheatre, near the area now occupied by the Guildhall (⊳ 102). Oval in shape, with high earth banks supporting wooden benches for some 5,000 spectators, it was used for entertainment (including executions) and could be hired for private functions. Wild animals were butchered in the arena for the audience's delight, but gladiatorial combats were the star attraction. These might involve a heavily armed fighter against one more lightly armed and more agile, or a contest between a *retiarius* (gladiator equipped with a net and trident) against an opponent with sword and shield. All the gladiators paraded round the arena together before fighting—often to the death, though a defeated gladiator could appeal to the crowd for mercy.

DEATH AND BAY LEAVES

A lavish sarcophagus discovered in the Spitalfields area of the City in 1999 was expected to be that of a powerful citizen of Roman London. When the lead casket inside was opened, however, it was found to contain the skeleton of a young woman. Buried around AD350 and in her 20s when she died, she clearly came from an extremely rich family. The sarcophagus was decorated with scallop shells, symbols of life after death. She had been wrapped in expensive garments of silk and wool, some shot through with gold thread. Also interred with her were glass and jet objects and, touchingly, her head had been put gently to rest on a pillow of fresh, sweet-smelling bay leaves.

THE ROYAL SAINT

Edward the Confessor (*c.*1003–66) was the only English king ever canonized. A deeply religious man, he gave his patronage to a Benedictine monastery on Thorney Island in the Thames marshes west of London, paying for its church to be rebuilt in the Romanesque style, which was fashionable in Normandy, and establishing a royal palace near the site. The monastery relics included fragments of the True Cross, blood from Christ's wounded side, some of the Virgin Mary's milk and one of St. Paul's fingers. When Edward died in 1066, leaving his kingdom without an heir and his throne in dispute, he was laid to rest there —behind the high altar of Westminster Abbey (⊳ 194–195).

London's importance was underlined when William I, 'the Conqueror' (1027–87), built the Tower of London to keep the city under control after the Norman conquest. Over the following centuries streets were paved for the first time, hospitals and prisons were built, and church spires studded the skyline. Rich merchant guilds took over the government of the city, which had its own mayor and aldermen. Merchants and financiers came to London from Germany, Denmark, France and Italy; until its expulsion in 1290 there was a flourishing Jewish community. Westminster, meanwhile, became a regular meeting place of Parliament, and magnates built houses along the river between the city and Westminster.

In 1500 London had a population of perhaps 50,000, which was quadrupled by immigration in the Tudor period. City merchants virtually monopolized England's foreign trade, with ships leaving the Port of London for the Mediterranean and the East, America and Africa. Bricks were used in more buildings and the most expensive houses had pumped water. Constables and marshals were employed to deal with crime and vagrancy. Disease was rife, but life was longer on average in London than elsewhere.

Above *The killing of Wat Tyler in front of King Ricahrd II, from the Chronicles of medieval historian Jean Froissart*

OLD LONDON BRIDGE

London's only bridge in the Middle Ages was a remarkable sight. People lived on it in houses along each side, from three to seven floors high. These were not finally removed until 1762. There were shops on the ground floors—more than a hundred of them—and at the core a two-storey chapel dedicated to St. Thomas à Becket. Below, the bridge's 19 arches created dangerous rapids. In 1390 the bridge was turfed over for a great tournament between English and Scottish champions. It had more gruesome uses too. The heads of executed traitors were parboiled in the gatehouse, dipped in tar and stuck on the gateway. One visitor in 1598 counted more than 30 on display.

THE ZOO IN THE TOWER

Until the 1830s the Tower of London (▷ 112–117) housed a royal collection of wild animals. Henry III (1207–72) had a polar bear which liked to fish in the Thames, three leopards sent by the Holy Roman Emperor, and an elephant, a gift from France, which caused great excitement when it arrived but survived for only two years. An official Keeper of the King's Lions and Leopards was appointed, and lions still lived in the Tower in the time of James I (1566–1625), who liked to set mastiffs on them. Around 1750 the zoo had lions, tigers, leopards, bears, monkeys, eagles, vultures and an ostrich.

Below left *London's first zoo, in the Tower of London*
Below right *The Globe Theatre depicted on Visscher's map of London, 1616*

THE KILLING OF WAT TYLER

In 1381 thousands of rebels objecting to a poll tax journeyed from Kent and Essex to London. The followers of the Peasants' Revolt—whose demands included the redistribution of church wealth—killed several government officials before the 13-year-old king, Richard II (1367–1400), agreed to meet them at Smithfield. After some initial dialogue there was a scuffle, as the Mayor of London, William Walworth, tried to arrest Wat Tyler, the rebel leader. Tyler struck at him with a dagger but Walworth, saved by the mail shirt under his clothes, ran Tyler through with his sword. Richard rode towards the rebels, proclaiming himself their true leader and the crowd fled. Poll taxes were not imposed again—until 1990 by Margaret Thatcher.

QUEEN ELIZABETH AT TILBURY

When the Spanish Armada sailed to invade England in 1588, Elizabeth I (1533–1603) insisted on visiting her troops at Tilbury. Accompanied by her courtiers, she arrived riding a white horse and wearing a steel corselet over her white velvet dress. Having dismounted, she walked through the ranks before delivering a stirring address. The Queen was a superb orator and her defiant speech is famous in English history. 'I know I have but the body of a weak and feeble woman,' she announced, 'but I have the heart and stomach of a king, and of a king of England too.' Elizabeth was still at Tilbury when news arrived of the Armada's defeat. It was the key turning point of the Anglo-Spanish War (1585–1604).

SHAKESPEARE AND THE GLOBE

Bankside in the time of William Shakespeare (1564–1616) was London's most notorious entertainment area, known for its drinking dens and 'stews' (brothels), its bull- and bear-baiting pits and its theatres. A new theatre called the Globe (▷ 78)—polygonal, thatched and built of wood—opened there in 1599 and staged many of Shakespeare's plays, including *Macbeth, Othello* and probably *Henry V* (with its veiled reference to the theatre as 'this wooden O'). Bottled ale sold well to the audiences, and buckets served as emergency toilets. When the theatre was destroyed by fire in 1613 the only person hurt was a man whose breeches were set alight, but he resourcefully quenched the flames with a bottle of beer.

When James VI of Scotland (1566–1625) arrived in London to be crowned James I of England in 1603, the city was 10 times the size of any other in the kingdom. The first horse-drawn cabs appeared on the streets in the 1620s, annoying the Thames watermen, who ran London's earliest taxi service, and the development of the West End as a fashionable quarter started in Covent Garden (⊳ 142–143). The city guarded its privileges jealously. When Charles I (1600–49) interfered with them he met with fierce opposition, which was to be a major factor of his defeat in the Civil War. The 11-year Commonwealth government brought further encroachments, and London rejoiced when Charles II (1630–85) rode through the streets to reclaim the throne in 1660.

Smart neighbourhoods developed, such as St. James's and Bloomsbury, but most of the medieval city was devoured by the Great Fire. Sir Christopher Wren (1632–1723) rebuilt St. Paul's Cathedral (⊳ 104–109) and the city churches, but his plan for new streets was rejected. The old layout was restored, though the new buildings were in brick. The city soon recovered its dominance and in 1694 the Bank of England (⊳ 101) was founded.

Clockwise from above *The Great Fire of 1666 destroyed most of London; Charles I facing the executioner's block in 1649; the great dome of St. Paul's Cathedral, Christopher Wren's most famous achievement*

GUNPOWDER, TREASON AND PLOT

A group of conspirators intent on restoring Roman Catholicism in England found a Yorkshire soldier of fortune named Guy Fawkes, who was ready to blow up Parliament, with the aim of killing James I and his ministers gathered for the State opening ceremony in 1605.

After renting a cellar that ran beneath the House of Lords, they filled it with 36 barrels of gunpowder and a quantity of iron bars, concealed under masses of rubbish. Word of the plot leaked out, however; the building was searched and Fawkes was found lurking there with a length of slow-match, tinder and a watch. After interrogation under torture in the Tower of London, he was hanged, drawn and quartered, as were his fellow plotters.

THE EXECUTION OF CHARLES I

The Civil War was at an end, and Charles I had been convicted of waging war against his own people. On a cold January afternoon in 1649 he donned an extra shirt—in case his shivers were mistaken for fear—and stepped through a window of the Banqueting House (▷ 175) in Whitehall on to a specially built scaffold, watched by a large crowd. The King pushed his hair up under his cap and knelt awkwardly at the block, which was only 26cm (10in) high. In complete silence he stretched out his arms as a signal to the executioner, who brought the axe down and severed the King's head with one stroke. A groan went up from the crowd, and one or two spectators passed out.

THE GREAT PLAGUE

An epidemic of bubonic plague in 1664–65, though less lethal than the Black Death, still killed around 100,000 people in London, a third of the population. People who could get out of town did so, though many doctors and clergy stayed to fulfil their duties. The disease was transmitted by fleas and spread by flea-ridden rats, but this was not understood at the time, and misguided remedies included a cull of dogs and cats. Plague-stricken houses had a cross daubed on the door, and the inhabitants were locked inside for 40 days' quarantine. To the cry of 'Bring out your dead', carts clattered through the streets collecting corpses, which were thrown into 'plague pits' and covered with a layer of quicklime.

THE GREAT FIRE

A catastrophic fire started in a bakery in Pudding Lane, near London Bridge, in the early hours of a September morning in 1666. Fanned by a strong wind and fuelled by wooden houses, it destroyed 80 per cent of the city's buildings and made more than 100,000 people homeless. The death toll remains a mystery—only five were recorded but there were probably more that went unregistered. Charles II sent diarist Samuel Pepys (1633–1703) to the scene to order the construction of fire breaks, and the next day the King and his brother, the future James II, took charge of operations. Flames raged up to 90m (300ft) high and threw out a rain of sparks. The navy was called in and houses were demolished. Finally the wind dropped and after four days the fire burned itself out.

BLOOD AND THE CROWN JEWELS

Colonel Thomas Blood was an adventurous Irishman who had his estates confiscated for supporting Parliament against Charles I. In 1671 he made an audacious attempt to steal the Crown Jewels, which were put on display in the Martin Tower of the Tower of London by the Keeper of Regalia, Talbot Edwards. Disguised as a clergyman, Blood befriended the Keeper and won his trust, returning later with three accomplices to steal the crown, orb and sceptre. They overpowered the Keeper and were making off with their booty when he recovered and raised the alarm. All three were caught, Blood with the crown under his parson's cloak. Charles II, apparently amused by the escapade, pardoned Blood and restored his Irish estate.

London's population grew towards the million mark as people from all parts of the country flocked in to seek their fortunes in the heart of England's political, commercial and artistic life. London covered more than twice as much ground in 1800 as in 1700. The villages of Knightsbridge, Kensington and Chelsea became extensions of the West End. Elegant squares and streets went up in Mayfair to house wealthy families with their servants. There were fashionable shops in Bond Street, Oxford Street and the Strand, smart coffee-houses and the Vauxhall and Ranelagh pleasure gardens to enjoy. The British Museum (▷ 134–139) and the Royal Academy of Arts (▷ 146) opened their doors, Handel's oratorios were premiered at Covent Garden (▷ 142–143) and exotic plants from around the world were grown at Kew Gardens (▷ 268–269).

It was also a London of smoke and stench, open sewers, high infant mortality rates and appalling slum 'rookeries'. Disease, drunkenness, prostitution and thieving were rife. Highwaymen, notably Dick Turpin, preyed on travellers into and out of London. There was no organized police force or fire brigade. Areas such as Seven Dials were avoided altogether by respectable citizens, who hired linkmen with torches to light them through the dark.

Clockwise from above *Houses in Bedford Square showing the symmetry and classical lines of Georgian architecture; the Egyptian Room of the British Museum; stone tablet marking the site of Tyburn tree*

AT THE CHESHIRE CHEESE

The Cheshire Cheese pub in Fleet Street has a list of famous past patrons. Lexicographer Dr. Samuel Johnson (1709–84) lived round the corner and came here or to the Turk's Head in Gerrard Street to gossip with his friends, writer James Boswell, painter Sir Joshua Reynolds, author Oliver Goldsmith and actor David Garrick. Johnson's memory has been saluted at the Cheshire Cheese by many later literary figures. Writer G. K. Chesterton once took his part at a Johnsonian dinner, and Irish poet W. B. Yeats and his contemporaries conducted a regular literary circle there in the 1890s.

THE ST. GILES ROOKERY

A rookery, sometimes also known as a stew, was an old colloquial term for a slum or ghetto. In about the middle of the 18th century the area round the church of St. Giles-in-the-Fields was one of London's worst slums. Its narrow streets, alleys and yards were synonymous with squalor, beggars, prostitution, crime and drink, with up to 50 people crammed into each ramshackle little house. Notorious taverns and gin-shops in the area included the Maidenhead Inn, in Dyott Street, and the Rat's Castle. When the nearby brewery's giant vat burst in 1814 and beer flooded the streets, the slum's inhabitants rushed out with jugs and cups. Even the children brought spoons, and some unfortunate people trying to lap beer from the gutters fell in and were drowned.

COLLECTORS ALL IN A ROW

Sir Hans Sloane (▷ 139) left his cornucopia of antiquities, artworks, manuscripts, natural history specimens and weird curiosities to the nation. The British Museum (▷ 134–139) was founded to house them and other treasures such as the Harleian Collection of manuscripts, assembled by the Earls of Oxford, and the Cotton family's books and antiquities. Money was raised by public lottery to pay for the building in Great Russell Street and the museum opened in 1759. In due course many more collections were purchased or donated, including Sir William Hamilton's antique vases, Egyptian antiquities, classical sculptures, the marble friezes removed from the Parthenon in Athens by Lord Elgin, and King George III's library.

TYBURN TREE

Marble Arch (▷ 216) stands on the site once occupied by the Tyburn gallows. Convicts were brought here to be hanged, travelling from Newgate prison three to a cart, sitting on their own coffins. On the way they were allowed to stop at taverns for free drinks and many, mercifully, arrived drunk. The hangman was sometimes in a similar condition. Huge crowds gathered to watch as the noose was fastened round the prisoner's neck, the horse was whipped up and the cart moved on, leaving the rope to drop. Friends would rush to tug on the dangling victim's legs and shorten the ordeal. From 1783 executions were conducted in Newgate, ending some 600 years of Tyburn hangings, which had claimed more than 50,000 souls.

THE LONDON MOB

In 1780 Member of Parliament Lord George Gordon (1751–93) led a huge demonstration to the Houses of Parliament (▷ 179–180) to protest against the relaxation of penalties on Roman Catholics. Some members of the crowd went on the rampage; Irish people and Roman Catholics were assaulted and their houses destroyed, and Roman Catholic chapels were looted to screams of 'No Popery'. Hoodlums poured out of the slums to drink, rape, kill and steal. Prisons were stormed and the prisoners released, and a mob armed with muskets attacked the Bank of England. After a week of mayhem the government called out the troops. In the ensuing suppression 285 people were killed. Gordon himself was acquitted of high treason, but 25 of the rioters were hanged.

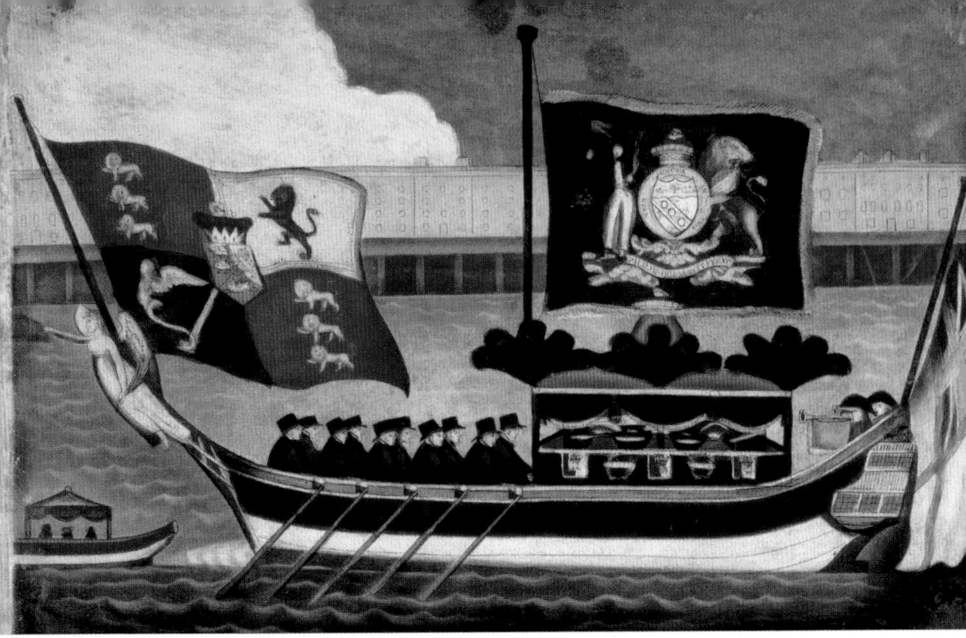

In the first half of the 19th century 'the great wen' (growth), as journalist William Cobbett called London, continued to expand. It was now the financial capital of the world and improved roads turned villages such as Hampstead and Highgate, Camberwell and Dulwich into suburbs for commuting businessmen. Meanwhile, as the docks expanded down the Thames, cheap housing spread through Whitechapel, Stepney and Bethnal Green in the East End. Architect John Nash (1752–1835) designed Regent's Park, Belgravia was laid out in style, Lord's cricket ground opened and London University was founded. London Zoo (▷ 219) opened and the National Gallery (▷ 182–187) and Nelson's Column were new landmarks in Trafalgar Square (▷ 190–191). Gas lighting made streets seem safer and in the 1820s and 1830s London acquired a police force and a fire brigade. The first horse-drawn omnibuses ran in 1829, and the railways arrived soon afterwards.

In stark contrast to such progress were the pressing problems of overcrowding and poverty, which spurred on the advocates of sweeping political and social reform.

Clockwise from above *Glass painting from the National Maritime Museum, Greenwich, showing Nelson's funeral barge; Madame Tussauds exhibition catalogue from 1883; to become a 'peeler'—police officer—men had to be 1.8m (6ft) tall and have a clean record*

LORD NELSON'S FUNERAL

Admiral Lord Horatio Nelson (1758–1805) died in action against the Napoleonic fleet at the Battle of Trafalgar. He was brought home in his flagship, HMS *Victory*, and his coffin taken by boat to Greenwich (▷ 256–257) and up the river. At the Admiralty in Whitehall it was placed on a funeral car made to resemble the *Victory*, with a winged figure of Fame at the prow. The Royal Scots Greys led the procession to St. Paul's. Bells tolled, guns boomed and fifes and drums played as the cortège moved through streets lined with people. A dozen sailors from the *Victory* bore the coffin. Darkness was gathering before the service was over and Nelson was lowered into a place of honour directly below the cathedral dome (▷ 107, 109).

THE PEELERS

As Home Secretary in 1829, Sir Robert Peel (1788–1850) introduced London's first effective police force. Called 'peelers' or 'bobbies' after their creator, the officers—many of them ex-soldiers—stepped on to the streets in blue uniforms and top hats, and made their Whitehall headquarters off Scotland Yard. At first the constables were regarded with suspicion and hostility by Londoners, who prized their freedom. 'Blue devils' was another popular nickname. Policemen were often attacked and when one was killed by rioters in 1831 the coroner's jury brought in a verdict of justifiable homicide. Gradually, under their Irish chief, Richard 'King' Mayne, who ran the force until his death in 1868, they acquired a reputation for discipline and restraint.

MADAME TUSSAUD AND THE WAXWORKS

Marie Tussaud (1761–1850), born Anna Maria Grosholtz in Strasbourg, arrived in England from her native France in 1802 with her two sons—having abandoned their father—and toured her waxworks show around the country until settling in London in 1835. In Paris, during the Terror that followed the French Revolution, she had been forced to make wax models of the severed heads of prominent victims of the guillotine, some of whom she had known personally. After fleeing the country she attracted wide attention for her display of lifesized likenesses of famous figures. Madame Tussaud's sons continued the business after her death and moved it to the present Baker Street site in 1884 (▷ 217).

NEWGATE'S DREADFUL WALLS

Newgate prison was the most famous and dreaded in the country, originally established in the city's west gatehouse in the 12th century. Charles Dickens wrote of 'Those dreadful walls of Newgate, which have hidden so much misery and such unspeakable anguish.' New arrivals were liable to be robbed of everything they had, including clothes, and were bullied by both seasoned inmates and prison officials. Occasionally rich prisoners could buy special treatment and live quite comfortably in an airy room, playing skittles or tennis and drinking in one of the taverns inside the walls. Most prisoners, however, endured grim cells, dirt, lice and vermin, an appalling stench and dreadful food. The prison was demolished in 1902.

THE MUDLARKS

Mudlarks were scavengers who lived by scouring the Thames shore after the tide had gone down to pick up any articles they could sell. They sometimes waded up to their waists in thick, greasy mud, mixed with a nauseating combination of raw sewage and the occasional dead animal. They ranged from small children to bent old women in clothes so tattered and filthy they were scarcely even rags. Most lived near the river and would come out soon after low tide and wait for the chance to scrabble about among barges and boats on the shore. They gathered pieces of coal, wood, rope or iron, bones, tools and copper nails, which were particularly valuable. Coal would be sold to their neighbours and other finds to the local rag-and-bone shops.

As the Great Exhibition of 1851 in Hyde Park displayed Britain to the world in the world's largest city, vigorous reform was under way. From the 1860s the Peabody Trust built new housing for the poor; in the 1870s slums were cleared to make way for Shaftesbury Avenue and Charing Cross Road, philanthropist Thomas Barnardo (1845–1905) opened his first homes for destitute children and the London School Board set out to give every London child an elementary education.

The population rose steeply, hitting 4 million by the end of the century. In the City and central districts, however, numbers fell as cheap transport allowed people to live farther from their places of work. With the introduction of underground trains and trams, London spread over yet more of the surrounding country, swallowing Hammersmith, Putney, Clapham, Stratford, Tottenham and Hornsey. London County Council was founded in 1888 to run an area of well over 260sq km (100sq miles). By the end of the century electricity lit the streets and new department stores were attracting custom, including Harrods (▷ 233) and Liberty (▷ 155–156).

Clockwise from above *The Great Exhibition of 1851 showcased industrial enterprise worldwide; Big Ben takes its nickname from the huge bell that chimes the hour; an 1880s photograph of Ludgate Hill looking down to St. Paul's Cathedral*

THE GREAT STINK

The Thames in 1858 was an open sewer for all the filth of London. That year's hot summer created a stench so horrific that it was dubbed the Great Stink. Noxious fumes penetrated the Houses of Parliament—and consequently something was done. Sir Joseph Bazalgette (1819–91), chief engineer of the new Metropolitan Board of Works, built 800km (500 miles) of main sewers and 21,000km (13,000 miles) of lesser drains, superbly constructed in brick and still working today. The Victoria Embankment (▷ 147) was built along the north bank of the river with a massive sewer inside as well as a tunnel for the new underground trains. On top were gardens and a new road to relieve London's traffic congestion. It was an engineering feat of genius and earned Bazalgette a knighthood.

JACK THE RIPPER

To this day no one knows the identity of the killer who stalked the cobbled, gas-lit alleys of Whitechapel in 1888, killing prostitutes. The body of Mary Anne Nicholls, the first undoubted victim of the Whitechapel Murderer—as he was known at first—was discovered in Durward Street, with her throat cut, and horribly mutilated. Four more victims were found over the following weeks. The murders caused a sensation in the press, especially when mocking letters signed 'Jack the Ripper' were sent to the police. The police's failure to catch the Ripper led to the resignation of the London Police Commissioner. Suspects have ranged from a deranged policeman to a Russian spy.

THE DIAMOND JUBILEE

Queen Victoria's 60 years on the throne were honoured in 1897 in a spectacular celebration of the British Empire. The little figure in black widow's dress was cheered by huge crowds lining the streets to see her driven in her state landau to a brief thanksgiving service on the steps of St. Paul's Cathedral. The sun blazed down on soldiers in glittering array from every corner of the globe—cavalry from India and Australia, Gurkhas and Sikhs, Africans, Chinese, and Dyaks from Borneo. Governors General of the colonies had a prominent place and were joined by foreign royalty and statesmen, but the main plaudits were for 'the Widow at Windsor', who could not restrain her tears.

BIG BEN

Edmund Beckett Denison, later Lord Grimthorpe (1816–1905), was one of the top barristers of his day. Savagely aggressive and sarcastic, he also knew more about clockmaking than anyone in the country. It was Denison who designed the 5-tonne timepiece in the new clock tower of the Houses of Parliament (▷ 179–180), equipped with its own revolutionary gravity escapement and a giant bell weighing more than 13 tonnes. The clock, nicknamed Big Ben, began operation in 1859. Denison was a difficult character and engaged in prolonged controversy with the architect of the Houses of Parliament, Sir Charles Barry (1795–1860), but his clock keeps excellent time to this day, and its chime is one of London's most familiar and evocative sounds.

ON THE FIRST TUBE

The world's first underground trains began running in 1863 on a line nicknamed 'the Drain', 6km (4 miles) long, between Paddington, Euston, King's Cross and Farringdon Street stations. The steam-powered trains caught on at once. Despite the smoke, grime and smell, Victorian gentlemen in stove-pipe hats rode them with perfect equanimity. The dark green carriages were well lit, trains ran every 10 minutes at peak times and tickets cost from three pence to six pence, depending on class of travel. Almost 10 million journeys were made in the railway's first year. More lines soon opened and in 1890 electric trains appeared in the City, on the first line to be called 'the Tube'. Nearly 150 years after the first Tube, the first air-conditioned carriages are about to enter service.

The London of 1900 was the capital of the largest empire the world had ever known. Suburban sprawl continued and by 1939 the population was 9 million. The Greater London Council was responsible for an area of 1,550sq km (600sq miles) from 1965 until its abolition in 1986, which left no central London authority. Motor cars and buses replaced horses and hansom cabs, though the average speed of travel in London in 1999 was no faster than in 1899. Damage in World War I was slight, but in World War II the winter Blitz of 1940–41 killed 20,000 people. Later, many more deaths were caused by flying bombs and rockets. Some underground stations served as air-raid shelters, where Londoners bedded down on the platforms.

The war was followed by exhaustion, austerity and the collapse of the London docks. Immigration was encouraged to fill the shortage of workers, and new arrivals from the West Indies, Pakistan and Bangladesh added to London's cultural mix. With recovering affluence in the 1960s came the youth culture of coffee bars, boutiques and 'swinging London'. Skyscrapers changed the skyline, while planners and architects replaced houses with concrete tower blocks.

Clockwise from above *The 1951 Festival of Britain; before the Clean Air Act people regularly resorted to masks to protect themselves from pollution in London's dense fogs; poppies are left round the Tomb of the Unknown Soldier in Westminster Abbey on Remembrance Day*

THE UNKNOWN SOLDIER

Garlanded with red poppies and set in the floor near Westminster Abbey's (▷ 194–195) west door is the Tomb of the Unknown Soldier. It contains the remains of a soldier selected at random from among those killed but never identified on the Western Front in World War I. He was reburied in the abbey on Armistice Day in 1920 as a memorial to a lost generation, lying in a coffin of British oak and interred in earth brought from France under a slab of marble from Belgium. The ceremony took place in the presence of King George V and many heads of state and military leaders, with a guard of honour formed by 100 holders of the Victoria Cross. Nearby is the Congressional Medal of Honor, conferred by the United States.

THE CAFÉ DE PARIS BOMB

The Café de Paris in Coventry Street was a well-known nightclub in the heart of the West End. One March night in 1941 customers were dining and dancing in the basement, advertised as 'the safest place to dance in town', when there was a blinding flash as two high-explosive bombs fell on the cinema above. The band leader Ken 'Snakehips' Johnson and some of his musicians were killed, as were entire parties seated at some tables. Survivors staggered up into the night, in shock, bleeding and covered with dust. Some of the first on the scene were looters, stealing wallets and wrenching rings off dead and dying fingers. In all, 34 bodies were eventually brought out.

THE FESTIVAL OF BRITAIN

A century after the Great Exhibition of 1851, the Festival of Britain was held to boost national morale after the war. In London it centred on a site on the South Bank, where 11ha (27 acres) of bomb-blasted Victorian buildings were cleared. The story of Britain's past was told, but the emphasis was on science, technology and the future. In the five months it lasted, 8.5 million people went to admire the futuristic Skylon sculpture and investigate the Dome of Discovery, the Design Review Pavilion, the 3-D polaroid cinema, the crazy Emmet railway and the new Royal Festival Hall (⊳ 87), as well as Battersea Park (⊳ 211). The festival's permanent legacy was the Southbank Centre (⊳ 79).

A CLEANER CITY

The 1956 Clean Air Act, which prohibited coal fires in central London, finally put an end to the city's famous fogs, which would cloak the whole town in thick, impenetrable, clammy mist. On the streets in a fearsome four-day 'pea-souper' smog in December 1952 it was hardly possible to see beyond the end of your outstretched arm. Traffic was brought to a virtual standstill and several people died of aggravated chest and lung complaints. In 1957 there were no fish in the Thames between Richmond and Tilbury. A campaign began to clean up the river, and was so effective that to general astonishment a salmon was caught in the Thames in 1974. Litter, however, remains a problem, and many visitors are quite shocked by the volume of discarded fast food wrappers and plastic bottles on the streets, as well as the free newspapers left on public transport.

MILLENNIUM PROJECTS

London reached the end of the 20th century in a blaze of activity, much of it focused around the Thames. Some projects were huge successes, while others struggled to achieve popularity. Firmly in the latter category was the Millennium Dome, a tent-like arena that hosted a short-lived exhibition, only to fall into disuse for several years. The Millennium Bridge (⊳ 77), which provides a new means for pedestrians to get from St. Paul's to the South Bank, wobbled when it first opened, but was eventually fixed. At the southern end of the bridge, the disused Bankside power station was converted into the magnificent Tate Modern (⊳ 80–81), which immediately pulled in huge crowds of awestruck art-lovers. Topping even Tate Modern in popularity was the London Eye (⊳ 75), a giant sightseeing wheel offering fabulous views over the city.

London hardly had time to draw breath after the excitement of the city's Millennium festivities before preparations for celebrating the Queen's Golden Jubilee (▷ 18) got under way. The city was host to another display of royal pageantry in the same year, when the Queen Mother died at the age of 101. Her ceremonial funeral was held in the majestic setting of Westminster Abbey.

Above *No. 30 St. Mary Axe, popularly known as 'the Gherkin', was opened in 2004 on the site of the old Baltic Exchange and is one of London's most distinctive skyscrapers*

A NAIL-BITING FINISH

In July 2005 the International Olympic Committee finally announced the winner of the race to host the 2012 Olympic Games. After a nail-biting 18-month race for the nomination, London won a two-way fight with Paris at the IOC meeting in Singapore, after bids from Moscow, New York and Madrid had been eliminated. The bid's chairman, Sebastian Coe, himself the winner of four Olympic medals, received a great deal of credit for the way he led London's bid.

It will be the first time the Olympics have been held in London since 1948, and the news was greeted with delight.

A DEFIANT CITY

London was brought crashing down to earth from its Olympic success by two waves of terrorist attacks. On 7 July 2005 four suicide bombers struck in central London in the morning rush hour, targeting Underground trains and a bus, and killing 52 people and injuring many more. Two weeks later, people were shocked by news of four attempted attacks, although this time no bombs exploded.

In the days and weeks that followed Londoners adapted to the disruptions to the transport system and heightened security measures. Many thought they saw a revival of the 'Blitz spirit' that prevailed in the city during World War II (▷ 38).

COUNTDOWN TO 2012

It wasn't only in Trafalgar Square that news of London's successful Olympic bid was greeted with jubilation. In Stratford, in east London, one of the most deprived areas in the UK, the news was also a cause of celebration. London's plans focus on transforming a 200ha (500-acre) swathe of land in the area into a futuristic Olympic Park, 10km (six miles) from Trafalgar Square. It will include an 80,000-seat athletics stadium, an aquatics centre, a velodrome, a BMX track and a hockey centre, as well as an athletes' village.

A number of existing venues will also be used for Olympic events, including the new stadium at Wembley (▷ 17) for soccer, Wimbledon for tennis and Lord's cricket ground for archery. Even the unloved Millennium Dome has been given a new lease of life as the O2 Arena, and will host the gymnastics and basketball competitions.

Construction of the Olympic Park will also involve huge investment in public transport. New track for the Channel Tunnel Rail Link, opened in November 2007, allowing central London to be reached from the Olympic Park in just seven minutes, and Heathrow airport's Terminal Five opened in 2008 at a cost of £4 billion. Progress on the various 2012 projects continues apace, despite the UK economy being among those worst affected by the global financial crisis.

ON THE MOVE

On the Move gives you detailed advice and information about the various options for travelling to London, before explaining the best ways to get you around the city once you are there. Handy tips help you with everything from buying tickets to renting a car.

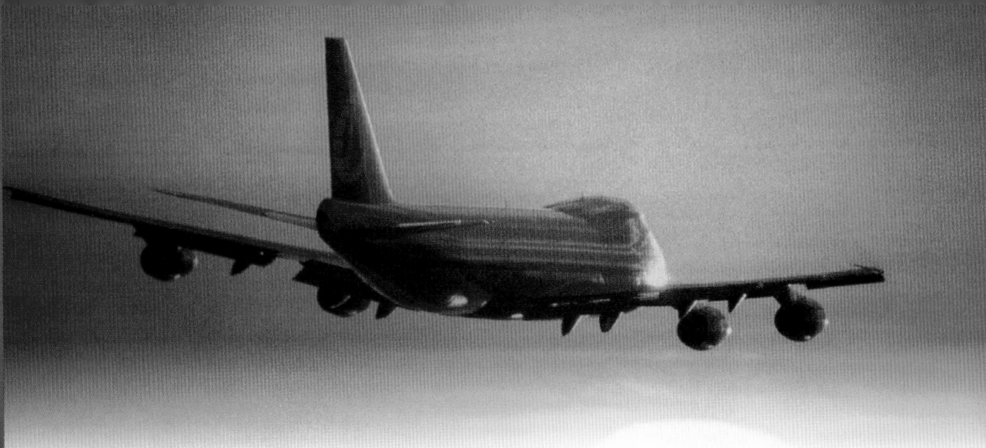

ARRIVING BY AIR

This is how most visitors enter the UK. London has air connections to all major world cities. If you are coming from another continent you will almost certainly arrive at either Heathrow, London's biggest airport and one of the busiest in the world, or at Gatwick, which is considerably farther away but the next in size. London's three other airports, Stansted, Luton and London City, serve mainly short-haul destinations. For security reasons there are no luggage lockers at any of the airports.

London Heathrow (LHR), is 19km (12 miles) to the west of central London.

There are five terminals: Terminals 1, 2 and 3 are located in the main central terminal complex; Terminal 4 is on the south side of the airport; Terminal 5 is to the west. Check which terminal you need at www.heathrowairport.com.

» **Terminal 1** serves BMI, Air New Zealand, South African Airways, Aer Lingus, Cyprus Airways, Transacro Airlines, Icelandair, Asiana Airlines, El Al, LOT, US Airways and United Airlines.

» **Terminal 2** serves most European airlines and some carriers from other continents.

» **Terminal 3** serves most long-haul flights from outside Europe.

» **Terminal 4** serves Qantas, several US carriers, a handful of other airlines and a few British Airways flights.

» **Terminal 5** is used exclusively by British Airways and serves more than 90 per cent of their flights.

All five terminals are linked to the London Underground, reached by well-signposted moving walkways and elevators. One station serves

GETTING TO CENTRAL LONDON FROM THE AIRPORT

AIRPORT (CODE)	HEATHROW (LHR)	GATWICK (LGW)
TAXI	£45–£70. 40 min–1 hour	£77. 1 hour 10 min
OVERLAND TRAIN	Heathrow Express to Paddington. Every 15 min 5.10am–11.25pm 365 days a year. £16.50 single, £32 return. Journey time: 15–20 min. Heathrow Connect to Paddington. Every 30 min 4.42am–11.08pm. Stops at 6 stations. £4.90–£7.40. Journey time: 25 min.	Gatwick Express to Victoria. Every 15 min 5am–12.35am, last train 1.35am, first train 4.30am. £16.90 one way, £28.80 return (under 16s £14.40). Journey time: 30 min. Southern trains to Victoria take slightly longer for £10.90 one way. First Capital Connect to London Bridge (£8.90), every 15 min, journey time 30 min, or to St. Pancras International.
TUBE (UNDERGROUND)	Piccadilly Line from Terminals 1, 2 and 3, Terminal 4 or Terminal 5 stations. Runs 5.15am–11.45pm daily. £4 adult/£2 child. Tickets available in all baggage reclaim areas. Journey time: 50 min.	N/A
BUS	National Express to Victoria Coach Station. Every 15–30 min. £10 one way. Journey time: 40 min–1 hour.	National Express from North and South Terminals to Victoria Coach Station. £6.60 one way. Every hour. EasyBus to Fulham Broadway station. From £2 one way online, £6 cash. Journey time: 1 hour 20 min.
CAR	Terminals 1, 2 and 3: junction 4, M4. Terminal 4: M4 junction 3. Travel eastbound along M4. Terminal 5: M25 junction 14.	Junction 9, M23. Travel northbound along M23.

Terminals 1, 2 and 3, while Terminals 4 and 5 each have their own station. American Airlines, BA and United Airlines now have check-in facilities at Paddington station. Passengers with connecting flights should follow the signs.

London Gatwick (LGW) is 48km (30 miles) to the south of central London. It has two terminals, North and South, linked by the Gatwick Transit, an efficient and free monorail. Trains run every three to four minutes from each terminal, with a journey time of just under two minutes. The South Terminal handles the bulk of Gatwick's traffic, serving domestic, international and charter flights. BA and American Airlines passengers can check luggage in at Victoria station, central London, which saves time at the airport.

London Stansted (STN), third in size, is 56km (35 miles) northeast of London, in Essex. The passenger terminal occupies a modern glass and steel building (1991) designed by British architect Sir Norman Foster. Driverless rapid transit trains shuttle between this and the airport's other two buildings. Stansted is London's fastest-growing airport.

London Luton (LTN) is 52km (32 miles) north of central London. A new passenger terminal opened in 1999, along with Luton Parkway railway station, from which there are frequent trains to King's Cross. It serves mainly low-cost charter flights, but some scheduled services operate from here.

London City Airport (LCA) is the capital's smallest airport, 10km (6 miles) from central London. Much used by business travellers, the airport has facilities such as meeting rooms and full secretarial services. The airport now has improved eating and shopping opportunities. Flights operate to over 30 European destinations and several British airports. Check-in time is only 20 minutes before departure. Expected growth at this airport will see passenger numbers rising up to 3.9 million a year by 2010.

On arrival, you have several choices of transport to central London. The table below compares the methods of transport from each of the airports, with costs, journey times and frequency.

TIPS

» When departing from Heathrow or Gatwick, check which terminal you will need, as it is cumbersome to move between them—particularly at Heathrow.

» Note that there are no black taxi cabs at Stansted.

STANSTED (STN)	LUTON (LTN)	CITY (LCA)
£99. 1–2 hours	£60–£65. 1 hour 45 min	£25. 20–30 min
Stansted Express to Liverpool Street (Central line). Change at Tottenham Hale for the Victoria line. Runs 5.30am–midnight. Every 15 min. £18 one way, £26.80 return (child £13.40). Journey time: 45 min.	Free shuttle bus from terminal to Luton Airport Parkway station (8 min). First Capital Connect services to St. Pancras International, City, Blackfriars and London Bridge. Every 15 min 7am–10pm. £11.50 one way. Journey time: 35 min.	London City Airport DLR station (known as the King George V extension). Trains run every few min 5am–12.30am (www.tfl.gov.uk for timetable and prices). Journey time: 22 min from Bank Station.
N/A	N/A	N/A
National Express A6 to Victoria Coach Station. Every 15 min. £10.50 one way (child £7.50). EasyBus to Victoria. From £2 online, £6 cash. Every 20 min. Journey time: 1 hour 30 min.	Greenline Bus No. 757 to Victoria Coach Station. Every 30 min peak, every hour off-peak. £11 one way (child £5.50, £1 off-peak). EasyBus to Victoria (as from Gatwick). Journey time: 1 hour 30 min.	N/A
Junction 8, M11. Travel southbound along M11.	2 miles (3km) from junction 10, M1. Travel southbound along M1.	N/A

ARRIVING BY TRAIN

Eurostar, the company that operates the Channel Tunnel rail service, links France (Paris and Lille) and Belgium (Brussels) directly to London in less than three hours. Since 2007, Eurostar's high-speed trains arrive in the state-of-the-art transport and retail complex at St. Pancras International station, which boasts Europe's longest champagne bar, a fresh daily farmers' market and world-class brasserie. Look for the 30ft (9m) high evocative statue *The Meeting Place* by artist Paul Day. The station is connected to King's Cross St. Pancras Underground station, which is served by the Northern, Victoria, Circle, Metropolitan and Hammersmith & City lines.

Passports are required for travel and you must check in at least 30 minutes before the train is due to depart. Only one item of hand luggage and two suitcases are allowed per person. Bear in mind that Eurostar trains are long, and it can be quite a walk down the platform to find your carriage.

On arrival you must clear passport control and customs. The Underground and buses are clearly marked or you can take a taxi from the rank immediately outside the station.

National trains arrive from other parts of Britain into one of London's 11 main railway stations (▷ 62). All stations have Underground links.

ARRIVING BY CAR

Eurotunnel operates the train service for cars, caravans and motorcycles through the Channel Tunnel. The journey between Calais and Folkestone takes 20 minutes, during which time drivers and passengers remain in their vehicles.

Upon arrival at Folkestone in the UK leave the terminal on the M20 motorway northbound, joining at junction 11a. Traffic permitting, the drive to London takes just over one hour.

ARRIVING BY FERRY

Eurostar and Eurotunnel have taken a lot of traffic away but taking a ferry can still be a cheaper way of crossing the Channel. Various ferry companies operate services between British ports and ports on the European continent. Trains run from ports on the south coast—Dover, Folkestone, Ramsgate, Newhaven, Portsmouth and Poole—to various London stations and from Harwich on the east coast to London Liverpool Street.

ARRIVING BY COACH

If you travel to London by long-distance coach you will probably arrive at Victoria Coach Station (VCS) on Buckingham Palace Road, near Victoria main railway station. The coach station is a few minutes' walk from the Underground station, which is on the Victoria, District and Circle lines. Alternatively, there is a taxi rank immediately outside the coach station.

USEFUL TELEPHONE NUMBERS AND WEBSITES

AIRPORTS

HEATHROW: tel 0870 000 0123, www.heathrowairport.com
- Lost Property: tel 020 8745 7727 (8am–4pm)
- Left Luggage: tel 020 8747 4599. Offices can forward luggage
- Train: Heathrow Express tel 0845 600 1515, www.heathrowexpress.com
- Bus: tel 08705 808080, www.nationalexpress.com
- Taxi: Terminal 1 tel 020 8745 7487. Terminal 2 tel 020 8745 5408. Terminal 3 tel 020 8745 4655. Terminal 4 tel 020 8745 7302

GATWICK: tel 0870 000 2468, www.gatwickairport.com
- Lost Property: tel 01293 503162
- Left Luggage: South Terminal tel 01293 502014, 24 hours. North Terminal tel 01293 502013.
- Trains: The Gatwick Express tel 0845 850 1530, www.gatwickexpress.com. First Capital Connect tel 0845 700 0125, www.firstcapitalconnect.co.uk Southern Railways tel 0845 127 2920
- Bus: tel 08705 808080, www.nationalexpress.com, www.easybus.co.uk
- Taxi: Checker Cars tel 0800 747737 or 01293 567700

STANSTED: tel 0870 000 0303, www.stanstedairport.com
- Lost Property: Items lost in the airport tel 01279 663293
- Left Luggage: tel 01279 663213
- Trains: The Stansted Express tel 0845 600 7245, www.stanstedexpress.com
- Bus: A6 tel 0870 580 8080, www.nationalexpress.com
- Taxi: Checker Cars tel 01279 661111

LUTON: tel 01582 405100, www.london-luton.co.uk
- Lost Property: tel 01582 395219
- Left Luggage: tel 01582 405100
- Trains: First Capital Connect tel 0845 700 0125, www.firstcapitalconnect.co.uk
- Bus: Greenline tel 0844 801 7261, www.greenline.co.uk
- Taxi: Cabco tel 01582 737777. Alpha Taxis tel 01582 595499. Taxi rank outside terminal building

LONDON CITY: tel 020 7646 0088, www.londoncityairport.com
- Lost Property: tel 020 7646 0088
- Left Luggage: tel 020 7646 0088
- Trains: tel 020 7646 0088
- Taxi: Taxi rank outside terminal building

GENERAL AIRPORT INFORMATION:
- www.worldairportguide.com

COACH AND TRAIN
- Coach Tourism Council: www.coachtourismcouncil.co.uk
- Eurolines: tel 08705 143219, www.eurolines.com
- Eurostar: UK tel 0870 518 6186. From outside UK tel 0044 1233 617575, www.eurostar.com
- Eurotunnel: tel 08705 353535, www.eurotunnel.com
- National Express: tel 0870 580 8080, www.nationalexpress.com
- National Rail enquiries: tel 0845 748 4950
- Victoria Coach Station: tel 020 7730 3466

LONDON TRANSPORT

London is a large city and at some stage you are bound to need to use its extensive public transport system, run by London Regional Transport (LRT). The Underground (Tube), buses and overground trains principally make up the network, with the Docklands Light Railway (DLR), riverboats and Tramlink as additional options.

Of the two main choices, Underground or bus, the Underground is certainly the quickest way to get around, but it is not always satisfactory and you will have to be patient at least once during your visit as a train is delayed or grinds to a halt for no apparent reason. It can also be very uncomfortable, hot and claustrophobic, involving long walks, escalators and staircases. Buses, on the other hand, offer views and a chance to get to grips with the geography of London.

Taxis are useful for short distances, but longer journeys are expensive.

For train travel and coach (long-distance bus) information, ▷ 61–63.

TRAVEL INFORMATION

» The main London Transport Information Centre, at Piccadilly Circus Underground station, is open Mon–Sat 7.30–9, Sun 8.15–8 and supplies free route maps and schedules as well as information brochures in several languages.

You can also phone for around-the-clock information (tel 020 7222 1234).

» Other travel information offices can be found at Heathrow Airport (Terminals 1, 2 and 3), Euston and Liverpool Street Underground stations and Victoria train and coach stations.

CHILDREN AND PUBLIC TRANSPORT

» Accompanied children under the age of five are travel free on all Underground and DLR services.

» All children under the age of 14 travel free on the buses and trams.

» Pushchairs (strollers) may need to be folded and placed in the storage areas on buses.

» Child fares apply to children aged 5 to 15.

» Children aged 14 or 15 need a child photocard to buy and use any child fare ticket or travel card. These are available from all Underground stations or London Transport Information Centres.

» Reduced rates for older children on the buses and children over 5 on the Underground apply with the Oyster Card (▷ 48).

DISCOUNTS

» Various reductions are available on weekly and monthly travelcards.

» Free travel for people over the age of 60 is available to London residents only with a Freedom Pass.

TICKETS

» You can buy tickets for all forms of public transport at most Underground stations, London Travel Information Centres and national rail stations, and at around 2,500 local ticket outlets, including many newsagents.

» If you know where you want to travel, use the ticket machines. Change is given. Touch-screen ticket machines at Underground stations also accept Electron and Solo cards.

» Ticket offices at Underground stations do close occasionally.

» One-day tickets can be bought four days in advance; try to order and collect tickets outside morning or evening rush hour.

» Underground stations and London Travel Information Centres accept personal cheques, supported by a cheque guarantee card, and credit cards.

» Monthly Oyster Travelcards are available through Ticketline (www.ticket-on-line.co.uk or www.ticket-on-line.com if you are buying tickets outside the UK).

» For further information on London fares, see the individual transport entries following or pick up a copy of the 'Fares and Tickets' leaflet from Underground stations and London Travel Information Centres.

TIPS

» If possible avoid travelling during the rush hour (weekdays 7.30 to 9.30am and 4.30 to 7pm). The Underground in particular gets extremely crowded and many buses are so full that waiting passengers are unable to board.

» Buy a Travelcard, which is valid for the entire transport network, or an Oyster Card if you don't require overground rail.

» Use common sense when travelling alone at night, but there is no need to be unduly concerned about the risk of mugging.

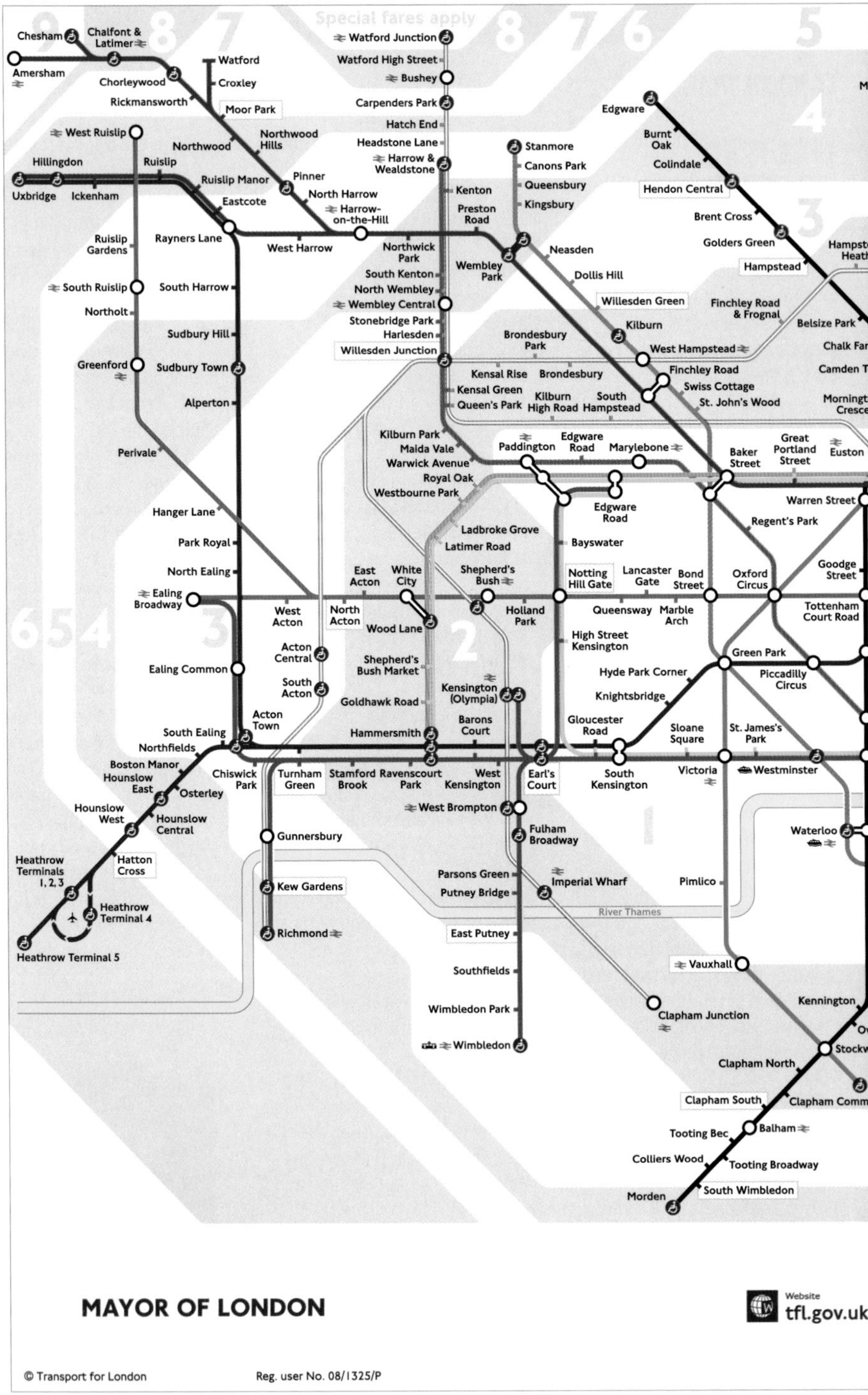
Special fares apply
9
8
7
6
5
4
3
2
1
654
3
Chesham
Chalfont & Latimer
Amersham
Chorleywood
Rickmansworth
Watford
Croxley
Moor Park
Watford Junction
Watford High Street
Bushey
Carpenders Park
Hatch End
Headstone Lane
Harrow & Wealdstone
Edgware
Burnt Oak
Colindale
Hendon Central
Brent Cross
Golders Green
Hampstead
Hampstead Heath
Stanmore
Canons Park
Queensbury
Kingsbury
West Ruislip
Northwood
Northwood Hills
Pinner
North Harrow
Harrow-on-the-Hill
Kenton
Preston Road
Hillingdon
Ruislip
Ruislip Manor
Eastcote
Uxbridge
Ickenham
Ruislip Gardens
Rayners Lane
West Harrow
Northwick Park
Wembley Park
Neasden
Dollis Hill
Willesden Green
Kilburn
West Hampstead
Finchley Road & Frognal
Belsize Park
Chalk Farm
Camden Town
South Ruislip
South Harrow
South Kenton
North Wembley
Wembley Central
Stonebridge Park
Harlesden
Willesden Junction
Northolt
Sudbury Hill
Greenford
Sudbury Town
Alperton
Brondesbury Park
Kensal Rise
Brondesbury
Kensal Green
Queen's Park
Kilburn High Road
South Hampstead
Finchley Road
Swiss Cottage
St. John's Wood
Mornington Crescent
Perivale
Kilburn Park
Maida Vale
Warwick Avenue
Royal Oak
Westbourne Park
Paddington
Edgware Road
Marylebone
Baker Street
Great Portland Street
Euston
Warren Street
Regent's Park
Edgware Road
Hanger Lane
Ladbroke Grove
Latimer Road
Bayswater
Park Royal
North Ealing
Ealing Broadway
East Acton
White City
Shepherd's Bush
Notting Hill Gate
Lancaster Gate
Bond Street
Oxford Circus
Goodge Street
Tottenham Court Road
West Acton
North Acton
Wood Lane
Holland Park
Queensway
Marble Arch
High Street Kensington
Green Park
Acton Central
South Acton
Shepherd's Bush Market
Goldhawk Road
Kensington (Olympia)
Hyde Park Corner
Piccadilly Circus
Knightsbridge
Ealing Common
Acton Town
South Ealing
Northfields
Hammersmith
Barons Court
Gloucester Road
Sloane Square
St. James's Park
Boston Manor
Hounslow East
Osterley
Chiswick Park
Turnham Green
Stamford Brook
Ravenscourt Park
West Kensington
Earl's Court
South Kensington
Victoria
Westminster
Hounslow West
Hounslow Central
West Brompton
Fulham Broadway
Waterloo
Gunnersbury
Heathrow Terminals 1, 2, 3
Hatton Cross
Heathrow Terminal 4
Heathrow Terminal 5
Kew Gardens
Richmond
Parsons Green
Putney Bridge
Imperial Wharf
Pimlico
River Thames
East Putney
Southfields
Wimbledon Park
Wimbledon
Vauxhall
Clapham Junction
Kennington
Oval
Stockwell
Clapham North
Clapham South
Clapham Common
Balham
Tooting Bec
Tooting Broadway
Colliers Wood
South Wimbledon
Morden
MAYOR OF LONDON
Website
tfl.gov.uk
© Transport for London
Reg. user No. 08/1325/P

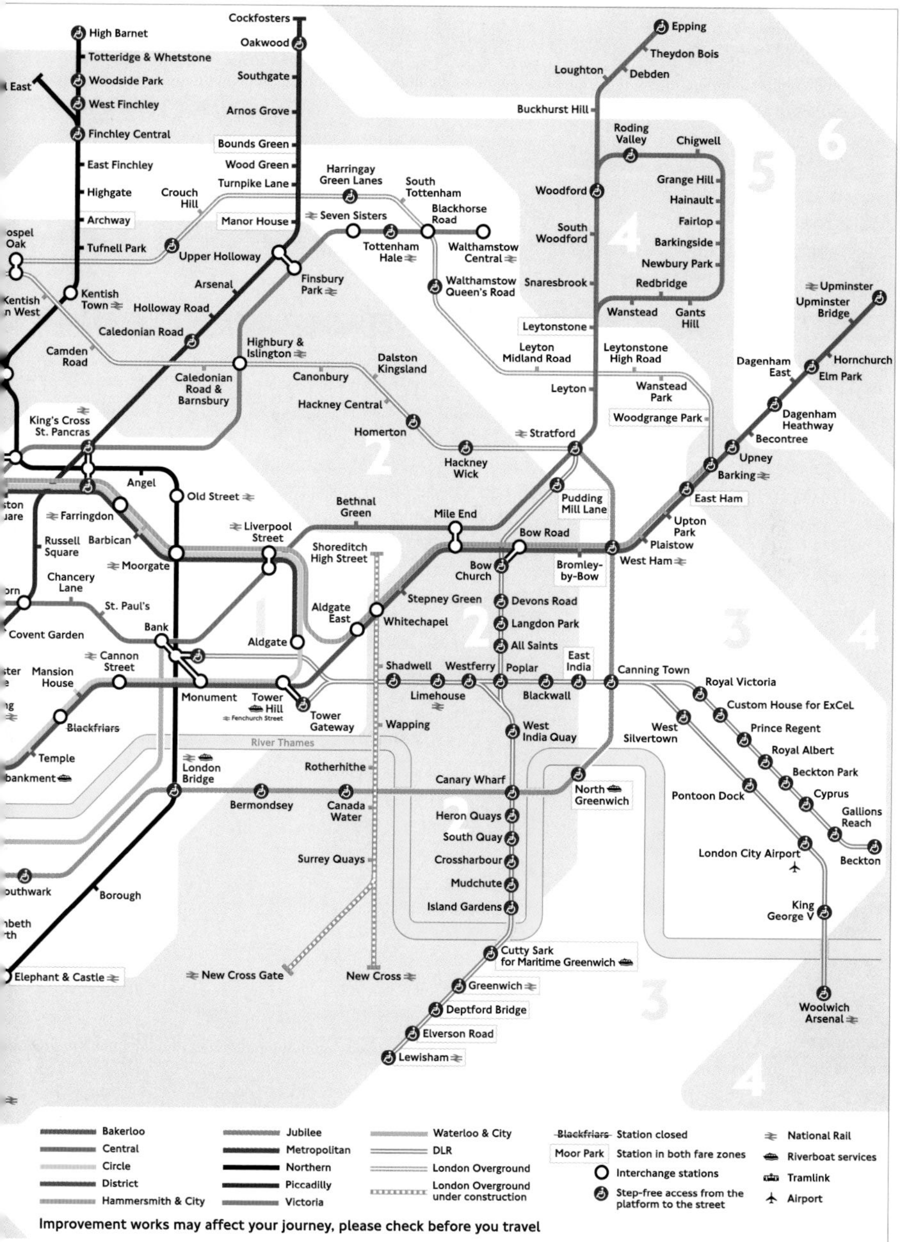

24 hour travel information 020 7222 1234

Transport for London UNDERGROUND

Version J TfL 12.09

Correct at time of going to print

TRAVELCARDS AND ZONES

» Travelcards are valid for the entire transport network in selected zones, including buses, Underground (Tube), Docklands Light Railway (DLR), Croydon Tramlink and suburban national rail services within the London area (excluding Heathrow Express).

» Travelcards give you unlimited travel within the zone area paid for, as well as one-third off most riverboat services. They are available from Underground stations, London Travel Information Centres, national rail stations (in the London area) and many newsagents across the capital. You can buy a Travelcard up to four days before you intend to use it.

» For the purposes of transport pricing the London area is divided into zones, central London occupying Zone 1 with Zones 2–6 following in a series of concentric rings (⊳ 46–47).

» The concept is simple. The more zones you want to travel in, the more you have to pay. Ensure that your ticket is valid for the zones that you travel in or through, or you may find yourself paying a fine.

TRAVELCARDS	VALID	ZONES AND PRICES	NOTES
1 Day Travelcard (Peak)	1am–4.30am the following day, Mon–Fri (except public holidays)	Zones 1 and 2: £7.20 adult, £3.60 child. Zones 1–4: £10 adult, £5 child. Zones 1–6: £14.80 adult, £7.40 child	If you are using only Underground, bus, Tramlink and DLR services, it is cheaper to use an Oyster Card
1 Day Travelcard (Off-Peak)	From 9.30am Mon–Fri and all day on Sat, Sun and public holidays until 4.30am the following day	Zones 1 and 2: £5.60 adult, £2 child (children must buy a Zone 1–6 ticket). Zones 1–4: £6.30 adult, £2 child. Zones 1–6: £7.50 adult, £2 child	If you are using only Underground, bus, Tramlink and DLR services, it is cheaper to use an Oyster Card
3 Day Travelcard (Peak)	1am–4.30am the following day, Mon–Fri (except public holidays)	Zones 1 and 2: £18.40 adult, £9.20 child. Zones 1–4: £42.40 adult, £21.20 child. Zone 1–6: £21.20 adult, £6 child. (Off-peak only available for zones 1–6)	
Oyster Card (a 'smartcard' that can store up to £90 pay as you go)	At all times. Underground trains run from approx 5.30am until 12.30am (time varies on the individual lines). Also for use on DLR, buses and trams	All zones and some national rail. A £3 refundable deposit is required on new cards. The £4 single journey in Zone 1 is £1.50 with an Oyster card. Other zones £1	Oyster Cards can be obtained online at www.tfl.gov.uk/oyster or at Underground stations and Oyster ticket shops. When making multiple journeys, the card caps payment at 50p less than the cost of a Travelcard
Weekly Travelcard	Valid, with a photocard only, for seven consecutive days and can be used at any time For travel on Underground, buses, Tramlink, DLR and most national rail services in the London area	Zones 1 and 2: £25.80 adult, £12.90 child. Zones 1–4: £36.80 adult, £18.40 child. Zones 1–6: £47.60 adult, £23.80 child	
Bus & Tram Pass	All-zone pass valid for one day, one week or longer	All zones.One day £3.80, one week £13.80. Children pay £1 per day if accompanied by an adult	

LONDON UNDERGROUND

London's Underground system is also known as the Tube. The earliest lines, dating from the mid-19th century, were constructed close to the surface using a technique known as 'cut and cover'; builders dug a trench, laid the tracks, then roofed over the trench and replaced the earth. The later, deeper lines were constructed using tunnel boring machines. These lines were called 'tubes', and the name stuck.

The London Underground system is the oldest and most extensive network of its kind in the world, with more than 500 trains and over 260 stations, and maintenance is an on-going challenge. Much of the track is old and subject to repairs, leading to breakdowns and delays. That said, the extended Jubilee line was opened in 1999, providing a state-of-the-art metro system between central and eastern London. It was Europe's biggest engineering project and the new stations built along the line are an attraction in their own right. Prominent architects were chosen to design the stations. Canary Wharf, for example, hailed as an 'underground cathedral', was designed by Sir Norman Foster.

Twelve lines make up the Greater London Underground system and each has its own name and is colour-coded on the Underground map (▷ 46–47. Stations with interchanges with other lines and with suburban rail are marked with a white circle on the map.

Trains run from approximately 5.30am Monday to Saturday (7am Sunday) to approximately midnight Monday to Saturday (11pm Sunday) every day except Christmas Day.

UNDERSTANDING THE UNDERGROUND MAP

TUBE STATION

A simple dash indicates a station with no interchanges

MAINLINE STATION

This symbol indicates a connection with a mainline station.

COLOUR-CODED LINES

Each line is colour-coded to make navigation easy.

STATION WITH INTERCHANGE

Interchanges with other lines and with suburban rail are marked with a white circle. Two white circles show more than one line interchange.

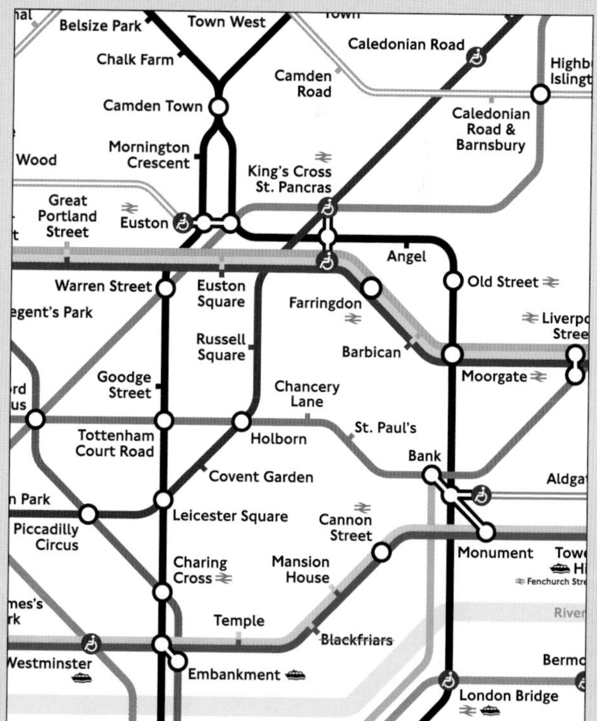

HOW TO USE THE UNDERGROUND

» Stand on the right on escalators so that people in a hurry can walk on the left.

» Be aware that if you cannot produce a valid ticket you will be given an on-the-spot fine of £10.

» Watch out for keys, security passes and some handbag clasps; they may cause magnetic interference and damage your ticket.

» If you are travelling with bulky items, pushchairs (strollers) or folding bicycles, use the special wide gates provided. Ask a member of staff to let you through.

» Stand clear of the train's closing doors. Obstructing them slows trains down and causes delays.

» Mind the gap between the platform and the train.

» Let passengers off the train first before embarking.

» Stand behind the yellow line on the platform when waiting for a train.

» Avoid taking too much luggage on the Underground. Storage space is limited, and there are no porters.

» Keep your bag with you at all times and report any unattended bags.

» Be prepared for heat in summer. There is no air-conditioning, and delays are not uncommon.

» Mobile phones are permitted, but don't expect to get a signal underground.

» Report threats and violent behaviour to members of staff.

» Watch out for pickpockets. Keep your bags securely fastened and don't carry valuables in back pockets or rucksacks. Keep an eye on your bags at all times.

TIPS

» Check the service update section of www.tfl.gov.uk to see if trains are running smoothly. A journey planner on the site helps you plan how to get from A to B in the easiest way.

» Also see www.tfl.gov.uk or tel 020 7222 1234 for up-to-date news and information. There are details on fares and tickets in 14 different languages.

» To avoid ending up at the wrong destination, be sure to check the indicator display on the platform and the front of the train displaying the final destination station.

» Pick up a pocket-size London Underground map, free at all Underground stations.

» Travel after 9.30am and at weekends for cheaper tickets.

» Buy tickets at the machines, or at a sales booth.

» Note that there are two types of machine. One has a few buttons for the most common fares (one destination, single or return ticket and travel cards), the other has lots of buttons, one for every station and ticket type.

» You will need your ticket to get out of the station, so don't throw it away.

Below *Central Underground stations are individually decorated, often with local themes, and frequently have street musicians playing*

A TYPICAL JOURNEY ON THE UNDERGROUND

SOUTH EALING

From South Ealing to Oxford Circus

Journey time: 42 min
Zones used: 1, 2, 3
Single fare: adult £4, child £2

Find a map and identify the colours of the lines you will need.

Buy a ticket for all the zones you will be travelling through.

Insert your ticket face upwards in the front of the machine at the gates. When it emerges from the top slot, take it out and the gates will open.

Follow signs for the **PICCADILLY LINE**, going down stairs or escalators where necessary.

Check the board between the two platforms and choose the platform for the train heading towards Green Park.

Wait for the **PICCADILLY LINE** train on the platform. The electronic display on the platform tells you when the train is due to arrive and where it terminates.

Get on the train heading for **COCKFOSTERS**, **ARNOS GROVE**, **OAKWOOD** or **KING'S CROSS ST. PANCRAS**. This information will be displayed on the electronic platform displays as the train arrives and on the front of the train.

Board the train quickly and carefully.

Track the number of stops until you need to change on the route map above the window in the train. On arrival at stations, announcements inform you of the connections available at each one. Stations are easily identified by the large Underground signs mounted on platforms and visible from inside the train. (34 min)

SOUTH EALING

Leave the train at **GREEN PARK**.
Change on to the **VICTORIA LINE**. Follow signs. (2 min)

Wait for the **VICTORIA LINE** train on the platform. (3 min)

Get on the train heading for **WALTHAMSTOW CENTRAL**, **SEVEN SISTERS** or **KING'S CROSS ST. PANCRAS**. (3 min)

OXFORD CIRCUS

Leave the train at **OXFORD CIRCUS**. When you complete your journey, your ticket will be retained in the machine at the exit.

Follow signs to the relevant exit for the street you want.

FARES

Fares for the Underground depend on the zones you wish to travel in. If you are travelling through many zones several times a day, consider purchasing a Travelcard or taking advantage of discounted fares (▷ 48). You will make substantial savings by purchasing an Oyster Card, which will also give savings for children. Child fares without any special discount tickets apply to children aged 5 to 15; children aged 14 or 15 require a photocard. Below are the full price fares without discounted special deals.

ZONES	ADULT (£)	CHILD (£)
Zone 1	4.00	2.00
Zones 2–6	3.20	1.60

BUSES

London's bright red double-decker buses, along with the black cabs (▷ 57), have become an icon. You cannot fail to notice them as you walk around the capital. Increasingly you will see other types of buses travelling around London as well. London bus routes run along most main roads in central London. For short journeys and if you are not in a hurry the buses can be a pleasant way of getting around. On longer journeys they are slower than trains or the Underground but they are always less expensive and quite comfortable.

» Daytime buses in London run Monday to Saturday from around 6am to midnight and Sunday from 7.30am to 11.30pm. In theory, buses run at least once every 10 to 15 minutes in each direction along the route, and much more frequently on heavily used routes. In practice, because of the traffic conditions, you can wait 30 minutes for a bus to arrive, and then three are likely to come along at once.

» Buses come in two styles, so-called Routemaster buses, with a conductor, and driver-only buses.

» Routemaster buses have been phased out and only the No. 9 and No. 15 remain on popular tourist routes. A conductor will sell you a ticket, and Travelcards are also valid.

» Driver-only buses have two doors: one at the front, where you board, and one midway, where you get off. Pay the driver when you board. You need to have change ready. Longer, 'bendy' buses operate on some routes.

» Drivers and conductors prefer the exact money, but they will give you change.

» On both types of bus you have to let the driver know you want to get off at a particular stop. Press the red button on a driver-only bus, or pull the cord at the side of the cabin on a Routemaster.

» Hold on to your ticket until the end of the journey, because inspectors regularly board the buses to check tickets and catch fare-dodgers.

TICKET OPTIONS

» The single adult cash bus fare in the whole of the London bus network is £2, or £1 with an Oyster Card.

» Children 5–13 go free on all buses. Children 14–15, and students up to 18, go free with an Oyster photocard.

» Remember that return fares are not available for bus services.

» On certain marked routes (including all 'bendy' buses) cash single fares are not available on the buses. If you do not hold a bus pass, an Oyster Card or a Travelcard, you must buy a cash single ticket or a one-day bus pass before boarding. Roadside ticket machines are located at all bus stops on routes where this system applies. Likewise, within Zone 1 you cannot pay cash on the bus.

» You can purchase day passes, priced at £3.80 for adults; children go free (14–18 only free with Oyster photocard). Week passes are £13.80 for adults, free for children (14–18 only free with Oyster photocard). However, these are not valid on the Underground.

» If you intend to use the Underground as well, you are better off buying an Underground travelcard or Oyster Card, as these are also valid on buses.

NIGHT BUSES

» Night buses (the number is preceded by 'N') run between 11pm and 6am on the main routes through London; the majority pass through Trafalgar Square.

» Night buses stop only at bus stops if requested.

» Fares are the same as daytime fares, except for children, who pay adult fares after 10pm.

TIP

» For advice on how to get around the city by bus, call London Transport or look online (tel 020 7222 1234, www.tfl.gov.uk).

UNDERSTANDING BUS STOPS

BUS NUMBERS

Each route is marked by a number on the front and the back of the bus corresponding to the numbers on the bus stops. The final destination of the bus is often displayed on the bus along with a brief list of the areas of London on the route.

TIMETABLES

Timetables can be found at bus stops either posted inside bus shelters or attached to individual bus stops. They show the first and last buses on the route you want and allow you to work out the frequency of the service, the times the bus will arrive at your stop and when it will reach the destination you require. The stop that you are standing at will be marked in bold on the timetable.

BUS STOP TYPES

- Bus stops are marked by a London Transport circular BUS STOP sign which has a line through the middle with either a white or red background.
- At main bus stops (signs show a red circle on a white background) you will find information on bus routes, route numbers and times. The bus will stop here automatically.
- At request stops (white circle on a red background) you must hail the bus.
- At night treat all stops as request stops.

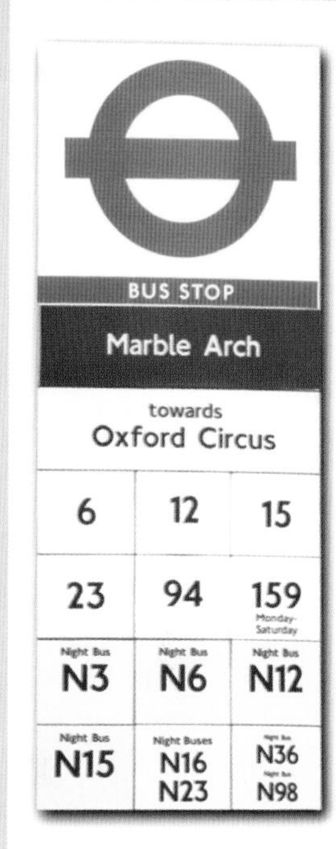

BUS STOP
Marble Arch
towards
Oxford Circus
6
12
15
23
94
159
Night Bus
N3
Night Bus
N6
Night Bus
N12
Night Bus
N15
Night Buses
N16
N23
N36
N98

MAIN VISITOR BUS ROUTES

Certain routes link key attractions or provide interesting views. Below are seven routes of particular interest.

BUS NO. 8

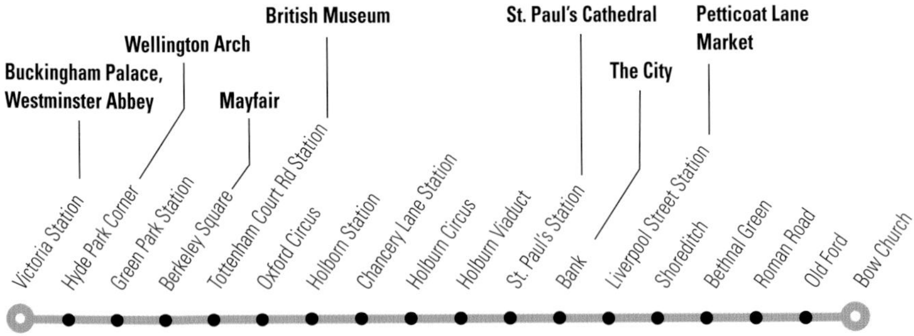
Buckingham Palace, Westminster Abbey
Wellington Arch
Mayfair
British Museum
St. Paul's Cathedral
The City
Petticoat Lane Market
Victoria Station
Hyde Park Corner
Green Park Station
Berkeley Square
Tottenham Court Rd Station
Oxford Circus
Holborn Station
Chancery Lane Station
Holburn Circus
Holburn Viaduct
St. Paul's Station
Bank
Liverpool Street Station
Shoreditch
Bethnal Green
Roman Road
Old Ford
Bow Church

BUS NO. 11

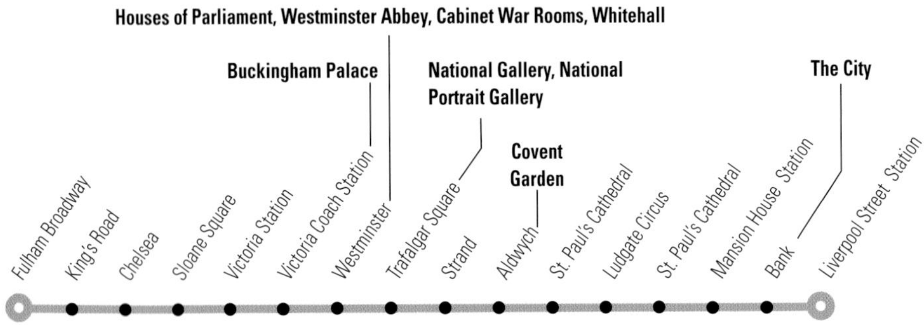
Houses of Parliament, Westminster Abbey, Cabinet War Rooms, Whitehall
Buckingham Palace
National Gallery, National Portrait Gallery
Covent Garden
The City
Fulham Broadway
King's Road
Chelsea
Sloane Square
Victoria Station
Victoria Coach Station
Westminster
Trafalgar Square
Strand
Aldwych
St. Paul's Cathedral
Ludgate Circus
St. Paul's Cathedral
Mansion House Station
Bank
Liverpool Street Station

BUS NO. 14

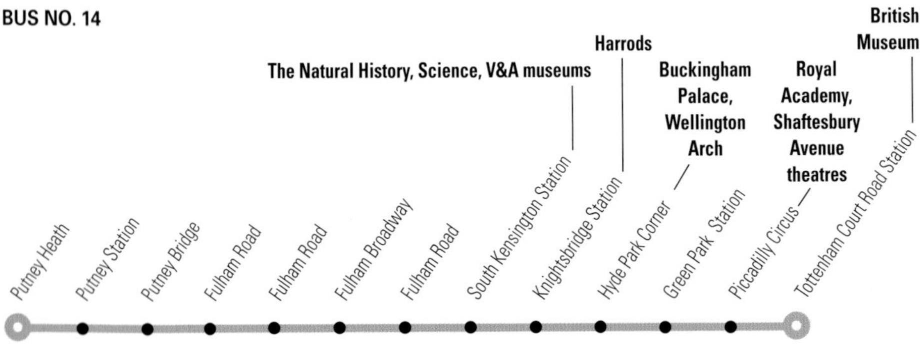
The Natural History, Science, V&A museums
Harrods
Buckingham Palace, Wellington Arch
Royal Academy, Shaftesbury Avenue theatres
British Museum
Putney Heath
Putney Station
Putney Bridge
Fulham Road
Fulham Road
Fulham Broadway
Fulham Road
South Kensington Station
Knightsbridge Station
Hyde Park Corner
Green Park Station
Piccadilly Circus
Tottenham Court Road Station

BUS NO. 15

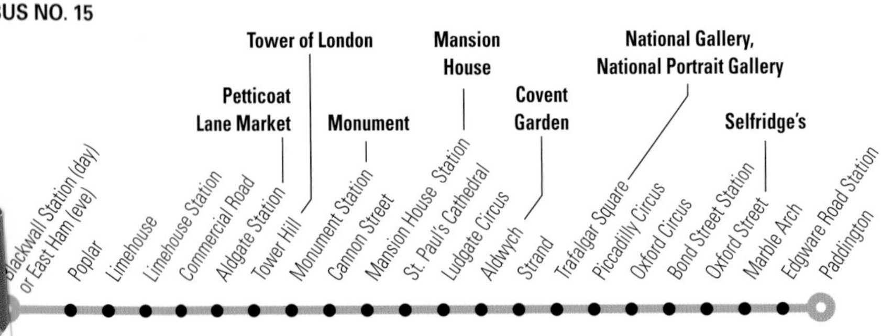
Petticoat Lane Market
Tower of London
Monument
Mansion House
Covent Garden
National Gallery, National Portrait Gallery
Selfridge's
Blackwall Station (day) or East Ham (eve)
Poplar
Limehouse
Limehouse Station
Commercial Road
Aldgate Station
Tower Hill
Monument Station
Cannon Street
Mansion House Station
St. Paul's Cathedral
Ludgate Circus
Aldwych
Strand
Trafalgar Square
Piccadilly Circus
Oxford Circus
Bond Street Station
Oxford Street
Marble Arch
Edgware Road Station
Paddington

BUS NO. 74

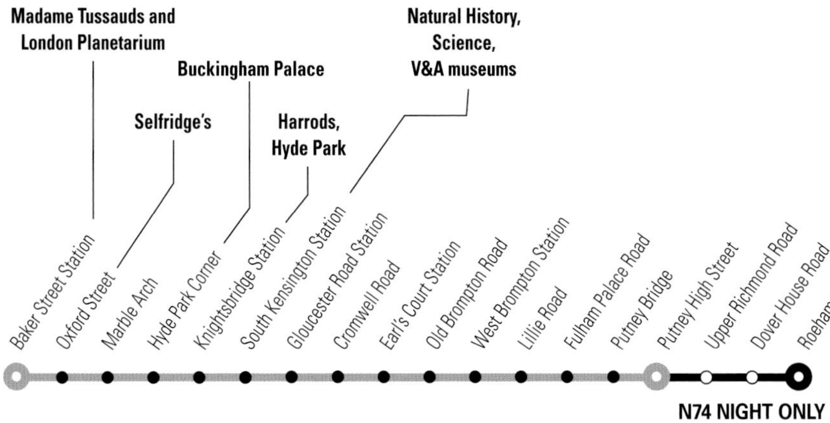

BUS NO. 188

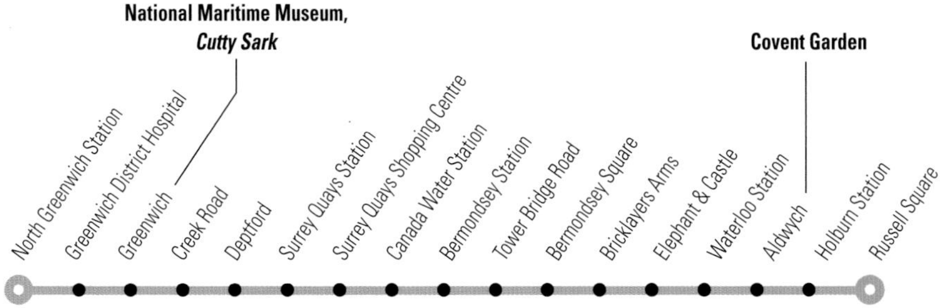

RV1 ROUTE

A bus service of particular interest to visitors is Riverside 1, which links the South Bank to the West End and the City. The route, aimed at boosting tourism, employment and accessibility for local communities, brings together more than 30 arts and visitor attractions, five Underground stations, three national rail stations and five river piers. The service runs from Tower Gateway past London Bridge station, Bankside and Waterloo station up to Covent Garden.

The buses, sporting the traditional red livery of London buses, carry a Riverside bus logo and a series of icons identifying the key destinations along the route. In addition, special information screens on board the bus alert passengers to approaching destinations and their attractions.

RV1 buses run daily every 10 minutes between 6am and midnight. On board, you can pick up a guide to local attractions.

For details visit www.southbank london.com/riverside.

BUS RV1

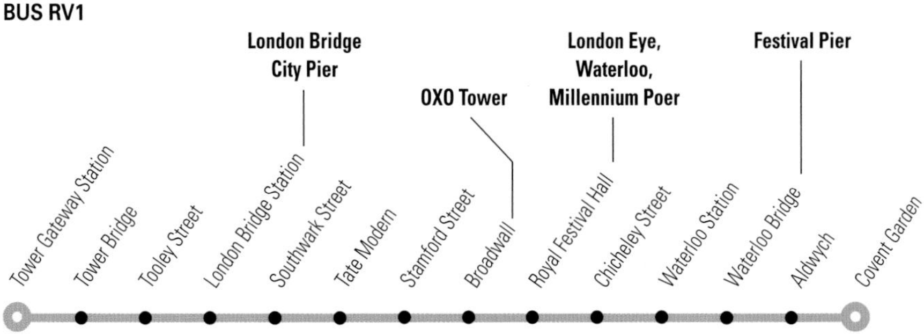

DLR AND RIVER BOATS

The Docklands Light Railway (DLR) and London's river transport network complement London's Underground and buses to provide an integrated public transport system.

DOCKLANDS LIGHT RAILWAY

» The computerized and driverless trains of the Docklands Light Railway (DLR) serve the Docklands area to the east of the City. For the most part they run on an elevated track, allowing panoramic views.
» The DLR is part of the Underground system, so Travelcards (▷ 48) may be used.
» From Bank or Tower Gateway station (near Tower Hill Underground station), the system runs south through the Isle of Dogs and Greenwich to Lewisham, north to Stratford, or east to Beckton and the King George V Docks (the station for London City airport).
» The DLR runs Monday to Friday 5.30am to 12.30am with a more limited service operating at the weekend.
» There is a 10 per cent discount for group single, return, One-Day Shuttle and Flyer tickets. They must be booked at least seven days in advance by calling DLR Customer Services (tel 020 7363 9700).
» For more information on the DLR contact DLR Customer Services or visit www.tfl.gov.uk.

LONDON RAIL AND RIVER ROVER TICKETS

» These allow you one full day unlimited hop-on hop-off travel on City Cruises River Boats and the Docklands Light Railway. It is possible to go by boat from Westminster to Greenwich, for example, and return on the DLR to Tower Hill.
» Tickets can be bought at all DLR stations except Bank and Canning Town: £13.50 for adults, £6.80 for ildren and £33 for a family. Group family tickets can be bought at a ount seven days in advance. r more information visit www. v.uk or tel 020 7363 9700.

RIVERBOATS

» Travelcard holders (▷ 48) receive a third-off discount on most riverboat services. Most services start and end at Westminster Pier, which is the midway point along the Thames.
» Boats operate from 6.30am to around 9pm but vary according to the route. The network extends from Hampton Court Palace (▷ 260–261) in the west to the Thames Barrier (▷ 263) in the east.
» You can travel on the river with a single, return or DLR River Rover ticket.
» There are ticket offices on the piers or on the boats themselves in some cases.
» Upriver, you can go from Westminster Millennium Pier to Hampton Court Pier via Kew and Richmond piers. This service operates, subject to tides, at 10.30am, 11am, noon and 2pm April to October. A round trip to Hampton Court can take between seven and eight hours. The last boat from Hampton Court is at 5pm. A single ticket is £13.50 and a return is £19.50. Children travel half price. For more information contact Westminster Passenger Services (tel 020 7930 2062).
» Downriver, you can go from Embankment Pier to Greenwich Pier via Waterloo Millennium Pier, Bankside Pier and Tower Pier. These services depart from Embankment every 30–45 minutes from 10am until 4.20pm. The last boat returns from Greenwich at 5.35pm. A return ticket costs between £4.90 and £9.80. Children (5–15) travel half price; under 5s free. Hopper passes cost £10.50 for adults, £5.25 for children. For more information contact Catamaran Cruisers (tel 020 7695 1800).

TRAMLINK

» Tramlink (www.tfl.gov.uk), the south London tram network, comprises three routes that run between the Wimbledon, Croydon, New Addington and Beckenham areas.
» Tickets must be bought before boarding at the automatic ticket machines at all Tramlink stops. Failure to do so could result in a £50 fine.
» See Travelcards and Zones (▷ 48) for more ticket information.

Below *A boat cruise passes the Thames Barrier*

TAXIS AND MINICABS

There are two types of taxi in London: black cabs and minicabs.

BLACK CABS

Like the buses, London's black cabs are world-famous. The black cabs' design remains distinctive despite the fact that cabs now have advertising and come in colours other than the traditional black. You can rely on a London cabbie (driver) to know where he's going. Drivers must be licensed and have to pass extensive exams, dubbed 'the Knowledge' (▷ 15), to demonstrate that they know the city well enough to take passengers anywhere in London following the most direct route.

» Cabs operate 24 hours a day, 365 days a year, but you will be hard pushed to find one on New Year's Eve, when the England football team is playing at home, or in a downpour when West End theatres and cinemas empty.

» Drivers must accept a fare of up to 19km (12 miles) in London, 32km (20 miles) if the journey is from Heathrow Airport, and journeys of up to one hour in Metropolitan and City districts. Although they may be willing, taxi drivers are not obliged to accept journeys outside this range. If they do accept, and the journey is wholly within the London area, the fare payable is shown on the meter.

» For more information on London taxis and charges, visit www.tfl.gov.uk.

TAXI FIRMS

Computer Cab: tel 020 7908 0207
Call-A-Cab: tel 020 8901 4444
Datacab: tel 020 7432 1540
Dial-A-Cab: tel 020 7253 5000
Lady Cabs: tel 020 7254 3501
Radio Taxi Cabs: tel 020 7272 0272

MINICABS

» These are saloon cars and must be booked by phone or from a minicab firm office. Do not hail a minicab in the streets, as drivers may be untrained or uninsured.

» Avoid taxi touts who operate at airports and stations as they overcharge and are even more likely to be unlicensed or uninsured. Take licensed black cabs from taxi ranks at airports and stations or ring a recommended minicab firm in advance to arrange for someone to pick you up.

TIPS

To get a cab:

» Hail one in the street. Only those with an illuminated TAXI sign are vacant and will stop.

» Go to a designated taxi rank, usually found outside railway stations and large hotels.

» Call London Black Cabs (tel 0871 871 8710), to book in advance. Booking charge.

CHARGES

» The cost of a cab journey is regulated through a metering system and is displayed inside the cab, at the front.

» Tariffs are calculated according to the distance you have travelled, unless the taxi speed drops below 10mph (16kph), when it is calculated per minute.

» Extra charges are made for telephone booking, travel during the Christmas and New Year period, and for additional luggage.

» It is common practice to tip 10–15 per cent of the total fare. Although this is not compulsory, drivers expect it.

Monday to Friday 6am to 8pm

£2.20 up to: 310.4m or 66.8 seconds. Then: additional 20p every 155.2m/33.4 seconds (up to £14.40)
Thereafter: additional 20p every 108.8m/23.4 seconds

Saturday and Sunday 6am to 8pm

£2.20 up to: 252m or 54.2 seconds. Then: additional 20p every 126m/27.1 seconds (up to £17.20)
Thereafter: additional 20p every 108.8m/23.4 seconds

Every night 8pm to 6am and all times on public holidays

£2.20 up to: 203.8m or 43.8 seconds. Then: additional 20p every 101.9m/21.9 seconds (up to £20.80)
Thereafter: additional 20p every 108.8m/23.4 seconds

Below *When the 'Taxi' sign is lit, the cab is available for hire*

DRIVING IN LONDON

A car can be a liability in London, and the best advice for anyone contemplating driving in the capital is simple: don't. Getting around will take you longer than travelling on public transport and parking is scarce and expensive. However, a car is one of the best ways of seeing the surrounding area and travelling farther afield. On the whole, motorists drive safely, roads are good and signposting very efficient.

THE LAW

» Traffic in the UK drives on the left.
» Wearing seat belts is obligatory, including those in the back if fitted.
» Motorcyclists must wear helmets.
» The speed limit in built-up areas is 30mph (48kph). Outside built-up areas it is 60mph (97kph) on single carriageways, and 70mph (113kph) on dual carriageways (two-lane highways) and motorways, unless a sign indicates otherwise.
» Do not drink any alcohol at all if you are planning to drive.
» Red routes are priority routes controlled by the city police where no stopping is allowed at any time. On the carriageway they are marked with red lines.
» Private cars are banned from bus lanes—watch out for signs.
» Give way to your right at roundabouts (see diagram below).

FUEL

» All large garages are self-service. They sell higher octane unleaded fuel, unleaded 95 octane and diesel.
» There are 24-hour fuel stations in central London at 38–46 Albert Embankment; 132 Grosvenor Road and 104 Bayswater Road.

CONGESTION CHARGING

» A congestion charge was introduced in central London in February 2003, covering broadly the same area as Zone 1 on the Underground. You can see a detailed map online at www.tfl.gov.uk.
» Every private car must pay £8 per day to drive into the congestion area between 7am and 6pm Monday to Friday, excluding public holidays.
» You can pay online (www.cclondon.com), by phone 24 hours a day (tel 0845 900 1234), in person at various outlets throughout the UK, including fuel stations and shops, by text message from a mobile phone, or by credit or debit card at self-service BT Internet kiosks inside the congestion area and other selected locations. You will need your vehicle details.
» You can pay before midnight on the day or up to 90 days before your journey into the congestion zone. Don't leave it too late—the charge rises to £10 if you pay after midnight on the day of travel.
» Fixed and mobile digital cameras check number plates and those in breach of regulations are fined £100 (£50 if paid within 14 days).

TIPS

» Know your route.
» Plan parking in advance.
» Avoid driving in the rush hour (weekdays 7.30 to 9.30am and 4.30 to 7pm).

PARKING

» Street parking in London is limited. Check roadside signs for any restrictions.

Never Park

» If you cannot comply with or don't understand the regulations—ignorance will not be accepted as an excuse if you are caught out.
» On a pedestrian crossing or area marked with zigzags.
» At the side of a road that has a central double white line.
» On a clearway (main road not allowing vehicles to stop).
» On a cycle or bus lane or a tramway.
» In bays reserved for doctors, ambulances, disabled drivers or other priority users.

Meters

» Meter parking in central London costs between £3–£4 per hour (20p and £1 coins accepted).
» Most areas have a maximum stay of 2 hours. You can pay for a particular bay once only and cannot return within an hour to top up the meter.
» Generally, meter parking is free after 6.30pm Monday to Friday and from 1.30pm on Saturday and all day Sunday, but there are exceptions, particularly in areas where parking

MAKING IT EASY AT ROUNDABOUTS

When reaching a roundabout give priority to traffic on your right, unless directed otherwise by signs, road markings or traffic lights. Look forward before moving off to make sure traffic in front has moved. Watch out for vehicles already on the roundabout; be aware they may not be signalling correctly or at all.

Approach mini roundabouts in the same way. Vehicles MUST pass round the central markings.

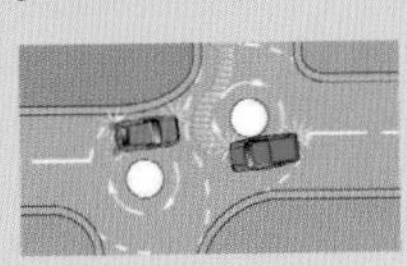

space is at a premium, so it is important always to check the instructions on the meter.

On-Street Pay and Display

» If you park in a 'pay and display' area you must buy a ticket from one of the machines located in the parking zone.

» Some machines require you to type in the first three numbers of your vehicle registration plate; if you don't do this correctly, you may be fined even if you buy a ticket correctly. You can then buy time as you require, within designated limits.

» Display the ticket clearly inside your vehicle.

Parking Restrictions

» Yellow lines on the road and curb and yellow plates on lamp-posts indicate on-street parking restrictions.

» A single line indicates that parking restrictions apply; notices explain exactly what these are.

» A double line means that no parking is allowed at any time.

» A broken line indicates limited restrictions.

» A single red line indicates that no stopping is permitted.

» Many streets are reserved for permit-holders only.

Car Parks

» The biggest car park operator in London is National Car Parks (NCP); car parks are recognizable by black-on-yellow signs with 'NCP' displayed prominently. Be aware that rates are very expensive. Further information from NCP (tel 0870 606 7050, www.ncp.co.uk).

» NCP parks include: Arlington House, Arlington Street SWIA 1RJ (tel 0870 242 7144), and 21 Bryanston Street W1H 7AB (tel 0870 242 7144).

» Masterpark (tel 020 7823 4567, www.masterpark.org.uk) also operates car parks in central London.

» There are several 24-hour parking garages in central London. Park Lane, below Marble Arch roundabout, is the biggest; there are usually spaces here even when all other car parks are full. Other 24-hour garages are at Brewer Street W1, Newport Place WC1 and Upper St. Martin's Lane WC1.

TRAFFIC WARDENS/FINES

» Metropolitan Police traffic wardens patrol London's streets. The current Fixed Penalty Notice for parking offences is £80 for less serious offences, £120 for more serious ones.

If You Get a Parking Ticket

» Don't ignore it. Many parking fines carry a 50 per cent discount if you pay within 14 days. The payment address is on the back.

» Appeal if you think the ticket is unfair. Write to the address on the back, giving as much tangible evidence as possible. Take notes and photographs at the scene.

STOPPING

» You may pick up and drop off passengers in restricted areas but not on clearways (eg red routes in London).

» Continuous loading/unloading is permitted except where curb markings indicate a loading ban, or on clearways.

» Check for notices on posts or walls to see when restricted hours apply.

CLAMPING AND TOWING AWAY

» If your car is parked illegally it may be immobolized by a wheel clamp; the notice posted on your windscreen explains how to get it released.

» Vehicles are usually released within one hour of payment (£45 plus the parking fine).

» If your vehicle is towed away, it will cost at least £200 to get it back. Vehicles must be collected in person and you must produce at least one form of identification such as your driver's licence.

CAR BREAKDOWN AND ACCIDENTS

» Several organizations in the UK can assist in the event of breakdown. Check whether membership in your home country entitles you to reciprocal help from a British organization.

At the Scene of an Accident

» If, as a driver, you are involved in a road-traffic accident, stop and remain at the scene for a reasonable period and give your vehicle registration number, your name and address, and that of the vehicle owner (if different), to anyone entitled to ask.

» If you do not exchange those details at the scene you must report the accident at a police station or to a police constable within 24 hours.

BREAKDOWN ORGANIZATIONS

The Automobile Association (AA) Lambert House, Stockport Road, Cheadle SK8 2DY, tel 0800 085 2721. You can become a member on the spot but it will cost you more than if you join beforehand.

The AA website (www.theaa.com) provides advice on what to do in the event of breakdown; a 'Route Planner', with maps and directions; traffic news and online road status reports. AA Roadwatch (tel 84322 from mobiles, charges vary, or 0906 888 4322 from land lines, up to 65p per minute) has the latest on traffic jams.

The Environmental Transport Association (ETA)
68 High Street, Weybridge, Surrey KT13 8RS. Tel 0800 212810. Open Mon–Fri 8–6, Sat 9–4, closed Sun. Breakdown number supplied on joining, which can be done around the clock at www.eta.co.uk.

The Royal Automobile Club (RAC)
Great Park Road, Bradley Stoke, Bristol BS32 4QN. Tel 0870 572 2722 (membership enquiries), tel 0800 828282 (breakdowns, 24 hours). Open Mon–Fri 7am–8.30pm, Sat–Sun 8.30–5, www.rac.co.uk

ROAD SIGNS AND DRIVING TIPS

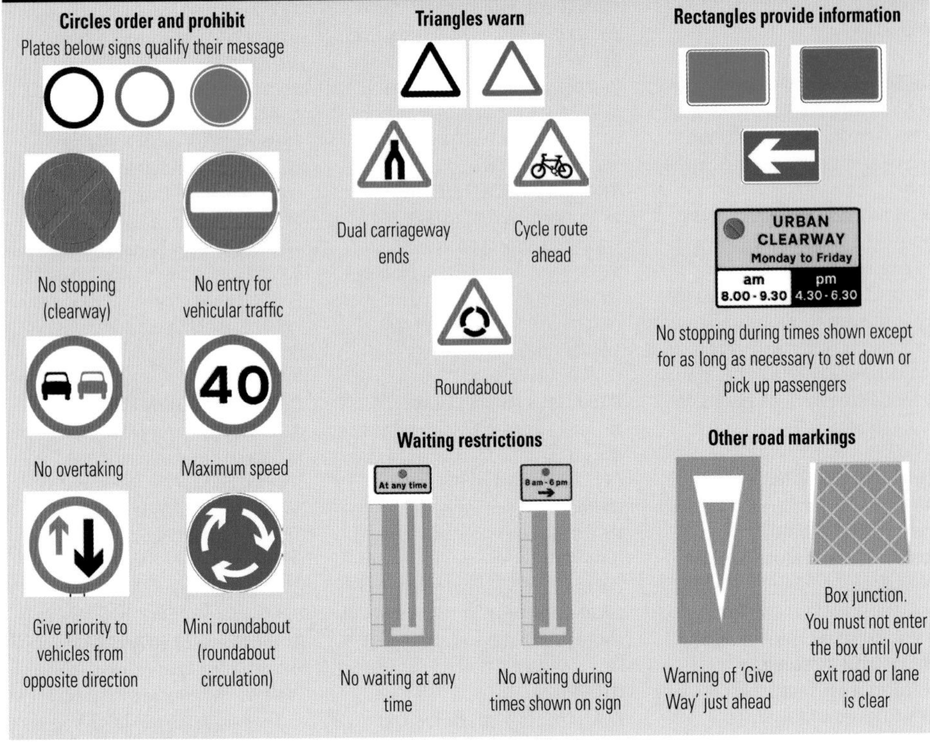

CYCLING IN LONDON

Cycling is a good alternative to often time-consuming and frustrating travel on the Underground or bus, but be prepared for the heavy traffic. Some roads and parks have designated cycle routes and it is possible to cycle along parts of the Thames Path and canal towpaths. A series of free cycling maps covers all of London (tel 020 7222 1234, www.tfl.gov.uk).

BICYCLES ON TRAINS

›› You can take your bicycle on the surface lines of the Underground network—District, Circle, East London, Hammersmith and City, and Metropolitan lines—but not on the deeper lines that have elevators and escalators. A map available from any Underground station shows which parts of the network you can use.

›› Folding bicycles can be taken on all lines, so long as they are folded up.

›› Many mainline train services allow bicycles. For long-distance services it is often necessary to book before you travel.

›› National Rail information (tel 0845 748 4950).

BICYCLE TOURS

The London Bicycle Tour Company, based in Gabriel's Wharf on the South Bank (www.londonbicycle.com), operates three guided tours of London. The company provides a bicycle for you to ride.

›› The Royal West Tour: Weekends, 14km (9 miles), 3.5 hours, £18.95.

›› The East Tour: Weekends (Sat only in winter), 14km (9 miles), 3.5 hours, £18.95.

›› Central London Tour: Daily, 10km (6 miles), 3 hours, £15.95 (on request).

SAFE CYCLING

›› Wear bright, colourful clothing. Use lights and wear fluorescent clothing at night.

›› Make other road-users aware of your movements.

›› Watch out for doors opening in stopped or parked cars.

›› Don't cycle down the inside of traffic when there is a left-turning junction ahead, as you may get cut up.

›› Wear helmets for extra safety, although they are not compulsory. Face masks filter out traffic pollution.

›› Always lock your bicycle to a fixed object.

LEAVING LONDON

BY TRAIN

London has 11 mainline rail stations, each serving a different region of the country as well as providing cross-city services (▷ 62). Most parts of the UK can be reached in a day from London: Intercity trains on major routes travel at 225kph (140mph), so journey times from one end of the country to the other can take just a few hours. Conversely, some trains stop at every station so travelling a relatively short distance can seem interminable.

Several different companies now operate the railway network, which can lead to some curious price anomalies as each company determines its own fare structure. It is worth checking whether another company serving the same region can offer an alternative route or price.

There are two classes of train travel: first and second. First is more expensive but does guarantee you a seat on crowded trains as well as complementary drinks and newspapers. Otherwise second class (standard) is perfectly acceptable and you can reserve a seat if you book in advance.

Sleeping compartments can be booked with Scotrail on some overnight services to and from Scotland (tel 0845 755 0033).

Tickets

» You can get a ticket for any company or any destination from any rail station, either from the ticket office or from automated machines. Most Underground stations sell rail tickets, too, as do travel agents. Tickets can also be booked and paid for over the phone or internet.

» Many different ticket options are available, so it pays to do some homework in advance, particularly as the cheapest options generally require that you buy tickets a week or more in advance.

» For a day trip, 'cheap-day' return tickets are the least expensive option, but check the restrictions on when you may travel.

» If you intend to leave London by train on several occasions, it may pay to buy a Network Railcard, valid for a year. It costs £25, for which you get a third off on fares to stations in southeast England for up to four people (www.railcard.co.uk).

» A young person's railcard (for those aged 16 to 25 and mature students in full-time education) costs £26 and gives a third off rail travel across the country (www.railcard.co.uk).

» Senior citizens' railcards cost £20 and give a third off fares.

» To buy railcards, you need a passport-size photo.

» Children under five travel free and 5- to 15-year-olds pay half price for most tickets—but check, as there are exceptions.

SUBURBAN TRAINS

The national rail network offers another way of getting across London and to the edges of the city. This service is particularly important in south and southeast London,

LONDON'S MAINLINE RAILWAY STATIONS

Map shows distribution of mainline stations and the interconnecting Underground lines.

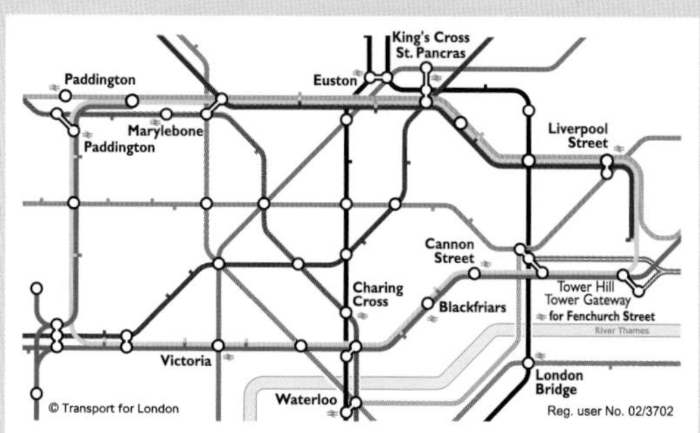

On Board

» Because many different train operators run services on the national network, the services and conditions on board trains vary depending on the service you use.

» All trains have toilets, and longer routes tend to have some form of catering service on board, usually a refreshments trolley.

» Ask the train operator about any lost property.

» No smoking. In July 2007 a complete smoking ban in enclosed spaces came into force.

» In some carriages, the use of mobile phones is prohibited.

Stations

» All but very small local stations have toilet and refreshment facilities.

» Few stations have left-luggage facilities for security reasons, but King's Cross and Paddington stations provide a good if expensive facility.

» Larger stations have information desks where you can report lost property.

» If you are changing trains, check information screens when you arrive to find the right platform for your connection. The destination of a train should be marked on screens on the platform or on the train.

MAINLINE STATIONS AND MAJOR DESTINATIONS				
STATION	REGIONS	MAJOR TRAIN OPERATORS	UNDERGROUND CONNECTIONS	MAJOR DESTINATIONS
Euston	Midlands, Northwest, Scotland	Virgin, First Scotrail, Silverlink	Northern, Victoria, Hammersmith & City, Metropolitan	Glasgow, Liverpool Manchester
St. Pancras	Midlands North	Midland Mainline, First Capital Connect, Eurostar	Northern, Victoria, Piccadilly, Hammersmith & City, Circle, Metropolitan	Edinburgh, Manchester
King's Cross	East Midlands, Yorkshire, Northeast, Scotland	GNER, Hull Trains	Northern, Victoria, Piccadilly, Hammersmith & City, Cirlce, Metropolitan	Cambridge, Edinburgh, York
Liverpool Street	East Anglia, Essex	Stansted Express, One	Hammersmith & City, Circle, Metropolitan, Central	Cambridge, Norwich
Fenchurch Street	Thames Estuary, Essex	c2c	Circle, District	Southend
London Bridge	Southeast	First Capital Connect, Southern, South Eastern	Jubilee, Northern	
Charing Cross	Southeast	Southern, South Eastern Trains	Northern, Bakerloo	Brighton, Canterbury, Dover
Waterloo	Southwest, Wales	South West Trains, Arriva	Northern, Bakerloo, Jubilee, Waterloo & City	Bournemouth, Exeter Portsmouth, Salisbury Winchester, Windsor
Victoria	Southern England	Gatwick Express, Southern	Victoria, District, Circle	Brighton, Canterbury
Paddington	South and West Midlands, West Country, Wales	First Great Western, Heathrow Express	District, Circle, Hammersmith & City, Bakerloo	Bath, Bristol, Oxford, Stratford-upon-Avon, Cardiff
Marylebone	Midlands	Chiltern Railways	Bakerloo	Birmingham

where the Underground system is less extensive, although there are many other routes providing efficient travel across the Greater London area. Travelcards (▷ 48) are valid on trains for journeys within the zone system (▷ 46–47).

TIPS

» If you want to be sure of a seat, avoid rush hour (weekdays 7.30 to 9.30am and 4.30 to 7pm). Thousands of London commuters use the services daily at that time.

» Telephone 0845 748 4950 for prices and timetables for all UK trains and destinations, or visit www.nationalrail.co.uk for timetables.

» Discount long-distance train fares can also be found through Megabus (▷ 63).

Left *Oyster Cards are convenient and offer considerable cost savings*

First Capital Connect

» First Capital Connect runs a service from Bedford, north of London, through London. This stops at five main London stations (St. Pancras International, Farringdon, City Thameslink, Blackfriars and London Bridge) and continues down to Brighton.

» The Thameslink service, run by First Capital Connect, also connects London with Luton Airport and Gatwick Airport (▷ 43).

Transport for London

» TFL are now running the former Silverlink Metro, a surburban route covering west, north and east London.

West Midlands Train Services

» West Midlands rail service connects London and Birmingham, stopping at Milton Keynes, Northampton, Hemel Hempstead and Watford.

BY COACH

» Coaches (long-distance buses) run from London to all parts of the country, leaving from Victoria Coach Station (VCS), 164 Buckingham Palace Road SW1W 9TP. They provide a much cheaper but slower alternative to rail travel (see below).

» VCS has a travel counter, open 8 to 7 Monday to Friday, 8 to 4.30 Saturday and 8 to 3 Sunday. Here you can buy or book airport coach tickets, tours and excursions, London Travelcards, theatre and concert tickets, rail tickets, ferry and hovercraft tickets and travel insurance. It is also possible to arrange Western Union money transfer.

National Express

» The largest bus company is National Express (tel 08705 808080), which operates to all regions of the UK and to Heathrow, Luton and Stansted airports.

» It is best to book your seat in advance. You can do so online at www.nationalexpress.com, or in person at the ticket hall at Victoria Coach Station, which is open 6am to 11.30pm daily. Telephone sales (tel 08705 808080) are open daily 8–8; all major credit and debit cards are accepted.

» You can get advance purchase coach tickets until two hours before departure. It is cheaper to book in advance and to travel mid-week.

Other Coach Services

» Oxford Express coaches run to and from Oxford (tel 01865 785400, www.oxfordbus.co.uk).

» Green Line coaches connect local cities and airports to the capital (tel 0844 801 7261, www.greenline.co.uk).

» Megabus offers extremely low fares to major destinations throughout the UK (tel 0900 160 0900, www.megabus.com).

COACH VERSUS TRAIN

Prices vary considerably depending on how tickets are booked and how far in advance. It is best to check online at the various websites. Significant savings can be made on train and bus tickets if they are purchased in advance. To ensure availability, bookings should be made at least 24 hours in advance.

For the relevant mainline stations, ▷ 62. All coaches leave from Victoria

BATH
Train 1 hour 25 min
Coach 3 hours 15 min

BRIGHTON
Train 50 min
Coach 2 hours

CAMBRIDGE
Train 45 min
Coach 2 hours

CANTERBURY
Train 1 hour 25 min
Coach 1 hour 50 min

NORWICH
Train 1 hour 50 min
Coach 3 hours

OXFORD
Train 1 hour 30 min
Coach 1 hour 40 min

STRATFORD-UPON-AVON
Train 2 hours 10 min
Coach 3 hours 30 min

WINDSOR
Train (from Waterloo) 56 min
(from Paddington change at Slough) 35min
Coach 1 hour 10 min

YORK
Train 2 hours
Coach 5 hours

VISITORS WITH A DISABILITY

Transport staff in London are aware of the needs of passengers with disabilities and generally go out of their way to help. It is best to phone in advance if you need special help or services. A good general source of information is www.tourismforall.org.uk

AIR

Most airlines have a department for making arrangements for passengers with special requirements; budget airlines may charge.

Designated disabled parking spaces are available in all BAA-run airports (tel 0870 000 1000).

Heathrow

Airport Coach Services (tel 020 7222 1234) vehicles and Heathrow Express (tel 0845 600 1515) trains are wheelchair-accessible.

Gatwick

Only certain train services are wheelchair-accessible. Information (tel 0875 301530).

Stansted

The Stansted Express train is wheelchair-accessible. Buses from Stansted to other airports and central London are not (tel 0845 600 7245). Coach/bus information, Airport Travel Line (tel 0870 574 7777).

Luton

The shuttle bus to Luton Airport Parkway is wheelchair-accessible and there are elevators at the station. Information (tel 01582 405100).

London City

Wheelchair-accessible shuttle buses run from the airport to Liverpool Street. Information (tel 020 7646 0088).

BUS

›› The Stationlink bus service that operates between major rail stations has low entrance ramps, low floors and spaces for wheelchairs.

›› All buses are now low-floor for accessibility. Information (tel 020 7222 1234).

COACH

›› Coaches tend to have high steep steps that may be difficult to negotiate. People who are sufficiently mobile may use coach services, but staff are not permitted to help passengers with boarding.

›› Manual wheelchairs can be carried, but only if folded and if there is room. Powered vehicles or wheelchairs are not permitted on coach services.

›› The National Express Disabled Persons travel helpline (tel 08717 818179).

DRIVING

Parking

The City of London Access Team (tel 020 7332 1995 or download from www.cityoflondon.gov.uk) produces a leaflet for people with disabilities.

Breakdown

The Automobile Association (AA) has a disability helpline for members with disabilities (tel 0800 262 0500).

EUROTUNNEL

The Shuttle has been designed with passengers with disabilities in mind. There is no need to get out of your car during the journey, but Eurotunnel does require prior notice of visitors with disabilities. Amenities in the passenger terminal buildings are wheelchair-accessible.

DOCKLANDS LIGHT RAILWAY

›› The DLR was constructed much more recently than the main Underground system, so is generally easier to use.

›› Most stations are accessible by elevator or ramp. Call the DLR Customer Services (tel 020 7363 9700) during office hours to check more details.

›› There are elevators, escalators and/or ramps on every station platform. All platforms are level with the trains for easy access. There is a designated wheelchair bay on every train.

›› Platforms have tactile edges for visually impaired passengers and passenger information displays show train information.

FERRY

Improvements have been made to UK ports to cater for passengers with disabilities, but it is still advisable to contact the port in advance.

RAIL

›› Portable ramps are available at most stations and some trains carry lightweight versions for use at unmanned stations.

›› Increasingly, accessible toilets are available on long-distance trains and many regional services.

›› Eurostar trains are wheelchair-accessible (as is the arrival point at St. Pancras International) with space for a maximum of two chairs per train. Reservations and information (tel 0870 518 6186).

TAXI

›› All taxis are wheelchair-accessible.

UNDERGROUND

›› The new Jubilee line trains are wheelchair-accessible from all the new stations between Westminster and Stratford.

›› For all enquiries (tel 020 7222 1234 24-hour Information Centre or tel 0845 330 9880 Customer Service Centre). An 'accessibility Tube map' is available from www.tfl.gov.uk.

›› Guide dogs are permitted on all forms of public transport in London.

REGIONS

This book is divided into five regions of London. Region names are for the purposes of this book only and places of interest are listed alphabetically in each region.

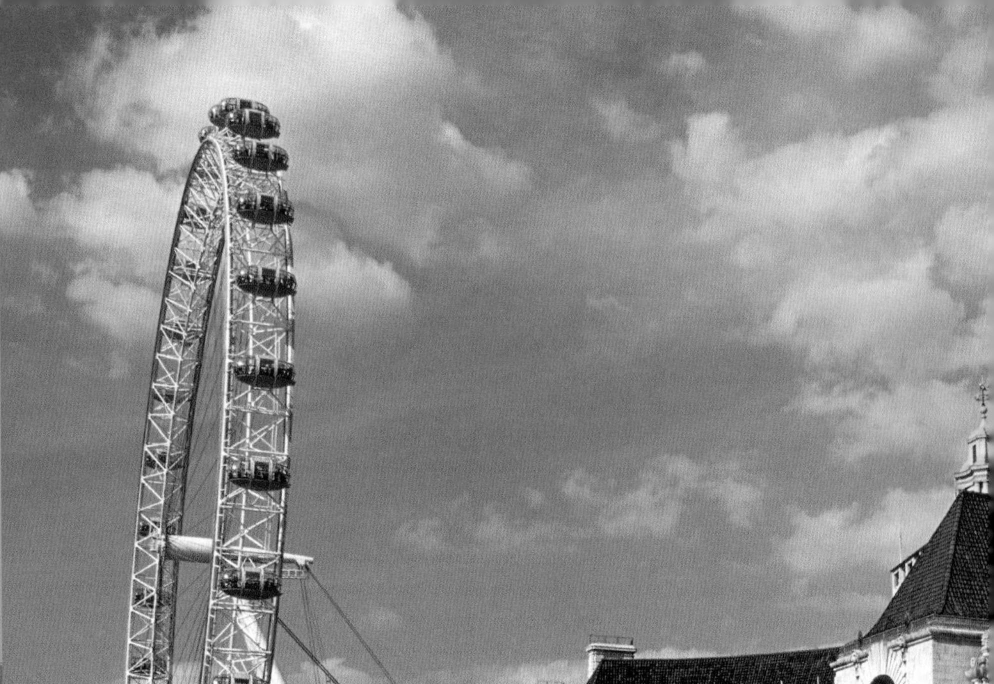
AQUARIUM

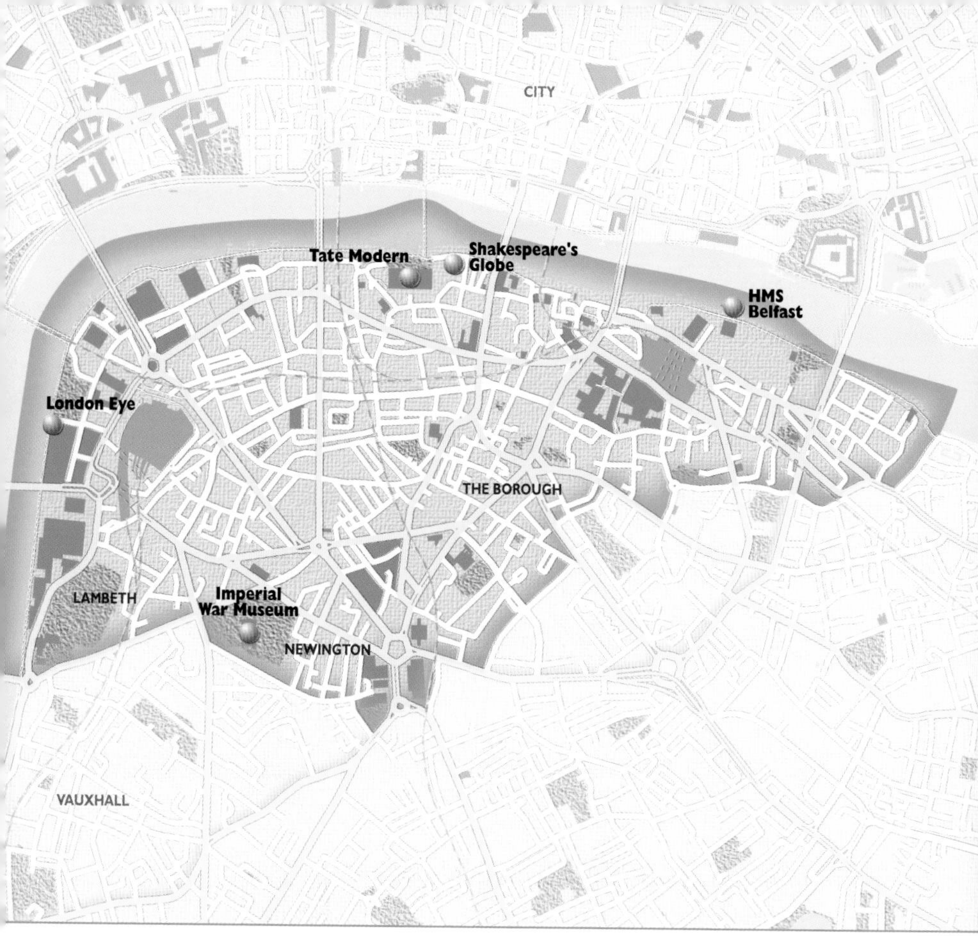

SOUTH BANK

Occupying the inner curve of the majestic bend that the River Thames traces through the centre of London, the South Bank wears several of the city's most iconic landmarks on its riverfront like jewels on a necklace, while concealing some of central London's most authentic working neighbourhoods in the warren of busy streets beyond. Spanning the northern ends of the boroughs of Lambeth to the west and Southwark to the east, the pedestrianized riverside itself constitutes ideal walking territory, especially from the hi-tech Ferris wheel of the London Eye, which stands proudly in front of imposing County Hall, to the southern end of picturesque Tower Bridge. En route you pass the South Bank cultural complex, the huge brick and glass edifice of the Tate Modern with its tall chimney, and the faithful reconstruction of Shakespeare's Globe Theatre, just as it was in the time of the bard himself.

Away from the river, sandwiched between the two busy railway terminals of Waterloo and London Bridge, the sights thin out, although the grand Imperial War Museum lies on the road from Westminster Bridge to the Elephant and Castle, the hub of south London's road system. What most fascinates the visitor here is the sudden transition to the gritty, urban feel of neighbourhoods such as Lambeth, Newington and Walworth, which have remained largely ungentrified despite their proximity to the centre. These are fine spots to wander aimlessly and take in a simple cafe meal or sip a pint in an unspoilt pub.

One area that has been transformed into something of a gourmet's paradise is Borough Market, which now boasts a fine range of quality food shops as well as trendy restaurants and bars.

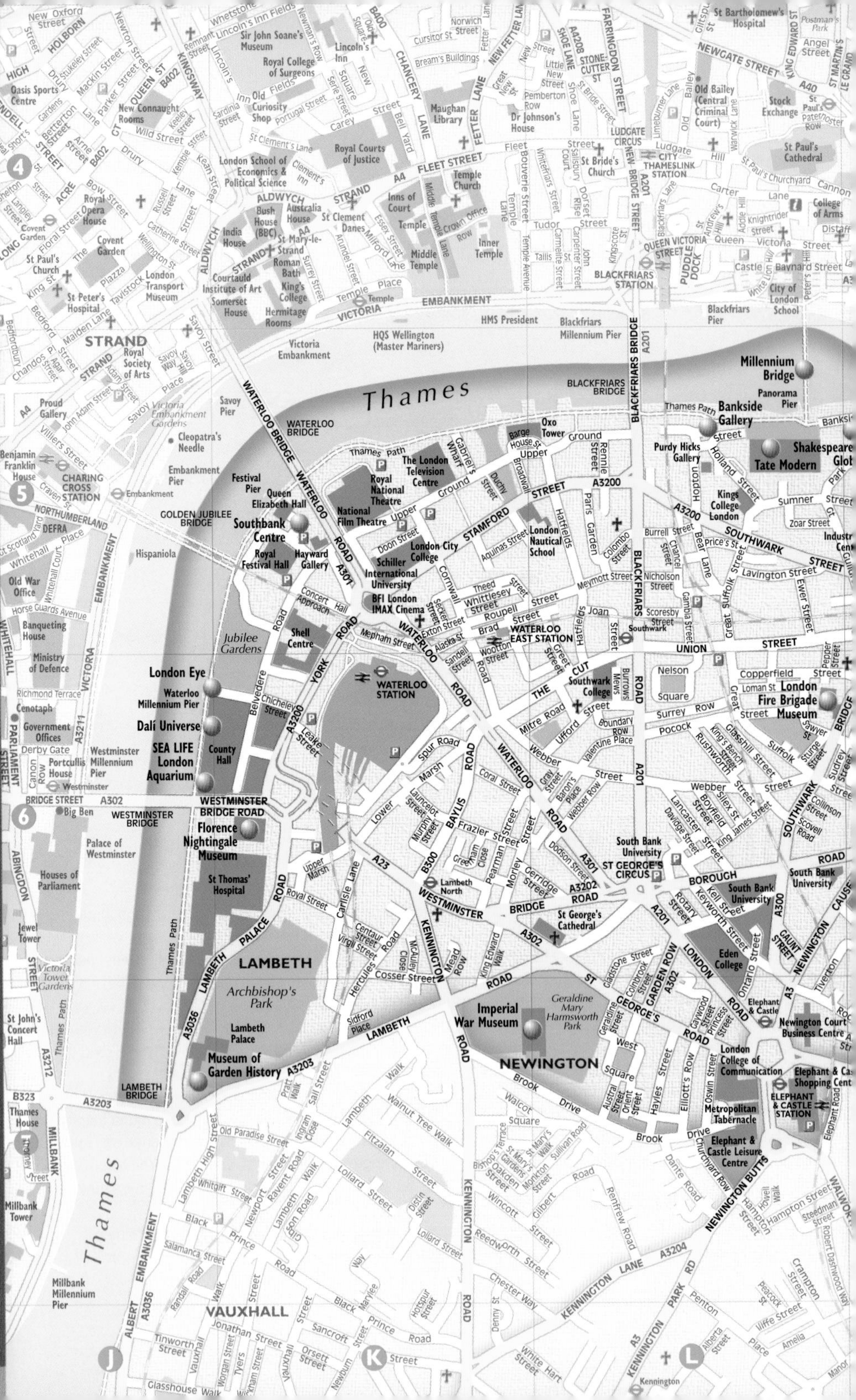
Thames
Waterloo Bridge
Blackfriars Bridge
Westminster Bridge
Lambeth Bridge
Golden Jubilee Bridge
Millennium Bridge
Southbank Centre
Royal Festival Hall
Hayward Gallery
Queen Elizabeth Hall
National Film Theatre
Royal National Theatre
The London Television Centre
Oxo Tower
Bankside Gallery
Tate Modern
Shakespeare's Globe
London Eye
Dalí Universe
SEA LIFE London Aquarium
County Hall
Florence Nightingale Museum
St Thomas' Hospital
Lambeth Palace
Museum of Garden History
Archbishop's Park
LAMBETH
Imperial War Museum
Geraldine Mary Harmsworth Park
NEWINGTON
St George's Cathedral
Waterloo Station
Waterloo East Station
BFI London IMAX Cinema
Shell Centre
Jubilee Gardens
London Fire Brigade Museum
South Bank University
London College of Communication
Metropolitan Tabernacle
Elephant & Castle Leisure Centre
Elephant & Castle Shopping Centre
Elephant & Castle Station
Palace of Westminster
Houses of Parliament
Big Ben
Jewel Tower
Victoria Tower Gardens
St John's Concert Hall
Millbank Tower
Millbank Millennium Pier
VAUXHALL
Old War Office
Banqueting House
Ministry of Defence
Cenotaph
Government Offices
Portcullis House
Westminster Millennium Pier
Charing Cross Station
Embankment Pier
Cleopatra's Needle
Savoy Pier
Royal Society of Arts
STRAND
Covent Garden
Royal Opera House
London Transport Museum
St Paul's Church
Somerset House
Courtauld Institute of Art
King's College
Royal Courts of Justice
London School of Economics & Political Science
Sir John Soane's Museum
Royal College of Surgeons
Lincoln's Inn
Old Curiosity Shop
Temple Church
Inner Temple
Middle Temple
Dr Johnson's House
St Bride's Church
Old Bailey (Central Criminal Court)
St Paul's Cathedral
Stock Exchange
College of Arms
Blackfriars Station
HMS President
HQS Wellington (Master Mariners)
Blackfriars Millennium Pier
Fleet Street
Victoria Embankment
Westminster Bridge Road
Kennington Road
Lambeth Road
St George's Road
Borough Road
Southwark Street
Stamford Street
Upper Ground
Union Street
The Cut
Kennington Lane
Newington Butts

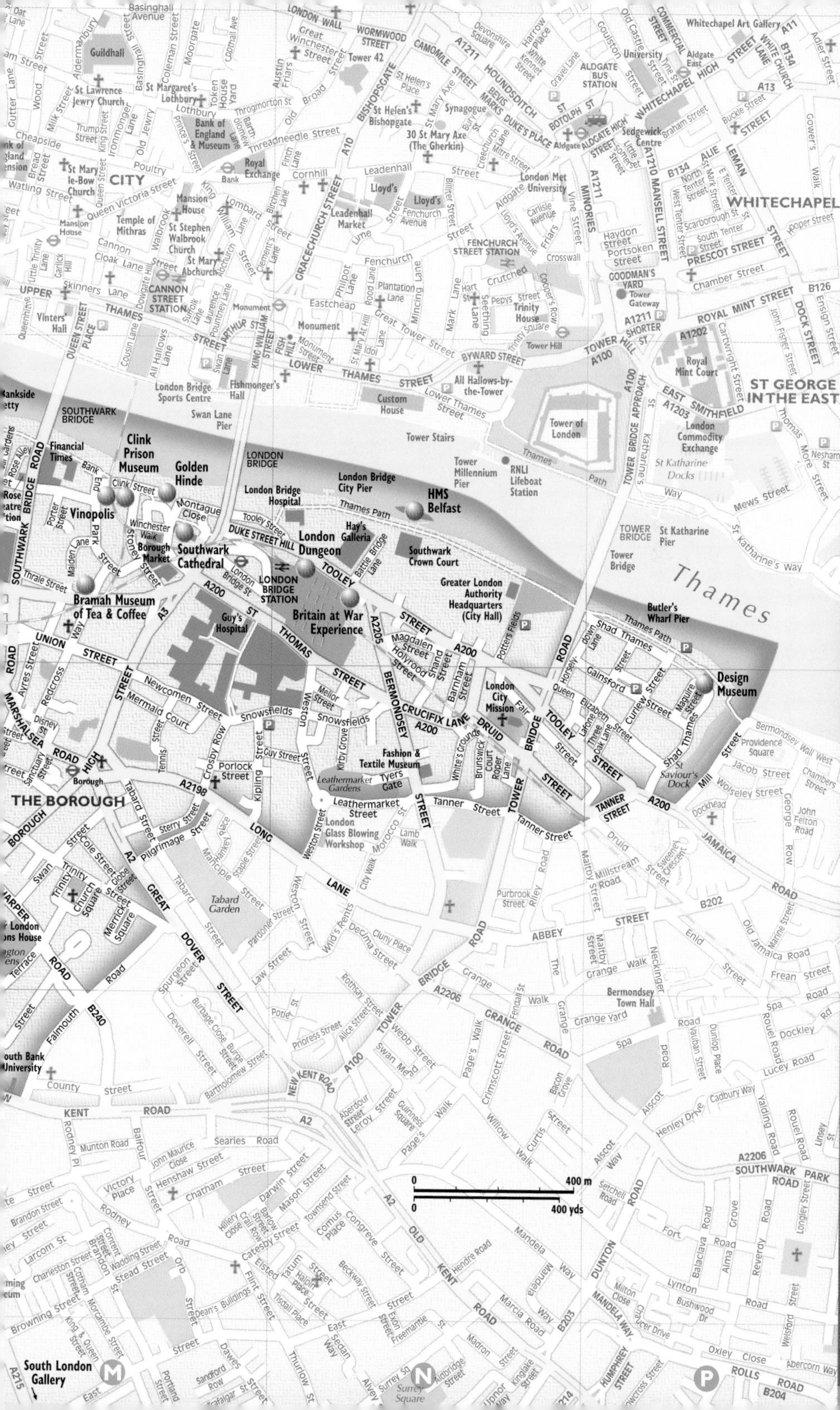
CITY
WHITECHAPEL
ST GEORGE IN THE EAST
THE BOROUGH
Thames
Guildhall
St Lawrence Jewry Church
St Margaret's Lothbury
Bank of England & Museum
Royal Exchange
St Mary le-Bow Church
Mansion House
Temple of Mithras
St Stephen Walbrook Church
St Mary Abchurch
CANNON STREET STATION
Vinters' Hall
Monument
Tower 42
St Helen's Bishopgate
Synagogue
30 St Mary Axe (The Gherkin)
Lloyd's
Leadenhall Market
London Met University
ALDGATE BUS STATION
Whitechapel Art Gallery
University
FENCHURCH STREET STATION
Trinity House
Tower Hill
GOODMAN'S YARD
Tower Gateway
Royal Mint Court
London Commodity Exchange
St Katharine Docks
London Bridge Sports Centre
Fishmonger's Hall
Custom House
All Hallows-by-the-Tower
Tower of London
Swan Lane Pier
Tower Stairs
Tower Millennium Pier
RNLI Lifeboat Station
SOUTHWARK BRIDGE
LONDON BRIDGE
TOWER BRIDGE
Tower Bridge
St Katharine Pier
Bankside Jetty
Financial Times
Clink Prison Museum
Golden Hinde
Vinopolis
Borough Market
Southwark Cathedral
Bramah Museum of Tea & Coffee
London Bridge Hospital
London Bridge City Pier
HMS Belfast
Hay's Galleria
London Dungeon
LONDON BRIDGE STATION
Britain at War Experience
Southwark Crown Court
Greater London Authority Headquarters (City Hall)
Guy's Hospital
Butler's Wharf Pier
Design Museum
London City Mission
Fashion & Textile Museum
Leathermarket Gardens
London Glass Blowing Workshop
Borough
Tabard Garden
Bermondsey Town Hall
South Bank University
South London Gallery
0 400 m
0 400 yds

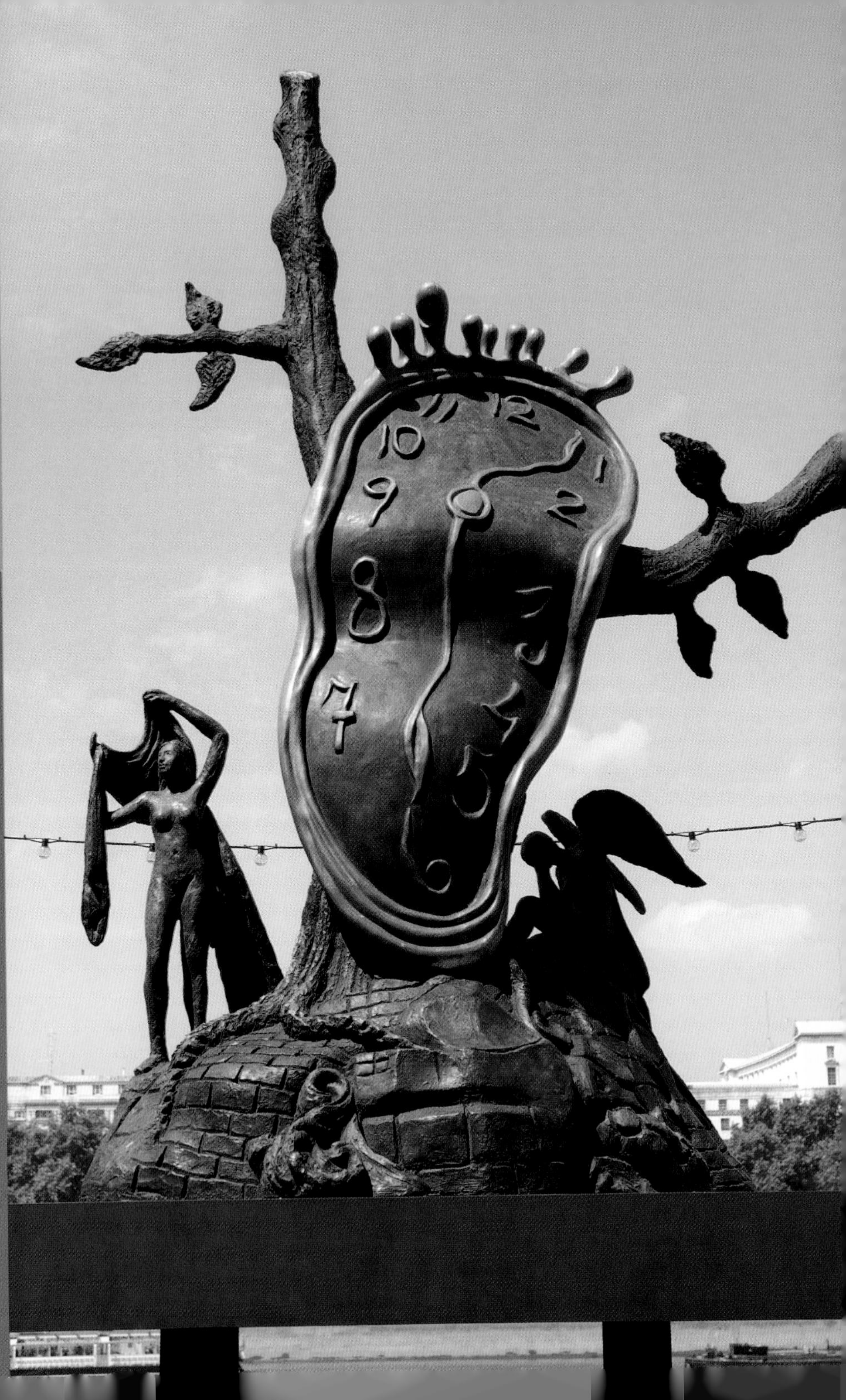

BANKSIDE GALLERY

www.banksidegallery.com

Two historic art societies have their homes in this south bank gallery near Tate Modern (▷ 80–81): the Royal Watercolour Society, the world's first institution to specialize in watercolours, and the Royal Society of Painter Printmakers, founded in 1880 to seek recognition for artists working in etching, engraving and mezzotint. Housed in the converted ground floor of a 1970s block of flats, the gallery showcases the activities of both societies with a mix of one-person shows and themed exhibitions of watercolours and prints.

68 L5 48 Hopton Street SE1 9JH 020 7928 7521 Daily 11–6 Free Mansion House, Southwark 45, 63, 100 Bankside Pier

BRAMAH MUSEUM OF TEA & COFFEE

www.teaandcoffeemuseum.co.uk

The stories of two of the world's most important commodities, tea and coffee, and their effect on our daily lives from the 17th century to the present day are told in this fascinating museum. Having spent a lifetime in the trade, Edward Bramah started the museum in 1992 with his own collection of teapots.

One section of the museum explains with prints, posters, maps and photographs how Britain developed into the world's largest tea-importing nation. It explores the history of tea, beginning with the East India Company (formed in 1600) and continuing through early 18th-century London tea gardens to smuggling, tea auctions, the Boston Tea Party, clipper ships and tea-growing in India and Sri Lanka.

The coffee story is traced from its first recorded use by a 9th-century Arab physician via the 19th-century espresso machine to instant coffee and automatic filters.

On show are tea and coffee sets, tea caddies, teaspoons, strainers and sugar tongs, kettles, giant tea urns and early Italian espresso machines. There are different types of tea to sniff and coffee beans to handle, and notes on such themes as the Japanese tea ceremony, tea bricks, tea dances and the 1950s London coffee bar phenomenon.

69 M5 40 Southwark Street SE1 1UN 020 7403 5650 Daily 10–6 Adult £4, child (under 14) £3.50, family £10 London Bridge 381, RV1

BRITAIN AT WAR EXPERIENCE

www.britainatwar.co.uk

Here you can learn what it was like to be on Britain's Home Front during World War II, the most turbulent period in the nation's 20th-century history. The Britain at War Experience is not a war museum devoted to the instruments of destruction but a tribute to ordinary people who lived their lives against the backdrop of air raids, the blackout, rationing and evacuation.

Begin your journey by taking an elevator down into the converted railway arches beneath London Bridge train station, where a mock-up of an underground air-raid shelter serves as a prelude to a huge collection of evocative photographs and assorted items ranging from rolls of toilet paper, ration books, gas masks and bombs to a complete Anderson shelter.

You can also see re-creations of a 1940s shopping arcade, a BBC radio studio, a theatre dressing room and a club for GIs.

Special effects re-create the sights, sounds, even smells of a London street during the Blitz, and you can walk through the shattered remains of a bombed department store, a cinema, a pub and homes.

69 N5 Churchill House, 64–66 Tooley Street SE1 2TF 020 7403 3171 Apr to mid-Nov daily 10–5; mid-Nov to end Mar daily 10–4.30. Adult £11.45, child (5–15) £5.50, under 5s free, family £20 London Bridge 47, 381, RV1

CLINK PRISON MUSEUM

www.clink.co.uk

A skeleton hanging in a cage marks the entrance to the gloomy basement housing the museum—a taste of what's to come. From the 12th century until 1780, when the building was burned down during the Gordon Riots (▷ 33), this was the site of the notorious Clink Prison, where clerics, heretics, debtors, prostitutes and an assortment of Bankside lowlife were imprisoned in appalling conditions. Its name is said to derive from the 'clinch' irons that were used to pin prisoners down, and 'the clink' has become a slang term for any prison. The museum covers the history of the prison using archive material, tableaux of torture scenes and displays of gruesome instruments.

69 M5 1 Clink Street SE1 9DG 020 7403 0900 Mon–Fri 10–6, Sat–Sun 10–9 Adult £5, child (in full-time education) £3.50, family £12 London Bridge 35, 43, 149, RV1

DALÍ UNIVERSE

www.daliuniverse.com

Laid out as a labyrinth of galleries at County Hall (the former headquarters of the Greater London Council on the South Bank), this stylish exhibition is dedicated to Spanish self-publicist and surrealist artist Salvador Dalí (1904–89). It has more than 500 of his works on loan from various European collectors, including sculpture, drawings, lithographs and gold and glass objects. Reflecting the major influences in his life and work, the exhibits are grouped into three themes: Sensuality and Femininity (where you'll find the famous bright red Mae West Lips sofa), Religion and Mythology and Dreams and Fantasy. Don't miss *Spellbound*, an oil painting created for the set of Sir Alfred Hitchcock's Hollywood movie (1945) of the same name.

68 K6 Riverside Building, County Hall, Westminster Bridge Road SE1 7PB Information line: 020 7620 2720 Mon–Thu 9.30–6, Fri–Sun 9.30–7 Adult £14, child (7–16) £7, under 7s free Waterloo, Westminster 3, 12, 148, 159 Westminster Millennium Pier, Waterloo Millennium Pier

Opposite *Dalí's* Nobility of Time *sculpture*

HMS BELFAST

Launched in March 1938, this huge warship had an active career during World War II and played a leading part both in the destruction of the German battle cruiser *Scharnhorst* at the Battle of North Cape and in the Normandy landings. She now floats off the south bank of the Thames near Tower Bridge, the only surviving example of an armoured warship from this era, and an awesome sight with her heavy armour and massive gun turrets.

TOURING THE DECKS

A self-guided tour starts on the quarterdeck, where officers and guests of honour were piped aboard and guards and bands paraded, and leads to the top of the bridge, with its four Bofors gun mountings, three of which can be aimed by hand (anyone can have a go). The tour then takes you down through nine decks to see the triple 6-inch gun turrets, the shell rooms and magazines and the cramped mess decks, officers' cabins, galley and sick bay. Life-size models represent members of the crew going about their business—a surprisingly realistic and disconcerting touch.

The operations room is manned by models, re-enacting the ship's part in the Battle of North Cape on 26 December 1943. It's a simple gimmick but an effective one, enhanced by photographs and memorabilia that emphasize the human cost of the conflict.

The ship's company galley dates from the period after HMS *Belfast*'s modernization in the 1950s, when meals were prepared by properly trained and qualified staff and served from the counter; more figures are shown dishing up and following the precise rules posted up around the galley. In the sickbay, a well-equipped operating room reflects the need for every kind of health care on a cruiser designed to spend long periods at sea.

The tour ends with a visit to the boiler and engine rooms, where massive boilers produced superheated steam at high pressure to be piped to the turbine engines, which in turn drove the propeller shafts. It took about four hours to raise sufficient steam for the ship to get under way.

Videos trace the history of each zone on the tour, and officers are on hand to answer questions and keep crowds flowing.

In the exhibition room you can see the signatures of 36 survivors from a crew of 1,963 on the *Scharnhorst*, sunk on Boxing Day 1943 off the coast of Norway.

INFORMATION

www.hmsbelfast.iwm.org.uk
69 N5 Morgan's Lane, Tooley Street SE1 2JH 020 7940 6300 Mar–end Oct daily 10–6; Nov–end Feb daily 10–5 Adult £9.95, child (under 16—must be accompanied by adult) free London Bridge, Tower Hill 36, 705, RV1 London Bridge City Pier, Tower Millennium Pier Visits take form of self-guided tours £3.25, in English, French, German Walrus Café in zone 3 Gifts, models and books with general war/armed forces theme

TIP

» If you are claustrophobic, you may not like the deeper regions, and the tour involves climbing down steep ladders without much headroom.

Above *Bristling with guns, the* Belfast *gives a comprehensive insight into the lives and work of her crew*

DESIGN MUSEUM

www.designmuseum.org

In 1989 a 1950s warehouse on Butler's Wharf was converted into the modernist Design Museum, the first in the world to be dedicated to 20th- and 21st-century design. One of London's most inspiring cultural attractions, it promises to be more than a conventional museum, with a mission 'to excite everyone about design'. An evolving permanent collection presents mass-produced design classics including cars, cameras, furniture, domestic appliances and office equipment, while temporary exhibitions range from retrospectives about great designers to thematic shows.

The first-floor Review Gallery showcases the most innovative contemporary designs and technologies from around the world.

69 P6 · 28 Shad Thames SE1 2YD · 020 7403 6933 · Daily 10–5.45 · Adult £8.50, child (under 12) free, family £16 · London Bridge, Tower Hill (or Tower Gateway for DLR) · 42, 47, 78, 188, 381 · St. Katharine's Pier

FLORENCE NIGHTINGALE MUSEUM

www.florence-nightingale.co.uk

Set in a modern annexe of St. Thomas's Hospital, where Florence Nightingale (1820–1910) established the first-ever nurses' training school in 1860, the museum covers her career and contribution to public health. Her work nursing soldiers during the Crimean War, which earned her the title 'the lady with the lamp', and her contribution to public health, are evoked with personal mementoes, clothing, furniture, books, letters, portraits and nursing equipment, plus audiovisuals and realistic reconstructions.

68 K6 · 2 Lambeth Palace Road SE1 7EW · 020 7620 0374 · Daily 10–5 · Adult £5.80, child (5–18) £4.80, under 5s free, family £16 · Westminster, Waterloo · 12, 148, 159, 211, 507, RV1 · Westminster Millennium Pier

GOLDEN HINDE

www.goldenhinde.com

Nestling in a small dock on Bankside is an exact full-scale replica of the galleon in which Sir Francis Drake (c1543–96) circumnavigated the globe between 1577 and 1580. In fact the replica has travelled further than the original, twice around the globe. The ship's cramped interior would have been home to more than 80 sailors. Its five decks include a gun deck that holds 22 cannons. During the holiday periods there are occasional tours led by well-versed guides dressed in Elizabethan costume, adding authenticity to your visit.

For those wanting to find out just what it was like to sleep aboard ship, it is possible to stay overnight as part of an educational visit from April to September.

69 M5 · St. Mary Overie Dock, Cathedral Street SE1 9DE · 0870 011 8700 · Daily 10–5.30 · Adult £7, child (4–18) £5, under 4s free, family £10 · London Bridge · 17, 35, 43, 47, 48, 133, 501 · London Bridge City Pier, Bankside Pier

IMPERIAL WAR MUSEUM

▷ 74.

LONDON DUNGEON

www.thedungeons.com

Hidden away in the vaults beneath London Bridge railway station is a grisly parade of life-size tableaux, complete with disturbing sound and special effects. Along with scenes of death from disease, early surgery, murder and various methods of torture, the museum presents re-enactments of some of the most horrific events in British history.

The Great Fire of London is a £1 million re-creation of the fire-ravaged streets of London in 1666; Traitor! Boat Ride to Hell and Extremis: Drop Ride are fearsome plummets into murky water and abyss respectively. Jack the Ripper takes you back to 1888 for a terrifying tour through the district of Whitechapel, following the bloody footsteps of the most infamous serial killer of his time.

One of the most spectacular and ambitious exhibitions, which opened in 2003, is the one about the Great Plague; it will certainly challenge the squeamish as it vividly and realistically re-creates the horrors of the plague that claimed more than 100,000 lives in 1665. Expect to see black rats (they carried the disease) running around, and to walk through a tunnel piled up with the ravaged corpses of plague victims.

Equally as frightening is Labyrinth of the Lost, where visitors find (or rather lose) themselves in a baffling mirror maze of eerie catacombs, live characters and spooky special effects.

Throughout the museum, actors in period costume help keep you constantly on edge.

69 N5 · 28–34 Tooley Street SE1 2SZ · 020 7403 7221, 0870 846 0666 · Daily 10–5.45 · Adult £21.95, child (5–15) £16.95, under 5s free · London Bridge · 35, 43, 47, 133, 149, 343, RV1

Below *The London Dungeon has been scaring visitors in historic Southwark since 1976*

IMPERIAL WAR MUSEUM

An imposing pair of naval guns guards the entrance to the country's most impressive military museum—just a taster of the diverse collection inside, which covers wars involving Britain or the Commonwealth since 1914. This includes not only World Wars I and II, but many other international conflicts, from Korea and Vietnam to Suez and the Arabian Gulf.

GROUND FLOORS

You're first confronted by a confusing array of military equipment in the airy Large Exhibits Gallery: Tanks, artillery, fighter planes, trucks and submarines are haphazardly parked—or suspended—in the domed space. Take time to wander among the vehicles, many of which have stories of bravery attached. There's the wooden dinghy *Tamzine*, for instance, the smallest surviving boat to have taken part in the evacuation of 200,000 troops from Dunkirk in 1940. Sometimes it's simply the sense of scale that impresses, in exhibits such as the colossal V2 rocket or the cramped World War II fighter cockpit.

On the lower ground floor are well-conceived re-creations of the 1940–41 Blitz and World War I trench warfare, complete with sound effects and smells. The section about the British Home Front is fascinating, and includes evocative touches such as posters exhorting the women of Britain to 'come into the factories', or 'dig for victory'.

Elsewhere on the labyrinthine lower floor, collections can easily be overlooked. World War II receives the fullest coverage, with detailed sections on the eastern front and war in northwest Europe and the Far East. Monty: Master of the Battlefield documents the life of Field Marshal Montgomery, opened to coincide with the 60th anniversary of the battle of El Alamein, which took place in 1942.

UPPER FLOORS

Move up to the first floor for the absorbing Secret War exhibition. Items on show include bottles of invisible ink used by German spies and one of the few remaining German Enigma machines used to encode messages.

The art galleries on the second floor are a popular section of the museum, with work by Paul Nash, Henry Moore and Stanley Spencer.

On the third floor is the distressing counterpoint to the martial display below. The Holocaust Exhibition examines the Nazi persecution of Europe's Jewish communities and other groups, such as gypsies and homosexuals, between 1933 and 1945. Exhibits include shoes collected from prisoners at Majdanek concentration camp in Poland.

INFORMATION

www.iwm.org.uk

68 K7 Lambeth Road SE1 6HZ General enquiries 020 7416 5320 Daily 10–6 Free (except for some special exhibitions) Lambeth North, Elephant & Castle, Southwark, Waterloo 3, 12, 344, C10 Audio tours available, £3.50 £3.50, in English only On ground floor, 10–5.30 Gifts with relevant themes

TIP

›› Note that curators don't recommend the Holocaust Exhibition for children under 14.

Below *World War I biplane on display in the Large Exhibits Gallery*

LONDON EYE

The world's largest observation wheel and London's most visible icon is four times wider than the dome of St. Paul's and more than 200 times larger than the wheel of an average racing bicycle. It offers a ride that's enthralling even for those who hate heights, offering spectacular views across the city in every direction.

RIDING HIGH

Passengers ride in one of 32 pod-like capsules that rotate smoothly in a slow-moving, 30-minute flight. Each capsule is fully enclosed and comfortably holds 25 people. Because the capsules are secured on the outside of the wheel (rather than hung from it, as they would be on a Ferris wheel), views through the large glass windows are totally unobstructed. And because the capsules are kept level by a motorized motion stability system, you can walk around inside them quite safely—although seating is provided. For additional safety, each capsule is in touch with the ground via camera and radio links. Note, however, that flights may be cancelled at the last minute owing to weather conditions. You can ask for a flight attendant to accompany you, to point out major landmarks. The wheel is in constant motion, revolving continuously at a quarter of the average walking speed and enabling you to walk straight on and off the moving capsules.

After dark, the trees lining the approach to the London Eye are bathed in green lights, and the boarding platform appears to float on a cloud of blue light. Sunset and after-dark flights are also available.

BACKGROUND

The British Airways London Eye was conceived by David Marks and Julia Barfield to celebrate the millennium, using a design that represents the turning of the century. It took seven years and the expertise of hundreds of people from five European countries to realize their vision, and over a week to lift the Eye upright from a horizontal position across the Thames—a procedure previously attempted only in oil-rigging operations. Although originally intended as a temporary structure, the Eye is so popular that it is unlikely that it will disappear from the skyline.

INFORMATION

www.ba-londoneye.com
68 J6 British Airways London Eye, Riverside Building, County Hall Westminster Bridge Road SE1 7PB
Bookings: 0870 500 0600 (between 8.30am and 8pm) May, Jun, Sep daily 10–9, Jul, Aug daily 10–9.30, Oct–end Apr 10–8 Adult £17, child (4–15) £8.50, under 4s free; 10 per cent discount available online Waterloo, Westminster, Embankment, Charing Cross 77, 211, 381, RV1 Waterloo Millennium Pier *Essential Eye Souvenir Book* and in-flight mini guide available from the ticket hall or shop £5, in English, French, German, Spanish, braille Café Manga in County Hall and outside in Jubilee Gardens In Jubilee Gardens, selling souvenirs and gifts, including Eye-inspired jewellery

TIPS

» Book ahead. Although not essential, it is recommended.
» Arrive 30 minutes before your flight, to allow time for boarding.
» You can always buy tickets on the day but may wait for over an hour.

Above *Survey London from the comfort of a stable pod on the Eye*

LONDON FIRE BRIGADE MUSEUM

www.london-fire.gov.uk

The Great Fire of 1666 marks the starting point for this journey through the history of firefighting in London. Exhibits housed in two buildings of the London Fire Brigade's Training Centre include original fire engines, pumps, uniforms and uncomfortable-looking breathing apparatus.

Among the museum's possessions are the personal belongings of Captain Eyre Massey Shaw. He was in charge of the brigade from 1861 and is credited as the father of the modern fire service. His silver helmet and KCB decoration are on display.

A collection of paintings by World War II firefighters shows telling scenes of the Blitz as they experienced it.

68 L6 Winchester House, 94A Southwark Bridge Road SE1 0EG 020 7587 2894 Visit by guided tour only (Mon–Fri 10.30 and 2) by prior arrangement Adult £3, child (7–14) £2, under 7s £1 Borough, Southwark, Elephant & Castle 344

MILLENNIUM BRIDGE

www.arup.com/millenniumbridge

Two of London's famous landmarks—St. Paul's Cathedral (▷ 104–109) in the City and the Tate Modern gallery (▷ 80–81) at Bankside—are connected by this bridge built in 2000, the first pedestrian crossing to be built over the Thames in more than a century.

Architect Norman Foster and engineer Ove Arup designed it to give the impression of a single sweeping 'blade of light', illuminated from deck level with an innovative light pipe system. The steel structure is 325m (1,066ft) high and carries 3,000 tonnes of horizontal force. After some celebrated teething troubles, during which it wobbled when people attempted to use it, it was adjusted and eventually reopened in 2002.

68 L5 Open access Free St. Paul's, Southwark 11, 15, 17, 45, 63, 344, RV1 Blackfriars Millennium Pier, Bankside Pier

MUSEUM OF GARDEN HISTORY

www.museumgardenhistory.org

The redundant parish church of St. Mary-at-Lambeth provides the setting for this collection of gardening tools and machinery, including everything from spades to cloches and mowers. Outside, in the church courtyard, a knot garden uses plants popular in the 17th century, including fragrant old roses.

Two major figures in the development of English gardening, John Tradescant the elder (1570–1638) and his son, John, gardeners to Charles I and II, are laid to rest here, A window in the church commemorates them.

68 J7 Lambeth Palace Road SE1 7LB 020 7401 8865 Daily 10.30–5 Suggested donation £3; guided tour £8 per person Lambeth North, Westminster 3, 344, 77, 507, C10

SEA LIFE LONDON AQUARIUM

www.sealife.co.uk/london

More than 3,000 forms of marine life can be found swimming around under the former offices of the Greater London Council in County Hall, one of Europe's largest aquariums. Laid out across three floors, the aquarium displays its residents in tanks representing a variety of environments, from ponds to rivers to oceans.

The aquarium is divided into 14 different zones, in which you will find sharks and stingrays gliding between giant, submerged Easter Island-style heads. There are countless gaudy fish to enjoy in the Reef and Corals and Indian Ocean exhibitions, and children get a thrill from stroking a stingray on the 'beach'. It takes 2 million litres (440,000 gallons) of Thames water and tons of imported salt to fill the tanks.

The aquarium is committed to conservation and as a way of raising money for research you're invited to adopt from a choice of over 20 different types of fish. Not surprisingly, the sharks, piranhas and rays are the most popular.

68 J6 County Hall, Westminster Bridge Road SE1 7PB 020 7967 8000 Daily 10–6 (opening hours may vary so check first) Adult £15.25, child (3–14) £11.75, students (15–17) £11.25 (with proof of age), family £45 Waterloo, Westminster, Embankment 12, 53, 159, 211, 381, RV1

Left *The Millennium Bridge is a handy way to reach to St. Paul's from the South Bank*
Below *Window in the Museum of Garden History*

INFORMATION

www.shakespeares-globe.org
68 M5 21 New Globe Walk SE1 9DT 020 7902 1400. Box office: 020 7401 9919; tours: 020 7902 1500
May–end Sep daily 9–12.30 (theatre tour and exhibition), 12–5 (exhibition and virtual theatre tour); Oct–end Apr daily 10–5 (theatre tour and exhibition). Performances most afternoons and evenings daily, May–end Sep
Exhibition and theatre tour: adult £10.50, child (5–15) £6.50, under 5s free, family £28. Performance: £15–£33, plus £5 (standing); advance booking essential
Cannon Street, London Bridge, Mansion House, St. Paul's, Southwark
15, 45, 63, RV1 Theatre tour May–end Sep daily 9–12.30; Oct–end Apr daily 10–5 *Shakespeare's Globe: The Guidebook*, £5, in English, French, German
Swan at the Globe has a bar (11am–late) on the ground floor for all-day eating and drinking. The Brasserie with its river view is for more substantial meals and for gourmet take-out. Light Theatre Bar menu also available Shakespeare- and Globe-related gifts and books

Below *Inside the reconstructed Elizabethan theatre*

SHAKESPEARE'S GLOBE

Bankside's original Globe was one of England's first true playhouses, built in 1599 by a company that included William Shakespeare. Before this, acting companies would tour the country, often performing in the courtyards of inns. Unfortunately, the Globe didn't last long—it was destroyed by fire during a production of *Hamlet* in 1613. A replacement was built, with a tiled roof, a year later but was demolished by the Puritans in 1642, and for the next three centuries the site remained empty.

After visiting Bankside in 1949, American film actor and director Sam Wanamaker (1919–93) was determined to create an accurate, functioning reconstruction of the Globe, built as near as possible to the original site and using materials, tools and craft techniques closely matching those of Elizabethan times. Although the project began in 1969, reconstruction wasn't started until 1987, and it was another 10 years before the new Globe's completion in 1997.

Small by modern standards, the Globe is an O-shaped, white-plastered building constructed with unseasoned oak and held together with 6,000 oak pegs. It's crowned with the first thatched roof to be built in the city since the Great Fire in 1666; the modern version plays it safe with a sprinkler system. In the middle, an elevated stage and a yard are surrounded on three sides by tiers of benches.

In the interests of authenticity, productions are held during the afternoon, much as in Shakespeare's day, without artificial lighting, and only in fine weather. As with the original, there is standing room in front of the stage, where groundlings (the term used in Shakespearean times for standing members of the audience) can heckle the actors in Elizabethan fashion.

UNDERGLOBE

Beneath the theatre, the huge space called the UnderGlobe houses the Shakespeare's Globe Exhibition. Here the roles of actor, musician and audience are brought to life through text, film, music and multimedia. You can learn about the techniques used to design and make the costumes in the Theatre Workroom, and in Special Effects you discover what was used for blood and how the sound of thunder in Macbeth was created.

Above *Come to Vinopolis to relive London's wine-trading history*

SOUTHBANK CENTRE

www.sbc.org.uk

London's premier centre for the performing arts sits on the south side of the river between the Hungerford and Waterloo bridges. It includes the Royal Festival Hall (▷ 87–88), a major concert venue, reopened in June 2007 after a major refurbishment; the National Film Theatre (▷ 87), with cinemas, a cafe and shop; the Queen Elizabeth Hall (▷ 87) and adjoining Purcell Room, staging smaller concerts and chamber music respectively; and a clutch of high-profile theatre spaces.

This was the site of the 1951 South Bank Exhibition, part of the Festival of Britain, held as a morale-booster during the post-war years. The only building to survive from that time is the Royal Festival Hall, where exhibitions and events are held in the huge open-plan foyer, and concerts and ballet productions take place in the auditorium above.

To the east is the Hayward Gallery (tel 020 7960 5226, Sun–Thu 10–6, Fri–Sat 10–10, adult £8, under 12s and members free, www.hayward.org.uk), a grim concrete bunker built in 1968, which hosts major contemporary art exhibitions, with the emphasis on British artists. Note that the Southbank Centre hosts many free foyer events so it's always worth asking what's on.

68 K5 Belvedere Road SE1 8XX General information 020 7921 0600. Ticket office 0871 663 2500 (9am–8pm) Foyer daily 10am–10.30pm Performances only Waterloo, Embankment 77, RV1

SOUTH LONDON GALLERY

www.southlondongallery.org

This renowned contemporary art gallery shows work by local, national and international artists. Acclaimed artists who have exhibited here include Tracy Emin, Barbara Kruger, Christian Boltanski and Keith Tyson. A permanent collection of nearly 2,000 works can be viewed by appointment.

Off map 69 M8 65 Peckham Road SE5 8UH 020 7703 6120 Tue–Sun 12–6 Free; admission charge to individual events Elephant & Castle, then bus 12, 171, P3; Oval then bus 36, 436 12, 36, 171 Peckham Rye

SOUTHWARK CATHEDRAL

www.dswark.org/cathedral

This stone building, originally built between 1220 and 1420 as part of a medieval priory, is tucked away near London Bridge on the south bank of the Thames. Prior to 1905, when it was given cathedral status, it was the parish church of St. Saviour. Inside the nave retains some original stonework and fascinating 15th-century ceiling bosses—look for the one which depicts the devil swallowing Judas Iscariot. It's also worth seeking out many of the tombs and memorials, including that of Shakespeare's brother, Edmund, who died in 1607. A monument to the playwright himself (who lived in Southwark from 1599 to 1611) depicts various characters from his plays.

69 M5 Montague Close SE1 9DA 020 7367 6700 Mon–Fri 8–6, Sat 9–5, Sun 12.30–5 and for services Free, but donations requested London Bridge 15, 35, 40, 133, 149, 344, 381, RV1

TATE MODERN

▷ 80–81.

VINOPOLIS

www.vinopolis.co.uk

London has a rich history of wine trading and this is the starting point for this unusual exhibition. Set in historic vaults that were once at the centre of Europe's wine trade, this multi-award-winning visitor attraction takes you on an encyclopaedic trawl from Alsace wines to Zinfandel grapes, visiting every major wine-producing region in the world. The basic tour (self-guided) includes sampling five different wines plus a cocktail—this must be the only museum in the world where you are actually encouraged to saunter around with a glass of wine in your hand. Touch-screen technology, audio-guides and assisted tastings aim to educate your taste buds.

69 M5 1 Bank End, Bankside SE1 9BU 020 7940 8300 Thu–Fri 12–10, Sat 11–10, Sun 12–6 Basic tours, tasting five wines plus a cocktail £19.50. More tours available London Bridge 17, 21, 35, 40, 43, 48, 133, 149, 343, 501, 521, RV1 Cantina Vinopolis ▷ 90

INFORMATION

www.tate.org.uk

68 L5 Bankside SE1 9TG 020 7887 8888; recorded information 020 7887 8008 Sun–Thu 10–6, Fri–Sat 10–10 (galleries open daily at 10.15) Free, donations welcome. Charge for special exhibitions Southwark, Mansion House, St. Paul's 45, 63, 100, 344, 381, RV1 Bankside Pier Choice of audiotours covering permanent collection, architecture, children's trail, tour for the visually impaired. Available from near the Turbine Hall information point and Level 3, £2, in English, French, German, Italian, Spanish Official guide £2.99, in English, French, German, Italian, Spanish, Japanese; handbook £16.99 Restaurant on Level 7 with exceptional views Cafe on Level 2; kiosk by the north entrance; bar on Level 4 Large shop on Level 1 with comprehensive range of art books, posters, prints, stationery and postcards

Above *States of Flux Room 2*

INTRODUCTION

Towering over the Millennium Bridge on the south bank of the Thames, Tate Modern opened in 2000 as one of the world's leading museums of modern art, and it's been pulling in huge crowds ever since.

By the early 1990s the Tate Gallery, now called Tate Britain (▷ 192–193), needed more space. Its international modern art collection had nearly doubled in 40 years, and the decision was made to divide the collection between British and other works of art. A major new gallery was planned to house the international work, and the venue chosen was a decommissioned power station, a huge 1950s brick and steel-frame building designed by Sir Giles Gilbert Scott (1880–1960). A competition was mounted for the best plan to transform the site, and the winners, out of 148 entrants, were Swiss architects Herzog & de Meron. Renovation began in 1995 and the gallery opened five years later. In March 2009 revised plans were announced for the museum to add the uniquely shaped Tate Modern 2 directly behind the current gallery. Using the old power house's oil tanks as its foundation, the design, also by Herzog & de Meron, will add 5,000sq m (54,000sq ft) of exhibition space. It is hoped to open during 2012.

You can use entrances on the western or the northern side of the former power station. On the west side there are two; the main entrance takes you down an access ramp into the enormous, airy Turbine Hall, which acts as a dramatic interior plaza for temporary installations. Another entrance on this side of the building gives level access to the second floor. The main shop and information point are on Level One (the basement) and escalators take you up to the galleries on the upper levels.

The collection is divided into four broad themes: Material Gestures, Poetry and Dream, Energy and Process, and States of Flux. Each has combinations of film media, installations, painting, photography and sculpture, linking historic works with contemporary. Every year there are additional special loan exhibitions and several shows focusing on a single artist, theme or period.

WHAT TO SEE

Tate Modern continues the story of art where the National Gallery (▷ 182–187) leaves off. Its displays are changed regularly, but they always include works by the most influential artists of the 20th century, such as Picasso, Matisse, Dalí, Moore, Bacon, Gabo, Giacometti and Warhol.

LEVEL 3

Material Gestures (Room 2)
***Venice Woman IX* by Alberto Giacometti**

Giacometti (1901–66) began to sculpt his series of emaciated human figures in the 1940s, providing a sober answer to the 'superman' philosophy of the pre-war Futurists. The fragility and dignity of this bronze piece, with all its resonance of human suffering, underlines Giacometti's own view that his thin sculptures were truer to humanity than larger works.

Poetry and Dream (Beyond Surrealism: Room 2)
***Naked Man with Knife* by Jackson Pollock**

Before developing his famous 'drip' technique, American artist Jackson Pollock (1912–56) painted this powerful work as he was beginning to assert his own style. The image of the interlocking figures conveys a brooding violence and was based on Mexican painter Orozco's lost work depicting Abel and Cain.

LEVEL 5

States of Flux (After Impressionism: Room 3)
***Reading Woman with Parasol* by Henri Matisse**

Matisse (1869–1954) painted this work in 1921, while staying in a house near Nice. It is typical of the artist's work in the 1920s and an excellent example of his mastery of everyday subjects. The colours are more subdued than in his early Fauvist works.

States of Flux (After Impressionism: Room 3)
***Girl in a Chemise* by Pablo Picasso**

During his Blue Period Picasso (1881–1973) produced several portraits of people from society's margins. This study of a melancholy, thin young girl is included in the Naked and Nude collection in contrast to the idealized nude. It's a poignant work, which goes beyond the depiction of a model and into the realms of social commentary.

States of Flux (Umberto Boccioni and Roy Lichtenstein: Room 1)
***Unique Forms of Continuity in Space* by Umberto Boccioni**

The Futurist movement was founded by writers and artists such as Umberto Boccioni (1882–1916) in the early 20th century, when industrialization was engulfing Italy and innovations such as cars and electricity seemed to promise a dynamic and thrusting age ahead. This 1913 sculpture shows the air in the wake of the moving figure, giving a vivid sense of speed and progress.

States of Flux (Cubism, Futurism and Vorticism: Room 3)
***Mandora* by Georges Braque**

Braque (1882–1963) was a leading light among the Cubists, whose experiments in form and perception revolutionized the art world. Braque collected early musical instruments and in this image of a mandora, a small lute, he uses his fragmented style to suggest rhythm and sound—a very active kind of still-life painting.

GALLERY GUIDE

LEVEL ONE
Turbine Hall: Sculpture by Henry Moore

LEVEL TWO
Starr Auditorium, Seminar Rooms

LEVEL THREE
Material Gestures (New Painting and Sculpture 1945–60)
Poetry and Dream (Surrealism & Beyond)

LEVEL FOUR
Changing exhibitions

LEVEL FIVE
Energy and Process (art inspired by transformation and natural forces)
States of Flux (Cubism, Futurism and Vorticism)

TIP

›› Tate Boat links Tate Britain, the London Eye and Tate Modern (every 10 min).

Below *The entrance lobby is in what used to be the turbine hall in the old power station*

ALONG THE SOUTH BANK

A walk past Westminster, Britain's seat of government, and London's premier centre for the performing arts, the South Bank, with spectacular views along the Thames.

THE WALK
Distance: 5km (3 miles)
Allow: 2 hours minimum
Start at: Westminster Underground station
End at: St. Paul's Underground station

HOW TO GET THERE
Jubilee, Circle or District line to Westminster
11, 12, 24, 453

★ This well-trodden route exudes a sense of space in an otherwise highly populated city.

Leave Westminster Underground station by exit 1 (Pier) to reach the bank of the Thames near Big Ben. You can take boat trips from here up and down the river (▷ 266–267).

Cross the road, skirt around the base of Big Ben and turn left along the Parliament Green side of the Houses of Parliament (▷ 179–180).

At the end of the complex of buildings you can see St. Stephen's Tower—make for this now. On your right you'll pass Westminster Abbey (▷ 194–195). When you come to the gardens on your left, enter and follow them to Lambeth Bridge. Turn left across the bridge, then left along the Thames path. Across the road to your right are Lambeth Palace and the Museum of Garden History (▷ 77).

❶ Since 1197 Lambeth Palace, a largely medieval complex of domestic buildings, has been the official residence of the archbishops of Canterbury. The medieval crypt and Great Hall, rebuilt in the 17th century, house the palace library (the first public library in England) and grand 19th-century reception rooms. Open for pre-arranged tours only—apply in writing.

Continue to the edge of Westminster Bridge by St. Thomas's Hospital, where you'll find the Florence Nightingale Museum (▷ 73). Cross the road and go down the steps to the former County Hall, now housing the London Aquarium (▷ 77) and Daíi Universe (▷ 71). Unless you want to visit either of these, continue straight on along the river path to reach the London Eye (▷ 75).

❷ Behind the wheel are the Jubilee Gardens, laid out in 1977 to commemorate Queen Elizabeth's silver jubilee. The former Shell Centre, behind them, has the largest clock facade in the world. *Jubilee Oracle*, the statue on the pavement by Alexander, was completed in 1980. Street performers are often here, entertaining passers-by.

Left *The London Eye and County Hall seen from Westminster Bridge*

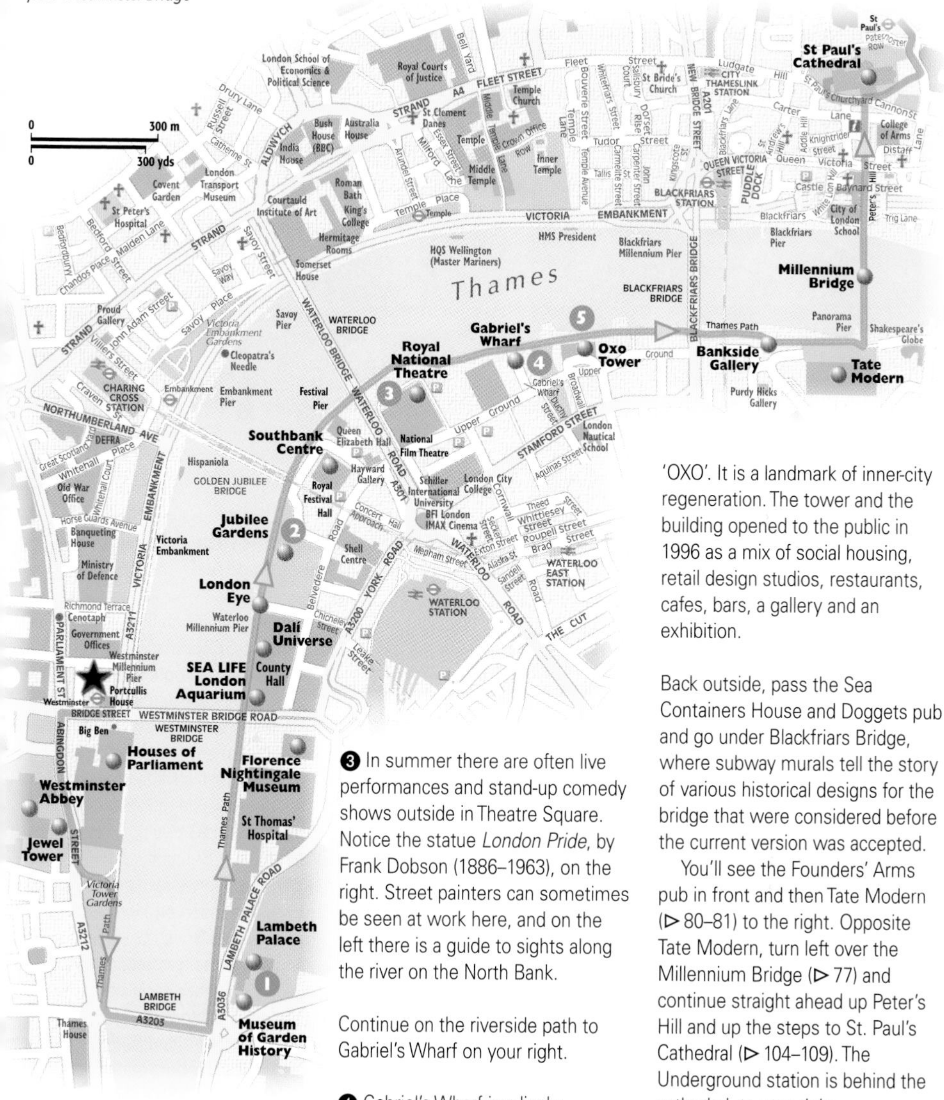

With the river on your left, continue under Hungerford Bridge (now officially the Golden Jubilee Bridge) and past the Royal Festival Hall and Festival Pier, another place where you could catch a boat along the river or over to Westminster.

Continue under Waterloo Bridge, where there is often an open-air book fair near the entrance to the National Film Theatre. Continue to the Royal National Theatre.

❸ In summer there are often live performances and stand-up comedy shows outside in Theatre Square. Notice the statue *London Pride*, by Frank Dobson (1886–1963), on the right. Street painters can sometimes be seen at work here, and on the left there is a guide to sights along the river on the North Bank.

Continue on the riverside path to Gabriel's Wharf on your right.

❹ Gabriel's Wharf is a lively collection of design workshops, restaurants and bars—a great place for unusual textiles, fashion, jewellery, ceramics and furnishings.

Continue past Bernie Spain Gardens and on to Oxo Tower Wharf.

❺ The Oxo Tower, former headquarters of the famous British stock-cube makers, is a witty 20th-century building with windows that spell out the word 'OXO'. It is a landmark of inner-city regeneration. The tower and the building opened to the public in 1996 as a mix of social housing, retail design studios, restaurants, cafes, bars, a gallery and an exhibition.

Back outside, pass the Sea Containers House and Doggets pub and go under Blackfriars Bridge, where subway murals tell the story of various historical designs for the bridge that were considered before the current version was accepted.

You'll see the Founders' Arms pub in front and then Tate Modern (▷ 80–81) to the right. Opposite Tate Modern, turn left over the Millennium Bridge (▷ 77) and continue straight ahead up Peter's Hill and up the steps to St. Paul's Cathedral (▷ 104–109). The Underground station is behind the cathedral, to your right.

WHEN TO GO

» Try to go early or late to see the sun rising or setting on the river.

» Gabriel's Wharf Market is open Tuesday to Sunday 11–6.

WHERE TO EAT

There are places to go for a drink all along the river. Consider EAT, behind the Oxo Tower, the National Film Theatre cafe or the Gourmet Pizza Company at Gabriel's Wharf.

SOUTHWARK SIGHTS

This section of the borough of Southwark covers a fascinating area just south of the Thames. It combines some interesting attractions and two lively markets with an authentic neighbourhood feel.

THE WALK
Distance: 5km (3 miles)
Allow: 2 hours
Start: Borough Underground station
End: London Bridge Station

HOW TO GET THERE
Northern line to Borough
35, 40, 153, 343, C10

★ The attraction of this walk is that it takes you from the bustle of Borough to Southwark's scenic eastern riverfront. The route also affords a glimpse into the evolving neighbourhood of Bermondsey, which was actually quite a rural haven during the Middle Ages, dominated by an abbey; the advent of the railways and spillover from the docklands saw social conditions deteriorate during the 19th century. While some of the area away from the Thames remains staunchly working class, as you approach the river you will come across trendy flats and loft conversions.

From Borough Underground station turn left to cross Marshalsea Road and continue along Borough High Street. Turn left onto Southwark Street. The Bramah Museum of Tea & Coffee is at No. 40, on the corner of Redcross Way.

❶ The fascinating Bramah Museum of Tea & Coffee (▷ 71) explores the history of the world's two favourite hot beverages through a series of displays and a fine collection of artefacts and paraphenalia. There is also a tea room, if you are in need of refreshment.

Turn right onto Redcross Way and immediately right onto Park Street, which brings you to the Borough Market on the opposite side of Stoney Street.

❷ Borough Market (▷ 86) is the last remaining early morning wholesale fruit and vegetable market in central London, where traders are joined on Thursdays, Fridays and Saturdays by a variety of specialist food retailers. Expect to see stalls selling anything from French cheeses and Cumbrian wild boar meat to barbecued burgers and organic vegetables. The enclave has now been enhanced by a few gourmet restaurants and the odd trendy bar.

From Borough High Street turn right onto St. Thomas Street, then take the second right onto Weston Street, until Leathermarket Street, where you turn left. (At the far end of Leathermarket Street, the Fashion & Textile Museum is on the opposite side of Bermondsey Street at No. 83.)

❸ The Fashion & Textile Museum (www.ftmlondon.org) was founded by renowned British designer Zandra Rhodes and occupies a building designed by Mexican architect Ricardo Legoretta. Situated in gentrified Bermondsey Village, the museum showcases constantly revolving exhibitions of cutting edge fashion, textiles and jewellery.

Turn right from Leathermarket Street onto Bermondsey Street (or head south from the Fashion & Textile Museum if you have stopped for a visit) until it meets Long Lane, where you turn left. Bermondsey Antiques Market is on the right.

❹ Bermondsey Antiques Market is a stalwart affair that operates on

Left *The fish on sale at Borough Market is temptingly fresh*

Friday only from 5am to 3pm. The serious traders have all done their business in the early hours before it opens, leaving tons of bric-a-brac for the average shopper to pore over later on. Confusingly, the place is sometimes still also referred to as the New Caledonian Market, as it has its roots in a pre-war flea market near the Caledonian Road in Islington.

Turn left onto Tower Bridge Road and then head north until Queen Elizabeth Street. Turn right onto that and left at the end onto Shad Thames. The Design Museum is at No. 28.

❺ The Design Museum (⊳ 73) is located in a converted 1950s warehouse and contains a growing permanent collection tracing developments in the design of items as diverse as cars, cameras and cabinets. There are also temporary exhibits on a range of themes related to all aspects of innovation in design.

From the river side of the Design Museum at the end of Shad Thames, turn left along the Thames Path, continuing underneath Tower Bridge. Turn left up Battle Bridge Lane and then right onto Tooley Street. London Bridge station is on the left.

❻ This section of the South Bank not only gives you a close-up view of the city's most iconic bridge, whose castle-like turrets rise above you as you admire them from below, but you will also pass in front of the lopsided beehive that is London's new City Hall, where the Mayor's offices are, and beside veteran battleship the HMS *Belfast* (⊳ 72). As you approach London Bridge station on Tooley Street there are two more highly popular attractions; the absorbing Britain At War Experience (⊳ 71) at Nos. 64–66 and the gruesomely entertaining and ever-popular London Dungeon (⊳ 73) at Nos. 28–34.

PLACES TO VISIT

FASHION & TEXTILE MUSEUM

✉ 83 Bermondsey Street
☎ 020 7407 8664
🕐 Wed–Sun 11–6

BERMONDSEY ANTIQUES MARKET

✉ 63 Bermondsey Street
☎ 020 7407 1096
🕐 Fri 5am–3pm

WHEN TO GO

The earlier you can set off on this walk the more of the genuine action you will catch at the two markets. For food buying and sampling, Borough Market is livelier at weekends, while Bermondsey Antiques Market only operates on Friday.

WHERE TO EAT AND DRINK

You're spoiled for choice at Borough Market. If you fancy a splurge, Roast in the Floral Hall at the market is a good choice, better if you've done the walk in reverse. Pubs along the way include quaint George Inn on Borough High Street and the Rose on Snowsfields.

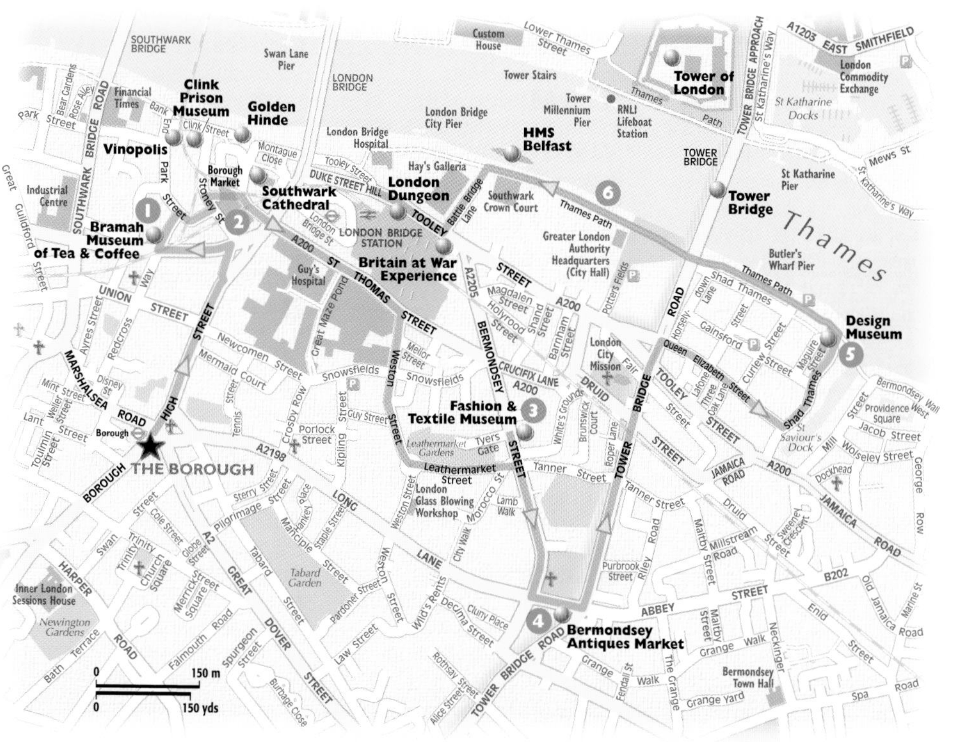

SHOPPING

BOROUGH MARKET

www.boroughmarket.org.uk

A wholesale fruit and vegetable market has operated here for many years, but there is now a very successful weekend international food market, with up to 70 stalls. It sells top-quality fish, meat, vegetables, cider, cheese, bread, coffee, cakes and patisseries to London's foodies and top chefs so you will be in good company.

95 M5 Borough High Street/Bedale Street/Stoney Street/Winchester Walk SE1 020 7407 1002 Thu 11–5, Fri 12–6, Sat 9–4 London Bridge 344, 381, RV1

FUNKI FRESH

www.funkifresh.co.uk

It's been a long road to this chic riverfront location for Funki Fresh from its 1997 beginnings at Portobello and Spitalfields markets. On offer are a range of fine ladies' garments, all individually handmade, from casual tops through evening attire to coats and hats.

94 K5 13 Gabriel's Wharf, 56 Upper Ground SE1 9PP 020 7928 1100 Mon–Sat 11–6 Waterloo, Southwark 4, 26, 59, 68, 76, 168, 171, 188, 243, 341, 521

GAME OF GRACES

www.gameofgraces.com

This very trendy and rather pricey boutique on up-and-coming Gabriel's Wharf deals in fashionable women's clothing. Colours are mostly muted—blacks and greys predominate and cerise is about as bright as blouses go, for example. It also doesn't cater to the larger lady—size 14 (US 12) is the maximum.

94 K5 6 Gabriel's Wharf, 56 Upper Ground SE1 9PP 020 7928 4050 Daily 11–6 Waterloo, Southwark 4, 26, 59, 68, 76, 168, 171, 188, 243, 341, 521

GANESHA

www.ganesha.co.uk

This delightful shop is at once fun and fair trade, importing high-quality home furnishings and accessories from co-operatives in India. Items include baskets, bedding, cushions, leather bags, silk scarves, shawls and woolly hats. There is also a range of scented candles, incense and even Bollywood CDs.

94 K5 3 Gabriel's Wharf, 56 Upper Ground SE1 9PP 020 7928 3444 Tue–Fri 11.30–6, Sat–Sun 12–6 Waterloo, Southwark 4, 26, 59, 68, 76, 168, 171, 188, 243, 341, 521

ENTERTAINMENT AND NIGHTLIFE

AMERSHAM ARMS

www.amersham-arms.co.uk

The performance space at this popular New Cross pub is small enough for intimacy but big enough to generate a decent atmosphere. The wide range of entertainment

Left *Prepare to be impressed at the 20m-high (65ft) IMAX screen*

here includes Monday comedy nights, alternative gigs, ukelele evenings, discos and student events. The beer and snacks are not bad either.
Off map 95 P8 388 New Cross Road SE14 6TY 020 84691499 Fri–Sat 10pm–3.30am Fri £2, free before 11pm; Sat £1, free before 11pm 21, 36, 136, 171, 177, 436, 453 New Cross Gate

GLOBE, SHAKESPEARE'S

▷ 78.

IMAX CINEMA

www.bfi.org.uk/imax

A 480-seat cinema in a space-age balloon, with the biggest film screen in Britain, showing exhilarating 2-D and 3-D movies.
94 K5 1 Charlie Chaplin Walk, South Bank SE1 8XR 0870 787 2525 Embankment, Waterloo 4, 68, 77, 171, 176, RV1

INDIGO2

www.theo2.co.uk/indigo2

Although the Indig02 is dwarfed by the huge arena that anchors the ex-Millennium Dome, it is beautifully designed and can hold up to 2,400 people. It has hosted a diverse range of acts from rock legends like The Who to more eclectic performers such as Daniel Johnson.
Off map 95 P6 The 02, Peninsula Square SE10 0DX 020 8463 2000 Daily 9am–late North Greenwich 108, 129, 132, 161, 188, 422, 472

MASS NIGHTCLUB

www.mass-club.com

This popular club in buzzing Brixton consists of three rooms over two levels. Mass Club hosts events such as Ibiza Underground and the Crimson fetish night, while Babalou is the stage for emerging bands and has more ambient trance nights.
Off map 94 L8 St. Matthew's Church, Brixton Hill SW2 1JF 020 7738 7875 Fri–Sat 9pm–6am £5–£15 Brixton 45, 59, 109, 118, 133, 159, 250, 333

MINISTRY OF SOUND

www.ministryofsound.com

Perhaps the most famous club in London, the Ministry is a huge place where you can experience every kind of house music. Never mind the unfriendly bouncers, long queues and high admission price: just party.
94 L6 103 Gaunt Street SE1 6DP 0870 060 2666 Fri 10.30pm–6.30am, Sat 11pm–7am £13–£20 Elephant & Castle 12, 188, 453, C10

NATIONAL FILM THEATRE (NFT)

www.bfi.org.uk

Part of the Southbank Centre (▷ 79), with two cinemas showing both British and international films. Focus of the London Film Festival (▷ 295).
94 K5 Southbank Centre, Belvedere Road SE1 8TL 020 7928 3232 Daily 11–11 £5–£9 Embankment, Waterloo 1, 26, 68, 76, 77, 168, 171, 176, 188, RV1

OLD VIC

www.oldvictheatre.com

Historic building (1818) where Britain's National Theatre began before transferring to the South Bank in the 1970s.
94 K6 The Cut, Waterloo Road SE1 8NB 0870 060 6628 £10–£50 Waterloo, Southwark 68, 168, 171, 176, RV1

PURCELL ROOM

www.southbankcentre.co.uk

Smallest of the three concert halls at the Southbank Centre (▷ 79). An intimate space for chamber music, accompanied singers, solo singers, musicians and more.
94 K5 Southbank Centre SE1 8XX 0871 663 2500 £10–£50 Embankment, Waterloo 68, 77, 171, RV1

QUEEN ELIZABETH HALL

www.southbankcentre.co.uk

The middle-sized of the three auditoriums at the Southbank Centre hosts small orchestral concerts, bands, small-scale opera and dance productions and chamber music.
94 K5 Southbank Centre SE1 8XX 0871 663 2500 £10–£50 Embankment, Waterloo 68, 77, 171, RV1

ROYAL FESTIVAL HALL

www.southbankcentre.co.uk

Part of the Southbank Centre (▷ 79). Major classical music performances,

Below *Food stalls at Borough Market*

with regular appearances by the Philharmonia and the London Philharmonic. Also jazz, ballet and other genres.
94 K5 Southbank Centre SE1 8XX 0871 663 2500 £15–£50 Embankment, Waterloo 68, 77, 171, RV1

ROYAL NATIONAL THEATRE
www.nationaltheatre.org.uk
There are three auditoriums here: the Cottesloe, accommodating 300, with no fixed seats or staging; the 890-seat proscenium Lyttleton; and the Olivier (1,080), which is named after Sir Laurence Olivier, the National Theatre's first director.
94 K5 South Bank SE1 9PX 020 7452 3000 £10–£50 Waterloo 68, 77, 171, 176, RV1

THE VENUE
www.thevenuelondon.com
Once this was a stage for the then-unknown band Radiohead; now the live acts are almost exclusively tribute bands. The Venue actually comprises six separate spaces, so there's something for most people.
Off map 95 P7 2a Clifton Rise, New Cross SE14 6JP 020 8692 4077 Fri 9pm–4am, Sat 9pm–4.30am Fri £7, £3 before midnight with flyer, ladies free before 11pm; Sat £12, £5 before 10pm with flyer 21, 36, 136, 171, 177, 436, 453 New Cross Gate

SPORTS AND ACTIVITIES

CHARLTON ATHLETIC FOOTBALL CLUB
www.cafc.co.uk
Currently aiming to get back into the Championship (football's second tier), having dropped two divisions from their Premier League heyday, the Addicks have always cultivated a friendly armosphere at their club.
Off map 95 P6 The Valley, Floyd Road, Charlton SE7 8BL 0871 226 1905 53 Charlton

CRYSTAL PALACE FOOTBALL CLUB
www.cpfc.co.uk
The Eagles have had mixed fortunes in recent decades, with a bumpy history of relegation (going down a division) and promotion. They have now played five straight seasons in the Championship.
Off map 94 J8 Selhurst Park, Whitehorse Lane, Selhurst SE25 6PU 020 8768 6000 468 Thornton Heath, Selhurst

CRYSTAL PALACE NATIONAL SPORTS CENTRE
www.gll.org
A venue for major athletics events, where world-class competitors do battle in the summer.
Off map 94 J8 Ledrington Road, Crystal Palace SE19 2BB 020 8778 0131 63, 322 Crystal Palace

MILLWALL FOOTBALL CLUB
www.millwallfc.co.uk
Don't be worried by any rumours you may have heard about the bad reputation of Millwall supporters. Since moving to the 20,000 all-seater New Den in 1993, the club has cultivated a more family-oriented atmosphere and are currently going well in League One, football's third tier.
Off map 95 P6 The New Den, Zampa Road, Bermondsey SE16 3LN 020 7232 1222 Surrey Quays 1, 21, 47, 53, 172, 188, 381, P12 New Cross, South Bermondsey

HEALTH AND BEAUTY

THE CLUB AT COUNTY HALL
www.theclubatcountyhall.com
Located on the south bank of the Thames between Westminster and the London Eye, this private club within the Marriott Hotel offers a 25m (82ft) pool, steam room, sauna, Jacuzzi, gym and beauty treatments.
94 K6 County Hall SE1 7PB 020 7928 4900 Mon–Wed 9–8, Thu–Fri 8am–9pm, Sat–Sun 10–6. Booking essential Day membership from £29 (as guest of member, or by separate negotiation) Westminster, Waterloo 12, 53, 159, 211

SOUTH BANK CLUB
www.southbankclub.co.uk
This huge health and fitness club has a great gym, equipped with state-of-the-art apparatus, where you can work out alone or in a class. There are also squash courts, sauna and steam facilities and a spa pool.
Off map 94 J8 124–130 Wandsworth Road SW8 2LD 020 7622 6866 Mon–Thu 6.30am–11pm, Fri 6.30am–9pm, Sat–Sun 8.30–8 Treatments from £30 77, 87 Wandsworth Road

FOR CHILDREN

ALL FIRED UP
www.allfiredupceramics.co.uk
This is a fun place to be creative and solve any gift or souvenir headaches at the same time. You can hand paint a range of durable ceramics from plates to piggy banks at very reasonable prices and collect them a few days later. There's a nice cafe too.
Off map 95 N8 34 East Dulwich Road SE22 9AX 020 7732 6688 Mon–Tue, Sat 9.30–6, Wed–Thu 9.30am–10pm, Sun 10.30–4.30 Adult £4.50 paint/fire ceramic pieces, child (3–16) £3, under 3s free. Price for ceramics varies 12, 40, 63, 78, 176, 185, 484 East Dulwich

NAMCO STATION
www.namcostation.co.uk
Action-packed interactive entertainment on three levels, from tenpin bowling to dodgems and every kind of video game and simulator imaginable, including downhill skiing, skateboarding, Grand Prix racing, martial arts, jet-skiing, soccer, horse-racing.
94 K6 County Hall, Riverside Building, South Bank SE1 7PB 020 7967 1066 Daily 10am–12am Free entry Waterloo, Westminster 77, RV1

NATIONAL FILM THEATRE
Weekend film screenings (▷ 87).
Adults £7.90, child (under 16) £5

TATE MODERN
Saturday workshops for over-fives, with storytelling and poets. 'Start' is on Sundays from 11 to 5 (tel 020 7887 3959 for more information), with Tate-related games and puzzles.
▷ 80–81.

PRICES AND SYMBOLS
The prices given are for a two-course set lunch (L) and a three-course à la carte dinner (D) for one person, without drinks. The wine price is for the least expensive bottle.

For a key to the symbols, ▷ 2.

BALTIC
www.balticrestaurant.co.uk
The vodka bar is trendy, the restaurant even trendier. White walls, steel chairs and abstract paintings provide a modern setting for predominantly traditional Eastern European cuisine. You might start with *kopytka* (potato dumplings) with tomato sauce, and follow with a leek and wild mushroom risotto made from *kasza*, a type of barley with a nutty taste. Jazz every Sun at 7pm.
94 L6 74 Blackfriars Road SE1 8HA 020 7928 1111 Daily 12–3.30, 6.30–11.15. Closed 25–26 Dec, 1 Jan, public hols L from £14.50, D from £27, Wine from £15 (carafe from £10.50) Southwark

BLUEPRINT CAFÉ
www.blueprintcafe.com
A bustling, stylish restaurant in the Design Museum (▷ 73) with unrivalled views over the River Thames to Tower Bridge and the City. The decor is sophisticated and simple, as is the menu, which changes daily. Modern European dishes are presented in a straightforward manner—for example, saffron risotto or chicken with hummus and raita. A splendid place for summer dining.
95 P6 The Design Museum, 28 Shad Thames SE1 2YD 020 7378 7031 Mon–Sat 12–3, 6–11, Sun 12–4. Closed 25–28 Dec, 1 Jan L from £25, D from £32, Wine from £17 Tower Hill, London Bridge

BUTLERS WHARF CHOP HOUSE
www.chophouse.co.uk
A traditional British restaurant on the River Thames, close to the Tower of London. Doors that run the length of the whole restaurant are opened during fine weather, and tables are set outside. Typical dishes are crab soup with sour cream and sippets (small pieces of toast), slow-roasted pork with prunes, and sticky toffee pudding. The bar area by the entrance has its own menu and requires no booking. Check out the bargain New World wines—always a popular choice.
95 P5 The Butler's Wharf Building, 36e Shad Thames SE1 2YE 020 7403 3403 Mon–Sat 12–3, 6–11, Sun 6–10. Closed Good Fri L from £22, D from £30, Wine from £22 Tower Hill, London Bridge 47, 188, 381, C10

CANTINA DEL PONTE
Lots of lusty Italian flavours are to be savoured at this modern riverside location. Apart from the tasty pizzas and pastas, there are traditional delights such as veal Milanese and excellent seafood. The outdoor

Above *Butlers Wharf Chop House is a great place to eat al fresco on a warm day*

seating has a huge canopy and patio heaters.
95 P5 The Butler's Wharf Building, 36c Shad Thames SE1 2YE 020 7403 5403 Mon–Sat 12–3, 6–11, Sun 6–10 L £10 (fixed 2 courses), £15 (fixed 3 courses), D £17.50 (fixed 3 courses), Wine from £15 Tower Hill, London Bridge 47, 188, 381, C10

CANTINA VINOPOLIS

www.cantinavinopolis.com

This vivacious, wine-themed restaurant with understated furnishings, bare brick walls, terracotta floor tiles and high ceilings is just a few minutes walk from the Thames and has a relaxed, brasserie style. Simple dishes with a strong Mediterranean influence are prepared in the open-view kitchen, and might include tian of smoked chicken and avocado with French vinaigrette or seared tuna with crushed new potatoes, sun-blushed tomatoes and salsa verde. There's an extensive and inspiring international wine list and a huge choice available by the glass.
95 M5 1 Bankside SE1 9BU 020 7940 8333 Mon–Sat 12–3, 6–10.30, Sun 12–4. Closed 25–26 Dec, 1 Jan L from £15, D from £30, Wine from £15.75 London Bridge

CHAMPOR-CHAMPOR

www.champor-champor.com

This is a small, wonderfully bohemian, southeast Asian restaurant in the Borough district. The name, which can be roughly translated from Malay as 'mix and match', is the key to the menu, which reflects Asian cuisines with roots in Malaysia plus a taste of the exotic. A two-course, fixed-price meal might include poached king prawns in Chinese rice wine followed by boneless quail, botok-botok, coconut rice and lemon grass gravy.
95 N6 62–64 Weston Street SE1 3QJ 020 7403 4600 Mon–Sat 6.15–10.15. Closed Sun, Easter, 24 Dec–2 Jan, public hols D from £29, Wine from £15 London Bridge

GEORGETOWN

www.georgetownrestaurants.co.uk

This upscale, colonial-style, Malaysian restaurant combines indigenous Malay cuisine with flavours imported by Mandarin Chinese and Tamil Indian immigrants. Nasi goreng, Mandarin tim sum and Chettinad koli typify the three culinary strands.
95 M5 10 London Bridge Street SE1 9SG 020 7357 7359 Mon–Sat 7–11, 12–3, 5.30–11, Sun 12–3 B from £4, L and D from £25, Wine from £18 London Bridge 35, 47, 48, 149, 381, 512, RV1

MAGDALEN

www.magdalenrestaurant.co.uk

The food here is basically British with European, especially French, influences, served in a warmly decorated, two-storey restaurant. Starters such as potted Devon crab can be followed by treats like roast pheasant with braised red cabbage, bacon and chestnuts. Round it all off with a sticky rum baba.
95 N5 152 Tooley Street SE1 2TU 020 7403 1342 Mon–Fri 12–2.30, 6.30–10.30, Sat 6.30–10.30 L £15.50 (fixed 2 courses), D £18.50 (fixed 3 courses), Wine from £17 London Bridge 47, 48, 149, 381, 512, RV1

THE OXO TOWER RESTAURANT

www.harveynichols.com

With its amazing views through floor-to-ceiling windows overlooking the River Thames and the City, this cubed tower tends to impress all those who visit. Cuisine is Modern European with elements of fusion; typical dishes on offer could be monkfish tail, pearl barley sauce with cauliflower and almond pureé

Below *The Oxo Tower Restaurant offers great food in an enviable location*

or venison saddle and shoulder with cranberries, celeriac cream and juniper jus. Desserts might include wild strawberry soufflé with milk ice cream.
94 L5 8th Floor, Oxo Tower Wharf, Barge House Street SE1 9PH 020 7803 3888 Mon–Sat 12–2.30, 4–11, Sun 4.30–10, 6.30–10. Closed 25–26 Dec L from £33 (3 courses), D from £45, Wine from £20 Blackfriars

LE PONT DE LA TOUR

Another modern riverside establishment in this revitalized wharf, offering splendid views of Tower Bridge. The upscale French menu includes delights such as celeriac soup with garlic croutons and Label Anglais chicken with braised cabbage and morel sauce. Impressive wine list too.
95 P5 The Butler's Wharf Building, 36d Shad Thames SE1 2YE 020 7403 8403 Mon–Fri 12–3, 6–11, Sat 12–4, 6–11, Sun 6–10 L from £21.50, D £39.50 (3 courses), Wine from £23 Tower Hill, London Bridge 47, 188, 381, C10

RSJ

www.rsj.uk.com
RSJ is set a block back from the river but is very handily placed for the South Bank theatre scene and convenient to Waterloo station. The Modern British food is top quality and excellent value (particularly the fixed-price dinner menu) and the charming, simple, modern and informal surroundings are very relaxing. Expect the likes of Caledonian rib-eye steak with grilled peppers, aubergine and courgettes.
94 K5 33 Coin Street SE1 9NR 020 7928 4554 Mon–Fri 12–2.30, 5.30–11, Sat 5.30–11. Closed Christmas, 1 Jan L from £15.95, D from £27, Wine from £16.50 Waterloo

PUBS

THE ANCHOR

This historic pub lies in the shadow of Shakespeare's Globe (▷ 78). Diarist Samuel Pepys supposedly watched the Great Fire of London from here in 1666, and regulars over the years have included writer Oliver Goldsmith and painter Sir Joshua Reynolds. There are excellent river views, black beams, faded plasterwork and a maze of tiny rooms. A varied menu includes pan-fried halibut with olives and cod in crispy bacon served on wilted spinach. Garden and patio overlooking the River Thames.
95 M5 Bankside, 34 Park Street SE1 9EF 020 7407 1577 Mon–Sat 11–11, Sun 12–10.30. Restaurant: Mon–Sat 12–2.30, 5–10, Sun 12–9.30 Bar meals from £6, D from £22.50 London Bridge, Mansion House

THE ANCHOR & HOPE

With two rosettes for its excellent food, good Eagle IPA beer and a family-friendly policy, this award-winning gastropub manages to appeal to most tastes without diluting its strengths. For sunny days there's a garden and street-seating. It is convenient for Waterloo station and the South Bank. Groups will also appreciate its innovative policy of pricing selected main courses for up to six diners (such as rib of beef, chips and Béarnaise sauce).
94 L6 36 The Cut SE1 8LP 020 7928 9898 Tue–Sun 11–11, Mon 5–11. Restaurant Tue–Sat 12–2.30, 6–10.30, Sun 12.30–5, Mon 6–10.30 Bar meals from £15, D from £30 Waterloo, Southwark

FOUNDERS ARMS

www.foundersarms.co.uk
This modern Youngs pub has a trendily designed interior and offers tasty bar food such as beer-battered fish and chips, steak and ale pie and pastas, salads and sandwiches. But the real attraction is the riverside patio, where you can watch a Waterloo sunset.
94 L5 52 Hopton Street, Bankside SE1 9JH 020 7928 1899 Mon–Thu 10am–11pm, Fri 10am–12am, Sat 9am–12am, Sun 9am–11pm; food served until 10pm Bar meals from £7.50 Southwark, Waterloo Blackfriars 45, 63, RV1

THE GEORGE INN

This 17th-century coaching inn is now owned by the National Trust. It has a lovely courtyard and fading plasterwork, black beams and a warren of tiny rooms inside. Food is along the tried and trusty lines of steak, ale-and-Guinness pie and traditional fish and chips, and they also serve some decent real ales (beers made in the barrel by the traditional method).
95 M5 77 Borough High Street SE1 1NH 020 7407 2056 Mon–Sat 11–11, Sun 12–10.30. Meals: daily 12–5. Closed 25 Dec Bar meals from £5.50, D from £20 London Bridge

KINGS ARMS

A hidden gem of a pub, tucked away in a lovely residential street only a few minutes' walk from Waterloo. There is a pleasant, down-to-earth atmosphere and a good range of real ales and lagers, as well as quality Thai food.
94 K5 25 Roupell Street, Waterloo SE1 8TP 020 7207 0784 Mon–Sat 11–11, Sun 12–10.30; food served Mon–Fri 12–3, 6–10.30, Sun 12–4 Meals from £8 Southwark, Waterloo 4, 26, 68, 139, 171, 176, 243, 381

THE OLD SALT QUAY

Popular pub with a riverside garden, a range of ales and tasty but pricey seafood and steak in the menu. Tends to get quite crowded so service can be a problem.
Off map 95 P6 163 Rotherhithe Street SE1 5QU 020 7394 7108 Mon–Sat 11am–2am, Sun 11–11 From £6.95 Rotherhithe 381, C10

THE ROYAL OAK

www.fancyapint.com/pubs/pub1228.html
This lovely Victorian pub stands in the heart of Borough and attracts many locals as well as City workers. The fine pub grub includes the likes of rabbit casserole, quality meat pies and proper Sunday roasts, which can all be accompanied by real ales or a range of fine wines.
95 M6 44 Tabard Steet SE1 4JU 0871 258 9747 Mon–Fri 11–11, Sat 12–11, Sun 12–6 Bar meals from £6 Borough 21, 35, 40, 133, 343, 344, 381

PRICES AND SYMBOLS

Prices given are the starting price for a double room for one night. Breakfast is included unless noted otherwise. All the hotels listed accept credit cards unless otherwise stated. Note that rates vary widely throughout the year.

For a key to the symbols, ▷ 2.

ALL SEASONS LONDON SOUTHWARK ROSE

www.southwarkrosehotel.co.uk

Very conveniently located for all the South Bank attractions, this modern hotel offers comfortable rooms at reasonable rates, as well as six spacious suites. All rooms have 32in flat-screen TVs and complementary WiFi. The stylish restaurant offers hearty British fare.

95 M5 47 Southwark Bridge Road SE1 9HH 020 7015 1480 Double from £185 78 London Bridge 344, 381, RV1

CANNIZARO HOUSE

www.cannizarohouse.com

Once frequented only by London's elite, this extremely elegant 18th-century mansion stands amid beautifully landscaped grounds in peaceful Wimbledon. Fine paintings, murals and fireplaces feature throughout the building and each room is furnished separately with the utmost attention to detail. The restaurant serves quality, largely organic produce.

Off map 94 J8 West Side, Wimbledon Common SW19 4UE 020 8879 1464 Double from £155 46 Wimbledon 93, 200

DEVONPORT HOUSE

www.devere.co.uk

Set in the leafy grounds of the Maritime Museum, there are few more imposing buildings to stay in than this World Heritage Site. The rooms have all been modernized tastefully to ensure comfort while maintaining character, and there are 22 meeting and training rooms. The restaurant is highly recommended.

Off map 95 P8 King William Walk, Greenwich SE10 9JW 020 8269 5400 Double from £129 94 Cutty Sark 129, 177, 180, 188, 199, 266, 386

EXPRESS BY HOLIDAY INN

www.exhisouthwark.co.uk

A good-value modern hotel, suitable for both families and business travellers. The rooms are simple but spacious, with Sky TV and power showers. Only the complimentary breakfast is served but there are pubs and restaurants nearby.

94 L5 103–109 Southwark Street SE1 0JQ 020 7401 2525 Double from £135 88 Southwark, London Bridge 344, 381, RV1

IBIS HOTEL GREENWICH

www.ibishotel.com

Modern hotel offering comfortable accommodation in bright and practical rooms. There's a self-service breakfast buffet and dinner is also available. Only minutes from the Royal Observatory, the vast park and the heart of trendy Greenwich.

Off map 95 P8 30 Stockwell Street, Greenwich SE10 9JN 020 8305 1177 Double from £98 82 Cutty Sark 129, 177, 180, 188, 199, 266, 386

LONDON BRIDGE HOTEL

www.londonbrigdehotel.com

Elegant, independently owned hotel enjoying a prime location on the edge of the City, next to London Bridge train station. Bedrooms include a number of spacious deluxe rooms and suites. The public

Left *The stylish entrance lobby at the London Bridge Hotel*

areas are small yet sophisticated. The Georgetown Asian restaurant offers Malaysian cuisine in a colonial setting and the stylish contemporary Borough bar is a good place for drinks and casual dining. There's a well-equipped gym on-site.
95 M5 8–18 London Bridge Street SE1 9SG 020 7855 2200 Double from £202 138 (10 smoking) London Bridge 47, 343, RV1

LONDON MARRIOTT HOTEL COUNTY HALL

www.marriott.com
Luxury hotel in an enviable position, occupying the riverside building that formerly housed the Greater London Council, the city's governing body. Bedrooms have excellent facilities and enjoy superb London views. Public areas include the library lounge and a crescent-shaped restaurant overlooking Westminster, which serves a range of contemporary cuisine. Residents here have access to the extensive spa and health complex.
94 K6 Westminster Bridge Road, County Hall SE1 7PB 020 7928 5200 Double from £289 200 Indoor Westminster, Waterloo 12, 77, 148, RV1

MAD HATTER HOTEL

www.fullershotels.com
Attractive hotel that has maintained the 19th-century facade of this former millinery factory. The stylish theme of the exterior is continued inside, with all the rooms decked out in lavish period furnishings. Unsurprisingly, as it is owned by the renowned west London brewery Fullers, there is an attached pub serving excellent beer and bar food.
94 L5 3–7 Stamford Street SE1 9NY 020 7401 9222 Double from £135 30 Waterloo, Southwark 45, 63, RV1

MERCURE LONDON CITY BANKSIDE

www.mercure.com
A contemporary hotel forming part of the South Bank rejuvenation. The air-conditioned bedrooms are spacious and there's modern dining in the stylish restaurant.
94 L5 71–79 Southwark Street SE1 0JA 020 7902 0800 Double from £225 144 (6 smoking) Waterloo, Southwark, London Bridge 381, 705

NOVOTEL LONDON CITY SOUTH

www.novotel.com
One of the Novotel chain's new generation, this location has a contemporary design, with smart, modern bedrooms and spacious public areas. Guests can relax in the sauna and steam room or work up a sweat in the gym.
95 M5 53–61 Southwark Bridge Road SE1 9HH 020 7089 0400 Double from £109 182 Southwark, London Bridge 344, 381, RV1

TRAVEL INN LONDON COUNTY HALL

www.premiertravelinn.com
The rooms here are simple but functional, neatly designed and quite comfortable. All have their own bathrooms and will accommodate up to two adults and two children (under 15) So, if all you really want is a bed for the night in the heart of central London (right next to the London Eye and opposite the Houses of Parliament, though sadly with no views in this direction) then you can't beat the value/location equation that this chain hotel offers. It occupies the modern part of the old County Hall, which was formerly the headquarters of the Greater London Council.
94 K6 County Hall, Belvedere Road SE1 7PB 0870 238 3300 Double from £99 313 Waterloo 77, RV1

Below *A room at the London Bridge Hotel*

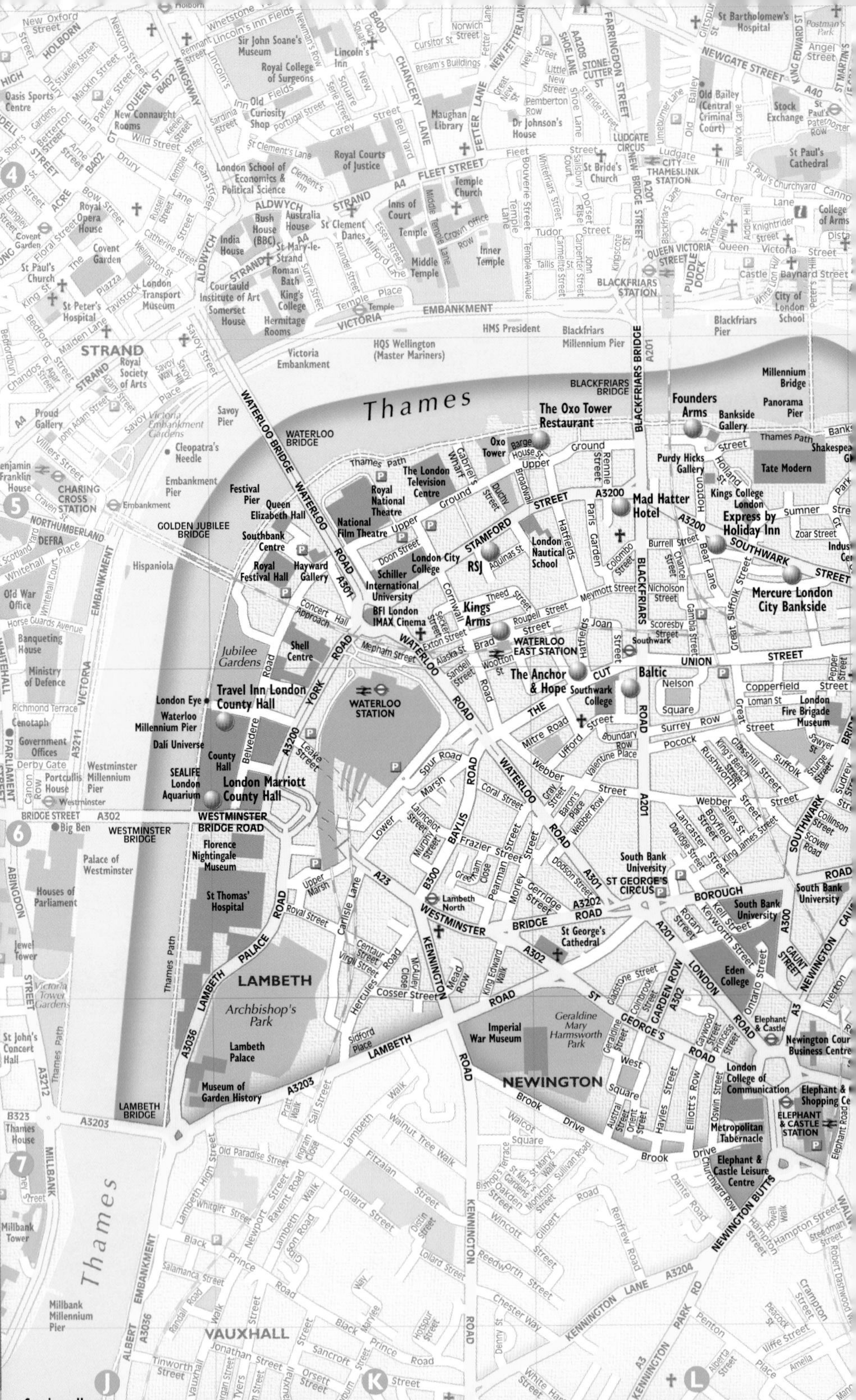
Thames
The Oxo Tower Restaurant
Founders Arms
Mad Hatter Hotel
Express by Holiday Inn
RSJ
Kings Arms
Mercure London City Bankside
The Anchor & Hope
Baltic
Travel Inn London County Hall
London Marriott County Hall
WATERLOO STATION
WATERLOO EAST STATION
BLACKFRIARS STATION
CHARING CROSS STATION
ELEPHANT & CASTLE STATION
CITY THAMESLINK STATION
Tate Modern
Royal National Theatre
National Film Theatre
Royal Festival Hall
Hayward Gallery
Queen Elizabeth Hall
Southbank Centre
BFI London IMAX Cinema
London Eye
County Hall
SEALIFE London Aquarium
Dalí Universe
Imperial War Museum
Florence Nightingale Museum
St Thomas' Hospital
Lambeth Palace
Museum of Garden History
Houses of Parliament
Palace of Westminster
Big Ben
St Paul's Cathedral
Royal Courts of Justice
Somerset House
LAMBETH
NEWINGTON
VAUXHALL
STRAND
WATERLOO BRIDGE
BLACKFRIARS BRIDGE
WESTMINSTER BRIDGE
LAMBETH BRIDGE
Millennium Bridge

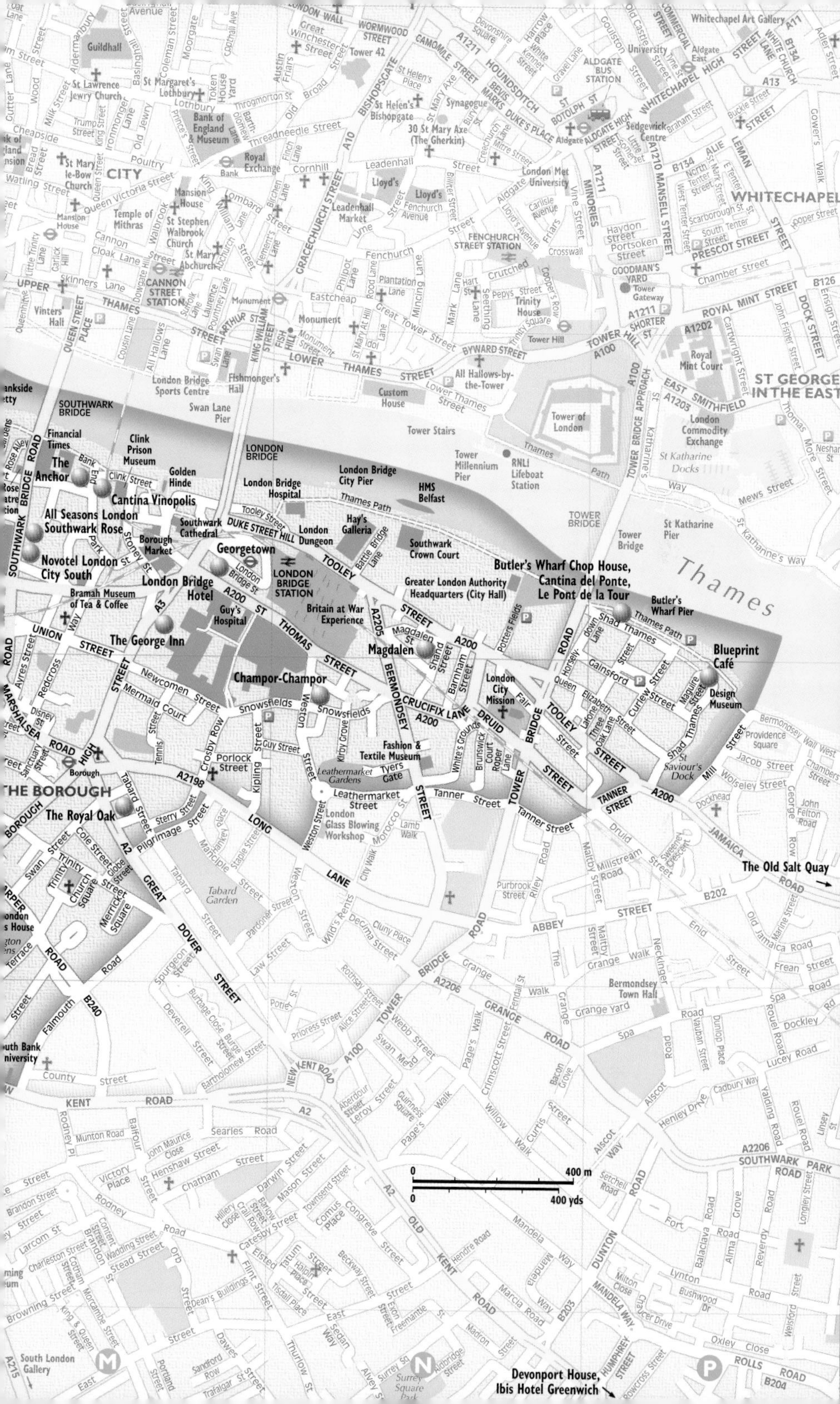

CITY
WHITECHAPEL
ST GEORGE IN THE EAST
THE BOROUGH
Thames
The Anchor
Cantina Vinopolis
All Seasons London Southwark Rose
Novotel London City South
Georgetown
London Bridge Hotel
The George Inn
Champor-Champor
Magdalen
Butler's Wharf Chop House, Cantina del Ponte, Le Pont de la Tour
Blueprint Café
The Royal Oak
The Old Salt Quay
Devonport House, Ibis Hotel Greenwich
Guildhall
Bank of England & Museum
Royal Exchange
Lloyd's
Leadenhall Market
30 St Mary Axe (The Gherkin)
Tower 42
Monument
Custom House
Tower of London
Tower Bridge
HMS Belfast
London Bridge
Southwark Bridge
London Bridge Station
Cannon Street Station
Fenchurch Street Station
Southwark Cathedral
Borough Market
Clink Prison Museum
Golden Hinde
London Dungeon
Hay's Galleria
Britain at War Experience
Guy's Hospital
Greater London Authority Headquarters (City Hall)
Design Museum
Fashion & Textile Museum
Bermondsey Town Hall
St Katharine Docks
Royal Mint Court
London Commodity Exchange
South London Gallery
Tooley Street
Long Lane
Tower Bridge Road
Old Kent Road
Jamaica Road
Great Dover Street
Borough High Street
Southwark Park Road
0
400 m
0
400 yds

ENTRY TO THE TRAITORS' GATE

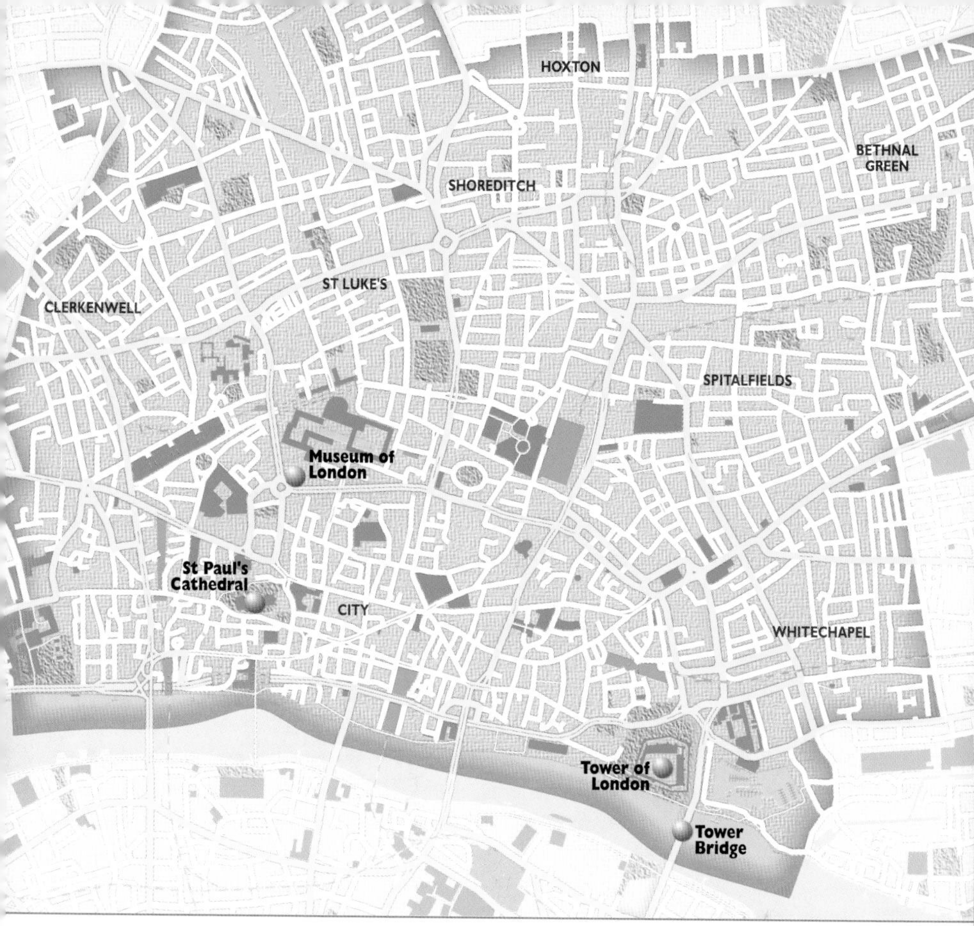

FLEET STREET TO THE TOWER

Nestling on the north bank of the Thames, the densely built-up area between the erstwhile home of the newspaper industry in Fleet Street and the hallowed turrets of the Tower of London encompasses some of the capital's oldest structures. It has at its core the traditional economic heart that is the City of London. Although the bowler hats are a thing of the past, there is still a palpable sense of purpose in the stride of the current generation of wheelers and dealers as they dart to and fro from their lairs in the tightly packed banks and other financial institutions. There might not be the mass of soaring skyscrapers as in Manhattan, but some of London's narrowest alleys run in maze-like fashion between these hives of money-making activity and, of the few high-rise buildings that do exist, the iconic post-millenial edifice at 30 St. Mary Axe has become affectionately known as the Gherkin because of its shape.

It's not all about business, though. The City has a soul too, exemplified in most dramatic fashion by the heaven-piercing dome of St. Paul's Cathedral, one of the world's great places of worship. At the far west end of Fleet Street, Britain's moral code is personified in the gilt statue of Justice that stands atop the Old Bailey criminal court. Justice of a more summary nature used to be meted out to traitors at the Tower of London, of course, usually in the form of an axe and chopping block. Another structure of historical note is the stone column known simply as the Monument, which marks the spot where the Great Fire started in 1666, while just north of the Tower and near the Barbican Centre you can see some of the best remains of the original Roman city walls.

400 m
400 yards
PENTONVILLE
CLERKENWELL
ST LUKE'S
SHOREDITCH
CITY
Thames
City University
The City University
Moorfields Eye Hospital
Wesley's Chapel, House & Museum
Honourable Artillery Company Headquarters
Mount Pleasant Postal Sorting Office
London Weather Centre
Gray's Inn
Inns of Court & School of Law
St John's Gate
St Bartholomew's Medical School
Charterhouse
Central London Markets (Smithfield)
The Barbican
Guildhall School of Music & Drama
City University Business School
Museum of London
St Bartholomew's the Great
St Bartholomew's Hospital
Exhibition Halls
Ironmonger Row Baths
Finsbury Leisure Centre
London Silver Vaults
Lincoln's Inn
Royal College of Surgeons
Maughan Library
Dr Johnson's House
Old Bailey (Central Criminal Court)
Stock Exchange
St Paul's Cathedral
Guildhall
Clock Museum
St Lawrence Jewry Church
Bank of England Extension
Bank of England & Museum
Royal Exchange
St Mary le-Bow Church
Mansion House
Temple of Mithras
St Stephen Walbrook Church
St Mary Abchurch
Royal Courts of Justice
Temple Church
Inns of Court
Middle Temple
Inner Temple
St Clement Danes
St Bride's Church
College of Arms
City of London School
Vinters' Hall
HMS President
HQS Wellington (Master Mariners)
Blackfriars Millennium Pier
Blackfriars Pier
Millennium Bridge
Bankside Jetty
Panorama Pier
London Bridge Sports Centre
Fishmonger's Hall
Swan Lane Pier
Tate Modern
Shakespeare's Globe
Bankside Gallery
Oxo Tower
Purdy Hicks Gallery
Financial Times
Clink Prison Museum
Rose Theatre Exhibition
Vinopolis
Golden Hinde
London Bridge Hospital
Southwark Cathedral
Borough Market
The London Television Centre
Royal National Theatre
National Film Theatre
Hayward Gallery
Royal Festival Hall
London City College
Schiller International University
London Nautical School
Kings College London
Industrial Centre
Bramah Museum of Tea & Coffee
Guy's Hospital
BFI London IMAX Cinema
Shell Centre
WATERLOO EAST STATION
LONDON BRIDGE STATION
OLD STREET STATION
FARRINGDON STATION
BARBICAN STATION
MOORGATE STATION
CITY THAMESLINK STATION
BLACKFRIARS STATION
CANNON STREET STATION
BLACKFRIARS BRIDGE
SOUTHWARK BRIDGE
LONDON BRIDGE
WATERLOO BRIDGE
VICTORIA EMBANKMENT
FLEET STREET
HOLBORN VIADUCT
NEWGATE STREET
LONDON WALL
CHEAPSIDE
QUEEN VICTORIA STREET
UPPER THAMES STREET
CITY ROAD
GOSWELL ROAD
PENTONVILLE ROAD

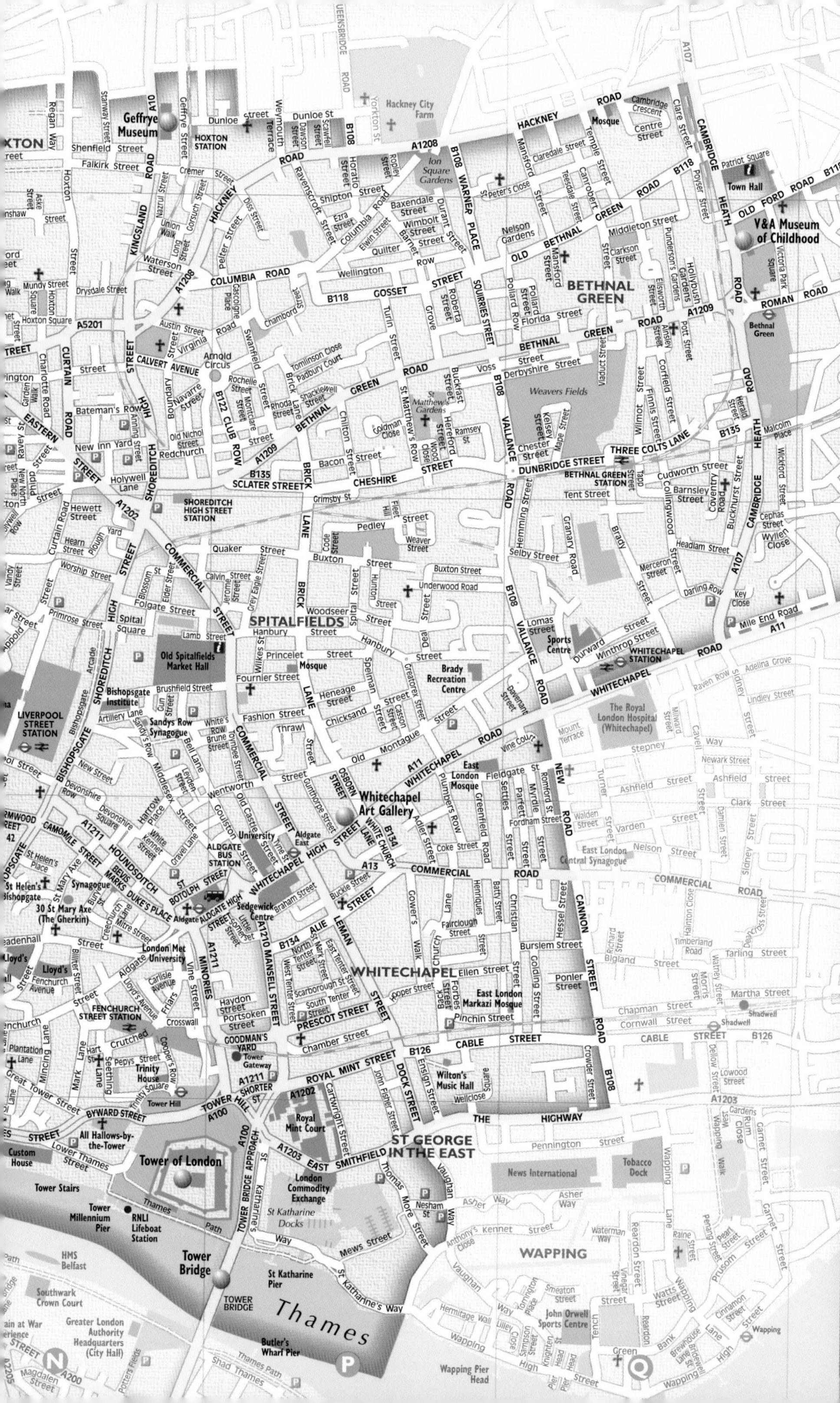
Geffrye Museum
HOXTON STATION
Hackney City Farm
Ion Square Gardens
Town Hall
V&A Museum of Childhood
BETHNAL GREEN
Bethnal Green
Arnold Circus
Weavers Fields
St Matthew's Gardens
Nelson Gardens
BETHNAL GREEN STATION
SHOREDITCH HIGH STREET STATION
SPITALFIELDS
Old Spitalfields Market Hall
Mosque
Brady Recreation Centre
Sports Centre
WHITECHAPEL STATION
The Royal London Hospital (Whitechapel)
Bishopsgate Institute
LIVERPOOL STREET STATION
Sandys Row Synagogue
East London Mosque
Whitechapel Art Gallery
University
ALDGATE BUS STATION
Aldgate East
Aldgate
East London Central Synagogue
St Helen's Bishopsgate
Synagogue
30 St Mary Axe (The Gherkin)
Sedgewick Centre
Lloyd's
London Met University
WHITECHAPEL
East London Markazi Mosque
FENCHURCH STREET STATION
GOODMAN'S YARD
Tower Gateway
Trinity House
Tower Hill
Wilton's Music Hall
Royal Mint Court
ST GEORGE IN THE EAST
All Hallows-by-the-Tower
Custom House
Tower of London
London Commodity Exchange
St Katharine Docks
News International
Tobacco Dock
Tower Stairs
Tower Millennium Pier
RNLI Lifeboat Station
WAPPING
HMS Belfast
Tower Bridge
St Katharine Pier
Thames
Southwark Crown Court
Greater London Authority Headquarters (City Hall)
Butler's Wharf Pier
John Orwell Sports Centre
Wapping Pier Head
Shadwell
Wapping
Mosque
COMMERCIAL ROAD
WHITECHAPEL ROAD
CABLE STREET
THE HIGHWAY
BETHNAL GREEN ROAD
HACKNEY ROAD
CAMBRIDGE HEATH ROAD
OLD BETHNAL GREEN ROAD
COLUMBIA ROAD
COMMERCIAL STREET
BRICK LANE
SHOREDITCH HIGH STREET
BISHOPSGATE
MINORIES
MANSELL STREET
LEMAN STREET
CANNON STREET ROAD
VALLANCE ROAD
MILE END ROAD
EAST SMITHFIELD
ROYAL MINT STREET
TOWER BRIDGE APPROACH
TOWER HILL
BYWARD STREET

BANK OF ENGLAND MUSEUM

www.bankofengland.co.uk/museum

The Old Lady of Threadneedle Street, the nation's central bank, occupies a massive, undistinguished, seven-storey office building designed and erected by English architect Sir Herbert Baker between 1925 and 1939. Sculptures on its facade of Britannia are by sculptor Sir Charles Wheeler (1892–1974), and inside there's a museum (entrance on Bartholomew Lane) tracing the history of the nation's finances from the bank's foundation in 1694 to today's high-tech environment. On display are a faithful restoration of the 1790s bank stock office, a late 18th-century banking hall by Sir John Soane (▷ 148–149) and chronological displays of minted coins, bank notes, gold bars from ancient times to the modern market bar, plus unexpected items such as pikes and muskets used to defend the bank. There are also documents relating to such famous customers as Horatio Nelson and George Washington.

Interactive displays reveal the intricacies of bank note design and production. A computerized simulation allows you to play at wheeling and dealing on the stock market. You also get the unusual chance to lift a genuine gold bar. Don't miss the £1-million note, used for accounting purposes only.

98 M4 Bank of England, Threadneedle Street EC2R 8 AH 020 7601 5545 Mon–Fri and day of Lord Mayor's Show (▷ 296) 10–5 Free Bank 8, 11, 25, 26, 47

THE BARBICAN

www.barbican.org.uk

This area of the city was once a maze of small streets and warehouses, before its devastation by bombs in December 1940. Today's Barbican complex, 14ha (35 acres) of concrete buildings, was built over the site between 1971 and 1982. It incorporates flats, an arts centre and premises for the Guildhall School of Music and Drama. At its heart is the D-shaped arts centre, Europe's largest multi-arts and conference venue and home of the London Symphony Orchestra. A wide range of innovative exhibitions of 20th-century and current art and design is staged in the gallery on Level 3 and in The Curve (ground floor). There's also a lively programme of jazz, classical, contemporary and world music, and two cinemas showing independent, art-house and mainstream films. Stage productions take place in the Barbican Theatre or the smaller Pit.

98 M3 Silk Street EC2Y 8DS 0207 7638 4141; 020 7638 8891 (box office) Mon–Sat 8am–11pm, Sun 11–11. Box office daily 9–8 Free; separate charges for productions and exhibitions in Level 3 gallery Barbican 4, 8, 11, 23, 26, 56, 153

DR. JOHNSON'S HOUSE

www.drjohnsonshouse.org

This large, dark-brick house buried in a maze of courtyards and passages is one of the few residential 18th-century buildings surviving in the City of London. It was the home and workplace of journalist, poet and lexicographer Dr. Samuel Johnson (1709–84) from 1748 to 1759, and it was here that Johnson compiled the first comprehensive English dictionary, published in 1755.

Restored to its original condition, with panelled rooms and a pine staircase, the house contains a collection of period furniture, prints and portraits, as well as first editions of the dictionary. While Johnson worked on his entries for the dictionary in his own corner of the house, six copyists stood in the garret to transcribe them.

98 K4 17 Gough Square EC4A 3DE 020 7353 3745 May–end Sep Mon–Sat 11–5.30; Oct–end Apr Mon–Sat 11–5 Adult £4.50, child (10–16) £1.50, under 10s free, family £10 Temple, Holborn, Chancery Lane (closed Sun) 4, 11, 15, 26, 76, 172

GEFFRYE MUSEUM

www.geffrye-museum.org.uk

A series of rooms decorated and furnished in period style takes you through 400 years of domestic life, starting with an oak-panelled, 17th-century room and passing through Georgian restraint and elaborate Victorian design eventually to reach a 20th-century converted warehouse space.

A 1998 extension brings displays up to the present, and includes modern furniture and interiors, as well as a temporary exhibition gallery and design centre. Changes in horticultural style are reflected in the gardens, arranged as outdoor rooms and including a walled herb garden.

The Geffrye Almshouses—14 houses and a chapel—are open on the first Saturday and the first and third Wednesday of the month. They were originally built for elderly and impoverished ironmongers and their widows in 1715 on land bequeathed by Sir Robert Geffrye, a former Lord Mayor of London.

99 N1 Kingsland Road, Shoreditch E2 8EA 020 7739 9893 Tue–Sat 10–5, Sun 12–5. Garden open Apr–end Oct during museum opening hours Free; almshouses £2 adult, children free Old Street, Liverpool Street 67, 149, 242, 243

Left *Dr. Johnson's House*

Right *A 19th-century drawing room in the Geffrye Museum*

GUILDHALL

www.cityoflondon.gov.uk

England's third-largest civic hall, begun in 1411, is the City's only secular stone structure to have survived the Great Fire of 1666 (▷ 31). The Corporation of London, which governs the City, still has its home here.

Beyond the unusual entrance, designed in 1788 with Gothic and Indian influences, is a medieval great hall with stained-glass windows and monuments to national heroes such as Lord Nelson, the Duke of Wellington and Sir Winston Churchill. Beneath is the most extensive medieval crypt in London and London's most important recent archaeological find, the remains of the capital's only Roman amphitheatre (▷ 27).

The Guildhall library contains prints, drawings and books about the history of London, as well as the Clock Museum, which has some 600 watches, 30 clocks and 15 marine timekeepers dating from the 15th to the 20th century.

Since the 17th century the Corporation has collected works of art, mostly portraits, and paintings of naval battles and views of historic London; a changing selection is displayed in the Guildhall art gallery.

98 M4 Gresham Street EC2P 2EJ 020 7606 3030 Mon–Sat 9–5. Closed during ceremonies/events. Art gallery Mon–Sat 10–5, Sun 12–4. For clock museum check ahead 020 7332 1868/1870 Guildhall and clock museum free; art gallery £2.50, child (under 16) free; free all day Fri and from 3.30pm Mon–Thu, Sat Bank, St. Paul's, Mansion House, Moorgate 8, 11, 15

MONUMENT

www.cityoflondon.gov.uk

The devastating Great Fire of 1666 (▷ 31) wiped out the medieval heart of London. The Monument commemorates this event and the later rebuilding. Built between 1671 and 1677 to a design by Sir Christopher Wren, chief architect of the new city, it stands on the northern bank of the Thames, east of London Bridge. The fluted column of Portland stone is 62m (203ft) high, which equals the distance from the start of the fire in Pudding Lane. At the top a flaming urn of copper symbolizes the fire.

The 311 steps of a steep internal spiral stairway lead to the viewing platform, 41m (133ft) up.

98 N4 Monument Street EC3R 8AH 020 7626 2717 Daily 9.30–5.30 Adult £2, child (under 16) £1 Monument 15, 21, 25 London Bridge City Pier

Above *Stained-glass window in the Order of St. John Museum, St. John's Gate*

MUSEUM OF LONDON

▷ 103.

OLD BAILEY (CENTRAL CRIMINAL COURT)

www.cityoflondon.gov.uk

Its correct title is the Central Criminal Court, but everyone knows the courthouse as the Old Bailey, a name borrowed from the nearby street. Major criminal trials from all over England and Wales are heard in this baroque building, erected in 1907 on the site of the notorious Newgate prison (▷ 35).

A bronze, gilded figure of Justice carrying her sword and scales (but not blindfolded) crowns the green copper dome, echoing the design of nearby St. Paul's Cathedral.

Public galleries are open for viewing of trials in session.

98 L4 Central Criminal Court, Old Bailey EC4M 7EH 020 7248 3277 Mon–Fri 10–1, 2–5 (approx); reduced court sitting Aug. No admission for children under 14 Free St. Paul's 8, 15, 25, 242

ST. JOHN'S GATE

www.sja.org.uk/museum

Clerkenwell's medieval priory of St. John was the base of the Knights Hospitallers, who sent men, money and supplies to hospitals on the great pilgrim routes in Europe. Today all that remain of the buildings are the crypt of the Norman church and the Tudor gatehouse, part of which houses a museum of the history of the Order of St. John, with exhibits such as Crusader coins and Turkish Ottoman mail armour.

Victorian pioneers began the St. John Ambulance voluntary first-aid movement here. Its service continues today, and an interactive gallery relates its history.

98 L3 St. John's Lane EC1M 4DA 020 7324 4005 Mon–Fri 10–5, Sat 10–4; tours Tue, Fri, Sat 11am, 2.30pm Donations requested for tours: adult £5, children and concessions £4 (St. John Ambulance members free) Farringdon 63, 55, 243

MUSEUM OF LONDON

Laid out in a striking, modern building near the Barbican (▷ 101), the Museum of London uses exhibits, film sequences, voice commentary and interactive tools to bring the city's past to life. The displays are organized over two floors around a central courtyard. You start on the upper floor and descend a series of ramps to explore the exhibitions of London's history from prehistoric times to the 20th century.

EARLY LONDON

The London Before London gallery looks at the lives of prehistoric settlers in the area. Finds include a 9,000-year-old antler mattock (an agricultural pickaxe) recovered near the present-day site of the New Scotland Yard police headquarters, and a stone axehead, probably imported 2,500 years ago from continental Europe. Objects found along the banks of the Thames—a vital resource for the prehistoric community—are displayed in the centre.

Most impressive is the Roman London gallery, which explains the founding of Londinium in about AD50 and traces its development until AD410, when the Roman army left Britain. Large models show the city's growth, and a huge array of ordinary items shows how people lived and worked. These range from leather shoes to a hoard of gold coins, each one representing a month's pay for a Roman soldier.

The Dark Ages, Saxon and Medieval London Gallery shows objects from recent excavations never displayed before, shedding light on the Dark Ages, then moving on through such diverse topics as Anglo-Saxon relics and the Black Death.

One of the most devastating events to hit London was the Great Fire in 1666. Following the Great Plague, the result of the fire on the city was catastrophic. The London's Burning exhibition follows the story and its impact on Londoners themselves. You can also learn how the cityscape was changed for ever.

NEW DEVELOPMENTS

The lower galleries are closed until 2010. Until then there are four sections to visit, from prehistory to the Great Fire of 1666. The future will see a new visitor centre, 25 per cent more exhibition space and a superb gallery devoted to London's modern history. Of special interest will be a state-of-the-art glass-fronted gallery, which will face the street and contain the stunning Lord Mayor's coach.

INFORMATION

www.museumoflondon.org.uk
98 M3 London Wall EC2Y 5HN 020 7001 9844 Mon–Sat 10–5.50, Sun 12–5.50; also until 9pm first Thu of each month Free Moorgate, Barbican, St. Paul's, Bank 4, 8, 25, 56, 100, 521 £7.95, in English, German, French, Italian, Japanese, Spanish Cafe on lower level Small shop with good selection of books on London

Below *The rather conspicuous Lord Mayor's coach, displayed on the lower level*

SIAE·ET·URBIS·CONDITOR·CHRISTOPHORUS·WREN·QUI·VIXIT·ANNOS·ULTRA·NO

INTRODUCTION

The first St. Paul's was built in AD604, possibly on the site of a Roman temple of Apollo. Rebuilt three centuries later after a Viking attack, the structure was replaced by a huge Gothic cathedral, now known as Old St. Paul's, built by the Normans in 1087. By the 17th century this had a dubious reputation as the home of several obscure cults, such as that of the odd bearded St. Uncumber, who was most likely a figment of somebody's imagination, and the site of horse fairs and secular entertainments. After the Civil War its nave was used as a cavalry barracks, and shops were set up in its portico.

Following its destruction in the Great Fire of 1666, Sir Christopher Wren (1632–1723) was commissioned to build a new version. His first design was rejected for proposing radical European elements and the second was abandoned; the final version was an uneasy compromise between the architect and the clergy. Even then, monetary problems plagued the project, which finally got off the ground in 1675 and was completed in 1710, during the reign of Queen Anne.

Since the first service was held in 1697, the cathedral has shared with Westminster Abbey some of the most momentous ceremonies in Britain's history. These include the funerals of Lord Nelson, the Duke of Wellington and Winston Churchill; Queen Victoria's Jubilee; peace ceremonies to mark the ends of both world wars; the wedding of Charles and Diana; and thanksgiving services for both the Golden Jubilee and the 80th birthday of Queen Elizabeth II. The noble structure survived attempts by Hitler's Luftwaffe to undo Wren's work during the Blitz, and photographs of St. Paul's standing unbent among the surrounding wreckage provided strongly symbolic images of the British people's resilience.

St. Paul's is the cathedral of the Diocese of London, comprising the five episcopal areas of London, Kensington, Willesden, Edmonton and Stepney, which together account for a large part of Greater London. The Bishop of London oversees four area bishops, who are assisted in turn by archdeacons and deacons, who themselves oversee groups of parishes. In 2004 special services were held at the cathedral to celebrate the 1,400th anniversary of the diocese.

A wide flight of steps leads up to the west front entrance, flanked by two clock towers. Wren's original Classical design, using a Greek cross with the dome over the central intersection, was modified to provide an impressive processional space for the clergy, and the first view on entering is of the three-bay-long nave provided for this purpose. To the left are All Souls' Chapel and the bell tower, then St. Dunstan's Chapel. To the right is the Chapel of St. Michael and St. George. Farther down, in one of the nave arches, is the Wellington memorial, and ahead is the massive dome. Nelson's memorial is to the right, in the south transept, and beyond it is the entrance to the crypt and shop. The choir stalls and the organ case are ahead, and behind the high altar is the American Memorial Chapel. Stairs at the southwest corner of the crossing lead up to the dome and its galleries.

WHAT TO SEE

THE DOME AND GALLERIES

Eight pillars support this huge structure, over 111m (364ft) high and weighing about 66,000 tonnes. It's a stiff climb up 259 steps to the Whispering Gallery, which runs around the dome's interior. Here, acoustics are such that someone standing on the opposite side of the gallery can hear your whispers quite clearly after several seconds' delay—though only early visitors have the peace

INFORMATION

www.stpauls.co.uk
98 L4 St. Paul's Churchyard EC4M 8AD 020 7326 4128 Mon–Sat 8.30–4. Times of daily services vary—call or check online for details St. Paul's, Mansion House 4, 11, 15, 23, 25, 26, 100, 242 Blackfriars, City Thameslink Cathedral, Crypt and Galleries: adult £11, child (6–16) £3.50, under 6s free, family £25.50. Services free Mon–Sat 11am, 11.30am, 1.30pm and 2pm. Adult £3, under 10s £1. Audiotours: £4, English, French, German, Italian, Spanish, Russian, Japanese, Mandarin £3.25, in English, French, German, Italian, Japanese, Spanish Refectory restaurant. Afternoon teas, roast lunch Sunday Crypt Café. Light and airy with good snacks and light lunches; licensed CDs of psalms, organ and choral music; guidebooks; religious merchandise; Christmas decorations

Opposite *The cathedral nave is a dramatic combination of vast space and elaborate decoration*
Below *The Millennium Bridge connects St. Paul's to the South Bank*

to test the theory properly. There are fine views down to the nave below and up to the frescoes of the dome above, where scenes from the life of St. Paul were painted by Sir James Thornhill between 1716 and 1719.

Another 119 steps lead to the Stone Gallery, which encircles the exterior of the dome's base, 53m (173ft) up. Climbing higher still you pass through the timberwork that rests on the inner dome, supporting the wooden skin of the outer, lead-covered dome. Between these two domes is a third: the brick cone supporting the elegant lantern that crowns the whole structure. This can be viewed from the Golden Gallery, the smallest of the galleries, which runs around the highest point of the outer dome, 85m (279ft) and 530 steps from ground level. A hole in the floor gives a dizzying view straight down to the cathedral floor. Above are the ball and cross at the very top, originally added in 1708 and replaced in 1821. For safety reasons visitors are not allowed into the interior of the ball.

THE CHANCEL

This part of the cathedral, near the choir and altar, is a riot of Byzantine-style gilding, with mosaics of birds, fish and animals, dating from the late 19th century. In the north choir aisle is a marble sculpture by Henry Moore (1898–1986), *Mother and Child*. French master metalworker Jean Tijou (*fl*1689–*c*1711) designed the wrought-iron gates and most of the cathedral's decorative metalwork.

A statue of the Virgin and Child, originally part of the Victorian altar screen, which was damaged by a bomb during World War II, stands in the south choir aisle. Also here is a marble effigy of poet John Donne (1572–1631), who was dean of the cathedral. This is one of few effigies to have survived the Great Fire of London in 1666, and you can still make out the scorch marks on its base.

Below *The dome behind one of the towers of the west front*

The organ is the third-largest in Britain, with 7,189 pipes, 5 keyboards and 138 organ stops. Its case was carved by Grinling Gibbons (1648–1721), as were the choir stalls. The high altar, made of marble and carved and gilded oak with a canopy based on a sketch by Wren, replaced its bomb-damaged predecessor in 1958.

WELLINGTON'S TOMB

The Duke of Wellington (1769–1852), military hero of the Napoleonic Wars and prime minister from 1828 to 1830, lies in a simple Cornish granite casket under the crossing. Designed in 1858 by F. C. Penrose, it has echoes of the style of Napoleon's tomb in Les Invalides in Paris. Banners made for Wellington's funeral procession hang around the tomb, but the Prussian flag that originally hung there was removed during World War I and has never been reinstated.

NELSON'S TOMB

Admiral Nelson (1758–1805), who died in action against Napoleon at the Battle of Trafalgar, lies in the middle of the crypt, one of around 200 tombs contained in this huge space, which was part of the medieval cathedral. Nelson's coffin—carved from the mast of a defeated French ship—went with him into battle and was kept handy behind his desk. After his death, Nelson was preserved in French brandy for the journey home, and at Gibraltar the coffin was placed into a lead-lined casket and steeped in distilled wine. Finally, his remains were

TIPS

» The cathedral sometimes closes for special events so it's wise to check before a visit.

» Buy guidebooks at the west end of the cathedral or from the shop in the crypt, or online.

» If you come to one of the free organ recitals at 5pm every Sunday, bring some loose change for the collection at the end.

» A good way to get a free glimpse of the cathedral and sample its atmosphere is to attend a service.

Above *Looking up at the dome's painted ceiling*

1 West Doorway
2 All Souls' Chapel
3 St. Dunstan's Chapel
4 Wellington Memorial
5 Font
6 Martyr's Chapel
7 Choir
8 High Altar
9 American Memorial Chapel
10 St. Mary's Chapel
11 Pulpit
12 Steps down to crypt
13 Nelson Memorial
14 Steps up to Whispering Gallery and Upper Galleries
15 Chapel of St. Michael and St. George

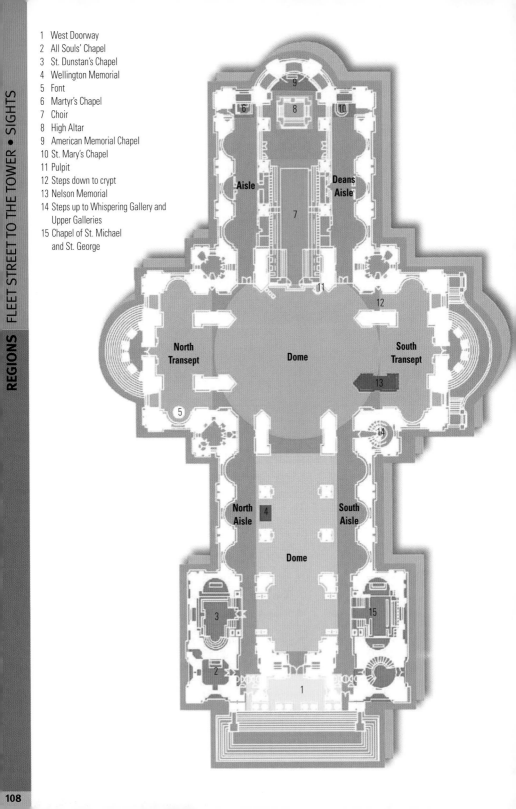

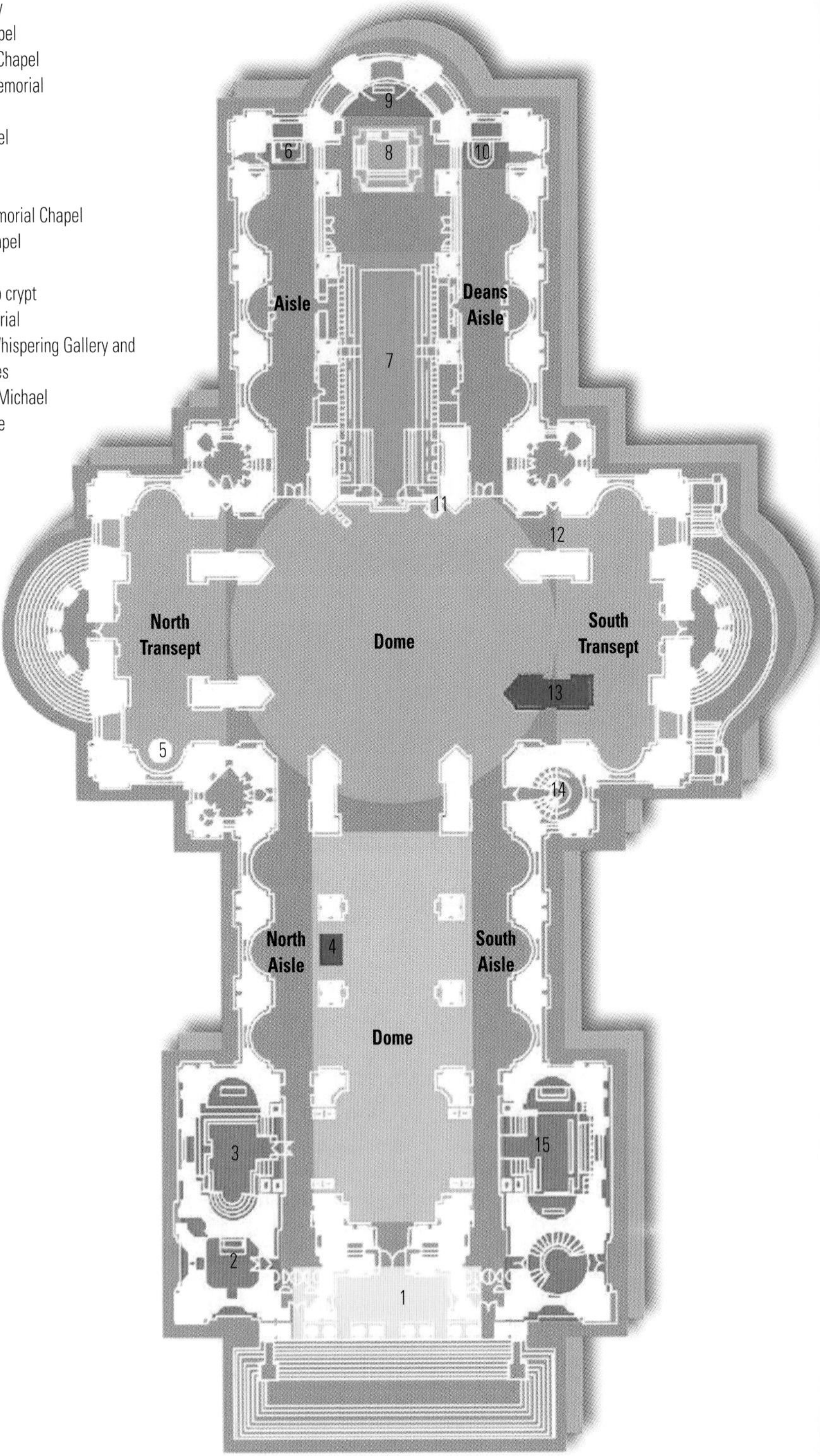

encased in two more coffins before being buried in the crypt under Cardinal Wolsey's 16th-century sarcophagus, which had remained empty since its confiscation by Henry VIII. The monument to Nelson shows two naval cadets being introduced to their hero by Britannia. It was sculpted by John Flaxman (1755–1826), an internationally famous artist in his time.

THE LIGHT OF THE WORLD

Quietly resplendent in the north transept, the cathedral's most famous painting makes for a good place to sit and reflect. The work in question is *The Light of the World* by pre-Raphaelite Holman Hunt, who in 1900 made this copy of his own original, which adorns the chapel of Keble College, Oxford. The painting is deeply symbolic, showing Christ knocking at the handleless, overgrown door of the human soul and awaiting the answer from within. Note how the lamp of the spirit gently radiates through the dark surroundings.

THE TREASURY

In the southwest section of the crypt, just before the entrance to the shop and restaurant, is the cathedral's collection of gold, silver and other precious objects. Much of the cathedral's original gold and silver was stolen during a robbery in 1810, and more than 200 of the ceremonial vessels and accessories in the current display are actually on loan from other London churches. One of St. Paul's own possessions is the 1977 Jubilee Cope, made for a thanksgiving service in honour of the 25th anniversary of Queen Elizabeth II's accession and worn by Gerald Ellison, the Bishop of London. Its ornate decoration depicts 73 embroidered London church spires. Other interesting exhibits are two effigies dating from before the Great Fire. Though they look like wood, these are stone effigies, originally painted in vivid colours. The heat of the fire fused the paint to the surface and turned them the colour of polished oak.

SIR CHRISTOPHER WREN'S MEMORIAL

A plain black slab gives tribute to the cathedral's architect, with the exhortation *'circumspice si monumentum requiris'* ('if you require a memorial, look about you'). It was inserted in the late 18th century by the surveyor of St. Paul's, Robert Mylne, after a heated debate about a suitable monument; a grand statue had also been proposed. It was Wren's son who provided the memorial's telling phrase. Other architects are commemorated nearby, along with artists including William Blake (1757–1827) and J. M. W. Turner (1775–1851).

MUSIC AT ST. PAUL'S

St. Paul's choir first appears in the records in 1127, when the Bishop of London, Richard de Belmeis, founded a choir school. To celebrate the opening of Wren's cathedral the choir sang an anthem composed by its leader, John Blow, accompanied by the new organ, described by diarist John Evelyn as the best in Europe. After 1860, when the screen that originally supported the organ was taken away, a bigger choir was needed as well as a new organ, to fill the now much larger space. The organ was built in 1872 and the choir increased to a total of 58 voices, which enabled it to establish a wider repertoire of works. Today the choir consists of 30 choristers (boy trebles), eight probationers (who will become choristers) and 18 adults—all chosen by audition. It still follows the monastic tradition of singing services: daily evensong and matins, eucharist and evensong on Sundays. It also has a busy schedule of concerts, broadcasts and recordings. The choirboys are given a normal schooling along with their musical training, which involves learning the piano and another instrument and attending two daily choral rehearsals.

Left *Both of the west front towers were originally intended to have a clock face*
Below *View from the choir of the elaborate canopy above the high altar*

TEMPLE, INNER AND MIDDLE
www.innertemple.org.uk
www.middletemple.org.uk
Two Inns of Court (▷ 140 and 144) make up the Temple, named after the crusading Knights Templar, who acquired the land in 1160. The 12th-century circular Temple Church still stands at the heart of this network of gardens and courtyards.

In addition to the church, you can visit the Inner and Middle Temple gardens and the 16th-century Middle Temple Hall, where the first recorded performance of Shakespeare's *Twelfth Night* took place. It has an impressive hammerbeam roof, Elizabethan tables and royal portraits.

Black-gowned lawyers stroll between their chambers and the Royal Courts of Justice (▷ 146–147) on the other side of Fleet Street.

98 K4 Inner Temple EC4Y 7HL; Middle Temple EC4Y 9BT Inner Temple 020 7797 8250; Middle Temple 020 7427 4800 Inner Temple Gardens Mon–Fri 12.30–3. Middle Temple Hall Mar–end Nov Mon–Fri 10–12, 3–4. Middle Temple Gardens May–end Jul, Sep Mon–Fri 12–3. Church Wed–Sat 11–4, plus services (020 7353 3470) Free Temple (closed Sun), Holborn, Chancery Lane (closed Sun) 11, 15, 23 Savoy Pier

TOWER BRIDGE
▷ 111.

TOWER OF LONDON
▷ 112–117.

V&A MUSEUM OF CHILDHOOD
www.vam.ac.uk
This museum has undergone major redevelopment since 2002. The magnificent 19th-century building has been restored and the galleries brought up to date. With nearly 6,000 exhibits spanning 400 years of childhood, this is one of the biggest and oldest collections of its kind in the world. The museum opened in 1872 as the east London branch of what would eventually become the Victoria & Albert Museum (▷ 224–228).

Exhibits include swaddling bands (cloth used to wrap babies) from the 16th century, dolls from the 17th (don't miss the Nuremberg Dolls' House, made in 1673—the only example of its type outside Germany), games from the 18th, toy theatres from the 19th, model trains from the 20th and construction kits from the 21st. Children's events and activities take place at weekends and during school holidays.

99 Q2 Cambridge Heath Road E2 9PA 020 8983 5200 Daily 10–5.45 Free, small charge for some activities Bethnal Green 106, 254, 309, 388, D6

WHITECHAPEL ART GALLERY
www.whitechapelgallery.org
Founded in 1901 to 'bring great art to the people of the East End of London', the gallery shows a changing programme of contemporary and 20th-century art, featuring new and acknowledged artists in solo shows, group exhibitions and commissions. Media range from painting and sculpture to video and photography.

The Arts and Crafts building, designed by Charles Harrison Townsend, provides over 2,230sq m (24,000sq ft) of gallery space, and was the first purpose-built British gallery to host changing exhibitions.

99 P4 77–82 Whitechapel High Street E1 7QX Recorded info: 020 7522 7878; other enquiries: 020 7522 7888 During exhibitions Tue–Wed, Fri–Sun 11–6, Thu 11–9 Free except one paying show per year; Tue free all year Aldgate East 15, 25, 67, 253 Liverpool Street

Left *Middle Temple Hall garden in the Inns of Court*

TOWER BRIDGE

London's best-known bridge, linking the Tower of London (▷ 112–117) and the South Bank promenade, has been a tourist attraction since 1982, with access to the upper walkways and engine rooms and a Tower Bridge exhibition tracing its history. There are stupendous views across London from the high-level walkway, 43m (140ft) above the Thames, and interactive computer displays help pick out the most famous buildings on the skyline, but the hydraulically operated bascules (from the French for 'see-saw') are the main attraction. Originally designed (in the late 19th century) to allow tall ships to sail through, they are still lifted more than 900 times a year for cruise liners and other large river craft. If you want to time your visit to coincide with the bridge opening, a list of times is posted daily in the entrance kiosk to the exhibition or you can call 020 7940 3984. Vessels have to give at least 24 hours' notice if they want to pass through.

The famous neo-Gothic towers, with their mock-medieval turrets, are an attraction in themselves. DVD shows and graphic display panels in the towers and on the walkways give an idea of the debates and controversies that led to the construction of the bridge, discussed since 1800 but not officially planned until 1876. Some of the designs submitted over the following seven years included a futuristic-looking structure with sliding roadways, a rolling bridge and a sub-riverain arcade. The winning design, submitted by Sir Horace Jones and adapted by engineer John Wolfe Barry, took eight years to build.

From the south tower, follow the blue guideline to the engine rooms, which house the beautifully crafted Victorian machinery used to power the bridge between 1894 and 1976.

PLANNING THE BRIDGE

Between 1750 and 1850 10 new bridges had been built along the Thames to cope with the increasing trade and traffic of a booming city. East of London Bridge, where the population had expanded to over a million by the late 19th century, there was no river crossing. Plans were delayed and disrupted by wharfingers and shipping traders, who feared the decline of river business, and by the need for 43m (140ft) of clearance for tall-masted ships. A competition was finally opened for a new design. The winning architect, Sir Horace Jones, died in 1887 before the foundations were complete, and the task was passed on to his assistant, George Daniel Stevenson, who had an even greater passion for the Victorian Gothic style.

INFORMATION

www.towerbridge.org.uk

99 P5 · Tower Bridge SE1 2UP · 020 7403 3761 · Apr–end Sep daily 10–6.30 (last entry 5.30), Oct–end Mar daily 9.30–6 (last entry 5) · Adult £6, child (5–15) £3, under 5s free, family tickets £10–£14 · Tower Hill, London Bridge · 15, 42, 78, 100, RV1 · Tower Millennium Pier · £2.50, in English, French, German, Dutch, Japanese · Tower Café under north tower; indoor and outdoor seating · Small kiosk in engine rooms selling limited range of souvenirs

Below *The bridge was given a royal opening in 1894, with a gun salute from the Tower of London to greet the first raising of the bascules*

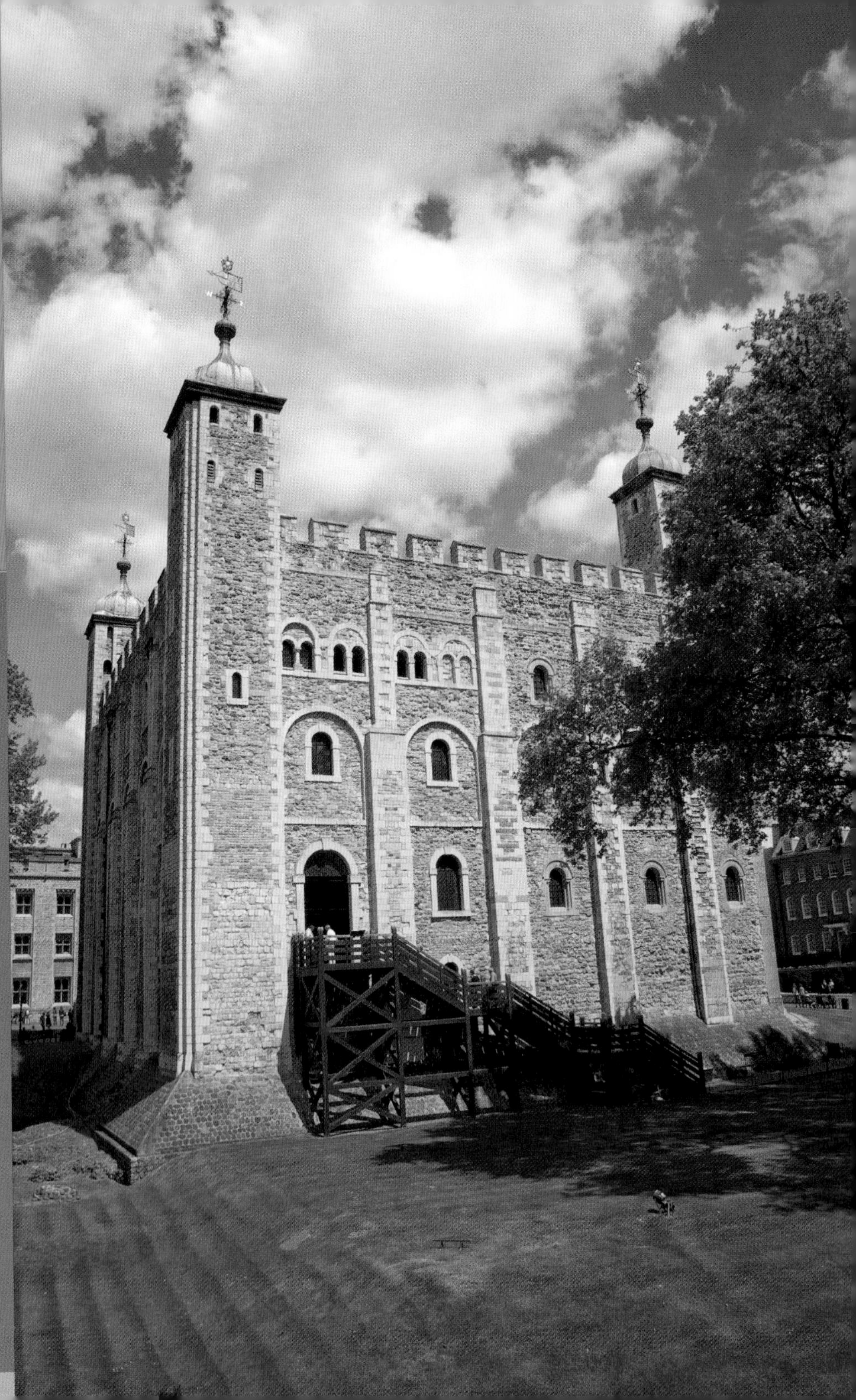

INTRODUCTION

The White Tower was built in the 11th century on a commanding site on the Thames, which probably had earlier royal significance. It was constructed over one of the defensive structures that William the Conqueror had hastily erected in the aftermath of the Battle of Hastings in 1066, when he had effectively won the succession to the English throne by defeating King Harold II. William saw the necessity of having a strong fortress from which to subdue the feisty people of London, already a huge city by medieval standards, and thus began the Tower's history proper. Between 1190 and 1285 it was encircled by two towered curtain walls and a moat, and in the 14th century the wharf was added. This major expansion, which saw the Tower more or less take the shape it retains to this day, was begun during the reign of Richard the Lionheart (1189–99), under the auspices of his chancellor, William Longchamp, while Richard went off on crusade. Henry III (r1216–72) then strengthened the defences after a group of rebellious barons made him seek refuge in the Tower in 1238.

It was left to his successor, Edward I (r1272–1307), however, to supervise the transformation of the fortress into Britain's largest and sturdiest concentric castle. During his reign the Tower was also used as a prison for the first time, setting in train the lengthy list of captives, many of them royal, who were incarcerated and often executed here. Among the most celebrated inmates were several of Henry VIII's wives, Catholic martyr Sir Thomas More and Guy Fawkes, mastermind behind the failed Gunpowder Plot of 1605 (▷ 30).

Further additions included the Chapel Royal and Queen's House, built in Henry VIII's reign, and the 17th-century New Armouries. Strong bastion though it was, the Tower could not protect Charles I and it was taken and controlled by Cromwell and the Parliamentarians throughout the Civil War (1642–49) and subsequently used mostly as a munitions store. The Tower was last used to assert power over people during the Chartist rebellion of the 1840s. Since then it has played a ceremonial and, finally, a touristic role. In 1988 the Tower of London was designated a World Heritage Site.

The Tower's layout illustrates its development from William the Conqueror's White Tower to the complex of defences completed by Edward I and Henry III and essentially unchanged today.

Entry to the Tower is through the Middle Tower in the southwest corner of the site. Once inside, you can wander at will. At the heart of the complex is the White Tower, 36m (118ft) across and 27m (88ft) high, with weathervanes topping the corner turrets. It is surrounded by 13th-century outer and inner walls, the latter punctuated by 12 towers.

A complex of later buildings within the inner wall includes the New Armouries, Waterloo Barracks and the Fusiliers' Museum.

WHAT TO SEE

WHITE TOWER

At the heart of the Tower is its oldest medieval building, thought to date from 1078 and probably marking a site of political significance for many centuries before that. It earned its name in the 13th century, when Henry III had the exterior whitewashed, but the original stone, brought over from Caen in Normandy, has mainly been replaced over the years with Portland stone from Dorset. The windows and doors are also replacements, added in the 17th and 18th centuries, and the turret roofs are a 16th-century feature.

The White Tower was built to serve as a fortress, armoury and a royal residence, and is split inside into three floors and a basement, where the

INFORMATION

www.hrp.org.uk
99 N5 London EC3N 4AB
0844 482 7777; tickets: 0844 482 7799 Tue–Sat 9–5.30, Sun–Mon 10–5.30. All buildings inside the gates close 30 min after last admission; Tower closes 1 hour after last admission. To watch the nightly Ceremony of the Keys apply in advance in writing enclosing an S.A.E. (▷ 295) Adult £17, child (5–16) £9.50, under 5s free, family £47 Tower Hill 15, 42, 78, 100, RV1 Tower Millennium Pier Tales of the Tower audio £3.50 in English, French, German, Italian, Spanish, Japanese, Russian, Mandarin £3.95, in English, French, Russian, Japanese, Spanish, Italian, German New Armouries restaurant Tower Café and kiosk on wharf Tower Shop at main entrance in the Salvin Pumphouse; Jewel House Shop in Lower Martin Tower; White Tower Shop, in basement of White Tower; Medieval Palace Shop; Beefeater Shop in Water Lane

Opposite *The White Tower, which replaced an earlier wooden building*

TIPS

» Crowds can be a problem in the summer. To save queueing, buy tickets in advance by calling 0870 756 7070 or online at www.hrp.org.uk and obtain a small discount as well.

» In the Martin Tower, there's a display on the making of the Crown Jewels.

» Check at the main entrance near the Middle Tower for times of free daily guided tours by Yeoman Warders.

Below *Forty Yeoman Warders have office at the Tower, all of whom have to have served in the armed forces and have a good record; in 2007 the first woman was appointed to a post*

Opposite *Armour on display in the White Tower*

11th-century well still holds fresh water. On the ground floor is an exhibition about small arms, from the Royal Armouries collection; spiral stairs lead to the first floor, with the gloriously simple Chapel of St. John the Evangelist, a double-height room original to the building. Used as chapel throughout the Middle Ages, from the 16th to the 19th centuries it stored state records. The adjacent large room may have been used for banquets and royal ceremonies.

Temporary exhibitions are held on the top floors and stairs lead to the turrets above, where Charles II's astronomer, John Flamsteed, observed the stars until a new observatory was built at Greenwich (⊳ 256–257).

JEWEL HOUSE

First stop for many visitors is the Jewel House (in the Waterloo Barracks), north of the White Tower. Here you pass through a series of displays giving a history of the Coronation Regalia (Crown Jewels) before reaching the treasury, where the collection is kept. An excellent visual story of the jewels entertains those waiting to view the exhibits, and it is possible to repeat the circuit round the actual jewels immediately for a second look at no extra cost.

The jewels mainly date from the restoration of the monarchy in 1660; the older regalia were melted down on Oliver Cromwell's orders, and only three swords and a coronation spoon survive. The sovereign's orb and sceptre (topped with a dove), made for Charles II in 1661, have been used in every coronation since, but there are also many later additions, such as the new sets

made for James II's wife, as queen consort, and for Mary II, crowned with William III but queen in her own right. Among the priceless stones used in the regalia are the world's biggest cut diamond, the 530-carat First Star of Africa, set in the head of the sceptre. The 317-carat Second Star of Africa diamond is part of the Imperial State Crown, made for the coronation of George VI in 1937 and set with no fewer than 2,868 diamonds, as well as 17 sapphires, 11 emeralds, 5 rubies and 273 pearls.

TOWER GREEN

Endlessly fascinating to visitors are the Tower's famous prisoners and their grisly deaths. Tower Green, west of the White Tower, is the main focus for stories of suffering and heroics: some of the tower's best-known prisoners were held in the buildings around this area of garden, including Sir Walter Raleigh, whose stay in the Bloody Tower led to the addition of a new floor to provide room for him and his family. The tower's name derives from the supposed murder of the two princes, Edward V and Richard, Duke of York, sons of Edward IV and allegedly the victims of their ambitious uncle, Richard III. They disappeared in 1483, aged around 13 and 10.

The Queen's House, a black-and-white, half-timbered building next to the Bloody Tower, was the scene of Guy Fawkes' interrogation in 1605 (▷ 30) and of a daring escape when the Earl of Nithsdale, imprisoned after the 1715

BEHEADED

The Scaffold Site in front of the Chapel of St. Peter ad Vincula saw the executions of the only five women to be beheaded for treason—four of them during Henry VIII's reign. First on the block was Anne Boleyn in 1536; she and the next victim, wife No. 5, Catherine Howard, were both accused of adultery. Catherine's lady-in-waiting Jane, Viscountess Rochford, met her fate along with her mistress. In 1541, 70-year-old Margaret Pole, Countess of Salisbury, was executed for her Catholic faith and Yorkist loyalty. Henry's daughter Mary I continued the family tradition by dispatching the fifth woman, Lady Jane Grey, proclaimed queen in 1553 in an attempt to secure a Protestant succession.

TRADITIONS

The Tower has many ancient traditions. One is the nightly Ceremony of the Keys (▷ 295), when the Chief Yeoman Warder locks the main gates of the Tower at 9.53pm, after which a bugler sounds the Last Post. This ceremony has scarcely changed in more than 700 years, except that it now takes place under floodlights with an audience.

Eight ravens live in the gardens, well cared for by the official Ravenmaster; legend has it that the Tower will collapse if they fly away, but in fact their wings are clipped so this will never happen.

On 21 May members of Eton College and King's College, Cambridge put white roses and lilies in Wakefield Tower in memory of Henry VI, who founded both institutions and who was murdered here in 1471.

Above left *Yeoman Warders carrying out the Ceremony of the Keys*
Above right *Anne Boleyn was one of those who passed through Traitors' Gate*

Jacobite rebellion, dressed as a woman and made his getaway. Particularly high-ranking prisoners were kept in the 13th-century Beauchamp Tower. In the upper chamber you can still see inscriptions carved by the prisoners, some with amazing skill and intricacy.

TRAITORS' GATE

Just beyond the entrance to the medieval palace, opposite the gateway of the Bloody Tower, is a great stone archway. Above it is Tudor timber-framing and below are the wooden watergates that gave direct access from the river. Its name derives from the number of prisoners accused of treason who were brought by boat through this entrance. Until the 1860s there was an engine in the pool behind the gate that used water power or horsepower to raise water to a tank on the roof of the White Tower.

WAKEFIELD TOWER

Next in size to the White Tower, this was built in the 13th century to house King Henry III's main private room and included a private river entrance, still visible in Water Lane. Its impressive upper chamber was the king's bedroom, and has been decked out according to accounts written in his son Edward I's reign, when it served as a throne room. The current throne is a copy of the Coronation Chair in Westminster Abbey, and sits flanked by candelabra under the magnificent vaulted ceiling. A painted timber screen divides the main room from the chapel, reputed to be the site of Henry VI's murder while at prayer, though like many of the Tower's legends this is probably more convenient than true (see side panel).

FUSILIERS' MUSEUM

King James II established the Royal Regiment of Fusiliers in 1685 to guard the Tower's arsenal. They took their name from the 'fusil', a then-state-of-the-art musket which they were the first to use. The museum and the regiment headquarters occupy a 19th-century building which was initially the officers' mess. Inside is a display tracing the Fusiliers' service in the American War of Independence, the Crimean War, World War I and World War II, among many other campaigns, up to their more recent peace-keeping missions in Northern Ireland and the Balkans.

Most of the items on display are uniforms, medals and paintings. Some of the quirkier exhibits include a metal boot worn by a soldier who had avoided action for more than three years during the Napoleonic Wars by putting a corrosive lotion on his leg to create an open sore. His leg was cured within days of the boot being fitted.

GUIDE TO THE TOWER

1 Middle Tower
2 Byward Tower
3 Bell Tower
4 Traitors' Gate
5 St. Thomas's Tower
6 Bloody Tower
7 Wakefield Tower
8 White Tower
9 Chapel of St. John the Evangelist
10 Queen's House
11 Gaoler's House
12 Tower Green
13 Scaffold Site
14 Beauchamp Tower
15 Royal Chapel of St. Peter ad Vincula
16 Waterloo Barracks with Crown Jewels
17 Devereux Tower
18 Flint Tower
19 Bowyer Tower
20 Brick Tower
21 Martin Tower
22 Fusiliers' Museum
23 Former Hospital
24 Workshop
25 Constable Tower
26 Broad Arrow Tower
27 Salt Tower
28 Lanthorn Tower
29 Cradle Tower
30 Well Tower
31 Develin Tower
32 Brass Mount
33 Legge's Mount
34 Tower Wharf
35 Queen's Stair

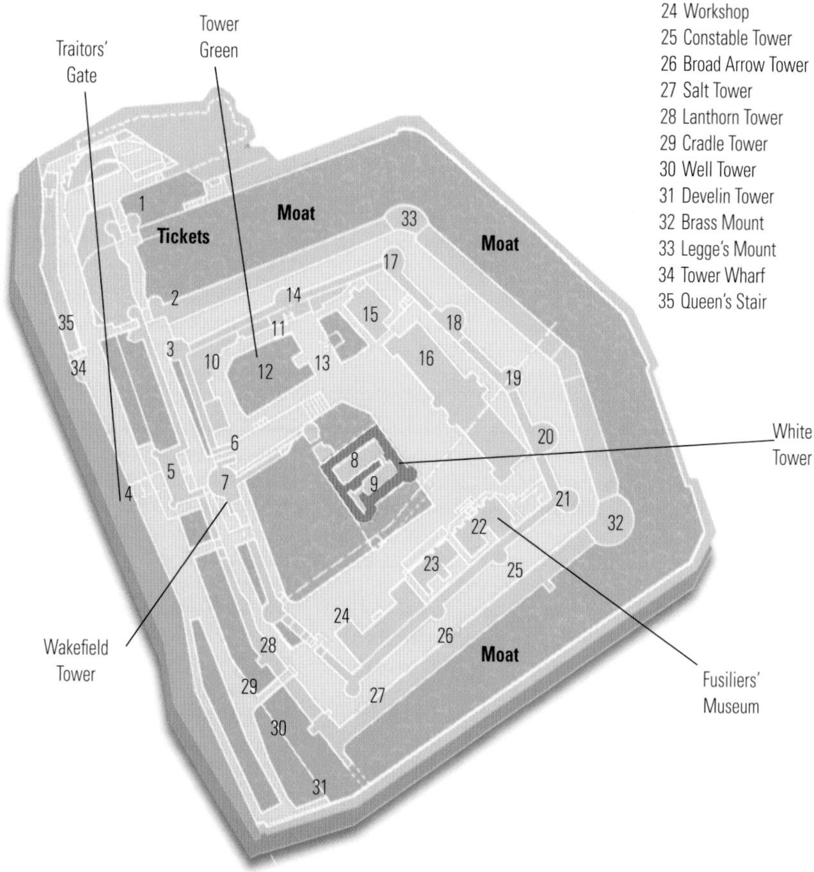

AROUND THE CITY

The City is the financial heart of Britain, a compact area of modern buildings, medieval lanes and churches designed by Sir Christopher Wren.

THE WALK
Distance: 2 miles (3km)
Allow: 2 hours minimum
Start at: Monument Underground station
End at: Bank Underground station

HOW TO GET THERE
Circle or District line to Monument 15, 35

★ The charm of this walk is that it covers one of the oldest parts of London, which at the same time is home to some of the city's most modern buildings.

Take the London Bridge/King William Street (south) exit from Monument station. Walk straight ahead past the Monument on your left and onto London Bridge for views along the river. Tower Bridge (▷ 111) is to your left, with HMS *Belfast* (▷ 72) moored nearby. To the west is the Tate Modern tower (▷ 80–81).

Return towards the Underground station and turn right onto Monument Street. Follow this to the Monument (▷ 102).

Climb Fish Street Hill to Eastcheap and then turn right. Pudding Lane, where the Great Fire of London started in 1666, is the next road on the right. Cross Eastcheap to turn left into Philpot Lane. The Lloyd's Building is ahead of you.

❶ Sir Richard Rogers (co-architect of the Pompidou Centre in Paris) designed this 'inside-out' building for insurance underwriters Lloyd's of London in 1978. The 14-storey glass, concrete and aluminium office block, with its exterior tangle of ventilation ducts and fire stairs, attracts admiration and derision in equal measure.

At the end of Philpot Lane, cross Fenchurch Street into Lime Street and follow the cobbled street on the left, Lime Street Passage, into Leadenhall Market.

❷ Leadenhall Market (▷ 120), now under a wrought-iron and glass roof, has been operating as a meat and fish market since the 14th century. Today its alleys are a mix of market stalls, as well as pubs and upmarket fashion shops. Have a drink or lunch at the Lamb Tavern (closed weekends).

Take Whittington Avenue from the market and turn right into Leadenhall Street by Lloyd's. Cross the road and an open square. To your right looms the startling 30 St. Mary Axe (aka the Gherkin). St. Helen's Bishopsgate is behind the tower block in the middle of the square.

❸ St. Helen's is a rare survivor of the Great Fire of London and is London's largest medieval church. It contains several fine memorials (open daily 9–5).

At the church turn left to follow Great St. Helen's to Bishopsgate.

Above *Leadenhall Market*
Left *The porticoed Mansion House*

Turn left here and at the traffic lights cross into Threadneedle Street. Continue past a statue of US philanthropist George Peabody on the left, and turn right down Bartholomew Lane alongside the Bank of England (▷ 101).

At the end of Bartholomew Lane turn left along Lothbury and into Gresham Street. Guildhall (▷ 102) is to your right, behind St. Lawrence Jewry Church. Facing away from Guildhall, cross Gresham Street into King Street and on to Cheapside. Turn right here and head for the steeple of St. Mary-le-Bow.

❹ Sir Christopher Wren designed 51 churches in the City, of which St. Mary-le-Bow is one. Its bells once sounded the curfew for Londoners, and to be born within earshot was the definition of a Cockney.

Go round the back of the church and turn right into Bow Lane. Williamson's Tavern is on the right. Turn left into Watling Street and as you turn look right to see the dome of St. Paul's Cathedral (▷ 104–109). According to tradition, Wren conducted his business in Ye Olde Watling Pub while he was building St. Paul's.

Follow Watling Street to a major junction and cross the intersection bearing left into Queen Victoria Street. Turn right into Bucklersbury to St. Stephen Walbrook Church.

❺ St. Stephen Walbrook is the Lord Mayor's official church, and considered to be Wren's finest City church. Its dome was probably built as a prototype (1672–79) for that of nearby St. Paul's. Centrally placed beneath it is the altar by English sculptor Henry Moore (1987). This asymmetrical lump of stone is at odds with its classical setting.

From the church turn left along Walbrook and then right at the end towards the Royal Exchange building at the far side of the junction. On the right is the Mansion House (open for organized groups only).

❻ This is one of London's grandest surviving Georgian town palaces, with magnificent interiors including elaborate plasterwork and carved timber ornament. Built in the mid-18th century, it is the home of the Lord Mayor of London.

Bank Underground station is at this road junction.

TIP

» Do this walk on a weekday, when the streets are busy with City workers. At weekends the area is deserted and some places close.

WHERE TO EAT

Stop at one of the cafes or pubs in Leadenhall Market, or at an outdoor cafe by the George Peabody statue. The Place Below, in the crypt of St. Mary-le-Bow (tel 020 7329 0789), serves good vegetarian food.

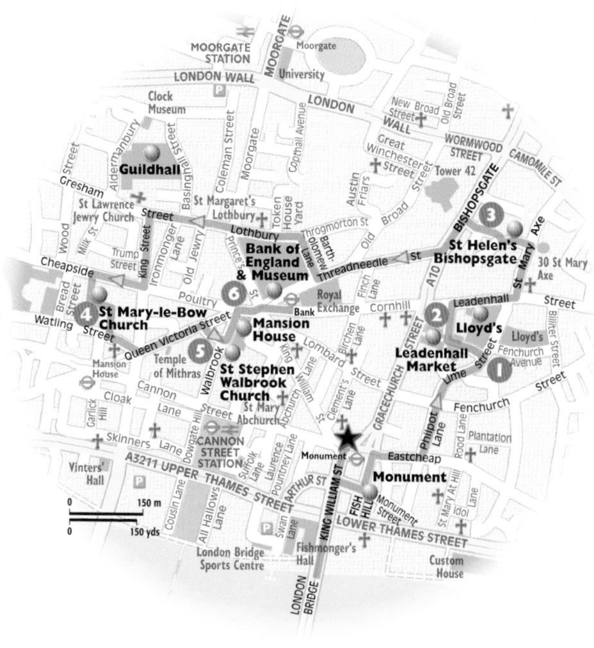

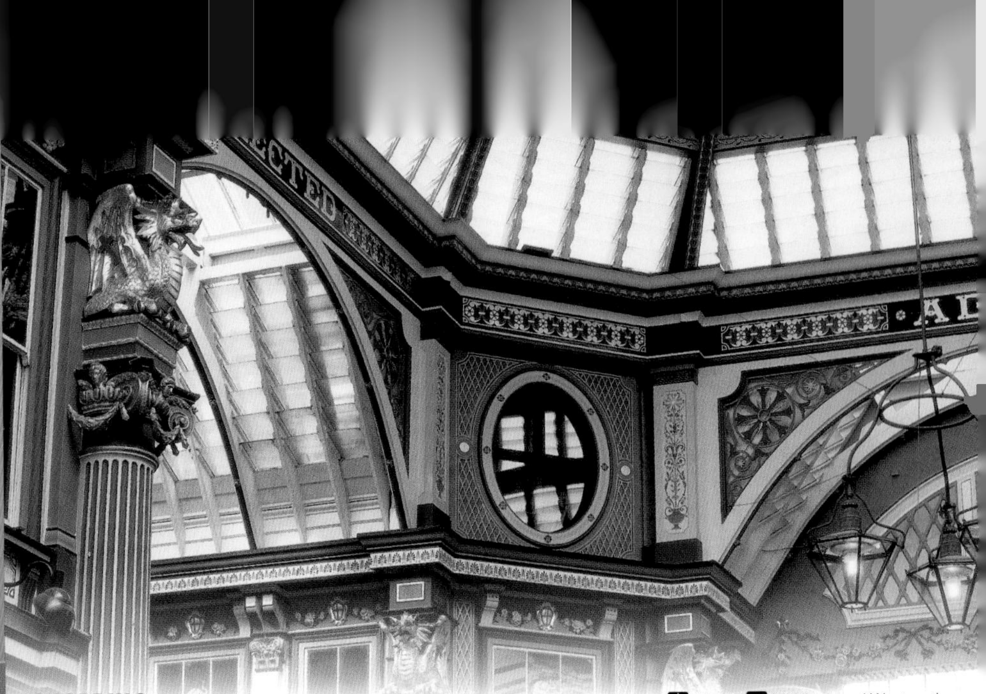

SHOPPING

BRICK LANE MARKET

Never mind the quality, feel the atmosphere at this vibrant multi-ethnic street market. Come for clothes (especially leather), furniture, fruits, kitchenware and kitsch. Or just follow the side streets to see where they lead and sift the jewels from the junk.
127 P2 Brick Lane/Cheshire Street/Sclater Street Sun 8–2 Liverpool Street, Aldgate East 23

LEADENHALL MARKET

www.cityoflondon.gov.uk
Probably the most chic of the city's markets, with meat, fish, poultry, cheese, wine and chocolate specialists. Worth visiting for the atmospheric building in the heart of the City (▷ 118), which really comes to life early lunchtime.
127 N4 Whittington Avenue EC3 020 7929 1073 Mon–Fri 11–4 Monument, Bank 8, 25, 40

MONT BLANC

www.montblanc.com
Superbly crafted pens and other writing implements are the signature items on sale at this plush boutique. However, there is also plenty in the way of watches, leather accessories, jewellery, eyewear and perfumes, all at prices that reflect the quality.
126 M4 10 Royal Exchange EC3V 3LL 020 7929 4200 Mon–Fri 9–5.30 Bank 8, 11, 15, 23, 25, 26, 43, 76, 344

ONEDEKO

www.onedeko.co.uk
This is a good place for high-end designer furniture that displays plenty of imagination and style. Quirky accessories such as flower-shaped and tube map mirrors, shoe racks and kitchen equipment are also available. Smaller gift items include the morse code tea towel and dog and cat holders to hang it on.
127 P3 103 Commercial Street E1 6BG 020 7377 5900 Mon–Fri 10.30–6, Sat 12–5.30, Sun 10.30–5.30 Liverpool Street, Aldgate East 15, 25, 67, 78, 254

PETTICOAT LANE

www.eastlondonmarkets.com
London's most famous market was named after the garments sold by French immigrants in the 1700s. Look for clothing at bargain prices—especially fabrics and leather jackets. Around 1,000 stalls.
127 N4 Middlesex and Wentworth streets E1 020 7377 8963 Mon–Fri 10–3, Sun 9–3 Liverpool Street, Aldgate, Aldgate East 8, 42, 344

R TWINING & CO

www.twinings.com
One of London's oldest firms, Twinings has been trading in tea for more than 300 years. This shop—still on its original site opposite the Royal Courts of Justice—sells a wide range of teas, fruit and herb infusions plus teapots, cups, mugs and biscuits. There's a small museum at the back.
126 K4 216 Strand WC2R 1AP 020 7353 3511 Mon–Fri 9–5, Sat 10–4 Temple 9, 11, 13, 15, RV1

ENTERTAINMENT AND NIGHTLIFE

333 MOTHER

www.333mother.com
This City club and bar offers a mix of styles that might include soul, funk, reggae, drum 'n' bass and hip-hop. Sunday is gay night.
127 N2 333 Old Street EC1V 9LE 020 7739 5949 Mon–Wed 8pm–3am, Thu, Sun 8pm–4am, Fri–Sat 8pm–1am £5–£10 Old Street 43, 55, 243

Left *Detail of the Victorian decoration at Leadenhall Market*

BARBICAN CENTRE

www.barbican.org.uk

A 2,000-seat concert hall in the confusingly laid-out arts complex (▷ 101). Home of the world-class London Symphony Orchestra and the English Chamber Orchestra.

126 M3 Silk Street EC2Y 8DS 020 7638 4141; box office 020 7638 8891 Tickets £6.50–£35 Barbican 4, 8, 11, 23, 26, 56, 153

CARGO

www.cargo-london.com

A very cool East End bar in a cavernous building. Restaurant with huge tables that you'll have to share. Not particularly friendly, but the top DJs and bands make it popular.

127 N2 83 Rivington Street, Shoreditch EC2A 3AY 020 7749 7844 Club: Mon–Thu 6pm–1am, Fri–Sat 6pm–3am, Sun 6pm–12am. Restaurant: Mon–Thu 12–11, Fri 12–12, Sat 6pm–12am, Sun 6pm–10pm £7–£15 Old Street, Liverpool Street 8, 43, 55, 243

CHARLIE WRIGHT'S INTERNATIONAL BAR

www.charliewrights.com

This lively Thai restaurant and bar is frequented by a diverse crowd. Music Friday to Sunday.

126 N2 45 Pitfield Street N1 6DA 020 7490 8345 Thu–Fri 12am–4am, Sat 6pm–4am, Sun 6pm–1am Free (Fri–Sat £4 after 10pm) Old Street 55, 203, 243

COMEDY CAFÉ

www.comedycafe.co.uk

Dine in comfort during shows by established stand-up acts—and a no-heckling policy. Dancing afterwards.

127 N2 66 Rivington Street, Shoreditch EC2A 3AY 020 7739 5706 Tue–Sat 6pm–2am £5–£14, Wed free Old Street 55, 243

FABRIC

www.fabriclondon.com

Fab superclub with mainly techno music, an easygoing 20-something crowd and less well-known DJs.

126 L3 77A Charterhouse Street EC1M 3HN 020 7336 8898 Fri 10pm–6am, Sat 11pm–8am, Sun 11pm–6am £12–£18 Farringdon 17, 45, 46, 63

HOME BAR

www.homebar.co.uk

Large basement where you can chill out without interruption and enjoy laid-back grooves and upbeat tunes (retro, hip-hop). The crowd is relaxed and the atmosphere friendly.

127 N2 100–106 Leonard Street EC2A 4RH 020 7684 8618 Wed–Fri 6pm–2am, Sat 7pm–3am Free Old Street 55, 205, 243

PLASTIC PEOPLE

www.plasticpeople.co.uk

This small basement club prides itself on the breadth and quality of its eclectic music, rotating the very best in latin, Afro jazz, hip hop, house, techno, soul, rock 'n' roll, punk, funk, even folk, plus genres you suspect they may have concocted, such as future jazz.

127 N3 147 Curtain Road, Shoreditch EC2A 3QE 020 7739 6471 Thu 10pm–2am, Fri–Sat 10pm–4am, Sun 8pm–11.30pm. £5–£8 Old Street, Liverpool Street 8, 11, 23, 26, 35, 42, 43, 47, 48, 55, 67, 76, 78, 100, 133, 141, 149, 214, 242, 243, 271, 344

SADLER'S WELLS THEATRE

www.sadlerswells.com

Europe's finest dance venue offers classical ballet, modern dance and opera. The building, opened in 1998, replaces the theatre founded by Lilian Bayliss in 1931.

126 L2 Rosebery Avenue EC1R 4TN 020 7863 8198; box office 0844 412 4300 £10–£40 Angel 19, 38, 341

SHOREDITCH ELECTRICITY SHOWROOMS

A great place with atmosphere where you drink at bashed-up tables and can't fail to notice the kitsch alpine scene across one wall. Full of City boys—macho business types—on weekdays but more mellow on Saturday and Sunday.

127 N2 39A Hoxton Square N1 6NU 020 7739 3939 Sun–Thu 12–12, Fri–Sat 12pm–late Phone for details Old Street 55, 205, 243

SPORTS AND ACTIVITIES

ARSENAL FOOTBALL CLUB

www.arsenal.com

Famous north London club that usually finishes near the top of the Premiership. The club relocated to the new Emirates Stadium at Ashburton Grove in 2006.

Off map 126 M1 Emirates Stadium, 75 Drayton Park, Highbury N5 1BU 020 7704 4000 Arsenal 4, 30

BROADGATE ICE ARENA

www.broadgateice.co.uk

This outdoor rink is home to the Broomball League, which plays a variation of ice hockey; matches Mon, Tue, Wed evenings (free).

127 N3 Broadgate Circle, Eldon Street EC2M 2QS 020 7505 4000 Oct–end Apr Mon–Fri 12–2.30, 3.30–5.30, Sat 11–1, 2–4, 5–7, Sun 11–1, 2–4, 5–7 £6 per session, child (under 16) £4, skate rental £2, child £1 Liverpool Street 8, 26, 35

TOTTENHAM HOTSPUR FOOTBALL CLUB

www.spurs.co.uk

A match at White Hart Lane is usually guaranteed to provide goals and entertainment, whether Spurs—one of England's most historic and stylish clubs, with an exceptionally fine tradition in Cup football—win, lose or draw.

Off map 127 N1 White Hart Lane, Bill Nicholson Way, High Road, Tottenham N17 0AP 0870 420 5000 White Hart Lane, Northumberland Park 76, 149, 259

WEST HAM UNITED FOOTBALL CLUB

www.whufc.com

The highly respected Hammers have returned to form in recent years and won promotion back to the Premiership (football's top flight) in 2005.

Off map 127 R2 Boleyn Ground, Green Street, Upton Park E13 9AZ 0870 112 2700 Upton Park 15, 115

PRICES AND SYMBOLS

The prices given are for a two-course set lunch (L) and a three-course à la carte dinner (D) for one person, without drinks. The wine price is for the least expensive bottle.

For a key to the symbols, ▷ 2.

1 LOMBARD STREET—THE FINE DINING RESTAURANT

www.1lombardstreet.com

A typical City building with large-scale windows, opposite the Bank of England. Behind the busy, informal brasserie is a fine dining area in a quiet back room, with formal service. The cooking is primarily French, with dishes such as seared foie gras with muscatel grapes in Armagnac; roasted turbot on the bone with woodland mushroom and herb ragoût; and *feuillantine* of caramelized Granny Smith apples with Guinness ice cream and glazed hazelnuts. The slightly cheaper sister restaurant, The Brasserie, within the same building, is also recommended.

126 M4 1 Lombard Street EC3V 9AA 020 7929 6611 Mon–Fri 12–2.30, 3, 6–10. Closed 25–26 Dec, 1 Jan, public hols L from £40, D from £65, Wine from £22 Bank

ALBA

www.albarestaurant.com

This contemporary restaurant, a short stroll from the Barbican, offers a taste of northern Italy. Like the olive-green walls and brightly hued prints, the menu is modern and has such daily specials as Piedmont ravioli and tagliolini with butter, sage and white truffles. Desserts include chocolate mousse cake on a base of amaretto-soaked panettone.

126 M3 107 Whitecross Street EC1Y 8JD 020 7588 1798 Mon–Fri 12–3, 6–11 L from £15.50, D from £18, Wine from £15 Barbican

LE CAFÉ DU MARCHÉ

www.cafedumarche.co.uk

Actually three cosy restaurants under one roof. Le Café offers a three-course fixed-price menu, accompanied by live jazz in the background every evening. The first floor Le Grenier laso has fixed-price menus and is strong on grilled meat and fish. Le Rendezvous is smaller and à la carte.

126 L3 Charterhouse Mews, Charterhouse Square EC1M 6AH 020 7608 1609 Mon–Fri 12–2.30, 6–10, Sat 6–10 L from £20, D from £31.50 Farringdon, Barbican

CANTEEN

www.canteen.co.uk

This unpretentious eatery in Spitalfields Market opened in 2006 to rave reviews and has heaved with an eclectic mix of foodies, locals and city types ever since. Glass-walled on three sides, it teams retro booth seating with long shared tables and prides itself on offering high-quality cuisine at reasonable prices. The all-day menu includes breakfast items and designated 'fast service' dishes, as well as a daily roast, home-made pies and fish options. Expect British classics conjured from the freshest of ingredients, plus a diet-busting array of comfort desserts, such as steamed syrup pudding and custard, or orange jelly with ice cream and shortbread.

127 N3 2 Crispin Place E1 6DW 0845 686 1122 Mon–Fri 8am–11pm, Sat–Sun 9am–11pm. Closed 24–26 Dec B from £7, L from £15, D from £20, Wine from £12.50 Liverpool Street

CLERKENWELL DINING ROOM & BAR

www.theclerkenwell.com

The sharp contemporary interior comes as a surprise after the blue and terracotta frontage. The cuisine

Left *Typically elegant City restaurant*

is modern European, featuring such goodies as lamb saddle served with tagliolini, mint, sweet pea emulsion and pea shoots, or halibut with baby squid with lemon and parsley, white cocoa bean purée, tomato and light curry sauce.
126 L3 69–73 St. John Street EC1N 4AN 020 7523 9000 Mon–Fri 12–2.30, 6–11, Sat 6–11 L and D from £30, Wine from £15 Farringdon 55, 153, 243

EYRE BROTHERS
www.eyrebrothers.co.uk
Tucked amid gentrified Shoreditch lofts, this dining spot boasts dark wood, cool leather and a long, trendy bar. The cuisine is a mixture of regional Portuguese and classic Spanish, featuring earthy flavours and bright colours. Try the seafood, potato, sweet pepper and saffron stew, or wild rabbit rice with red wine chorizo, broad beans and globe artichokes.
127 N2 70 Leonard Street EC2 4QX 020 7613 5346 Mon–Fri 12–3, 6.30–11, Sat 6.30–11. Closed Christmas–New Year L from £18, D from £23, Wine from £15 Old Street

HAZ
www.hazrestaurant.com
A buzzing, slickly run place in the heart of the City, this Turkish restaurant is popular with business types and visitors alike. Perfect for meat lovers but with plenty of choices for vegetarians. The meals are served at long communual tables so this is not the place for quiet romantic meals for two. The set meals are particularly good value. Tasty meze dishes and more filling casseroles are also on offer.
127 N4 9 Cutler Street E1 7DJ 020 7929 7923 Daily 11.30–11.30 L from £10, D from £20, Wine from £14 Liverpool Street

MEHEK
www.mehek.co.uk
Stunningly decorated by a Bollywood designer, there is more room inside this popular Indian restaurant than appears from the hole-in-the-wall exterior. The cuisine is mostly standard north Indian with a modern twist, and some dishes from other parts of the subcontinent, such as guinea fowl in Bengali herbs and Goan fish curry.
126 M3 45 London Wall EC2M 5TE 020 7588 5043 Mon–Fri 11.30–3, 5.30–11 L from £12, D from £25, Wine from £16 Moorgate, Liverpool Street

MORO
www.moro.co.uk
Value for money is the key at this lively and always busy Spanish/North African restaurant. The menu changes weekly but many of the dishes are inspired by the wood-fired oven, ranging from simple grilled chicory with ham and sherry vinegar to roasted turbot with roast beetroot, lentils and spicy red chili *churrasco* sauce. Warm goat's cheese with pine nuts, raisins and orange blossom water in filo pastry might provide an interesting and unusual dessert. The wine list is largely Spanish.
126 K2 34–36 Exmouth Market EC1R 4QE 020 7833 8336 Mon–Sat 12.30–2.30, 7–10.30. Closed Sun, 25–26 Dec, 1 Jan, public hols L from £25, D from £35, Wine from £11 Farringdon, Angel

RHODES TWENTYFOUR
www.rhodes24.co.uk
This latest addition to the empire of celebrity chef Gary Rhodes sits on the 24th floor of the NatWest Tower enjoying panoramic views across the City. Friendly, casually dressed staff serve starters such as warm goat's cheese tartlet and spinach soup, and main courses such as buttered organic salmon with smoked bacon oyster champ. Note that security is tight here and reservations are essential.
127 N4 Tower 42, 25 Old Broad Street EC2N 1HQ 020 7877 7703 Mon–Fri 12–2.30, 6–9. Closed 24 Dec–2 Jan L from £30, D from £42, Wine from £20 Bank, Liverpool Street

ST. JOHN
www.stjohnrestaurant.com
Approached through an archway and big iron gates, with a cafe/bakery below, this restaurant has a menu that nods to traditional British meat cuisine and has a pig motif with butchery markings. There's plenty of offal—salted kid's liver, rabbit's heart, kidneys and liver—and unusual ingredients such as smoked eel with bacon and mash, sausage and chickpeas, and the freshest of game in season. If the meat-fest gets too much, you could go for oysters, and there's always at least one vegetarian dish on the menu.
126 L3 26 St. John Street EC1M 4AY 020 7251 0848 Mon–Sat 11–11. Closed 25–26 Dec, 1 Jan, Easter L from £25, D from £35, Wine from £20 Farringdon, Barbican, Chancery Lane

SMITHS OF SMITHFIELD
www.smithsofsmithfield.co.uk
This sizeable building started life as a warehouse in around 1886 before the completion of the Smithfield Meat Market that lies next door. The upper floors have panoramic views that take in the City, St. Paul's Cathedral (▷ 118–119) and the Old Bailey (▷ 102). The organic and additive-free Modern British cooking includes the likes of crisp belly of pork, mashed potato and green sauce, roast monkfish with baby leeks, game chips and caviar butter sauce.
126 L3 Top Floor, 66–67 Charterhouse Street EC1M 6HJ 020 7251 7950 Mon–Fri 7am–11.30pm, Sat 10am–11.30pm, Sun 9.30am–11.30pm. Closed 25–26 Dec, 1 Jan B from £2.50, L from £12.50, D from £30, Wine from £20 Farringdon, Barbican

TATSUSO
Tatsuso is known for its authentic Japanese food. Upstairs is the teppan-yaki dining room, with chefs cooking at the table in front of the customers, and downstairs is the more traditional Japanese à la carte and separate sushi bar. An appetizer here might be lightly breaded scallops marinated in vinegar with

a seaweed salad and thin strips of beef, with a main course of *yakitori*—skewered pieces of grilled chicken with a soy-based sauce.
127 N3 32 Broadgate Circle EC2M 2QS 020 7638 5863 Sun–Thu 11.30–2.30, 6.30–11, Fri–Sat 11.30–2.30, 6.30–12. Closed 25–26 Dec, 1 Jan, public hols L from £38, D from £50, Wine from £15 Liverpool Street

PUBS

THE BLEEDING HEART TAVERN

www.bleedingheart.co.uk/tavern
The original tavern opened in 1746 and was named in memory of Elizabeth Hatton, murdered in nearby Hatton Garden 100 years earlier. The rustic scrubbed tables sit well with the wooden flooring. Ales are from Adnam's Brewery, there's an impressive wine list and a menu of traditional pub food with a contemporary flavour, such as spit-roast, grilled gammon steak and rib-eye steak with Béarnaise sauce. No children.
126 L3 19 Greville Street EC1N 8SQ 020 7242 8238 Mon–Fri 11–11. Restaurant: 12–3, 6–10.30. Closed 24 Dec–2 Jan, public hols Bar meals from £10, D from £20 Farringdon

THE CROWN

In this carefully restored 1860s building, everything from the reclaimed building materials used in the restoration and the second-hand furniture to the organic menu and wine list is green—based on sound environmental practices. The menu changes with the seasons, and is a mix of European dishes, such as leek and parsnip soup, shoulder of lamb stuffed with anchovies, garlic and rosemary, and pan-fried chicken livers with sage, walnuts and noodles. The bitter chocolate mousse makes a delicious end to the meal. There's also a garden in which food is served.
Off map 127 Q2 223 Grove Road E3 5SN 020 8880 7261 Mon 5–11, Tue–Fri 12–11, Sat–Sun phone for times. Restaurant: Tue–Sun 12.30–3, Mon–Sun 7–10pm. Closed 25 Dec Bar meals from £8, D from £23 Mile End

THE DUKE OF CAMBRIDGE

www.dukeorganic.co.uk
This stylishly modernized building in a residential street in trendy Islington was one of London's first pubs to specialize in organic food, wine and beer. Changing blackboard menus might include seasonal modern European dishes such as pumpkin and sage soup or grilled asparagus with anchovy. Try to leave space for desserts such as rhubarb fool with shortbread and the sumptuous pear and chocolate soufflé cake. Garden and patio.
Off map 126 L1 30 St. Peter's Street N1 8JT 020 7359 3066 Tue–Sun 12–11, Mon 5–11. Restaurant: 12.30–3, 5.30–10. Closed 25–26 Dec, 1 Jan Bar meals from £13, D from £20 Angel

THE EAGLE

On the fringe of Clerkenwell, London's focus on cool, The Eagle was one of Britain's first pubs to concentrate on the quality of its food. The pub has even published its own cookbook, *Big Flavours and Rough Edges*. The straightforward, rustic blackboard menu favours a Mediterranean style. The post-work City buzz can be truly intoxicating.
126 K2 159 Farringdon Road EC1R 3AL 020 7837 1353 Mon–Fri 12.30–3, 6.30–10.30, Sat–Sun 12.30–10.30 Meals from £8 Angel, Farringdon

THE JERUSALEM TAVERN

This dimly lit bar dates from 1720, when it was a merchant's house, and it has often been used as a film set. It derives its name from the Priory of St. John, originally on the site. There are bare floorboards, rustic tables and a selection of magazines and newspapers. Bar food is simple—speciality sandwiches, sausage baguettes and beef casserole. Try one of the pub's own excellent cask ales.
126 L3 55 Britton Street EC1M 5NA 020 7490 4281 Mon–Fri 11–11. Meals: 12–3. Closed 25 Dec, Good Fri, Easter Mon Bar meals from £7 Farringdon

THE OLD BANK OF ENGLAND

London's grandest pub, with tall ornate ceilings, this magnificent building, formerly the Law Courts branch of the Bank of England, lies by legend between the site of Sweeney Todd's barbershop and his mistress's pie shop; it was in the tunnels and vaults below the present building that his hapless victims were butchered before being cooked and sold in Mrs Lovett's pies. Don't let that put you off, especially as the pub does great pies. The menu ranges from light snacks to more substantial traditional English offerings. No children allowed.
126 K4 194 Fleet Street EC4A 2LT 020 7430 2255 Mon–Fri 11–11. Meals: 12–8. Closed public hols Bar meals from £8 Aldwych, Chancery Lane

THE PEASANT

www.thepeasant.co.uk
Here, the original Victorian features have been restored, including an inlaid mosaic floor, horseshoe bar and conservatory. The peasant-style food with a Mediterranean leaning includes pan-fried Barbary duck with Israeli couscous or roast halibut with sweet potato. Children are not allowed in the bar area. Terrace.
126 L2 240 St. John Street EC1V 4PH 020 7336 7726 Mon–Sat 12–11, Sun 12–10.30. Restaurant: Tue–Fri 12.30–3.30, 6.30–11 Bar meals from £10, D from £24 Angel, Farringdon

YE OLDE CHESHIRE CHEESE

This rambling institution is full of nooks and crannies and has a long history of entertaining literary greats such as Sir Arthur Conan Doyle and Charles Dickens. It was the haunt of journalists when Fleet Street was the hub of Britain's newspaper world and is still one of the few remaining chop houses rebuilt after the Great Fire of 1666. Come here for Olde English pub food.
126 L4 Wine Office Court, 145 Fleet Street EC4 2BU 020 7353 6170 Mon–Sat 11–11, Sun 12–3. Restaurant: 12–10. Closed 25–26 Dec, public hols Bar meals from £8, D from £17 Blackfriars, Aldwych, Chancery Lane

PRICES AND SYMBOLS

Prices given are the starting price for a double room for one night. Breakfast is included unless noted otherwise. All the hotels listed accept credit cards unless otherwise stated. Note that rates vary widely throughout the year.

For a key to the symbols, ▷ 2.

ANDAZ

www.andaz.com

This is the largest hotel in the City, newly transformed with designer rooms that include WiFi and iPod docking stations. The choice of restaurants includes the elegant 1901 for fine dining, Catch for seafood, Miyako, a Japanese restaurant, and Eastway for quick snacks. There is also a gym with treatment rooms, a steam room and personal trainers on request.

127 N3 Liverpool Street EC2M 7QN 020 7618 5000 Double from £135 267 (5 smoking) Liverpool Street 8, 26, 35, 42, 47, 48, 78, 149, 242, 344

THE CHAMBERLAIN

www.thechamberlainhotel.com

Lavishly converted from early 20th-century offices, this hotel is ideally placed for the City and Tower Bridge (▷ 111). The bedrooms are stylish and the bathrooms modern and fitted with TV. A popular pub is on the premises, along with an unusual split-level dining room. Parking and discounted sports facilities for hotel guests are close by.

127 N4 130–135 Minories EC3N 1NU 020 7680 1500 Double from £155 64 Fenchurch Street, Aldgate, Tower Hill 15, 25, 42, 78, 100

THE HOXTON

www.hoxtonhotels.com

An innovative new hotel opened in 2006. Roaring fires give a country-lodge feel, while cool cocktails and flat-screen TVs add a contemporary edge. The guest rooms provide luxury at a budget price and include sumptuous duck-down duvets, Frette linen and great power showers. The Hoxton Grille is a mix of Paris chic and New York vibe. There are plenty of good bars, pubs, clubs and restaurants within the area. The hotel has easy access to the Underground, which will quickly transport you to all the city's major attractions.

127 N2 81 Great Eastern Street EC2A 3HU 020 7550 1000 Double from £165 205 Old Street 55

MALMAISON CHARTERHOUSE SQUARE

www.malmaison.com

Maintaining the same focus on quality service and cuisine as other hotels in this small but classy chain, this establishment has the advantage of being central yet situated in a leafy square. The rooms are decorated in mute tones and come with power showers, CD players and free internet access.

126 L3 18–21 Charterhouse Square, Clerkenwell EC1M 6AH 020 7012 3700 Double from £125 97 Barbican, Farringdon 4, 56, 153

THISTLE CITY BARBICAN

www.thistle.com

This hotel offers a free shuttle bus to local Tube stations at peak times from its location on the fringe of the City. The rooms are modern and well equipped, with some deluxe options. Public areas include a sleek bar, decent restaurant and the smart Otium leisure club.

126 M2 Central Street, Clerkenwell EC1V 8DS 0870 333 9101 Double from £95 463 Old Street, Barbican, Moorgate 4, 55, 56, 243

Above *The Chamberlain Hotel*

0 400 m
0 400 yards
The Duke of Cambridge
PENTONVILLE
PENTONVILLE ROAD
A501
CITY ROAD
GOSWELL ROAD
ST JOHN STREET
City University
Thistle City Barbican
Moorfields Eye Hospital
OLD STREET STATION
SHOREDITCH
The City University
The Peasant
Moro
CLERKENWELL
The Eagle
Mount Pleasant Postal Sorting Office
FARRINGDON ROAD
ROSEBERY AVENUE
ST LUKE'S
OLD STREET
Ironmonger Row Baths
Finsbury Leisure Centre
Wesley's Chapel, House & Museum
Honourable Artillery Company Headquarters
Alba
Exhibition Halls
St John's Gate
Clerkenwell Dining Room & Bar
Malmaison Charterhouse Square
St Bartholomew's Medical School
The Jerusalem Tavern
Le Café du Marché
St John
FARRINGDON STATION
BARBICAN STATION
City University Business School
The Barbican
Guildhall School of Music & Drama
FINSBURY SQUARE
CHISWELL STREET
London Weather Centre
Gray's Inn
Inns of Court & School of Law
The Bleeding Heart Tavern
Smiths of Smithfield
Central London Markets (Smithfield)
St Bartholomew's The Great
Museum of London
MOORGATE STATION
Mehek
LONDON WALL
HOLBORN CIRCUS
HIGH HOLBORN
Chancery Lane
London Silver Vaults
Lincoln's Inn
Royal College of Surgeons
HOLBORN VIADUCT
St Bartholomew's Hospital
Postman's Park
Old Bailey (Central Criminal Court)
NEWGATE STREET
Stock Exchange
Clock Museum
Guildhall
St Lawrence Jewry Church
St Margaret's Lothbury
Bank of England & Museum
Royal Exchange
Maughan Library
Dr Johnson's House
Ye Olde Cheshire Cheese
The Old Bank of England
FLEET STREET
Royal Courts of Justice
Temple Church
Inns of Court
Middle Temple
Inner Temple
St Bride's Church
LUDGATE CIRCUS
CITY THAMESLINK STATION
St Paul's Cathedral
Bank of England Extension
Cheapside
St Mary-le-Bow Church
CITY
Mansion House
I Lombard Street
Temple of Mithras
St Stephen Walbrook Church
St Mary Abchurch
College of Arms
BLACKFRIARS STATION
PUDDLE DOCK
City of London School
CANNON STREET STATION
Monument
UPPER THAMES STREET
VICTORIA EMBANKMENT
HQS Wellington (Master Mariners)
HMS President
Blackfriars Millennium Pier
Blackfriars Pier
Vintners' Hall
Fishmonger's Hall
London Bridge Sports Centre
Swan Lane Pier
Millennium Bridge
Panorama Pier
Bankside Jetty
SOUTHWARK BRIDGE
LONDON BRIDGE
BLACKFRIARS BRIDGE
Thames
WATERLOO BRIDGE
Oxo Tower
Bankside Gallery
Tate Modern
Shakespeare's Globe
Financial Times
Clink Prison Museum
Golden Hinde
Rose Theatre Exhibition
Vinopolis
Southwark Cathedral
Borough Market
London Bridge Hospital
The London Television Centre
Royal National Theatre
National Film Theatre
Hayward Gallery
Royal Festival Hall
London City College
Schiller International University
London Nautical School
Purdy Hicks Gallery
Kings College London
Industrial Centre
SOUTHWARK STREET
STAMFORD STREET
Bramah Museum of Tea & Coffee
LONDON BRIDGE STATION
Guy's Hospital
BFI London IMAX Cinema
WATERLOO EAST STATION
Shell Centre
UNION STREET

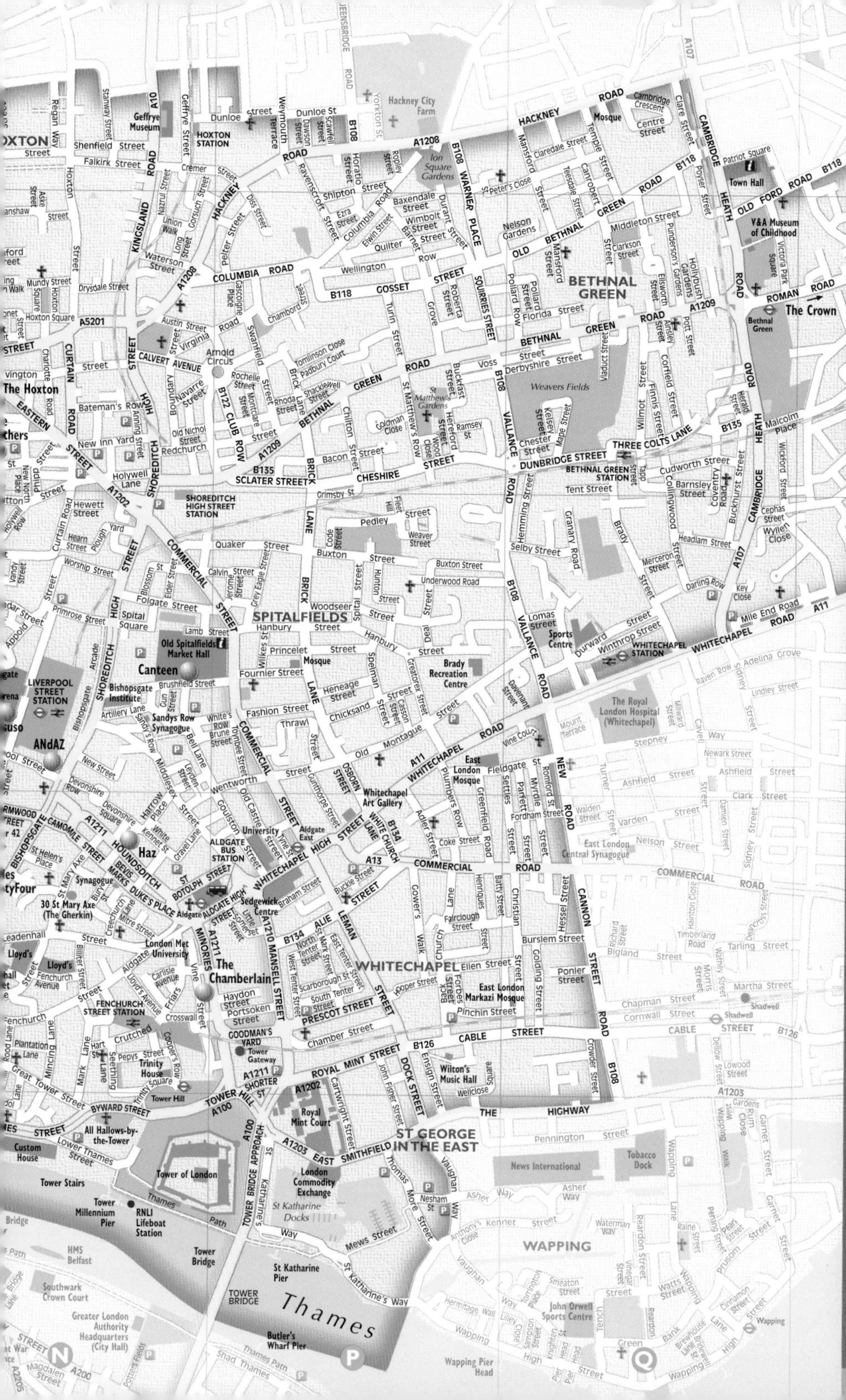
HOXTON
Hackney City Farm
Geffrye Museum
HOXTON STATION
HACKNEY ROAD
Ion Square Gardens
Cambridge Crescent
Mosque
Town Hall
V&A Museum of Childhood
OLD FORD ROAD
ROMAN ROAD
The Crown
Bethnal Green
BETHNAL GREEN
OLD BETHNAL GREEN ROAD
Nelson Gardens
COLUMBIA ROAD
GOSSET STREET
WARNER PLACE
SQUIRRIES STREET
BETHNAL GREEN ROAD
Weavers Fields
Arnold Circus
CALVERT AVENUE
KINGSLAND ROAD
HACKNEY ROAD
St Matthew's Gardens
VALLANCE ROAD
THREE COLTS LANE
DUNBRIDGE STREET
BETHNAL GREEN STATION
CAMBRIDGE HEATH ROAD
The Hoxton
EASTERN STREET
CURTAIN ROAD
SHOREDITCH HIGH STREET
SHOREDITCH HIGH STREET STATION
SCLATER STREET
CHESHIRE STREET
BRICK LANE
COMMERCIAL STREET
SPITALFIELDS
Old Spitalfields Market Hall
Canteen
Bishopsgate Institute
LIVERPOOL STREET STATION
ANdAZ
Mosque
Brady Recreation Centre
Sports Centre
WHITECHAPEL STATION
WHITECHAPEL ROAD
Mile End Road
The Royal London Hospital (Whitechapel)
Sandys Row Synagogue
East London Mosque
Whitechapel Art Gallery
Aldgate East
ALDGATE BUS STATION
Haz
Synagogue
30 St Mary Axe (The Gherkin)
Lloyd's
Sedgewick Centre
London Met University
The Chamberlain
FENCHURCH STREET STATION
WHITECHAPEL
East London Central Synagogue
COMMERCIAL ROAD
CANNON STREET ROAD
East London Markazi Mosque
CABLE STREET
Shadwell
Tower Gateway
Trinity House
Tower Hill
Wilton's Music Hall
THE HIGHWAY
Royal Mint Court
All Hallows-by-the-Tower
Custom House
ST GEORGE IN THE EAST
News International
Tobacco Dock
Tower of London
Tower Stairs
Tower Millennium Pier
RNLI Lifeboat Station
London Commodity Exchange
St Katharine Docks
TOWER BRIDGE APPROACH
WAPPING
HMS Belfast
Tower Bridge
St Katharine Pier
TOWER BRIDGE
Thames
Southwark Crown Court
Greater London Authority Headquarters (City Hall)
Butler's Wharf Pier
John Orwell Sports Centre
Wapping Pier Head
Wapping

COVENT GARDEN MARKET
PUNCH & JUDY
COVENT GARDEN
REAL FOOD MARKET

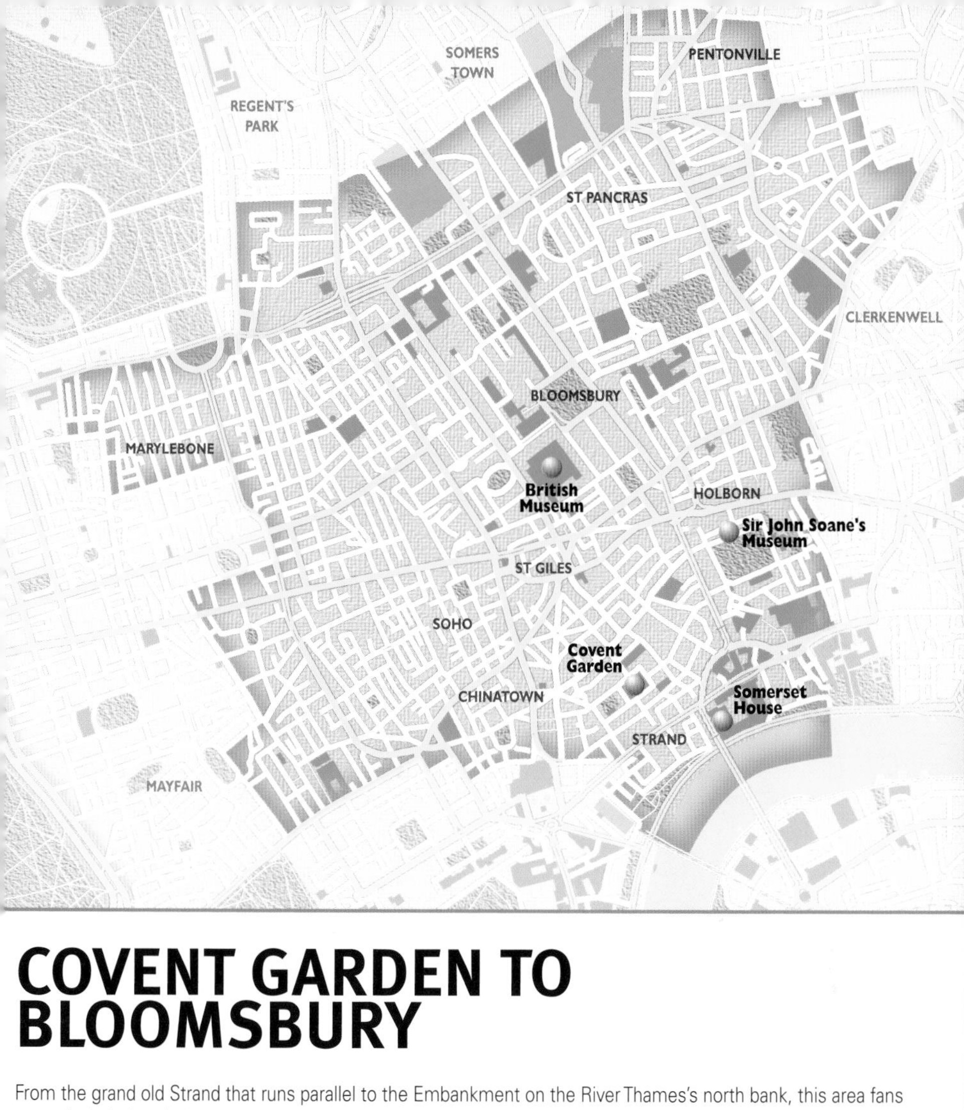

COVENT GARDEN TO BLOOMSBURY

From the grand old Strand that runs parallel to the Embankment on the River Thames's north bank, this area fans out to include London's principal entertainment and commercial districts, Covent Garden and Soho. Here you will find the vast majority of the city's renowned theatres, as well as many of its more mainstream nightlife venues and a dazzling selection of shops. Covent Garden itself is blessed with more attractive streets and buildings than its brash neighbour, all centred upon its famous Piazza, a haven for tourists, street performers and the odd pickpocket following in the footsteps of Charles Dickens's Fagin.

Across the other side of Charing Cross Road, famous for its bookshops, the architecture is a tad more functional throughout most of Soho, although its main hubs of Leicester Square and Piccadilly Circus, presided over by the impish Eros, always manage to attract hordes of visitors, if not that many Londoners. Just to the north, the city's modest Chinatown provides a colourful break and the chance of grabbing an inexpensive bite to eat. Continuing north from here, the rest of Soho develops a split personality, partly a seedy series of sex shops, partly an elegant set of streets around Soho Square, interspersed with more upscale restaurants and pubs.

Forming a distinct northern boundary to this part of the city is London's most famous consumer honeypot, Oxford Street, where most of the huge department stores vie for business. To the east and north of here, beyond the West End's lone skyscraper, Centre Point, you will find a completely different atmosphere in the classy area of Bloomsbury. With the magnificent British Museum as its cultural centrepiece and several leafy squares, the surprisingly quiet streets contain some of the capital's most desirable and expensive property.

Regent's Park
0
400 m
0
400 yds
St John's Lodge
Open Air Theatre
Queen Mary's Garden
The Holme
Regent's College
Clarence Gate
Sherlock Holmes Museum
Madame Tussauds
Royal Academy of Music
Regent's Park Barracks
REGENT'S PARK
Royal College of Physicians
Park Square
Regent's Park
The London Clinic
Royal National Orthopaedic Hospital
Great Portland Street
University of Westminster
Euston Tower
National Temperance Hospital
EUSTON STATION
SOMERS TOWN
Community Sports Centre
Drummond Crescent
University College
University College London
University College Hospital
Petrie Museum of Egyptian Archaeology
BT Tower
UCL
LISSON GROVE
MARYLEBONE
Central Synagogue
Wallace Collection
Wigmore Hall
All Saints' Church
West End Great Synagogue
Marble Arch
Speakers Corner
Bond Street
Shopping Centre
Oxford Circus
Handel House Museum
St George's Church
US Embassy
Roosevelt Memorial
MAYFAIR
Faraday Museum
Royal Academy of Arts
Burlington Arcade
Piccadilly Circus
Eros
London Trocadero
SOHO
CHINATOWN
St James's Church
Green Park
Hyde Park
Carlton House
Duke of York Column
YMCA
Tottenham Court Road
OXFORD STREET
REGENT STREET
PICCADILLY
EUSTON ROAD
MARYLEBONE ROAD
TOTTENHAM COURT ROAD
SHAFTESBURY
HAYMARKET
PALL MALL
PARK LANE
1
2
3
4
5
F
G
H

London Canal Museum
PENTONVILLE
King's Cross Thameslink Station
St Pancras Station
King's Cross Station
British Library
ST PANCRAS
Royal National Throat, Nose & Ear Hospital
Thomas Coram Foundation (The Foundling Museum)
Coram's Fields
Brunswick Shopping Centre
Eastman Dental Hospital
Mount Pleasant Postal Sorting Office
Charles Dickens Museum
CLERKENWELL
The City University
St Bartholomew's Medical School
Charterhouse
National Hospital for Sick Children (Great Ormond St)
National Hospital for Neurology & Neurosurgery
BLOOMSBURY
Royal London Homeopathic Hospital
London Weather Centre
Farringdon Station
Gray's Inn
Inns of Court & School of Law
The Method Studio
British Museum
The Cartoon Museum
HOLBORN
Holborn Circus
Central London Markets (Smithfield)
St Bartholomew's The Great
St Bartholomew's Hospital
City Temple
Sir John Soane's Museum
Lincoln's Inn
Royal College of Surgeons
London Silver Vaults
Oasis Sports Centre
New Connaught Rooms
Old Curiosity Shop
Maughan Library
Dr Johnson's House
Old Bailey (Central Criminal Court)
Stock Exchange
St Paul's Cathedral
London School of Economics & Political Science
Royal Courts of Justice (Law Courts)
Temple Church
St Bride's Church
City Thameslink Station
Royal Opera House
Covent Garden
St Paul's Church
London Transport Museum
St Peter's Hospital
Bush House (BBC)
Australia House
India House
St Clement Danes
St Mary-le-Strand
Roman Bath
King's College
Courtauld Institute of Art
Inner Temple
Middle Temple
Blackfriars Station
STRAND
Hermitage Rooms
Somerset House
Victoria Embankment
HQS Wellington (Master Mariners)
HMS President
Blackfriars Millennium Pier
Blackfriars Pier
Thames
BLACKFRIARS BRIDGE
WATERLOO BRIDGE
Royal Society of Arts
National Portrait Gallery
St Martin-in-the-Fields
Proud Gallery
Savoy Pier
Cleopatra's Needle
Embankment Pier
Trafalgar Square
Nelson's Column
Benjamin Franklin House
Charing Cross Station
Embankment
Golden Jubilee Bridge
Government Offices
DEFRA
Hispaniola
Festival Pier
Queen Elizabeth Hall
Southbank Centre
Royal Festival Hall
Hayward Gallery
Royal National Theatre
National Film Theatre
The London Television Centre
Oxo Tower
London City College
Schiller International University
London Nautical School
Bankside Gallery
Purdy Hicks Gallery
Tate Modern
Kings College London
J
K
L

Fine Quality
Silver & Jewellery

ALL SAINTS' CHURCH

www.allsaintsmargaretstreet.org.uk

All Saints' soars up from its crowded site north of Oxford Street. Designed by William Butterfield (1814–1900) in 13th-century Gothic style, its lofty architecture and lavish interior of granite, marble and polychrome tiles make it one of the most impressive Victorian churches in London. At 69m (227ft), the cross-banded spire is the second highest in the city. Visit after dark if possible, as the church looks its best in candlelight.

130 H4 7 Margaret Street W1W 8JG 020 7636 1788 Daily 7–7 Free Oxford Circus 7, 8, 10, 176

BRITISH LIBRARY

www.bl.uk

Britain's national library, formerly housed in the British Museum (▷ 134–139), gained its own purpose-built complex in 1998—the UK's biggest 20th-century public building. This stunning new package consists of a spacious piazza, three public galleries, new public artworks, a restaurant, a cafe, a shop and plenty of activities and tours. Eight of its fourteen floors are above ground, six below; beneath these are basements extending to a depth of 25m (82ft).

Before entering the galleries, go up the steps by the information desk and walk around the floor-to-ceiling central glass shaft to enjoy some of the beautiful bindings of the King's Library, George III's 60,000 volumes donated by his son George IV in 1823. The outer walls store the British Library's stamp collection—the world's finest—and you can pull out the vertical trays of stamps to examine specimens.

The John Ritblat Galleries display more of the library's treasures, including various editions of the Magna Carta (the 13th-century charter of public liberties), Leonardo da Vinci's notebooks and the only surviving manuscript in Shakespeare's own hand. You can listen to recordings of rare bird song or a speech by Sir Winston Churchill.

Above *The British Library occupies striking modern premises in St. Pancras*
Left *Luxury goods tempt passers-by in the covered Burlington Arcade*

The Workshop of Words, Sounds and Images explains how books and newspapers are created and printed and how sound is recorded. Finally, the Pearson Gallery interprets the library's great collections and stages special exhibitions.

The reading rooms are accessible only to pass-holders, who can consult any work from the collection, including every book printed since 1911. There are currently about 150 million items in more than 400 languages; some 8,000 titles are added each working day.

131 J2 96 Euston Road NW1 2DB 020 7412 7332 Public areas, galleries and bookshop: Mon, Wed–Fri 9.30–6, Tue 9.30–8, Sat 9.30–5, Sun 11–5. Reading rooms open to readers only Public areas, galleries, bookshop free King's Cross, St. Pancras, Euston, Euston Square 10, 30, 73, 91

BRITISH MUSEUM

▷ 134–139.

BURLINGTON ARCADE

www.burlington-arcade.co.uk

Leather goods, bespoke shoes, antique and contemporary jewellery, cashmere garments, perfumery and unusual gifts can all be found behind the Regency-style mahogany shop-fronts of this Piccadilly arcade. Built in 1819 with a central, timberframe glass canopy, its original purpose was to prevent passers-by tossing rubbish into the garden of Burlington House (see Royal Academy of Arts, ▷ 146). Former soldiers of the regiment of the 10th Hussars were recruited to keep order. 'Beadles' in Edwardian frock coats and top hats still enforce Regency laws of courtesy and decorum, which forbid whistling, singing, hurrying and carrying large packages.

130 H5 Piccadilly W1 Mon–Wed, Fri 8–6.30, Thu 8–7, Sat 9–6.30, Sun 11–5 Free Green Park, Piccadilly Circus 8, 9, 14, 19 38

THE CARTOON MUSEUM

www.cartoonmuseum.org

This is London's first dedicated cartoon museum. The collection conserves and displays a fascinating range of British cartoons, caricatures and comics. The reference library contains some 4,000 books on cartoons and aspects of the art, as well as more than 2,500 comics. The museum hosts lectures and workshops for adults and children.

131 J3 35 Little Russell Street WC1A 2HH 020 7580 8155 Tue–Sat 10.30–5.30, Sun 12–5.30 Adult £5.50, child (under 18) free Tottenham Court Road, Holborn 7, 38, 91, 188

INTRODUCTION

Wealthy physician Sir Hans Sloane (1660–1753) spent his life collecting assorted coins, books and natural history specimens, which by his death amounted to some 80,000 items. The government bought this collection and it was first put on display as the British Museum in 1759, at Montague House, which occupied the museum's present site. However, augmented by donations from benefactors, travellers, historians and archaeologists, the museum soon outgrew its home and Sir Robert Smirke's classical building (1823–47) was constructed to replace Montague House. As the museum continued to grow, more galleries were added, but space was still a major problem and by the late 20th century it became clear that a more radical solution had to be found. So in 1998 the British Library (▷ 133), which had occupied the Reading Room, was moved to St. Pancras and the Great Court was given a complete overhaul.

There are two entrances to the museum: one (the main entrance) on Great Russell Street (south) and the other on Montague Place (north). Both lead into the covered Great Court, which is the hub of the museum, forming the crossroads between all the galleries. It also serves as the main information centre and the location of the shops and eateries.

The museum's collections are arranged by geography, culture and theme, but the layout and sheer size of the place can still be bewildering. Note that collections from the same culture are not necessarily on the same floor (▷ 138). The best way to tackle the museum is to focus on the highlights or on one or two collections.

WHAT TO SEE

GREAT COURT AND READING ROOM

Entering Sir Robert Smirke's imposing, neoclassical building has become a pleasure in itself since the addition in 2000 of Sir Norman Foster's glorious, curved glass canopy over the central Great Court, turning the previously dark and confusing area cluttered with storerooms into a huge, light space—now Europe's largest covered square. It's worth lingering here to enjoy the sculpture displays set around the Great Concourse Gallery (such as the Easter Island statue and a reconstructed chariot) while deciding which galleries to visit.

In the middle of the court is the circular Reading Room, completed in 1857 to the design of Smirke's brother, Sydney. Karl Marx and other intellectuals once worked here. From a viewing area at the front, you can enjoy the domed ceiling, restored to its original colour scheme of blue, cream and gold, the low-lit desks and the floor-to-ceiling bookcases. There's an information desk near the entrance.

MAIN FLOOR

Rosetta Stone (Room 4)

Though not particularly impressive to look at, the Rosetta Stone was instrumental in solving many of the puzzles of the ancient Egyptian world. The slab of black basalt, discovered by Napoleon's army in the Nile Delta in 1799, reproduces the same (not very exciting) text in three languages: Greek, Demotic and Egyptian. This offered the first opportunity for modern scholars to crack the code of Egyptian hieroglyphics by comparing them with known scripts.

Elgin Marbles (Room 18)

The question of where they should be—in Greece or in Britain—still causes passionate debate. In fact, such is the controversy raging around them that

INFORMATION

www.britishmuseum.org
131 J3 Great Russell Street WC1B 3DG 020 7323 8000
Sat–Wed 10–5.30, Thu–Fri 10–8.30. Great Court Sun–Wed 9–6, Thu–Sat 9–8.30. Check times for temporary exhibitions. Late views: selected galleries only; check ahead Free; charges for some temporary exhibitions Holborn, Tottenham Court Road, Russell Square, Goodge Street 6, 7, 10, 19, 38, 59, 68, 91, 188 'Highlights' 90-minute tours: daily 10.30, 1, 3, adult £8. For foreign language tours call 020 7323 8181. 'eyeOpener' 30–40-minute introductory tours; choose from Japan, Ancient Greece, Ancient Iraq, Africa, China, Enlightenment Gallery, North America or Mexico, Art of the Middle East, The World of Money, Ancient Egypt, Early Medieval Europe, Assyrian reliefs. Daily starting at 11 until 3.45; free. Various audiotours in several languages, £3.50 A good selection for adults and children from £5 to £16.99. Available in English, French, German, Italian, Spanish, Korean, Chinese, Japanese Court restaurant on upper floor of Great Court serves hot and cold meals, morning coffee, afternoon tea, evening dinner. Open Sat–Wed 11–5 (last orders), Thu–Fri 11–10.30. Reservations: 020 7323 8990 Court cafe (east and west) serving hot drinks, light meals. Open Sun–Wed 9–5.30, Thu–Sat 9–9. Gallery cafe, next to Room 12, serving hot and cold light meals, morning coffee and afternoon tea. Open daily 10–5 Bookshop on north side of Great Court concourse, selling titles on art, history, archaeology etc. Children's shop on east side of Great Court concourse. Souvenir and guide shop on west side of Great Court concourse. Grenville shop on east side of the main entrance, next to Room 3, selling replica sculpture, jewellery, silk scarves and ties

Opposite *Iron and gilt bronze helmet from the ship burial at Sutton Hoo, dating from the 7th century*

the marbles' quality can be overlooked. These frieze reliefs, taken from the Parthenon, the temple to Athena on the Acropolis at Athens, are some of the finest sculptures of antiquity. Displayed in a vast room, they are best viewed as a kind of cartoon strip depicting a festival to commemorate Athena's birthday.

Following a visit to Athens in 1800 Lord Elgin, then British ambassador in Constantinople, obtained a licence from the Turkish Sultan to remove the stones, which had suffered severe damage during a skirmish between the Turks and a Venetian fleet in 1687. Arguing that the marbles would not survive if they remained in Greece, Elgin had them transported to Britain. The eventful journey involved a shipwreck and Elgin's detention in France.

Assyrian Reliefs (Rooms 6–10)

Vivid carved figures carrying pots and weapons, taking part in daily activities or military campaigns, were cut into panels for the Assyrian kings' palaces and temples, and have survived since about 880–612BC. Originally set on the buildings' mud-brick walls—some to a height of 2.6m (8.5ft), they were coloured with paint, traces of which can sometimes still be seen. Like comic strips, they relate their stories from one end of a wall to the other. Some of the most striking friezes come from the great palace—known as the Southwest Palace—of King Sennacherib, who came to the throne of Assyria in 704BC and moved his capital from Dur-Sharrukin (modern Khorsabad) to the ancient city of Nineveh, which he rebuilt in magnificent style. The palace was his great showpiece, many of its rooms covered with alabaster wall reliefs.

UPPER FLOORS

Portland Vase (Room 70)

This ancient cameo-glass vase was probably made in Rome between AD5 and AD25. Nothing is known about it prior to its appearance in the description of Cardinal del Monte's art collection in Italy in 1601. After passing to a series of buyers, it eventually reached the hands of the 3rd Duke of Portland in 1786.

Above *Smirke's Greek-inspired colonnaded facade on Great Russell Street*

He lent it to potter Josiah Wedgwood, who copied its cameo design and made it world-famous. The 4th Duke deposited it in the British Museum, which eventually bought it outright in 1945.

Love and marriage are the themes of its decoration, with a mythological slant, and one theory is that it was made as a wedding gift, at a time when glass-blowing was a relatively new technique.

Sutton Hoo Treasure (Room 41)
This comprises the collection of treasures from an Anglo-Saxon royal burial ship that survived intact in Suffolk and was excavated in 1939. The ship was probably a monument to Raedwald, the last great pagan king of East Anglia, who died in about AD625. Besides fine gold jewels, the boat contained a sceptre, a gold purse, silver bowls and plates, mounted silver drinking horns, bronze cauldrons and silver and gold ship fittings. Among a number of weapons were a shield, a sword with jewelled gold hilt, and an iron helmet with bronze and silver fittings and 'eyebrows' edged in garnets (▷ 134).

Lewis Chessmen (Room 42)
Carved from the tusks of walruses, these squat, sometimes comical-looking little figures were discovered on the island of Lewis in the Outer Hebrides of Scotland in 1831 by a crofter while working his land. Scandinavian in origin, they depict the figures used on a chess board and are believed to date from the mid-12th century. There are 80 pieces in all.

Mildenhall Treasure (Room 49)
A farmer ploughing his field near Mildenhall in Suffolk in 1942 unearthed an entire set of late-Roman silver tableware. There were no coins, so it was not easy to date, but the collection's design suggests it was used during the 4th century AD, by someone of high standing. The level of decoration on the platters, ladles and spoons, bowls and dishes is superb, and includes handles shaped like dolphins and depictions of Bacchus, god of wine—a fashionable touch in silver dining sets throughout the Roman period.

TIPS

- Get your bearings in the Great Court, where you can pick up plans and information.
- Don't expect to see everything in a day; focus on what interests you and make for one or two galleries.
- Make a trip here in the evening on Thursday to Saturday, when the Great Court's restaurants and shops remain open. On Thursdays and Fridays the major galleries stay open late.

Left *Detail from the Elgin Marbles*
Below right *Norman Foster's glass-covered Great Court, opened in 2000*

GALLERY GUIDE

UPPER FLOOR

Rooms 41–48: Europe
Room 49: Roman Britain
Room 50: Britain and Europe 800BC–AD43
Room 51: Ancient Europe–prehistory
Rooms 52–59: Ancient Near East
Rooms 61–66: Egypt
Room 68: Money and medals
Rooms 69–73: Greece and Rome
Room 90: Changing exhibitions
Rooms 92–94: Asia

GROUND FLOOR

Room 1: Enlightenment
Room 2: Changing museum
Room 3: Special exhibitions
Room 4: Egypt
Room 5: Special exhibitions
Rooms 6–10: Ancient Near East
Rooms 11–23: Greece and Rome
Rooms 26–27: The Americas
Rooms 33–33a: Asia
Room 34: The Islamic World
Room 35 and King's Library: temporary exhibitions

RAISED LEVEL

Room 67: Korea
Room 95: Chinese ceramics

LOWER FLOORS

Clore Education Centre
Room 25: Africa
Room 77: Greek and Roman architecture
Room 78: Classical inscriptions
Rooms 82–85: Wolfson Galleries
Room 88: Holy Land
Room 89: Assyrian Life

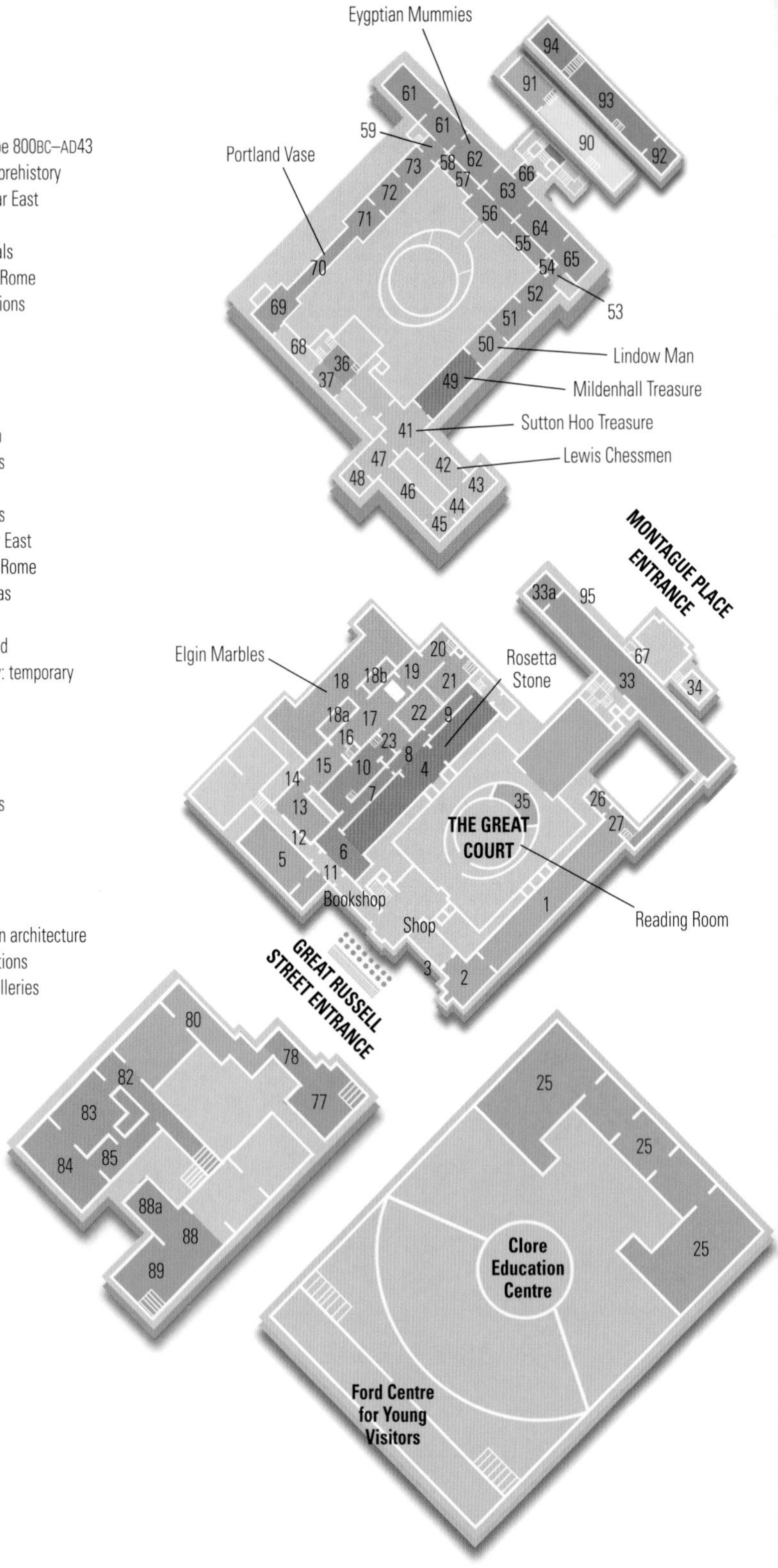

Egyptian Mummies (Rooms 62–63)
One of the most popular displays in the British Museum is that of Egyptian mummies and sarcophagi. Row after row of preserved bodies, wrapped in bandages and surrounded by their prized possessions and favourite food, exercise a gruesome fascination, especially for children. Most disturbing of all is the preserved body of 'Ginger', a Predynastic Egyptian from 3400BC in a reconstructed grave pit. Not just people were mummified: there are also elaborately wrapped cat mummies which were buried by pious Egyptians in special cat cemeteries. The craftsmanship and elegance of the items surrounding and celebrating the dead are superb—such as the intricately painted wooden coffin of Passenhor, its body busy with figures and texts, its head painted to represent a serene, young face framed by a headdress. Discovered in Thebes, it was created in about 700BC.

Lindow Man (Room 50)
Nicknamed 'Pete Marsh' by the archaeologists who found him in a waterlogged peat bog in Cheshire, the Lindow Man is an almost perfectly preserved—albeit somewhat leathery—2,000-year-old corpse. Among the current theories is one that he was sacrificed during a Druid ceremony. There are signs of a blow to his head and a wound to his throat, and mistletoe grains were found in his gut, suggesting that he was fed a hallucinatory meal before being knocked out, strangled and drowned.

Percival David Collection (Room 95)
This outstanding collection of Chinese ceramics dates was amassed by scholar and collector Sir Percival David, who acquired pieces sold off by the Chinese imperial household in the 1920s. He presented the collection, along with his extensive library of books relating to Chinese art and culture, to the University of London in 1950, and for many years both were housed in an elegant Georgian town house in Gordon Square. Lack of funding forced the Percival David Foundation to close in 2007, but in 2009 the ceramics were installed on permanent loan in a specially built new gallery in the British Museum.

In all there are about 1,700 Chinese ceramics, reflecting court taste and dating mainly from the 10th to the 18th centuries. Items range from bowls, teapots, cups and vases to incense burners and perfume baskets, spittoons, garden seats, flower-holders, lamp stands and candleholders, animal figurines and figures of Buddhas and deities.

Highlights include a collection of stoneware from the Song (960–1279) and Yuan (1279–1368) dynasties, as well as blue and white, polychrome and monochrome porcelains.

SIR HANS SLOANE

Having developed a keen interest in nature as a child in Ireland, Hans Sloane studied chemistry and botany in London, and medicine in France. A three-month voyage to Jamaica as physician to the new governor, the 2nd Duke of Albermarle, gave him the chance to observe the local fauna and flora, customs and natural phenomena such as earthquakes, and to collect plants, molluscs, insects and fish. He was intrigued by a popular local drink, cocoa, and concocted a variation adding milk to reduce its bitterness. On his return to England Sloane's version was sold as a medicine before passing to Messrs. Cadbury, who turned it into their famous drinking chocolate. Sloane continued his career as a distinguished physician while collecting curiosities and publishing works on his travels and studies. By the time of his death at the age of 93, his precious collection took up a large part of his house, and was looked after by a full-time curator.

Above *Monumental figures in the Egyptian Sculpture Gallery*

CHARLES DICKENS MUSEUM

www.dickensmuseum.com

Charles Dickens (1812–70), the prolific novelist and commentator on Victorian society, lived at no fewer than 15 addresses during his life. This Georgian terraced house in Bloomsbury is where he lived from 1837 to 1839. Now a museum of his life and work, it houses original manuscripts, first editions, personal effects, memorabilia, including the Dickens family tree, and 19th-century paintings, and includes the study where Dickens completed his first full-length novel, *The Pickwick Papers*, and later the famous *Oliver Twist* and *Nicholas Nickleby*.

The cluttered drawing room where the novelist entertained has been restored to its original Regency style, while reconstructions in the basement wash house and wine cellar convey a little more of the atmosphere of Dickensian London.

131 K3 48 Doughty Street WC1N 2LX 020 7405 2127 Mon–Sat 10–5, Sun 11–5 Adult £6, child (under 16) £3, family £15 Russell Square, King's Cross, Chancery Lane (closed Sun) 19, 38, 45, 55, 243

CHINATOWN

This vibrant enclave around pedestrianized Gerrard Street is crammed with dozens of Asian shops and eateries. Since the 1950s Chinese immigrants have made the area their own and the community congregates here to shop and socialize. Ornate gateways stand at either end of the pedestrian area, and even the phone boxes have pagoda-style roofs. At Chinese New Year (late January/early February, ▷ 294), huge papier-mâché lions dance through the streets against a background of firecrackers and exuberant street events.

130 H4 Open access Free Leicester Square, Tottenham Court Road 14, 19, 24, 38, 176

CLEOPATRA'S NEEDLE

www.akhet.co.uk/cleo.htm

This pink granite obelisk—the twin of the one in New York's Central Park—was constructed for the Egyptian Pharaoh Tuthmose III in about 1500BC, and its elaborately carved hieroglyphics and inscriptions were added to mark the victories of Rameses II. Its association with Cleopatra began when it was moved to Alexandria. In the 19th century, it was given to the British by the Egyptian viceroy, but its weight made shipment impossible for several decades.

Plaques mounted round the base of the obelisk give a brief history of the needle and commemorate the men who died during its transportation, when the ship carrying it ran into a storm in the Bay of Biscay. It was placed here beside the Thames in 1879, flanked by two Victorian bronze sphinxes. Nearby benches are also decorated with an Egyptian motif of winged sphinxes.

131 J5 Open access Free Embankment 68, 171, 176, 188, RV1 Embankment Pier

COVENT GARDEN

▷ 142–143.

FARADAY MUSEUM

www.rigb.org/heritage/faradaypage.jsp

Two rooms in the basement of the 18th-century Royal Institution building just north of Piccadilly house a small museum devoted to scientist Michael Faraday (1791–1867), discoverer of electro-magnetic induction, electro-magnetic rotations, the magneto-optical effect and much else besides. His original laboratory shows reconstructions of experimental set-ups and historical equipment, including his first electric generator and magneto-spark apparatus.

The Royal Institution was founded in 1799 to promote and popularize scientific research, and is the oldest independent research body in the world.

130 G5 The Royal Institution of Great Britain, 21 Albemarle Street W1S 4BS 020 7409 2992 Mon–Fri 9–9 Free Green Park, Piccadilly Circus 8, 14, 19, 38

GRAY'S INN

www.graysinn.org.uk

Gray's Inn is one of the four Inns of Court (along with Lincoln's Inn, ▷ 144, and Inner and Middle Temple, ▷ 110) established in the 14th century to provide accommodation for lawyers and their trainees. Together they now serve as the home of London's legal profession.

Although wartime bombing destroyed much of Gray's Inn, the most important buildings have been well restored. These include the 17th-century gateway on High Holborn, which gives access to the gardens, the only part open to the public. Known as the Walks, the gardens were first laid out in 1606 by English philosopher and statesman Sir Francis Bacon (1561–1626) when he was treasurer here.

Paths lead through quadrangles of varying character: Red-brick Georgian buildings line South Square, a quiet precinct with lawns and a statue of Bacon; late 17th-century houses and a chapel are found in Gray's Inn Square; and 18th-century houses distinguish Field Court.

131 K3 The Honourable Society of Gray's Inn, 8 South Square, Gray's Inn WC1R 5ET 020 7458 7800 Public access to gardens Mon–Fri 12–2.30. Chapel Mon–Fri 10–6 Free Chancery Lane (closed Sun), Holborn, Farringdon 8, 17, 25, 45, 243, 521

Right *Ornamental gates mark the entrances to Chinatown*

Below *Blue plaque at No. 48 Doughty Street, one-time home of Charles Dickens*

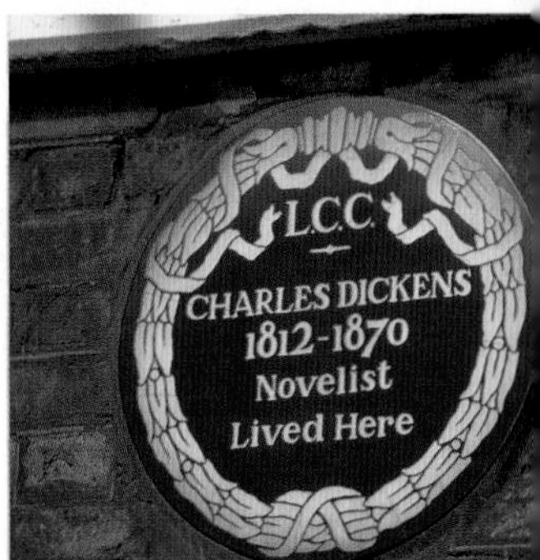

倫敦華埠
倫肆還臨英帝苑
HAIRDRESSERS
SALOON

INTRODUCTION

Covent Garden Piazza was London's first residential square, laid out in the 1630s by architect Inigo Jones and the model for numerous other squares around the city. Jones has been commissioned by the Earl of Bedford to model its Palladian-style arcades on the central piazza of Livorno in Italy. It was an immediate hit as promenading territory with the upper echelon of England's Renaissance society but it gradually metamorphosed into a thriving fruit and vegetable market, renowned for its flower-sellers and for the costermongers (a term originally meaning 'apple-sellers'), who effortlessly balanced towering stacks of baskets on their heads. This transformation ironically returned the area to its earlier usage, when it served as kitchen garden of the Convent ('covent' in Middle English) of St. Peter during the medieval period. Subsequent centuries saw the area's reputation decline further as brothels supplemented the market stalls, and it remained the province of pimps, whores and lowlifes well into the Victorian era. Indeed, this was the location chosen by playwright George Bernard Shaw for his character Henry Higgins to find the perfect cockney accent as spoken by flower-seller Eliza Doolittle in *Pygmalion*.

INFORMATION

www.coventgardenlife.com
131 J4 Open access Free
Covent Garden 9, 13, 23, 87, 139, 176, RV1

Above *The converted cellar area at the heart of the Piazza is filled with shops and cafes*

WHAT TO SEE

THE PIAZZA

When the traders moved out to Nine Elms near Vauxhall, south London, in the 1970s, the market area was transformed into the Piazza, a mix of specialist shops, stalls and eating places, with street entertainers to amuse the crowds. The central halls, still covered with their 1870s iron roofs and fronted at the eastern end, the original entrance, by grand stone columns, form the heart of this buzzing area.

Steps lead down to the converted cellar area of the halls, now housing more shops and the Punch and Judy pub. It was here that diarist Samuel Pepys made the first recorded mention of seeing a Punch and Judy puppet show in

May 1662. Shoppers sitting at the outdoor tables or leaning on the balcony above are entertained by street performers who must prove their worth by audition before being let loose on the public.

Retailers, too, are carefully chosen for their suitability to the Covent Garden spirit, so the Piazza's shops all have a certain character—such as Culpeper the Herbalist, or Benjamin Pollock's Toy Shop, which specializes in toy theatres, Punch and Judy, antique toys, miniatures and games.

There's still a daily market here (10.30–6.30), set up in the North Hall and collectively known as the Apple Market. More than 200 stallholders are registered to trade in it, and because most exhibit only once or twice a week, there is always an enormous variety of crafts, jewellery, clothing and accessories (Tue–Sun). On Mondays, the market is turned over exclusively to stalls selling antiques and collectables.

AROUND AND BEYOND THE PIAZZA

On the northeast corner of the Piazza is the magnificently refurbished Royal Opera House (▷ 158). Its design incorporates the original iron framework of the market's Floral Hall. Across the Piazza is the former Flower Market, now the site of the refurbished London Transport Museum (▷ 145), while the Italianate St. Paul's Church (▷ 147), on the west side of the Piazza, is about the only building not to have changed its purpose. The area in front of it is another space often devoted to street performances. To the east are two of the area's famous theatres, the elegant Theatre Royal Drury Lane (▷ 160) and the Lyceum (▷ 158), on Wellington Street.

The area known as Covent Garden spreads well beyond the Underground station and into the narrow streets leading off the Piazza, themselves full of arty specialist shops. Long Acre is a particularly good hunting ground, as is King Street and the small roads that radiate out from Seven Dials, to the northwest.

TIP

›› Petty thieves operate more around Covent Garden than in any other part of London, so you should guard your valuables against sleight of hand.

Left *Old buses on display at the London Transport Museum*
Below *Crowds gather to watch street entertainers on the Piazza*

LEICESTER SQUARE

www.officiallondontheatre.co.uk/tkts for cut-price tickets

By night, particularly on a Friday or Saturday, this pedestrianized central London square is one of the most crowded places in the city, teeming with people on their way to or from cinemas, nightclubs, restaurants, fast-food outlets and bars. By day its tiny central garden is a popular lunchtime resting place. In the middle of the garden is the marble Shakespeare Memorial Fountain (1874) by Giovanni Fontana, facing a bronze statue of Charlie Chaplin (1981) by John Doubleday. Around the perimeter are busts of some of the square's former local residents—Sir Joshua Reynolds, Sir Isaac Newton, William Hogarth and John Hunter.

The tkts ticket booth in the clock tower building on the south side of the square is the best place to buy discounted theatre tickets.

130 H5 Leicester Square WC2H 7NJ Open access to the square. Cut-price tkts ticket booth: Mon–Sat 10–7, Sun 2–3 Free Leicester Square 24, 29, 176

LINCOLN'S INN

www.lincolnsinn.org.uk

The buildings of Lincoln's Inn, one of London's four Inns of Court (▷ 110 and 140), cover 400 years and a number of architectural styles. The 15th-century Old Hall, where the Court of Chancery sat between 1733 and 1873, is the setting for the protracted Jarndyce v Jarndyce case in Charles Dickens' novel *Bleak House*. A 17th-century chapel built above a beautiful open undercroft has massive pillars and dramatic vaulting, and gas lamps still light the 17th-century houses in New Square. The mock-Tudor Great Hall, with its red brick and black frame, is a 19th-century addition.

An archway at the northwest corner of New Square leads to Lincoln's Inn Fields, at 5ha (12 acres) the largest square in London and once a popular venue for fighting duels. Today lawyers battle it out instead on the tennis courts here in their lunch hour. On the north side is Sir John Soane's Museum (▷ 148–149).

131 K4 Lincoln's Inn WC2A 3TL 020 7405 1393 Mon–Fri 9–6. Chapel 12–2.30 Free Chancery Lane (closed Sun), Holborn 8, 25, 242, 521

LONDON CANAL MUSEUM

www.canalmuseum.org.uk

Here on Regent's Canal, within striking distance of one of the city's busiest areas, you can see inside a narrowboat cabin, trace the history of London's canals and learn about the cargoes they carried and the people who lived and worked on the waterways when they formed the nation's commercial arteries. The museum is housed in a former warehouse built for famous ice-cream-maker Carlo Gatti, and also explores the history of the ice trade and ice cream. Don't miss the opportunity to look down into the Victorian ice well.

131 J1 12–13 New Wharf Road, King's Cross N1 9RT 020 7713 0836 Tue–Sun 10–4.30 Adult £3, child (8–15) £1.50, under 8s free King's Cross 10, 46, 73, 205 King's Cross

Left *Charlie Chaplin's statue in Leicester Square*

LONDON TRANSPORT MUSEUM

www.ltmuseum.co.uk

Covent Garden's former Flower Market (▷ 142–143) now houses the London Transport Museum, which tells the story of the city's transport since the early 1800s and explores its impact on the growth of the capital and the lives of Londoners.

The museum's permanent displays draw from more than 375,000 items—the most comprehensive collection of historic urban transport in the world. Fulfil your childhood fantasies by clambering into the driving seat of a bus or operating a simulated Tube train, and admire the handsomely designed horse-drawn and electric trams. Discover the story of wartime London when the city's transport workers played a key role.

In addition to the vehicles themselves, there are maps, posters, models, uniforms, signs and other equipment. Touch screens provide more information, and there are many working models and hands-on exhibits.

The museum reopened in November 2007 after a £22 million refurbishment. It still tells the history of transport in the city but there is also an emphasis on future developments, including other major city projects in Delhi, New York, Paris, Shanghai and Tokyo. The museum will take a major role over the coming decades in the debate on the environmental impact of transport in the city and its effect on the inhabitants.

131 J4 Covent Garden Piazza, Covent Garden WC2E 7BB 020 7379 6344 or 020 7565 7299 (24-hour recorded information) Sat–Thu 10–6, Fri 11–6 Adult £10, under 16s accompanied by an adult free Covent Garden, Leicester Square, Holborn, Charing Cross 6, 9, 15, 13, 23, 139, RV1 The Upper Deck cafe

PETRIE MUSEUM OF EGYPTIAN ARCHAEOLOGY

www.petrie.ucl.ac.uk

This collection, kept in the University of London's Institute of Archaeology building, consists of about 80,000 Egyptian and Sudanese items. It was started by Victorian enthusiast Amelia Edwards and expanded by Professor William Flinders Petrie (1853–1942), who excavated dozens of major sites. Treasures include finds from the Roman cemeteries at Hawara, famous for its beautiful mummy portraits, El-Amarna, the city of king Akhenaten, and the first true pyramid, at Meydum. A new museum building is being planned to open in 2011, where the whole collection can be displayed at once.

130 H3 University College London, Malet Place WC1E 6BT 020 7679 2884 Tue–Fri 1–5, Sat 11–2 Free. Donations welcome Euston, Euston Square, Warren Street, Goodge Street 18, 24, 29, 73

Above *Street artists congregate in Leicester Square and will rustle you up a portrait on the spot; they vary in quality, so choose carefully*

PHOTOGRAPHERS' GALLERY

www.photonet.org.uk

Britain's first independent photographic gallery, founded in 1971, is now a leading venue for contemporary shows with a full schedule of exhibitions and educational events. Temporary exhibitions cover aspects of the history of photography. (The portrait painter and founder of the Royal Academy, Sir Joshua Reynolds, lived here in the 18th century.) Two buildings off Charing Cross Road accommodate the three galleries, a bookshop and a cafe.

131 J4 5 and 8 Great Newport Street WC2H 7HY 020 7831 1772 Galleries: Tue–Wed, Sat 11–6, Thu–Fri 11–8, Sun 12–6 Free Oxford Circus 12, 24, 29, 176

Above *Statue of Eros in Piccadilly Circus*

PICCADILLY CIRCUS

One of the world's busiest traffic circles, formed by the junction of five streets in the West End, the Circus has become a byword for urban clamour and crowds. It was created by John Nash as part of a scheme to link St. James's with Regent's Park. Neon advertisements flash above the constant flow—or crawl—of traffic and the tourists, workers and shoppers who throng the area at all hours.

Its focal point is the aluminium statue known as Eros, above a bronze fountain erected in 1892 as a memorial to the philanthropic 7th Earl of Shaftesbury. Sir Alfred Gilbert, the designer, intended it as an angel of Christian charity rather than the Greek god of love, and was so dismayed by changes to his design that he refused to attend the unveiling.

Piccadilly is believed to take its name from a 16th-century frilly collar called a pikadil. A dressmaker who made his fortune selling these fashion items built his house nearby.

130 H5 Open access Free Piccadilly Circus 9, 12, 15, 19, 23, 139, 159

ROYAL ACADEMY OF ARTS

www.royalacademy.org.uk

Burlington House, on Piccadilly, was built as a Palladian palazzo (mansion) for the Earl of Burlington around 1720. Since 1768 it has been the home of the Royal Academy of Arts, the country's first formal art school. English portrait painter Sir Joshua Reynolds (1723–92) was the first president and painters John Constable (1776–1837) and J. M. W. Turner (1775–1851) were among the first students.

In March 2004 the Royal Academy opened its splendid 18th-century Neo-Palladian suite of John Madejski Fine Rooms to provide a permanent display space for major works by Reynolds, Gainsborough, Constable, Spencer and Hockney. Here too is the outstanding *Taddei Tondo*, a circular relief of the Madonna and Child with the infant St. John, carved by Michelangelo in 1504–05. It is one of only four marble sculptures by the artist outside Italy.

Major international exhibitions on loan from collections around the world fill two suites of galleries and draw huge crowds. The top floor of the building (the Sackler Wing, reached by glass lift or steps) was remodelled by Sir Norman Foster, himself an Academician, in 1991, and is used for smaller exhibitions, including shows by living artists.

The Royal Academy Summer Exhibition (Jun to mid-Aug) is a hugely popular show of work by amateurs and professionals (▷ 21), any of whom can submit pieces for consideration. In 1987 a painting entitled *Farm Buildings in Norfolk* was entered under the name of Arthur George Carrick, an alias of Prince Charles, who is a keen artist.

130 H5 Burlington House, Piccadilly W1J 0BD General enquiries 020 7300 8000, 020 7300 5760 (recorded information) Exhibitions Sat–Thu 10–6, Fri 10–10. Fine Rooms Tue–Fri 1–4.30, Sat–Sun 10–6 Prices vary according to exhibitions; adult from £9, child (12–18) from £4, (8–11) from £3. Fine Rooms free, under 9s free. Tours free Green Park, Piccadilly Circus 9, 14, 19, 22, 38

ROYAL COURTS OF JUSTICE (LAW COURTS)

Crowds, cameramen and reporters eager for a verdict often congregate outside the Royal Courts of Justice, at the end of the Strand. The country's most important and high-profile civil cases are tried in this elaborate neo-Gothic building, designed by George Edmund Street in the 1870s. A concoction of spires and pinnacles, it houses more than 50 courtrooms. Public galleries are open to anyone, but security is very tight and to enter you'll have to undergo stringent checks.

On reaching the Main Hall ask for a plan and guide to the complex at

the information desk. Cases being heard that day are posted here. An exhibition in the minstrels' gallery traces the history of lawcourt dress.
131 K4 Strand WC2A 2LL 020 7947 6000 Mon–Fri 10–4.30. Cases start around 10am and break for lunch at 1pm Free Chancery Lane, Temple 4, 11, 15, 76

ST. CLEMENT DANES

This small and elegant building surrounded by traffic in the middle of the Strand is the latest in a succession of churches on the site. The 11th-century church was first rebuilt by William the Conqueror, then again in the 14th century, demolished and rebuilt by Wren in 1680–82 and virtually destroyed by bombs in 1941, leaving only the steeple (1719) and walls. The interior was rebuilt and dedicated to the Royal Air Force in 1958, and daily prayers and memorial services are held here for its members. Don't miss the black Welsh slate badges of units of the RAF set into the church floor.
131 K4 Strand WC2R 1DH 020 7242 8282 Daily 8–4.30; Sun service 11am Free Temple (closed Sun), Charing Cross 4, 11, 15, 76

ST. PAUL'S CHURCH

St. Paul's was conceived as an integral feature of Inigo Jones's 17th-century Italianate piazza, Covent Garden (▷ 142–143), and its Tuscan pillars and columns still dominate the west side of the square. This portico was never used as the church's main entrance is on Bedford Street.

With the Theatre Royal Drury Lane (▷ 160) and the Royal Opera House (▷ 158) nearby, St. Paul's has always been associated with the theatre and is consequently known as the actors' church. Dozens of plaques commemorate distinguished figures of the thespian world, such as London-born film actor and director Charlie Chaplin (1889–1977).

Other memorials in the church include those for artist J. M. W. Turner, baptized here in 1775, and woodcarver Grinling Gibbons, buried here in 1721.

The space in front of the church is used by all kinds of street performers—clowns, fire-eaters, musicians and acrobats. At the costermongers' harvest festival (▷ 295), cockney market stall-holders converge, dressed for charity in the outfits of pearly kings and queens.
131 J4 Bedford Street WC2E 9ED 020 7836 5221 Mon–Fri 8.30–4.30, Sat–Sun check for times Free Covent Garden, Leicester Square 9, 11, 13, 15, 23, RV1

SIR JOHN SOANE'S MUSEUM

▷ 148–149.

SOMERSET HOUSE

▷ 150–151.

THOMAS CORAM FOUNDATION (THE FOUNDLING MUSEUM)

www.foundlingmuseum.org.uk
The Thomas Coram Foundation was set up in 1739 to provide shelter and education for orphaned and abandoned children. The founder was sea captain and philanthropist Thomas Coram, with the composer Handel and artist William Hogarth as governors and benefactors.

The Foundling Museum was founded in 1998 and after a major refurbishment opened as a state-of-the-art museum in 2004. It tells the story of the Foundling Hospital and displays a fine collection of art and social history. It is next to the Foundation now known as the Coram Family, which continues the work of helping vulnerable children.
131 J2 40 Brunswick Square WC1N 1AZ 020 7841 3600 Tue–Sat 10–5, Sun 11–5 Adult, £5, under 16s free Russell Square, King's Cross 10, 19, 45, 68, 73, 168, 243

VICTORIA EMBANKMENT

The Victoria Embankment, built in the late 1860s to 1870s, was a massive engineering project, reclaiming land from the north bank of the River Thames to create a buffer against flooding. This is where you'll find Cleopatra's Needle (▷ 140), the city's oldest monument, dating from around 1500BC.
131 K5 Open access Free Embankment, Charing Cross 3, 11, 12, 15, 88, 148

Below *Italianate St Paul's Church in Covent Garden dates from 1633*

INFORMATION

www.soane.org

131 K4 13 Lincoln's Inn Fields WC2A 3BP 020 7405 2107 Tue–Sat 10–5; first Tue each month also 6–9pm Free; donations box provided Chancery Lane (closed Sun), Holborn 8, 25, 242, 521 Museum tour Sat 11am, £5 £1, in English and French (includes floor plan) Salespoints selling books on art and architecture, cards

Above *Sir Thomas Lawrence's portrait of Sir John Soane (1827) dominates the library/dining room*

INTRODUCTION

From the moment you arrive it's apparent that this is a museum unlike any other. The entrance is through the front door of No. 12; don't be disconcerted if it's shut—just climb the steps and knock for admission. This is one of three town houses containing the vast collection of sculptures, paintings, carvings and curios amassed by Sir John Soane (1753–1837).

Soane was Professor of Architecture at the Royal Academy (▷ 146) and made his collection of curios, casts and models available to his students and to enthusiastic amateurs. For that purpose he demolished and rebuilt three houses in succession on the north side of Lincoln's Inn Fields between 1792 and 1824, keeping 12 Lincoln's Inn Fields as a family home and office and using 13 and 14 as his museum. The house was open to visitors the day before and the day after each of his lectures, and by 1827 was already known as the Academy of Architecture.

It's possible to wander at will, but a floorplan suggests the route Soane recommended. This starts with the dining room and library and continues to the study and dressing room, crammed with antique marble fragments. You're now overlooking Monument Court, a central light well with relics rescued from demolished buildings. Across the corridor full of marbles and casts is the picture room, on the site of No. 14's old stableyards. A staircase then leads down to the basement, with the Monk's Parlour and yard and the crypt, full of plaster prototypes of classical monuments. Stairs lead back up to the ground floor and the colonnade, which overlooks the basement under a high dome.

The trail leads on through the New Picture Room; the peaceful breakfast parlour; a dining room housing changing exhibitions as the Soane Gallery; another breakfast parlour, and up the curved staircase to the spacious first-floor drawing rooms, where you can see a pencil sketch of Mrs. Soane and portraits of Soane and of his sons, John and George; the sons both proved to be a disappointment to him, which is why Soane in due course left his collection to the nation.

WHAT TO SEE

THE PICTURE ROOM

This small room is crowded with paintings, most prominently William Hogarth's two series of satirical fables, *A Rake's Progress* (1733) and *An Election* (1754)—the original paintings on which his popular engravings were based. By using hinged screens instead of walls Soane managed to fit more than a hundred works into this room; the screens are opened regularly to show the paintings on the other sides. Three works by Canaletto, the pride of Soane's collection, are displayed in the New Picture Room, upstairs.

SARCOPHAGUS OF PHARAOH SETI I

Taking pride of place in the atmospheric crypt is this huge stone coffin, covered in delicate hieroglyphs and bought by Soane in 1824. The sarcophagus dates from around 1370BC and was considered an extremely important archaeological find—one of the finest items of its kind outside Egypt, in fact. Nevertheless, the British Museum turned down the opportunity to add the sarcophagus to its collection before Soane put in his bid.

TIMEPIECES

Among the items in the museum is an important collection of clocks and timepieces, going back to the 17th century. Included are a calendar watch presented to Sir Christopher Wren by Queen Anne in the 1690s; one of five astronomical clocks made by Raingo of Paris for the Prince Regent and his brothers; clocks by Benjamin Lewis Vulliamy and Thwaites and Reed in cases designed by Soane himself; and a late 18th-century eight-day marine chronometer designed by Thomas Mudge for the Duke of Marlborough. This last item was No. 10 of a series of 15 chronometers made to Mudge's design by his son, and regarded as the finest in existence.

CAST COLLECTION

Soane's collection of casts made from scultpures and other pieces, mainly kept in the crypt, is an invaluable guide to the methods of cast-manufacturing in the early 19th century. This busy trade involved casting work from private and public collections, and Soane provided a useful archive by recording the makers in his journals and ledgers. Included in his extensive collection are rare life-masks of the artist Thomas Banks and actress Sarah Siddons, but one of the most noteworthy sections is the group of 91 casts made by the workshop of sculptor Antonio Canova (1757–1822) in Rome. These include items from temples, churches and from the sculpture collection of Polish Prince Poniatowsky. Soane obtained the collection in 1834.

TIPS

» Tuesday evening tours are very atmospheric as part of the museum is candlelit. Queues are likely.
» Visit as early as possible on Saturday to avoid queueing.

Below left *Busts, urns and architectural fragments are all clustered together under the dome*
Below right *The breakfast room at No. 13*

INFORMATION

www.somersethouse.org.uk
131 K4 The Strand WC2R 1LA
020 7845 4600 (recorded information), Courtauld Gallery 020 7848 2526, Gilbert Collection 020 7420 9400, Hermitage Rooms 020 7845 4630 Daily 10–6; extended hours apply to Courtyard, River Terrace and restaurant Somerset House: free. Courtauld Gallery, Gilbert Collection (each): adult £8, child (12–17) £6, under 12s free. Hermitage Rooms: adult £5, under 18s free. Free admission to Courtauld Gallery Mon 10–2 except public hols Temple (closed Sun), Covent Garden, Holborn 6, 9, 11, 13, 15, 23, 91, 176 Embankment Pier Admiralty restaurant River Terrace summer cafe; Courtauld Cafe; take-away food/courtyard lunches at delicatessen near Seamen's Hall Gifts and gallery merchandise in Courtauld Gallery, Hermitage Gallery and Gilbert Collection; Somerset House shop next to Navy Office entrance

INTRODUCTION

Somerset House was built between 1776 and 1786 on the site of the Duke of Somerset's Tudor palace, which was demolished in 1775. There is evidence that the site had been used for various churches, cloisters and chapels before the palace was constructed, and it is likely that the area was covered in primitive wood and mud block buildings from the earliest times of London's settlement. The new Somerset House was used to accommodate offices of state such as the Navy Office and the Exchequer, and later became a warren of civil servants' offices. The Strand Block was set aside for 'useful learning and polite arts', and taken over by institutions such as the Royal Academy of Arts, the Royal Society and the Society of Antiquaries. In more recent times it was best known to most Britons as the location of the General Registry of Births, Marriages and Deaths, which had displaced learned societies by 1900.

Following the exit of this registry and several other government departments from the complex in the late 1990s, Somerset House was given a major overhaul and gained a new lease of life as a combination of art galleries, exhibitions and public leisure areas.

You can enter through one of two entrances. The Great Arch on Victoria Embankment gives access to the Embankment Galleries and Terrace Rooms; the Strand Block entrance leads to the Courtauld Institute of Art's collection. Only the Courtauld Gallery has a permanent collection, though some of its famous works are occasionally lent out to other institutions. The Embankment Galleries, which replaced the Gilbert Collection when it moved to the Victoria & Albert Museum in 2009, and the Terrace Rooms house temporary exhibitions, usually with a themes like fashion, photography and modern media.

Other areas accessible from the riverside are Seamen's Hall, where you will find general information booth for the whole complex and a range of guidebooks, and the King's Barge House. In this underground space you can see a gilded 18th-century barge, which used to enter here from the Thames before the Embankment was built, as well as a host of interesting displays concerning the history of the building as a royal palace; unfortunately, it is only accessible when there is an exhibition on in the Embankment Galleries. At the heart of the complex is a granite-paved courtyard, occupied by fountains and cafe tables in summer and an ice rink in winter. The 55 water jets that play in the courtyard were the first major public fountains to be commissioned in London since those made for Trafalgar Square in 1845. This space is also used for occasional concerts and functions as an open-air cinema—check the website for details. Other popular activities include free guided tours and workshops for children and families.

WHAT TO SEE

COURTAULD GALLERY

The Courtauld Gallery contains six private collections, featuring Old Masters, Impressionist and post-Impressionist paintings, sculpture and applied arts, and was started in 1931 by textile magnate Samuel Courtauld (1876–1947). The first floor's grand rooms house European art from the early Italian Renaissance to 18th-century British portraiture and include a room full of sumptuous paintings by Rubens, including a portrait of his family. Farther up the spiral staircase, a suite of softly top-lit rooms contains a stunning array of Impressionist and post-Impressionist paintings, including eight Cézanne canvases and several by Van Gogh and Gauguin. Other rooms display British 20th-century pictures.

Adam and Eve (1526)
Lucas Cranach (1472–1553) created strikingly original religious works, portraying the subjects with detailed intensity and working the background into the whole, instead of using it as a scenic backdrop. Here he depicts a very real and human couple struggling with uncertainty and temptation.

Self-Portrait with Bandaged Ear (1889)
Vincent Van Gogh (1853–90) painted this portrait of himself after cutting off a piece of his right ear following a quarrel with fellow artist Paul Gauguin when both were living in Arles. Later in the same year he was admitted to an asylum in St. Rémy.

A Bar at the Folies-Bèrgere (1882)
Édouard Manet (1832–83) captured the mood of Paris in the late 18th century perfectly in one of his last works, depicting a barmaid standing in front of the long mirror behind the bar, with herself and the crowd of revellers reflected in it.

EMBANKMENT GALLERIES

This huge space in the riverside block has been completely revamped to house temporary exhibitions, usually of three months' duration. The general remit is to showcase cutting-edge developments in areas such as fashion, design and architecture. Nick Knight's late 2009 SHOWstudio, which explored the influence of hi-tech and multimedia on the fashion world, is a good example of the type of show you will find here.

TERRACE ROOMS

The compact Terrace Rooms, which lead off from the main lobby of Seaman's Hall, also house temporary exhibitions of contemporary work, often displays of photography on a topical theme.

TIPS

» The riverfront terrace is a great place to bring your own picnic and enjoy it in peaceful surroundings.

» Check the schedule of events, which includes guided tours, events and lectures for each collection and workshops for all ages. These are very popular and tend to fill up so book as early as possible.

GALLERY GUIDE
COURTAULD GALLERY

Ground Floor
Gallery 1: Early medieval art and objects

First Floor
Galleries 2–4: Early Impressionists, Impressionists and post-Impressionists
Gallery 5: Italian Renaissance; 18th-century British art
Galleries 6–7: Major European schools: Rubens, Brueghel the Elder, Tiepolo, Kokoschka

Second Floor
Galleries 8–14: 20th-century collections
Gallery 11: Roger Fry and the Bloomsbury Group

Opposite *Jets of water spout from the courtyard in summer*
Below *The Courtauld Gallery's elegant Nelson Staircase*

THROUGH MAYFAIR

Laid out in the early 18th century by courtiers and aristocrats, Mayfair was named after a fair held here annually in May. It is one of the city's most expensive and exclusive areas, with many commemorative Blue Plaques and shops bearing the royal warrant (▷ 19).

THE WALK
Distance: 5km (3 miles)
Allow: 2 hours
Start at: Piccadilly Circus Underground station
End at: Oxford Circus Underground station

HOW TO GET THERE
Bakerloo or Piccadilly line to Piccadilly Circus 10, 14, 15, 453

★ This walk through the smartest part of London takes you back to a more gracious era.

Leave Piccadilly Circus Underground station by Subway 3, the Piccadilly (south side) exit, and walk left along Piccadilly to St. James's Church on the left.

❶ St. James's was designed by Sir Christopher Wren and consecrated in 1684. Inside, the ceiling is decorated with ornate gold leaf. English poet and painter William Blake (1757–1827), best known for his *Songs of Innocence and Experience*, was baptized here.

Continue past Princes Arcade, Hatchards bookshop (▷ 198) and Fortnum and Mason (▷ 198). Cross Piccadilly to the Royal Academy of Arts (▷ 146). Burlington Arcade (▷ 133) is ahead; go through the arcade and turn right into Burlington Gardens, then left onto Savile Row.

❷ Savile Row has become a byword for gentlemen's tailoring; Gieves and Hawkes (No. 1), the oldest outfitters, was founded in 1785.

The Beatles made their last public performance at No. 3, on the roof of the Apple building, in 1969.

Continue along Savile Row and take the next turning left. Follow Clifford Street to New Bond Street at the far end. Turn left into a pedestrianized zone.

❸ In 1995, to mark the 50th anniversary of the end of World War II, *Allies*, a bronze sculpture of British Prime Minister Winston Churchill and US President Franklin D. Roosevelt was unveiled here.

Walk down New Bond Street onto Old Bond Street. At No. 28 turn right into the Royal Arcade and pass through to Albemarle Street. Turn right. Across the street is Brown's Hotel (▷ 166), where Eleanor and Franklin Roosevelt honeymooned.

At the end of the street turn left and follow Grafton Street onto Dover Street. Turn right down Hay Hill and cross at the bottom onto Lansdowne Row. Continue to Curzon Street, passing the Geo F. Trumper barber shop on the right. Cross the road and go through the covered entrance onto Shepherd Market.

❹ The market was built in 1735 by architect Edward Shepherd.

Left *Gentlemen's outfitters line Savile Row*
Right *A Blue Plaque marks Handel's house*

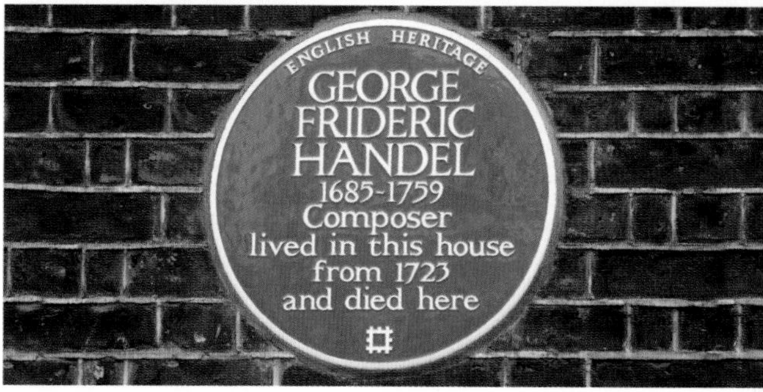

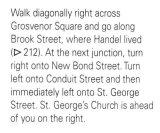

It earned notoriety as a red-light district, but now its lanes are lined with cafes, unusual shops and eateries.

At Ye Grapes pub turn right through a pedestrianized zone. Cross cobbled Trebeck Street and continue along Shepherd Market Road. Turn right up Hertford Street to Curzon Street, turn left then right onto Chesterfield Street. Turn left onto Charles Street at the top. Go right at the Red Lion onto Waverton Street and right again onto Hay's Mews. Take the next right onto Chesterfield Hill and at the end turn left, back onto Charles Street. Follow this to Berkeley Square.

❺ Berkeley Square was laid out in the mid-18th century with long lines of houses on the east and west sides, but today only those on the west survive. In the central gardens are 30 huge plane trees (▷ 24), planted in 1789.

At the northwest corner of the square, turn left onto Mount Street, then left again onto Mount Street Gardens, where there is an entrance to the Church of the Immaculate Conception.

❻ The church was founded by Jesuit exiles from Liège, Belgium. The altar is by Augustus Pugin.

Go to the end of the gardens, then turn right up South Audley Street to Grosvenor Square. On the left is the US Embassy.

❼ The embassy is a modern block among the square's period buildings. Statues commemorate presidents Roosevelt and Eisenhower.

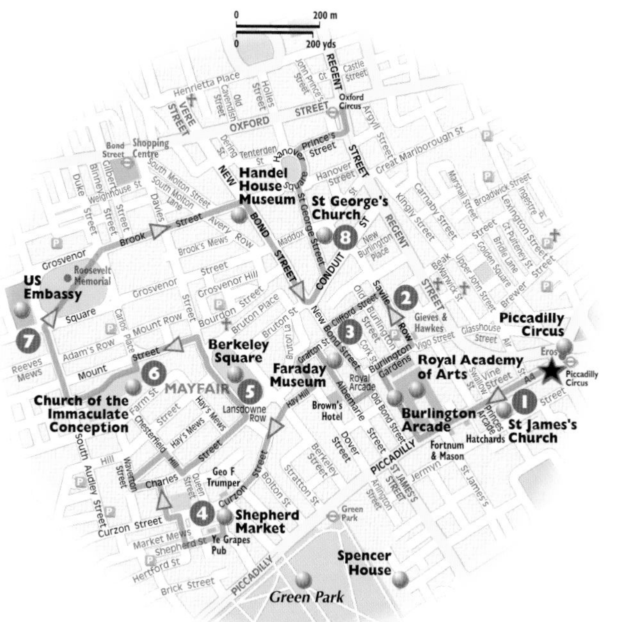

Walk diagonally right across Grosvenor Square and go along Brook Street, where Handel lived (▷ 212). At the next junction, turn right onto New Bond Street. Turn left onto Conduit Street and then immediately left onto St. George Street. St. George's Church is ahead of you on the right.

❽ St. George's Church was, and is, a fashionable wedding venue. British Prime Minister Benjamin Disraeli, US President Theodore Roosevelt and English poet Percy Bysshe Shelley were all married in this church.

Continue to the end of St. George Street to reach Hanover Square. Take Princes Street from the northeast corner onto Regent Street. Turn left to reach Oxford Circus station.

TIP

» Take this stroll in the week, as some shops close on Sundays and churches may be booked for weddings on Saturdays.

WHERE TO EAT

Lansdowne Row has several cafes and snack bars, and there are plenty of places to eat and pleasant pubs in Shepherd Market.

PLACES TO VISIT

ST. JAMES'S PICCADILLY

☎ 020 7381 0441

Lunchtime concerts (1.10pm, £3 donations suggested) Mon, Wed, Fri, and evenings Thu, Fri, Sat, often with star artists from around the world (prices vary; telephone for details).

SHOPPING

ALGERIAN COFFEE STORES

www.algcoffee.co.uk

This splendid Soho shop has been around since 1887 and is one of the oldest in the country. It offers around 140 blends of coffee and 200 types of tea. The shop retains its original wooden floorboards, fixtures and fittings and the wonderfully old-fashioned window display looks as if it has changed little in decades.

168 H4 52 Old Compton Street W1D 4PB 020 7437 2480 Mon–Wed 9–7, Thu–Fri 9–9, Sat 9–8 Leicester Square, Piccadilly Circus 10, 14, 19, 25, 38

ANDERSON & SHEPPARD

Established in 1906, Anderson's is a very traditional establishment, with wooden counters and tape measures. Superlative classic English gentlemen's suits are hand-crafted here by expert tailors at a cost of nearly £2,000 per suit. They also sell blazers and overcoats to complete the outfit.

168 G4 30 Savile Row W1S 3PT 020 7734 1420 Mon–Fri 8.30–5.30 Piccadilly Circus, Oxford Circus 12, 13, 15, 23, 139

THE ASTROLOGY SHOP

www.londonastrology.com

Those curious about the cosmic forces will find this shop rather fascinating. Books, games, maps and other astrology-related products are available, and you can have your star chart prepared while you wait.

169 J4 78 Neal Street WC2H 9PA 020 7813 3051 Mon–Sat 11–8, Sun 12–6 Covent Garden 1, 9, 11, 13,15

BENJAMIN POLLOCK'S TOY SHOP

www.pollocks-coventgarden.co.uk

Benjamin Pollock started selling theatrical sheets—a penny plain, twopence coloured—to children in the 19th century, and this extraordinary shop carries on the tradition of selling beautifully made toy theatres, as well as old-fashioned, hand-crafted items such as Punch and Judy puppets, dolls, paper gifts and unusual toys.

169 J4 44 The Market, Covent Garden WC2E 8RF 020 7379 7866 Mon–Sat 10.30–6, Sun 11–4 Covent Garden 6, 9, 13, 23, RV1

BERWICK STREET

This fruit and vegetable market tucked away in Soho also sells cheese, bread, herbs and spices. Loud stallholders, media and fashion folk plus a few shady characters set a lively scene. Best at lunchtime.

168 H4 Berwick Street W1 Mon–Sat 9–6 Piccadilly Circus 10, 14, 19, 25, 38

BLACKWELL'S

www.blackwell.co.uk

Set on a corner of the book-lover's paradise, Charing Cross Road, Blackwell's is part of an Oxford-based chain that stocks academic titles as well as fiction and general interest. This outlet is particularly strong in history, philosophy, fiction, medical and computing titles.

169 J4 100 Charing Cross Road WC2H 0JG 020 7292 5100 Mon–Sat 9.30–8, Sun 12–6 Leicester Square 14, 19 24, 29, 176

CHAPPELL OF BOND STREET

www.chappellofbondstreet.co.uk

Established in 1811 and once frequented by Beethoven, Richard Strauss and Charles Dickens, this store has the largest selection of classical and popular printed music in the UK. Also keyboards and brass/woodwind instruments.

Left *Hamleys toyshop celebrated its 250th birthday in 2010*

168 H4 152–160 Wardour Srreet W1F 8YA 020 7432 4400 Mon–Fri 9.30–6, Sat 9.30–5.30 Oxford Circus 8, 10, 25, 55, 73

COVENT GARDEN
www.coventgardenlondonuk.com
Well worth a visit just to see the street performers and soak up the lively atmosphere. The central area, the Piazza, hosts an antiques and collectables market on Mondays and an arts and crafts market selling jewellery, clothing, silverware and pottery the rest of the week (▷ 142–143).
169 J4 Office: 41 The Market WC2E 8RF 020 7836 9136 Daily 10–6 Covent Garden 9, 11, 13, 15, RV1

CULPEPER THE HERBALIST
www.culpeper.co.uk
A reliable brand for herbs, oils, gifts and food. You can make your own cosmetics by adding essential oils to the store's face, hand, body and bath products.
169 J4 8 The Market, Covent Garden WC2 8RB 020 7379 6698 Mon–Fri 10–7, Sat 10–8, Sun 10–6 Covent Garden 6, 9, 13, 23, RV1

FENWICK
www.fenwick.co.uk
Unintimidating department store with five floors of fashions and accessories, lingerie and housewares, and a dedicated personal shopping suite.
168 G4 63 New Bond Street W1A 3BS 020 7629 9161 Mon–Wed, Fri–Sat 10–6.30, Thu 10–8 Bond Street 8, 10, 14, 19

FOOTE'S
www.footesmusic.com
Huge selection of drums, percussion, woodwind, brass and string instruments to buy new or second-hand, or just to rent, and at reasonable prices.
168 H4 10 Golden Square W1F 9JA 020 7437 1811 Mon–Fri 9–6, Sat 10–6 Piccadilly Circus 14, 19, 38

FOYLES
www.foyles.co.uk
This enormous bookshop stocks a massive 1.4 million titles—and a promise that you're more likely to find that elusive title here than in any other bookshop. It has an active schedule of literary luncheons, a big music section, a snazzy jazz cafe and a section of books for, by and about women.
168 H4 113–119 Charing Cross Road WC2H 0EB 020 7437 5660 Mon–Sat 9.30–9, Sun 11.30–6 Tottenham Court Road 14, 19, 24, 29, 176

GERRY'S
www.gerrys.uk.com
Whatever your tipple, Gerry's probably stocks it, and if it doesn't you'll find more than enough to catch your eye in the extraordinary collection of wines and spirits. This classic store encapsulates the spirit of Soho (pardon the pun). Friendly expert service.
168 H4 74 Old Compton Street W1D 4UW 020 7734 4215 Mon–Thu 9–6.30, Fri 9–8, Sat 9–10 Leicester Square, Piccadilly Circus 10, 14, 19, 25, 38

HAMLEYS
www.hamleys.com
The 'World's Finest Toyshop' and great fun for all ages. Five large floors full of the latest playthings—soft toys, dolls, dressing up, computer games, train sets, kites, LEGO and much more. The switched-on staff demonstrate the latest gadgets.
168 H4 188–196 Regent Street W1B 5BT 0870 333 2450 Mon–Fri 10–8, Sat 9–8, Sun 12–6 Oxford Circus 8, 10, 12, 13

HAROLD MOORES RECORDS
This shop may have England's largest and most comprehensive selection of classical music LPs and CDs, both new and second-hand. Perfect for browsing.
168 H4 2 Great Marlborough Street W1F 7HQ 020 7437 1576 Mon–Sat 10–6.30, Sun 12–6 Oxford Circus 8, 10, 12, 13, 23

HEAL'S
www.heals.co.uk
A top destination for contemporary interior design and furnishings for the past two centuries, with striking, high-quality furniture, rugs, beds, furnishing fabrics, bed linen and home accessories. The main store, on Tottenham Court Road, is immense.
168 H3 The Heal's Building, 196 Tottenham Court Road W1T 7LQ 020 7636 1666 Mon–Wed 10–6, Thu 10–8, Fri 10–6.30, Sat 9.30–6.30, Sun 12–6 Goodge Street 11, 19, 22, 211, C1

JAMES SMITH & SONS
www.james-smith.co.uk
This very traditional old London shop, established in 1830, manufactures umbrellas by hand—a real craft. You'll also find shooting sticks, parasols and walking sticks in which you can keep dice—or a dram of whisky.
169 J4 53 New Oxford Street WC1A 1BL 020 7836 4731 Mon–Fri 9.30–5.15, Sat 10–5.15 Tottenham Court Road 8, 14, 98

JOHN LEWIS
www.johnlewis.co.uk
Largest by far of this popular and respected chain of department stores, this is the place to shop for household goods, from batteries and towels to furniture and entire kitchens. Very good quality, clearly and logically set out and 'never knowingly undersold'. Also sells beauty products and conservatively priced clothing.
168 G4 Oxford Street W1A 1EX 020 7629 7711 Mon–Wed, Fri 9.30–8, Thu 9.30–9, Sat 9.30–7, Sun 12–6 Oxford Circus, Bond Street 8, 10, 12, 23, 73

LIBERTY
www.liberty.co.uk
Mock-Tudor building, complete with creaky timber staircase and sloping ceilings, actually built in the 1920s. The interior contains an eclectic stock ranging from ornaments and rugs that seem to have been gathered on some explorer's travels

to designer apparel. Menswear boutique with shirts and ties of every colour imaginable.
168 G4 210–220 Regent Street W1B 5AH 020 7734 1234 Mon–Sat 10–9 Oxford Circus, Piccadilly Circus 8, 10, 12, 13, 23

LILLYWHITE'S

www.sportsdirect.com
A department store dedicated entirely to sports, Lillywhite's can outfit you for virtually any pastime, from golf to skiing. Particularly strong on footwear.
168 H5 24–36 Lower Regent Street SW1Y 4QF 0870 333 9600 Mon 10–9, Tue–Sat 10–9.30, Sun 12–6 Piccadilly Circus 9, 14, 19, 22

MRS KIBBLE'S OLDE SWEET SHOPPE

Step back in time for a taste of nostalgia at this adorable little time warp in the middle of Soho. Wall-to-wall jars are filled with sweets from the past that will bring back childhood memories: sugar mice, bon-bons, flying saucers, toffee apples, and lots more. Mrs. Kibble Jnr. runs the shop and extends an old-fashioned welcome, as well.
168 H4 57a Brewer Street W1F 9UL 020 7734 6633 Mon–Thu 11–6, Fri–Sat 11–7, Sun 11–4 Piccadilly Circus 9, 14, 19, 22, 38

MULBERRY COMPANY

www.mulberry.com
Ready-to-wear fashions for men and women, plus accessories, bags, luggage and items such as camera cases, all in top-quality leather. Founder Roger Saul originally started out as a belt designer. This flagship store has three floors and is fitted out in oak, amber glass, bronze and, of course, leather.
168 G4 41–42 New Bond Street W1S 2RY 020 7491 3900 Mon–Sat 10–6, Thu 10–7 Bond Street 8, 10, 14, 19

NEAL'S YARD DAIRY

www.nealsyarddairy.co.uk
The queen of cheese shops in Covent Garden concentrates on cheese made by small-scale makers in the British Isles. Owners Randolph Hodgson and Jane Scotter buy direct from farms and sell around 60 to 70 varieties in the dairy, a wonderful place displaying vast round cheeses, where you can sample the wares.
169 J4 17 Shorts Gardens WC2H 9AT 020 7240 5700 Mon–Sat 10–7 Covent Garden 6, 9, 13, 23, 87

PAPERCHASE

www.paperchase.co.uk
The most design-led stationer in the UK carries a huge range of art papers and materials, including handmade Japanese papers. This is the vast flagship store.
168 H3 213–215 Tottenham Court Road W1T 7PS 020 7467 6200 Mon–Sat 9.30–7, Thu 9.30–8, Sun 12–6 Goodge Street 10, 24, 29, 73, 134

PLAYIN' GAMES

Central London's only indoor games specialist. Set a stone's throw from the British Museum and among a number of fine bookshops and print galleries. The store offers board games, and classic, family and role-playing games.
169 J3 33 Museum Street WC1A 1LH 020 7323 3080 Sun–Fri 10–6.30, Sat 10–7 Tottenham Court Road 7, 188

SOTHEBY'S

www.sothebys.com
Since its beginnings in 1744, when Samuel Baker sold several hundred rare books, Sotheby's has branched out to every aspect of fine and decorative art, dealing in everything from Old Masters and Impressionists to contemporary art.
168 G4 34–35 New Bond Street W1A 2AA 020 7293 5000 Mon–Fri 9–6 Bond Street 8, 10, 14, 19

ENTERTAINMENT AND NIGHTLIFE

100 CLUB

www.the100club.co.uk
Billed as Europe's most famous live music venue. Opened in 1942, the 100 Club originally focused exclusively on jazz until the 1960s, when the Rolling Stones and The Kinks played here. Music from soul, funk and jazz to R&B, swing and Latin.
168 H4 100 Oxford Street W1D 1LL 020 7636 0933 £6–£20 Tottenham Court Road 7, 8, 10, 25, 55, 73

ADELPHI THEATRE

www.adelphitheatre.co.uk
The Adelphi was built in 1806, but its cool black livery dates back to 1930. It stages popular shows and long-running musicals.
169 J5 Strand WC2E 7NA 0870 403 0303 £16–£49.50 Charing Cross 9, 11, 13, 15, 23

ALDWYCH THEATRE

www.aldwych-theatre.co.uk
For 22 years the London home of the Royal Shakespeare Company (1960–82), the Aldwych now stages plays and musicals under Michael Codron's watchful eye.
169 K4 49 Aldwych WC2B 4DF 020 7379 3367 £25–£59.50 Covent Garden, Charing Cross 6, 9, 13, 23, RV1

AMBASSADORS THEATRE

www.theambassadorstheatre.co.uk
The West End's smallest theatre mounts an interesting programme of drama by contemporary artists. Seats 400.
169 J4 West Street WC2H 9ND 0870 060 6627 £25–£45 Leicester Square 14, 19, 38

BAR CODE

A cruisey, gay men's bar with a lively, sweaty basement dance floor, plus fruit machines and a pool table. The crowd is flirtatious and easy-going. Comedy camp on Tuesdays.
168 H4 3–4 Archer Street W1D 7AP 020 7734 3342 Mon–Sat 4pm–1am, Sun 4pm–10.30pm Free Piccadilly Circus 14, 19, 38

BORDERLINE

www.meanfiddler.com
Famous venue (capacity 275) that has seen many big names in its

time. Music is from country to heavy metal and beyond.
168 H4 Orange Yard, Manette Street W1D 4JB 020 7734 5547, box office 0870 060 3777 £6–£16 Tottenham Court Road 8, 10, 14, 24

CAFÉ DE PARIS
www.cafedeparis.com
Elegant and original nightspot established in 1924, with velvet sash curtains and a long sweeping staircase to the dance floor and bar. Live jazz and cabaret nightly. Drinks are expensive and there is a strict door policy; no sportswear. There's also a restaurant if you want to eat first.
168 H5 3–4 Coventry Street W1D 6BW 020 7734 7700 Club nights Fri, Sat 10pm–3am (restaurant 6–9pm) £20 Leicester Square, Piccadilly Circus 9, 12, 13, 15, 23

CAMBRIDGE THEATRE
www.cambridgetheatre.co.uk
Tucked away on Seven Dials and normally home to short-lived musicals, the Cambridge Theatre was restored in 1987 to its 1930s gold and silver art deco splendour.
169 J4 Earlham Street WC2 9HU 0844 412 4652 £20–£50 Tottenham Court Road, Covent Garden 14, 19, 38

CANDY BAR
www.candybarsoho.com
This leading lesbian and bisexual bar in central London attracts a large crowd and has DJs every night. Gay male guests are also welcome. Decidedly relaxed atmosphere, and there is no dress code.
168 H4 4 Carlisle Street, off Dean Street W1D 3BJ 020 7494 4041 Mon–Thu 5pm–11.30pm, Fri–Sat 5pm–2am, Sun 5pm–11pm Free Sun–Thu, £5 Fri–Sat after 9pm Tottenham Court Road 14, 19, 24, 29, 176

CHUCKLE CLUB
www.chuckleclub.com
Student bar with cheap drinks and an established comedy club that pulls in some of the best in the business.
169 K4 Three Tuns Bar, London School of Economics, Houghton Street WC2A 2AE 020 7476 1672 Sat 7.45pm–3am £8–£10 Holborn 8, 59, 168, 188

CINEWORLD SHAFTESBURY AVENUE AT THE TROCADERO
www.cineworld.co.uk
Seven-screen multiplex from this major cinema chain.
168 H5 13 Coventry Street W1V 7FE 0871 200 2000 Leicester Square, Piccadilly Circus 14, 19, 22, 38

COMEDY STORE
www.thecomedystore.co.uk
The best in stand-up comedy features improvised sketches from the Comedy Store Players. Big British TV and radio names who cut their teeth here include Rik Mayall, Ade Edmonson, Ben Elton, Julian Clary, Josie Lawrence, Paul Merton and Steve Coogan. Over-18s only.
168 H5 1a Oxendon Street SW1Y 4EE 0870 060 2340 Tue–Thu, Sun 8pm–10.15pm, Fri–Sat 8pm–10.15pm, 12am–2.15am £12–£15 Piccadilly Circus, Leicester Square 14, 19, 38

COMPTON'S OF SOHO
www.comptons-of-soho.co.uk
This is a gay London institution, legendary for being cruisey. The club sprawls over two floors and gets very crowded.
168 H4 53 Old Compton Street W1D 6HJ 020 7479 7961 Mon–Fri 12–11pm, Sat 11–11, Sun 12–10pm Free Leicester Square, Tottenham Court Road 14, 19, 24, 29, 176

COWARD THEATRE
www.noel-coward-theatre.co.uk
Dating from 1903 and formerly called the Albery, the Coward Theatre has an impressive roll-call of stars from Olivier to Izzard.
169 J4 85–87 St. Martin's Lane WC2N 5AU 0870 950 0920 £10–£50 Leicester Square 24, 29, 176

DONMAR WAREHOUSE THEATRE
www.donmarwarehouse.com
Housed in a refurbished 19th-century warehouse in trendy Covent Garden, the Donmar Warehouse was led for a decade by Sam Mendes, attracting the starriest of casts. Since 2002 Michael Grandage has continued its eclectic programming, including classic drama and new plays.
169 J4 Earlham Street WC2H 9LX 0870 060 6624 £15–£50.50 Covent Garden 14, 19, 38

EGG
www.egglondon.net
One of London's newest nightspots attracting an up-for-it, up-to-the-minute crowd who come for the live bands as well as DJs playing house, techno and electro. Intimate Mediterranean atmosphere.
169 J1 200 York Way, King's Cross N7 9AX 020 7609 8364 Fri–Sat 10pm–late, Sunday Breakfast 4am–12pm £15 King's Cross

EMPIRE
www.empirecinemas.co.uk
Large central cinema showing new releases.
168 H4 190 J4 5–6 Leicester Square WC2H 7NA 0871 471 4714 Leicester Square, Piccadilly Circus 14, 24, 29

GARRICK THEATRE
www.garrick-theatre.co.uk
Small theatre named after the 18th-century actor and entrepreneur David Garrick (1717–79).
169 J5 Charing Cross Road WC2H 0HH 0870 890 1104 £20–£45 Leicester Square, Charing Cross 24, 29, 176

GIELGUD THEATRE
www.delfontmackintosh.co.uk
Opened in 1906, the Gielgud was known as the Globe until the mid-1990s, when, with Shakespeare's Globe about to open on the South Bank, it changed its name to honour Sir John Gielgud (1904–2000), who frequently performed here. The theatre stages high-profile works and was refurbished in 2007.
168 H4 33 Shaftesbury Avenue W1V 8AR 0870 890 1105 £20–£49.50 Piccadilly Circus 14, 19, 38

GUANABARA

www.guanabara.co.uk

Decadent Latino cocktails and exotic Brazilian dance music—you could well be in Rio. Restaurant.

169 J4 New London Theatre, Parker Street WC2B 5PW 020 7242 8600 Mon–Sat 5pm–2.30am, Sun 5pm–midnight £5–£10; free before 9pm Covent Garden 6, 9, 13, 23, 87

LONDON COLISEUM

www.eno.org

Home to the English National Opera (who always sing in English) with regular visits from Welsh National Opera, Opera North and the Royal Festival Ballet. ENO aims to offer opera to the widest possible audience and is known for some innovative productions.

169 J5 St. Martin's Lane WC2N 4ES 020 7632 8300 £5–£70 Charing Cross, Leicester Square 24, 29, 176

LONDON PALLADIUM

www.londonpalladium.co.uk

A colossal theatre built in 1910, the Palladium has been home to the biggest musicals (including a flying car in *Chitty Chitty Bang Bang*) and a series of television specials.

168 H4 Argyll Street W1F 7TF 020 7494 5020 £25–£55 Oxford Circus 8, 10, 73, 453

LYCEUM THEATRE

www.lyceum-theatre.co.uk

Once a concert hall, and then a waxworks, the Lyceum's famous colonnaded entrance opened in 1996, and now is home to Disney's *The Lion King*.

169 J4 21 Wellington Street WC2 E7DA 0870 243 9000 £15–£55 Charing Cross 9, 13, 23

LYRIC THEATRE

www.the-lyric-theatre.co.uk

The oldest of the four fine, if faded, Victorian theatres on Shaftesbury Avenue, the Lyric opened in 1888 and now stages entertaining dramas and musicals.

168 H4 29 Shaftesbury Avenue W1V 7HA 0870 890 1107 £20–£50 Piccadilly Circus 14, 19, 38

MARKET PLACE

www.marketplace-london.com

Market Place, set on two floors, is a classic London DJ bar, popular with Londoners after work, with panelled walls and very good food. Downstairs is larger, with room to dance and alcove tables.

168 H4 11 Market Place W1W 8AH 020 7079 2020 Mon–Wed 11am–12am, Thu–Fri 11am–1am, Sat 12pm–1am, Sun 1pm–1am Free–£7 Oxford Circus 7, 8, 10, 73, 176

NOVELLO THEATRE

www.novellotheatre.com

The Novello was built as a pair with the Aldwych Theatre in 1905. Seats 1,067.

169 K4 Aldwych WC2B 4LD 0870 060 2335 £15–£45 Covent Garden, Temple 9, 11, 13, 23

ODEON LEICESTER SQUARE

www.odeon.co.uk

Famous central mega-cinema and West End showpiece used for many film premieres. Six screens show new-release blockbusters in luxurious comfort.

169 J5 22–24 Leicester Square WC2H 7JY 0871 224 4007 Leicester Square, Piccadilly Circus 24, 29, 176

PICCADILLY THEATRE

www.piccadillytheatre.co.uk

Tucked behind Piccadilly Circus, and principally the home of comedies and musicals, the likes of Al Jolson, Evelyn Laye and Henry Fonda have trod the boards at the Piccadilly Theatre.

168 H4 16 Denman Street W1D 7DY 0870 060 6630 £20–£55 Piccadilly Circus 14, 19, 38

PIZZA EXPRESS JAZZ CLUB

www.pizzaexpress.co.uk

All kinds of modern and contemporary jazz in a basement under the main branch of Pizza Express in Soho. A popular combination, so book ahead.

168 H4 10 Dean Street W1D 3RW Jazz club 020 7439 8722; restaurant 020 7437 9595 £15–£20 Tottenham Court Road 8, 10, 14, 24, 73

Right *Bronze ballerina outside the Royal Opera House*

PRINCE CHARLES

www.princecharlescinema.com

Central independent cinema offering seats at lower than usual West End prices. Foreign-language films shown with English subtitles.

168 H4 7 Leicester Place WC2H 7BP Box office 0870 811 2559 Leicester Square, Piccadilly Circus 24, 29, 176

RENOIR

Independent two-screen cinema showing art-house and foreign-language films (English subtitles) and classics from the repertory.

169 J2 Brunswick Centre, Brunswick Square WC1 1AU 020 7837 8402 Russell Square 7, 17, 45, 46, 188

RONNIE SCOTT'S

www.ronniescotts.co.uk

Britain's top jazz venue and one of the most famous jazz clubs in the world. The best players line up to perform here.

168 H4 47 Frith Street W1D 4HT 020 7439 0747 £26–£36; more for special gigs Tottenham Court Road 8, 10, 14, 24, 73

ROYAL OPERA HOUSE

www.roh.org.uk

The principal venue for world-class opera and ballet was reopened in 1999 after extensive redevelopment. The building, in Covent Garden, hosts major operatic productions and is home to the Royal Ballet. The Opera House also stages regular exhibitions of costumes and memorabilia of former stars.

169 J4 Bow Street WC2E 9DD 020 7304 4000 £3–£180 Covent Garden 4, 9, 13, 15, 176, RV1

SAVOY THEATRE

www.thesavoytheatre.co.uk

Built in 1881 by Richard D'Oyly Carte to stage operettas by Gilbert and Sullivan. Redesigned in the 1920s. Seats 1,100.

169 J5 Strand WC2R 0ET 0870 164 8787 £40–£55 Charing Cross 9, 11, 13, 15, 23, 176

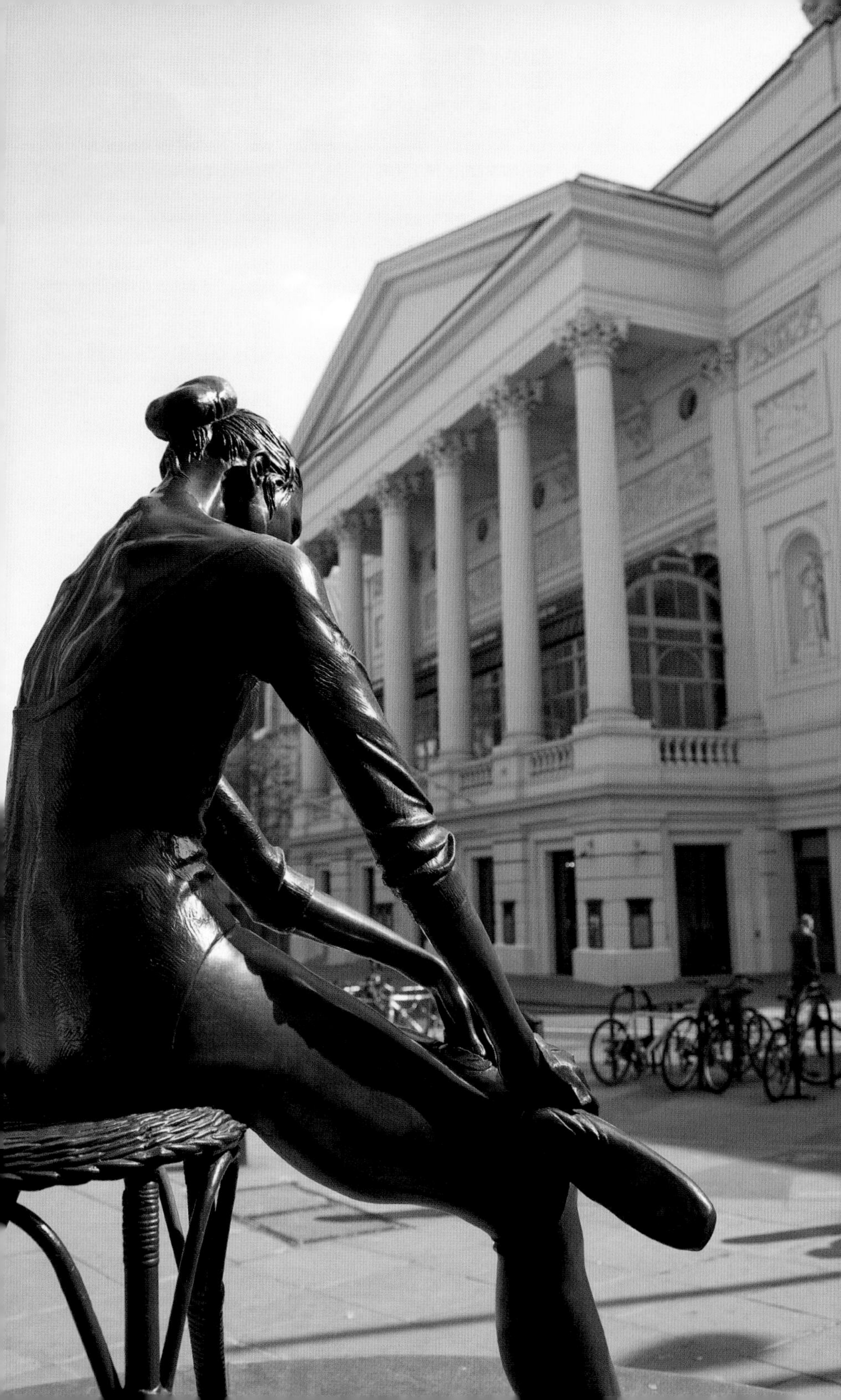

THE SCALA
www.scala-london.co.uk
This former cinema turned clubbing venue with three floors and several bars hosts hip-hop and breakbeat nights. Friday is Popstarz, a gay indie night attracting many straights. Phone or check website for live music nights in week.
169 J1 275 Pentonville Road N1 9NL 020 7833 2022 Mon–Thu 7pm–11pm, Fri–Sat 10pm–6am £8–£15 King's Cross 30, 73, 214

SHADOW LOUNGE
www.theshadowlounge.co.uk
This pretentious gay club in the heart of Soho, more like an overcrowded bar, is one of the few gay venues with a straight bar-style dress code—that is, smart and fashionable. Over-21s only.
168 H4 5 Brewer Street W1F 0RF 020 7287 7988 Mon–Sat 9pm–3am £3–£10 Leicester Square 12, 13, 15, 23, 139

SHAFTESBURY THEATRE
www.shaftesbury-theatre.co.uk
Independent theatre built in 1902 on the corner of Shaftesbury Avenue, staging mainly musicals and comedies. Seats 1,000.
169 J4 210 Shaftesbury Avenue WC2H 8DP 0870 906 3798 £22–£62 Covent Garden 14, 19, 38

SHAW THEATRE
www.theshawtheatre.com
Named after Irish playwright George Bernard Shaw, once a local councillor here. Now refurbished and associated with the next-door hotel, the Shaw Park Plaza. Stages family shows and international dance productions.
169 J2 100–110 Euston Road NW1 2AJ 020 7388 2555; box office 0871 594 3123 £8–£35 King's Cross, Euston 10, 30, 73, 168

SMOLLENSKY'S ON THE STRAND
www.smollenskys.co.uk
Central bar-cum-restaurant with live music every night, including jazz, modern, Latin, soul and salsa. Great atmosphere and lots of variety.
169 J4 105 The Strand WC2R 0AB 020 7497 2101 £7–£10; jazz menu £17–£21 Charing Cross 9, 11, 13, 15, 23

STRAWBERRY MOONS
www.strawberrymoonsbar.co.uk
Just off Regent Street, at the top of a charming cobbled square, Strawberry Moons is a great place to party. The decor is very pink and cocktails are the focus, while dancing to resident DJ's cheesey music goes on late into the night.
168 H5 15 Heddon Street W1B 4BF 020 7437 7300 Mon–Wed 5pm–late, Thu–Sat 5pm–3am Free most nights Piccadilly Circus, Oxford Circus 12, 13, 15, 23

THEATRE ROYAL DRURY LANE
www.rutheatres.com
The present theatre, built in 1812, is the fourth on this site and stages mostly musicals. And there are ghosts—the Man in Grey walks around the Upper Circle during successful productions. Seats 2,205.
169 J4 Catherine Street WC2B 5JF 0870 890 1109 £15–£60 Covent Garden 6, 9, 13, 23, RV1

VAUDEVILLE THEATRE
This small venue, which opened in 1870, was the third theatre to occupy this site. It stages musicals and comedy. Seats 714.
169 J5 404 Strand WC2B 4LD 0870 890 0511 £17–£39–50 Charing Cross 9, 11, 13, 23, 176

VILLAGE SOHO
www.village-soho.co.uk
A young, relaxed crowd enjoys this stylish, late, gay cafe-bar, which fills two floors in an L-shaped building. The dance bar downstairs plays funky house and chart music.
168 H4 81 Wardour Street, Soho W1D 6QD 020 7539 4089 Mon–Sat 4pm–1am, Sun 4pm–11.30pm Free–£2 Piccadilly Circus 12, 14, 19, 38

VUE WEST END
www.myvue.com
Nine-screen multiplex in the heart of London's 'movieland'.
168 H4 3 Cranbourn Street WC2H 7AL Bookings 0871 224 0240 Leicester Square 24, 29, 176

WALKABOUT@LIMELIGHT
www.walkabout.eu.com
One of London's more unusual clubs in a small converted chapel, where the original alcoves combine with state-of-the-art light and sound. DJs play 1960s to the present day rock, pop and commercial dance music.
169 J4 136 Shaftesbury Avenue W1D 5EZ 020 7255 8630 Mon–Fri 12pm–2am, Sat 10am–2am, Sun 12–12 £3–£8 Leicester Square 9, 12, 13, 15, 23

THE YARD BAR
www.yardbar.co.uk
This friendly gay haven in the middle of frenetic Soho is a good place for a pre-club drink. The central outdoor courtyard makes a welcome change from crammed bars and there's an upstairs loft bar. Reasonable prices, good food and friendly staff.
168 H4 57 Rupert Street W1V 7HN 020 7437 2652 Mon–Thu 1pm–11.30pm, Fri–Sat 1pm–12am Free Piccadilly Circus, Leicester Square 12, 14, 19, 38

SPORTS AND ACTIVITIES

CENTRAL YMCA
www.ymca.co.uk
The original site of the first YMCA (established 1844) houses a huge sports centre, offering almost any kind of physical activity you want—gym, pool, sports hall, playing fields, dance studio, climbing wall and more.
168 H4 112 Great Russell Street WC1B 3NQ 020 7343 1700 Mon–Fri 6.30–10, Sat 10–8, Sun 10–6.30 Day membership £15, weekly £45 (use of all facilities) Tottenham Court Road 7, 10, 24, 73

THE GYM COVENT GARDEN
www.jubileehallclubs.co.uk
Central, well-equipped gym which also offers classes. Gym and sports centre are open access. Also offers a range of beauty therapies and treatments. Book ahead.

169 J4 30 The Piazza, Covent Garden WC2 8BE 020 7836 4007 Mon–Fri 7am–10pm, Sat 9–9, Sun 10–5 £6.50–£8 Covent Garden 6, 9, 13, 23, RV1

OASIS SPORTS CENTRE

Indoor and outdoor swimming pools, sauna, gym, massage, squash, badminton, martial arts and fitness training.

169 J4 32 Endell Street WC2H 9AG 020 7831 1804 Mon–Fri 6.30am–10pm, Sat, Sun 9.30am–6pm Call for details Covent Garden 14, 19, 38, RV1

SOMERSET HOUSE

In winter, the central courtyard of this magnificent building becomes an ice rink (▷ 150–151).

HEALTH AND BEAUTY

CHARLES WORTHINGTON

www.cwlondon.com

Award-winning but never intimidating, this chic salon in a Georgian town house wants to make you feel at ease and offers a drink and snacks as you sit down. Four other London salons. Booking essential.

168 H3 7 Percy Street W1T 1DQ, 020 7631 1370 Mon–Thu 8–7.45, Fri 10.15–6.45, Sat 9.15–5.45, Sun 10–4.45 Cut and blow dry from £50 Goodge Street, Tottenham Court Road 10, 24, 29, 73, 134

THE SANCTUARY

www.thesanctuary.co.uk

This famous women-only Covent Garden spa has an atrium pool complete with swing, and a relaxation area with a koi carp pool.

169 J4 12 Floral Street WC2E 9DH 0114 243 0330 Mon–Fri 9.30–6, Sat–Sun 9.30–8. Booking essential Treatments from £40 Covent Garden 6, 9, 11, 13, 15, 24, 29, 87, 91, 176

FOR CHILDREN

CORAM'S FIELDS

Outdoor fun for young and older children. Lawns for running, games and picnics, plus a sand pit, Astro Turf football pitch, basketball court, climbing equipment. Adults without children are not allowed.

169 J2 93 Guilford Street WC1N 1DN 020 7837 6138 Mon–Fri 9–7, Sat–Sun 9–6 Free Russell Square 17, 46, 59, 91

COVENT GARDEN

Punch and Judy shows using hand-operated puppets have been staged here since the 17th century (▷ 142–143). There's also an excellent range of children's shops, such as Benjamin Pollock's Toy Shop (▷ 154).

HAMLEYS

The world's most famous toy shop (▷ 155).

TROCADERO

www.troc.co.uk, www.funland.co.uk

Seven storeys of tenpin bowling, indoor bumper cars, computer games and simulator rides.

168 H5 7–14 Coventry Street W1D 7DH 020 7292 3642 Sun–Wed 10am–midnight, Thu–Sat 10am–1am Bowling from £4 per person Piccadilly Circus 9, 14, 19, 22, 38

***Below** The Sanctuary atrium pool*

PRICES AND SYMBOLS

The prices given are for a two-course set lunch (L) and a three-course à la carte dinner (D) for one person. The wine price is for the least expensive bottle.

For a key to the symbols, ▷ 2.

ACORN HOUSE

www.acornhouserestaurant.com

Acorn House is widely regarded as the first truly eco-friendly restaurant in London, dedicated to the use of organic and recycled material, and offering local people training in hospitality. Only the best seasonal ingredients are used and Roux-trained chef Arthur Potts Dawson produces a cuisine he calls 'Modern London'. Lunchtime takeaways include hot soup and wholesome sandwiches. The dining room is stark but the food is utterly appetizing—and make sure you leave room for the scrumptious desserts.

✚ 169 K2 ✉ 69 Swinton Street WC1X 9NT ☎ 020 7812 1842 🕑 Mon–Fri 12–3, 6–10, Sat 5.30–10. Closed 23 Dec–2 Jan, public hols ✋ L from £29.50, D from £39.50, Wine from £20 🚇 King's Cross, Russell Square

THE ADMIRALTY RESTAURANT

www.theadmiraltyrestaurant.com

Set within historic Somerset House (▷ 150–151), this French brasserie-style restaurant has seen a rebirth with its previously colourful interior now a cool relaxed grey. The menu features French regional and contemporary dishes including starters such as gratin of Cornish crab with tarragon and lemon tagliatelle; main dishes featuring delights such as salmon fillet with roasted almonds; and tasty desserts, which might include passion fruit crème brûlee.

✚ 169 K4 ✉ Somerset House, The Strand WC2R 1LA ☎ 020 7845 4646 🕑 Mon–Fri 12–3.30, 5.30–9.30, Sat 12–4. Closed 24–26 Dec, public hols ✋ L from £14, D from £20, Wine from £18 🚇 Charing Cross

ALLORO

www.alloro-restaurant.co.uk

A chic traditional Italian restaurant with an adept staff. The interconnecting bar and restaurant are long and narrow with a glass front and leather banquette seating. The selection of antipasti, fresh pasta and risotti precedes desserts such as *tortino tiepido di aranca* (an orange sponge cake made with olive oil) and home-made ice cream. Main courses include fresh egg tagliatelle with fresh tomato and basil sauce—a classic.

✚ 168 G5 ✉ 19–20 Dover Street W1S 4LR ☎ 020 7495 4768 🕑 Mon–Fri 12–2.30, 7–11, Sat 7–11. Closed 25–26 Dec, 1 Jan, public hols ✋ L from £28, D from £35, Wine from £20 🚇 Green Park

ARBUTUS

www.arbutusrestaurant.co.uk

This Soho-based restaurant opened to great acclaim in 2006 and it continues to please. The brainchild of Will Smith and Anthony Demetre, both highly respected chefs, it features classic seasonal dishes with a definite modern twist. This includes smoked eel, sea bass, saddle of rabbit and the most delectable English plum sorbet you could wish to try.

✚ 168 H4 ✉ 63–64 Frith Street W1D 3JW ☎ 020 7734 4545 🕑 Mon–Sat 12–2.30, 7–10.30, Sun 12–3, 5.30–10.30 (pre-theatre 7–11). Closed 24–26 Dec, 1 Jan ✋ L from £35, D from £35, Wine from £15 🚇 Tottenham Court Road, Leicester Square

Left *The sophisticated dining space at L'Escargot*

ARCHIPELAGO

www.archipelago-restaurant.co.uk

Archipelago dares to be different. The international dishes on the menu are inspiring and adventurous, transporting diners to the four corners of the globe. It's not the best place for the timid, with exotic concoctions like spiced Australian kangaroo fillet with spinach and pak choi, peanut crusted wildebeest or African crocodile bites.

168 H3 110 Whitfield Street S1T 5ED 020 7383 3346 Mon–Fri 12–2.30, 6–10.30, Sat 6–10.30. Closed 2 weeks at Christmas, public hols L from £25, D from £35, Wine from £20 Warren Street

BENTLEY'S OYSTER BAR AND GRILL

www.bentleys.org

Bentley's has had a makeover by renowned chef Richard Corrigan, who purchased the restaurant in 2005. It still serves oysters and seafood in much the same way as it did in 1916. The fish, and the meat and game on the grill, are of the finest quality. Typical dishes include steamed Welsh lamb pudding and wild sea bass with herbs.

168 H5 11–15 Swallow Street W1B 4DG 020 7734 4756 Grill: Mon–Sat 12–3, 6–11, Sun 11.30–3.30, 6–10. Oyster and champagne bar: Mon–Sat 12–12, Sun 12–10. Closed 25–26 Dec, 1 Jan L from £25, D from £30, Wine from £19 Piccadilly Circus

CHRISTOPHER'S

www.christophersgrill.com

Christopher's is based on the grand steak and lobster restaurants of the US and is set in an elegant Victorian town house with curving staircase and high ceilings. The simpler dishes on the Modern American menu are particularly successful, with plenty of flavour in the Maryland crab cake and a really succulent Aberdeen Angus steak. Desserts include fresh fruity sorbets and classic US cheesecakes. The modern wine list includes a very good selection by the glass.

169 J4 18 Wellington Street WC2E 7DD 020 7240 4222 Mon–Fri 12–3, 5–11.30, Sat 11.30–3.30, 5–11.30, Sun 11.30–3.30, 5–10.30. Closed Easter, 25–26 Dec L from £19.50, D from £27, Wine from £18 Embankment

CIGALA

www.cigala.co.uk

Tucked away in the back streets of Holborn, this popular Spanish restaurant is regularly crowded with local customers in both the light, understated upstairs restaurant and the basement tapas bar. The open-plan kitchen keeps things slightly steamy and turns out dishes such as *venado asado*—fillet of venison wrapped in ham, potato bake and wild mushrooms. A good range of Spanish wines.

169 K3 54 Lamb's Conduit Street WC1N 3LW 020 7405 1717 Mon–Sat 12–10.45, Sun 12–9.30. Closed 25–26 Dec, 1 Jan, Easter, public hols L from £17, D from £30, Wine from £15 Holborn

L'ESCARGOT—THE GROUND FLOOR RESTAURANT

www.whitestarline.org.uk

A Soho landmark, L'Escargot has been serving classy French cuisine since 1927. This was the first restaurant to offer fresh snails in Britain and they're still a speciality. Alongside starters such as *asparagus velouté* or *pâté forestière*, you might find snail ravioli accompanied by parsley purée. Fine art decorates the walls—the collection includes original works by Joan Miró, Henri Matisse, David Hockney and Andy Warhol.

168 H4 48 Greek Street W1D 4EF 020 7437 6820 Mon–Fri 12–2.15, 6–11.30, Sat 6–11.30. Closed 25–26 Dec, 1 Jan L from £20, D from £30, Wine from £20 Tottenham Court Road, Leicester Square

THE GALLERY AT SKETCH

www.sketch.uk.com

Public art gallery by day, sophisticated dining room by night, nothing about this restaurant is conventional. Housed in a Grade II-listed building, the 360-degree modern art projections and bold mix of old cutlery and white Louis XV chairs with Formica table tops reflect the challenging, experimental style of the imaginative menu, with dishes like aubergine and white chocolate, spiced duck magret served with raw miso tuna and mandarin sorbet. Fine dining is available in the lecture room.

168 G4 9 Conduit Street W1S 2XG 020 7659 4500 Mon–Sat 7–10.30pm (bar open until 2am) D from £50, Wine from £20 Oxford Circus, Piccadilly

HAKKASAN

One of the most stylish restaurants in London, with exceptional Cantonese cuisine. A winding marble staircase leads to a lobby lined with pink orchids and incense bowls; the spacious dining area is partitioned with dark wood lattice screens. The dim sum platter is a highlight at lunch; fried rice with dried shrimp, Chinese sausage and shiitake mushrooms served in a lotus leaf is also worth a try. Nice cocktails.

168 H4 8 Hanway Place W1T 1HD 020 7927 7000 Mon–Fri 12–3, 6–11.30, Sat–Sun 12–5, 6–12.30. Closed 25–26 Dec L from £30, D from £50, Wine from £26 Tottenham Court Road

THE IVY

www.the-ivy.co.uk

There's still a buzz at the Ivy; people clearly want to be heard as well as seen here. In the heart of theatreland, the V-shaped building opens into a small bar, which leads on to the main room with leaded windows and coloured glass. The menu offers simple dishes, ranging from snacks to a main meal, with international influences.

169 J4 1–5 West Street, Covent Garden WC2H 9NQ 020 7836 4751 Daily 12–3, 5.30–12. Closed L 27 Dec, D 24 Dec, 25–26 Dec, 1 Jan, Aug public hol L from £25, D from £35, Wine from £21 Leicester Square, Covent Garden

J. SHEEKEY

www.j-sheekey.co.uk

This much-loved establishment, off the beaten track in theatreland, is in a class of its own when it comes to fish. The freshness of the catch is second to none. Look for Cornish fish stew, roast whole gilthead bream with herbs and olive oil and grilled sardines *piri piri*. Oak panelling, portraits of theatre stars and bench seating set the scene. Reserve well in advance.

169 J4 28–32 St. Martin's Court WC2N 4AL 020 7240 2565 Mon–Sat 12–3, 5.30–12, Sun 12–3, 6–11. Closed D 24 Dec, 25–26 Dec, 1 Jan, public hols L from £26, D from £35, Wine from £18 Leicester Square

MELA

www.melarestaurant.co.uk

An unusual Indian restaurant that uses traditional Indian cooking methods and spices and combines them with Western ingredients, for example, the *batakh sula shashlik*—chargrilled chunks of duck supreme marinated in yoghurt and spices, served on a skewer with onions, courgettes (zucchini), tomatoes and peppers. All dishes are freshly prepared and service is friendly and prompt. The simple, minimalist decor makes a pleasant backdrop.

169 J4 152–156 Shaftesbury Avenue WC2H 8HL 020 7836 8635 Mon–Sat 12–11.30, Sun 12–10.30. Closed L 25–26 Dec L from £10, D from £14, Wine from £11 Leicester Square

MON PLAISIR

www.monplaisir.co.uk

This is the oldest French restaurant in London, run by the same family for 50 years. An unassuming entrance leads to a maze of comfortable rooms, including a mezzanine-style loft, brightly decked with modern abstract paintings. The menu mixes classics such as *cassoulet d'escargots* and *coquilles St.-Jacques* with more contemporary fare such as steamed sea bass with broccoli and shellfish sauce. All desserts are handmade by the chef patissier. Bustling, friendly French service with closely packed tables creating a Gallic atmosphere.

169 J4 19–21 Monmouth Street WC2H 9DD 020 7836 7243 Mon–Fri 12–2.15, 5.45–11.15, Sat 5.45–11.15. Closed 25–26 Dec, 1 Jan, public hols L from £15, D from £35, Wine from £16 Covent Garden, Leicester Square, Tottenham Court Road

MOSAICO

www.mosaico-restaurant.co.uk

Mosaico is a stylish traditional Italian restaurant with a bar area, huge flower arrangements, brown leather seating and lots of pale wood. The menu is in Italian with English translations and is dotted with some of the most popular Italian dishes: veal Milanese with fresh tomato and rocket, linguine with fresh clams in wine, and green tagliolini with Parma ham—some of which is especially labelled '24 months aged'. The wines are all Italian, with options by the glass.

168 G5 13 Albermarle Street W1S 4HJ 020 7409 1011 Mon–Fri 12–2.30, 6.30–10.30, Sat 6.30–10.30 L from £25, D from £35, Wine from £18 Green Park

ORRERY

www.danddlondon.com

Orrery is in the heart of Marylebone and one of the smartest restaurants in London, with huge, round windows and long rows of tables attended by professional French staff. The menu is Modern European with dishes such as terrine of *foie gras* with Sauternes *gelée*, fillet of bream with roast artichokes and truffles or saddle of venison with black pudding.

168 F3 55–57 Marylebone High Street W1M 3AE 020 7616 8000 Mon–Sat 12–2.30, 6.30–10.30, Sun 12–2.30, 6.30–10. Closed 25–26 Dec, 1 Jan, Good Fri L from £24 (3 courses), D from £45, Wine from £22 Baker Street, Regents Park

ORSO

www.orsorestaurant.co.uk

Covent Garden cellar restaurant with designer-free interior. A bilingual menu, broadly Tuscan, offers seasonal cooking. Small pizzas (perhaps with wild mushrooms, goat's cheese and garlic), penne with courgettes (zucchini), basil and pecorino cheese, calves' liver with endive and pancetta and sardines dusted with Parmesan are all simply presented on colourful Italian pottery.

169 J4 27 Wellington Street WC2E 7DA 020 7240 5269 Daily 12–12. Closed 24–25 Dec L from £20 (Sat–Sun only, including cocktail), D from £30, Wine from £15 Covent Garden

OZER

www.sofra.co.uk

Huseyin Ozer's restaurant is stylish and contemporary, with a rich bold interior tempered with neutral linens, cool tiles and intricate lighting. Dishes are Mediterranean, but with strong North African and Middle Eastern accents. A wide choice of menus and dishes makes selecting tricky as they cover grills, seafood, casseroles, vegetarian, set menus and hot or cold mezes as either starters or main courses.

168 G3 5 Langham Place W1B 3DG 020 7323 0505 Daily 12–12 B from £3, L from £13, D from £15, Wine from £14 Oxford Circus

RASA SAMUDRA

www.rasarestaurants.com

The name means 'a taste of the ocean', and this authentic Indian restaurant specializes in the home cooking of the coastal state of Kerala in southwest India, particularly fish and seafood. The exterior is hard to miss, with its bold pink, and the interior is decorated with bright silks and vibrant oil paintings. Try a crab *varuthathu* cooked dry with ginger, curry leaves, chilli and mustard seeds accompanied by rice tossed in lemon juice, curry leaves and mustard seeds.

168 H3 5 Charlotte Street W1T 1RE 020 7637 0222 Mon–Sat 12–3, 6–11, Sun 6–11. Closed 2 weeks Dec L from £20, D from £30, Wine from £15 Tottenham Court Road, Goodge Street

LA TROUVAILLE
www.latrouvaille.co.uk
A busy, bustling French bistro offering good value and rustic French cooking with intense flavours. Dishes range from poached cassoulette of snails with Bayonne ham, garlic and red wine sauce to fillet of Galway beef to roasted saddle of rabbit and pan-fried *fois gras*. For dessert you might be able to enjoy chocolate fondant with ginger ice cream or an Earl Grey tea crème brûlée.
168 H4 12a Newburgh Street W1F 7RR 020 7287 8488 Mon–Sat 12–3, 6–11. Closed 25–26 Dec, public hols L from £16.50, D from £35, Wine from £16 Oxford Circus

VEERASWAMY RESTAURANT
www.realindianfood.com
The oldest Indian restaurant in London has been given a contemporary spin. Multi-hued lacquered walls with a creative use of glass, chrome and gold leaf add to the smart, yet informal, surroundings. The menu picks up on southern and northern Indian specialities. A starter of mussels in coconut and ginger might be followed by apple *dopiaza*, a tender lamb dish of caramelized onion and apples.
168 H5 Victory House, 99 Regent Street W1B 4RS 020 7734 1401 Mon–Fri 12–2.15, 5.30–10.30, Sat 12.30–3, 5.30–10.30, Sun 12.30–2.30, 6–10.30. Closed D 25 Dec L from £22, D from £22, Wine from £18 Piccadilly Circus

PUBS

THE ARGYLL ARMS
There has been a tavern here since 1740, but the present building is mid-Victorian and notable for its stunning floral displays. There's a range of sandwiches and the hot food menu might offer vegetarian moussaka, beef and Guinness pie, traditional haddock and chips or the popular lasagne. Children are not allowed in the bar area.
168 G4 18 Argyll Street W1F 7TP 020 7734 6117 Mon–Sat 11am–11.30pm, Sun 12–10.30. Meals: daily 12–10. Closed 25 Dec Bar meals from £13 Oxford Circus

CITTIE OF YORKE
A pub has stood on this site since 1430. In 1695 it was rebuilt as the Gray's Inn Coffee House and the large cellar bar dates from this time. The panelled front bar has an original chandelier and portraits of illustrious locals, including Charles Dickens and Sir Thomas More. Bar food includes sandwiches, salads and soups, plus a handful of hot dishes.
169 K3 22 High Holborn WC1V 6BN 020 7242 7670 Mon–Sat 11.30–3, 5–9. Meals: 11.30–9. Closed 25–26 Dec Bar meals from £6 Holborn

THE FRENCH HOUSE
www.frenchhousesoho.com
Notable for its custom of serving only half pints of beer, this small Soho bar holds an annual Pint Day dedicated to the long-established British charity, the National Society for the Prevention of Cruelty to Children (NSPCC). The bar remains much as it was in the 1950s, when it was popular with writers and artists such as Brendan Behan, Dylan Thomas and Francis Bacon. Weekly changing menus might feature navarin of lamb or roasted monkfish with ham. No children.
168 H4 49 Dean Street W1D 5BG 020 7437 2477 Mon–Sat 11–11, Sun 12–10.30. Restaurant: Mon–Sat 11–3, 5–7, Sun 11–3. Closed 25 Dec Bar meals from £6, D from £26 Tottenham Court Road

THE LAMB
This traditional watering hole, with a distinctive green-tiled facade, was built around 1729 and sends you back in time the minute you walk in the door, with its dark polished wood, original sepia photographs of music hall stars, rare glass 'snob screens', and an old phonograph in the bar that can be wound up to play discs by request. Home-cooked bar food covers all bases, including vegetarian choices, a fish dish, light bites and traditional meals such as sausage and mash. No children allowed in the bar area. Meals are served on the patio.
169 J3 94 Lamb's Conduit Street WC1N 3LZ 020 7405 0713 Mon–Sat 12–12, Sun 12–10.30. Meals: 12–3, 5.30–9 Bar meals from £7, D from £18 Holborn, Russell Square

THE LAMB AND FLAG
The oldest pub in Covent Garden, its cosy atmosphere attracts city workers and vistors to partake of a beer or some traditional pub grub.
169 J4 33 Rose Street WC2E 9EB 020 7497 9504 Mon–Sat 11–11, Sun 12–10.30. Meals: Mon–Fri 12–3.30, Sat–Sun 12–5 Bar meals from £7 Covent Garden

THE PERSEVERANCE
www.the-perseverance.moonfruit.com
A central London haven of good food, fine wine and conviviality. The elegant, candlelit dining room upstairs offers starters such as home-made gnocchi, courgettes (zucchini) and mussels, mackerel with sweet pepper relish, and main dishes such as sea bream with artichokes, confit potatoes and red wine sauce, and pork with mushroom casserole. Good but small wine list. Book in advance if you're coming for Sunday lunch.
169 J3 63 Lamb's Conduit Street WC1N 3NB 020 7405 8278 Mon–Thu, Sat 12–11, Fri 12–12, Sun 12–6. Restaurant: Mon–Sat 12–10, Sun 12–6. Closed 25–26 Dec Bar meals from £5, D from £18 Holborn, Russell Square

THE SEVEN STARS
The clientele of this pub, built in 1602, is drawn from the adjacent Law Courts. This highly individual free house serves fresh, home-made dishes. A changing selection of options might include oysters, steak, herrings and Caesar salad. Adnam's ales. No children.
169 K4 53 Carey Street WC2A 2JB 020 7242 8521 Mon–Fri 11–11, Sat–Sun 12–11. Meals: 12–9. Closed 25–26 Dec, 1 Jan, Easter Mon Bar meals from £8, D from £19 Chancery Lane

PRICES AND SYMBOLS

Prices given are the starting price for a double room for one night. Breakfast is included unless noted otherwise. All the hotels listed accept credit cards unless otherwise stated. Note that rates vary widely throughout the year.

For a key to the symbols, ▷ 2.

ASHLEE HOUSE

www.ashleehouse.co.uk

Stylish and rather funky, this hostel is just two minutes' walk from King's Cross Station. Safe and clean accommodation and the friendly staff make it a popular choice for backpackers. It is close to London's nightlife action and well positioned for access to most of the city's major sights. Single, twin and multi-bedded rooms are available. There's a lounge for chilling out, WiFi internet access and a laundry room. Continental breakfast is included in the price.

169 J2 261–265 Gray's Inn Road 020 7833 9400 Double from £50, beds from £16 25 King's Cross 17, 45, 46

THE BONNINGTON IN BLOOMSBURY

www.bonnington.com

A smart hotel central to the city, the British Museum (▷ 134–139) and Covent Garden (▷ 142–143). The public areas, all with plenty of space, include the Malt Bar, Waterfalls Restaurant and a comfortable lobby lounge. Bedrooms include a number of superb new executive rooms and suites.

169 J3 92 Southampton Row WC1B 4BH 020 7242 2828 Double from £290 214 Russell Square, Holborn 7

BROWN'S HOTEL

www.brownshotel.com

Reopened for business in late 2005 after a major refurbishment, Brown's is famous for its English country-house style, traditional furnishings and quality fixtures and fittings. Accommodation is excellent and rooms are particularly spacious for Mayfair. The elegant Grill, in 1930s design with banquette booths, offers British classics with a modern twist, creating an intriguing mix. The English Tea Room is popular for afternoon tea.

168 G5 Albemarle Street W1S 4BP 020 7493 6020 Double from £367 118 Green Park 8

EURO

www.eurohotel.co.uk

This friendly bed-and-breakfast enjoys an ideal location in a leafy Georgian crescent. Russell Square Underground station, which links direct to Heathrow Airport, is only a few minutes' walk away. Many bedrooms have private bathrooms. Breakfast is served in the attractive dining room, but note that there are no meals in the evening. Tennis courts.

169 J2 51–53 Cartwright Gardens, Russell Square WC1H 9EL 020 7387 4321 Double from £95 (ensuite) £76 (no ensuite) 34 Russell Square 7, 59, 68, 91, 168, 188

GRANGE BLOOMS

www.grangehotels.com

The Grange Blooms is part of an 18th-century row of town houses in Bloomsbury, just round the

Left *Vast flower arrangements are a talking point of One Aldwych's lobby bar*

corner from the British Museum (▷ 134–139). Bedrooms are furnished in Regency style, and there are several day rooms: a lobby lounge, a garden terrace, a breakfast room and a cocktail bar, all decorated with antiques and adorned with huge flower arrangements. The lounge menu is also available as room service.
169 J3 7 Montague Street WC1B 5BP 020 7323 1717 Double from £180 26 Holborn, Russell Square 7, 68, 188

GUILFORD HOUSE

www.guilfordhotel.activehotels.com
Within walking distance of the British Museum (▷ 134–139), Guilford House has single, double, triple and family rooms, all with private shower. Continental breakfast.
169 K3 6 Guilford Street WC1N 1DR 020 7430 2504 Double from £74 12 Russell Square, King's Cross 17, 45, 46

KINGSWAY HALL

www.kingswayhall.co.uk
Close to Covent Garden, this is a modern, stylish and comfortable hotel. Air-conditioned bedrooms have such extra facilities as a safe deposit box and an iron. The compact lounge bar serves drinks and light snacks and the Harlequin Restaurant provides more formal dining on the premises. There's a fitness centre in the basement.
169 J4 66 Great Queen Street WC2B 5BX 020 7309 0909 Double from £159 170 Holborn 1, 59, 68, 91, 168, 171, 188

MENTONE HOTEL

www.mentonehotel.com
This impressive bed-and-breakfast in a row of Victorian houses overlooking pleasant gardens in Bloomsbury is close to many central London attractions and a few minutes' walk from Russell Square Undergound station. All bedrooms have private bathrooms; five provide facilities for visitors with disabilities. Breakfast is taken in the downstairs dining room and free internet access is available. Tennis courts opposite. No evening meals.
169 J2 54–55 Cartwright Gardens WC1H 9EL 020 7387 3927 Double from £90 45 King's Cross, Russell Square, Euston 10, 30, 73, 91, 205

ONE ALDWYCH

www.onealdwych.com
One Aldwych is well known for its chic and contemporary style set in an Edwardian building. There's a host of interesting features: a swimming pool with underwater music in the health club, the dramatic amber city mural in the lofty Axis Restaurant—acclaimed for its Modern British cooking—and the contemporary lobby bar where American martini cocktails are the thing to drink. Live jazz on Tuesday and Wednesday evenings. Bedrooms are no less stylish, with giant pillows, down duvets and granite bathroom surfaces.
169 J4 1 Aldwych WC2B 4RH 020 7300 1000 Double from £340 (exc. breakfast) 105 (38 smoking) Indoor Charing Cross, Covent Garden 521

RADISSON EDWARDIAN HAMPSHIRE HOTEL

www.radissonedwardian.com
This popular hotel is in central Leicester Square. The public areas have all been elegantly refurbished, with wood-panelled lounges and sitting rooms. Bedrooms and suites are air-conditioned. There is an excellent restaurant and you can have drinks in the elegant high-backed chairs of the Hampshire Bar.
169 J5 31–36 Leicester Square WC2H 7LH 020 7839 9399 Double from £270 (exc. breakfast) 124 (13 smoking) Leicester Square 24, 29, 176

REGENCY

www.regencyhotelwestend.co.uk
The Regency Hotel is close to Madame Tussauds (▷ 217) and the West End. The bedrooms are well furnished and include some suitable for families. Breakfast is served in a light and cheerful basement breakfast room.
168 F3 19 Nottingham Place W1U 5LQ 020 7486 5347 Double from £89 20 (1 smoking) Euston, King's Cross, Baker Street 2, 13, 27, 30, 74, 82, 113, 139, 189

THE SAVOY

www.the-savoy.com
At the time of writing the Savoy was still undergoing a £100 million restoration, due to be completed in 2010. The finished product will retain Edwardian features and enhance later art deco additions in the new Beaufort Bar and River Restaurant. All the back rooms overlook the river. Check for prices and other details.
169 J5 Strand WC2R 0EU 020 7836 4343 Indoor Charing Cross, Covent Garden 6, 9, 11, 13, 15, 23, 87, 91, 176

STRAND PALACE

www.strandpalacehotel.co.uk
At the heart of theatreland, the Strand Palace is a vast hotel, with rooms that vary in style, including Club rooms with enhanced facilities and exclusive use of the Club lounge. The extensive public areas include four places in which to eat and a popular cocktail bar.
169 J4 372 The Strand WC2R 0JJ 020 7379 4737 Double from £290 (exc breakfast) 783 Charing Cross

THE WESTBURY

www.westburymayfair.com
The Westbury, which recently underwent a £25 million refurbishment, is right in the heart of London's finest shopping area. Standards of accommodation are high throughout. The public spaces offer a variety of eating and drinking options, including the Polo Bar for cocktails.
168 G4 Bond Street W1S 2YF 020 7629 7755 Double from £249 249 Bond Street 8

Regent's Park
0
400 m
0
400 yds
REGENT'S PARK
SOMERS TOWN
LISSON GROVE
MARYLEBONE
MAYFAIR
SOHO
CHINATOWN
Hyde Park
Regency
Orrery
Archipelago
Rasa Samudra
Ozer
Hakkasan
The Argyll Arms
Arbutus
L'Escargot
La Trouvaille
The Gallery at Sketch
The French House
The Westbury
Veeraswamy
Mosaico
Alloro
Brown's Hotel
Bentley's
EUSTON STATION
National Temperance Hospital
University College London
University College Hospital
Petrie Museum of Egyptian Archaeology
Royal National Orthopaedic Hospital
Royal College of Physicians
Royal Academy of Music
Madame Tussauds
Sherlock Holmes Museum
Wallace Collection
Wigmore Hall
Central Synagogue
All Saints' Church
BT Tower
University of Westminster
Euston Tower
Handel House Museum
St George's Church
Royal Academy of Arts
Burlington Arcade
St James's Church
US Embassy
Roosevelt Memorial
Speakers Corner
West End Great Synagogue
London Trocadero
Regent's College
Open Air Theatre
Queen Mary's Garden
The Holme
St John's Lodge
Regent's Park Barracks
The London Clinic
Piccadilly Circus
Eros
Green Park
Oxford Circus
Bond Street
Marble Arch
Baker Street
Great Portland Street
Warren Street
Goodge Street
Tottenham Court Road
Euston Square
MARYLEBONE ROAD
EUSTON ROAD
OXFORD STREET
REGENT STREET
PICCADILLY
PARK LANE
BAKER STREET
TOTTENHAM COURT ROAD
GREAT PORTLAND STREET
PORTLAND PLACE
GOWER STREET
HAMPSTEAD ROAD
ALBANY STREET
SHAFTESBURY AVENUE
HAYMARKET
PALL MALL
NEW BOND STREET
WIGMORE STREET
MORTIMER STREET
GOODGE STREET
GRAFTON WAY
CONDUIT STREET
MARYLEBONE HIGH STREET
PADDINGTON STREET

PENTONVILLE
London Canal Museum
ST PANCRAS
BLOOMSBURY
HOLBORN
CLERKENWELL
STRAND
St Pancras Station
King's Cross Station
King's Cross Thameslink Station
British Library
Royal National Throat, Nose & Ear Hospital
Ashlee House
Acorn House
Euro
Mentone Hotel
British Medical Association
Thomas Coram Foundation (The Foundling Museum)
Coram's Fields
Brunswick Shopping Centre
Eastman Dental Hospital
Mount Pleasant Postal Sorting Office
Guilford House
Charles Dickens Museum
The Lamb
National Hospital for Sick Children (Great Ormond St)
National Hospital for Neurology & Neurosurgery
Cigala
The Perseverance
Royal London Homeopathic Hospital
The Method Studio
The Bonnington in Bloomsbury
British Museum
Grange Blooms
The Cartoon Museum
Inns of Court & School of Law
Cittie of Yorke
Sir John Soane's Museum
London Silver Vaults
Lincoln's Inn
Royal College of Surgeons
Kingsway Hall
New Connaught Rooms
Oasis Sports Centre
Mon Plaisir
Old Curiosity Shop
The Seven Stars
Royal Courts of Justice (Law Courts)
London School of Economics & Political Science
Royal Opera House
Covent Garden Piazza
Christopher's
One Aldwych
Bush House (BBC)
India House
Australia House
St Clement Danes
St Mary-le-Strand
Courtauld Institute of Art
King's College
The Admiralty Restaurant
Somerset House
The Lamb & Flag
Orso
Strand Palace
St Peter's Hospital
J Sheekey
Royal Society of Arts
The Savoy
Waterloo Bridge
Victoria Embankment
Victoria Embankment Gardens
Cleopatra's Needle
Embankment Pier
Golden Jubilee Bridge
Charing Cross Station
Trafalgar Square
Nelson's Column
Benjamin Franklin House
Government Offices
DEFRA
Hispaniola
St Martin-in-the-Fields
Temple Church
Inner Temple
Middle Temple
Maughan Library
Dr Johnson's House
St Bride's Church
City Thameslink Station
Blackfriars Station
HMS President
HQS Wellington (Master Mariners)
Blackfriars Millennium Pier
Blackfriars Pier
Blackfriars Bridge
Thames
Oxo Tower
The London Television Centre
Royal National Theatre
National Film Theatre
Queen Elizabeth Hall
Southbank Centre
Royal Festival Hall
Hayward Gallery
Festival Pier
London City College
Schiller International
London Nautical School
Bankside Gallery
Purdy Hicks Gallery
Tate Modern
Kings College London
The City University
St Bartholomew's Medical School
St John's Gate
Charterhouse
Farringdon Station
Central London Markets (Smithfield)
Holborn Circus
City Temple
St Bartholomew's Hospital
Old Bailey (Central Criminal Court)
Stock Exchange
St Paul's Cathedral
Ludgate Circus
PENTONVILLE ROAD
KING'S CROSS ROAD
GRAY'S INN ROAD
EUSTON ROAD
ROSEBERY AVENUE
FARRINGDON ROAD
THEOBALD'S ROAD
HIGH HOLBORN
KINGSWAY
CHANCERY LANE
FLEET STREET
STRAND
ALDWYCH
VICTORIA EMBANKMENT
NEW OXFORD STREET
SHAFTESBURY AVENUE
CHARING CROSS ROAD
ST MARTIN'S LANE
SOUTHAMPTON ROW
WOBURN PLACE
RUSSELL SQUARE
HOLBORN VIADUCT
NEWGATE STREET
FARRINGDON STREET
NEW BRIDGE STREET
STAMFORD STREET
SOUTHWARK STREET
GOSWELL ROAD
ST JOHN STREET

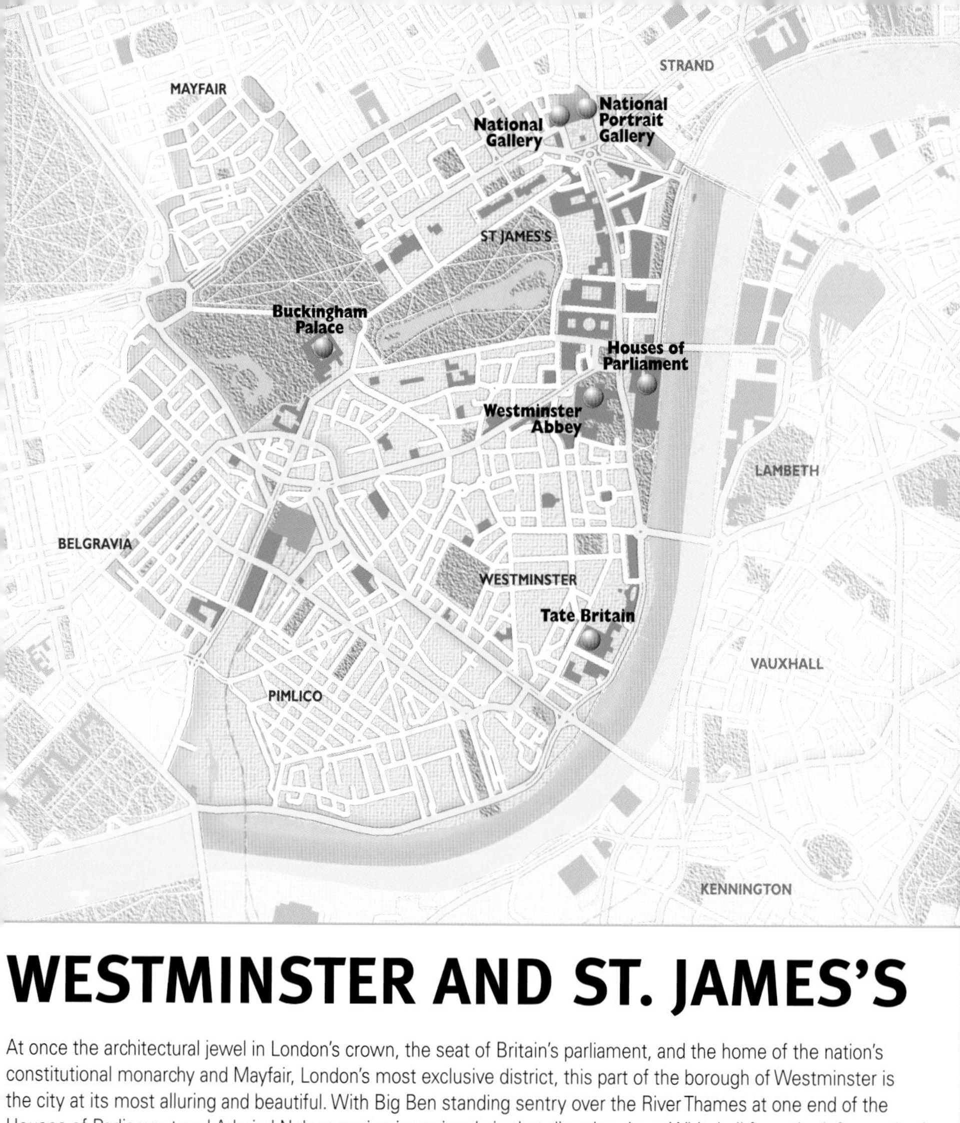

WESTMINSTER AND ST. JAMES'S

At once the architectural jewel in London's crown, the seat of Britain's parliament, and the home of the nation's constitutional monarchy and Mayfair, London's most exclusive district, this part of the borough of Westminster is the city at its most alluring and beautiful. With Big Ben standing sentry over the River Thames at one end of the Houses of Parliament and Admiral Nelson gazing imperiously in that direction down Whitehall from the lofty perch of his column in Trafalgar Square, you could barely ask for a more imposing introduction to the area. And yet these are only two of the magnificent structures that catch the eye wherever you turn. On the far side of Parliament Square from the famous clock stands the medieval masterpiece of Westminster Abbey, while behind Nelson at the top of Trafalgar Square, the stylish facade of the National Gallery heralds the wealth of artistic treasures within. Some way southwest down the river, the Tate Britain holds another world-class collection of art.

Passing from Trafalgar Square through Edward VII's colossal Admiralty Arch, you can stroll down Pall Mall, as the green expanse of St James's Park unfolds to your left and the outline of Buckingham Palace comes gradually into focus in front of you. As you near the official residence of Queen Elizabeth II and the royal family, another fine patch of nature, Green Park, stretches out to the right, lined by a row of splendid mansions. It's a shame, however, not to detour at least for a little while, so that you can stand on the small footbridge that spans the elongated lake in St. James's Park and be rewarded by the breathtaking view as the grandeur of the city manifests itself all around.

Hyde Park
The Serpentine
Serpentine Road
0
400 m
0
400 yards
5
6
7
8
E
F
G
MAYFAIR
KNIGHTSBRIDGE
BELGRAVIA
PIMLICO
US Embassy
Roosevelt Memorial
Grosvenor Square
Faraday Museum
Royal Academy of Arts
Burlington Arcade
Green Park
Spencer House
St James's Palace
Clarence House
Lancaster House
Apsley House
Wellington Arch
Hyde Park Corner
Queen Mother Gate
Albert Gate
Edinburgh Gate
Brook Gate
Grosvenor Gate
Green Park
Constitution Hill
Queen Victoria Memorial
Buckingham Palace
Buckingham Palace Gardens
Queen's Gallery
Royal Mews
Wellington Barracks
Westminster City School
Westminster Cathedral
London Tourist Board
VICTORIA BUS STATION
VICTORIA STATION
Victoria Place Shopping Centre
VICTORIA RAIL/AIR TERMINAL
The Colonnades Shopping Centre
UK Passport Office
VICTORIA COACH STATION
Queen Mother Sports Centre
Harrods
Knightsbridge
Holy Trinity Church
Sloane Square
Saatchi Gallery
Duke of York's Headquarters
Royal Hospital Museum
Burtons Court
Royal Hospital
The Infirmary Royal Hospital
Ranelagh Gardens (site of Chelsea Flower Show)
National Army Museum
The Lister Hospital
Chelsea Physic Garden
Thames
CHELSEA BRIDGE
GROSVENOR BRIDGE
CHELSEA EMBANKMENT
PICCADILLY
PARK LANE
GROSVENOR PLACE
BELGRAVE SQUARE
EATON SQUARE
SLOANE STREET
KING'S ROAD
BUCKINGHAM PALACE ROAD
VICTORIA STREET
VAUXHALL BRIDGE ROAD
EBURY BRIDGE ROAD
PIMLICO ROAD
ROYAL HOSPITAL ROAD
GROSVENOR ROAD
BROMPTON ROAD
A4
A3212
A3216
A3214
A302
A202
A315
A4202

Thames
National Portrait Gallery
National Gallery
St Martin-in-the-Fields
Trafalgar Square
Nelson's Column
Benjamin Franklin House
Charing Cross Station
Embankment
Strand
Royal Society of Arts
Savoy Pier
Waterloo Bridge
Victoria Embankment
Victoria Embankment Gardens
Cleopatra's Needle
Embankment Pier
Festival Pier
Golden Jubilee Bridge
Queen Elizabeth Hall
Southbank Centre
Royal Festival Hall
Hayward Gallery
National Film Theatre
Royal National Theatre
The London Television Centre
Oxo Tower
HMS President
HQS Wellington (Master Mariners)
Somerset House
Hermitage Rooms
London City College
Schiller International University
BFI London IMAX Cinema
London Nautical School
Waterloo East Station
Waterloo Station
Shell Centre
Jubilee Gardens
London Eye
Waterloo Millennium Pier
Dalí Universe
County Hall
London Aquarium
Hispaniola
Admiralty Arch
Institute of Contemporary Arts (ICA)
Carlton House
Duke of York Column
Old Admiralty
Government Offices
Old War Office
Horse Guards Parade
Banqueting House
Ministry of Defence
St James's
St James's Park
Privy Council Office
Foreign & Commonwealth Office
Cenotaph
Churchill Museum & Cabinet War Rooms
Treasury
Portcullis House
Westminster Millennium Pier
Westminster
Big Ben
Westminster Bridge
Queen Elizabeth II Conference Centre
Middlesex Guildhall
Central Hall
St James's Park
Caxton Hall
New Scotland Yard
Department of Trade & Industry
St Margaret's Westminster
Westminster Abbey
Palace of Westminster
Houses of Parliament
Jewel Tower
Church House
Westminster School
Victoria Tower Gardens
Florence Nightingale Museum
St Thomas' Hospital
Lambeth
Archbishop's Park
Lambeth Palace
Museum of Garden History
Lambeth Bridge
Civil Service Recreation Centre
St John's Concert Hall
RHS New Hall
Thames House
Westminster
Millbank Tower
The Greycoat Hospital
Tate Britain
Millbank Millennium Pier
Chelsea College of Art & Design
Pimlico
Vauxhall Bridge
Vauxhall
Vauxhall Station
Vauxhall City Farm
St George Wharf
Pimlico Gardens
Lambeth North
St George's Cathedral
Geraldine Mary Harmsworth Park
Imperial War Museum
Newington
The Oval Cricket Ground
Ken Barrington Centre
Kennington
Covent Garden Flower Market

BANQUETING HOUSE

www.hrp.org.uk

The Banqueting House is all that remains of Whitehall Palace, the sovereign's main residence from 1530 until its destruction by fire in 1698. English architect Inigo Jones (1573–1652) amazed the public with his Palladian design of three central bays and Ionic columns, giving London (and Britain) its first glimpse of neoclassical architecture. State occasions, plays and masques were held in the magnificent main hall in which the painted ceiling by Peter Paul Rubens allegorically glorifies the reign of James I, and a less propitious period for the monarchy was marked when Charles I stepped out of the first-floor balcony to face his execution in 1649.

The undercroft, designed as a drinking den for James I, now houses a small exhibition and video on the history and use of the building.

173 J5 Whitehall SW1A 2ER 0870 751 5178 Mon–Sat 10–5. May close at short notice for state functions Adult £4.80, child (under 16) free Westminster, Embankment 11, 24, 53, 88, 159 Lunchtime concerts

BENJAMIN FRANKLIN HOUSE

www.benjaminfranklinhouse.org

Opened to the public on Franklin's 300th birthday (he was born on 16 January 1706) after extensive restoration, this house, built around 1730, holds a Grade I architectural listing for its many original features, including 14 fireplaces, ceilings, shutters, floors and a lovely central staircase.

Franklin lived here from 1757 to 1775, and it is the only home of his remaining in the world. The museum highlights the many accomplishments and inventions of this brilliant man, some of which were discovered here. The Historical Experience combines the latest technology with lively performances to show Franklin's integral role in politics, science and philosophy. The interests of this highly social and gregarious man ranged from bifocal spectacles and an energy-saving oven to health issues such as inoculation and cures for the common cold.

The museum holds key artefacts such as bones studied at the anatomy school run by Dr. William Hewson, who lived here during Franklin's stay. The house is also home to the Student Science Centre, which through hands-on experiments demonstrates Franklin's significant discoveries such as electricity and medical processes studied by Dr. Hewson.

173 J5 36 Craven Street WC2N 5NF 020 7839 2006 Wed–Sun 12–5. Shows at 12, 1, 2, 3.15, 4.15 (arrive 10 min before start Adult £7, child (under 16) free Charing Cross, Embankment 6, 11, 13, 15, 23, 91, 176 (to Strand)

BUCKINGHAM PALACE

▷ 176–177.

CHURCHILL MUSEUM AND CABINET WAR ROOMS

www.iwm.org.uk

Nowhere is the personal experience of war and the sense of crisis more keenly felt than in these cramped underground rooms in Whitehall, where the most senior figures of Britain's government and armed forces worked and slept during World War II. Most interesting of those rooms open to the public are the Map Room, its walls covered in pinhole-riddled maps as the progress of the war was tracked; the Cabinet Room, where the work of government carried on during bombing raids; the Transatlantic Telephone Room, which had direct communication with Washington's White House; and the Prime Minister's Room, where Sir Winston Churchill broadcast to the nation. More rooms make up the world's first major museum dedicated to the life of Winston Churchill.

A free audio-guide navigates you through corridors that reverberate to the sound of sirens and the voices of guards as bombs explode and fires rage outside.

173 J6 Clive Steps, King Charles Street SW1A 2AQ 020 7930 6961 Daily 9.30–6 Adult £15, child (under 16) free Westminster, St. James's Park 3, 11, 12, 24, 53, 88

Opposite *The main hall of the Banqueting House, with its superb Rubens ceiling*
Below *The Map Room in the Cabinet War Rooms has been left as it was in August 1945*

INFORMATION

www.royal.gov.uk
172 G6 Buckingham Gate SW1A 1AA 020 7766 7300 Aug–end Sep (precise dates vary) 9.45–6 (last entry 3.45); timed ticket system with admission every 15 min Adult £15, child (5–17) £8.50, under 5s free, family £38.50 Victoria, Green Park, Hyde Park Corner 11, 211, 239, C1, C10 £5.25, in English, French, German, Italian, Japanese, Spanish In palace garden during summer opening, selling guides, books, souvenirs

Above *The Changing of the Guard outside the palace is always a popular spectacle*

INTRODUCTION

The palace so familiar to millions from newsreels and postcards took shape comparatively recently, after centuries of piecemeal architectural changes. Originally plain Buckingham House, it was built as the Duke of Buckingham's country mansion at the western end of St. James's Park and Green Park. George III snapped it up as a private residence in 1761 and work began on embellishments and additions to the shell of the Duke's old home. When Queen Victoria and Prince Albert moved into the palace in 1837 a whole new wing was added to accommodate their fast-growing family.

The palace is owned by the British state, as is Windsor Castle, and is not the private property of the monarch, like Sandringham House or Balmoral Castle. Consequently there was not much the Queen could do about the decision—controversial to some—made in 1993 to generate funds for the restoration of Windsor Castle after fire damage by opening the State Rooms to the public. Until now they have only been open in August and September, when the royal family is not in residence, but the urgent need for extra funds to conduct repairs on the palace itself led to a government proposal in May 2009 to open up for longer periods.

Without even entering the grounds at all, you can enjoy the Changing of the Guard through the surrounding railings. This splendid bit of pomp takes place at 11.30am daily from May to July and on alternate days the rest of the year.

WHAT TO SEE

THE STATE ROOMS

You enter the palace through the Ambassadors' Court, in the south wing, and go through John Nash's dramatic Grand Hall to climb the curving Carrara marble stairs of the Grand Staircase to the first-floor State Rooms. Beyond the small Guard Room, hung with Gobelin tapestries, is the Green Drawing Room, an antechamber to the Throne Room, where official visitors gather before being presented to the Queen. Ahead is the Throne Room, a theatrical space leading up to the Chairs of State under a baroque proscenium arch.

From here you go into the Picture Gallery, 47m long (155ft), hung with works by Rubens, Rembrandt, Canaletto and Van Dyck. The Silk Tapestry Room, with its monumental French pedestal clock, links the Picture Gallery with the East Gallery, part of Queen Victoria's new block, leading into the Ball Supper Room and the vast Ballroom, now used for investiture ceremonies and state banquets.

More Gobelin tapestries are displayed in the smaller West Gallery, which leads to the State Dining Room, vividly decorated in white and gold with deep-red walls and carpet. Next comes the sumptuous Blue Drawing Room, with a dazzling ceiling by John Nash and huge Corinthian columns. The opulent decoration continues in the Music Room, with its vaulted, domed ceiling and columns of lapis lazuli scagliola (imitation stone, made of glue and plaster).

A blaze of white and gold greets you in the White Drawing Room, where there are more pieces of wonderful French furniture. The intricately designed Minister's Staircase leads back to the ground floor and the Marble Hall, displaying statues of nymphs and portraits of Victoria's relations. From the Bow Room tours exit into the garden.

Other visitor attractions are the Queen's Gallery (▷ 181) and the nearby Royal Mews (▷ 181). Combined tickets are available.

TIPS

» To avoid the queues, book a timed ticket in advance.

» For same-day tickets on the day go to the Visitor Entrance, Buckingham Palace Road.

Left *The Royal Guards do not just guard the Queen but are also serving soldiers*
Below *The Grand Staircase takes you up to the State Rooms*

GREEN PARK

www.royalparks.org.uk

Henry VIII bought this swathe of land for hunting, along with Hyde Park (▷ 212) to the west and St. James's Park (▷ 181) on the other side of The Mall. Famous for its mature trees and avenues, Green Park's 16ha (40 acres) are less formal than London's other royal parks. In the southwest corner is the Wellington Arch (▷ 191).

172 G6 020 7930 1793 Open access Free Green Park, Hyde Park Corner 8, 14, 19, 82

GUARDS MUSEUM

www.theguardsmuseum.com

The Guards are the monarch's personal bodyguard, made up of soldiers from the Grenadier, Coldstream, Scots, Irish and Welsh Guards. Their 350-year regimental history is explored using more than 30 displays of uniforms, weapons and tableaux depicting famous battles from the 17th-century English Civil War to the present day.

All this is found under the parade ground at the east end of Wellington Barracks, whose classical facade overlooks St. James's Park (▷ 181).

173 H6 Wellington Barracks, Birdcage Walk SW1E 6HQ 020 7414 3428 Daily 10–4. Closed on ceremonial days Adult £3, under 16s free St. James's Park 11, 24, 148, 211

HOUSES OF PARLIAMENT

▷ 179–180.

INSTITUTE OF CONTEMPORARY ARTS (ICA)

www.ica.org.uk

English art critic and historian Sir Herbert Read (1893–1968) established the ICA soon after World War II. Originally housed in Dover Street, it was moved in 1968 to Carlton House Terrace, a long and elegant white-stone building fronted by neoclassical columns and designed by John Nash (1752–1835). Behind its formal facade the Institute presents contemporary films, exhibitions of avant-garde art, talks and dance productions.

173 H5 The Mall SW1Y 5AH 020 7930 3647 Mon–Wed 12–11, Thu–Sat 12pm–1am, Sun 12–9. Gallery daily 12–70; until 9pm on Thu (during exhibitions) Day membership £2 weekdays, £3 weekends; check ahead for individual events/exhibitions Charing Cross, Piccadilly Circus 3, 9, 11, 12, 13, 19, 23, 88

JEWEL TOWER

www.english-heritage.org.uk

The three-storey red-brick Jewel Tower was built in about 1365 as part of the original Palace of Westminster and used to store Edward III's treasures. A moat surrounded it at that time.

On the first floor an exhibition records the history of Parliament from 1066 to the present day, and on the second floor a 50-minute video explains the workings of government, and a virtual tour takes you round the Houses of Parliament.

173 J6 Abingdon Street SW1P 3JX 020 7222 2219 Apr–end Oct daily 10–5; Nov–end Mar daily 10–4 Adult £3, child (5–16) £1.50, under 5s free Westminster 3, 12

Below *The Canada Memorial fountain in Green Park*

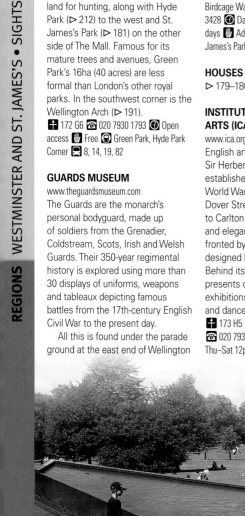

HOUSES OF

INTRODUCTION

Despite their Gothic appearance, the present Houses of Parliament, the headquarters of state power, are quite recent. The medieval Palace of Westminster was virtually destroyed by fire in 1834, and a competition was held to design a replacement in the Elizabethan style. It was won by architect Charles Barry (1795–1860) and his assistant, Augustus Pugin (1812–52).

WHAT TO SEE

PARLIAMENT

At the State Opening of Parliament (▷ 296) the Queen processes through the building on a route that can be followed on a public tour during the summer recess, when Members of Parliament take their annual break. After passing through the Norman porch, tours enter the Queen's Robing Room, a dazzle of gold and crimson. The Royal Gallery comes next, hung with portraits of monarchs. Huge Victorian portraits of the Tudors decorate the Prince's Chamber. From here you enter the Lords' Chamber, where the Queen addresses Parliament and the Lord Chancellor takes up position on the Woolsack, a wool-stuffed cushion representing British prosperity.

This is the end of the Queen's journey, but visitors continue through the Peers' Lobby to the Central Lobby, between the two Chambers. This is where members of the public can come face to face with their political representatives to plead their particular cause—that is, to lobby. From here a corridor leads into the Commons Lobby, with a red line marking the boundary between Government and Opposition members—traditionally seated at just over two swords' lengths apart, for safety's sake. Although there is not much

INFORMATION

www.parliament.uk

173 J6 Parliament Square SW1A 0AA House of Commons 020 7219 4272, House of Lords 020 7219 3107, tickets for summer tours 0870 906 3773 Tour during summer recess, Aug Mon–Tue, Fri–Sat 9.15–4.30, Wed–Thu 1.15–4.30; Sep–end Oct Mon, Fri–Sat 9.15–4.30, Tue–Thu 1.15–4.30. Clock Tower by request only Strangers' Gallery and Clock Tower free; for tours see below Westminster 3, 11, 12, 24 Westminster Millennium Pier Tour during summer recess: adult £12, child (4–16) £5, under 4s free, family £30. Foreign-language tours in French, Spanish, German or Italian at set times Free 'Brief Guides' in several languages. Various souvenir guidebooks Jubilee Café in Westminster Hall Gift shop in Westminster Hall

Above *The Houses of Parliament at dusk*

chance of a violent confrontation between opposing MPs these days, it is common for some pretty barbed comments to be cast back and forth during the more heated debates, leading to the frequent demands for 'Order! Order!' from the Speaker of the House. Next comes St. Stephen's Hall, on the site of the original chapel, and finally the 11th-century Westminster Hall, now used only occasionally for ceremonial occasions.

Free tours are available throughout the year for UK residents, while foreign visitors can only book tickets during summer recess. You can attend debates in the House of Commons or the House of Lords. You can also watch committees and judicial hearings. Wait outside St. Stephen's Entrance, but note that queues can be long for the most interesting debates or for Prime Minister's Questions. UK residents can arrange free tickets for entry in advance by contacting their local MP's office or a Lord. If you're visiting from overseas, you must apply to your embassy or high commission in the UK for a card of introduction, which permits entry during the early afternoon. Each embassy may issue only four cards per day so book well in advance. To arrange a tour of the Big Ben clock tower, UK residents can contact their MP; overseas visitors should write, at least three months in advance, to Clock Tower Tours, Parliamentary Works Services Directorate, 1 Cannon Row, London SW1A 2JN.

BIG BEN

If it's the Astronomer Royal at the Meridian a few miles east in Greenwich that sets the time, then it is the clock tower of the Houses of Parliament that keeps it in most people's minds. Better known as Big Ben, the most famous clock in the world is renowned for keeping remarkably accurate time and, as its chimes are broadcast by the BBC, people all over Britain and beyond set their watches by it. Completed in 1859, its four ornate faces, made of gilt and cast iron and 7m (23ft) in diameter, are positioned about four-fifths of the way up th 96m (315ft) Gothic Revival tower. It remains a matter of debate whether it is named after the former Commissioner of Works, Benjamin Hall, or a popular boxer of the period, Benjamin Caunt. To be exact, the name Big Ben only refers to the huge 13-ton bell inside, not the rest of the clock or tower. The hammer weighs 200kg (440lb) and when struck the great bell emits the musical note E in an unhurried, ponderous manner. This is the sound that thousands of revellers, waiting half a mile away in Trafalgar Square, see the New Year in by every 31 December. Indeed, it is worth making a point of seeing Big Ben at least once when it is lit up at night, whatever the date is.

Right *The octagonal Central Lobby is decorated with mosaics of St. George, St. Andrew, St. David and St. Patrick*
Below *Marochetti's* Richard the Lionheart *(1860), one of several statues around the Houses of Parliament*

NATIONAL GALLERY

▷ 182–187.

NATIONAL PORTRAIT GALLERY

▷ 188–189.

QUEEN'S GALLERY

www.royal.gov.uk

In the course of 500 years or so British royalty has amassed a huge collection of fabulous art and treasures. Items from that collection, held in trust for the nation by the Queen, are on show at this gallery in Buckingham Palace (▷ 176–177). The changing selection includes paintings by Canaletto, Frans Hals and Leonardo da Vinci; French, English and Asian porcelain, including Sèvres china; a dazzling array of snuff boxes; exquisite Fabergé eggs and flowers; furniture; and personal pieces selected from the collection of Queen Elizabeth, the Queen Mother (1900–2002).

The gallery itself was built in the 1960s from the ruins of the private chapel on the west front of Buckingham Palace, damaged by bombs during World War II. After massive redevelopment, it was reopened by the Queen in her golden jubilee year, 2002.

172 G6 Buckingham Palace Road SW1A 1AA 020 7766 7301 Daily 10–5.30 (timed ticketing) Adult £8.50, child (5–17) £4, family £20 Victoria, Green Park, Hyde Park Corner 11, 211, 239, C1, C10

ROYAL MEWS

www.royal.gov.uk

Run as a working stables, the Royal Mews gives a fascinating glimpse of daily life in one of Buckingham Palace's royal household departments. The royal family's state vehicles are on permanent display, including the fairy-tale gold state carriage, commissioned by George III in 1762. Gilded in 22-carat leaf and weighing in at 4 tonnes, this ornate colossus needs eight horses to draw it and is apparently a most uncomfortable ride.

You can also usually see the 30 or so carriage horses stabled here for much of the year. Most are Cleveland Bays, the only British breed of carriage horse, and Windsor greys, which, by tradition, draw the Queen's carriage.

172 G6 Buckingham Palace Road SW1A 1AA 020 7766 7302 Apr–end Oct daily 11–5 Adult £7.50, child (5–17) £4.80, family £20 Victoria, Green Park, Hyde Park Corner 11, 211, 239, C1, C10

Above *The Jewel Tower is one of the two surviving sections of the medieval Palace of Westminster; it was detached from the main buildings so survived the great fire of 1834*

ST. JAMES'S PARK

www.royalparks.org.uk

St. James's Park is the most attractive of all London's green spaces. From the footbridge that crosses the lake at its heart there are uninterrupted views westwards to the facade of Buckingham Palace, while to the east is the rear of Sir George Gilbert Scott's classical government offices, and the turrets and onion domes of the National Liberal Club.

Three palaces surround the park: The oldest, Westminster, is now the Houses of Parliament (▷ 179–180); St. James's Palace, across The Mall, remains the official court; and since 1837 the monarch has lived at the third, Buckingham Palace (▷ 176–177), at the southern end. Clarence House, on the park's northwestern edge, was the home of Queen Elizabeth, the Queen Mother, and is now the home of Prince Charles (Aug–end Sep daily 10–5.30 by timed tour, must be pre-booked, tel 020 7766 7303). Admiralty Arch, at the northern tip of the park, marks the other end of The Mall.

The park's central feature is the pleasant lake, created by John Nash from the canal originally excavated from the marshy land for Charles II. Charles was responsible for introducing the geese, pelicans and waterfowl whose descendants still live here. Duck Island is their sanctuary, maintained as a wildlife reserve; for information on guided tours of the island contact the park office.

On the west side of the island are the park's resident pelicans, a gift to Charles II from a Russian ambassador. It's since become something of a tradition for ambassadors to offer a pelican to the park. You can watch the pelicans being fed every day at 3pm near Duck Island Cottage.

Inn The Park is a restaurant with a landscaped roof with a seating area and a timbered promenade.

173 H6 5am–midnight Free St. James's Park, Green Park 11, 12, 53, 88, 211 Park Office, The Store Yard, Horse Guards Approach, St. James's Park

INTRODUCTION

The National Gallery was born in 1824, when the government decided that London needed a national art collection to compete with such European galleries as the Uffizi in Florence and the Louvre in Paris. The Pall Mall house of John Julius Angerstein was for sale at the time, along with his collection of 38 paintings, including works by Raphael and Rembrandt. The government paid £57,000 for the house and pictures, and used the house as the first gallery, until the present building was completed in 1838. The spot, at the crossroads of the city, could be easily reached by the rich in the west and the poor in the east. William Wilkins' neoclassical design attracted much criticism, but plans to replace it altogether were shelved. A new wing built in 1876 added seven new exhibition rooms at the east end, including the impressive dome.

In 1907 barracks behind the Gallery were cleared and work began on five new galleries. Between 1928 and 1933 the National Gallery commissioned Boris Anrep to lay three mosaics in the vestibule of the main hall to illustrate the Labours of Life and the Pleasures of Life; another, laid in 1952, depicts Modern Virtues. The northern extension opened in 1975, and the Sainsbury Wing, funded by Lord Sainsbury, was opened in 1991.

The collection is clearly arranged by period in four wings on the main floor, with other works in the collection shown in the lower floor galleries A to G (lower gallery A is always open on Wednesday afternoons). All the paintings in the collection are on display, except those on loan and those being reframed or repaired, and it would take several long visits to see them all.

Tate Modern (▷ 80–81) tells the story of art from the 20th century—and is a good place to visit after exploring the preceding centuries here.

WHAT TO SEE

THE SAINSBURY WING

The Wilton Diptych

The grey stone arches and plain walls of the Sainsbury Wing are a perfect backdrop for the vivid gold and blue lapis lazuli of this medieval painting on two hinged panels, created in about 1395–99. On one panel Richard II is shown dedicating his kingdom to the Virgin Mary and kneeling to receive her blessing, accompanied by St. John the Baptist, King Edmund and Edward the Confessor. On the other panel we see Mary and the Christ Child surrounded by the heavenly host. The work glitters with gold leaf, all finely punched; Christ's halo, for instance, is decorated with a design of thorns, foreshadowing the crown of thorns that he will eventually wear.

Jan van Eyck (*c*1389–1441), *Arnolfini Portrait*

One of the secular works in the Sainsbury Wing's collection is the famous *Arnolfini Portrait* by Van Eyck, sometimes misleadingly called *The Arnolfini Wedding*. His depiction of an affluent Italian merchant and his wife in the Netherlands was painted in the mid-15th century and shows the couple surrounded by the ordinary furnishings of domestic life: the bed, a few oranges on a side table, discarded wooden sandals and a little dog. Every texture, including the velvets, silks and furs of their clothes, is immaculately conveyed, and a circular mirror at the back of the room repeats it all in tiny, convex reflection, above which the artist has declared 'Jan van Eyck was here, 1434'.

Sandro Botticelli (*c*1445–1510), *Venus and Mars*

Created in Florence in 1485, Botticelli's beautifully composed image of the gods of love and war shows them lying on the grass, Mars clearly exhausted

INFORMATION

www.nationalgallery.org.uk

173 J5 Trafalgar Square WC2N 5DN 020 7747 2885 Daily 10–6, Fri 10–9. Temporary exhibitions may have extended opening hours Free; donations box provided Charing Cross, Leicester Square 6, 9, 11, 12, 13, 24, 176, 453 Free guided tours daily 11.30am and 2.30pm. Tours leave from the Sainsbury Wing Information Desk. Free family talks Sat 11.30am and 2.30pm. Free Family Sundays every week with themed activities, tours and trails. Check meeting place on arrival. Audio-guides with themed tours, each looking at about 20 paintings. Portable CD-ROM audio-guide with information on more than 1,000 paintings (a label next to a picture displays a number that calls up the appropriate commentary). Highlights tour in six languages: English, French, German, Spanish, Italian, Japanese. Security or deposit requested. Payment by voluntary contribution Guides from £4.95, in several languages The National Dining Room that provides classic dishes and English comfort food is on the Sainsbury Wing's first floor, with spectacular views over Trafalgar Square and Nelson's Column. Open daily 10–5 (Wed until 8pm). Reservations: 020 7747 2525. The National Café has its own entrance on St. Martin's Lane and boasts a modern European menu. Also snacks and quick meals. Open Mon–Fri 8am–11pm, Sat 10am–11pm, Sun 10–6. Reservations dinner only: 0207 7747 2525 The Espresso Bar is on Level 0 directly below the Central Hall. Open daily 10–5 (Fri until 8.45) Central shop selling National Gallery publications, art books, gifts, cards and CDs is on Level 2 by the main entrance. On Level 0, reached by the Sir Paul Getty entrance, the latest shop sells art magazines, guidebooks, gifts and cards. On Level 0 of the Sainsbury Wing is the gallery's largest shop, selling books, jewellery, gifts, postcards and posters

Opposite *The refurbished Victorian North Wing*

by love and Venus ready for more. Between them three child-satyrs, one wearing Mars's helmet, try in vain to wake Venus's lover. The satyrs have stolen Mars's lance—a joke to show that he is now disarmed. The crisp colours and Venus's contemporary dress give this scene from classical mythology an irresistible freshness, and the gentle humour of the theme suggests that it might well have been painted as a gift for a newly married couple. The wasps (*vespe* in Italian) may be a pun on Vespucci, the name of a family who sometimes commissioned Botticelli, or they may be a reference to the stings of love.

THE WEST WING

Hieronymus Bosch (c1450–1516), ***Christ Mocked***

The only work by the great Belgian painter in the gallery, it shows an ethereal and calm-looking Christ being crowned with thorns by four grotesque figures. The artist employs various techniques to increase the emotional intensity and the contrast between Christ and his tormentors. Note the spiked dog collar worn by the figure top right (centuries before punk) and the, to us, incongruous combination of the crescent moon of Islam and the Star of David on the headdress of the man pictured bottom left.

Hans Holbein (1497–1543), ***The Ambassadors***

Painted in 1533, this enormous panel shows full-length portraits of two Frenchmen, Jean de Dinteville, ambassador to England, and Georges de Selve, bishop of Lavaur. The two men lean on each side of a table cluttered with objects, each one symbolizing their life and interests—a globe, a compass, a musical score, a book. There's a more profound theme, however, than worldly interests. The transience of life and its occupations are represented by a lute with a broken string and, strangest of all, a distorted shape between the men's feet, which turns out to be a skull. In the top left corner, a barely visible crucifix symbolizes eternal life beyond death.

Above *The National Gallery seen from Trafalgar Square; the columns of the central portico come from Carlton House, the Prince Regent's house, which was demolished in 1825*

THE NORTH WING

Rembrandt van Rijn (1606–69), *Belshazzar's Feast*

One of the Dutch master's more dramatic creations, this painting was commissioned by a wealthy Jewish patron. It depicts the biblical scene from Daniel Chapter 5, where Belshazzar, king of Babylon, throws a lavish feast for his nobles, during which he blasphemously uses the sacred goblets his father Nebuchadnezzar had looted from Jerusalem Temple. Using his trademark technique of drawing attention to the important features of the canvas by illuminating them in stark contrast to the dark background, Rembrandt shows the moment when the hand of God appears and phrophesies the king's imminent death with the inscription on the wall. This, incidentally, is the origin of the phrase 'the writing is on the wall'.

Pieter de Hooch (1629–84), *The Courtyard of a House in Delft*

This domestic scene dating from 1658 is a masterpiece of composition and light, showing a woman and child in a brick courtyard, a passage along the side of a burgher's house and another woman looking out towards the canal and the neighbour's house. The contrasts of light and colour in the red and yellow

TIP

›› Visit on a Friday if your schedule is tight. There's an extra tour at 6.30pm and late opening to 9pm.

›› Paintings are moved around so check at the desk or call first to find your favourite.

Below *Vincent van Gogh's* Sunflowers *(1888) was one of many pictures of the same subject painted to decorate his yellow house in Provence*

GALLERY GUIDE
SAINSBURY WING
Basement: Special exhibitions
Lower ground floor: Sainsbury Wing Theatre
Ground floor: Entrance, shop, information
First floor: Micro Gallery, restaurant
Second (main) floor, Rooms 51–66: Early Renaissance work, 1250–1500, including Van Eyck, Masaccio, Duccio, Piero della Francesca, Botticelli, Leonardo da Vinci, Raphael

NORTH WING
Rooms 14–32: Paintings 1600–1700, focusing on Dutch work and including Rubens, Van Dyck, Rembrandt, Vermeer, and Caravaggio

WEST WING
Rooms 2, 4–12: Paintings 1500–1600, including Titian, Cranach, Michelangelo, Bronzino

EAST WING
Rooms 33–46: Paintings 1700–1900, including the Impressionists, Gainsborough, Constable and Van Gogh

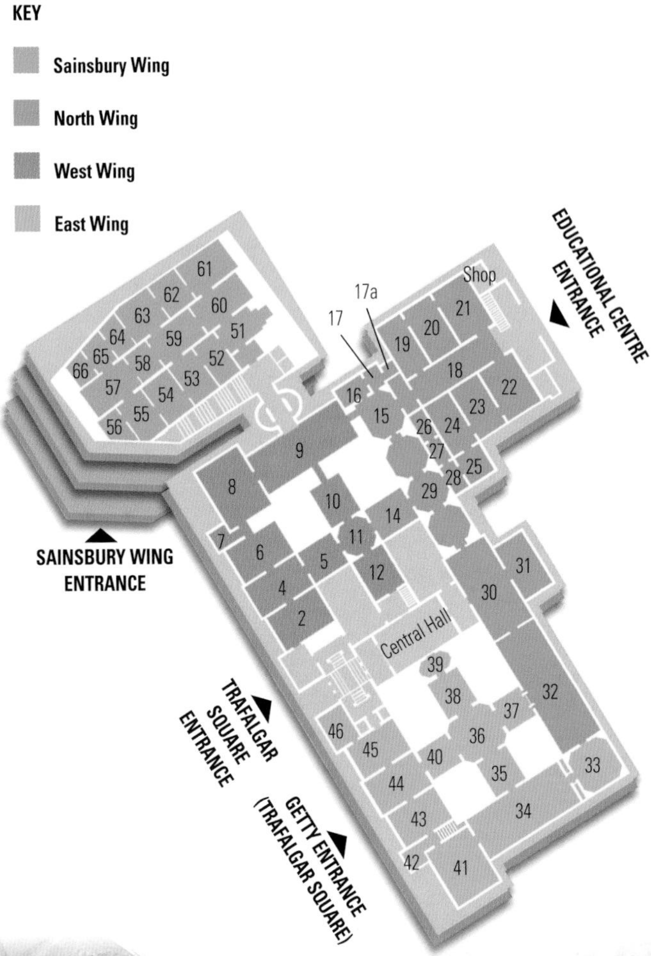

Below The Beach at Trouville *by Claude Monet (1870). The grains of sand visible in the thick oil paint suggest that the work was at least partly executed on the beach*

brick, the tiled passage floor and the daylight beyond are a perfect illustration of a Dutch master's work at its best. A stone plaque is set over the arched entrance to the passage; its inscription, which starts 'This is in St. Jerome's vale', is a clue to the real tablet, which originally hung over the entrance to the Hieronymusdale cloister in Delft, Holland.

THE EAST WING

Joseph Wright of Derby (1734–97), *An Experiment on a Bird in the Air Pump*

Joseph Wright was a painter of the new industrial age, using dramatic lighting techniques inspired by artists such as Caravaggio to show blacksmiths at work, cotton mills and furnaces and, as in this work, scientists. The gruesome experiment taking place by candlelight involves placing a bird in a vacuum; everyone in the small group gathered to watch reacts in a different way—including a couple (representing Mary Barlow and Thomas Coltman, friends of Wright) who are interested only in each other.

J. M. W. Turner (1775–1851), *The Fighting Temeraire*

In his depiction of the old warship (which saw action at the Battle of Trafalgar in 1805) being towed to a ship-breaking yard in 1838, Turner makes the most of his innovative treatment of light and colour, which foreshadowed the new optical techniques of the Impressionists. Pale and spectral, the old ship—redundant in the age of steam—sails to its end against a blazing sunset, reflected in the shimmering surface of the water.

Vincent van Gogh (1853–90), Room 45

A fine collection of paintings by Vincent Van Gogh includes such works as *Sunflowers* (1888), in rich shades of gold and yellow, and *Chair* (1888), a still life that illustrated his belief in the direct relationship of art to nature and daily life. *A Wheatfield, with Cypresses,* painted in 1889, when Van Gogh was in the St. Rémy mental asylum, conveys the movement of clouds and wind with bold, swirling brush strokes. Seen together, Van Gogh's paintings are a perfect illustration of the bright colours and apparently spontaneous strokes that revolutionized art in the late 19th century.

ART THROUGH THE AGES

The gallery's chronological display reveals how artists' methods and materials developed over the centuries. Most of the earliest works—in the Sainsbury Wing—are painted on wood, using either tempera (pigments in egg yolk) or slow-drying oils applied to a chalk or gesso background. Some also use gold leaf, which was beaten from coins into wafer-thin sheets. By 1510, when the West Wing's collection starts, oils were the main medium, painted onto sailcloth, or canvas, which could be rolled up and shipped off to international patrons. In the 17th century, subjects tended to be secular and domestic, and painters such as Caravaggio perfected techniques of realistic light and shadow. New synthetic paints had a huge influence on art after 1800, and the fact that they were stored in flexible metal tubes and sold via merchants (rather than made up by the artists themselves) made it possible to leave the workshop and work alone, virtually anywhere that inspiration struck.

Above *The Central Hall was designed in the 1880s by Sir John Taylor, a distinguished architect of royal palaces*

INFORMATION

www.npg.org.uk
173 J5 St. Martin's Place WC2H 0HE 020 7312 2463 Sat–Wed 10–6, Thu–Fri 10–9 Free. Charge for some special exhibitions Leicester Square, Charing Cross 24, 29, 176 National Portrait Gallery Sound Guides £2 Visitor's Guide £5 The Portrait Restaurant on the top floor (▷ 201); tea from 3pm The Portrait Café in the basement Art-themed books, posters, cards, jewellery, frames, stationery, book shop (basement), selling titles on British history, art, portraiture, photography, costume, literature and biography. Exhibition shop outside Wolfson Gallery

Above *The Statesmen's Gallery contains portraits and busts of eminent Victorians*

INTRODUCTION

The National Portrait Gallery was founded in 1856 by the 5th Earl Stanhope, historian, politician and trustee of the British Museum, to collect the likenesses of famous British men and women. After 40 years of being moved around London to a succession of unsuitable homes it was finally given a permanent new gallery on St. Martin's Place. After several appeals for permission to increase the gallery space it was agreed in 1928 that a new wing could be built along Orange Street, and in the 1990s there was further expansion into the old Royal Dental School (now home to the Heinz Archive and the reference library).

In 2000 the Queen opened the Ondaatje Wing, named after benefactor Christopher Ondaatje.

The gallery entrance is a surprisingly modest doorway tucked away at the back of the National Gallery (▷ 182–187). Exhibits are arranged chronologically, but a little confusingly, over three floors, with the selection beginning on the second floor and ending on the ground floor.

To reach the start of the collection, take the escalator up from the main hall to the Tudor Galleries, the 17th century and work from the 18th century, which follows themes such as the Kit-Cat Club, the arts, and science and industry. The Victorians, their art and their achievements occupy most of the first-floor rooms, including daguerreotypes (early photographs). Rooms 30–33 cover the period from World War I to 1990 and include a collection of portraits of the royal family. The Balcony Gallery, also on the first floor, covers 1960–90 with photographs, busts and figurines, and back on the ground floor, Britain since 1990 is represented in a constantly changing exhibition of contemporary portraits, with new acquisitions also displayed here.

WHAT TO SEE

SECOND FLOOR

The Tudor Galleries

A magnificent series of royal, aristocratic and family portraits makes this whole, compact section of the gallery a must-see. Among the most stunning works is the dazzling Ditchley Portrait of Elizabeth I by Marcus Gheeraerts the Younger (1592), a tour de force of political propaganda. Gheeraerts shows the Queen triumphantly standing on a map of Britain with storm clouds behind her to the right, intended to represent the defeated Spanish Armada, and bright skies to the left, signalling a glorious future under the Virgin Queen's reign. Look out too for the huge ink-and-watercolour cartoon of Henry VIII by Hans Holbein—a preparatory work for the mural showing Henry, his parents and his third wife, Jane Seymour, which hung in Whitehall Palace until its destruction by fire in 1698; Rowland Lockey's group portrait of Sir Thomas More and his household and five generations of descendants; the full-length portrait of Catherine Parr by Master John; and a fiery-cheeked Sir Francis Drake, by an unknown artist.

George Villiers, Duke of Buckingham (Jacobean Court)
William Larkin's sumptuous full-length portrait of James I's handsome favourite was painted in 1616, when its subject was 24 years old. Villiers is almost upstaged by the lush red velvet of his cape and the bronze folds of silk drapery above him. These curtains were, in fact, green until 1985, when experts found traces of the original paint and removed the top layer to reveal the artist's rich shades, now displayed as he had intended.

FIRST FLOOR

The Brontë Sisters (Victorian Rooms)
Branwell Brontë (1817–48) painted this portrait of his sisters Anne (1820–49), Emily (1818–48) and Charlotte (1816–55) in about 1834. Growing up in a remote North Yorkshire parsonage, the siblings shared a vivid imaginary world, and the three young women went on to produce passionate and dark novels including *The Tenant of Wildfell Hall* (Anne), *Wuthering Heights* (Emily) and *Jane Eyre* (Charlotte). Branwell failed in his attempts to make his name as a writer and as an artist, and succumbed to drink and opium. A poignant outline, clearly seen between Emily and Charlotte, shows where he has painted out the self-portrait that originally completed the group. Technically the painting may not be impressive but the image of three remarkable 19th-century novelists is fascinating.

Zandra Rhodes (Balcony Gallery)
Andrew Logan's sculpture of the larger-than-life fashion designer is one of several late 20th- and early 21st-century pieces in the National Portrait Gallery using unconventional materials and forms to bring out the personalities of their subjects. Logan has opted for resin and bright, theatrical colours to express Rhodes' extrovert character and flamboyant style. It makes a striking contrast to the gallery's earlier sculptures, mainly in marble or bronze, as well as to contemporary works such as the cool ceramic figure of Coco Chanel.

Left *Historian and politician Thomas Macaulay (1800–59) is commemorated on the facade of the building*

TIP

» Rent the CD guide in the ground floor entrance hall to hear contemporary sitters talking about their portraits.

GALLERY GUIDE

GROUND FLOOR

Rooms 34–41: Britain since 1990; new acquisitions

FIRST FLOOR

Rooms 21–29: The Victorians. Introduction: Queen Victoria, Statesmen's Gallery, Expansion and Empire, Early Victorian Arts, Portraits and Politics, Portraits by G. F. Watts, Late Victorian Arts, Turn of the Century

Room 30: We Are Making A New World: Britain 1914–18
Room 31: A National Portrait: Britain 1919–1959 and Britain and the World 1939–59.
Room 32 (Balcony Gallery): Late 20th-century portraits
Room 33: Diana, Princess of Wales

SECOND FLOOR

Rooms 1–3: Tudor Galleries. The Early Tudors, The Elizabethan Age, Miniatures Gallery
Rooms 4–8: 17th century. The Jacobean Court, Charles I and the Civil War, Science and the Arts in the 17th century, Charles II: the Restoration of the Monarchy, The Later Stuarts
Rooms 9–14: 18th century. The Kit-Cat Club, The Arts in the Early 18th Century, Britain in the Early 18th Century, The Arts in the Later 18th Century, Science and Industry in the 18th Century, Britain becomes a World Power, Landing, William Hazlitt's Spirit of the Age
Rooms 17–20: The Regency Weldon Galleries. Royal Celebrity and Scandal; Art, Invention and Thought: The Romantics; Art, Invention and Thought: Making the Modern World; The Road to Reform

Above *Looking across Trafalgar Square to the graceful spire of St. Martin-in-the-Fields*

ST. MARTIN-IN-THE-FIELDS

www.stmartin-in-the-fields.org

Steps lead up to the magnificent Corinthian portico of the church of St. Martin-in-the-Fields, at the northeastern corner of Trafalgar Square. Many considered this lovely church to be the square's finest building. Scottish architect James Gibbs (1682–1754) designed it in the 1720s, and the lavish interior is decorated with ornate Italian plasterwork. Officially the parish church of Buckingham Palace, St. Martin's has strong royal connections—George I was a warden here, and there's a royal box to the left of the high altar. For some 40 years there has been a Chinese congregation at the church with regular Sunday services.

The St. Martin-in-the Fields £36 million building project has almost reached its conclusion, with only the exterior of the church to be finished. Inside the church restoration is magnificent, the perfect setting for a lunchtime or evening concert. The Café in the Crypt offers an escape from the hustle of London's streets.

173 J5 Trafalgar Square WC2N 4JJ 020 7523 6644 Mon–Sat 8–6.30, Sun 8–7.30; brass-rubbing Mon–Wed 10–7, Thu–Sat 10–9, Sun 11.30–6 Free; brass-rubbing from £4.50 Charing Cross, Leicester Square 9, 11, 12, 13, 15, 24, 453

SPENCER HOUSE

www.spencerhouse.co.uk

Built in the mid-18th century for Earl Spencer (an ancestor of the late Diana, Princess of Wales), Spencer House is London's finest surviving Palladian mansion.

To see the interior you must take a guided tour, which leads into eight state rooms restored to their original style by the current owners, the Rothschilds. Company executives occupy the rest of the building.

Interior decor is lavish, to say the least, from the ornate green and gold ceiling in the Great Room to the classical murals in the Painted Room. A highlight is the Palm Room, where gilded columns and painted fronds stretch out like palm trees.

During spring and summer the magnificent 18th-century gardens are also open occasionally.

172 H5 27 St. James's Place SW1A 1NR 020 7514 1958 By guided tour only: Sun 10.30–5.45 (last tour 4.45); closed Jan, Aug. Times vary, so phone ahead Adult £9, child (10–16) £7. No admission to under 10s Green Park 9, 14, 19, 22, 38

TATE BRITAIN

▷ 192–193.

TRAFALGAR SQUARE

www.london.gov.uk/trafalgarsquare

One of the world's most famous squares sits at the northern end of Whitehall (▷ 191), where it was laid out to John Nash's design between 1829 and 1841, as a commemoration of Admiral Lord Nelson's victory against the French at the 1805 Battle of Trafalgar.

Feeding the pigeons in Trafalgar Square, once a must for any visitor to London, is now forbidden (▷ 24).

Nelson towers on his 56m (185ft) column at the centre of the square. The statue itself, though 5m (17ft) high, can be seen only from strategic viewpoints such as the National Portrait Gallery's top floor restaurant (▷ 201), but the four huge bronze lions that guard him, sculpted in the 1860s by Sir Edwin Landseer, are clearly on view, as well as the reliefs around the base of the column, showing Nelson's naval victories. A 17th-century equestrian monument commemorating Charles I, by Hubert Le Sueur (1633), stands on a traffic island.

At the square's corners are four great plinths. Three support more statuary: George IV, again on horseback, by Chantrey and T. Earle

(1834), originally meant for Marble Arch; Sir Henry Havelock, by William Behnes (1861), and Sir Charles Napier, by G. G. Adams (1855)—both celebrating military heroes of their time. The fourth is now devoted to hosting modern sculpture, which will periodically change. Marc Quinn's striking white marble sculpture of disabled artist Alison Lapper—naked and pregnant—was the first.

The famous fountains, decorated with sculptings of mermaids and men, sharks and dolphins, were installed in the 19th century and embellished by Sir Edwin Lutyens in 1939.

Leaping into the water during New Year celebrations is another tradition that has now been ruled out on grounds of safety. However, the water still plays in the fountains from 10am daily.

173 J5 Open access Free Charing Cross, Leicester Square 3, 9, 11, 12, 24, 88, 176, 453

WELLINGTON ARCH

www.english-heritage.org.uk

England's answer to the Arc de Triomphe in Paris is a neoclassical arch erected in 1826 to celebrate the Duke of Wellington's victories in the Napoleonic Wars. A huge equestrian statue of the Duke was added 20 years later.

At one time the rooms inside the arch housed a police station; now there's a permanent exhibition on the statues and memorials of London, and you can enjoy the views from the platform beneath the sculpture.

172 G6 Hyde Park Corner W1J 7JZ 020 7930 2726 Apr–end Sep Wed–Sun 10–5; Nov–end Mar Wed–Sun 10–4 Adult £3.50, child (5–16) £1.80, under 5s free Hyde Park Corner 2, 8, 9, 10, 14, 16, 19

WESTMINSTER ABBEY

▷ 194–195.

WESTMINSTER CATHEDRAL

www.westminstercathedral.org.uk

Britain's premier Roman Catholic church is a striking Westminster landmark with its 83m (273ft) bell tower and striped patterning of red brick and white stone. Designed in Byzantine style by Victorian architect John Francis Bentley (1839–1902), it echoes the Basilica of St. Mark in Venice. Bentley's brief was that the church should have an extra wide nave to accommodate large congregations, and that it should bear no resemblance to the nearby Protestant Westminster Abbey. You can take a lift to the top of the bell tower for views of Big Ben, Buckingham Palace and Nelson's Column.

172 H7 Victoria Street SW1P 1QW 020 7798 9055 Mon–Fri 7–7, Sat 8–7, Sun 8–7.45; campanile Apr–end Nov daily 9.30–5; Dec–end Mar Thu–Sun 9.30–5 Free; lift to campanile adult £2, under 18s £1, family £5 Victoria 11, 24, 148, 211, 507

WHITEHALL

Whitehall is the broad avenue connecting Trafalgar Square (▷ 190) with Parliament Square—and the heart of the British government—to the south. Heading south, the first building on the right is the Admiralty.

Next is Horse Guards, where two members of the Household Cavalry mount guard on horseback between 10 and 4—a tradition that persists although all that remains of the former royal palace is the Banqueting House (▷ 175), opposite. The soldiers keep to their stations without moving or making eye contact with passers-by.

Beyond Horse Guards is the gated entrance to Downing Street. This has been the official residence of the Prime Minister (No. 10) since 1731. No. 11 is the official home of the Chancellor of the Exchequer.

Farther along is the poignant Portland-stone Cenotaph, designed by Sir Edwin Lutyens and unveiled in 1920 to commemorate the victims of World War I. This provides the focus of the Remembrance Day celebrations held annually since 1918 on the Sunday nearest 11 November.

173 J5 Open access Free Charing Cross, Westminster 11, 12, 24, 53, 88, 159, 453

Left *Nelson on his column stands high above bustling Trafalgar Square*

Below *Westminster Cathedral was founded by Cardinal Vaughan in 1895*

INFORMATION

www.tate.org.uk
173 J7 Millbank SW1P 4RG
020 7887 8888, 020 7887 8008 (recorded information) Daily 10–5.50
Free but donations welcome; charge for special exhibitions Pimlico, Vauxhall, Westminster 2, 3, C10, 36, 87, 88, 185 Mon–Fri 11, 12, 1.15, 2, 3, Sat–Sun 12, 3, free. Tate Audioguider highlights (free), in English, French, German Catalogues to specific collections available in the shop for £20–£30 Rex Whistler Restaurant Excellent selection of art books, plus related souvenirs

Above *John Constable's* Flatford Mill *(1817)*

INTRODUCTION

The story of the Tate begins with Henry Tate (1819–99), the sugar millionaire, who was determined that London should have a showcase for British art. He offered his own collection of Victorian paintings to get it going (including Millais's *Ophelia*), together with funds for a gallery. Finally, the government took up his idea and Sidney Smith's building was constructed between 1812 and 1821 on the north bank of the Thames, a short way south of the Houses of Parliament. The grim Millbank Penitentiary prison once occupied the site; across the Embankment, steps lead down to the Thames, where convicts condemned to transportation boarded ships bound for Australia. The prison was closed and demolished in the 1890s.

Piecemeal additions and donations followed, including the central cupola and sculpture galleries given by art dealer Joseph Duveen and his son, Lord Duveen, in 1937, and the restaurant, with its landscape murals (*The Pursuit of Rare Meats*, 1920s) by Rex Whistler, in 1983. A northwestern extension was built in the 1970s, and in 1987 the Clore Galleries, designed by Sir James Stirling, were opened.

Since the transfer of its international collection to Tate Modern (▷ 80–81) in 2000, the Tate's British collection has been able to spread out in its Millbank premises. Despite this, the gallery still owns far more than it can display at once, and the pictures on show are changed regularly every year. Generally, the art is displayed chronologically, with rooms devoted to specific artists or themes, but because of the annual rehangs it's impossible to say with any certainty what can be seen where.

There are three entrances to the gallery. The Manton Entrance, on Atterbury Street (left of the main steps), leads to special exhibitions on Level One. The Clore Gallery Entrance leads through the sculpture garden (right) and up to rooms 35–45 on Levels Two and Three (the Clore Galleries), devoted to works by J. M. W. Turner (1775–1851) and his contemporaries. The Millbank Entrance provides the main access, up the riverside steps, taking you into the main part of the collection, on Level Two.

Rooms are set out chronologically, starting with 16th-century works in Room 1 at the top of the Manton Staircase.

WHAT TO SEE

LEVEL TWO

The Cholmondeley Ladies (Room 2)

This intriguing and touching portrait painted by an unknown artist some time between 1600 and 1610 shows two straight-backed young women sitting up in bed side by side, dressed in intricate white dresses with large collars and headdresses, each holding a baby wrapped in rich red christening robes. At first glance mothers and children seem exactly alike, but you could spend hours exploring the subtle differences: in eye colour, jewellery and even in the minute detail of the lace edging on their clothes.

The Great Day of His Wrath by John Martin (Room 9)

Swirling black clouds and fiery red light are used in one of a triptych of 'judgement pictures' painted in 1851–53 by John Martin (1789–1854), inspired by the Book of Revelation in the New Testament. Martin developed Turner's ideas about the power of nature to the full, using dramatic scenes like this to convey the weakness of humanity. Here he gives a faithful depiction of the Bible's account of the Last Judgement: 'there was a great earthquake and the sun became black as sackcloth of hair and the moon became as blood. And the heaven departed as a scroll…and every mountain and island were moved out of their places.'

Recumbent Figure by Henry Moore (Room 1)

This powerful, abstract figure of a woman lying on her side was sculpted by Moore (1898–1986) from Hornton stone in 1938. The stone, which is formed in shallow beds, had to be laminated together in three pieces to make the block. It was commissioned by architect Serge Chermayeff and kept on his garden terrace in the Sussex Downs, creating a link between the rolling countryside and his modern house. Moore and his contemporaries were particularly keen on using local materials and making their work a part of the landscape, in the way of prehistoric figures and monuments.

The Golden Stairs by Sir Edward Coley Burne-Jones (Room 15)

Burne-Jones (1833–98) produced this beautifully composed scene of 18 women in white descending a staircase in 1880. The theme of the painting is something of a mystery, as were many of his works, whose medieval and mythical escapism was particularly popular in the late Victorian industrial age. The late 19th century, with its dizzying technological progress and industrialization, produced a reaction in artists such as Burne-Jones and the Pre-Raphaelite Brotherhood (formed in 1848), who romanticized the Middle Ages as a time when objects and pictures were individually produced by craftsmen and imbued with the value of their involvement and labour.

TIPS

» Pick up a gallery plan from the information desks to see what's on show where.

» To be sure of seeing a particular work, check with the gallery that it is on display.

» Late at Tate is held each Friday at 8pm, with free exhibitions, talks, music and films.

GALLERY GUIDE

LEVEL ONE

Sculpture Garden
Special exhibitions

LEVEL TWO

Rooms 1–17: British art from 1500 to 1900, covering Tudor and Stuart portraiture, works by William Hogarth, George Stubbs, John Constable and William Blake, plus Victorian paintings

Rooms 18–28: British art from 1900 to the present day, including bronze casting, sculpture and works by Henry Moore, Francis Bacon, Tracey Emin and John Piper, plus new exhibits

CLORE GALLERIES

LEVELS TWO AND THREE

Rooms T1–T10: Works by J. M. W. Turner

Below *New and refurbished galleries lie behind the Victorian facade*

INFORMATION

www.westminster-abbey.org 173 J6 Parliament Square SW1P 3PA 020 7222 5152 Mon–Sat 9.30–3.30. Sun worship only. Chapter House, Pyx Chamber, accessible only on a viewing platform. Abbey museum, Mon–Sat 10.30–4. Cloisters daily 8–6 subject to availability, closed during special events. College garden Apr–end Sep Tue–Thu 10–6; Oct–end Mar Tue–Thu 10–4. Free lunchtime band concerts Jul–end Aug Wed 12.30–2pm Adult £15, child (11–16) £6, under 11s (max of 2 children per paying adult) free, family £30–£42. Services free. Museum £1 (free with abbey church ticket). Cloisters, college garden free, donations welcome for upkeep of garden St. James's Park, Westminster 11, 12, 24, 159, 211 90-min tours, £3 per person. For bookings and further details 020 7654 4758. Audio-guides free with entry ticket at North Door £3, in English, French, German, Spanish, Italian, Russian, Japanese Stall in north cloister and outside west towers; hot and cold drinks, light snacks, sandwiches Outside west door exit; souvenirs, postcards, gifts, history, religious books

Above *The main entrance is through the great triple doors on the north front*

INTRODUCTION

Benedictine monks occupied this marshy site on the bank of the Thames from the middle of the 10th century, but it was Edward the Confessor who began the present building—the Collegiate Church of St. Peter in Westminster—as a new church for the abbey in 1050. Having died a week after its consecration, on 6 January 1066, he was the first monarch to be buried here. Almost a year later, William the Conqueror was crowned here, confirming the royal status of the church, which has seen the coronation of every subsequent English monarch with the exception of Edward V and Edward VIII.

Edward the Confessor was later canonized, and Henry III embarked on large-scale rebuilding in 1245 to make a shrine fit for the veneration of the sainted king. Today's church, greatly influenced by the French Gothic cathedrals of Amiens and Reims, was the result. In 1503 the Lady Chapel at the east end was rebuilt by Henry VII, who added his name to the chapel, making it into the architectural high point of the church. The west front was not completed until 1745, when the two towers were built to Nicholas Hawksmoor's design.

The abbey forms the south side of Parliament Square. You enter by the north transept, through one of three great doorways beneath the large rose window, whose pattern is repeated in the floor tiles of the chapter house. Inside, turn left to take a one-way, clockwise tour of the church and cloisters, passing a succession of chapels with a bewildering throng of tombs and monuments, before leaving by the west door.

WHAT TO SEE

STATESMEN'S AISLE

The north transept by which you enter the abbey became known as Statesmen's Aisle after the burial of prime minister William Pitt the Elder in 1778. He is actually one of the few famous personages commemorated here whose mortal remains actually lie within their tombs. Other major political figures whose graves or memorials are to be found here include William Gladstone, Lord Palmerston, Benjamin Disraeli and Sir Robert Peel, founder of the police force. Some of the best funerary artwork is actually on display within the three side chapels off Statesmen's Aisle. Most striking of all is the monument in St. Michael's Chapel, sculpted by Rubiliac in honour of Lady Elizabeth Nightingale, who died in childbirth. It shows her husband trying to ward off the skeletal figure of Death, who is rising from below to claim her.

HENRY VIII'S LADY CHAPEL

North of the sanctuary is the Lady Chapel, where you can view the white-marble effigy of Elizabeth I (died 1603), who shares a tomb with her half-sister, Mary I (died 1558). From the aisle you enter the main part of the chapel, with its exquisite fan-vaulted ceiling. It makes an impressive setting for the royal tombs arranged around the altar and aisles. Among the finest of these is the tomb of Henry VII, in front of the altar, and of his mother, Lady Margaret Beaufort, near the south aisle altar. They died in the same year (1509), and their tombs are the work of the Florentine sculptor Pietro Torrigiano (1472–1522), who, as a boy, was often involved in fights with Michelangelo. Note the carvings on the stall misericords (1512): Subjects include mermaids, monsters and a wife beating her husband.

POETS' CORNER

The south transept, also known as Poets' Corner, is where, since the 16th century, great poets, authors, artists and actors have been honoured with memorials. Here are the remains of poet Geoffrey Chaucer (*c*1345–1400), who lived in the abbey precincts while a royal clerk of the works (or buildings inspector). William Shakespeare's monument is here too, though his statue and assumed likeness date from 1740, over a century after his death.

Among the best monuments are the busts of 17th-century poets John Dryden, Ben Jonson and John Milton, and poet and artist William Blake (1757–1827)—the last sculpted in bronze by Sir Jacob Epstein in 1957.

THE QUIRE AND SANCTUARY

This is the ceremonial heart of the church, where services and royal coronations take place. The high altar is a relatively late addition, designed by Sir Gilbert Scott in 1867. The nearby mosaic of the Last Supper was created by Antonio Salviati. Standing to the sides of the altar are four large statues of Moses, King David, St. Peter and St. Paul, while in front of the high altar is the Cosmati Pavement, a mosaic made of glass and precious stones such as onyx, porphyry and serpentine. It was laid by Italian craftsmen in 1268.

CHAPTER HOUSE, PYX CHAMBER AND ABBEY MUSEUM

A door in the south quire aisle leads to the cloister, with its flowing tracery and superb views of the flying buttresses supporting the nave. The chapter house is an octagonal building of 1253, whose floor is still covered in its original tiles. The Norman undercroft, which survives from Edward the Confessor's original church (▷ 27), houses the abbey museum, where you can see macabre wax effigies, including those of Queen Elizabeth I, Charles II and Lord Nelson, made using their death masks and real clothes.

The Pyx Chamber, also part of the original abbey, contains the building's oldest altar, dated at around 1240. It's now home to original pyxes (money chests) and the abbey's church plate.

THE NAVE

Here you can enjoy the majestic nave roof, 32m (105ft) high. The complex patterning carries the eye eastwards; only by looking up can you appreciate the enormous length of the building, since at ground level the view is blocked by the 19th-century choir screen, where Sir Isaac Newton and other scientists are remembered. The Tomb of the Unknown Soldier (▷ 38) and St. George's Chapel are near the west door. Just outside the chapel is a portrait of Richard II (r1377–99), the oldest known true portrait of an English monarch.

TIPS

- » Attend a service and hear the choirboys, accompanied by the abbey organ on which composer Henry Purcell (1659–95) once played.
- » Note that the cloisters are free, entered through Dean's Yard.

A ROYAL TOUR

A walk through the original bastion of royal power in England, taking in three royal residences. You'll pass the former house of three prime ministers, skirt Whitehall and walk along Constitution Hill to see its poignant war memorial.

THE WALK
Distance: 2 miles (3km)
Allow: 2 hours minimum
Start at: St. James's Park Underground station
End at: Hyde Park Corner Underground station

HOW TO GET THERE
District or Circle line to St. James's Park; bus 11, 24, 148, 211

★ The huge art deco building above St. James's Park station is the London Underground headquarters.

Start from St. James's Park station by turning immediately left after the ticket barriers and emerging into Petty France. Cross the road and continue ahead down Queen Anne's Gate. Pass through the black gates at the end of the road and cross Birdcage Walk to the entrance to St. James's Park (▷ 181).

❶ In the park, look for noticeboards with a map, history and guide to bird life. James I is said to have housed an 'ellefant' here, plus crocodiles and other beasts, all gifts from foreign princes. The 'ellefant' was given a gallon of wine every day.

Continue straight ahead to reach the lake. Cross the bridge and turn immediately right. At the fork go left and look over to your right to see Big Ben (▷ 37). Walk on to the far northeast corner of the park and exit onto the Mall.

❷ To the right of the Mall, beyond Admiralty Arch, are Trafalgar Square (▷ 190–191) and Whitehall (▷ 191). To the left is Buckingham Palace (▷ 176–177). Royal and parliamentary Britain come together at least once a year when the Queen leaves the palace and passes down the Mall on her way to open Parliament (▷ 296).

Cross the Mall to the Institute of Contemporary Arts (▷ 178). With a day pass you can return later for a drink. Go around to the left of the ICA and up the steps to Waterloo Place.

❸ Statues here commemorate the Duke of York (1763–1827), second son of George III; Florence Nightingale (▷ 73); Edward VII; and Robert Falcon Scott, the British Antarctic explorer who died in 1912 on an expedition to the South Pole. Scott's wife, Lady Kathleen, was the sculptor.

Leave Waterloo Place by the northern side and turn left down Pall Mall and right onto St. James's Square.

❹ As you walk counterclockwise round the square, look for the former home of Nancy Astor (1879–1964), the second woman to be elected to Parliament and the first to take her seat. It's now the In-and-Out Club, one of St. James's private societies. Part of Chatham House was home to three former British prime ministers: William Pitt (1708–78), the Earl of Derby (1799–1869) and William Gladstone (1809–98). The gardens in the square are open Monday to Friday 10 to 4.30.

Continue past the East India Club and turn right into King Street. Here you'll find Christie's auction house (▷ 233). At the end of the street, cross St. James's Street and go down towards St. James's Palace in front of you.

❺ St. James's Palace, former home of Prince Charles, is closed to the public. It was built for Henry VIII in 1532 on the site of a former lepers' hospital, and remained the principal royal residence until Queen Victoria moved to Buckingham Palace.

Take the first right into Little St. James's Street and follow the road round to Bridgewater House. In front of you across the little square is the entrance to Clarence House, home of Prince Charles (▷ 181).

Continue round along the side of St. James's Palace into Marlborough Street, past the guard, to the Queen's Chapel.

❻ The Queen's Chapel was designed by Inigo Jones in 1627 for Charles I's French wife, Henrietta Maria.

Walk past the statue of Queen Alexandra on the left and rejoin the Mall at the bottom of the street. Turn right and continue to Buckingham Palace (▷ 176–177). If the Queen is in residence, the Royal Standard will be flying.

Above *Spring is a lovely time of year to stroll in St. James's Park*
Opposite *The Wellington Arch*

A detour around the far side of the palace takes you to the Guards Museum (▷ 178) and the Queen's Gallery (▷ 181).

Otherwise, bear right and head up Constitution Hill.

❼ At the top of Constitution Hill are the 2002 Memorial Gates, a testament to the 5 million volunteers from the Indian subcontinent, Africa and the Caribbean who died in the two world wars.

Cross over to the Wellington Arch (▷ 191). The walk ends here, by Hyde Park Corner Underground station.

WHERE TO EAT

Stop by the bandstand in St. James's Park. Deckchairs cost £1.50 for 2 hours or £2 for 4 hours Apr–Oct. For further information tel 020 7486 8117. There are refreshment stalls in the parks, and the Institute of Contemporary Arts has a good cafe.

PLACES TO VISIT

QUEEN'S CHAPEL (CHAPEL ROYAL)

✉ Queen's Chapel, Marlborough Road SW1A 1BG ☎ 020 7930 4832 🕐 Visitors are welcome to attend regular services of worship every Sunday, 11.15am Easter Day–end July (Queen's Chapel), early Oct–Good Friday (Chapel Royal)

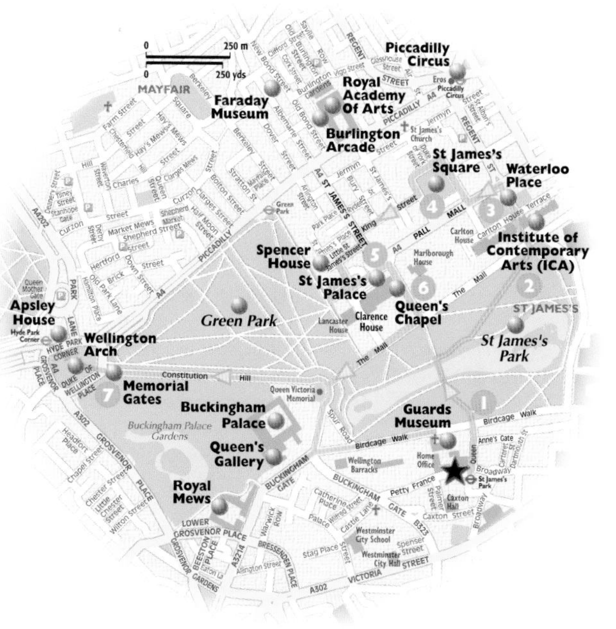

SHOPPING

BERRY BROS & RUDD

www.bbr.com

Holding two royal warrants, this is perhaps the oldest wine merchant in the world, established in 1698. The firm offers 2,500 different types of wine, maintaining perfect climate control in its warehouse in Hampshire. The St. James's Street shop is a beautiful, very old building with sloping floors.

204 H5 3 St. James's Street SW1A 1EG 0800 280 2440 Mon–Fri 10–6, Sat 10–5 Green Park, Piccadilly Circus 9, 14, 19, 22, 38

FLORIS

www.florislondon.com

Established in 1730, Floris is known for its perfumes, toilet waters, bath salts, scented soaps, shaving accessories and aftershave.

204 H5 89 Jermyn Street SW1Y 6JH 020 7930 2885 Mon–Fri 9.30–6, Sat 10–6 Green Park, Piccadilly Circus 9, 14, 19, 22, 38

FORTNUM AND MASON

www.fortnumandmason.co.uk

Founded in 1707 as a grocery, this famous store is wood-panelled and lit with chandeliers. The ground-floor food hall is particularly good. Treat yourself to a snack in the Fountain Restaurant or classic British food in the St. James restaurant. Outside, the clock chimes the hour and Mr. Fortnum and Mr. Mason emerge and bow.

204 H5 181 Piccadilly W1A 1ER 020 7734 8040 Mon–Sat 10–8, Sun (Food Hall Lower Ground Floor and Patio Restaurant only) 12–6 Green Park, Piccadilly Circus 9, 14, 19, 22, 38

HATCHARDS

www.hatchards.co.uk

John Hatchard started his bookshop in 1797 and moved it to the current site in 1801. Hatchards will find you any book in print in Britain. Stocked categories include everything from art and architecture to philosophy and sports.

204 H5 187 Piccadilly W1J 9LE 020 7439 9921 Mon–Sat 9.30–7, Sun 12–6 Piccadilly Circus 9, 14, 19, 22

POILÂNE

www.poilane.com

An English outpost of a truly Parisian boulangerie pâtisserie. Poilâne uses an enormous wood-fired oven to bake 80 loaves of its delicious and famously expensive sourdough bread every two hours. Have a look at the extraordinary bread chandelier, the original of which was made by artist Salvador Dalí.

204 G7 46 Elizabeth Street SW1W 9PA 020 7808 4910 Mon–Fri 7.30–7, Sat 7.30–6 Sloane Square 11, 19, 22, 211, C1

ST. JAMES'S CHURCH PICCADILLY

There is an antiques market on Tuesdays in the church courtyard (▷ 199), and a general market with arts and crafts Wed to Sat.

204 H5 197 Piccadilly W1J 9LL 020 7734 4511 Tue 10–6, Wed–Sat 11–6 Piccadilly Circus 9, 14, 19, 22, 38

TURNBULL & ASSER

www.turnbullandasser.com

The place to buy men's shirts off the peg or bespoke is set among other similar shops. Turnbull & Asser makes Prince Charles's shirts and used to make them for Edward VIII when he was Prince of Wales. Opened in 1885, the shop occupies a fine old building with a wood-panelled interior.

204 H5 71–72 Jermyn Street SW1Y 6PF 020 7808 3000 Mon–Fri 9–6,

Left *The Theatre Royal Haymarket in all its Regency glory*

Sat 9.30–6 Green Park, Piccadilly Circus 9, 14, 19, 22, 38

WATERSTONE'S

www.waterstones.com

This flagship branch of the major chain is Europe's biggest bookshop, with specialist floors focusing on fiction, academic titles, children's books and other subjects.

205 H5 203–206 Piccadilly W1V 1LE 020 7851 2400 Mon–Sat 9–10, Sun 12–6 Piccadilly Circus 9, 14, 19, 22

ENTERTAINMENT AND NIGHTLIFE

APOLLO WEST END

www.apollocinemas.co.uk

See the latest releases from the comfort of luxury reclining armchairs. Five screens offer the best quality in movie presentation.

205 H5 19 Regent Street SW1Y 4LR 0871 220 6000 Piccadilly Circus 8, 10, 12, 13, 23

CURZON MAYFAIR

www.curzoncinemas.com

Well-known art-house cinema with two screens and a bar.

204 G5 38 Curzon Street W1Y 7TY 020 7495 0500 Green Park 8, 10, 14, 19

HEAVEN

www.heaven-london.com

London's most famous gay club. Popcorn on Monday, no-attitude-party playing commercial and funky house; Wednesday is pop, funk and R'n'B; Friday and Saturday nights are explosive, with commercial house.

205 J5 The Arches, Villiers Street WC2N 6NG 020 7930 2020 Mon, Sat 11pm–6am, Tue–Fri 11pm–5am £2–£12 Embankment, Charing Cross 9, 11, 13, 15, 23

INSTITUTE OF CONTEMPORARY ARTS (ICA)

www.ica.org.uk

The ICA (▷ 178) stages avant-garde, experimental, movement-based performances. Hosts Dance Umbrella (www.danceumbrella.co.uk), one of the world's top contemporary dance festivals.

205 H5 The Mall SW1Y 5AH 020 7930 3647 £6–£9; day membership £1.50 (Mon–Fri) or £2.50 (Sat–Sun) gives equivalent discount plus admission to galleries and bar/cafe Charing Cross, Piccadilly Circus 3, 9, 11, 12, 13, 19, 23, 88

PACHA LONDON

www.pachalondon.com

Set in a 1920s building, the London offshoot of the Ibiza legend shuns the industrial look with original oak panelling, a stunning stained-glass ceiling and a balustraded gallery overlooking the main dance floor.

204 G7 Terminus Place, Victoria SW1V 1JR 0845 371 4489 Fri–Sat 11pm–5am £15–£20 Victoria 11, C1, C10

PIGALLE

www.thepigalleclub.com

An old cinema beautifully converted into a sophisticated 1940s-inspired supper club, with staff dressed in 1940s style. The mezzanine restaurant overlooks the stage so you can dine while enjoying the live performances. The atmosphere here is incredible; the clientele is older than in most other clubs, and later in the evening casts from the nearby musicals come and join the crowd.

205 H5 215–217 Piccadilly W1J 9HN 020 7644 1420 Mon–Wed 7pm–2am, Thu–Sat 7pm–4am £10–£30 Piccadilly Circus 14, 19, 38

ST. JAMES'S CHURCH PICCADILLY

www.sjpconcerts.org

This active church, designed by Christopher Wren and consecrated in 1684, offers popular lunchtime and evening choral and orchestral concerts in its sumptuous interior.

204 H5 197 Piccadilly W1J 9LL 020 7734 4511 £10–£30 Piccadilly Circus 9, 14, 19, 22

ST. JOHN'S, SMITH SQUARE

www.sjss.org.uk

This handsome deconsecrated church is a major classical music venue, often featuring the Sainsbury Organ, one of the finest in the UK. Superb acoustics for choirs, orchestras and solo recitals.

205 J7 Smith Square SW1P 3HA 020 7222 1061 £10–£20 Westminster 3, 87, 88, 507, C10

ST. MARTIN-IN-THE-FIELDS

www.smitf.org

Baroque music is the focus here of the free lunchtime concerts (donations appreciated) and evening concerts, which are always by candlelight.

205 J5 Trafalgar Square WC2N 4JJ 020 7766 1100 £10–£22 Leicester Square, Charing Cross 9, 24, 29, 176

THEATRE ROYAL HAYMARKET

www.trh.co.uk

With its handsome colonnaded entrance (courtesy of John Nash, 1821), opulent mirrors and gilding, the Theatre Royal dates back to Handel's day in 1720. It still prides itself on having the classiest casts and best-dressed audiences.

205 H5 Haymarket SW1Y 4HT 0870 901 3356 £20–£60 Piccadilly Circus 14, 19, 38

TRADER VICS

www.tradervics.com

This Tahitian-inspired bar will transport you from London to the South Pacific. The amazing tropical drinks menu includes the Mai Tais created by the legendary Trader Vic himself. It may be overpriced but it's great fun and a must see.

204 G5 London Hilton, 22 Park Lane W1Y 1BE, 020 7208 4113 Mon–Fri noon–1am, Sat 6pm–3am, Sun 6pm–11pm Free Hyde Park Corner 9, 14, 16, 19, 74

TRAFALGAR STUDIOS (AT THE WHITEHALL THEATRE)

www.theambassadors.com/trafalgarstudios

This art deco-style theatre is famous for the pre-war Whitehall Farces and for its post-war musical revues.

205 J5 14 Whitehall SW1A 2DY 0870 060 6632 £10–£42.50 Charing Cross 11, 12, 24

PRICES AND SYMBOLS

The prices given are for a two-course set lunch (L) and a three-course à la carte dinner (D) for one person, without drinks. The wine price is for the least expensive bottle.

For a key to the symbols, ▷ 2.

LE CAPRICE RESTAURANT

www.le-caprice.co.uk

Tucked away behind the Ritz in the exclusive St. James's district, but sleek and glamorous in black, white and chrome, Le Caprice is decorated with portraits of the rich and famous by renowned British photographer David Bailey. The food is uncomplicated and international, with dishes such as Thai baked sea bass, chicken *alla Milanese* and steak Americaine. Sunday brunch choices range from eggs Benedict to smoked salmon and bagels. You may well spot someone famous as Le Caprice is popular with the media set.

204 G5 Arlington House, Arlington Street SW1A 1RJ 020 7629 2239 Mon–Sat 12–3, 5.30–12, Sun 12–5, 6–11. Closed D 24 Dec, 25–26 Dec, L 27 Dec, 1 Jan, Aug public hols L from £25, D from £35, Wine from £21 Green Park

THE CINNAMON CLUB

www.cinnamonclub.com

Set in the former Westminster Library, the Cinnamon Club has a sophisticated look with its shelves of old books, brown leather armchairs, crisp white linen and parquet floor. Traditional Indian cooking gets surprising twists here—just taste the wild prawns baked with *kasundi* mustard and lemon rice or chargrilled duck breast with cloves and star anise. Try the above-average desserts. Impressive wine list.

205 J6 The Old Westminster Library, 30–32 Great Smith Street SW1P 3BU 020 7222 2555 Mon–Sat 12–2.45, 6–10.45. Closed 25–26 Dec, Easter L from £20, D from £24, Wine from £20 Westminster

IL CONVIVIO

www.etruscarestaurants.com

Deep red, cream and brickwork walls combine stylishly with light wooden flooring to create a chic setting for this bustling, friendly, Modern Italian restaurant. The menu offers dishes such as spaghetti with lobster and spring onions, baby monkfish wrapped in pancetta and lamb with a basil and pine kernal crust and baked aubergine. Desserts might include nougat parfait pyramid, and there's a range of Italian organic cheeses. The waiters are professional and helpful.

204 G7 143 Ebury Street SW1W 9QN 020 7730 4099 Mon–Sat 12–3, 7–11. Closed 25 Dec, 1 Jan L from £18, D from £22, Wine from £18 Victoria

GREENHOUSE

www.greenhouserestaurant.co.ukl

A chic, modern Mayfair-mews restaurant that is stylishly kitted out in neutral tones and natural textures, and dotted with classy art nouveau decorative glass. Chef Antonin Bonnet lends a spin to French and Mediterranean classics. Expect such delights as crab and daikon ravioli with spicy Korean red chilli pepper, seared grey mullet with swede purée and Alenois watercress, and clementine and jasmine tea ice cream. Great wine list.

204 G5 27a Hay's Mews, W1J 5NY 020 7499 3331 Mon–Fri 12–2.30, 6.45–11, Sat 6.45–11pm. Closed 25–26 Dec, 1 Jan, public hols L from £29, D from £65, Wine from £22 Green Park

JUST ST. JAMES

www.juststjames.com

In this former bank, whose customers have included Napoleon

Left *L'Oranger's classy decor matches its superb cuisine*

III and William Pitt the Younger, the ground floor now houses an airy restaurant with suede seating and cushions in bright, earthy tones. Lit by large storm lanterns, tables are surrounded by swathes of open space. The food is simple and eye-catching, with modern British dishes such as baked wild halibut with herb crust, or medallions of monkfish with braised oxtail, potato rosti and watercress purée.
204 H5 · 12 St. James's Street SW1A 1ER · 020 7976 2222 · Mon–Sat 12–3, 6–11.30, Sun 12–3. Closed 25–26 Dec · L from £20, D from £30, Wine from £21 · Green Park

KEN LO'S MEMORIES OF CHINA

www.memories-of-china.co.uk

Bamboo wallpaper and flooring contrast with red seating and grey slate screens. The cooking is Pekinese and Szechuan—some of the best in London—and speciality dishes are all beautifully prepared. Try fragrant braised aubergine (eggplant), sautéed salt and pepper prawns and fresh scallops steamed in their shells with black bean sauce, or the more well-known Imperial Peking duck. Best of all is the tender tasty lobster or handmade noodles.
204 G7 · 67–69 Ebury Street SW1W 0NZ · 020 7730 7734 · Mon–Sat 12–2.30, 7–12, Sun 7–10.30pm. Closed 25 Dec, public hols · L from £19.50, D from £30, Wine from £19.50 · Sloane Square, Victoria

MATSURI

www.matsuri-restaurant.com

This sophisticated Japanese restaurant occupies a basement divided into small dining areas, a sushi bar (some of the best in London) and teppan-yaki tables, where chefs cook to order raw slivers of tuna, salmon, sea bass, lobster tail and sirloin steak before you. Clear soup with chicken, prawn, tofu, lemongrass and coriander, and prawn and vegetable tempura all use fresh, high-quality ingredients. Finish off your meal with a pot of green tea.
204 H5 · 15 Bury Street SW1Y 6AL · 020 7839 1101 · Mon–Sat 12–2.30, 6–10.30, Sun 12–3, 6–10. Closed public hols · L from £15, D from £35, Wine from £20 · Green Park

NOBU

www.noburestaurants.com

Launched in 1997, Nobu remains at the forefront of new-style Japanese cooking and still brings A-list celebrities and well-heeled Londoners flocking to its doors. The food, the setting, the waiters and often the fellow diners make dining here a real event, but try to exercise some self-restraint as the prices can be stratospheric. Book well in advance. Try the six-course tasting menu to really do the place justice.
204 G5 · 1st Floor, Metropolitan Hotel, 19 Old Park Lane W1Y 4LB · 020 7447 4747 · Mon–Thu 12–2.15, 6–10.15, Fri 12–2.15, 6–11, Sat 12.30–2.30, 6–11.15, Sun 12.30–2.30, 6–9.45 · L from £26, D from £30, Wine from £26 · Hyde Park Corner

L'ORANGER

www.loranger.co.uk

Natural light spills on to the modern furnishings from a large skylight, and there's a courtyard in summer. Fish, prepared and presented simply, is the focus, and desserts are of a high standard. The wine list is predominantly French and very pricey. No children under six.
204 H5 · 5 St. James's Street SW1A 1EF · 020 7839 3774 · Mon–Fri 12–2.30, 6–11, Sat 6–11pm. Closed 25–26 Dec, public hols, one week in Aug · L from £24, D from £50, Wine from £30 · Green Park, Piccadilly Circus

THE PORTRAIT RESTAURANT

www.npg.org.uk

This unique restaurant at the top of the National Portrait Gallery (▷ 188–189) offers chic British cuisine along with some of the best views in London. Staple British classics are given a modern interpretation and prepared with skill and precision. The menu changes frequently but may include ham hock and flat parsley terrine, pot roast lamb shank with lentils and mashed potato, and bluberry and almond tart.
205 J5 · National Portrait Gallery, St. Martins Place WC2H 0HE · 020 7312 2490 · Sat–Wed 11.45–2.45, Thu–Fri 11.45–2.45, 5.30–8.30 (last order). Closed 25–26 Dec · L from £22, D from £35, Wine from £16 · Leicester Square, Charing Cross

TAMARIND

www.tamarindrestaurant.com

The gold pillars, copper place settings and solid leather chairs at Tamarind make a stylish basement venue for exquisite Michelin-starred northwest Indian tandoor food. Dishes might include tandoori prawns marinated with ginger, yoghurt, and paprika, or delicious curries concocted from lamb, chicken or seafood. The choices of dessert include dumplings of milk and semolina and tandoori *ananas*—pineapple with star anise, honey and saffron served with coconut ice cream. No children under 10.
204 G5 · 20 Queen Street W1J 5PR · 020 7629 3561 · Mon–Fri 12–2.45, 5.30–11.30, Sat 5.30–11.30, Sun 12–2.45, 6–10.30. Closed 25–26 Dec, 1 Jan · L from £15, D from £35, Wine from £24 · Green Park

THE WOLSELEY

www.thewolseley.com

The winner of the AA London Restaurant of the Year for 2005 and Time Out Best New Restaurant 2004, The Wolseley is housed in an opulent art deco building that was designed in the 1920s to be a showroom for Wolseley cars. Nowadays the resplendent chandeliers and marble pillars are the backdrop for the first-class Modern British café-style food that is served throughout the day— this is an ideal choice for afternoon tea.
204 G5 · 160 Piccadilly W1J 9EB · 020 7499 6996 · Mon–Fri 7am–12am, Sat 8am–12am, Sun 8am–11pm. L 12–2.30, D 5.30–12 · B from £7.50, L from £16.50, D from £25, Wine from £18 · Green Park

STAYING

PRICES AND SYMBOLS

Prices given are the starting price for a double room for one night. Breakfast is included unless noted otherwise. All the hotels listed accept credit cards unless otherwise stated. Note that rates vary widely throughout the year.

For a key to the symbols, ▷ 2.

ATHENAEUM

www.athenaeumhotel.com

A well-loved hotel in the heart of Mayfair with excellent hospitality. Some bedrooms have views over Green Park (▷ 178). A row of Edwardian houses next to the hotel has several spacious apartments. Public spaces include the Damask Restaurant, the Garden Room and a cocktail bar specializing in malt whisky. Sauna, massage room and spa.

204 G5 116 Piccadilly W1J 7BJ 020 7499 3464 Double from £310 (exc. breakfast) 157 (8 smoking) Green Park 8, 9, 14, 19, 22, 38

CAVENDISH LONDON

www.thecavendish-london.co.uk

This smart, stylish hotel occupies an enviable location in the prestigious St. James's area, just off Piccadilly. The bedrooms are fresh and contemporary, with larger executive rooms and suites available. There is a spacious first-floor lounge, as well as function rooms amd the highly rated David Britton restaurant.

204 H5 81 Jermyn Street SW1Y 6JF 020 7930 2111 Double from £250 230 Green Park, Piccadilly Circus 9, 14, 19, 38

COLLIERS HOTEL

www.colliershotel.co.uk

This small hotel offers basic but comfortable accommodation at very reasonable prices, in a pleasant row of houses not far from Buckingham Palace (▷ 176–177).

204 G7 95–97 Warwick Way SW1V 1QL 020 7828 0210, 020 7834 6931 Double from £55 20 Victoria 24

DOVER

www.dover-hotel.co.uk

A modern, home-from-home hotel with a 24-hour reception desk. Bedrooms have private showers and WCs with cribs for babies up to 12 months old. Tea- and coffee-making facilities, TV, a hairdryer, safety deposit box and luggage storage space are all provided in the bedrooms. Breakfast is served in the cozy lower ground-floor dining room. Special rates have been negotiated with the local car park, just a two-minute walk away. Convenient for Victoria station.

204 G7 42–44 Belgrave Road SW1V 1RG 020 7821 9085 Double from £65 (Sun–Thu), £75 (Fri–Sat) 33 Victoria 24

THE GORING

www.goringhotel.co.uk

The centrally situated Goring is convenient for the city's royal parks and principal shopping areas. It has the largest private garden of any of the central London hotels. Bedrooms are traditionally furnished, each to an individual design and decoration. The garden bar and drawing room are both popular for afternoon tea and cocktails. The restaurant menu has a well-deserved reputation for its contemporary British cuisine. Membership to a health club close by is included in the room rate.

204 G6 Beeston Place, Grosvenor Gardens SW1W 0JW 020 7396 9000 Double Mon–Fri from £350 (exc. breakfast) 74 Victoria 8, 16, 38, 52, 73, 82

Left *The Halkin Hotel is a model of gracious Georgian styling—all Portland stone and arched windows, with a garden at the back*

GRANGE ROCHESTER

www.grangehotels.com

Overlooking leafy Vincent Square, this small hotel is not far from some of London's finest shops, theatres and attractions. Bedrooms are stylishly furnished and quiet. Some have views (and balconies) overlooking the square. Public spaces are relatively small, but this is offset by the advantage that you can get something to eat at any time of the day.

205 H7 69 Vincent Square SW1P 2PA 020 7828 6611 Double from £150 80 Victoria 2, 36, 185

THE HALKIN HOTEL

www.halkin.como.bz

This one-of-a-kind contemporary hotel is in a peaceful area just a pleasant stroll away from Hyde Park. The stylish, air-conditioned bedrooms combine comfort with practicality and many include state-of-the-art facilities including TV, video and CD player, voice mail/internet access and in-room fax. There's also a gym, with personal trainers and yoga instructors on hand if required. You'd expect impressive food from this chic hotel, and it certainly delivers. The restaurant, Nahm, is run by chef David Thompson, whose way with Thai cuisine has even earned him a role as an advisor to one of Thailand's leading cooking institutes.

204 G6 Halkin Street, Belgravia SW1X 7DJ 020 7333 1000 Double from £390 41 Hyde Park Corner 9, 10, 14, 19, 22, 52, 74, 137

MELBOURNE HOUSE HOTEL

www.melbournehousehotel.co.uk

Refurbished in 2007, this convenient family-run bed-and-breakfast is an easy walk from Victoria mainline train station. Rooms are modern and some are suitable for families. Breakfast is served in the basement dining room. No visitors allowed in rooms.

205 H8 79 Belgrave Road SW1V 2BG 020 7828 3516 Double from £95 17 Pimlico 24

PREMIER INN LONDON VICTORIA

www.premierinn.com

This hotel is one of the most central of the Premier's 20 London branches and typifies the group's reputation for providing quality accommodation at very fair prices. The modern rooms may not have many frills but they are comfortable. There is a bar and restaurant on site too.

204 G7 82–83 Eccleston Square SW1P 1VS 0870 423 6494 Double from £90 107 Victoria 2, 24, 36, 185, 436

THE RITZ

www.theritzlondon.com

Synonymous with style, sophistication and attention to detail, the Ritz continues its stately progress into the 21st century, having recaptured much of its former glory. All bedrooms are furnished in Louis XVI-style, with marble bathrooms and every imaginable comfort and facility. A choice of elegant reception rooms includes the Palm Court, with its legendary afternoon tea, the beautifully refurbished Rivoli Bar and the sumptuous Ritz Restaurant, complete with delicate gold chandeliers and extraordinary trompe-l'oeil decoration.

204 G5 150 Piccadilly W1J 9BR 020 7493 8181 Double from £400 (exc. breakfast) 133 (20 smoking) Green Park, Piccadilly Circus 8, 9, 14, 19, 22, 38a

THE RUBENS AT THE PALACE

www.rubenshotel.com

If you want to stay near Buckingham Palace, this is the hotel for you. Right opposite the Royal Mews, it has stylish, air-conditioned bedrooms with state-of-the-art entertainment systems and high-speed internet access. There is a choice of rooms and suites, including the pinstripe-walled Savile Row rooms, which follow a tailoring theme, and the opulent royal rooms, which are named after different monarchs. Two dining rooms and a plush bar complete the facilities. Families and pets welcome.

204 G6 39 Buckingham Palace Road SW1W 0PS 020 7834 6600 Double from £174 (exc. breakfast) 161 (15 smoking) Victoria

SIDNEY

www.sidneyhotel.com

A pleasant hotel conveniently located close to Victoria train station. Several bedrooms are suitable for family use. The public areas include a bar lounge and an airy breakfast room. No evening meals.

204 H8 68–76 Belgrave Road SW1V 2BP 020 7834 2738 Double from £125 82 Victoria, Pimlico 24

THE STAFFORD

www.thestaffordhotel.co.uk

From the pristine, tastefully decorated and air-conditioned bedrooms, to the highly professional yet friendly service, this classically styled boutique hotel maintains the highest standards and retains an air of understated luxury. The American Bar is a fabulous venue in its own right, festooned with an eccentric array of celebrity photos, caps and ties. Afternoon tea is a long-established tradition here. The stylish Stafford Mews has been added, offering 26 stunning mews suites. Tucked away behind Green Park in a quiet corner of St James's, the Stafford is in an ideal position for excellent shopping and visiting the main sights.

204 H5 16–18 St. James's Places SW1A 1NJ 020 7493 0111 Double from £345 105 (5 smoking) Green Park 8, 19,14, 19, 22, 38

WINDERMERE

www.windermere-hotel.co.uk

A relaxed and informal family-run hotel within easy reach of Victoria mainline train station. The Pimlico Restaurant serves renowned evening meals and good breakfasts.

204 G8 142–144 Warwick Way SW1V 4JE 020 7834 5163 Double from £145 22 Victoria 24

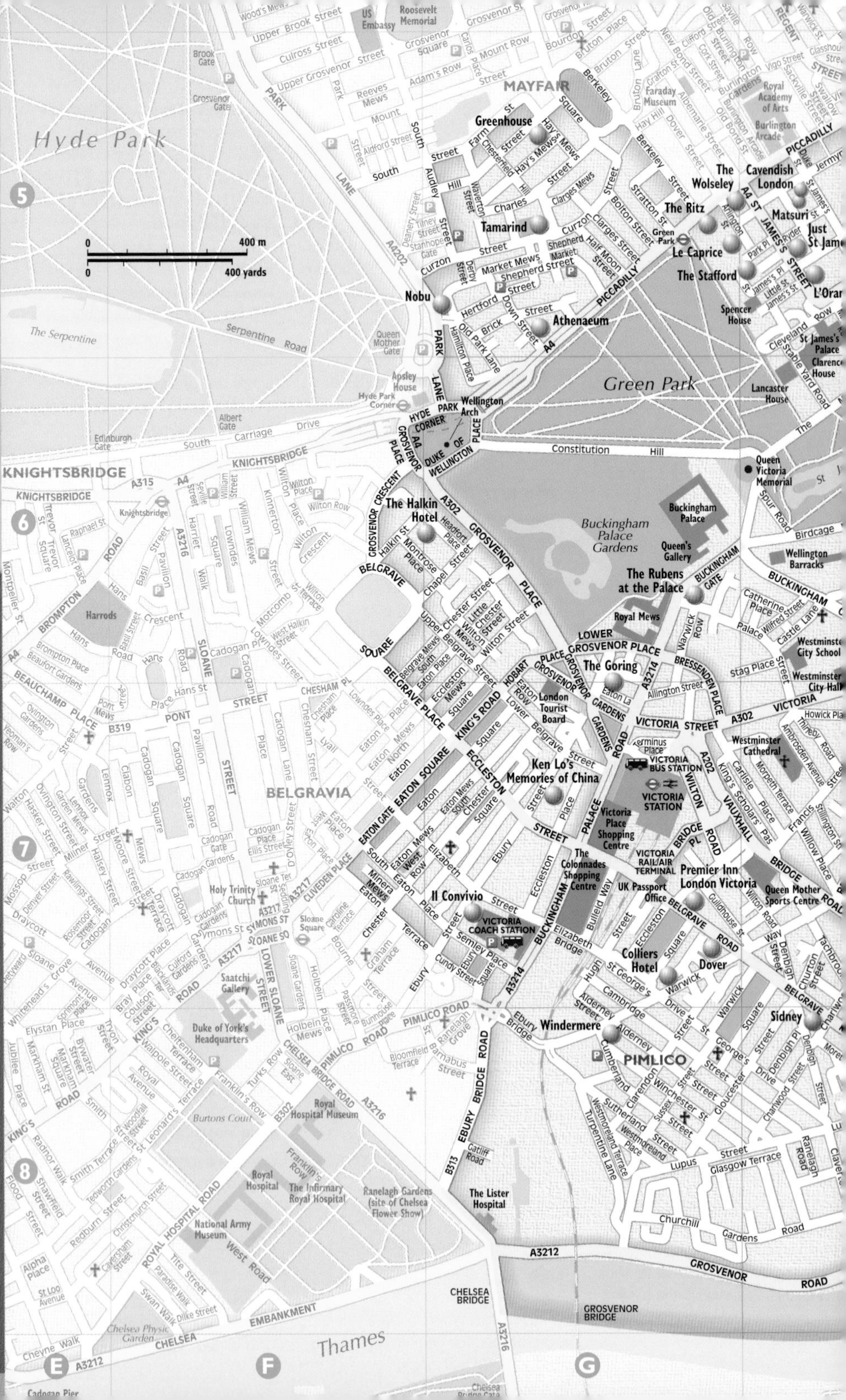
Hyde Park
The Serpentine
Serpentine Road
0
400 m
0
400 yards
MAYFAIR
KNIGHTSBRIDGE
BELGRAVIA
PIMLICO
Green Park
Buckingham Palace Gardens
Buckingham Palace
Queen's Gallery
Royal Mews
Queen Victoria Memorial
Wellington Barracks
St James's Palace
Clarence House
Lancaster House
Spencer House
Royal Academy of Arts
Burlington Arcade
Faraday Museum
US Embassy
Roosevelt Memorial
Apsley House
Wellington Arch
Hyde Park Corner
Harrods
Holy Trinity Church
Saatchi Gallery
Duke of York's Headquarters
Burtons Court
Royal Hospital Museum
Royal Hospital
The Infirmary Royal Hospital
Ranelagh Gardens (site of Chelsea Flower Show)
National Army Museum
Chelsea Physic Garden
The Lister Hospital
Westminster Cathedral
Westminster City School
Westminster City Hall
London Tourist Board
Victoria Bus Station
Victoria Station
Victoria Place Shopping Centre
Victoria Rail/Air Terminal
The Colonnades Shopping Centre
UK Passport Office
Victoria Coach Station
Queen Mother Sports Centre
Greenhouse
Tamarind
Nobu
Athenaeum
The Wolseley
Cavendish London
The Ritz
Matsuri
Just St James
Le Caprice
The Stafford
L'Oran
The Halkin Hotel
The Rubens at the Palace
The Goring
Ken Lo's Memories of China
Il Convivio
Premier Inn London Victoria
Colliers Hotel
Dover
Windermere
Sidney
PICCADILLY
PARK LANE
CONSTITUTION HILL
GROSVENOR PLACE
BUCKINGHAM PALACE ROAD
VICTORIA STREET
EBURY BRIDGE ROAD
KING'S ROAD
SLOANE STREET
CHELSEA BRIDGE ROAD
ROYAL HOSPITAL ROAD
CHELSEA EMBANKMENT
GROSVENOR ROAD
CHELSEA BRIDGE
GROSVENOR BRIDGE
Thames
Cadogan Pier
5
6
7
8
E
F
G

London Trocadero
Piccadilly Circus
Leicester Square
National Portrait Gallery
The Portrait Restaurant
National Gallery
Trafalgar Square
St Martin-in-the-Fields
Nelson's Column
Benjamin Franklin House
CHARING CROSS STATION
STRAND
Royal Society of Arts
HQS Wellington (Master Mariners)
HMS President
Victoria Embankment
Thames
Savoy Pier
WATERLOO BRIDGE
Victoria Embankment Gardens
Cleopatra's Needle
Embankment Pier
Embankment
GOLDEN JUBILEE BRIDGE
Festival Pier
Queen Elizabeth Hall
Southbank Centre
Royal Festival Hall
Hayward Gallery
National Film Theatre
Royal National Theatre
The London Television Centre
Oxo Tower
London City College
Schiller International University
BFI London IMAX Cinema
London Nautical School
WATERLOO EAST STATION
WATERLOO STATION
Shell Centre
Jubilee Gardens
London Eye
Waterloo Millennium Pier
Dali Universe
County Hall
London Aquarium
Hispaniola
Admiralty Arch
Institute of Contemporary Arts (ICA)
Duke of York Column
Carlton House
Old Admiralty
Government Offices
DEFRA
Old War Office
Horse Guards Parade
ST JAMES'S
Banqueting House
Ministry of Defence
Privy Council Office
St James's Park
Foreign & Commonwealth Office
Cenotaph
Government Offices
Churchill Museum & Cabinet War Rooms
Treasury
Portcullis House
Westminster Millennium Pier
Westminster
Guards Museum
Queen Elizabeth II Conference Centre
Middlesex Guildhall
Big Ben
WESTMINSTER BRIDGE
Florence Nightingale Museum
Central Hall
Palace of Westminster
St Margaret's Westminster
Houses of Parliament
St Thomas' Hospital
St James's Park
Caxton Hall
Department of Trade & Industry
Westminster Abbey
New Scotland Yard
Church House
Westminster School
Jewel Tower
LAMBETH
The Cinnamon Club
Victoria Tower Gardens
Archbishop's Park
Lambeth North
St George's Cathedral
Geraldine Mary Harmsworth Park
Imperial War Museum
Civil Service Recreation Centre
St John's Concert Hall
Lambeth Palace
RHS New Hall
Museum of Garden History
NEWINGTON
Thames House
LAMBETH BRIDGE
WESTMINSTER
Grange Rochester
Millbank Tower
Gordon Hospital
The Greycoat Hospital
Tate Britain
Millbank Millennium Pier
Chelsea College of Art & Design
Melbourne House Hotel
VAUXHALL
Pimlico
VAUXHALL BRIDGE
VAUXHALL STATION
Vauxhall City Farm
St George Wharf
Pimlico Gardens
The Oval Cricket Ground
Ken Barrington Centre
Covent Garden Flower Market
KENNINGTON

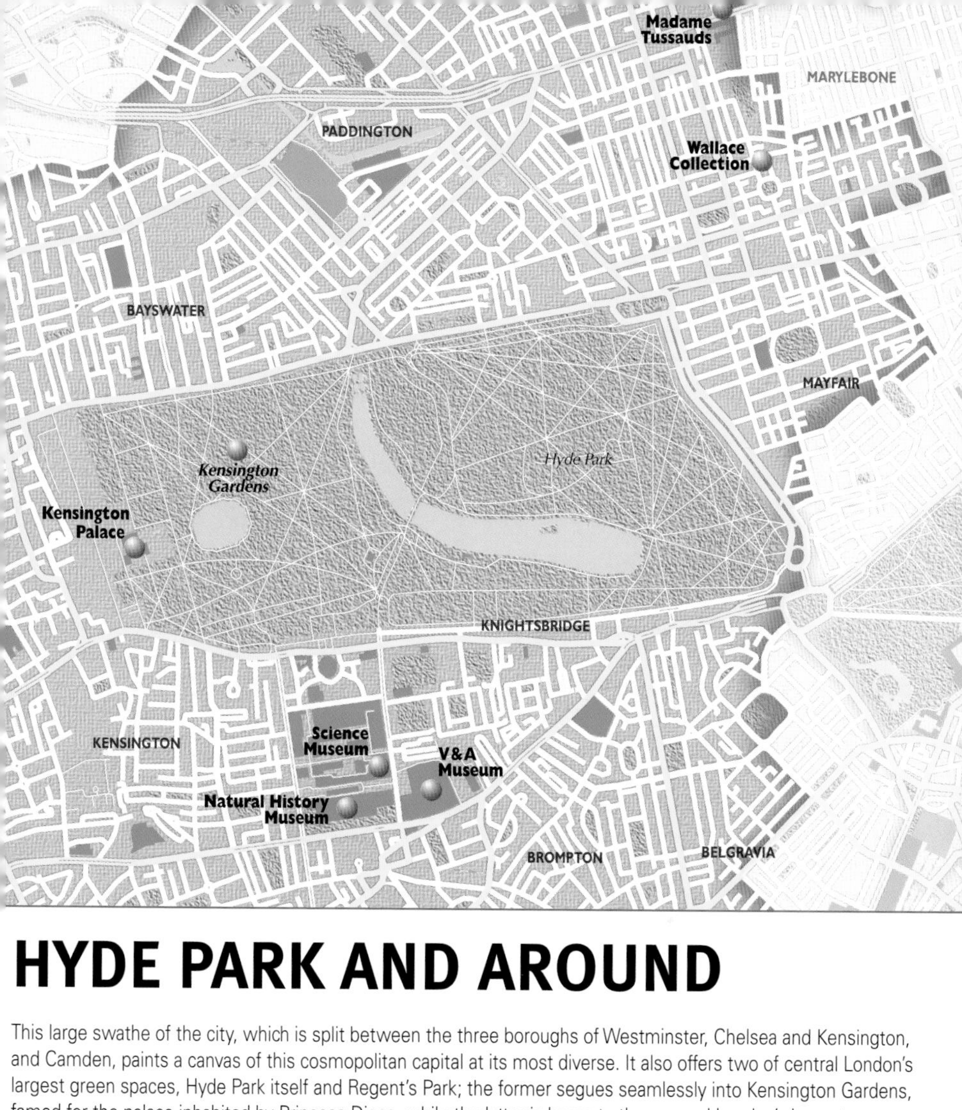

HYDE PARK AND AROUND

This large swathe of the city, which is split between the three boroughs of Westminster, Chelsea and Kensington, and Camden, paints a canvas of this cosmopolitan capital at its most diverse. It also offers two of central London's largest green spaces, Hyde Park itself and Regent's Park; the former segues seamlessly into Kensington Gardens, famed for the palace inhabited by Princess Diana, while the latter is home to the zoo and London's largest mosque. Cultural, ethnic and social diversity abound in the various neighbourhoods, from the quiet, classy bastions of old money in Belgravia and Chelsea, through the Afro-Caribbean community that still holds its annual carnival in Notting Hill and the high percentage of Middle Eastern immigrants and wealthy visitors in parts of Kensington, Bayswater and Edgware Road to the young punks and eccentrics who frequent Camden Lock and its fantastic market, where you can find quirky souvenirs and quality clothing and handicrafts from all over the world.

Eager shoppers have plenty more to choose from: the twin meccas of Harrods and Harvey Nichols are both in Knightsbridge, while the environs of nearby King's Road and Sloane Square are still packed with trendy boutiques. Kensington High Street offers more mainstream goods, like a mini Oxford Street, while lovers of art can cruise the Bayswater Road, on the north side of Hyde Park, every Sunday for works direct from the artist. As if all that wasn't enough, South Kensington is home to a trio of London's greatest museums—the Natural History Museum, the Science Museum and the Victoria & Albert Museum. The whole area also contains a profusion of lesser sights and even one of the world's great performance spaces in the rotund Albert Hall, opposite the memorial of Queen Victoria to her beloved consort.

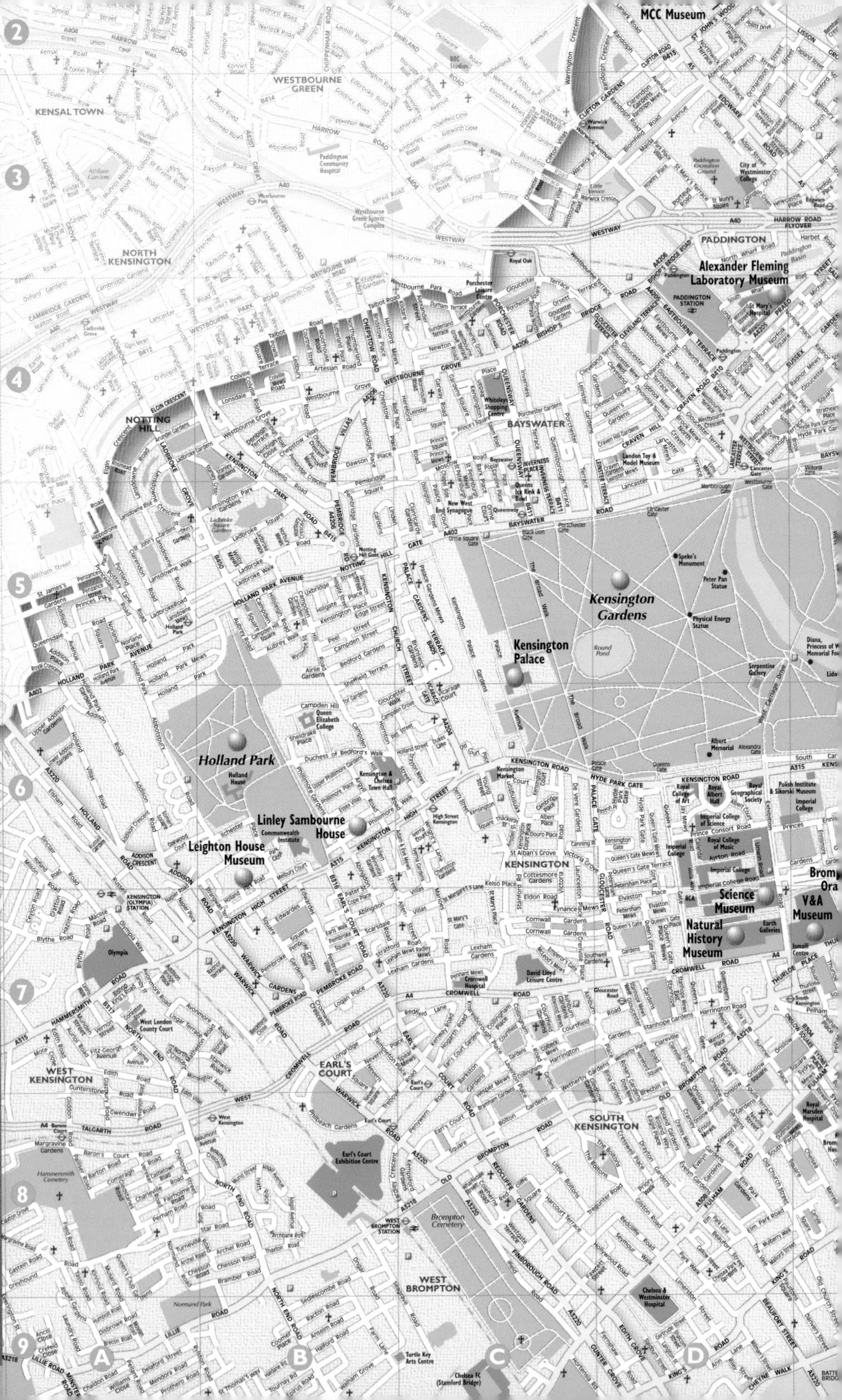
MCC Museum
WESTBOURNE GREEN
KENSAL TOWN
NORTH KENSINGTON
PADDINGTON
Alexander Fleming Laboratory Museum
Paddington Station
NOTTING HILL
BAYSWATER
London Toy & Model Museum
Queens Ice Rink & Bowl
New West End Synagogue
Whiteleys Shopping Centre
Kensington Gardens
Speke's Monument
Peter Pan Statue
Physical Energy Statue
Round Pond
Kensington Palace
Serpentine Gallery
Diana, Princess of Wales Memorial Fountain
Albert Memorial
Holland Park
Holland House
Queen Elizabeth College
Kensington & Chelsea Town Hall
Linley Sambourne House
Commonwealth Institute
Leighton House Museum
Royal Albert Hall
Royal College of Art
Royal Geographical Society
Polish Institute & Sikorski Museum
Imperial College
Royal College of Music
Science Museum
Natural History Museum
V&A Museum
KENSINGTON
Olympia
Kensington (Olympia) Station
David Lloyd Leisure Centre
Cromwell Hospital
West London County Court
WEST KENSINGTON
EARL'S COURT
Earl's Court Exhibition Centre
SOUTH KENSINGTON
Hammersmith Cemetery
West Brompton Station
Brompton Cemetery
WEST BROMPTON
Royal Marsden Hospital
Chelsea & Westminster Hospital
Normand Park
Turtle Key Arts Centre
Chelsea FC (Stamford Bridge)
A B C D
2 3 4 5 6 7 8 9

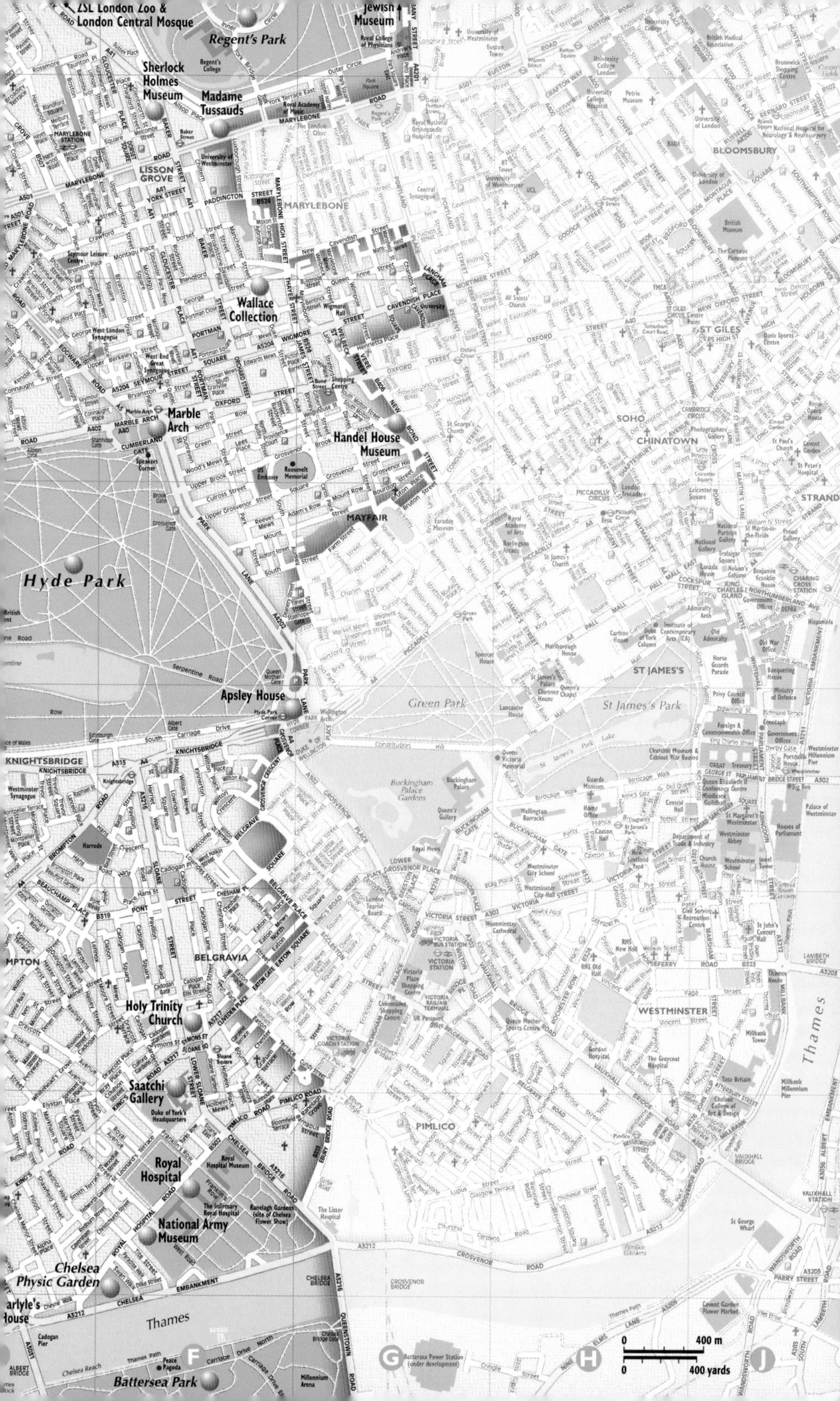
ZSL London Zoo & London Central Mosque
Regent's Park
Jewish Museum
Sherlock Holmes Museum
Madame Tussauds
MARYLEBONE
LISSON GROVE
BLOOMSBURY
Wallace Collection
ST GILES
SOHO
CHINATOWN
Marble Arch
Handel House Museum
MAYFAIR
STRAND
Hyde Park
ST JAMES'S
Apsley House
Green Park
St James's Park
KNIGHTSBRIDGE
BELGRAVIA
WESTMINSTER
Thames
Holy Trinity Church
Saatchi Gallery
PIMLICO
Royal Hospital
National Army Museum
Chelsea Physic Garden
Carlyle's House
Battersea Park
F
G
H
J
0
400 m
0
400 yards

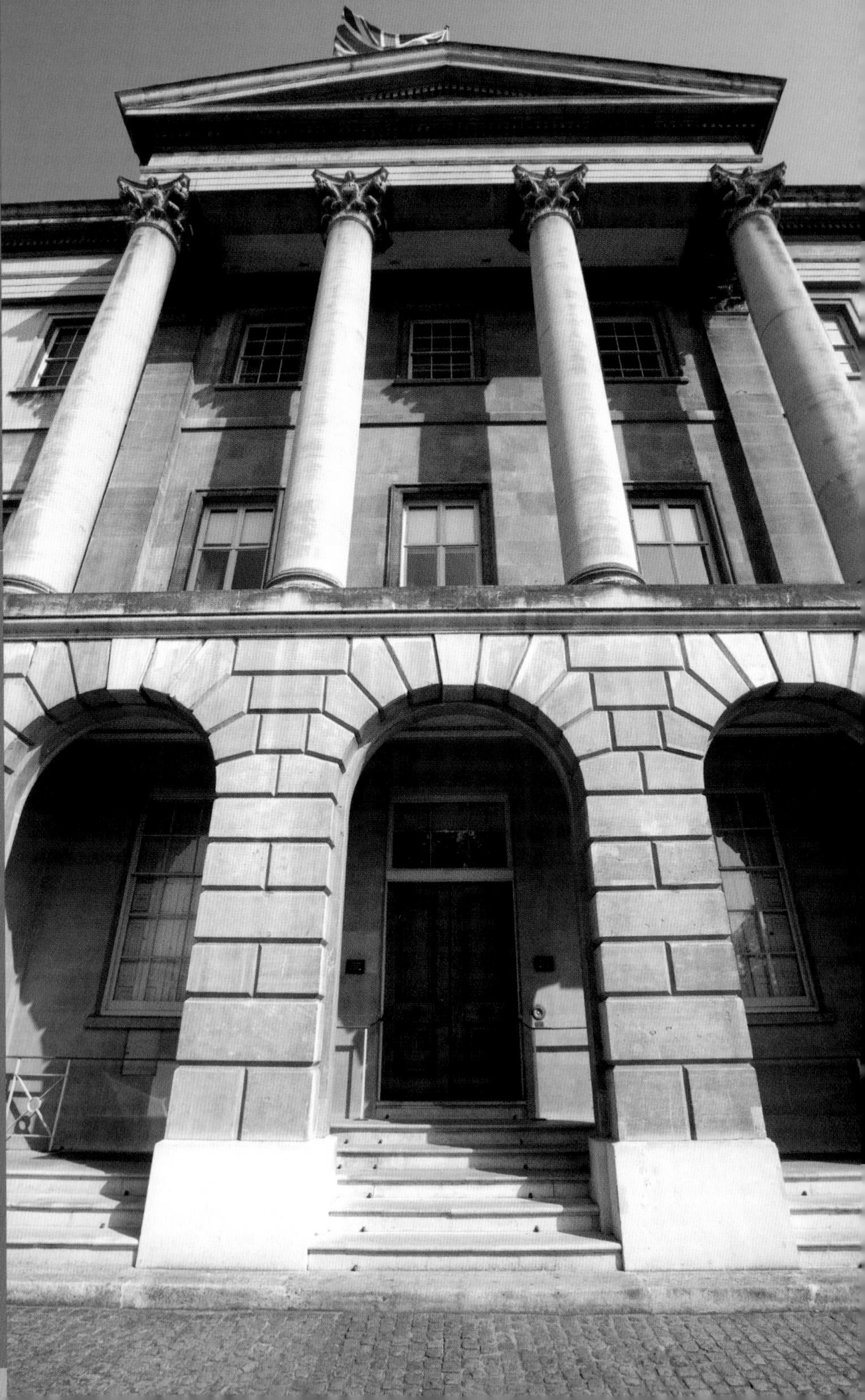

ALEXANDER FLEMING LABORATORY MUSEUM

www.imperial.uhs.uk

In 1928 Scottish bacteriologist Alexander Fleming (1881–1955) discovered penicillin while working in St. Mary's Hospital, next to Paddington Station. In the hospital's small museum, you can see the cramped laboratory where he cultivated the naturally antibiotic mould that revolutionized medicine. Museum volunteers are on hand to relate their personal experiences of the impact of antibiotics, and displays and a video tell Fleming's story and trace the role of penicillin in the fight against disease.

208 D4 St. Mary's Hospital, Praed Street W2 1NY 020 7886 6528 Mon–Thu 10–1, other times by prior appointment Adult £2, child £1 Paddington 7, 15, 27, 36

APSLEY HOUSE

www.english-heritage.org.uk

Designed by Robert Adam in 1771, this aristocratic town house at the western end of Piccadilly became the London home of war hero and future prime minister Arthur Wellesley, 1st Duke of Wellington, in 1817.

Known as 'No. 1 London', because it was the first house within the city toll gates on the western approach, it houses the Duke's outstanding collection of paintings, porcelain, silver, sculpture, furniture, medals and memorabilia—including his own death mask, and the Sèvres 'Egyptian' dessert service that Emperor Napoleon gave as a divorce present to Josephine, who rejected it. The Waterloo Gallery, 27m (90ft) long, contains the Duke's magnificent art collection, with works by Goya, Rubens and Murillo. Between 1992 and 1995 the interior of the house was restored to its early 19th-century appearance.

Although the 7th Duke gave the house and its contents to the nation in 1947, several apartments were retained for use as the family home.

209 F6 149 Piccadilly W1J 7NT 020 7499 5676 Apr–end Oct Wed–Sun 11–5; Nov–end Mar Wed–Sun 10–4 Adult £5.30, child (under 18) £2.70. Free entry on Waterloo Day (18 Jun) Hyde Park Corner 8, 9, 10, 14, 74

BATTERSEA PARK

www.batterseapark.org

Officially opened in 1858 by Queen Victoria, this riverside park was created on marshy common land known as Battersea Fields, partly to rid it of a reputation for illegal racing, drinking and gambling.

It has since become one of London's most popular parks, with three million visitors a year. Attractions include the original Victorian carriage drives, sports facilities, an art gallery, two playgrounds, a boating lake, sculptures by Henry Moore and Barbara Hepworth and a Japanese Peace Pagoda, given to London in 1985 by the Buddhist Order as a symbol of peace. Cycling has been a popular pastime here since 1896.

A £10.3 million revamp is currently under way to re-emphasize the Victorian layout, construct a riverside promenade to original designs and restore the 1951 Festival Gardens.

209 F9 Battersea Park SW11 4NJ 020 8871 7530 Daily 8am–dusk Free Sloane Square, then bus East of park (Queenstown Road) 137; west of park (Battersea Bridge Road) 19, 49; south of park (Battersea Park Road) 45, 344, 345 Battersea Park, Queenstown Road Cadogan Pier

BROMPTON ORATORY

www.bromptonoratory.com

Standing next door to the V&A (▷ 224–228) is the flamboyant Brompton Oratory (London Oratory of St. Philip Neri), an Italian baroque church designed by Herbert Gribble in 1876. This was the first new Roman Catholic church to be built in London after Henry VIII broke away from papal authority. Its design imitates Gesù Church in Rome, with nave and side chapels instead of aisles, and sumptuous statuary and decoration. Dominating the nave are Giuseppe Mazzuoli's gigantic 17th-century marble statues of the Apostles, originally from Siena Cathedral.

Above *Broad, tree-lined carriage drive in Battersea Park*
Opposite *Colonnaded Apsley House*

On a more intimate scale is the Chapel of St. Wilfrid, with a triptych by English artist Rex Whistler (1905–44).

208 E7 Brompton Road SW7 2RP 020 7808 0900 Daily 6.30am–8pm Free South Kensington 14, 74, 414, C1

CARLYLE'S HOUSE

www.nationaltrust.org.uk

Scottish historian and essayist Thomas Carlyle (1795–1881) lived in this Queen Anne house off the Chelsea Embankment from 1834 until his death. Inside you'll find Victorian furniture, pictures, portraits and books as they were during Carlyle's lifetime. He wrote many of his scholarly and historical works in the top-floor garret study, built specially for him in 1853.

Other literary figures of the day met at the house, including novelist Charles Dickens and poet Robert Browning.

209 E9 24 Cheyne Row SW3 5HL 020 7352 7087 Easter–end Oct Wed–Fri 2–5pm, Sat–Sun 11–5 Adult £4.50, child (5–16) £2.30, under 5s free Sloane Square, South Kensington 11, 19, 22 Cadogan Pier

CHELSEA PHYSIC GARDEN

www.chelseaphysicgarden.co.uk

Founded in 1673 by the Society of Apothecaries of London to study plants for medicinal purposes, this is Britain's second-oldest botanical garden after Oxford's, which predates it by 52 years. It is still used for medical and botanical research.

The walled plot (1.5ha/4 acres) holds around 5,000 species and many rare trees, as well as the largest fruiting olive tree growing outdoors in Britain. A rock garden was created in 1773 with basaltic lava brought back from Iceland by English botanist Sir Joseph Banks (1744–1820), who accompanied Captain James Cook on his 1768 expedition around the world on the *Endeavour*.

Flowering shrubs and rare peonies grow in a wilder area of the garden. Interesting specific gardens include the Pharmaceutical Garden and the Garden of World Medicine.

209 F8 66 Royal Hospital Road SW3 4HS 020 7352 5646 Apr–late Oct Wed–Fri 12–5, Sun 12–6 (also Jul, Aug Wed till 10). Also for snowdrops: first and second Sun in Feb, 11–3; Chelsea Flower Show: mid-May Mon–Fri 12–5; Chelsea Festival: mid-Jun Mon–Fri 12–5 Adult £7, child (5–15) £4, under 5s free Sloane Square 11, 19, 22, 211, 239

HANDEL HOUSE MUSEUM

www.handelhouse.org

No. 25 Brook Street was the Mayfair home of German-English composer George Frederick Handel (1685–1759) from 1723 until his death. It was here that he composed some of his best-loved works, including the *Messiah, Zadok the Priest* and the *Music for the Royal Fireworks*. Portraits of Handel and his contemporaries, scores, prints and sculpture are on display. Part of No. 23, next door (▷ 19), provides space for exhibitions and live music.

209 G4 25 Brook Street W1K 4HB 020 7495 1685 Tue, Wed, Fri, Sat 10–6, Thu 10–8, Sun 12–6. During busy periods, tickets may be timed Adult £5, child (5–15) £2, under 5s free Bond Street, Oxford Circus 3, 8, 25, 55, 176

HOLLAND PARK

www.rbkc.gov.uk

World War II bombing badly damaged Holland House, the Jacobean mansion that stood in the 22ha (55 acres) of parkland here. What's left is now a youth hostel, and the park itself is a busy public area with playgrounds, sports facilities, cafe and an ecology centre, as well as formal and informal gardens. An outdoor theatre on the terrace of the house stages a 10-week summer season of opera. The Japanese Kyoto Garden on the west side of the park was created for the 1991 London Festival of Japan.

208 B6 Daily dawn–dusk 020 7361 3003 Free Holland Park, High Street Kensington 9, 10, 27, 28, 31 C1

HOLY TRINITY CHURCH

www.holytrinitysloanesquare.co.uk

Built between 1888 and 1890 to a design by John Dando Sedding, Chelsea's Holy Trinity is regarded as one of London's best examples of the Arts and Crafts style, which grew up in the late 19th century as part of a reaction against mass-produced goods. Sir John Betjeman (1906–84), poet and writer, described the church as a 'cathedral of the Arts and Crafts movement', particularly admiring the ornate wrought-iron chancel gates. Artist Edward Burne-Jones and designer William Morris produced the huge east window with 48 panels depicting saints.

209 F7 Sloane Street SW1X 9BZ 020 7730 7270 Mon–Fri 8–5.30, Sat 10–4.30, Sun 8–1 (Sun services at 8.45 and 11) Free Sloane Square, Knightsbridge 19, 22, 137, C1

HYDE PARK

www.royalparks.gov.uk

Together with Kensington Gardens (▷ 213), Hyde Park forms a wide sweep of green to the southwest of Marble Arch. Henry VIII originally claimed it as hunting ground, but it was opened to the public by James I at the beginning of the 17th century. In the 1730s Queen Caroline, George II's wife, created the artificial lake known as the Serpentine for boating and bathing. Today the park is still used as a recreation area, with rowing boats and pedal boats for hire on the lake in summer. Cycling, rollerblading and skateboarding are allowed on designated tracks in the park.

North of the Serpentine is the Diana, Princess of Wales Memorial Fountain, opened by the Queen in July 2004. This controversial work, likened unkindly to a storm drain, more kindly called 'an oval of water', is nothing like a conventional fountain.

Speakers Corner (▷ 15), near Marble Arch, has for centuries provided an open-air forum where anyone can air their views.

Rotten Row—a linguistic corruption of *route du roi* (king's road)—was built to link rural Kensington Palace (▷ 214–215) to Piccadilly and St. James's Palace. Members of the Household Cavalry Brigade, among others, now exercise their horses along it, and at around 10.30am (9.30am on Sunday) and noon you can see them riding to and from the Changing of the Guard ceremonies at Buckingham Palace and Horse Guards (▷ 176–177).

209 E5 Daily 5am–midnight Free Hyde Park Corner, Marble Arch, Lancaster Gate 9, 14, 16, 19, 22, 36, 52, 74, 436

JEWISH MUSEUM

www.jewishmuseum.org.uk

At the time of writing, the museum was closed for a major redevelopment project which will triple its size and use state-of-the-art technology to present the history of Britain's Jewish community, in addition to its existing exhibits.

Off map 209 G2 Raymond Burton House, 129–131 Albert Street NW1 7NB 020 7284 1997 Call or check website for opening hours and prices

KENSINGTON GARDENS

London's greenery extends westwards from Hyde Park (▷ 212) into Kensington Gardens, but the two parks have quite different characters. Unlike the former hunting ground of Hyde Park, which still has an open informality, Kensington Gardens were created to a formal plan as the grounds of Kensington Palace, which sits at their western boundary. Much of the layout dates from work carried out for Queen Caroline, wife of George II, in the early 18th century, when the upper reach of Hyde Park's artificial lake, the Serpentine, was claimed and renamed the Long Water. At its northern end is a paved garden with a pavilion and four fountains and on its east bank stands an arch sculpted by Henry Moore in 1979 from Roman travertine.

The Serpentine Gallery, in the park's southern section, hosts changing exhibitions of contemporary art (tel 020 7402 6075, open daily 10–6 during exhibitions, free). It was built in 1908 and formerly served as a fashionable tea pavilion.

North of here are two sculptures: *Physical Energy* (1904), an equestrian bronze by George Frederick Watts (1817–1904), and *Peter Pan* (1912) by Sir George Frampton (1860–1928), commemorating the hero of J. M. Barrie's 1904 play. Nearby is the Diana, Princess of Wales Memorial Playground (▷ 236).

AROUND THE ALBERT MEMORIAL

Kensington Gardens entered a new phase of their history when they were opened to the public in 1841, during Queen Victoria's reign. The Queen's beloved husband, Prince Albert, is commemorated in a flamboyant monument (▷ 231) by Sir George Gilbert Scott (1811–78), southwest of the Serpentine Gallery. At its centre is Albert himself, holding the catalogue for the 1851 Great Exhibition, which he organized (▷ 36). Across Kensington Gore Road is another monument to the Prince—the domed Royal Albert Hall (▷ 231, 235).
Behind the Albert Memorial the Flower Walk runs east to meet the Broad Walk, which runs north between Kensington Palace and the Round Pond, west of the Serpentine Gallery. Created in 1728, the pond is where children and adults traditionally come to sail model boats. There's a bandstand to its south, where music is sometimes performed on summer days.

INFORMATION

www.royalparks.gov.uk
208 D5 · Daily 6am–dusk · 020 7298 2141 · Free · Lancaster Gate, High Street Kensington, Queensway, Bayswater · 9, 10, 27, 31, 49, 52, 70, 148

Above *Peaceful Kensington Gardens were laid out to an elegant plan*

INFORMATION

www.hrp.org.uk

208 C5 Kensington Palace State Apartments, Kensington Gardens W8 4PX 0870 751 5170 Mar–end Oct daily 10–6; Nov–end Feb daily 10–5 Adult £12.50, child (5–15) £6.30, under 5s free, family £34 High Street Kensington, Queensway 9, 10, 49, 52, 70, 148 Sound guide included in entry; guidebook £3.95, in English and German The Orangery (▷ 239) Kensington Palace Shop, the Yellow Drawing Room Shop

Above *Sir Christopher Wren re-orientated the palace to face west*

INTRODUCTION

In 1689 the asthmatic William III set up home in Kensington Palace to escape from the damp and smoke of riverside Whitehall Palace. He bought the existing 1605 Jacobean mansion named Nottingham House and had it enlarged by Sir Christopher Wren (1632–1723); the renowned architect saved time by simply adding new blocks to the four corners so the king's entourage could be accommodated. William's wife Mary subsequently had the Queen's Gallery added to her apartments, while the South Front was added during William's reign. His successor Queen Anne bequeathed the nation the Orangery, while George I had further extensions added to the palace in the 1720s.

The palace has been home to many members of the royal family, but is most famously where Diana, Princess of Wales, lived until her death in 1997; it was her marital home before her marriage to Prince Charles ended.

WHAT TO SEE

DRESS COLLECTION AND STATE APARTMENTS

On the ground floor the Royal Ceremonial Dress Collection presents a superb array of finery from the 18th to the 20th centuries, including a permanent collection of dresses belonging to Diana, Princess of Wales. You're taken through the elaborate process of dressing for court, from a replica of a shop where materials are chosen to a visit to the seamstress for a final fitting. First of the State Apartments, upstairs, are the Queen's Apartments, the largest of which is the 26m (85ft) Queen Mary's Gallery, a panelled room hung with royal portraits. Several smaller rooms are decorated with

17th-century furnishings and pictures, including the State Bed, in Queen Mary's Bedchamber, with its original hangings.

By contrast, the King's Apartments are very opulent. Italianate in style, the rooms have magnificent ceiling paintings by William Kent (*c*1685–1748). Most impressive is the Cupola Room, with its pillars, figures of Greek and Roman deities, and busts of Roman emperors and ancient philosophers. Queen Victoria was baptized here.

Courtiers and visitors would have used the King's Grand Staircase, designed by Wren, with its scrolled wrought-ironwork by Jean Tijou and walls and ceiling coated in Venetian-style paintings by Kent. The trompe-l'oeil wall painting of a gallery crowded with figures includes many contemporary portraits of George I's courtiers and servants.

THE GARDEN

Don't miss the pretty sunken garden, made in 1909 in an area previously occupied by potting sheds. It was modelled on a similar garden at Hampton Court, with lime trees trained to form a hedge on three sides and flower beds framing the central lily pond (to which there is no public access).

TIPS

» Look for access to the palace from the Broad Walk in Kensington Gardens.

» Check for current and future special exhibitions.

Left *The garden is at its best between April and October, when the beds are planted with vibrant flower displays*

Below *Leaf and flower detail from the wrought-iron gates*

Above *Victorian masterpieces on display in Leighton House Museum*

LEIGHTON HOUSE MUSEUM

www.rbkc.gov.uk

Victorian artist Frederic, Lord Leighton (1830–96) had this red-brick studio-house built to his own design on the edge of Holland Park. The result was a private palace devoted to art, equipped with only one bedroom as he didn't want to be bothered with house guests. Every room has been restored in period style; the most remarkable is the Arab Room, complete with pool and marble pillars and based on a Moorish banqueting hall in Palermo, Sicily. Islamic tiles collected by Leighton on his travels through Damascus, Cairo and Rhodes cover the walls and floor.

Other rooms, less exotically finished with red walls and ebonized wood, are hung with paintings by Leighton and many of his Pre-Raphaelite contemporaries, including John Everett Millais, Edward Burne-Jones and George Frederick Watts. Picnics are allowed in the walled garden.

In 2008 the museum closed for extensive renovation, reopening in 2010.

208 B6 12 Holland Park Road W14 8LZ 020 7602 3316 Under refurbishment at time of writing; call for times and prices High Street Kensington 9, 10, 27, 49

LINLEY SAMBOURNE HOUSE

www.rbkc.gov.uk

A mass of paintings, cartoons and photographs covers the walls in the Victorian house occupied by political cartoonist and illustrator Edward Linley Sambourne (1844–1910) from 1874 until his death.

The family continued to use the house until 1980, when it was opened as a museum. It remained almost totally unaltered during the intervening years, preserving its over-furnished, late 19th-century appearance, complete with original William Morris wallpapers, Asian rugs, stained-glass windows and heavy, Gothic-inspired furniture.

208 B6 18 Stafford Terrace W8 7BH 020 7602 3316 Guided tours Wed 11.15, 2.15, Sat–Sun 11.15. Reservations advised Adult £6, under 18s £1 High Street Kensington 9, 10, 27, 49, 52, 70

LONDON CENTRAL MOSQUE

www.iccuk.org

The showpiece Islamic Culture Centre and mosque, opened in 1978 on the eastern side of Regent's Park, provides a focus for London's Muslim communities, with lecture and conference facilities, a bookshop and a library. About 4,000 worshippers can be accommodated in the mosque, which has marble floors and intricate mosaics. Sir Frederick Gibberd (1908–84) designed the building with its splendid golden dome, 25m (82ft) high, and white minaret.

Off map 209 E2 146 Park Road NW8 7RG 020 7725 2218 Mon–Fri 9–5 Free Baker Street, Marylebone 13, 82, 113, 274

LORD'S TOUR AND MCC MUSEUM

www.lords.org

Cricket divides the British nation between devoted fans on the one hand and those who find it baffling and boring on the other. Lord's historic cricket ground has a wider appeal, however, and tours of the Marylebone Cricket Club (MCC) give an intriguing behind-the-scenes glimpse of a venue which has been in use since the 18th century.

In the Long Room, the cricket-watching room at the heart of the Pavilion, an art gallery contains portraits of the game's celebrities. You can also take a look in the players' dressing rooms and visit the MCC Museum, where pictures and mementoes trace 400 years of cricketing history and you can see the tiny, delicate Ashes urn.

The Brian Johnston Memorial Theatre shows footage of matches.

Off map 208 D2 Lord's Cricket Ground, St. John's Wood NW8 8QN 020 7616 8595/6 Tours daily 10, 12, 2, Apr–end Oct; 12, 2, Nov–end Mar. No tours during major matches or on preparation days. On other match days, only the 10am tour enters the Pavilion. MCC Museum included in tours Adult £14, child (5–16) £8, under 5s free, family £27 Marylebone, St. John's Wood 139, 189

MADAME TUSSAUDS

▷ 217.

MARBLE ARCH

John Nash designed this elegant monument of white Carrara marble in 1828 as the main entrance to Buckingham Palace (▷ 176–177), but it was moved to its current site next to Speakers Corner in Hyde Park (▷ 212) when the palace was extended in 1851. At the time it was intended to form the park's principal entrance, but it now stands isolated on a grassy traffic island and the central gates remain closed most of the time. To this day, only members of the royal family are allowed to drive through.

The triple-arched design was inspired by the Constantine Arch in Rome and is carved with intricate reliefs of winged, wreathed Victories, a Roman warrior and Justice, Peace and Plenty, plus representations of England, Scotland and Ireland.

209 F4 Open access Free Hyde Park Corner, Marble Arch, Bond Street, Green Park 10, 36, 54, 74, 137, 148, 274, 436

MADAME TUSSAUDS

Madame Tussaud's waxworks collection, a quirky eccentricity just beyond the southeast corner of Regent's Park, is one of London's most popular attractions. More than 2 million visitors come here every year to spot the likenesses of famous figures and pose beside heroes of sports and entertainment. The collection changes all the time: Celebrities know they've made it when their waxwork appears here, and they know they've had their day when their likeness is melted down to be turned into another rising star. Unlike fame, however, the techniques used to make the models are timeless and have barely changed since Madame Tussaud started her business 200 years ago. The hair used is real and the wax is similar to candlewax, which would melt in the heat of sunlight—thus explaining why the displays have to be kept in darkened rooms.

The oldest figure on display is Sleeping Beuaty, made in 1765 and based on Louis XV's mistress, Madame du Barry, but the highlight of a visit for many is the ghoulish Chamber Live, a chamber of horrors complete with live actors to terrify visitors even more. Exhibits here include such historical figures as Vlad the Impaler (the real-life Count Dracula); Joan of Arc, burning at the stake; Guy Fawkes, hanged, drawn and quartered (▷ 30); objects from London's brutal Newgate Prison (▷ 35); Jack the Ripper (▷ 37); and a scene that would certainly have been familiar to Madame Tussaud herself—execution by guillotine.

Tours end with a Spirit of London time-travel trip in a taxicab (complete with sounds and smells) from Elizabethan times through the Plague and Great Fire to the Blitz and on to the Swinging Sixties.

Latest attractions feature Pirates of the Caribbean and a chat with Davina in the Big Brother diary room. The interactive Sports Zone enables you to test your sporting skills or team up with the greats. You can even practise your golf with Tiger Woods.

As you go round, keep an eye out for the anonymous-looking 'tourists', sitting on benches or standing around chatting. You'll find yourself caught out more than once.

INFORMATION

www.madame-tussauds.com
209 F3 Marylebone Road NW1 5LR General enquiries 0870 999 0046; 0870 400 3000 (booking only; fee applies) Mon–Fri 9.30–5.30 (until 7 in school summer holidays), Sat–Sun 9–6 Prices vary according to time of visit or if booked online. Adult from £22.50, child (5–16) from £18.50 Baker Street 13, 27, 74, 82, 139 £4, in English, French, German, Italian, Spanish

STARDOME

Stardome, housed in the former London Planetarium, presents the Wonderful World of Stars, the brainchild of Aardman Animations. The intense visual effects contribute to the pleasure of the experience. As the saucers, stars and galaxies fly by, the audience is treated to a genuine sensation of hurtling through space with a bizarrely comical collection of extraterrestrials.

Above *The Beatles forever young at Madame Tussauds*

NATIONAL ARMY MUSEUM

www.national-army-museum.ac.uk

The British army's story is traced from the Middle Ages and the 1415 Battle of Agincourt to modern conflicts including the Falklands War, the Gulf War, Kosovo and Iraq. Although wartime experience is naturally to the fore, space is also given to peacetime military life.

In addition to describing campaigns and battles, the museum focuses on the lives of ordinary soldiers, using paintings, photographs, uniforms and equipment along with reconstructions and life-size models.

In 2006 changes included creating new themed galleries bringing military history up to date. They convey the British army's role as a peace-keeping force throughout the world.

Weekend special events follow a different theme every month, with uniformed interpreters, specialist lectures and children's workshops all making for an entertaining day out.

209 F8 Royal Hospital Road, Chelsea SW3 4HT 020 7881 2455 Daily 10–5.30 Free Sloane Square 11, 19, 22, 137, 239 (Mon–Sat) to museum Cadogan Pier

NATURAL HISTORY MUSEUM

▷ 220–221.

REGENT'S PARK

www.royalparks.gov.uk

Originally part of Henry VIII's royal hunting grounds, Regent's Park came into its own during the reign of the Prince Regent, later George IV, who gave the park its name. The original, grandiose plans, devised by John Nash, were to include a palace to the south in St. James's and a triumphal route up to the pleasure gardens. The park itself was to be girded by grand, stuccoed houses. Money ran out before the plans could be fully realized, but the park, some of the terracing and the first part of the triumphal route—Regent's Street—were completed before work came to a halt.

The York Gate entrance, near the Baker Street Underground station, lies just beyond the world-famous Madame Tussauds (▷ 217). As you walk up to the park you'll notice, on the right, the Royal Academy of Music, founded in 1822, where some of the world's finest musicians, singers and composers have trained.

On York Bridge, look back to see St. Mary's Church, on Marylebone High Street. When Nash laid out Regent's Park he deliberately aligned the York Gate axis to take in a view of the church, with its majestic Corinthian portico and circular tower. York Bridge continues past Regent's College, on the left, now a centre for European studies. Beyond lie Queen Mary's Gardens. Here, Nash had intended a temple dedicated to the memory of all who had contributed to British history and culture. Instead, the 6.8ha (17-acre) circle contains London's finest rose garden, planted to honour George V's wife, Queen Mary, and the Open-Air Theatre (▷ 235), founded in 1932.

To the west is the Y-shaped boating lake, and a walk around the upper part of the lake brings you to Hanover Gate, where the park's newer buildings are found. The London Central Mosque (▷ 216) is to the north, easily spotted with its golden dome, and to the south, fronting the Outer Circle, are Quinlan Terry's neo-Nash villas of 1992.

209 F2 Daily 5am–dusk Free Baker Street, Marylebone, Regent's Park, Great Portland Street, Camden Town 27, 82, 113, 274, C2

ROYAL HOSPITAL

www.chelsea-pensioners.co.uk

Chelsea's Royal Hospital was built by Sir Christopher Wren at the behest of Charles II in the late 17th century as almshouses for veteran soldiers. It still serves that purpose today, and the Chelsea Pensioners, as the residents are known, are a familiar sight in the area. Their dress uniform is the scarlet tunic of the Duke of Marlborough, worn with blue trousers and a tricorn hat; at other times you may see them in blue tunics. To catch them in their ceremonial garb, come here on Oak Apple Day (29 May), when they commemorate the Battle of Worcester—from which Charles II escaped by hiding in an oak tree in 1651—by festooning his statue in the central courtyard with oak leaves.

In the small museum you can see the pensioners' uniforms and medals, the barrel-vaulted chapel and the panelled Great Hall. Outside,

Below *Queen Mary's Gardens in Regent's Park; as well as the famous rose garden, there's an ornamental lake and the national delphinium collection*

Above *Fountains in front of the spacious new premises of the Saatchi Gallery—unique among contemporary art galleries of its size in offering free entry*

you can wander in the south grounds, site of the annual Chelsea Flower Show (▷ 295) since 1913, and Ranelagh Gardens, to the east of the main complex.
209 F8 Royal Hospital Road SW3 4SR 020 7881 5303 Mon–Sat 10–12, 2–4; May–end Sep Sun 2–4 Free Sloane Square 11, 137, 170, 239

SAATCHI GALLERY

www.saatchi-gallery.co.uk

The gallery moved in October 2008 to its smart new Chelsea premises, which provide a state-of-the-art showcase for the work of young unknown artists, and for artists of international repute who are not normally exhibited in the UK.
209 F7 Duke of York's Headquarters, King's Road SW3 4SQ 020 7823 2363 Daily 10–6 Free Sloane Square 11, 19, 22, 49, 211

SCIENCE MUSEUM

▷ 222–223.

SHERLOCK HOLMES MUSEUM

www.sherlock-holmes.co.uk

Fictional detective Sherlock Holmes, created by Sir Arthur Conan Doyle (1859–1930), 'lived' at 221b Baker Street together with his friend and colleague Dr. Watson between 1881 and 1904. This 1815 house is actually No. 239 Baker Street, but 221b is now the number on the door. Dedicated to the life and times of Holmes, the house has been carefully furnished to reflect descriptions in Conan Doyle's stories, with Holmes's study overlooking Baker Street on the first floor.

'Personal' belongings include the detective's deerstalker hat, magnifying glass, violin and chemistry equipment, and papers include a variety of exhibits from Holmes's cases, and the 'diary' of Dr. Watson. The third-floor exhibition rooms house wax models of characters and scenes from the stories.
209 F3 221b (239 postal address) Baker Street NW1 6XE 020 7935 4430 Daily 9.30–6 Adult £6, under 16s £4 Baker Street, Marylebone 13, 82, 274, 453

VICTORIA & ALBERT MUSEUM

▷ 224–228.

WALLACE COLLECTION

▷ 229.

ZSL LONDON ZOO

www.zsl.org

Occupying 15ha (37 acres) of the northeast corner of Regent's Park (▷ 218) and straddling the Regent's Canal, the London Zoological Gardens opened in 1828. It was the world's first institution dedicated to the scientific study of animals, and in its heyday in the 1950s attracted over 3 million visitors per year. Today conservation and study take preference over public display. Nonetheless, it is still a very popular and important visitor attraction offering the chance to see around 5,000 animals drawn from 650 species, many of which are endangered in the wild.

Highlights in the zoo include the famous Snowdon Aviary, designed by Lord Snowdon in 1964. There are plenty of new attractions too, such as the Clore Rainforest Lookout and Nightzone where small nocturnal animals scurry about in a moonlight world; and the wonderful Gorilla Kingdom, opened in March 2007, a £35 million enclosure for a colony of western lowland gorillas.

Near the entrance, you'll find the noisy primates, the silent world of the aquarium and the reptile house. The mountain-like Mappin Terrace (with wallabies and emus) was designed by Sir Peter Chalmers Mitchell (1864–1945), then secretary of the London Zoological Society, and J. J. Joass (1868–1952) in 1913; Joass also designed a new aquarium for the zoo in 1924. The modernist Penguin Pool, always crowded at feeding time, was designed by Berthold Lubetkin (1901–90) in 1931.
Off map 209 E2 Outer Circle, Regent's Park NW1 4RY 020 7722 3333 Early Mar–late Oct daily 10–5.30; late Oct–early Mar daily 10–4 Adult £14.50, child (3–15) £11, under 3s free, family £45.50 Camden Town 274, C2 London Waterbus Company (020 7482 2550) runs scheduled services from Camden Lock and Little Venice: Apr–end Sep daily 10–5

INFORMATION

www.nhm.ac.uk
208 D7 Cromwell Road SW7 5BD
020 7942 5000 Daily 10–5.50. Wildlife Garden May–end Sep daily 12–5
Free. Charge for some temporary exhibtions South Kensington 14, 49, 70, 74, 345, 414, C1 £4.50, in English only. Free floorplans and map
Restaurant: self-service meals and snacks Cafe, snack bar, coffee bar
Museum shop, Dino Store, Earth shop

Above *The Natural History Museum's main entrance, with its twin towers, on Cromwell Road*

INTRODUCTION

Built on land purchased by Prince Albert from money raised at the Great Exhibition of 1851 (▷ 36), the huge French Romanesque Natural History Museum was designed by Alfred Waterhouse (1830–1905) to house the British Museum's natural history collection, and opened to the public in 1881. Relief panels in terracotta showing animals, fossils, plants and insects run the whole length of the facade; living species of the time are shown to the left of the entrance, extinct ones to the right.

Thousands of animal, plant and mineral specimens were bequeathed by Sir Hans Sloane (▷ 139), including more than 10,000 animal specimens and 338 volumes of pressed plants. Sir Joseph Banks, who accompanied Captain Cook on his first voyage around the world in the 1760s, was another important benefactor. Today the museum owns more than 65 million specimens and more than a million books and manuscripts.

The main entrance, approached via a grand flight of stone steps from Cromwell Road, leads straight into the huge and richly decorated Central Hall, which has been likened to the nave of a cathedral. The hall leads off to the left to the Blue Zone, which has exhibitions on dinosaurs, mammals, creepy crawlies (including a robotic scorpion), fish and other marine life, plants and minerals, meteorites and the story of evolution. To the right and up the main stairs is the Green Zone, concentrating on ecology and evolution.

The museum's side entrance leads into the Red Zone, opened in 1996 and housed in rooms on the ground, mezzanine, first and second floors, linked by a central escalator which travels through a huge globe. State-of-the-art displays tell the story of the Earth's formation, with sections on volcanoes and earthquakes, hands-on stations demonstrating the forces of wind, water and heat, and galleries focusing on the Earth's natural geological treasury of gemstones and discussing ways of protecting our world for the future.

Outside the museum, the Wildlife Garden, in the Orange Zone, planted in 1993 on the west lawn, provides both peace and quiet and the chance to study some of Britain's habitats, from oak woodland to reedbeds, and their associated plants and animals. The Darwin Centre is also in this zone.

WHAT TO SEE

BLUE ZONE

Dinosaurs

This is one of the most popular galleries, with a high-level walkway bringing you eye to eye with some of the ancient monsters. The lighting is low and atmospheric, and there is an animatronic re-creation of the creatures in action, including one of the world's most advanced models of its kind, a terrifying 4m-high (13ft) *Tyrannosaurus rex*, now the subject of debate as to whether it was a hunter or a scavenger. Soaring staircases provide a views of the hall's detailed decoration (note the monkeys scrambling up and down the arches) and look down on the plaster-cast skeleton of *Diplodocus carnegii* (which comes from Wyoming), 150 million years old, 26m (86ft) long, and one of the largest animals ever to have roamed the earth.

The Blue Whale

Suspended from the ceiling in the Mammals section is another giant—a life-size model of a blue whale almost 28m (93ft) in length and dwarfing the African elephant, the largest land mammal.

GREEN ZONE

Ant Colony

The museum has its very own labour force of leafcutter ants, and you can watch as members of the thousands-strong colony grow and tend the fungus that provides its food, cut up the leaves collected from their feeding area and are guarded as they work by the soldier ants with vicious-looking jaws.

Giant Sequoia

One of the most intriguing exhibits is a passage cut through this enormous tree (*Sequoiadendron giganteum*) displayed on the stairs to the first floor. This particular specimen was cut down in 1892, by which time it was 84m (276ft) tall and measured 15m (49ft) around the girth. A tree ring count indicates that it was 1,335 years old when felled, having started its life in California in AD557.

RED ZONE

The Power Within/Earthquake

This unnerving series of displays has become one of the museum's top attractions. The exhibition explores the powerful forces of heat and pressure that are constantly on the move between the ground that we inhabit and the centre of the Earth. A simulator gives you some idea of how it feels to be in an earthquake; film footage of the Kobe earthquake in Japan in 1995 shows the terrors of the real thing, as a supermarket is shaken to its foundations. Volcano eruptions are re-created, and you can keep an update of the most recent earthquake occurrences around the world.

TIP

›› If the queues at the main entrance are very long, make for the side entrance on Exhibition Road.

GALLERY GUIDE

BLUE ZONE

GROUND FLOOR

Dinosaurs, Fishes, Amphibians, Reptiles
Marine Invertebrates
Human Biology
Mammals

GREEN ZONE

Wonders of the Natural History Museum
Fossil Marine Reptiles
Fossils from Britain
Ecology
Creepy Crawlies
Bird Gallery
Lasting Impressions (natural phenomena showing passage of time)

FIRST FLOOR

Our Place in Evolution
Minerals
Meteorites
Primates
Plant Power
(stairs): Giant Sequoia

RED ZONE

GROUND FLOOR

Visions of Earth
Today and Tomorrow

MEZZANINE FLOOR

Earth Lab

FIRST FLOOR

From the Beginning
Earth's Treasury

SECOND FLOOR

The Power Within/Earthquake
Restless Surface

ORANGE ZONE

Wildlife Garden
Darwin Centre: Life-science laboratories and collections

INFORMATION

www.sciencemuseum.org.uk
208 D7 Exhibition Road SW7 2DD 0870 870 4868 Daily 10–6 Main museum free; IMAX adult £8, child (under 16) £6.30, family £18.50–£25.50; SimEx Simulator adult £2.50, child £2; charges for some special exhibitions South Kensington 9, 10, 14, 74, 345, 360, 414, 430, C1 Science Museum Guide £2, in English, French, German, Italian, Japanese, Spanish; children's trail guides Deep Blue Café in the Wellcome Wing; Revolution Café in Energy Hall on ground floor Waterstone's bookshop; Science Museum Store selling educational toys, games, stationery

INTRODUCTION

The Science Museum grew out of the early scientific acquisitions of what would eventually become the V&A (▷ 224–228), which included ship models from the Admiralty, scientific instruments and a science library, plus important British Industrial Revolution inventions. In 1909 the science collection was hived off on its own. The main building of 1913 was designed by Sir Richard Allison as a combination of office block (outside) and department store (inside).

The museum is arranged over seven floors of the main building and in the new four-storey Wellcome Wing, which is connected to the old building at each level. Look out for the touch-screen computers that guide you from section to section.

The basement houses a popular hands-on gallery exploring the basic concepts of science, with separate interactive exhibitions for younger children (3–6) and 7- to 11-year-olds. There's also an exhibition explaining the technology behind ordinary domestic gadgets.

On the ground floor are displays on power and space, with three main exhibition areas. The Energy Hall is filled with engines of all kinds, and explores steam power. Exploring Space traces the story of the space rocket. Exhibitions on the first floor cover pretty much every material known to man, plus a series of themed displays on aspects of communications, agriculture and weather. A variety of exhibits on the second and third floors look at more areas of the appliance of science in daily life plus the exploration of sea and air, and a sound studio explains the mechanics behind radio. Galleries on the fourth and fifth floors tell the story of medicine and veterinary history with objects including an Egyptian mummy, leech jars and Louis Pasteur's microscope.

The Wellcome Wing has three floors of high-tech, interactive exhibitions about current science.

WHAT TO SEE

GROUND FLOOR

Apollo 10 (Making the Modern World)

One of the museum's main attractions is the full-size replica of the Apollo 10 command module. This was the command module that took astronauts Tom Stafford, John Young and Gene Cernan around the moon and returned them to Earth in May 1969, as a rehearsal for the first manned lunar landing two months later. Its outer surface was scorched during re-entry into the Earth's atmosphere. Visitors who are inspired by the module can even have a go at designing a spacecraft; a computer display will show whether the end result takes to the skies or comes down to earth with a bump.

Stephenson's *Rocket* (Making the Modern World)

This pioneering rail locomotive was Robert Stephenson's winning design in trials held at Rainhill in 1829 to decide how to power the Liverpool & Manchester Railway. Despite being a breakthrough in railway engine design, the Rocket was substantially rebuilt within 18 months to keep up with fast-developing technology and laid aside within 10 years. Nevertheless, it made history as the prototype for all future steam locomotives.

Babbage's Difference Engine No. 1 (Making the Modern World)

Charles Babbage was designing computers in the early 19th century, creating his Difference Engine No. 1, the first successful automatic calculator, in 1832. One section remains (the rest was melted for scrap), consisting of 2,000 parts and still in working order. His Difference Engine No. 2 was built here in 1991 to his original designs.

Atmospheric Engine by Francis Thompson (Energy Hall)

The atmospheric engine was invented at the start of the 18th century, but this one, dating from 1791, is the oldest engine of its type to survive complete. It burned coal to produce condensed steam to create a vacuum in a cylinder so that atmospheric pressure drove the piston. The engine was used to pump water from mines and remained operational for a record 127 years.

FIRST FLOOR

Cooke and Wheatstone's Telegraph (Telecommunications)

Patented in 1837 by William Cooke (1806–79) and Charles Wheatstone (1802–75), this five-needle telegraph was the first successful electric telecommunication device. It was put to use on the new railways and within a year was sending public telegrams and railway messages between London and West Drayton, 21km (13 miles) to the west. In 1845 the needle telegraph relayed a description of a murderer, who was arrested as he left the train.

THIRD FLOOR

Alcock and Brown's Vickers Vimy (Flight)

Pilot and navigator John Alcock and Arthur Whitten Brown made the first non-stop flight across the Atlantic in this aircraft in June 1919. The Vimy was made of wood and fabric, based on a British World War I bomber and driven by Rolls-Royce engines. Its journey from Newfoundland, Canada, to Clifden, Ireland, took 16 hours.

TIP

» Head for the higher, quieter floors to escape the crowds.

GALLERY GUIDE

BASEMENT

Children's science sections and domestic gadgets

GROUND FLOOR

Spacecraft, engines, important inventions. Wellcome Wing: IMAX cinema, Simex Simulator, science and technology news. Who am I? gallery

FIRST FLOOR

Telecommunications, materials, agriculture, surveying, weather, time. Wellcome Wing: genetics and psychology

SECOND FLOOR

Weighing and measuring, lighting, printing, physics, chemistry, mathematics, computing and technology, ships. Inside the Spitfire. Wellcome Wing: digital technology

THIRD FLOOR

Optics, 18th-century science, photography, health, temperature, geophysics and oceanography, night skies, recording studio, flight. Wellcome Wing: future developments

FOURTH AND FIFTH FLOORS

Medical and Veterinary History

Opposite *Well-presented, modern displays make the Science Museum appealing to all ages*

INFORMATION

www.vam.ac.uk
208 E7 Cromwell Road SW7 2RL 020 7942 2000 Sat–Thu 10–5.45, Fri 10–10 (selected galleries) Free, except for some exhibitions and events Free introductory tours daily (1 hour) 10.30–3.30; also free gallery talks on Thu at 1, Sun at 3; meet in the Grand Entrance V&A guidebook £4.99, in English, French, German, Japanese; The British Galleries at the V&A £4.95, in English only South Kensington 14, 74, 414, C1 Morris, Gamble & Poynter Rooms café on Level 1; open daily 10–5.15 (Fri until 9.30) Shop on Level 1 selling gifts and books inspired by objects in the museum; small shop selling postcards and children's items next to the cafe

Above *Room 23 is dedicated to garden sculpture, which became very popular in Britain in the 18th century*

INTRODUCTION

The V&A was founded in 1852 with profits from the Great Exhibition of 1851. Its aim was to give the working classes access to great art and to inspire British manufacturers and designers. Originally housed in Marlborough House, near Buckingham Palace, it was moved to the present site in 1857 as the South Kensington Museum. It was given its current name in 1899, when Queen Victoria laid the foundation stone of a new building that later opened in 1909.

Contemporary glass sculptor Dale Chihuly's extraordinary chandelier in twisted, colourful blown glass dominates the V&A's entrance hall and provides a sense of what's ahead—displays of tens of thousands of items, including fashion and textiles, furniture and paintings, jewellery, ceramics, glass, silver and ironwork.

The main entrance on Cromwell Road is on Level 1, but the galleries start (numerically) one level down (Level 0) with the European collection. On Level 1 are sculpture, plaster casts and photography; Islamic and Asian and more European collections; the Raphael Gallery, and the fashion collection.

The museum's 15 British Galleries begin on Level 2 and continue on Level 4. Level 3 features the Materials and Techniques galleries, including ironwork, jewellery, musical instruments, paintings, tapestries and silver; glass objects are on show on Level 4 and ceramics on the museum's top floor, Level 6.

WHAT TO SEE

EUROPEAN COLLECTION

The Becket Casket

Part of the medieval treasury, this gilt copper and blue enamel reliquary was made in about 1180. It is the oldest and largest of about 50 items associated with Thomas à Becket's martyrdom that survive from the workshops of the Limoges enamellers—experts at making beautiful goods with hard-wearing and cheap materials. The murder of Becket, the Archbishop of Canterbury who incurred Henry II's wrath and was assassinated at the cathedral altar, is pictured on the front; one of the knights can be seen hacking off the martyr's head. The lid of the casket shows Becket's funeral.

The Burghley Nef

This dazzling salt-holder is one of the boat-shaped objects (known as nefs) that were all the rage in 16th-century France. It was made in Paris in about 1527, with a rare nautilus shell serving as the salt bowl and set into the 'hold' of an elaborate silver sailing ship, resting on a golden-haired mermaid. The intricately worked details on the ship include two tiny figures playing chess—representing Tristan and Iseult, the legendary ill-fated lovers associated with the tales of King Arthur and Camelot.

Raphael Cartoons

Although their name conjures up images of *Peanuts*, these cartoons are actually works of extreme skill, painted in glue distemper as prototypes to be hung in the Sistine Chapel at the Vatican. The seven pieces were most likely completed in 1516 and then sent to Brussels for the weaving process. The cartoons portray various scenes from the Gospels and Acts.

ASIAN AND ISLAMIC COLLECTION

Chinese Pagoda

The centrepiece of the Gerard Godfrey Gallery of Chinese Export Art (Room 47) is a brightly coloured 2.7m (9ft) porcelain model of a 17-tier Chinese pagoda, one of only 10 of its kind believed to have survived. Each of the progressively smaller tiers is decorated with exquisitely delicate blues and golds and shows a tiny figure looking through an open window, shaded by green and silver canopies. At the time of its creation—between 1800 and 1815—trade was booming between Europe and China, and mass production of souvenirs for European buyers was at a peak. This pagoda was specially made to an individual order, rather than put together on an assembly line, and is based on the 15th-century pagoda of Nanking (destroyed in 1853).

TIPS

» Colour-coded signs and banners, corresponding to key areas of the museum, help you find your way around.

» Take advantage of the late-night opening until 10pm every Friday.

Below *The main facade was created by Austin Webb, who won a competition in 1891 to design the museum expansion*

PHOTOGRAPHY AT THE V&A

Only four years after the opening of the V&A, when photography was still in its infancy and regarded as strictly inferior to other art media, the museum began a collection of photographic work. One of its first exhibitions was a display of life studies by Clementina, Lady Hawarden (1822–65), who took many photographs of her daughters in their home at South Kensington in London. Her experiments with light, shade and reflection give added interest to these early examples of photography as an art form.

The V&A has now amassed more than 500,000 works in its photographic collection.

Below *The V&A cafe occupies the museum's three original refreshment rooms; the centre one was designed by James Gamble in Renaissance style*

Tipu's Tiger

One of the V&A's best-known objects is kept in the Nehru Gallery of Indian Art (Room 41). The 18th-century model of a tiger savaging a man, complete with mechanically produced growls and screams, was made for Tipu Sultan, son of Haidar Ali Khan, ruler of the state of Mysore. Known as the Tiger of Mysore, Tipu had the tiger emblem worked into many of his surroundings and possessions, but this example, with its sound-effects organ built into the brightly coloured tiger's side, is unique. It may represent the actual fate of the son of General Sir Hector Munro in Bengal. Tipu suffered defeat at the hands of the British at Seringapatam in 1799, and his tiger was brought back as booty to be put on show in the East India Company Museum, later to be transferred to the Victoria & Albert.

BRITISH GALLERIES

Writing Box

Henry VIII owned this portable stationery set, made in 1525 and elaborately decorated. Inside the lid of the box, the gilded leather lining shows the coat of arms of the king and Catherine of Aragon, cherubs and copies of a German woodcut of Venus and Mars; other parts of the box are illustrated with miniature profiles and intricate motifs and designs. Drawers and compartments are built into the design, which incorporates a Latin inscription wishing Henry triumph over his adversaries.

The Great Bed of Ware

Celebrated in literature and lore, the Great Bed of Ware was made between 1590 and 1600 for an inn in Ware, Hertfordshire, as a kind of marketing ploy, enticing travellers with its unusually large dimensions and ornamental carving—which would originally have been picked out in vivid colours. To

Above *The Italian Cast Court is full of plaster reproductions of major masterpieces*
Left *The Jewellery Gallery displays 3,500 jewels from the museum's jewellery collection*

modern eyes, the bed itself may not seem remarkably large, but the frame is certainly massive. It includes panels made by German immigrant craftsmen and Dutch-influenced marquetry. The bed had fulfilled its promotional function by 1601, when it warranted a mention in Shakespeare's play *Twelfth Night*.

Strawberry Thief by William Morris (1834–96)

In reaction against the dehumanizing processes of 19th-century mass industry, William Morris and his contemporaries in the Arts and Crafts movement sought to revive the craftsmanship of the Middle Ages. *Strawberry Thief*, a repeated design of thrushes stealing fruit among leaves and flowers used on fabric and wallpaper, is an example of Morris's attempt to bring individualism and beauty into middle-class homes. He produced it using an ancient indigo-discharge printing technique; for the first time, with this pattern, he used red and yellow along with blue and white, a long and difficult process that made this one of his firm's costliest cottons. Despite the high price, this design was to be one of the most popular and successful produced by Morris & Company.

THE FASHION COLLECTION

Sack-Back Gown

A finely worked satin gown made in France in the 1770s illustrates the way fashion developed in high society, incorporating casual dress (which sack-back gowns originally were) and combining old and new. The bodice, with its front fastening, is the height of contemporary style, while the square, wide 'saddle-bag' hoops and elbow-length, ruffled sleeves harked back 20 years or so. Delicate blue padded satin and chenille lace are used to decorate the ivory-coloured gown and petticoat, along with embroidered floral sprigs and gathered ribbon.

Bar Suit, Christian Dior (1905–57)

Dior's New Look designs hit the fashion shows in 1947 and created an immediate sensation among women accustomed to the pared-down, austere styles of wartime Europe. The bar suit has a cream silk jacket nipped in to show off a 46cm (18in) waist; a full black wool crêpe skirt flares out beneath it, with a hem measuring 7.3m (24ft) in circumference. Topping the ensemble is a low-brimmed hat, adding the finishing touch to an overall image of elegant chic.

GALLERY GUIDE
MAIN FLOORS
LEVEL 6
Rooms 137–145: Ceramics

LEVEL 4
Rooms 118–125: British galleries
Rooms 127–128a: Architecture
Rooms 129–131: Glass gallery

LEVEL 3
Rooms 65–69 and 70a: Silver galleries
Rooms 70–73: Gold, silver and mosaics
Rooms 74 and 76: 20th-century
Rooms 81, 82, 87–88a: Paintings
Rooms 83–84: Sacred silver and stained glass
Room 90: Prints and drawings
Room 90a: Portrait miniatures
Rooms 91–93: Jewellery gallery
Room 94: Tapestries
Rooms 95–100: Textiles
Room 101: Furniture
Rooms 107 and 109: Frescoes by Victorian artist Frederic, Lord Leighton
Room 111: Sculpture
Rooms 113–114e: Ironwork
Room 116: Metalware

LEVEL 2
Rooms 52–58: British galleries, tracing the history of British design from the Tudor era to 1900
All other rooms are for exhibitions.

LEVELS 0 AND 1
Rooms 1–9, 16a and 21–28: European displays (Rooms 21–24 Sculpture)
Rooms 17–20: Asian sculpture
Room 38a: Photography
Room 40: Fashion
Rooms 41–42, 44–45 and 47a–g: Asian and Islamic works
Room 46: Medieval
Rooms 46a and 46b: Cast courts
Room 48: Raphael gallery

HENRY COLE WING
LEVELS 4 AND 5
Study rooms
Lecture rooms

LEVEL 3
Temporary displays

LEVEL 2
Frank Lloyd Wright gallery

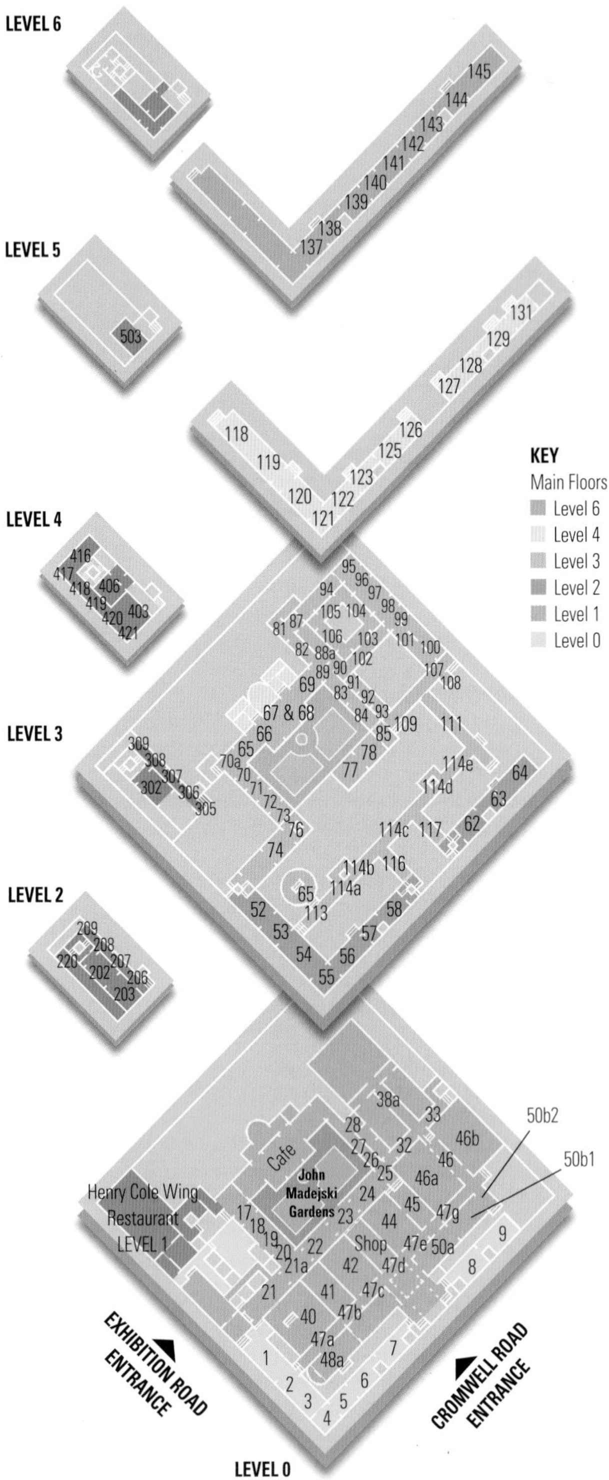

WALLACE COLLECTION

Four generations of the Hertford family amassed this world-class collection of art, on show in Hertford House, a beautiful 18th-century mansion. It was started when the 4th Marquess of Hertford, living as a recluse in Paris with his illegitimate son, Richard Wallace, during the French Revolution, bought French 18th-century paintings, porcelain and furniture to add to his inheritance of Sèvres porcelain and paintings by Canaletto and Gainsborough. Richard inherited the collection in 1870 and brought it to England, escaping the unstable political situation in France. He in turn added many fine examples of Renaissance ceramics, bronzes, armour and jewellery, and his widow left the collection to the nation in 1897, on condition that it remained intact and was never removed from central London.

FROM ARTWORKS TO ARMOUR

The rooms are packed with all sorts of beautiful objects, from paintings, furnishings and fittings originally made for the palaces of Fontainebleau and Versailles to 18th-century saucepans.

About 70 paintings from the 17th and 18th centuries hang in the Great Gallery. Most famously, these include *The Laughing Cavalier* by Frans Hals (1624), a portrait of an unknown young man (although he is neither a cavalier nor laughing) seated in sumptuous surroundings with a rural backdrop, and a marvellous portrait of King George IV by Sir Thomas Lawrence (1769–1830).

There's also a superb display of European arms and armour, much of it made by specialist metalworkers and embellished with fine inlay decoration. Seek out the late 15th-century set of armour for a man and his horse, made in Germany.

INFORMATION

www.wallacecollection.org

209 F4 Hertford House, Manchester Square W1U 3BN 020 7563 9500 Daily 10–5 Free Bond Street, Baker Street 2, 10, 13, 30, 74, 82, 94 Free guided tours weekdays 1pm, also Sat 11.30am, Sun 1pm, 3pm £7, in English only The Wallace Restaurant (Sun–Thu 10–5, Fri–Sat 10am–11pm) Gifts and books, many exclusive to the collection

Below *The Wallace Collection is housed in a Georgian mansion*

THE SEVEN WONDERS OF KENSINGTON

South Kensington became London's museum district in the 19th century. This simple route highlights the architectural masterpieces that were built here, drawing freely on Renaissance and Romanesque style.

THE WALK
Distance: 4km (2.5 miles)
Allow: 1hr
Start/end at: South Kensington Underground station

HOW TO GET THERE
District, Circle or Piccadilly line to South Kensington 14, 74, 414, C1

★ This walk captures the spirit of the Great Exhibition of 1851, which was organized by Prince Albert, the Queen's Consort. The exhibition was so successful that it inspired him to establish a permanent centre for the study of the applied arts and sciences. He proposed that some of the profits from the exhibition should be used to buy land in South Kensington. The result was the concentration of world-class museums in South Kensington, and Imperial College.

From South Kensington Tube, cross Thurloe Street and turn left into Exhibition Road. Cross the road at the traffic lights.

On the right-hand corner is the Victoria & Albert Museum.

❶ The Victoria & Albert Museum (▷ 224–228) is regarded as one of the world's greatest museums. As it has more than 11.5km (7 miles) of galleries, it's hard to know where to begin. Take your time and wander around slowly. Your patience will be rewarded by the extraordinary visual input of the thousands of items on display, mostly decorative items and period clothing.

Cross the road to the splendid Natural History Museum.

❷ The neo-Gothic architecture of the Natural History Museum (▷ 220–221) is extraordinary. Designed by Alfred Waterhouse, it uses the decorative terracotta that was so fashionable in the Victorian era (see also the Royal Albert Hall, above and opposite) to full effect. A series of lion sculptures also feature in the design.

The walk continues along Exhibition Road past the Science Museum, on the left, followed by Imperial College (for science, technology and medicine).

❸ The Science Museum (▷ 222–223) is less impressive from the outside—even some of its staff say that it resembles a small Selfridges. In the early stages it was a humdrum assortment of wooden buildings. The chief architect, Sir Richard Allison, had been asked to maintain strict economy in the

Left *The design of the Royal Albert Hall was inspired by Roman amphitheatres; the continuous terracotta frieze that runs around the outside of the dome shows allegorical figures engaged in various cultural activities*

new building, which was on a grand scale, as was the rambling hulk that is Imperial College.

Turn left into Prince Consort Road, which is home to the 600 students of the Royal College of Music.

❹ If you see some oddly shaped rucksacks and bags, they probably belong to a musician or student at the Royal College of Music, which provides courses for performers and composers. In the concert hall is an organ donated by composer Hubert Parry, who taught here, as did Charles Villiers Stanford and Ralph Vaughan Williams.

Halfway along Prince Consort Road, on the right, there are some steps that lead up to the round Royal Albert Hall, with its familiar glass-domed roof.

❺ Completed in 1871, 10 years after the death from typhoid of Queen Victoria's Prince Consort, the imposing auditorium of the Royal Albert Hall (▷ 235) had actually been planned during his lifetime. The project was funded by selling seats on 999-year leases, which theoretically still exist today. The venue hosts all sorts of musical styles, most famously the summer series of classical Proms concerts (▷ 294–295).

At the top of the steps bear right to reach the main road, Kensington Road (in this short stretch known as Kensington Gore). Cross this at the traffic lights for a closer look at the Albert Memorial.

❻ The grandiose Albert Memorial was finished in 1876 in honour of Victoria's late husband. The pediment hosts a crowd of 169 life-size figures of famous men, while elsewhere bronzes and mosaics represent the different sciences and arts. Four surrounding marble groupings stand for the continents. Amid all of this sits a gilt statue of Albert himself, as if embarrassed by all the fuss.

Spend some time beyond the memorial and wander through the lovely Kensington Gardens.

❼ In effect the eastern half of Hyde Park, Kensington Gardens (▷ 213) are generally more serene. They were first opened to the public during the reign of George II but only on Sunday, and formal garb was de rigueur. The prettiest section of the Serpentine, here known as Long Water, the statue of Peter Pan and, of course, the grandeur of Kensington Palace are among the attractions here.

Retrace your steps back to the Royal Albert Hall. With the building on your left, continue along Kensington Gore, past the rather dull exterior of the Royal College of Art, until you reach Queen's Gate. Turn left, pass the Gore Hotel and cross Prince Consort Road. On the left is the other end of Imperial College and soon you'll see the wildlife garden of the Natural History Museum, behind the railings where Queen's Gate meets Cromwell Road.

Turn left along Cromwell Road and then take the right turn to take you back to South Kensington Underground station.

WHERE TO EAT AND DRINK

All the museums along this walk have either a cafe or a restaurant. The cafe at the V&A serves wine and beer, the food is particularly fresh and the surroundings opulent. Alternatively, you could wait until the end of the walk and take your pick of the pubs on Earl's Court Road, such as the Blackbird at No. 209.

WHEN TO GO

As this walk features such popular museums, it is best done on a weekday morning, when the crowds should be smaller, especially out of season. If you only concentrate on the outdoor section, however, then a sunny afternoon enhances the beauty of the tree-lined streets and the park.

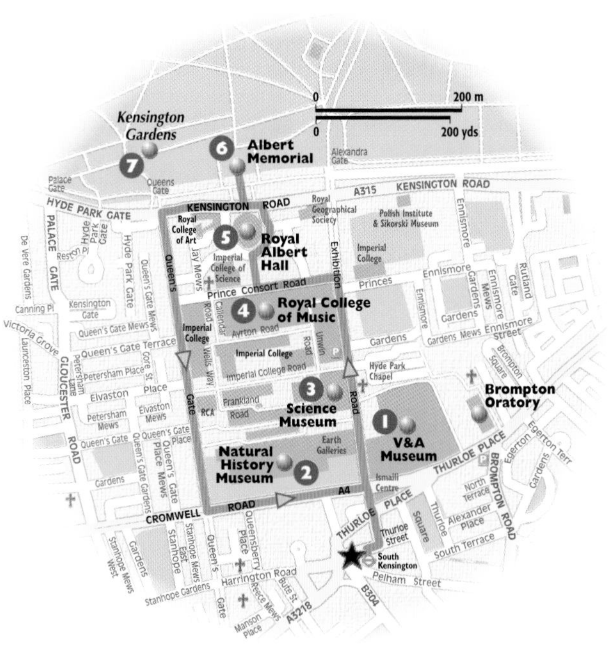

SHOPPING

AGENT PROVOCATEUR

www.agentprovocateur.com

This boudoir-style shop in otherwise very proper Belgravia sells seductive and even quite raunchy underwear.
247 F7 16 Pont Street SW1X 9EN 020 7235 0229 Mon–Sat 10–6 Knightsbridge, Sloane Square 19, 22, 137, C1

ALFIE'S ANTIQUE MARKET

www.alfiesantiques.com

London's largest antiques market, Alfie's is home to 100 dealers specializing in art deco, silver, furniture, paintings and prints, jewellery, ceramics, vintage clothing and lots more. You'll be competing against dealers and may well spot some celebrity faces too.
246 E3 13–25 Church Street, Marylebone NW8 8DT 020 7723 6066 Tue–Sat 10–6 Marylebone, Edgware Road 6, 13, 16, 82, 98, 139, 189, 274

BONHAM'S

www.bonhams.com

Operating since 1793, this international auction house deals in a wide variety of interesting lots—including football and cricket memorabilia. Fine art, furniture, carpets and silver and plate are among their auction themes.
247 E6 Montpelier Street SW7 1HH 020 7393 3900 Mon–Fri 9–5.30 Knightsbridge 9, 10, 14, 74, C1

BOOSEY & HAWKES @ BRITTENS MUSIC

www.boosey.com

This place stocks a huge range of musical instruments, many made by the company. Specializes in 20th-century composers.
247 G4 16 Wigmore Street W1U 2RF 0800 731 4778 Mon–Fri 9.30–6, Sat 10–5 Bond Street 8, 10, 73, C2

BRORA

www.brora.co.uk

Cashmere heaven. Beautiful, soft classics for all the family in sometimes startling hues, plus blankets, tweedy bags and slippers. Not cheap, but great quality.
246 E8 344 King's Road SW3 5UR 020 7352 3697 Mon–Sat 10–6, Sun 12–5 South Kensington, Sloane Square 11, 19, 22, 211, 328

BROWNS

www.brownsfashion.com

The latest and funkiest labels for women makes this smart boutique look intimidating, and it isn't cheap, but the people here know what's in vogue. See Browns Focus (No. 38) across the road for younger lines and Browns Labels for Less (No. 50) along the street for sale items. Small men's selection.
247 G4 23–27 South Molton Street W1K 5RD 020 7514 0016 Mon–Wed 10–6.30, Thu–Sat 10–7 Bond Street 8, 10, 12, 73, 139

CAMDEN LOCK MARKET

www.camdenlockmarket.com

This vibrant market, in a lovely setting around Camden Lock, has expanded and sprawled over the years to fill every patch of space from the canal back to Camden Lock Place. You'll find everything from high-quality designer clothes to art, food and furniture.
Off map 247 G1 Camden Lock Place/ Chalk Farm Road NW1 020 7485 7963 Daily 10–6 (Thu till 7) Camden Town 24, 27, 29, 31, 74, 134

CATH KIDSTON

www.cathkidston.co.uk

Cath Kidston's pretty and now famous floral designs, inspired by 1950s patterns, are available on fabrics, wallpapers, bed linen,

Left *Sloane Street is lined with branches of many exclusive fashion names—including Jimmy Choo, Dior, Prada and Armani*

table linen, vintage jewellery and ornaments in this charming Chelsea Green shop. The original store is at Clarendon Cross, Holland Park, and there are others around town.
247 E8 12 Cale Street SW3 3NS 020 7584 3232 Mon–Sat 10–6, Sun 12–5 Sloane Square, South Kensington 11, 19, 22, 211, 319

CHRISTIE'S

www.christies.com
James Christie conducted his first sale in 1766 and went on to hold the greatest auctions of his time. Christie's salerooms are world famous, auctioning major works such as Rembrandt's *Portrait of a Lady*—sold in 2000 for more than £19 million. Most auctions are free and public; book tickets for those that require one.
246 D7 85 Old Brompton Road SW7 3LD 020 7930 6074 Mon 5–7.30, Tue–Fri 9–5, Sat–Sun 10–4 South Kensington 14, 70, 74, 414, C1

THE CONRAN SHOP

www.conran.com
Housed in the magnificent Michelin Building, The Conran Shop was the pioneer of bringing late 20th-century design to the everyday household. Beautiful displays include furniture, kitchenware, books, gadgets, ceramics, fabrics and just about everything for the home.
246 E7 Michelin House, 81 Fulham Road SW3 6RD 020 7589 7401 Mon–Tue, Fri 10–6, Wed–Thu 10–7, Sat 10–6.30, Sun 12–6 South Kensington 14, 49, 360

GENERAL TRADING COMPANY

www.general-trading.co.uk
A stylish emporium stocking furniture, tableware and ornaments. Since 1920 it's provided stylish wedding gifts and holds all current royal warrants. You might spot a celebrity or two in the cafe.
247 F7 2–6 Symons Street SW3 2GT 020 7730 0411 Mon–Sat 10–7, Sun 11.30–5.30 Sloane Square 19, 22, 211, C1

GIORGIO ARMANI

www.giorgioarmani.com
Comparatively understated fashion. This shop is one of a number of showcases of big Italian names along this street, also including Alberta Ferretti at No. 205 and Prada at No. 43.
247 F6 37–42 Sloane Street SW1X 9LP 020 7235 6232 Mon–Tue, Thu–Sat 10–6, Wed 10–7, Sun 12–6 Knightsbridge 19, 22, 137, C1

GRAYS ANTIQUE MARKET

www.graysantiques.com
A labyrinth of alleys concealed within an attractive 19th-century building. More than 200 dealers specialize in diverse items dating from 40BC to the 20th century. Keep your eyes open for a bargain.
247 G4 58 Davies Street W1K 5AB 020 7629 7034 Mon–Fri 10–6 Bond Street 6, 7, 8, 10, 12, 13, 15, 88, 98, 134, 137, 159

GUINEVERE

www.guinevere.co.uk
The original antiques emporium on this now famous strip of the King's Road, and probably the best. The 10 rooms give a vastly eclectic selection of fine antiques, ranging as much in price as in age and origin.
Off map 246 D9 574–580 King's Road SW6 2DY 020 7736 2917 Mon–Fri 9.30–6, Sat 10–5.30 Fulham Broadway 11, 14, 22

HARRODS

www.harrods.com
More than just a department store, Harrod's is a miniature kingdom. The vast, terracotta building occupies 6ha (15 acres)—a far cry from its origins as a small grocer's shop in 1849. Its Latin motto is *omnia, omnibus, ubique*—'everything for everyone, everywhere'. Pick up the Store Guide at the entrance for details of exhibitions and demonstrations. For many, the first-floor food halls are the highlight, partly for the range of good foods on display, but also for W. J. Neatley's tiled ceilings (1902). Equally lavish art deco ceramics decorate both the men's hairdressing rooms and the women's toilets. The elaborate central escalator is inspired by the art of Ancient Egypt.
247 E6 87–135 Brompton Road SW1X 7XL 020 7730 1234 Mon–Sat 10–8, Sun 11.30–6 Knightsbridge 9, 10 14, 74, C1

HARVEY NICHOLS

www.harveynichols.com
Chic department store with marvellous window displays and an ultra-trendy beauty bar that can even sell you 10 minutes of fresh air! Six floors of clothing, housewares and a food market on the fifth floor. Stylish cafe, restaurant and sushi bar.
247 F6 109–125 Knightsbridge SW1X 7RJ 020 7584 0011 Mon–Sat 10–8, Sun 11.30–6 Knightsbridge 9, 10 14, 74, C1

HEAL'S

www.heals.co.uk
A top destination for contemporary interior design and furnishings for the past two centuries, with striking, high-quality furniture, rugs, beds, fabrics, bed linen and home accessories. The main store, on Tottenham Court Road, is immense.
247 E8 234 King's Road SW3 5UA 020 7349 8411 Mon–Wed 10–6, Thu 10–8, Fri 10–6.30, Sat 9.30–6.30, Sun 12–6 Sloane Square, Goodge Street 11, 19, 22, 211, C1

HMV

www.hmv.com
The nationwide chain's megastore offers a wide selection of music styles.
247 G3 150 Oxford Street W1D 1DJ 0845 602 7802 Mon–Sat 9–8.30 (Thu till 9), Sun 11.30–6.30 Bond Street 6, 7, 10, 12, 13, 15, 23, 94, 98, 113, 137, 139, 159

JIMMY CHOO

www.jimmychoo.com
The best place in the Western hemisphere to find sexy high-heeled shoes, this store is in Knightsbridge,

the playground of the beautiful rich. Your wallet could be stretched by these fabulous items, but trying them on costs nothing and they make you feel like a superstar.
247 F5 32 Sloane Street SW1X 9NR 020 7823 1051 Mon–Sat 10–6, Wed 10–7, Sun 1–5 Knightsbridge 19, 22, 137, C1

JO MALONE
www.jomalone.co.uk
A wonderful shop full of luxury face creams, scented candles and divine perfumery. You can also come here for luxury facials.
247 F7 150 Sloane Street SW1X 9BX 020 7730 2100 Mon–Tue, Sat 9.30–6, Wed–Fri 9.30–7, Sun 12–5 Sloane Square 19, 22, 137, C1

LULU GUINNESS
www.luluguinness.com
Opened in 1996, this sleek, modern shop sells quirky 1950s handbags, hats and shoes. Lulu studied art in Paris and decided to push the boundaries of the bag—hence the handbags in the shape of flower baskets, spiders' webs and even castles.
247 F7 3 Ellis Street SW1X 9AL 020 7823 4828 Mon–Fri 10–6, Sat 11–6 Sloane Square 11, 19, 22, 211, C1

MARKS & SPENCER
www.marksandspencer.com
The flagship store of a venerable British institution famous for its good quality, reasonably priced clothing for men and women, homeware and top-of-the range convenience foods. The best women's fashions are in the Per Una and Limited collections.
247 F4 458 Oxford Street W1C 1AP 020 7437 7722 Mon–Fri 9–9, Sat 9–8, Sun 12–6 Marble Arch 6, 7, 10, 12, 13, 15, 23, 73, 94, 98, 113, 137, 139, 159

MOLTON BROWN
www.moltonbrown.co.uk
A seductive aroma greets you as you cross the threshold to look for shampoos, oils and scented candles. Set among tempting fashion shops and cafes.
247 G4 58 South Molton Street W1K 5SL 020 7499 6474 Mon–Sat 10–6.30, Sun 11–5 Bond Street 8, 10, 14, 19

PETER JONES
www.peterjones.co.uk
While the branch in Oxford Street is the largest John Lewis store, PJ (as it's affectionately known) is a more personal part of the chain, and an excellent choice for housewares and middle-market clothing.
247 F7 Sloane Square SW1W 8EL 020 7730 3434 Mon–Sat 9.30–7 (Wed till 8), Sun 11–5 Sloane Square 11, 19, 22, 211, C1

PORTOBELLO ROAD
www.portobelloroad.co.uk
Famous street market with hundreds of stalls selling antiques, vintage clothing, objets d'art and, at the northern end, fresh fruit and vegetables, baked goods and meat. It's not cheap and there is a lot of junk, but it's fun and you might spot a famous face or two. Runs along Portobello Road from Pembridge Road (Notting Hill Underground station) north up to Westbourne Park Road (Ladbroke Grove Underground station). Come early if you want to find a bargain.
246 B4 Office: 72 Tavistock Road W11 1AN 020 7727 7684 Market Sat only 8–7. Shops Mon–Sat, hours vary Notting Hill Gate 7, 12, 23, 27, 28, 31, 70, 94, 328

PURDEY
www.purdey.com
Founded in 1814, this glorious Victorian shop has supplied guns to every British monarch since Queen Victoria. Each shotgun and rifle is manufactured by hand.
247 F5 57–58 South Audley Street W1K 2ED 020 7499 1801 Mon–Fri 9.30–5.30, Sat 10–5 Green Park, Marble Arch, Hyde Park Corner 10, 16, 73, 74, 137

RIGBY & PELLER
www.rigbyandpeller.com
There is nothing the women at the Queen's corsetier do not know about undergarments. They can tell what size you are without a tape measure and have underwear for every size and shape of woman. There's a huge selection of swimwear and, of course, corsets.
247 E6 2 Hans Road SW3 1RX 020 7589 9293 Mon–Tue, Thu–Sat 9.30–6, Wed 9.30–7, Sun 12–6 Knightsbridge 14, 74, C1

ROCOCO
www.rococochocolates.com
Incredible chocolates, mostly handmade on the premises. Choose from hundreds of different varieties including quails' eggs (pralines), marzipans, violet creams and great big bars. Situated on a pleasant row of shops about 20 minutes' walk from Sloane Square.
246 D8 321 King's Road SW3 5EP 020 7352 5857 Mon–Sat 10–6.30, Sun 12–5 South Kensington, Sloane Square 11, 19, 22, 211, 319

SELFRIDGE'S
www.selfridges.com
A Victorian facade hides this popular store, now a modern emporium filled with designer clothes, accessories and a huge beauty hall. Also has a food hall with eclectic foodstuffs from around the globe.
247 F4 400 Oxford Street W1A 1AB 0800 123400 Mon–Sat 9.30–9, Sun 12–6 Marble Arch, Bond Street 6, 7, 10, 12, 13, 15, 23, 73, 94, 98, 113, 137, 139, 159

TRADITIONAL TOYS OF CHELSEA
As the name suggests, this is the place to come for traditional wooden toys, as well as soft toys, dressing-up costumes for children, fairy-tale dolls and puppets.
247 E8 53 Godfrey Street SW3 3SX 020 7352 1718 Mon–Sat 10–6 South Kensington, Sloane Square 11, 19, 22, 211

ENTERTAINMENT AND NIGHTLIFE

CINÉ LUMIÈRE
www.institut-francais.org.uk
Part of the French government's centre of language and culture.

Shows French films and other European and world cinema productions, including premieres, recent releases, classics, rare movies and visits by directors, screenwriters and actors.
246 D7 Institut Français, 17 Queensberry Place SW7 2DT 020 7073 1350 South Kensington, Gloucester Road 49, 70, 74, 345

ELECTRIC CINEMA
www.the-electric.co.uk
Originally opened in 1910, the Electric Cinema later turned to repertory cinema, showing old classics and independent films. Also has a brasserie.
246 B4 191 Portobello Road W11 2ED 020 7908 9696 Ladbroke Grove, Notting Hill Gate 23, 52, 94

THE GATE
www.gatetheatre.co.uk
Tiny (70–80 seats) but well established theatre above a pub. All work is translated from languages and cultures other than British.
246 B5 11 Pembridge Road W11 3HQ 020 7229 0706 £10–£15 (Mon, 30 'pay what you can' seats available) Notting Hill Gate 27, 28, 31, 328

GATE CINEMA
www.picturehouses.co.uk
Converted from a coffee palace in 1910, this is now a leading art-house venue.
246 B5 87 Notting Hill Gate W11 3JZ 0871 704 2058 Notting Hill Gate 12, 70, 94, 148

HOLLAND PARK THEATRE
www.operahollandpark.com
Catching an opera in the park on a balmy summer evening might just be the highlight of your visit to London. You might also catch a shower, however, so be prepared. There is a special Champagne bar and you can even book a picnic (starting at £40), though it's cheaper to pack your own!
246 B6 Holland Park, Kensington High Street W8 6LU 0845 230 9769 £10–£54 High Street Kensington, Holland Park 9, 94, 148

NOTTING HILL ARTS CLUB
www.nottinghillartsclub.com
This bohemian basement spot, with projected images on whitewashed walls and fabrics, is a pioneering music and arts venue. The Cuban rum and beer are both great, and the drinks are reasonably priced. Impressive DJs play funky tunes. Frequent live bands and special happenings.
246 B5 21 Notting Hill Gate W11 3JQ 020 7598 5226 Mon–Fri 6pm–2am, Sat 4pm–2am, Sun 4pm–1am, last entry one hour before closing £5–£8 Notting Hill Gate 12, 28, 31, 52

ODEON WHITELEYS
www.odeon.co.uk
Eight-screen multiplex cinema in a shopping complex.
246 C4 2nd Floor Whiteleys Shopping Centre, Queensway, Bayswater W2 4YL 0871 224 4007 Bayswater, Queensway 12, 23, 70

OPEN-AIR THEATRE
www.openairtheatre.org
The New Shakespeare Company performs in this 1932 amphitheatre in Regent's Park (Jun–Sep). Take warm clothes, cushion and picnic.
Off map 246 F1 Regent's Park NW1 4NP 0870 060 1811 £10–£35 Baker Street, Regent's Park 18, 27, 30

PIZZA ON THE PARK
See good mainstream jazz performers every night, some well-known international names, in the dining area below. Book ahead.
247 F6 11 Knightsbridge SW1X 7LY 0845 602 7017 £10–£20 Hyde Park Corner 9, 10, 14, 19, 74

ROYAL ALBERT HALL
www.royalalberthall.com
The immense domed building just south of Kensington Gardens can seat 5,200. It is a venue for major concerts, ballets in summer and the summer Proms (▷ 294–295).
246 D6 Kensington Gore SW7 2AP 020 7589 3203, bookings 0845 401 5045 £6–£100 South Kensington, High Street Kensington 9, 10, 52, 70

ROYAL COURT/JERWOOD THEATRE UPSTAIRS
www.royalcourttheatre.com
High artistic reputation; presents only new work by leading or emerging playwrights—a bookshop sells play texts. The main theatre seats 400 and the studio 60.
247 F7 Sloane Square SW1W 8AS 020 7565 5000 £7.50–£26 Sloane Square 11, 19, 22, 211, C1

SCIENCE MUSEUM IMAX
▷ 223.

SCREEN ON BAKER STREET
www.screencinemas.co.uk
Two-screen chain cinema showing a mix of repertory pictures and new-release mainstream films.
247 F3 96–98 Baker Street W1U 6TJ 020 7486 0036, bookings 0870 066 4777 Baker Street 2, 13, 74, 82

WIGMORE HALL
www.wigmore-hall.org.uk
London's favourite intimate concert and recital venue, with acoustics of legendary perfection. Opened in 1901 as the Bechstein Hall. The architectural elegance (marble and plaster with cupola) matches the peerless quality of the great classic performances.
247 G4 36 Wigmore Street W1U 2BP 020 7935 2141 £10–£35 Bond Street 8, 10, 73, C2

SPORTS AND ACTIVITIES

CHELSEA FOOTBALL CLUB
www.chelseafc.co.uk
Glamorous club, reinvigorated since 2003 by the money of Russian oil tycoon Roman Abramovich, and the 2005 and 2006 Premier League champions.
246 C9 Stamford Bridge, Fulham Road SW6 1HS 0871 984 1905 Fulham Broadway 11, 414

CHELSEA SPORTS CENTRE
www.courtneys.co.uk/chelsea
Refurbished in 2007 to provide modern facilities in a building that retains its early 1900s charm. Sports hall, swimming pool, gym and dance studio.

247 E8 2 Chelsea Manor Street, SW3 5PL 020 7352 6985 Mon–Fri 6.30am–10pm, Sat 8–8, Sun 8am–10pm £3.50–£8 (depending on activity) Sloane Square, South Kensington 11, 19, 22, 49, 319

FULHAM FOOTBALL CLUB
www.fulhamfc.co.uk
A snug little ground by Premier League standards, where the team owned by Harrod's owner, Mohammed Fayed, play entertaining football. They were rewarded in 2009 by their highest league finish (seventh) and a place in the Europa League.
Off map 246 C8 Craven Cottage, Stevenage Road SW6 6HH 0870 442 1234 Putney Bridge 49, 94, 148

HYDE PARK
www.royalparks.org.uk
The Serpentine, an 11ha (27-acre) lake, has facilities for rowing, canoeing and hiring paddle boats (▷ 212).
247 E5 The Ranger's Lodge, Hyde Park W2 2UH 020 7298 2100 Hyde Park Corner, Marble Arch, Knightsbridge 9, 10, 12, 14, 73

REGENT'S PARK LAKE
www.royalparks.org.uk
In addition to boating facilities, the lake has islands, a heronry and waterfowl (▷ 218).
247 F2 Storeyard (Inner Circle), Regent's Park NW1 4NR 020 7486 7905 Baker Street, Marylebone, Regent's Park, Great Portland Street, Camden Town 27, 82, 205, 274, C2

SERPENTINE LIDO
www.serpentinelido.com
Hyde Park's lido has been in existence for more than 100 years. You can swim in the Serpentine or sunbathe in a deckchair. Playground, small pool for children, and facilities for changing and for people with disabilities.
247 E5 Hyde Park W1J 7NT 020 7706 3422 Jun–end Sep daily 10–6 Adult £4, child (under 15) £1, family £8, under 3s free Hyde Park Corner 9, 10, 14, 19, 22, 52, 74, 137

HEALTH AND BEAUTY

BALANCE
www.balancetheclinic.om
Peaceful retreat offering health treatments—including nutrition advice, colonics and lymph drainage—as well as massages.
247 E8 The Courtyard, 250 King's Road SW3 5UE 020 7565 0333 Mon–Thu 9–8, Fri 9–7, Sat 9–6, Sun 9–5.30. Booking advisable Treatments from £20 South Kensington, Sloane Square 11, 19, 22, 49, 211, 319

BHARTI VYAS
www.bharti-vyas.com
Holistic beauty centre offering treatments such as aromatherapy, acupressure and massage, tailored for individual customers.
247 F3 5 and 24 Chiltern Street W1U 7QE 020 7935 5312 Mon–Sat 9–6 (Wed, Fri till 7). Booking essential Facial from £75 Baker Street 2, 13, 30, 74, 82, 113, 139, 189, 274

BLISS LONDON
www.blissworld.com
Originally opened in New York, this salon promises highly trained experts. The glass of wine and rich chocolate brownies you're given before a treatment is surely bliss!
247 E7 60 Sloane Avenue SW3 3DD 020 7590 7109 Mon–Fri 9.30–8, Sat 9.30–6.30, Sun 12–6. Booking essential Manicure from £25 South Kensington 14, 49, 345

PORCHESTER SPA
West London's best-value spa includes three Turkish hot rooms, two Russian steam rooms, a cold plunge pool, a whirlpool bath and an art deco swimming pool.
246 C4 Porchester Centre, Queensway W2 5HS 020 7792 3980 Daily 10–10. Women only Tue, Thu, Fri, Sun (10–4). Men only Mon, Wed, Sat. Mixed couples Sun 4–10 From £15. Mixed couples ticket £28.25 Bayswater, Queensway 7, 15, 27, 36

VIDAL SASSOON
www.sassoon.com
The famous salon from the Swinging Sixties is now a slick modern operation with a unique three-year training school and six salons throughout London.
247 G4 60 South Molton Street W1Y 1HH 020 7491 8848 Mon–Wed, Fri 9–6, Thu 9–6.45, Sat 9–5.15, Sun 12–4.30. Booking advisable Cut and blow dry from £62 Bond Street 8, 10, 15, 73, 139

FOR CHILDREN

DIANA, PRINCESS OF WALES MEMORIAL PLAYGROUND
www.royalparks.gov.uk
Creative fun for children up to the age of 12. The playground has a Peter Pan theme and includes a pirate ship, crocodile, fountains and wigwams.
246 E5 Kensington Gardens W2 2UH 020 7298 2141 Daily 10am–dusk Free Lancaster Gate, High Street Kensington, Queensway 9, 10, 12

HOLLAND PARK ADVENTURE PLAYGROUND
www.rbkc.gov.uk
Ropes and swings, activity games and sports and ecology centre. It's open to children aged 5 to 15, but there's an under-8s area available.
246 B6 Holland Park W8 6LU 020 7471 9813 Daily dawn–dusk; under-8s area 12.30–4 Free Holland Park, Kensington High Street 9, 10, 94, C1

NATURAL HISTORY MUSEUM
▷ 220–221.

QUEENS ICE BOWL
A supermodern ice rink, plus 12 lanes of tenpin bowling, hi-tech video games and amusements.
246 C5 17 Queensway W2 4QP 020 7229 0172 Daily 10am–10.45pm Prices vary Bayswater, Queensway 7, 23, 27, 70

SCIENCE MUSEUM
There are interactive sections here aimed at specific age groups, and popular sleepover nights for 8- to 11-year-olds. ▷ 222–223.
246 D6 Science Nights sleepovers once a month: minimum five children and one adult (020 7942 4747)

Above *Babylon restaurant is known for its sumptuous seafood*

PRICES AND SYMBOLS

The prices given are for a two-course set lunch (L) and a three-course à la carte dinner (D) for one person, without drinks. The wine price is for the least expensive bottle.

For a key to the symbols, ▷ 2.

AMAYA

www.amaya.biz

Brainchild of the team behind Chutney Mary, this Indian restaurant scooped nearly every available award in 2005 by taking regional Indian food and bringing it bang up to date. Most of the food is prepared in full view of customers, ensuring absolute freshness as well as a great atmosphere. The seafood platter is a particular highlight, or try the Caesar salad with chicken tikka and an ever-changing small selection of in-season curries, soups and biryanis. Booking essential.

247 F6 Halkin Arcade, Motcomb Street SW1X 8JT 020 7823 1166 Mon–Sat 12.30–2.15, 6.30–11.30 (10.30 Sun) L from £16.50, D from £25, Wine from £20 Knightsbridge

ASSAGGI

A relaxed and traditional Italian restaurant with bare floorboards, wooden tables and plenty of yellow and terracotta, set above the Chepstow pub. Starters may include buffalo mozzarella, *fregola con arselle* (fregula pasta with clams) and *calamari ripieni* (stuffed squid). Main courses include *quaglia ripiena* (stuffed roasted quail) and *filetto di vitello al rosmarino* (pan-roasted fillet of white veal, rosemary and glazed baby onions). Perfectly accompanied by a selection of Italian and Sardinian wines.

246 C4 39 Chepstow Place W2 4TS 020 7792 5501 Mon–Sat 12.30–2.30, 7.30–11. Closed public hols L/D from £54, Wine from £21.50 Notting Hill Gate, Bayswater (W of Lancaster Gate)

AUBERGINE

www.auberginerestaurant.co.uk

In a quiet side street off Fulham Road, Aubergine has the feel of a chic neighbourhood restaurant with an unpretentious atmosphere. The cooking is accomplished and refined and very French. Try the seven-course tasting menu, or choose from a variety of faultless dishes from the à la carte one, such as seared scallops, *assiette* of corn-fed duck, or irresistible banana parfait with banana ice cream. The serious wine list offers few bargains but superb quality.

246 D8 11 Park Walk SW10 0AJ 020 7352 3449 Mon–Fri 12–2.15, 7–11, Sat 7–11. Closed 24 Dec–3 Jan, public hols L from £29 (3 courses inc. half bottle wine), D from £68, Wine from £27 South Kensington, Fulham Broadway

BABYLON

www.roofgardens.com

Superb roof-garden restaurant. Proceed through the cavernous marble foyer, hop into the lift and then walk past the fishtanks that form a wall of the small bar area. The generous and varied menu may offer delights such as tender baby squid bursting with king prawns and Cornish bourride perfumed with ginger and spring onions. Desserts might well include sliced exotic fruits and lychee sorbet.

246 C6 The Roof Gardens, 99 Kensington High Street W8 5SA 020 7368 3993 Mon–Sat 12–2.30, 7–11, Sun 12–2.30. Closed 25 Dec L from £18, D from £45, Wine from £20 High Street Kensington (SW of Lancaster Gate)

BIBENDUM

www.bibendum.co.uk

Housed in the large remarkable art deco Michelin building, this restaurant is light and airy with fabulous stained-glass windows depicting Bibendum, the Michelin Man, riding his bicycle, kick-boxing and drinking champagne. The Bibendum motif is also picked up on the glasses, decanters, vases, tables and even the chair legs. Great emphasis is placed on wine service, with guidance from the sommeliers through the list of some 600 wines. The less formal Oyster Bar opens all day (from noon) serving all manner of crustacea, plus salads and daily specials.

247 E7 Michelin House, 81 Fulham Road SW3 6RD 020 7581 5817 Mon–Fri 12–2.30, 7–11, Sat 12.30–3, 7–11, Sun 12.30–3, 7–10.30. Closed 25–26 Dec, 1 Jan L from £25, D from £50, Wine from £22 South Kensington

BOXWOOD CAFÉ

www.gordonramsay.com

A cross between fine dining in an elegant Knightsbridge hotel and the not-so-humble cafe experience, this Gordon Ramsay-inspired venture is one of London's most popular hotel eateries thanks to its combination of expert cooking, top-class service and relaxed atmosphere. Dishes are upmarket brasserie fare and often quite expensive, but you may be able to go for something as simple as grilled sardines with tomatoes and black olive dressing.

247 F6 The Berkeley Hotel, Wilton Place SW1X 7RL 020 7235 1010 Mon–Fri 12–3, 6–11, Sat 12–4, 6–11, Sun 12–4, 6–9.30 L from £21 (3 courses), D from £25. Wine from £22 Hyde Park Corner, Knightsbridge

CAMBIO DE TERCIO

www.cambiodetercio.co.uk

Voted the best Spanish restaurant outside Iberia in 2003, this attractive, friendly venue serves up exquisite Modern Spanish cooking. Dishes range from the innovative—Cuba libre of foie (duck liver mousse, coca-cola and rum gelée) lemon snow—to the classic such as beef solomillo, oxtail or grilled tuna, albeit with a modern twist. The desserts are superb: leave room for the creamy thyme-lemon ice cream. The wines are all Spanish, and are expensive.

246 D8 163 Old Brompton Road SW5 0LJ 020 7244 8970 Mon–Fri 12–2.30, 7.30–11.30, Sat 1–3, 7.30–11.30, Sun 1–3, 7–11 L from £23, D from £30, Wine from £25 Gloucester Road (W of South Kensington)

CARAFFINI

www.caraffini.co.uk

Friendly service greets you at this popular neighbourhood Italian restaurant. The pale yellow painted walls are hung with mirrors and prints and the pale wood floors contrast with Venetian blinds, rattan-style chairs, banquettes and plants. The lengthy menu includes a risotto with fresh baby artichokes and prawns and an excellent tiramisu. There's a good selection of vegetarian dishes and a range of Italian wines.

247 F8 61–63 Lower Sloane Street SW1W 8DH 020 7259 0235 Mon–Sat 12.15–2.30, 6.30–11.30. Closed 25–26 Dec, public hols L from £18, D from £30, Wine from £14 Sloane Square

CHEZ BRUCE

www.chezbruce.co.uk

This small, unassuming place—that looks more like a bistro from the outside rather than Wandsworth's culinary star—is set in a parade of shops overlooking the common, and is heaving most of the time. First-timers should look for the large maroon-coloured planters bursting with flowers outside, or just follow the savvy crowd who are full of admiration for Bruce Poole's memorable classic regional French cuisine with a twist. Noteworthy flavours, perfect balance and impeccable skill make for a memorable time.

Off map 246 D9 2 Bellevue Road SW17 7EG 020 8672 0114 Mon–Sat 12–2, 6.30–10.30, Sun 12–3, 7–9.30. Closed 24–26 Dec, 1 Jan L from £26 (3 courses), D from £40 (for 3 courses), Wine from £22 Balham Wandsworth Common

CHUTNEY MARY

www.chutneymary.com

This popular King's Road Indian restaurant has a sophisticated, contemporary look and a changing menu that combines established dishes with exciting new specialities, such as buttered crab (popular in Mumbai) and the restaurant's own *foie gras* dish cooked with seared mango and mild chilli marsala jelly. Don't miss one of the interesting and unusual desserts, such as the crème brûlée with strawberries and marsala spice.

Off map 246 D9 535 King's Road SW10 0SZ 020 7351 3113 Mon–Fri 6.30–11, Sat 12.30–2.30, 6.30–11, Sun 12.30–3, 6.30–10.30. Closed 25 Dec L from £25, D from £30, Wine from £20 Fulham Broadway

CIBO

www.ciborestaurant.net

Cibo is at once exciting and relaxing. The cooking is straightforward and concentrates mainly on seafood; there is a fine selection of grilled fish and shellfish and Modern Italian specialities such as lobster risotto or baked rack of lamb on a potato crust with baby artichokes. The wine list is interesting, with some hidden classics from overlooked regions. Set lunches are reasonably priced and the atmosphere is quieter than in the evening. The staff are friendly at all times.

246 A6 3 Russell Gardens W14 8EZ 020 7371 2085 Mon–Sat 12–3, 7–11, Sun 12–3. Closed 25–26 Dec L from £20, D from £33, Wine from £15 Kensington Olympia, Shepherd's Bush

THE COLLECTION

www.the-collection.co.uk

Take the long neon-lit catwalk from the Brompton Road entrance to this former fashion warehouse and you will find a bustling ground-floor bar and balcony restaurant. Black-clad staff, crisp linen, brick walls and high-backed contemporary seating

set the tone for the Modern British menu, which includes seared tuna sashimi with shiitake mushroom and cucumber salad; chargrilled rib steak with Béarnaise sauce; and mango carpaccio with coconut sorbet. Good selection of wines to complement the courses.
247 E7 264 Brompton Road SW3 2AS 020 7225 1212 Mon–Fri 5–11.30, Sat–Sun 12–3, 5–11.30. Closed 25–26 Dec, 1 Jan L from £24, D from £30, Wine from £13.50 South Kensington

LE GAVROCHE RESTAURANT

www.le-gavroche.co.uk

No other restaurant in Britain is as faithful to classic French tradition as the long-established Le Gavroche, the name now synonymous with the French Roux brothers. Tables are set with crystal and silver and the staff are professional and well informed. Dishes might include scallops baked in their shells and perfumed with truffles; lobster salad with mango, avocado, basil and lime; Scotch fillet of beef and foie gras, port sauce and truffled macaroni cheese; whole baked sea bass stuffed with fennel and wild rice. Desserts include a choice of soufflées and the famous Roux brothers' ice creams and sorbets. For a suitable accompaniment to your meal, choose from one of the most comprehensive wine lists in London. Male diners will need to wear a jacket.
247 F5 43 Upper Brook Street W1K 7QR 020 7408 0881 Mon–Fri 12–2, 6.30–11, Sat 6.30–11. Closed 25–26 Dec, 1 Jan, public hols L from £50 (3 courses), D from £70, Wine from £20 Marble Arch

LANGTRY'S

www.langtrysrestaurant.com

Named after the famous actress Lillie Langtry, who lived in this house, now the Cadogan Hotel. This new restaurant, with its modern British menu from chef Robert Lyons, is a welcome addition to the London hotel dining scene. The food served in the historic dining room offers fine cooking using the best seasonal ingredients. Start with delights such as Welsh cockle soup, move on to main dishes including toad-in-the-hole with crackling and finish off with yummy (if tooth-rotting) sticky toffee and date pudding with caramel sauce.
247 F7 21 Pont Street SW1X 9SG 020 7201 6619 Mon–Fri 7–10.30, 12–2.30, 6–10.30, Sat 8–11, 12–2.30, 6–10.30, Sun 8–11, 12–2.30. Closed 25 Dec B from £10, L from £25, D from £45 (set dinner £25), Wine from £16 Knightsbridge, Sloane Square

LEVANT

www.levant.co.uk

The perfume of roses drifts up the stairs to greet you at this Lebanese restaurant. Downstairs it is modern with polished stone floors and subtle lighting. Meze selections include spicy Armenian sausages, fried auberine (eggplant) with pomegranate dressing, and of course hummus and falafel. Made to share, they're eaten with warm pitta bread. Staff are happy to guide newcomers, and be prepared for the belly dancer.
247 G4 Jason Court, 76 Wigmore Street W1H 9DQ 020 7224 1111 Mon–Wed, Sun 12pm–12.30am, Thu–Sat 12pm–2.30am. Closed 25–26 Dec, 1 Jan L from £10, D from £25, Wine from £18 Bond Street

MAZE

www.gordonramsay.com

Yet another member of the Gordon Ramsay stable, bringing chef Jason Atherton from Ramsay's Dubai restaurant. He delivers a modern French approach with Asian influences, producing highly accomplished dishes such as slow roast quail with walnut purée and pickled lemons, white bean and Madeira sauce. There's a wide range of wines by the bottle and half bottle, and more than 25 choices by the glass.
247 F4 10–13 Grosvenor Square W1K 6JP 020 7107 0000 Daily 12–2.30, 6–10.30. Closed public hols L from £28.50 (4 courses), D from £60, Wine from £32 Bond Street

THE ORANGERY

www.digbytrout.co.uk

The quintessential English tea venue. Take tea or a light lunch in the beautiful Orangery designed for Queen Anne in 1704. You eat on the terrace or in the dining room in elegant surroundings overlooking the formal palace gardens. You can start with breakfast—from Continental to full English or even one with champagne. Lunch offers British delights such as steak or salmon followed by strawberry tart with lavender cream. For many, afternoon tea is the speciality—cucumber sandwiches or scones with cream and jam.
246 C6 Kensington Palace, Kensington Gardens W8 4PX 020 7938 1406 Daily 10–5. Closed 24–26 Dec B from £3.95, L from £9, full tea from £13.70, Wine from £15 High Street Kensington, Queensway

ORIGINAL TAGINES

www.original-tagines.com

As you would expect from the name, this Moroccan restaurant in Marylebone serves many versions of the eponymous dish among its main courses. Other specialities include a range of couscous dishes. Friendly staff and a warm, welcoming atmosphere. The charcoal grill is visible through a glass wall.
247 F3 7a Dorset Street W1H 3FE 020 7935 1545 Daily 11am–12am L from £15, D from £30, Wine from £10.50 Baker Street

RACINE

It doesn't get much more Gallic this side of the English Channel than in this popular Knightsbridge brasserie just opposite the South Kensington museums. There's an authentic bustle and a rather masculine look of dark wood and deep brown leather. Expect hearty bourgeois fare with big flavours such as grilled rabbit with mustard sauce and smoked bacon.
247 E7 239 Brompton Road SW3 2EP 020 7584 4477 Daily 12–3, 6–10.30 (Sun till 10). Closed 25 Dec

L from £17, D from £30, Wine from £20 South Kensington

RESTAURANT GORDON RAMSAY

www.gordonramsay.com

Attention to detail characterizes the whole of the slick operation here. There's an abundance of staff plus plenty of stylish features, such as salted and unsalted butter served on silver and marble plates, with a sprinkling of pepper on the salted. This is the mothership of famous British chef Gordon Ramsay's growing empire. If available, try pan-fried fillets of John Dory with Cromer crab, caviar, crushed new potatoes and a basil vinaigrette. Desserts include lime parfait with melon sorbet, honeycomb and chocolate sauce.

247 F8 68 Royal Hospital Road SW3 4HP 020 7352 4441 Mon–Fri 12–2.30, 6.30–11. Closed 2 weeks Christmas and New Year, public hols L from £45 (3 courses), D from £90, Wine from £32 Sloane Square

THE RIVER CAFÉ

www.rivercafe.co.uk

At this waterside restaurant you will be served some of the most authentic Italian food in London by staff selected for their personality above everything else. The menu might include spaghetti with crabmeat, olive oil and lemon, or squid chargrilled with chilli and served on rocket. Whole pigeon is cooked in the wood oven and accompanied by roasted pumpkin, fennel, celeriac (celery root) and carrots. Desserts are typically Italian, such as pannacotta or tiramisu.

Off map 246 A9 Thames Wharf, Rainville Road W6 9HA 020 7386 4200 Mon–Sat 12.30–2.30, 7–9.15, Sun 7–9.15. Closed 22 Dec–3 Jan, Easter, public hols L from £39, D from £55, Wine from £12.50 Hammersmith (10-minute walk)

SALLOOS RESTAURANT

Salloos is a long-established, family-run Pakistani restaurant tucked away in a secluded Belgravia mews. The food is prepared to order, so expect up to a 30-minute wait. The exquisite *aloo paratha*, a spicy potato dish, is a blend of the subtle and the spicy, and could be followed by melt-in-the-mouth charcoal-grilled kebabs. House specials, such as the king prawn *karahi*, come with very good basmati rice cooked with a mildly spiced stock. No children under six.

247 F6 62–64 Kinnerton Street SW1X 8ER 020 7235 4444 Mon–Sat 12–2.30, 7–11. Closed 25–26 Dec, public hols L from £20, D from £35, Wine from £20 Knightsbridge, Hyde Park Corner

SIX-13

www.six13.com

Named after the 613 Jewish disciplines, London's first Kosher fusion restaurant serves an eclectic mix of European, Pacific Rim and Jewish-influenced dishes. So, expect the likes of orange-glazed duckling on sauteéd Chinese vegetables, roulade of cod wrapped in savoy cabbage with bouillon and a citrus tomato salsa and gourmet spicy lamb burger. The desserts are equally intriguing concoctions.

247 G4 19 Wigmore Street W1U 1PH 020 7629 6133 Mon–Thu 12–2.30, 5.30–9.30. Closed 25 Dec, 1 Jan, Jewish holidays L from £20, D from £35, Wine from £18.50 Oxford Circus, Bond Street

TOM AIKENS

www.tomaikens.co.uk

London's top restaurant for 2005, according to the authoritative *Restaurant* magazine, Tom Aikens is the capital's newest gastronomic big-hitter. His cuisine is Modern French with inventive dishes that are intricately designed and superbly presented. The Chelsea setting is clean, modern and stylish. For visiting gourmets on a budget, lunch here is an irresistible proposition.

247 E8 43 Elystan Street SW3 3NT 020 7584 2003 Mon–Fri 12–2.30, 6.45–11. Closed 2 weeks over Christmas and New Year, last 2 weeks of Aug and public hols L from £23 (3 courses), D from £65, Wine from £18 South Kensington

YUMI RESTAURANT

Yumi is typically Japanese in its use of minimalist surroundings, with a sushi bar and the usual private rooms in both the main restaurant and the basement. The food is mostly along the familiar Japanese lines of sushi, sashimi, tempura and grilled beef or chicken with *teriyaki* sauce, although the chef's recommendations often offer something more unusual. Portions are tiny, though, so don't come if you're starving.

247 F4 110 George Street W1U 8NY 020 7935 8320 Daily 5.30–11 D from £40, Wine from £15 Marble Arch

ZAFFERANO

www.zafferanorestaurant.com

Hidden away behind fashionable Sloane Street, this chic Italian restaurant attracts a well-heeled crowd of tourists and shoppers. Starters might include seared tuna with blood orange, fennel and mint or thinly sliced Scotch beef with rocket and parmesan. For the main course there are unusual pasta options typified by pheasant ravioli with rosemary, as well as plenty of meat and fish dishes.

247 F6 15 Lowndes Street SW1X 9EY 020 7235 5800 Daily 12–2.30, 7–11 (Sun till 10.30). Closed 25–26 Dec, 1 Jan, public hols L from £29.50, D from £44.50, Wine from £18 Knightsbridge, Hyde Park

ZUMA

www.zumarestaurant.com

The clutch of awards, stylish Japanese surroundings, stunning food and long waiting list lead many people to compare Knightsbridge's Zuma with Nobu (▷ 201). The atmosphere is relaxed yet electric, the service unobtrusive yet well-informed and the food delicious and expensive. The melt-in-the-mouth scallops, feather-light lobster tempura and well-marbled *wagyu* beef all come highly recommended. Mouth-watering desserts include Zuma sorbet with king lychee and coconut biscuit. There is even a sake sommelier. Booking is essential.

247 E6 5 Raphael Street SW7 1DL 020 7584 1010 Mon–Fri 12.30–2.15, 6–11, Sat 12.30–3.15, 6–11, Sun 12.30–3.15 6–10. Closed Closed 25–26 Dec, 1 Jan L from £30, D from £50, Wine from £25 Knightsbridge

PUBS

THE ADMIRAL CODRINGTON

www.theadmiralcodrington.co.uk

Affectionately known as The Cod, this old Chelsea pub now incorporates a smart but homelike restaurant. Starters might include crispy squid tartlet, *foie gras* and chicken liver parfait, and main choices such as shoulder of lamb or crispy salmon fishcake. In the separate bar, which has its own distinct identity, you can have a meal such as home-made linguine with fresh salmon or just a sandwich or filled ciabatta bread. Garden with food served outside.

247 E7 17 Mossop Street SW3 2LY 020 7581 0005 Mon–Sat 11.30am–12am, Sun 12–10.30. Restaurant: Mon–Sat 12–2.30, 6.30–11, Sun 12–4, 7–10.30 Bar meals from £10.80, D from £30 South Kensington

THE ATLAS

www.theatlaspub.co.uk

This Victorian pub has a contemprorary twist, offering traditional ales along with quality restaurant food and business facilities. Food is mainly Mediterranean, with regularly changing dishes; some of the most popular are wild rocket and salmon risotto and Moroccan lamb tagine. Twelve wines, which change by the season, are offered by the glass. Children are welcome, and food is also served in the walled garden—only a handful of pubs in London have such gardens. The joy of this pub is that it offers restaurant-style meals without compromising its traditional origins.

246 B8 16 Seagrave Road SW6 1RX 020 7385 9129 Mon–Sat 12–11, Sun 12–10.30. Meals: Mon–Fri 12–2.30, 6–10, Sat 12–4, 6–10, Sun 12–10. Closed 24 Dec–1 Jan, Easter Bar meals from £7, D from £22 West Brompton

THE CHELSEA RAM

A busy neighbourhood gastropub near Chelsea Harbour, offering fresh produce including fish and meat from Smithfield's Market. Monthly changing menus have eclectic starters like crispy Thai duck salad or ballotine of chicken with pancetta and artichokes. Main dishes include special market selections from the blackboard, ranging from braised lamb shanks with olive oil mash to bangers and mash with roasted field mushrooms and spinach. No children after 8.30pm unless they are eating.

Off map 246 D9 32 Burnaby Street SW10 0PL 020 7351 4008 Mon–Sat 11–11, Sun 12–10.30. Restaurant: Mon–Sat 12–2.30, 7–10, Sun 12–5, 7–9.30 Bar meals from £8, D from £17 Earl's Court

THE CHURCHILL ARMS

Thai food is the speciality at this 200-year-old pub, with strong emphasis on exotic chicken, beef and pork dishes. Try Thai rice noodles with ground peanuts, spicy sauce and a choice of pork, chicken or prawns. Oak beams, log fires and a conservatory. Five Fullers ales and a buzzing atmosphere abound, especially when there's a big game on.

246 B5 119 Kensington Church Street W8 7LN 020 7727 4242 Mon–Sat 11–11, Sun 12–10.30. Restaurant: Mon–Sat 11–10, Sun 12–9.30 Bar meals from £6, D from £18 Notting Hill Gate

THE CROSS KEYS

www.thexkeys.co.uk

This pub, dating from 1765, which has attracted the rich and famous since the 1960s, includes a banqueting room and open-plan conservatory—complete with tree growing in the middle—plus a restaurant and modern art gallery. The menu leans towards the Modern European school, with smoked duck, king scallops fricassee in vol-au-vent and blueberry crème brûlée. More choice in the evening.

246 E9 1 Lawrence Street SW3 5NB 020 7349 9111 Mon–Sat 12–11, Sun 12–10. Restaurant: Mon–Sat 12–3, 7–10.30, Sun 12–3. Closed 25–26 Dec, 1 Jan, Easter Mon Bar meals from £6, D from £23 Sloane Square

THE GRENADIER

Regularly used as a film set, once the Duke of Wellington's officers' mess and much frequented by King George IV, the ivy-clad Grenadier stands in a cobbled mews behind Hyde Park Corner. The food ranges from solid, traditional fish and chips and beef Wellington to Belgravia salmon, named after the fashionable London district.

247 F6 18 Wilton Row SW1X 7NR 020 7235 3074 Mon–Sat 12–11, Sun 12–10.30. Restaurant: daily 12–2.30, 6–9.30 Bar meals from £9, D from £23 Hyde Park Corner

THE LADBROKE ARMS

The Ladbroke is on busy Ladbroke Road, with a front courtyard and split-level dining area to the rear. The menu changes daily and offers imaginative but not scary choices. Try confit tuna with garlic lentils as a starter, then linguine with sweet tomato and basil, or pan-fried salmon with prosciutto, pea and mint risotto.

246 B5 54 Ladbroke Road W11 3NW 020 7727 6648 Mon–Sat 11.30–11, Sun 12–10.30. Restaurant: daily 12–2.30, 7–9.30. Closed 25 Dec Bar meals from £10, D from £25 Holland Park

NAG'S HEAD

In a quiet mews near Harrods, this old pub once claimed to be the smallest pub in London. Enjoy looking through the What the Butler Saw kinescope; donations for its use go to Queen Charlotte's Hospital in London. The menu gives a good choice of plain, home-cooked food such as chicken and ham pie, vegetable quiche and chilli con carne.

247 F6 53 Kinnerton Street SW1X 8ED 020 7235 1135 Mon–Fri 11.30–11, Sat 11am–12am, Sun 11–7. Meals: daily 12–9 Bar meals from £8 Knightsbridge

STAYING

PRICES AND SYMBOLS

Prices given are the starting price for a double room for one night. Breakfast is included unless noted otherwise. All the hotels listed accept credit cards unless otherwise stated. Note that rates vary widely throughout the year.

For a key to the symbols, ▷ 2.

22 YORK STREET

www.22yorkstreet.co.uk

This elegant five-storey, Georgian terraced town house is a charmer, set in a quiet corner in the heart of central London, near Baker Street Tube. Rooms are individually furnished in a homey and elegant style, with wooden floors, rugs, French antiques and quilts. The Continental breakfast, taken around a large antique dining table, is one of the tastiest and healthiest in town. Tea or coffee and biscuits are always available in the comfy lounges.

247 F3 22 York Street W1U 6PX 020 7224 2990 Double from £120 18 (no children under 5) Baker Street

BARRY HOUSE

www.barryhouse.co.uk

A smart, friendly, family-run property that offers bed-and-breakfast near Hyde Park, Marble Arch and many of London's main sights. Two-night minimum stay at weekends.

246 D4 12 Sussex Place, Hyde Park W2 2TP 020 7723 7340 Double from £85 17 Paddington, Lancaster Gate 7, 15, 23, 27, 36

THE BEAUFORT

www.thebeaufort.co.uk

An attractive town house in a tree-lined cul-de-sac just a few minutes' walk from Knightsbridge. Air-conditioned bedrooms are well furnished and equipped with chocolates, CD players and free internet and satellite TV, including Sky movies. Complimentary drinks and afternoon tea are served in the attractive drawing room. A good Continental breakfast is served in guests' rooms.

247 E7 33 Beaufort Gardens SW3 1PP 020 7584 5252 Double from £210 (exc. breakfast) 29 South Kensington, Knightsbridge 14, 74, C1

BERJAYA EDEN PARK HOTEL

www.berjayaresorts.com

An elegant 1860 Bayswater town house, on a tree-lined terrace a few minutes' Tube ride from Oxford Street and the West End. Rooms are simply furnished. Suites have private entrance and adjoining family living room or private patio and sitting room area, including sofa bed.

246 C4 35–39 Inverness Terrace W2 3JS 020 7221 2220 Double from £69 113 (30 smoking) Bayswater, Queensway 12, 70, 94

THE BERKELEY

www.the-berkeley.co.uk

The Knightsbridge Berkeley never fails to impress. Ongoing refurbishment ensures an excellent range of bedrooms, each one furnished with perfect attention to detail. The public spaces are decorated with magnificent flower arrangements and the Blue Bar is strikingly furnished, its blue tones and white ceiling, complete with opulent chandelier, setting the scene for a relaxed pre-dinner drink. The health spa offers a range of treatments and there's an open-air rooftop pool. Two restaurants provide a contrast of styles: choose from the upmarket brasserie at Boxwood Café (▷ 238) and the Michelin-starred haute cuisine Pétrus.

247 F6 Wilton Place SW1X 7RL 020 7235 6000 Double from £289

Left *Claridge's imposing frontage*

214 (28 smoking) Hyde Park Corner 9, 10, 14, 19, 22, 52, 74, 137

BLAKEMORE

www.starcrown.com

This bed-and-breakfast enjoys a quiet yet central position just a few minutes' walk from Hyde Park (▷ 212). The bedrooms are neatly decorated and the executive rooms have been tastefully refurbished. Spacious public areas include the Rossetti bar lounge, smart lobby and the attractive Wellington restaurant.

246 C4 30 Leinster Gardens W2 3AN 020 7262 4591 Double from £104 163 Bayswater 12, 70, 94

BYRON

www.byronhotel.co.uk

This hotel in a row of Georgian houses has been restored to provide comfortable accommodation and to retain a number of original features. Bedrooms vary in size, but all are tastefully furnished and equipped with modern facilities. There's a dining room where you can have breakfast, and a guest lounge.

246 C4 36–38 Queensborough Terrace W2 3SH 020 7243 0987 Double from £155 45 Bayswater

THE CADOGAN HOTEL

www.cadogan.com

This Victorian hotel in Chelsea overlooks the gardens in Cadogan Place. Bedrooms are mostly air-conditioned and stylishly furnished. The elegant drawing room is popular for afternoon tea, and the grand Langtry's restaurant (▷ 239) serves traditional British dishes. There are tennis courts.

247 F7 75 Sloane Street SW1X 9SG 020 7235 7141 Double from £205 (exc. breakfast) 65 Sloane Square 19, 22, 137, C1

CAPITAL

www.capitalhotel.co.uk

This small, family-owned hotel near Harrods (▷ 233) has individually designed, fresh and light bedrooms with antique furniture and marble bathrooms. A highlight of any visit to this hotel is dinner in the two-Michelin-star Capital restaurant, where head chef Eric Chavot serves innovative French-inspired dishes.

247 F6 22 Basil Street SW3 1AT 020 7589 5171 Double from £305 49 rooms Knightsbridge 19, 22, 137, C1

CLARIDGE'S

www.claridgeshotel.com

Impressive standards of luxury, style and service are upheld at this iconic bastion of British hospitality. The sumptuously decorated, air-conditioned rooms have Victorian or art deco themes to reflect the architecture of the building. Gordon Ramsay at Claridge's, the hotel restaurant, is run by the renowned British chef; the food and service are superb. The sleek cocktail bar is a popular meeting place, and the lobby is a stylish place to have afternoon tea.

247 G4 Brook Street W1K 4HR 020 7629 8860 Double from £289 203 (20 smoking) Bond Street 8

THE DORCHESTER

www.dorchesterhotel.com

One of London's finest hotels, The Dorchester is sumptuous. The bedrooms all have individual design schemes, are beautifully furnished and have huge, luxurious bathrooms. Leading off from the lobby, The Promenade is perfect for afternoon tea or drinks. In the evening you can catch live music in the bar, and enjoy a cocktail or an Italian meal. The main restaurant is the traditional Grill Room, which looks almost exactly as it did in 1931 when the hotel first opened. A new restaurant was added in 2007 with Alain Ducasse at the helm. The Dorchester Spa includes health club, gym, beauty services, sauna and Jacuzzi.

247 F5 Park Lane W1K 1QA 020 7629 8888 Double from £485 244 (60 smoking) Hyde Park Corner, Marble Arch 2, 10, 16, 36, 73, 74, 82, 137, 148

FOUR SEASONS HOTEL

www.4seasonshotel.co.uk

Not to be confused with the Four Seasons London Hotel on Park Lane, this small family-run hotel is on the edge of Regent's Park (▷ 218) and within easy walking distance of London Zoo (▷ 219) and Madame Tussauds (▷ 217). Breakfast is served in the pretty conservatory, which gives the impression of being away from the bustling city.

247 F3 173 Gloucester Place, Regent's Park NW1 6DX 020 7724 3461 Double from £115 16 Baker Street, Marylebone 2, 13, 30, 74, 82, 113, 139, 189, 274

THE GAINSBOROUGH

www.eeh.co.uk

This Georgian town house is in a quiet street in South Kensington, near the Natural History Museum (▷ 220–221). The bedrooms have been individually designed and are decorated with fine fabrics and quality furnishings. There is a small public lounge and 24-hour room service is available.

246 D7 7–11 Queensberry Place SW7 2DL 020 7957 0000 Double from £182 49 South Kensington 14, 49, 70, 74, 345, 360, 414

THE GALLERY

www.eeh.co.uk

This stylish property, close to Kensington and Knightsbridge, offers friendly hospitality, attentive service and sumptuously furnished bedrooms, some with a private terrace. Public areas include several lounges (one with internet access) and an elegant bar. Room service is available 24 hours a day. There are no evening meals.

246 D7 8–10 Queensberry Place SW7 2EA 020 7915 0000 Double from £188 34 South Kensington 14, 49, 70, 74, 345, 360, 414

HART HOUSE

www.harthouse.co.uk

This elegant Georgian house, occupied by French nobility during the French Revolution of 1789, enjoys a prime location, a few

minutes' walk from Oxford Street's shops and Madame Tussauds (▷ 217). Both bedrooms and public areas are well furnished and stylishly decorated and have been carefully restored to retain much of the original character of the house. Excellent service and a warm welcome. English breakfast; no evening meals are served.
247 F3 51 Gloucester Place W1U 8JF 020 7935 2288 Double from £125 16 Baker Street, Marble Arch 2, 13, 30, 74, 82, 113, 139, 189, 274

HOTEL 167
www.hotel167.com
An attractive Victorian terraced house that has retained its character, conveniently located for Harrods and the South Kensington museums. All the light and airy en-suite rooms are equipped with mini-fridges and in-house video. There is a warm, country-house atmosphere, and breakfast is taken in the charming lobby. You need to book early to get in.
246 C8 167 Old Brompton Road SW5 0AN 020 7373 3221 Double from £99 19 Gloucester Road, South Kensington 49, 74

HOTEL ORLANDO
www.hotelorlando.co.uk
A small hotel in a row of Victorian houses, with a variety of bedroom styles. Breakfast is served in the basement dining room. No evening meals.
Off map 246 A9 83 Shepherd's Bush Road W6 7LR 020 7603 4890 Double from £60 14 Hammersmith 266, 267

JUMEIRAH CARLTON TOWER HOTEL
www.jumeirahcarltontower.com
In the heart of Knightsbridge and with the Cadogan Place gardens on its doorstep. Rooms are smooth and sleek, and one of the hotel's restaurants (the Club Room—noted for its healthy buffet) has panoramic views over London through large picture windows. There's also the Rib Room and the Chinoiserie for light meals. The swimming pool has a glass roof, and there are treatment rooms, gym, sauna, spa and Jacuzzi, and tennis courts, too.
247 F6 Cadogan Place SW1X 9PY 020 7235 1234 Double from £299 220 Indoor Sloane Square 19, 22, 137, C1

KENSINGTON HOUSE
www.kenhouse.com
This beautiful 19th-century property has been elegantly restored to provide contemporary accommodation in the heart of Kensington. The Tiger Bar provides an airy, informal setting for light snacks and meals all day. Bedrooms vary in style but are light and stylish and thoughtfully equipped. Guests have access to a health club close by for a small charge.
246 C6 15–16 Prince of Wales Terrace W8 5PQ 020 7937 2345 Double from Mon–Fri £180, Sat–Sun £140 41 (3 smoking) High Street Kensington 9, 10, 27, 28, 49, 328

KINGSWAY PARK
www.kingswaypark-hotel.com
Central bed-and-breakfast in an elegant Victorian building offering good value for money. Interesting modern artwork features in all the public spaces, including the basement dining room.
246 D4 139 Sussex Gardens W2 2RX 020 7723 5677 Double from £70 22 Paddington 705

THE LANDMARK LONDON
www.landmarklondon.co.uk
One of the last truly grand railway hotels, the Landmark is close to Hyde Park and Regent's Park. It has a number of stunning features, the most spectacular of which is the central eight-storey atrium, complete with palm trees, that forms the focal point of the hotel. There is a huge choice of bars and restaurants. The Cellars serves sophisticated bar meals; the Winter Gardens serves a varied menu all day. Bedrooms are stylish, spacious and air-conditioned, with luxurious marble bathrooms offering deep tubs and separate showers. Guests have access to a sauna, spa and Jacuzzi.
247 E3 222 Marylebone Road NW1 6JQ 020 7631 8000 Double from £299 299 (52 smoking) Indoor Marylebone, Baker Street 18

THE LANESBOROUGH
www.lanesborough.com
Occupying an enviable position on Hyde Park Corner, this elegant hotel has an ageless charm. Bedrooms and public rooms reflect the highest levels of comfort. The public areas are lavishly furnished and have magnificent flower arrangements. Service is equally impressive; a personal butler attends to guests' every need 24 hours a day. The conservatory restaurant is popular for innovative international cuisine and famous for afternoon tea. There is a spa.
247 F6 Hyde Park Corner SW1X 7TA 020 7259 5599 Double from £475 95 (40 smoking) Hyde Park Corner 9, 10, 14, 19, 22, 52, 74, 137

THE LEVIN
www.thelevinhotel.co.uk
Newly opened after a complete refurbishment, this sophisticated boutique hotel now has a fresh, modern look in classic English style. The pleasing bedrooms offer understated elegance with the very latest in lighting and technology combining with sumptuous fabrics and furnishings. Almost next door to Harrods, The Levin boasts a superb position in one of the most elegant corners of London, near to all the sights the capital has to offer.
247 F6 28 Basil Street SW3 1AS 020 7589 6286 Double from £260 12 Knightsbridge 19, 22, 137, C1

LINCOLN HOUSE
www.lincoln-house-hotel.co.uk
This friendly, family-owned Georgian B&B is set in a town house near Oxford Street and has been impressively renovated. A full English breakfast is served in the cottage-style dining room, and

Continental breakfast can be served in bedrooms. No evening meals.
247 F3 33 Gloucester Place W1U 8HY 020 7486 7630 Double from £115 (exc. breakfast) 24 Marble Arch 2, 13, 30, 74, 82, 113, 139, 189

THE MANDEVILLE
www.mandeville.co.uk
This elegant Edwardian building is only a short stroll from Oxford Street. Its de Ville restaurant has floral wallpaper, perspex (Lucite) and vibrant colours that give a retro feel, and the de Vigne bar offers cocktails. 24-hour room service available. Popular with foreign guests as the staff speak several languages.
247 G4 Mandeville Place W1U 2BE 020 7935 5599 Double from £316 (exc. breakfast) 142 Bond Street 3, 25, 53, 55, 176

MARANTON HOUSE HOTEL
www.marantonhousehotel.com
This stylish redbrick Victorian Earl's Court guest house has been owned and run by the same family for the last 20 years and you can be assured of a warm welcome and efficient friendly service. It overlooks an attractive garden square just a short walk from the Tube station. Rooms are simple but attractively furnished. There is a bar but no restaurant.
246 C7 14 Barkston Gardens SW5 0EN 020 7373 5782 Doubles from £92 16 Earls Court 16, 234

MARBLE ARCH INN
www.marblearch-inn.co.uk
Modern bed-and-breakfast a few minutes' walk from Hyde Park and Oxford Street. All rooms have TV, hairdryer, tea and coffee bar, wash basin and fridge, and most have a private shower and WC. The reception is open 24 hours a day. Minimum stay of three nights from Friday or two nights from Saturday.
247 E4 49–50 Upper Berkeley Street, Marble Arch W1H 5QR 020 7723 7888 Double from £70–£85 en suite 29 Marble Arch 6, 7, 15, 16, 23, 36, 98

MORNINGTON HOTEL
www.bw-morningtonhotel.co.uk
Fine Victorian building on a quiet road close to Hyde Park with direct Underground service to the West End. Bedrooms at this Best Western hotel provide comfortable, up-to-date accommodation. There are two lounges and an attractive dining room where an English breakfast is served. No evening meals.
246 D4 12 Lancaster Gate W2 3LG 020 7262 7361 Double from £129 66 Lancaster Gate 46, 94, 148

NEW LINDEN
www.mayflower-group.co.uk
Housed in a smart, gleaming-white Georgian building typical of this trendy area, this friendly hotel is a comfortable and very convenient base for many of the city's top attractions. It is just a short walk from Portobello Road, close to Kensington Palace Gardens and Hyde Park. All the rooms offer a comfortable retreat at the end of the day and the friendly staff are on hand to make you feel at home.
246 C4 59 Leinster Square, Notting Hill W2 4PS 020 7221 4321 Double from £115 51 Bayswater, Queensway 12, 27, 28, 31

NORFOLK PLAZA
www.norfolkplazahotel.co.uk
This popular hotel in the heart of Paddington is within easy walking distance of the West End. Bedrooms provide good facilities and include a number of split-level suites. The public areas include a smartly decorated bar and lounge and an attractive restaurant where breakfast is served. No dinner.
246 E4 29–33 Norfolk Square W2 1RX 020 7723 0792 Double from £130 87 Paddington 7, 27, 36, 436

PARK INN
www.parkinn.com
Centrally located in Lancaster Gate, this landmark building, with its stucco facade, has been a hotel since 1817 and retains an air of gentility. It offers modern, air-conditioned bedrooms and public spaces, and a fitness centre.
246 D5 66 Lancaster Gate W2 3NZ 020 7262 5090 Double from £140 188 Lancaster Gate, Queensway 46, 94, 148

ROYAL LANCASTER
www.royallancaster.com
Overlooking Hyde Park and Kensington Gardens, this is a well-established hotel with an excellent range of public facilities, including impressive conference rooms with a theatre to seat 1,500, a 24-hour business centre and car parking. The authentic and well-known Nipa Thai is among a good choice of drinking and eating options. Bedrooms are modern, with upper floors providing views across London.
246 D4 Lancaster Terrace W2 2TY 020 7262 6737 Double from £159 416 (60 smoking) Lancaster Gate, Paddington 46, 94, 198

RUSHMORE HOTEL
www.rushmore-hotel.co.uk
This private hotel is conveniently close to the exhibition halls of Earl's Court. Bedrooms are individually themed and include some rooms suitable for families. A Continental buffet breakfast is served in the conservatory. No evening meals.
246C7 11 Trebovir Road SW5 9LS 020 7370 3839 Double from £89 22 Earl's Court 74, 328, C1, C3

VICARAGE HOTEL
www.londonvicaragehotel.com
A family-run hotel offering warm and friendly hospitailty. This handsome Victorian house retains many original features, such as the sweeping cast-iron staircase in the hallway. It is in a quiet, tree-lined square, just off Kensington Church Street and only a short stroll from Kensington Palace. The bedrooms are small but immaculate, and retain a period style; some are en suite. The Vicarage breakfast is a highlight.
246 C6 10 Vicarage Gate W8 4AG 020 7229 4040 Double from £80, with bathroom from £122 18 High Street Kensington 9, 10, 12, 52, C1

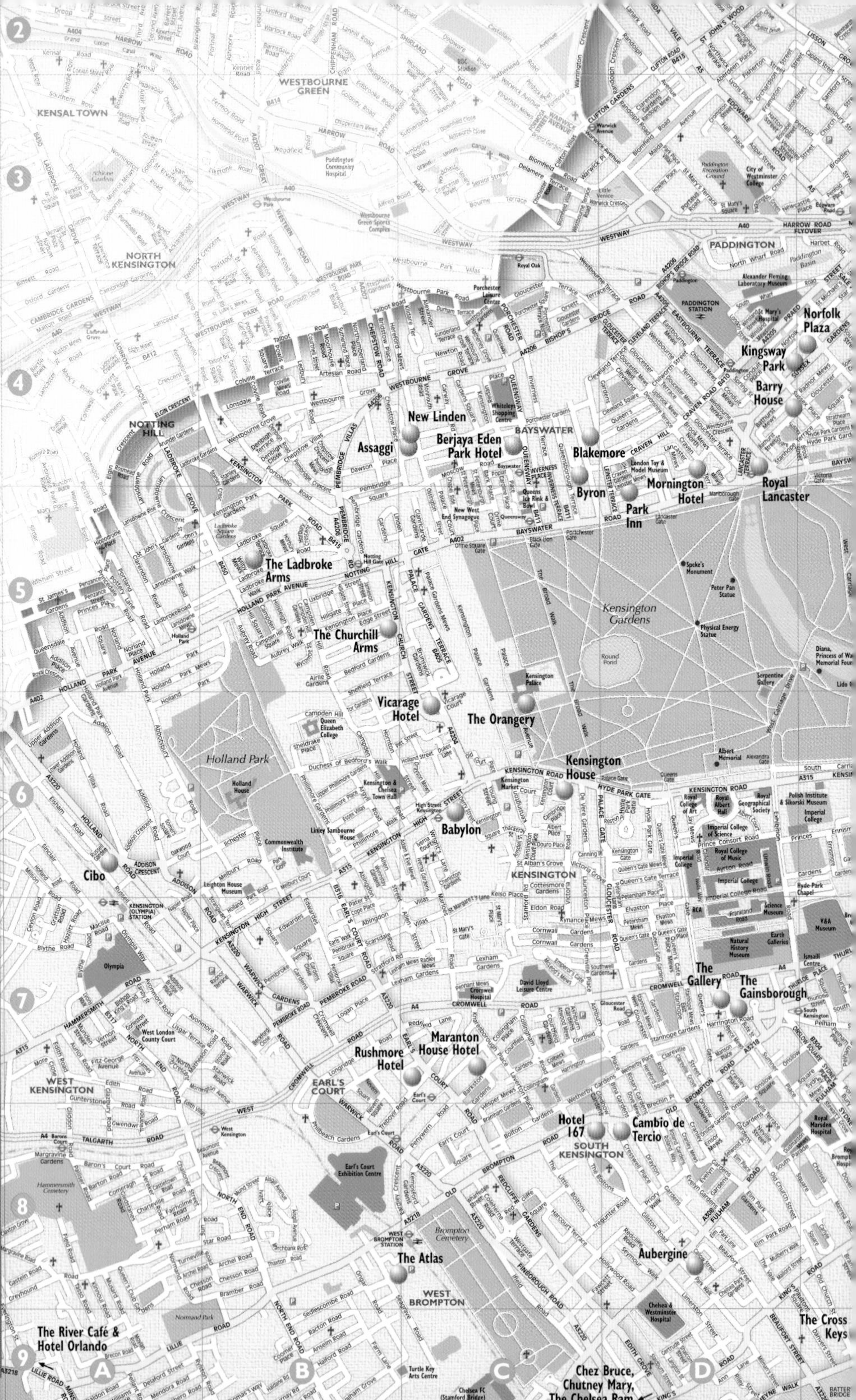
Norfolk Plaza
Kingsway Park
Barry House
New Linden
Berjaya Eden Park Hotel
Assaggi
Blakemore
Byron
Mornington Hotel
Royal Lancaster
Park Inn
The Ladbroke Arms
The Churchill Arms
Vicarage Hotel
The Orangery
Kensington House
Babylon
Cibo
The Gallery
The Gainsborough
Maranton House Hotel
Rushmore Hotel
Hotel 167
Cambio de Tercio
The Atlas
Aubergine
The Cross Keys
The River Café & Hotel Orlando
Chez Bruce, Chutney Mary, The Chelsea Ram
KENSAL TOWN
WESTBOURNE GREEN
NORTH KENSINGTON
NOTTING HILL
PADDINGTON
BAYSWATER
Kensington Gardens
Holland Park
KENSINGTON
WEST KENSINGTON
EARL'S COURT
SOUTH KENSINGTON
WEST BROMPTON
A
B
C
D
2
3
4
5
6
7
8
9

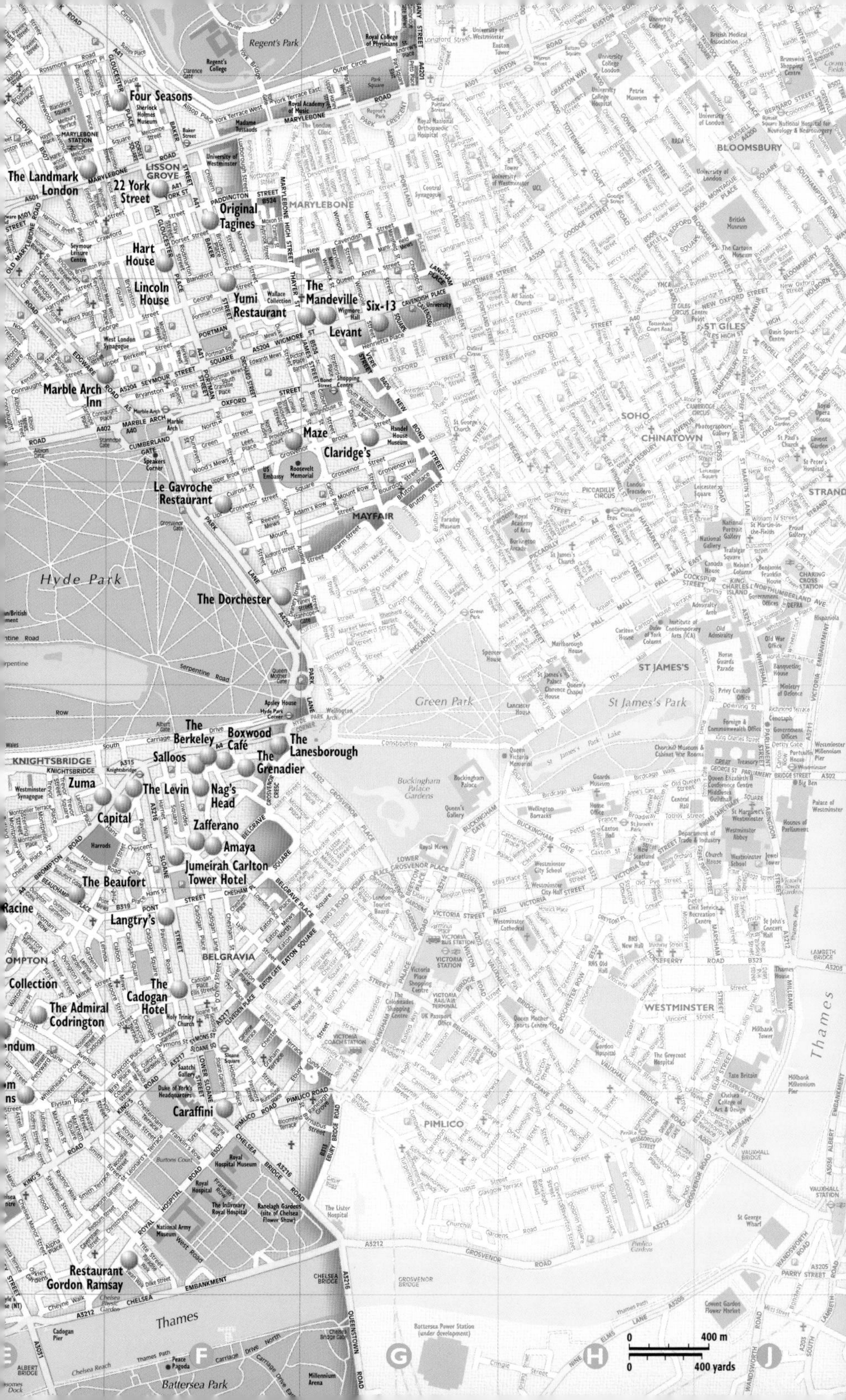
Four Seasons
The Landmark London
22 York Street
Original Tagines
Hart House
Lincoln House
Yumi Restaurant
The Mandeville
Six-13
Levant
Marble Arch Inn
Maze
Claridge's
Le Gavroche Restaurant
The Dorchester
The Berkeley
Boxwood Café
The Lanesborough
Salloos
The Grenadier
Zuma
The Levin
Nag's Head
Capital
Zafferano
Amaya
Jumeirah Carlton Tower Hotel
The Beaufort
Racine
Langtry's
Collection
The Cadogan Hotel
The Admiral Codrington
Caraffini
Restaurant Gordon Ramsay
Regent's Park
Hyde Park
Green Park
St James's Park
MARYLEBONE
BLOOMSBURY
MAYFAIR
SOHO
CHINATOWN
ST GILES
ST JAMES'S
KNIGHTSBRIDGE
BELGRAVIA
PIMLICO
WESTMINSTER
Thames
0 400 m
0 400 yards

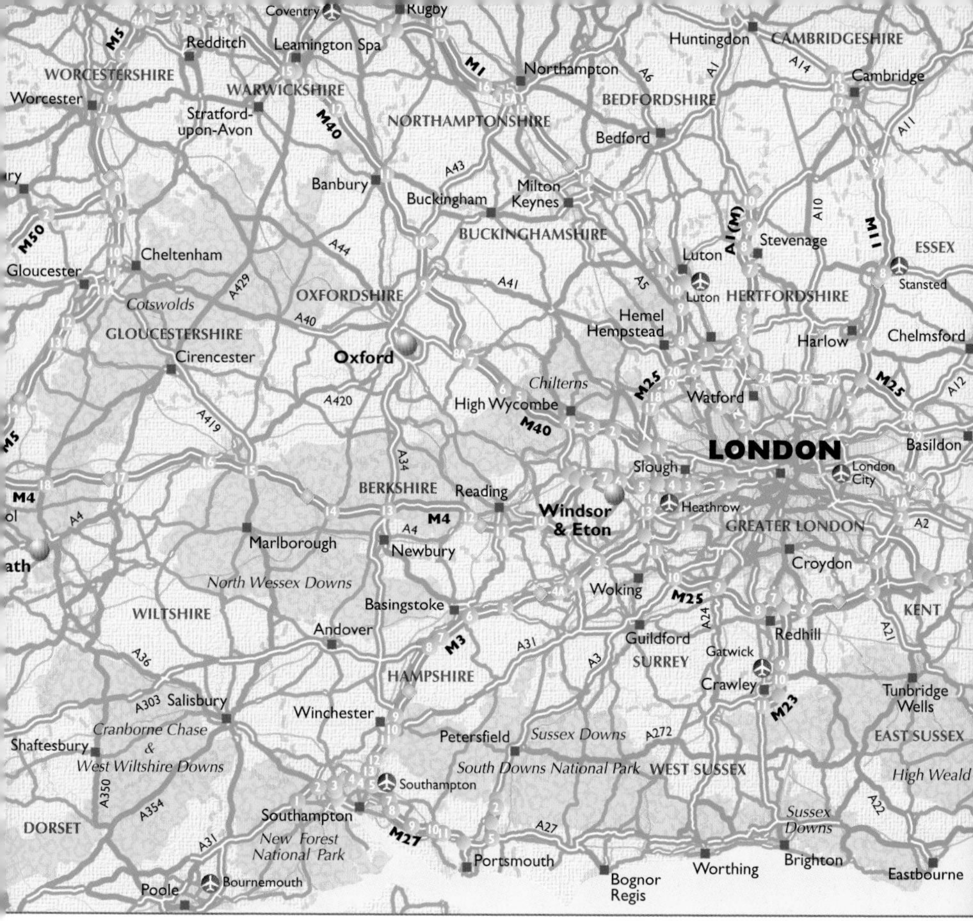

EXCURSIONS

Although central London has enough to keep you occupied for months, it is worth getting a feel for the city a little way farther out. There are many lesser-known attractions that can be visited in a couple of hours, such as Dulwich Picture Gallery or Horniman Museum, which double up nicely. These are still within city postcodes, as is Greenwich, which easily merits a full day's exploration on its own. The site of the Meridian boasts a beautiful riverside setting, as well as a bustling market, the vast maritime museum, the Royal Observatory and the Millennium Dome, now the O2 Arena, a huge entertainment complex. About the same distance on the north side of the centre, Hampstead offers a couple of minor sights and untrammelled beauty on its sprawling heath.

In the outlying suburban boroughs you can choose between famous royal residences of the past and present at Hampton Court and Windsor Castle, the latter sitting squatly across the river from Eton, a quaint place renowned for its exclusive public (that is, private) school. The River Thames itself offers a rich vein for exploration on tours both east and west of the centre. In the southwestern suburbs, an unmissable sight for any horticulturalist is the Botanical Gardens at Kew, only a couple of miles from the huge expanse of Richmond Park, still home to wild deer.

For a real getaway from the London area, perhaps best done as an overnight stay although both can be reached easily within a couple of hours, two standout options are Oxford and Bath. Oxford is dominated by the leisurely academic atmosphere emanating from the medieval spires and courtyards of its university colleges, while Bath has its roots in Roman times but impresses most for its exquisite Georgian architecture.

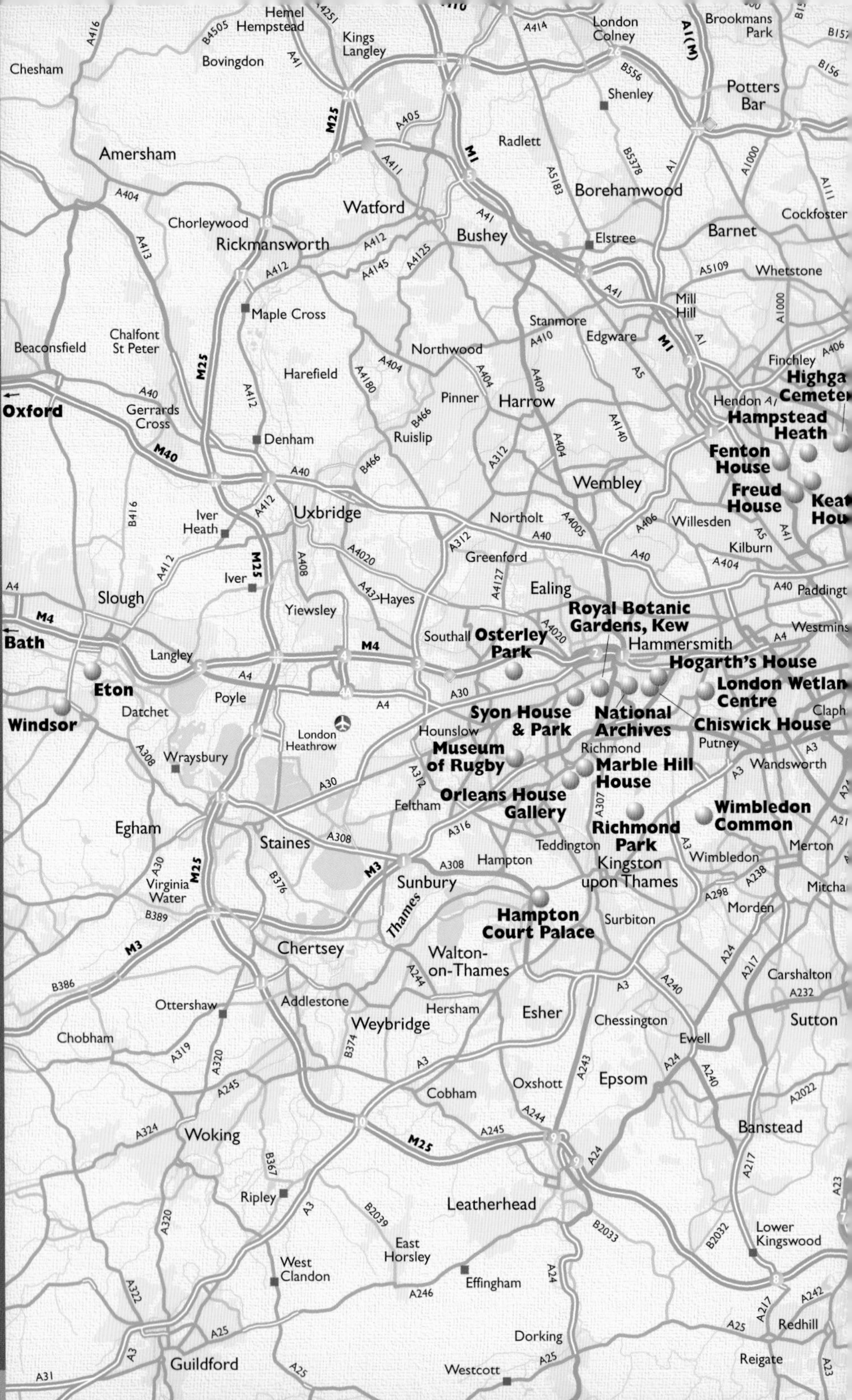
Royal Botanic Gardens, Kew
Osterley Park
Hogarth's House
London Wetland Centre
Syon House & Park
National Archives
Chiswick House
Museum of Rugby
Marble Hill House
Orleans House Gallery
Richmond Park
Wimbledon Common
Hampton Court Palace
Highgate Cemetery
Hampstead Heath
Fenton House
Freud House
Keats House
Eton
Windsor
Oxford
Bath
Hemel Hempstead
Kings Langley
London Colney
Brookmans Park
Chesham
Bovingdon
Shenley
Potters Bar
Amersham
Radlett
Borehamwood
Watford
Chorleywood
Rickmansworth
Bushey
Elstree
Barnet
Cockfosters
Whetstone
Maple Cross
Mill Hill
Stanmore
Edgware
Beaconsfield
Chalfont St Peter
Northwood
Harefield
Finchley
Pinner
Harrow
Hendon
Gerrards Cross
Denham
Ruislip
Wembley
Uxbridge
Iver Heath
Northolt
Willesden
Kilburn
Greenford
Iver
Slough
Ealing
Paddington
Yiewsley
Hayes
Westminster
Southall
Hammersmith
Langley
Poyle
Datchet
Hounslow
London Heathrow
Richmond
Putney
Wandsworth
Clapham
Wraysbury
Feltham
Egham
Staines
Teddington
Hampton
Kingston upon Thames
Wimbledon
Merton
Virginia Water
Sunbury
Thames
Morden
Mitcham
Surbiton
Chertsey
Walton-on-Thames
Carshalton
Addlestone
Ottershaw
Hersham
Esher
Chessington
Sutton
Chobham
Weybridge
Ewell
Epsom
Oxshott
Cobham
Banstead
Woking
Ripley
Leatherhead
Lower Kingswood
East Horsley
West Clandon
Effingham
Redhill
Dorking
Guildford
Reigate
Westcott
M25
M1
M4
M40
M3
A1(M)

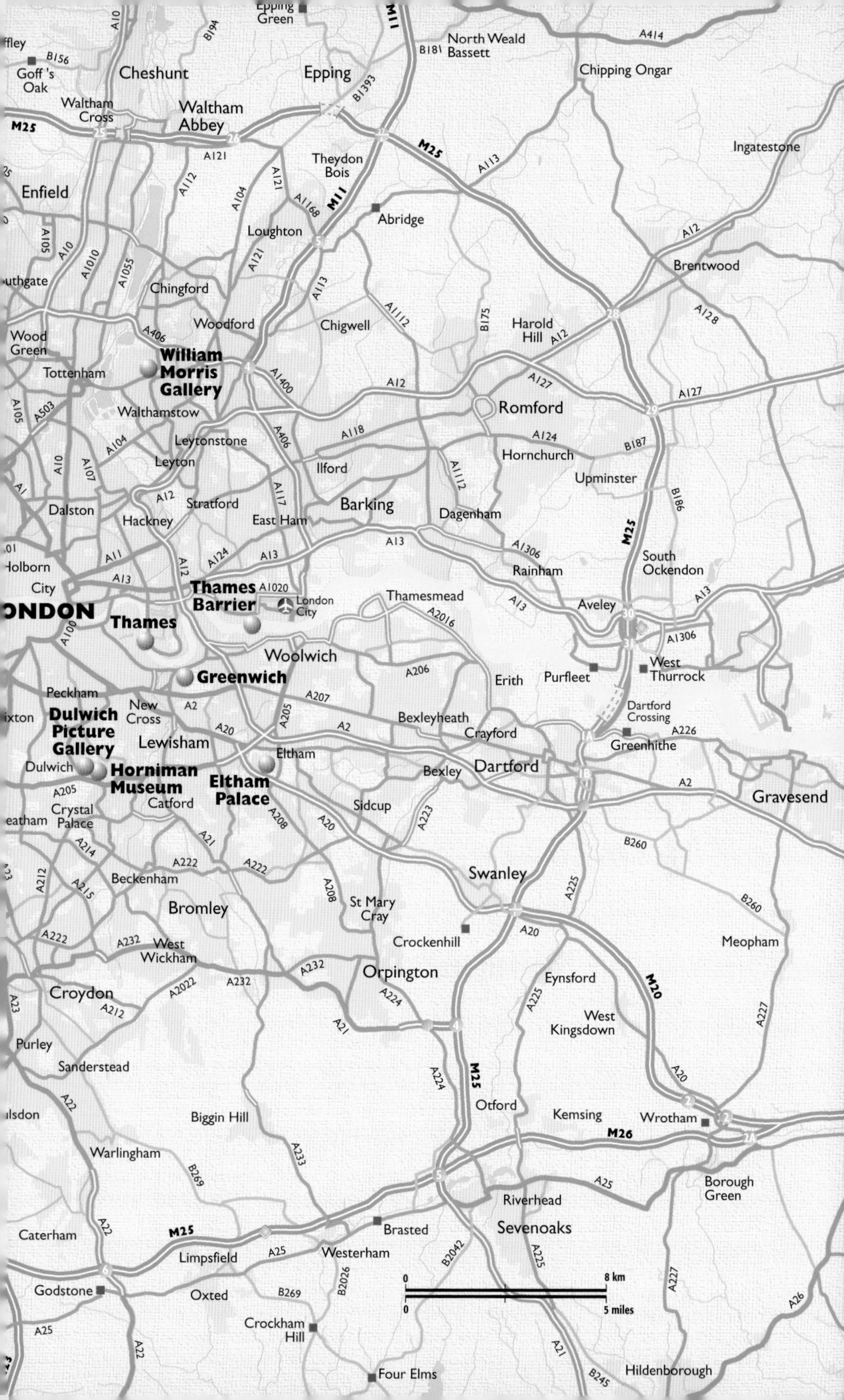

Epping Green
North Weald Bassett
Goff's Oak
Cheshunt
Epping
Chipping Ongar
Waltham Cross
Waltham Abbey
Ingatestone
Theydon Bois
Enfield
Abridge
Loughton
Brentwood
Chingford
Woodford
Chigwell
Harold Hill
Wood Green
William Morris Gallery
Tottenham
Romford
Walthamstow
Leytonstone
Hornchurch
Leyton
Ilford
Upminster
Dalston
Stratford
Barking
Hackney
East Ham
Dagenham
South Ockendon
Holborn
Rainham
City
Thames Barrier
London City
Thamesmead
Aveley
LONDON
Thames
Woolwich
West Thurrock
Greenwich
Erith
Purfleet
Peckham
New Cross
Dartford Crossing
Dulwich Picture Gallery
Lewisham
Bexleyheath
Crayford
Greenhithe
Eltham
Dulwich
Horniman Museum
Bexley
Dartford
Eltham Palace
Catford
Sidcup
Gravesend
Crystal Palace
Swanley
Beckenham
Bromley
St Mary Cray
Crockenhill
Meopham
West Wickham
Orpington
Croydon
Eynsford
West Kingsdown
Purley
Sanderstead
Otford
Kemsing
Wrotham
Biggin Hill
Warlingham
Borough Green
Riverhead
Sevenoaks
Brasted
Caterham
Limpsfield
Westerham
Godstone
Oxted
Crockham Hill
Four Elms
Hildenborough
M25
M11
M20
M26
A2
A12
A13
A20
A21
A22
A25
A127
A206
A207
B260
0
8 km
5 miles

INFORMATION

Tourist information office
www.visitbath.co.uk
✉ Abbey Chambers, Abbey Church Yard, Bath BA1 1LY ☎ 0906 711 2000

HOW TO GET THERE

Bath is 130km (80 miles) west of London
🚆 Paddington to Bath Spa (1 hour 25 min)
🚌 National Express from Victoria Coach Station (3 hours 20 min)
🚗 M4 west, exit junction 18, then A46 (2 hours)

Above *The Roman Baths are right next to Bath Abbey*

INTRODUCTION

A World Heritage Site, Britain's most complete Georgian city was built around the country's only natural hot springs—in use for thousands of years.

Bath's hot springs were known long before the Roman occupation and, according to legend, were used by King Lear's father, but it was in AD44 that the Romans began to exploit their supposed healing effects by establishing the spa resort of Aquae Sulis.

Medieval Bath prospered from the wool trade, but its hot springs fell into neglect until their rediscovery in 1755, when they were made fashionable by talented dandy Beau Nash. London's high society migrated here every year to take the waters and enjoy the balls and assemblies that made the city a byword for elegance and style. Bath responded by transforming itself in the grandest manner. Its best-known examples of Georgian townscape are The Circus, a circular piazza (1754–70) designed by John Wood; the Royal Crescent (1765–75), by his son John Wood the Younger; and Pulteney Bridge over the River Avon, surmounted by tiny Palladian houses by Robert Adams (1769–74).

WHAT TO SEE

The city has more than 20 museums and historic sites. In the very centre, the Roman Baths and Pump Room (daily; adult £10.25, child £6.50) represent Bath's *raison d'être*. The Georgian chandelier-hung Pump Room, overlooking the cloistered King's Bath, has its own chamber trio during afternoon tea; an elaborate drinking fountain issues samples of the hot spa water. Beyond, passages lead into the Roman bath complex, set up around the water temple of the goddess Minerva, whose bust presides over the scene.

Close by, Bath Abbey (daily) is a crowning example of the Perpendicular style, with its ornately carved west front representing the dream of angels that inspired the abbey's reconstruction by Bishop Oliver in 1499. The impressive east window depicts 56 scenes from Christ's life.

Off the Circus, the Assembly Rooms and Fashion Museum (daily 11–4), one of the most celebrated museums of its kind, is a look back at fashion across 400 years. Number 1 Royal Crescent (mid-Feb to end Nov Tue–Sun) displays a superb Bath townhouse interior (1767–74) with period furnishings. In Gay Street the Jane Austen Centre (daily) traces the life and works of the novelist, who paid two long visits to Bath in the 1700s and lived here from 1801 to 1806. The city features extensively in her first novel, *Northanger Abbey*, and also in her last, *Persuasion*.

In the elegant Holburne Museum of Art (Tue–Sat and Sun pm) at the end of Great Pulteney Street you can see the silver, paintings and porcelain collected by Sir William Holburne (1793–1874). Exquisite jade and porcelain from China is excellently displayed and labelled in the Museum of East Asian Art in Bennett Street (Tue–Sat 10–5 and Sun pm).

To find out how Bath became the place it is, visit the Building of Bath Museum in the Paragon (mid-Feb to end Nov Tue–Sun 10.30–5), where you'll find a detailed model of the city. Close by is the Museum of Bath at Work (Easter–end Oct daily; Nov–Easter Sat, Sun).

Museums aside, Bath is well known for its specialist shops and galleries. Other attractions include the botanical gardens in Victoria Park and the Themae Bath Spa near Kingsmead Square (opened in 2006). Consisting of new and restored Georgian buildings, it has a rooftop pool.

Sally Lunn's Refreshment House in North Parade Passage is thought to be Bath's oldest house.

NEARBY

Just over 3km (2 miles) southeast of the city, at Claverton, the American Museum in Britain (end Mar–end Oct Tue–Sun pm) occupies a gracious 18th-century manor house and shows re-creations of American homes from different states between the 17th and the 19th centuries, as well as folk art and exhibits on Shakers and Native Americans. There are also formal gardens.

A mile (1.6km) south of the city centre, Prior Park Landscape Garden (Mar–end Oct Wed–Mon 11–dusk; Nov–end Feb Sat–Sun 11–5.30), owned by the National Trust, is an 18th-century creation by Lancelot 'Capability' Brown (1716–83).

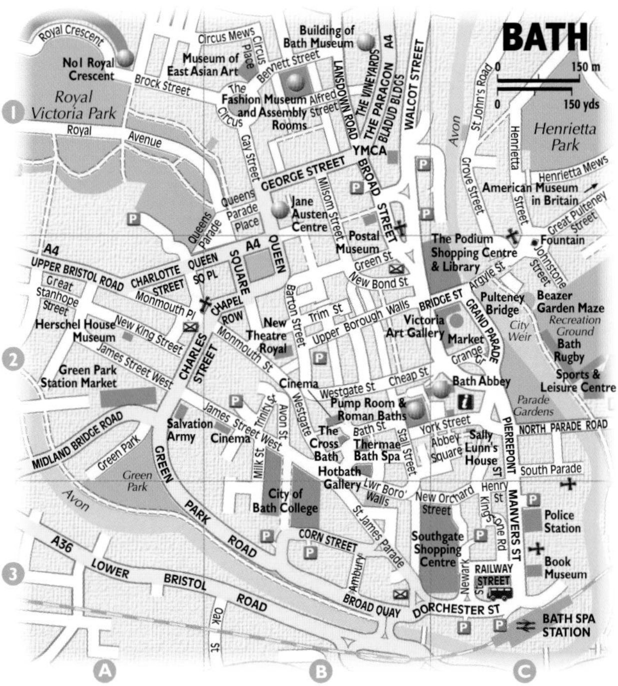

TIPS

» Explore on foot—the city is small enough. Free guided walks are available from the tourist information office.

» Take an open-top bus tour (no booking required). They are available throughout the day all year round from Pulteney Weir and the abbey.

» Enjoy the River Avon on a boat trip from Pulteney Bridge; daily during the summer.

WHERE TO EAT

FIREHOUSE ROTISSERIE

www.firehouserotisserie.co.uk

Pacific Southwestern grills, gourmet pizzas and vegetarian dishes served from an open kitchen. Relaxed atmosphere.

2 John Street, Bath BA1 2JL

01225 482070 Mon–Sat 12–2.30, 6–11 L/D £15–£20, Wine from £11.95

MOODY GOOSE

www.moodygoose.co.uk

Michelin-starred restaurant serving British and French dishes such as salmon galantine and poached saddle of rabbit.

7A Kingsmead Square, Bath BA1 2AB

01225 466688 Mon–Sat 12–1.30, 7–9.30 L from £22.50, D from £35, Wine from £14

WOODS RESTAURANT

www.woodsrestaurant.com

Popular brasserie in an elegant Georgian setting serving good-quality British, French and international dishes.

9–13 Alfred Street Bath BA1 2QX

01225 314 812 12–2.30, 6–10.30 L from £15, D from £30, Wine from £14.50

CHISWICK HOUSE

www.english-heritage.org.uk

This superb example of Palladian architecture is the work of Richard Boyle, 3rd Earl of Burlington (1694–1753), who made it his mission to promote the style in Britain. The perfectly symmetrical exterior, with its octagonal central dome and classical portico with six Corinthian columns, gives no clue to the sumptuously decorated rooms inside. Don't miss the gilding in the Blue Velvet Room or the domed saloon, lit from the drum windows, which were derived from the Roman Baths of Diocletian. The classical Italianate gardens were laid out to complement the architecture.

10km (6 miles) W of Tralfagar Square ✉ 50 Burlington Lane W4 2RR ☎ 020 8995 0508 🕐 Easter–end Oct Sun–Wed 10–5; Nov–20 Dec prebooked appointments ✋ Adult £3.50, child (6–18) £3, under 6s free Ⓤ Turnham Green 🚌 27, 190, 391 🚆 Turnham Green, Chiswick ☕ Daily summer, weekends winter 🎁

DULWICH PICTURE GALLERY

www.dulwichpicturegallery.org.uk

More than 300 masterpieces make up this exceptional art collection, most painted in the 17th and 18th centuries and including works such as Van Dyck's *Madonna and Child*, Poussin's *Return of the Holy Family from Egypt* and Rembrandt's portrait of *Jacob III de Gheyn*, stolen several times from the gallery but recovered on each occasion. The neoclassical building, designed by Sir John Soane in 1811, was England's first purpose-built art gallery. A striking addition by Rick Mather, opened in 2000, provides more exhibition space, an education centre for children and adults, and a cafe overlooking the large garden.

The gallery also serves as a mausoleum: At the rear of the building are the tombs of Noel Desenfans, who was responsible for putting the collection together in the 1790s, and Sir Francis Bourgeois, who bequeathed it to Dulwich College in 1811.

8km (5 miles) SE of Trafalgar Square ✉ Gallery Road, Dulwich Village SE21 7AD ☎ 020 8693 5254 🕐 Tue–Fri 10–5, Sat–Sun 11–5. Free tours Sat–Sun 3pm (normal admission charge) ✋ Adult £5, under 16s £3. Exhibitions adult £8, child (under 16) free 🚌 P4 from opposite Brixton Tube or Lewisham bus station; 3 to West Dulwich station; 37 to North Dulwich station 🚆 West Dulwich, North Dulwich ☕ 🎁

ELTHAM PALACE

www.english-heritage.org.uk

Moated parkland surrounds the remains of one of England's largest but least known royal medieval palaces and the flamboyant house built next door by film director Stephen Courtauld in the 1930s and furnished in art deco style. Inside it's fitted out with the modern conveniences of the day, including an electrically operated central vacuum cleaner, loudspeakers relaying jazz to the ground floor, and an internal phone system. Check out the dining room with its pink leather upholstered chairs and black-and-white doors, Virginia Courtauld's exotic bathroom lined with onyx and gold mosaic and featuring a bust of Psyche, and the centrally heated cage once occupied by the Courtaulds' pet lemur. The grounds include a rose garden and colour-themed planting.

19km (12 miles) SE of Trafalgar Square ✉ Off Court Road, Eltham SE9 5QE ☎ 020 8294 2548 🕐 Apr–end Oct Sun–Wed 10–5; Nov–23 Dec, Feb–end Mar Sun–Wed 11–4. Palace and grounds closed 23 Dec–31 Jan ✋ House and gardens: adult £8.30, child (5–16) £4.20, family £20.80 🚌 132, 161, 162, 233, 286, 314 to Eltham station 🚆 Eltham ☕ 🎁

FENTON HOUSE

www.nationaltrust.org.uk

This red-brick house built in 1695 is one of the best of its kind surviving in London. Period furnishings are complemented by a fine collection of ceramics, Georgian furniture and 17th-century needlework. The Benton Fletcher Collection of keyboard instruments from the 17th and 18th centuries is regularly put to use for concerts given in the house. Outside, roses grow in the charming walled garden, and there's an orchard and vegetable garden as well.

8km (5 miles) NW of Trafalgar Square ✉ Hampstead Grove, Hampstead NW3 6SP ☎ 020 7435 3471, general information 01494 755563 🕐 Mar Sat–Sun 2–5; Easter–end Oct Sat–Sun 11–5, Wed–Fri 2–5 ✋ Adult £5.70, child (5–16) £2.80, under 5s free, family £14.20 Ⓤ Hampstead 🚌 46, 268 🚆 Hampstead Heath

FREUD'S HOUSE AND MUSEUM

www.freud.org.uk

Sigmund Freud (1856–1939), Austrian neurologist and founder of psychoanalysis, lived at 20 Maresfield Gardens in south Hampstead from 1938 (when he escaped from Nazi-occupied Vienna). His youngest daughter, Anna, herself a psychoanalyst, continued to live there up until her death in 1982. The house is now a museum devoted to Freud's life and work, and contains his famous couch, along with his collection of antiquities, books, letters, diaries and other personal mementoes.

8km (5 miles) NW of Trafalgar Square ✉ 20 Maresfield Gardens NW3 5SX ☎ 020 7435 2002 🕐 Wed–Sun 12–5 ✋ Adult £5, under 12s free Ⓤ Finchley Road 🚌 13, 82, 113 🚆 Finchley Road and Frognal, Hampstead Heath 🎁

Opposite *Dulwich Picture Gallery*
Below *Red-brick Fenton House, Hampstead*

INFORMATION

www.cuttysark.org.uk
www.oldroyalnavalcollege.org
www.nmm.ac.uk
www.english-heritage.org.uk (for Ranger's House)
11km (7 miles) SE of Trafalgar Square on the south bank
✉ Cutty Sark: Visitor Centre, Cutty Sark Gardens SE10 9HT. Old Royal Naval College: entrance from King William Walk. National Maritime Museum: Greenwich Park, SE10 9NF. Ranger's House: Chesterfield Walk, Blackheath, SE10 8QX ☎ Cutty Sark Visitor Centre: 020 8858 3445. Old Royal Naval College: 020 8269 4747. National Maritime Museum: 020 8858 4422, recorded information 020 8312 6565. Ranger's House: 020 8853 0035 Cutty Sark Visitor Centre: Sun–Tue 11–5. Old Royal Naval College: daily 10–5, grounds 8–6. National Maritime Museum: daily 10–5 Cutty Sark Visitor Centre: free. Old Royal Naval College: free; guided tours £4. National Maritime Museum: free, charge for special exhibitions. Ranger's House: adult £5.50, child (5–15) £2.80, under 5s free Greenwich 188 River boat from Westminster Millennium Pier (1hr 10 min) DLR to Island Gardens, then walk through the tunnel Regatta Café and Paul Coffee Bar, Level 2 of National Maritime Museum Level 1 of National Maritime Museum; two shops at the Royal Observatory

INTRODUCTION

This lively riverside town is home to some of London's finest buildings, set against a backdrop of beautiful parkland, and the largest maritime museum in the world. In North Greenwich the space-age Millennium Dome has been transformed into the huge O2 entertainment complex, containing performance spaces, clubs, shops, restaurants and the British Music Experience.

The best way to reach Greenwich is by river, as the view from the riverside is one of the finest in London. Most people come here to admire the assembly of historic buildings—the former Royal Naval College, the National Maritime Museum in the Queen's House and the Old Royal Observatory, in Greenwich Park. It's also worth browsing the craft stalls at the covered weekend market and sampling some of the many good pubs and restaurants.

An off-beat place worth visiting is the Fan Museum at 12 Croom's Hill (Tue–Sat 11–5, Sun 12–5), dedicated to the ancient art of fan-making. There are over 3,500 fans in the collection, dating from the 11th century onwards, on show in changing, themed exhibitions and in permanent displays.

WHAT TO SEE

CUTTY SARK

This sleek tea clipper anchored by Greenwich Pier was built in 1869 to carry cargoes between Britain and the Orient. In 1871 she broke the world record for sailing between London and China, completing the trip in only 107 days. Following a devastating fire in May 2007, the ship is closed for restoration until autumn 2010. It is possible to go to the Visitor Centre to learn all about the clipper.

OLD ROYAL NAVAL COLLEGE

This monumental group of buildings was laid out by Sir Christopher Wren in 1664 as a hospital for infirm and aged seamen. After the hospital closed in 1869, the complex was taken over by the Royal Naval College, training officers from all over the world, and it's now used by the University of Greenwich and the Trinity College of Music.

Two areas are open to the public: the Painted Hall and the chapel. The Painted Hall, created by Sir James Thornhill in 1707–17, features the largest painting in Great Britain, *Triumph of Peace and Liberty*, showing joint monarchs William (1650–1702) and Mary (1662–94) surrounded by allegorical figures. It measures 32 x 15m (106 x 51ft), and Thornhill and his assistants worked on it for some 20 years and received a fee of £6,685—then a princely sum—for their labours. The chapel (1718–25), restored by James Stuart after a fire in 1779, is in neo-Grecian style. The vast altar painting, *St. Paul Shaking Off the Viper*, is by American artist Benjamin West (1738–1820).

NATIONAL MARITIME MUSEUM

A suite of stunning galleries centred on the glass-roofed Neptune Court, and opened for the Millennium, gives the museum more space to tell the story of Britain's maritime history from the failed 16th-century invasion of the Spanish Armada to the 19th century. It focuses on exploration, trade and empire and explores themes such as luxury liners and naval heroes. Among the huge collection of ships (including hundreds of models), paintings, navigational instruments and the relics of sailors and explorers, seek out the luxurious state barge made for Frederick, Prince of Wales, in 1732, and the jacket Nelson was wearing when he was fatally wounded at the Battle of Trafalgar in 1805.

The museum's central building, the Queen's House, was England's first example of the neoclassical Palladian style, brought from Italy by Inigo Jones (1573–1652). Begun in 1616 as a palace for James I's wife, Anne of Denmark, it was not completed until 1635 in the reign of Charles I for his queen, Henrietta Maria. Inside, the best feature is the Tulip Stair, named after the pattern on its balustrade.

Also in the care of the National Maritime Museum is the Old Royal Observatory, founded by Charles II in 1675 to tackle the problem of finding longitude at sea. The original building, Flamsteed House, was designed by Sir Christopher Wren for John Flamsteed, the first Astronomer Royal. The Royal Observatory has undergone a £15 million redevelopment with new galleries, an education centre and the Peter Harrison Planetarium, with its excellent Star Life show (tel: 020 8312 8575; Mon–Fri 1, 2, 3, 4, Sat–Sun 11, 12, 1, 2, 3, 4; adult £6, child £4).

The large Gate Clock measures Greenwich Mean Time, the standard by which time is set all round the world. In the courtyard you can straddle the eastern and western hemispheres by standing astride the simple brass strip that marks the Greenwich Meridian.

RANGER'S HOUSE

At the southern end of Greenwich Park is the 18th-century Ranger's House, which became the official residence of the 'Ranger of Greenwich Park'. It's now a showcase for the Wernher Collection, formerly at Luton Hoo in Bedfordshire, which belonged to diamond and gold merchant Sir Julius Wernher. There are more than 700 works of art including paintings, tapestries, furniture, ceramics, ivories and jewels from the 16th and 17th centuries.

BRITISH MUSIC EXPERIENCE

London's newest museum is a highly entertaining history of pop culture and music tracing developments from the 1940s to the present day. It concentrates mainly on UK artists and bands, while showing their US influences and counterparts when appropriate. There are seven chronological sections, fetauring plenty of paraphernalia like original stars' instruments and garb. Other highlights are the Gibson Interactive Studio and Dance the Decades display. Your visit starts and ends with lively (and loud) video presentations. One excellent feature is that you can bookmark any info that especially interests you by touching your smart ticket onto the electronic pads, to be retrieved at your leisure on the museum's website.

✉ 02 complex, North Greenwich SE10 0DX ☎ 020 8463 2000 ⏲ Daily 10–8 (last entry 6.30) ✋ Adult £15, child (5–16) £12, under 5s free, family £40 Ⓤ North Greenwich 🚌 108, 129, 132, 161, 188, 422, 472

Above *Compass on the dome of the Old Royal Naval College*
Opposite *Greenwich Park and the Royal Observatory*
Below *The* Cutty Sark *is being restored to its former glory*

HAMPSTEAD HEATH

www.cityoflondon.gov.uk

Hampstead Heath is a wonderfully diverse public open space of 320ha (790 acres), with areas of ancient woodlands, bogs, hedgerows and natural grassland. Londoners come to walk, jog, ride horses, enjoy picnics, fly kites, play petanque and swim in the three ponds. Just east of the ponds is Parliament Hill, offering views over London. Local legend claims that Queen Boadicea (Boudicca), who led her Iceni people against the Roman occupiers (▷ 27), lies buried here.

At the northern end of the heath is Kenwood House (Apr–end Oct daily 11–5; Nov–end Mar 11–4), built in 1616 and remodelled by Robert Adam in 1764–79 for the Earl of Mansfield. It was left to the nation in 1927 by the 1st Earl of Iveagh, along with its outstanding collection of paintings. Here you will find Rembrandt's *Portrait of the Artist* (*c*1665), Vermeer's *The Guitar Player* (*c*1676) and Gainsborough's fine portrait of *Mary, Countess Howe* (*c*1764), among other important works by English and Dutch masters.

Open-air lakeside concerts are held in the grounds in June, July and August, with fireworks as a spectacular finale to some performances.

8km (5 miles) NW of Trafalgar Square
Hampstead Heath Information ☎ 020 8348 9908 ⓘ Open access ✋ Free
Ⓤ Hampstead 🚌 46, 210, C11
🚆 Hampstead Heath

HAMPTON COURT PALACE

▷ 260–261.

HIGHGATE CEMETERY

www.highgate-cemetery.org

During the 19th century everyone who was anyone in London was laid to rest in Highgate Cemetery. When it fell out of use, the main buildings became dilapidated and the landscape choked with brambles and sycamores. In the 1980s volunteers rescued and restored the grounds, clearing the tombs and graves but leaving enough greenery to create a romantic air.

The cemetery is divided in two by Swain's Lane: the original West Cemetery, Victorian Gothic in style, and the newer East Cemetery, peaceful, leafy and less visited. You can visit the West Cemetery by guided tour only; don't miss the Egyptian Avenue and Terrace Catacombs here. The exceptional collection of Victorian funerary architecture here includes the graves of about 850 famous figures, including German political theorist Karl Marx (1818–83), novelist George Eliot (1819–80) and chemist Michael Faraday (1791–1867, ▷ 140), plus 18 Royal Academicians, six Lord Mayors of London and 48 Fellows of the Royal Society. The surroundings are laid out as a mixed woodland of hornbeam, exotic lime, oak, hazel, sweet chestnut, tulip and field maple.

8km (5 miles) N of Trafalgar Square
✉ Friends of Highgate Cemetery, Swain's Lane N6 6PJ ☎ 020 8340 1834 ⓘ Eastern Cemetery: Apr–end Oct Mon–Fri 10–4.30, Sat–Sun 11–5; Nov–end Mar Mon–Fri 10–4, Sat–Sun 11–4. Closed during funerals. Western Cemetery: Admission by tour only. Apr–end Oct Mon–Fri 2pm, Sat–Sun 11, 12, 1, 2, 3, 4; Nov–end Mar last tour 3pm. No weekday tours Dec–end Feb; special tours can be arranged by request. No children under 8 ✋ Eastern Cemetery £3 (no video cameras). Western Cemetery standard tour £5 (no video cameras or tripods) Ⓤ Archway 🚌 143, 210, 271 to Lauderdale House 🚆 Upper Holloway 🎁

HOGARTH'S HOUSE

www.hounslow.info

Today, Hogarth's House stands close to a busy roundabout, but when the 'little country box by the Thames' was used as a summer home by artist and satirical engraver William Hogarth (1697–1764), it was set in open fields. The simple rooms are hung with copies of his work, including the moral tales *Marriage à la Mode* (1745) and *The Rake's Progress* (1735).

10km (6 miles) W of Trafalgar Square
✉ Hogarth Lane, Great West Road, Chiswick W4 2QN ☎ 020 8994 6757
ⓘ Apr–end Oct Tue–Fri 1–5, Sat–Sun 1–6; Oct–end Dec, Feb–end Mar Tue–Fri 1–4, Sat–Sun 1–5 ✋ Free; donation welcomed
Ⓤ Turnham Green 🚌 27, 190, 391
🚆 Turnham Green

HORNIMAN MUSEUM

www.horniman.ac.uk

A real gem, whose elegant clock tower stands proudly on the hilltop as you approach Forest Hill from Dulwich, this museum is named after Victorian tea merchant Frederick John Horniman, who

Below *The epitome of Georgian elegance, Marble Hill House is surrounded by public parkland*

originally displayed the many items he had collected during his travels in his house before founding the museum in 1901. It underwent a comprehensive refurbishment between 1999 and 2002. The main collections, which have grown tenfold in the ensuing century, cover Horniman's favourite subjects of natural history and anthropology. The former still largely consists of old-fashioned cases crammed full of stuffed and mounted creatures, with the noble exception of the small but delightful aquarium, but the displays on human culture and ethnology are first rate and up to date. There is also a massive collection of musical instruments with some interactive features.

10km (6 miles) S of Trafalgar Square
✉ 100 London Road, Forest Hill SE23 3PQ
☎ 020 8699 1872 ⏲ Daily 10.30–5.30
✋ Free 🚉 Forest Hill 🚌 176, 185, 197

KEATS HOUSE

www.keatshouse.org.uk

Poet John Keats (1795–1821) came to live here in 1818, fell in love with the girl next door, Fanny Brawne, and became engaged to her in 1819. In 1820 he left for Italy for health reasons; it was there that he died in 1821. During his brief time in this house he wrote some of his best-loved poems, including *Ode to a Nightingale*; the plum tree under which he wrote it has gone, but a replacement in the garden marks the spot.

The newly refurbished house displays letters, manuscripts and furnishings, synonymous with the period style.

8km (5 miles) NW of Trafalgar Square
✉ Keats Grove, Hampstead NW3 2RR
☎ 020 7435 2062 ⏲ Tue–Sun 1–5. Regular guided tours ✋ Adult £5, under 16s £2; entry to garden free 🚇 Belsize Park, Hampstead 🚌 46, C11 🚉 Hampstead Heath

LONDON WETLAND CENTRE

www.wetlandcentre.org.uk

The world's first wetland habitat created within a capital city sprawls over 42ha (105 acres) on the site of the former Barnes Elms reservoirs. Among the cleverly designed attractions are 14 different wetland environments, such as New Zealand whitewater, African floodplains, northern Tundra and Hawaiian lavaflow, and a Pond Zone; you will also find sustainable gardens, a trail and, of course, plenty of wildlife, including frogs, newts, damselflies and dragonflies. At the visitor centre you can see a film about the environment called *Planet Water*.

10km (6 miles) SW of Trafalgar Square
✉ Queen Elizabeth's Walk, Barnes SW13 9WT ☎ 020 8409 4400 ⏲ Apr–end Oct daily 9.30–6, Jan–end Mar 9.30–5 ✋ Adult £9.50, child (4–16) £5.30, under 4s free, family £26.60 🚇 Hammersmith 🚌 283 Duck Bus from Hammersmith Underground to Wetland Centre; 33, 72, 209 to Red Lion pub 🚉 Barnes

MARBLE HILL HOUSE

www.english-heritage.org.uk

Built to make the most of the views over the river towards Richmond Hill, Marble Hill House is an exemplary Palladian villa. It was designed as a rural retreat for Henrietta Howard, mistress of the Prince of Wales, the future George II, in 1724; later it was given to another royal consort, Mrs Fitzherbert, who was secretly married to the future George IV in 1785 but had to give way to Caroline of Brunswick.

As with all Palladian villas, the main rooms are on the second floor. The Great Room is a perfect cube, in keeping with the Palladian love of geometry. It is furnished as it would have been in Henrietta Howard's time, when regular visitors included the writers John Gay, Horace Walpole and Alexander Pope, who advised on the layout of the garden, with its groves of statuesque trees and manicured lawns. Today the grounds provide an atmospheric riverside backdrop for a series of outdoor concerts.

16km (10 miles) SW of Trafalgar Square
✉ Richmond Road, Twickenham TW1 2NL
☎ 020 8892 5115 ⏲ Apr–end Oct Sat 10–2, Sun and bank hol Mon 10–5. Tel for additional opening times ✋ Adult £4.40, child (5–16) £2.20, under 5s free, family £11 🚇 Richmond 🚌 65, 371 🚉 St. Margarets

MUSEUM OF RUGBY

www.rfu.com

Rugby Union fans will love this collection of memorabilia dating back to the 1800s. You can see the Calcutta Cup, the oldest rugby jersey in existence and use the interactive touch-screen computers to learn about the history of the game. Or test your strength on the scrum machine, relive the greatest-ever tries, and witness the highs and lows of the world's most prestigious competitions in the audiovisual theatre.

18km (11 miles) SW of Trafalgar Square
✉ Twickenham and Twickenham Stadium Tours, Rugby Road, Twickenham TW1 1DZ
☎ 0870 405 2001 ⏲ Tue–Sat 10–5, Sun 11–5. Closed Sun after match days
✋ Museum and stadium tour: adult £14, child (5–16) £8, family £40; museum only (match day ticket-holders only): £3
🚇 Richmond, then R68, R70 to Twickenham centre; Hounslow East, then 281 🚌 33, 110, 267, 281, 290, 490, H22, R68, R70
🚉 Twickenham

NATIONAL ARCHIVES

www.nationalarchives.gov.uk

All central government records, from the Norman Conquest in 1066 to the present day, are stored here, as well as all law court records, stacked away on 167km (104 miles) of shelving. There's a public display of some of the most significant pieces, such as the Domesday Book, the great land survey of 1086, plus curiosities such as letters from murderer Jack the Ripper, the last telegram sent from *Titanic* before it sank and pop star Elton John's change of name (from Reginald Dwight) by deed poll.

15km (9 miles) W of Trafalgar Square
✉ Ruskin Avenue, Kew TW9 4DU ☎ 020 8876 3444 ⏲ Mon, Wed, Fri 9–5, Tue, 10–7, Thu 9–7, Sat 9.30–5 ✋ Free 🚇 Kew Gardens 🚌 65, 237, 267, 391, R68 🚉 Kew Gardens ⛴ Kew Pier

INFORMATION

www.hrp.org.uk
21km (13 miles) SW of Trafalgar Square
East Molesey, Surrey KT8 9AU
Recorded information: 0844 482 7777; bookings: 0844 482 7799
Palace, maze Easter–end Oct daily 10–6; Nov–Easter daily 10–4.30. Gardens close 1–2 hours earlier
Adult £14, child (5–15) £7, under 5s free, family £38. Maze only: adult £3.50, child £2.50, family £10
111, 216, 411, 416, 451, 513, R68
Hampton Court
Summer services from Westminster Pier
Tours, audio-guides, exhibitions
£4.95
Privy Kitchen Coffee Shop; Tiltyard Tea-room, palace gardens
Barrack Block Shop in former palace barracks; Garden Shop; Base Court Shop, between Base Court and Clock Court; Tudor Kitchens Shop, next to Tudor Wine Cellar

INTRODUCTION

Hampton Court is one of the oldest and most interesting of London's royal palaces, with beautiful riverside gardens.

Cardinal Thomas Wolsey, Archbishop of York and chancellor to Henry VIII, built Hampton Court in 1514 as a country residence, almost completely obliterating all traces of the previous country manor belonging to the Knights Hospitallers of St. John of Jerusalem, which dated from the 13th century. In 1528 he made an unsuccessful bid to retain the king's favour by handing over his new home. Henry spent around £62,000 extending it, turning it into a royal palace with features such as a huge communal dining room, a chapel, bowling alleys, tennis courts and a hunting park. Apart from a few minor alterations by Elizabeth I and later the Stuarts, the layout remained unchanged until the 1690s, when William and Mary employed Sir Christopher Wren to make further modifications and additions. The main alterations were completely new apartments for both the king and the queen, costing a startling £113,000. The result was the striking mix of Tudor and baroque styles still in evidence today.

WHAT TO SEE

AROUND THE PALACE

You approach the palace through the Trophy Gates, surrounded by all manner of turrets and castellations, with the Tudor Great Gatehouse ahead, now only half the size it was during Cardinal Wolsey's day. Terracotta roundels, originally painted and gilded, depict Roman emperors in the two side turrets. Carved on the opposite gateway are the intertwined initials 'H' and 'A'—Henry and Anne. Having declared his marriage to Catherine of Aragon invalid, Henry married Anne Boleyn in 1533, but the marriage lasted only four years, and Anne was beheaded at the Tower (▷ 112–117).

Clock Court comes next, named after the huge astronomical clock (1540) on the gateway's inner side. This was made in 1540 for Henry VIII and was used to calculate the high tide at London Bridge, essential for working out when to move the king's entourage downstream. On the left is Henry VIII's Great Hall, with its hammerbeam roof, oriel window, minstrels' gallery and splendid tapestries depicting the story of Abraham. It was constructed during 1534 in great haste at the king's bidding, the workers toiling away by candlelight. Nearby, in the Tudor kitchens, more than 200 staff cooked for 600 people at a time. Opposite, through Wren's elegant colonnade, you enter Henry VIII's State Apartments (1689–94), decorated with paintings, furnishings and tapestries. Jean Tijou (*fl*1689–*c*1711), a French blacksmith, made the ironwork balustrades of the staircases, Grinling Gibbons (1648–1721) carved the woodwork and Antonio Verrio (*c*1639–1707) painted many of the ceilings. Two of the most interesting rooms in this section of the palace are the Great Watching Chamber, with its fine ceiling of gilded oak, and the Haunted Gallery, so named as it is supposedly the home of Henry's fifth wife, executed Catherine Howard. From here it is a few steps to the beautiful Chapel Royal, where regular services, open to the public, are still held.

Elsewhere, accessed by the grand King's Staircase, are William III's apartments, which include the Guard Chamber, complete with 3,000 pieces of armoury, the Privy Chamber with its imposing throne, and the Great Bedchamber, boasting a throne of a different sort—the king's velvet toilet. The smaller Queen's Apartments look over Wren's Fountain Court, and the public rooms look out on to avenues, canals and fountains. Inside, the opulent Queen's Drawing Room contains an impressive array of paintings, including a rather self-aggrandizing ceiling portrait of Anne herself as Justice. The Georgian Rooms include the Cumberland Suite, inhabited by George II before he acceded to the throne, the Cartoon Gallery, designed by Wren to accommodate the Raphael Cartoons, now in the Victoria & Albert Museum (▷ 224–228), and the Queen's Private Chapel. Finally, the four early Tudor Wolsey Rooms serve as reminders of the cardinal's original palace, although they now display works from the monarchy's huge Royal Collection.

THE GARDENS

Today's formal landscaping of avenues and lakes originated in William and Mary's time. To the south, the Privy Garden was for the use of the royal family and was separated from the river by Tijou's wrought-iron screen. Nearby are Henry VIII's Pond Garden and an Elizabethan knot garden of aromatic herbs. The Great Vine, planted in 1768 by Capability Brown, still produces black Hamburg grapes.

North of the palace are the Rose Gardens, formerly the tiltyards, where jousting took place, and the Wilderness, 4ha (10 acres) of natural woodland. The Maze, laid out in the 1690s, is in the top corner and covers 60sq m (645sq ft). The most famous labyrinth in the world is for many people the best-known feature of Hampton Court and the principal reason for coming here. Its original hornbeam hedges were replaced by yew as visitor numbers grew exponentially in the 1960s, as yew withstands wear and tear better. Although not the most elaborate maze in the world, it is still deceptively tricky and many visitors find themselves spending more time inside than they had planned. In 2005, an arts group was commissioned to install a sound work called *Trace*, which employs sensors to release short bursts of birdsong, laughter or music at certain points. It's a gimmicky but nonetheless amusing means of enhancing the whole experience.

TIPS

» Take a free introductory tour from one of the guides.

» Buy a combined train and palace entry ticket—it gives 10 per cent off admission.

Opposite *The mellow red brick of Hampton Court seems to glow in the sun*
Below *The unicorn statue outside faces his lion counterpart*

Above *Classical Roman statues decorate the rooms of 16th-century Syon House*
Opposite *The Thames Barrier was built to protect London against flooding*

ORLEANS HOUSE GALLERY

www.richmond.gov.uk

All that remains now of 18th-century Orleans House is the Octagon, a garden room built in 1720. The building, together with modern extensions at the back, houses a public gallery, workshops and temporary exhibitions.

The newly renovated Stables Gallery stages around seven contemporary and community-based exhibitions a year.

18km (11 miles) SW of Trafalgar Square
Riverside TW1 3DJ 020 8831 6000
Oct–end Mar Tue–Sat 1–4.30, Sun 2–4.30; Apr–end Sep Tue–Sat 1–5.30, Sun 2–5.30. Gardens 9am–dusk Free
33, 290, 490, H22, R68, R70
Twickenham

OSTERLEY PARK

www.nationaltrust.org.uk/osterley

One of London's largest surviving estate parks, with an elegant neoclassical villa at its heart, Osterley feels a thousand miles from the bustle of central London. The original Elizabethan villa was built by Thomas Gresham in 1576 and remodelled by Robert Adam in the late 18th century for Sir Francis Child, head of Child's Bank. Don't miss the Eating Room, with its elaborately decorated plaster ceiling, statues and paintings, or the Gobelin tapestries in the Tapestry Room.

The house is surrounded by pleasure gardens, ornamental lakes and parkland, and the 16th-century stables are now a cafe.

19km (12 miles) W of Trafalgar Square
Jersey Road, Isleworth TW7 4RB
020 8232 5050; infoline 01494 755566
House, Jersey Galleries, gardens: mid–Mar to end Oct Wed–Sun 11–5. Park and pleasure grounds: Apr–end Oct daily 8–7.30; Nov–end Mar daily 8–6; park closes early before major events House and gardens: adult £7.60, child (5–16) £3.80, under 5s free, family £20. Garden only: adult £3, child £1.50. Jersey Galleries and park: free Osterley H28, H91 Syon Lane

OXFORD

▷ 264–265.

RICHMOND PARK

www.royalparks.gov.uk

Originally enclosed as a hunting ground by Charles I in 1637, Richmond Park is, at 1,011ha (2,500 acres), London's largest open space. Its diverse landscape takes in grassland, areas of bog and bracken, wetland, woodland and ancient parkland trees, and herds of fallow (350) and red (300) deer still graze here—but in safety, nowadays. In spring, when camellias, magnolias, azaleas and rhododendrons come into flower, the Isabella Plantation is a treat to visit.

15km (9 miles) W of Trafalgar Square
Park Office, Holly Lodge, Richmond Park, Richmond, Surrey TW10 5HS 020 8948 3209 Open access during daylight hours Free Richmond, then bus 371 to Lass of Richmond Hill stop 72 85, 371, K3 Richmond, then bus 371 to Lass of Richmond Hill stop

THE RIVER THAMES

▷ 266–267.

ROYAL BOTANIC GARDENS, KEW

▷ 268–269.

SYON HOUSE AND PARK

www.syonpark.co.uk

Outside, this historic seat of the Dukes of Northumberland looks forbidding, but the battlemented mid-16th-century building contains some of the most elegantly decorated rooms in England. Robert Adam (1728–92) remodelled the interior between 1761 and 1768 using marble, gilded statues and plasterwork.

Among the duke's private rooms, now on view, are the Green Drawing Room with its splendid Adam fireplace, rescued from Northumberland House in the Strand when it was demolished in 1874. Upstairs is the suite of rooms furnished for the young Princess Victoria, to whom the 3rd Duchess of Northumberland was governess.

Capability Brown landscaped the grounds of Syon House between 1767 and 1773 by creating an idyllic version of the countryside, with lakes, lawns and fine specimen trees. The centrepiece, linking lake and garden, is the Great Conservatory, built between 1820 and 1827 by Charles Fowler, the architect of Covent Garden market (▷ 142–143). Several different planting environments are housed here, ranging from damp fernery to the hot, dry cactus beds.

The rose garden was replanted in 1995 with more than 8,000 roses.

Farther off, a stroll around the lakes takes in many moisture-loving plants, flowering shrubs and unusual trees.

In the Tropical Forest (separate admission charge, open daily 10–5.30, www.tropicalforest.co.uk, tel 020 8847 4730), rescued exotic animals, including monkeys, lemurs, snakes, lizards, baby crocodiles and more, are kept in near-natural habitats. Within the grounds there is also a giant indoor adventure playground, a garden centre, a trout fishery and an Edinburgh Woollen Mill outlet.

15km (9 miles) W of Trafalgar Square ✉ Syon Park, Brentford, Middlesex TW8 8JF ☎ 020 8560 0881 ⏲ House: Mar–end Oct Wed–Thu, Sun 11–5; gardens daily 10.30–5 or dusk if earlier; miniature steam railway open late Jun–late Aug Sun, and Apr–end Aug bank hol weekends ✋ House, gardens, Great Conservatory and rose garden: adult £9, under 16s £4, family £20; gardens and Great Conservatory: adult £4.50, child £2.50, family £10 🚇 Gunnersbury, then bus 🚌 237, 267 to Brentlea Gate 🚆 Kew Bridge or Gunnersbury, then bus ☕ 🎁

THAMES BARRIER

www.environment-agency.gov.uk

In 1953, 300 people died when the Thames broke its banks and flooded London. Since then the river has risen by another 50cm (20in)—and it will continue to rise by about 1m (3ft) every hundred years. The Thames Barrier was opened in 1984 to prevent further flooding, and its spectacular stainless steel gates, 61m (200ft) wide, are now a familiar landmark. Electrically powered hydraulic power packs, housed immediately below the stainless steel roofs, rotate the gates, which are regularly closed and reopened for experiments and inspection. Exhibits explain river tides, anti-pollution strategies and the return of river wildlife. In the information office there's a working model of the barrier and a re-creation of the great Victorian stench.

16km (10 miles) E of Trafalgar Square ✉ 1 Unity Way, SE18 5NJ ☎ 020 8305 4188 ⏲ Apr–end Sep daily 10.30–4.30; Oct–end Mar daily 11–3.30 ✋ Adult £3.50, under 16s £2 🚇 Greenwich 🚌 177, 180 🚆 Charlton Barrier Pier ☕ 🎁

WILLIAM MORRIS GALLERY

www.lbwf.gov.uk/wmg

This is the only public museum devoted to the designer, craftsman, writer and socialist William Morris (1834–96). Along with his contemporaries in the Arts and Crafts movement, he reintroduced craftsmanship into everyday domestic objects as a reaction against industrialization. Their work and Morris's life and influence are illustrated with displays of their fabrics, rugs, carpets, wallpapers, furniture, stained glass and painted tiles. There are also examples of Arts and Crafts furniture, textiles, ceramics and glass from the 1880s to the 1920s.

15km (9 miles) NE of Trafalgar Square ✉ Lloyd Park, Forest Road, E17 4PP ☎ 020 8496 4390 ⏲ Wed–Sun 10–5 ✋ Free; donations welcome 🚇 Walthamstow Central 🚌 34, 97, 123, 215, 275, 357 to Bell Corner 🚆 Walthamstow Central 🎁

WIMBLEDON COMMON

www.wpcc.org.uk

Together with Putney Lower Common, this slice of greenery covers about 461ha (1,140 acres). Among the areas of woodland, scrubland, heathland and recreation parks are a nature trail, an 18-hole golf course, cricket pitches, 26km (16 miles) of bridle paths, soccer and rugby pitches and athletics facilities.

A restored 1817 windmill now houses a museum (Apr–end Oct Sat 2–5, Sun 11–5) with models, flour-grinding machinery and a collection of woodworking tools.

East of the common, on Church Road, is the All England Lawn Tennis Club, venue for the annual Wimbledon championships (▷ 294). The excellent Tennis Museum, opened in 2006, provides a chronicle of the game of tennis from its origins in the 1860s to the present day (daily 10.30–5; closed middle Sun of championships, Mon after championships). In the cinema you can see footage of championship matches.

13km (8 miles) SW of Trafalgar Square ✉ The Ranger's Office, Windmill Road, Wimbledon Common SW19 5NR ☎ 020 8788 7655 ⏲ Open access ✋ Free 🚇 Putney Bridge, Southfields, Wimbledon 🚌 93 🚆 Wimbledon ☕

WINDSOR AND ETON

▷ 270–271.

INFORMATION

Tourist information office

www.visitoxford.org

15–16 Broad Street, Oxford OX1 3AS

01865 252200

HOW TO GET THERE

Oxford is 92km (57 miles) northwest of London

from Paddington (1 hour)

Victoria Coach Station: National Express service OXX90 (1 hour 40 min)

M4 west, then M40 to junction 7 (1 hour 15 min)

Above *The Radcliffe Camera, part of the Bodleian Library, with Brasenose College on the left and All Souls on the right*

INTRODUCTION

Home of one of the world's oldest universities, Oxford is a vibrant city of ancient buildings and riverside walks, with excellent shopping.

Everywhere in this city of spires and greenery there's a sense of the long tradition of learning. There's been a university here since the arrival in 1167 of a number of English scholars expelled from the Sorbonne in Paris after a dispute between the English and French kings.

Every student is attached to one of the 39 individual colleges. They are all different in character but most have their buildings, including a chapel and a high-ceilinged dining hall, set around quadrangles (quads). Most of the central colleges have medieval origins and display an interesting mixture of architectural styles from Renaissance to Victorian.

Oxford is not huge, but its layout can be confusing. High Street, which students call the High, runs from Carfax Tower east to Magdalen Bridge over the River Cherwell, dividing the city into north and south. To get your bearings, climb the towers of St. Michael's Church, in Cornmarket Street, the city's oldest building; the University Church of St. Mary the Virgin, High Street, dating from 1280 and serving the university; or the Carfax Tower, a remnant of the 14th-century St. Martin's Church, at the busy crossroads known as Carfax.

WHAT TO SEE

COLLEGES

Christ Church, St. Aldate's, founded in 1525, is the largest and most visited college and has the biggest quadrangle. Its chapel is Christ Church Cathedral, which predates the college and is England's smallest cathedral. Christ Church Picture Gallery includes works by Dürer and Michelangelo.

To the south and east spreads the bucolic Christ Church Meadow (entrances at St. Aldate's, Rose Lane and Merton Street), still grazed by cattle—a pocket of green countryside in the heart of the city. You can walk from the meadow or the High into the Oxford Botanic Garden (daily), the oldest botanic gardens in Britain, founded in 1621 and filled with plants from around the world.

Magdalen College (pronounced 'maudlin') is one of the richest and most spacious colleges, founded in 1458 and with its own deer park. Also worth a visit are Merton College, its peaceful gardens partly enclosed by the old city wall; New College, famous for its handsome hall, cloister and gardens; the Queen's College, with buildings by Christopher Wren (1632–1723) and Nicholas Hawksmoor (1661–1736); and, farther out in Parks Road, Keble College, a relative newcomer whose red-brick buildings are a Victorian tour de force.

UNIVERSITY BUILDINGS

Between Broad Street and High Street is a trio of eye-catching university edifices. The Sheldonian Theatre (built between 1664 and 1669), the first major architectural work by Sir Christopher Wren, assumes the shape of a Roman theatre and hosts university functions and concerts. Nearby are several buildings housing the Bodleian Library, the world's oldest library, opened in the 14th century and now housing over 6 million books (tours Mon–Sat). The circular, domed Radcliffe Camera, completed in 1749, serves as one of the library's reading rooms.

MUSEUMS

The pick of the museums is the Ashmolean in Beaumont Street (Tue–Sun), Britain's oldest public museum, opened in 1683, which contains Oxford University's priceless collections from the time of early man to 20th-century paintings. The cavernous and old-fashioned Pitt Rivers Museum in Parks Road (daily) has a celebrated anthropology collection of more than 250,000 objects, among them masks and shrunken heads. Next door is the University Museum of Natural History (daily), in a splendid neo-Gothic building.

For a succinct survey of the city from prehistoric times to the present, from mammoths to Morris Minor motor cars, visit the Museum of Oxford, St. Aldate's (Tue–Fri, Sun pm).

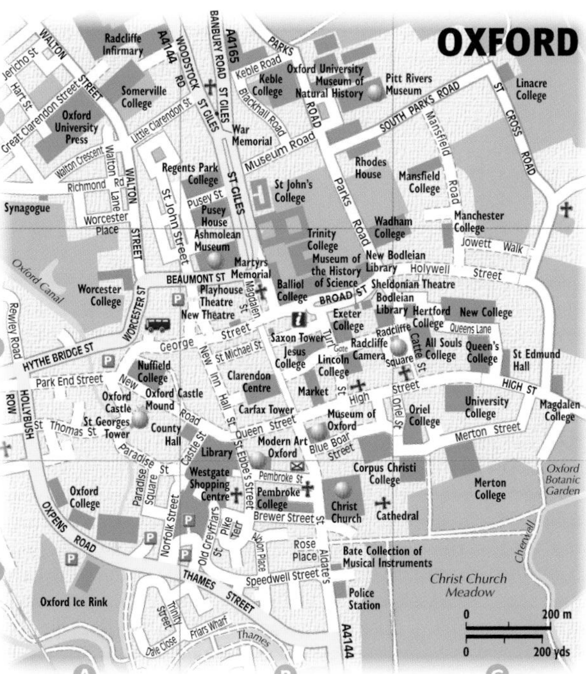

TIPS

- To get the real atmosphere, visit in term time.
- Use the park-and-ride on the outer ring road and take a bus into the heart of the city. The centre is pedestrianized and parking is expensive.
- Feel free to wander into many of the university and college buildings. Some charge for admission, and most have a notice indicating which areas are open and at what times.
- For an overview, join a guided walking tour of the city and colleges at the tourist information centre. Tickets are sold on a first come, first served basis.
- Hire a punt or rowing boat from the Cherwell Boathouse in Bardwell Road for a classic boating trip.

WHERE TO EAT

LE PETIT BLANC

www.lepetitblanc.co.uk

Authentic provincial French cuisine from monkfish, scallop and shellfish ragout to confit of rabbit leg.

✉ 71–72 Walton Street, Oxford OX2 6AG ☎ 01865 510999 L from £12, D from £15, Wine from £12.95 Daily noon–10.30

QUOD RESTAURANT AND BAR

www.quod.co.uk

A place that's buzzy all day long. Its Italian brasserie menu includes pizzas, pastas and risottos, plus heavenly desserts.

✉ Old Bank Hotel, 92–94 High Street, Oxford OX1 4BN ☎ 01865 202505 L from £10, D from £25, Wine from £11 Daily 11.30–11

INFORMATION

Tourist information offices

Kingston: ✉ Market House, Market Place, Kingston upon Thames KT1 1JS
☎ 020 8547 5592

Richmond: ✉ Old Town Hall, Whittaker Avenue, Richmond TW9 1TP
☎ 020 8940 9125

Southwark: ✉ Tate Modern, Level 2, Bankside SE1 9TG
☎ 020 7401 5277

Greenwich: ✉ Pepys House, 2 Cutty Sark Gardens, Greenwich SE10 5LW
☎ 0870 608 2000

HOW TO GET THERE

Embankment Pier

Circle, District, Bakerloo or Northern line to Embankment

9, 11, 12, 24

Westminster Pier

Circle, District or Jubilee line to Westminster

11, 12, 24, 453

INTRODUCTION

A cruise along the Thames is a leisurely way to see the city. It gives a new perspective to London's development and history, which is inextricably linked with this long and majestic river.

As the Thames flows west to east into Greater London, on the last stages of its 346km (215-mile) journey to the sea, it loops around Hampton Court Park and the 16th-century palace of Hampton Court itself (▷ 260–261), a reminder of the Tudor era. It's a fitting introduction to the river's course through the capital and recalls a period when the Thames was a place of regal processions, magnificent mansions and palaces, and thriving trade.

But the river's significance in the commercial and royal life of the nation goes back much farther—probably to the Bronze Age and earlier—and, having turned northwards, the river flows past Kingston upon Thames, the site of many Saxon coronations.

WHAT TO SEE

TEDDINGTON TO KEW

Navigating the river and its ebb and flow was a problem for centuries, alleviated with the building of locks and weirs such as those at Teddington, a little farther north at the point between the non-tidal and tidal sections of the river.

During the 17th and 18th centuries the lush banks of this stretch of the river became a fashionable setting for aristocratic homes and gardens. You pass Ham House, Marble Hill House (▷ 259) and Syon House (▷ 262) as the river makes its way past the affluent town of Richmond and up past Kew Gardens (▷ 268–269) to the Hanoverian Kew Palace.

KEW TO BATTERSEA

From here the Thames winds through Chiswick, with its lovely Georgian riverside houses, and past Barnes, now home of the London Wetland Centre (▷ 259), passing under the elaborate Victorian suspension bridge at Hammersmith. Fulham Palace (Museum/Gallery Mon–Tue 12–4, Sat 11–2, Sun 11.30–3.30; gardens daily dawn–dusk), private residence of the Bishops of London, is on the approach to the last southern dip of the river—where the Oxford and Cambridge Boat Race (▷ 295) starts at Putney—before it flows under Battersea Bridge and between the Chelsea Embankment and Battersea Park (▷ 211).

BATTERSEA TO BANKSIDE

This marks the point where the river enters central London and becomes a working highway, until recently lined with shipping, docks and warehouses. Today this is tourist London proper: The Thames flows between Lambeth Palace (▷ 82) and the Houses of Parliament (▷ 179–180) and past the London Eye (▷ 75) and the Southbank complex of concert, theatre and film venues (▷ 79), making a northern loop past the Victoria Embankment (▷ 147) and towards the Millennium Bridge (▷ 77), linking St. Paul's Cathedral (▷ 104–109) and Tate Modern (▷ 80–81).

BANKSIDE TO THE THAMES BARRIER

Beyond Shakespeare's Globe (▷ 78) and Southwark Cathedral (▷ 79) the river reaches London Bridge, the modern crossing that replaced the 1831 version, itself replacing its arched medieval predecessor, which was crammed with houses and shops. The next crossing is Tower Bridge (▷ 111), designed to allow tall ships passage between the city and the sea. Guarding the north bank is the Tower of London (▷ 112–117), William the Conqueror's fort placed strategically to protect access to the Port of London.

From this point the river passes through an area once dominated by shipping docks and now redeveloped as smart office and residential blocks.

Seafaring is the theme from here onwards, as the Thames reaches Greenwich (▷ 256–257) before continuing its course to the Thames Barrier (▷ 263) at Woolwich Reach and beyond the Greater London boundaries towards Gravesend and the sea.

RIVERBOATS

Sailing times vary with seasons and conditions.

From Embankment Pier:
Bateaux London Catamaran
www.hospitalityline.co.uk
Regular circular/hop-on, hop-off services, Embankment–Waterloo–Bankside–Tower–Greenwich, summer daily 10–5, winter daily 10–4.
☎ 020 7695 1800

From Westminster Pier:
Crown River Cruises
City Cruises
www.citycruises.com
Downriver Westminster to Tower Pier (30–40 min), Westminster to Greenwich (1 hour 30 min). Sailings about every 40 min, summer daily 8.40–6 (Westminster–Tower until 8.50), winter daily 10–6.
☎ 020 7740 0400
www.crownriver.com
Hop-on, hop-off between Westminster and St. Katharine's Pier, from 11am.
☎ 020 7936 2033

Thames River Services
www.thamesriverservices.co.uk
Downriver Westminster to Greenwich (50 min, leaves every 30 min) or Thames Barrier (1 hour 30 min, leaves on the hour); daily 10–5 (more services in summer).
☎ 020 7930 4097

Westminster Passenger Service Association
www.wpsa.co.uk
Upriver Westminster to Hampton Court (3 hours 30 min), Mar–end Oct daily 10.30, 11.15, 12 to all destinations, 2pm to Kew Gardens only.
☎ 020 7930 2062

Opposite *Cruise boat at Westminster Pier*
Above *Cruise boat passing under the Millennium Bridge*

INFORMATION

www.kew.org
13km (8 miles) W of Trafalgar Square
✉ Kew, Richmond, Surrey TW9 3AB
☎ 020 8332 5655 ⌚ Apr–end Aug Mon–Fri 9.30–6.30, Sat–Sun 9.30–7.30; Sep–end Oct daily 9.30–6; Nov–end Jan daily 9.30–5 or dusk; Feb–end Mar daily 9.30–5.30 Adult £12.25, under 17s free Kew Gardens 65, 391 Kew Bridge, Kew Gardens £4.95, in English only Victorian Terrace Café The Orangery; White Peaks restaurant; The Pavilion (Feb–end Oct only) At Victoria Gate and White Peaks

Above *The Temperate House*

INTRODUCTION

Kew has a royal palace, magnificent glasshouses, mature trees and—above all—120ha (300 acres) of spectacular gardens.

The gardens were created by combining two royal estates in 1772. Under the patronage of George III they developed into one of the world's foremost centres of horticultural research, largely thanks to botanist Sir Joseph Banks (▷ 220), who became the King's adviser in 1773 after his voyage around the world with Captain Cook. The early botanic garden occupied just a small area; the rest was landscaped by Capability Brown (his lake and Rhododendron Dell remain) and dotted with fanciful buildings to amuse courtly visitors.

WHAT TO SEE

The oldest building is the 10-storey pagoda, built in 1761–62 to the designs of William Chambers. Kew began to change after 1841, when the gardens were handed over to the State, and several greenhouses were added. The Palm House, designed by Decimus Burton, opened in 1848. It was thoroughly refurbished in 1985. Apart from a bewildering variety of palms and other tropical species, its basement hides the fascinating Marine Display, which includes examples of coral reefs, mangrove swamps, rocky shores and salty marshes.

Next was the Temperate House, also by Decimus Burton, begun in 1859. On completion, 40 years later, it was the world's largest greenhouse. From its elevated gallery you get a good view of the plants, including the Chilean wine palm, planted in 1846 and now claimed to be the largest greenhouse plant in existence.

The Princess of Wales Conservatory opened in 1987. Much of it is below ground level (for insulation) and is lit by a series of low, tentlike glass roofs. You pass through different climate zones, from arid desert at one end to orchid-filled tropics at the other.

British native wild flowers are the theme at Queen Charlotte's Cottage and Gardens on the southwestern fringes of the site, named after George III's queen. This is now a woodland nature reserve, as requested by Queen Victoria. Also tucked in a secluded corner of the gardens is the Rhododendron Dell, one of the few features left pretty much as it was in Capability Brown's original design, the other being the lake. The dell contains an amazing 700 varieties of the colourful shrub and is at its best in May, though flowering spans most of the year from November to August.

Apart from these more famous attractions, there are plenty more horticultural delights that can easily stretch your visit into a full day. The Bamboo Garden has 120 specimens from all over the world, some up to 3m (10ft) high, and is a good year-round exhibit. The Aquatic Garden, opened in 1909, comprises a set of tanks filled with water lilies, rushes and sedges; it is at its best when the plants bloom in summer. The beautifully landscaped Rock Garden, on the other hand, dates from 1882 and was redesigned in modern times to incorporate a bog garden and cascade. It is arranged into six geographical areas, showcasing mainly Alpine, Mediterranean and woodland plants, so there will always be something in flower. Finally, especially constructed around the 18th-century Ice House for grey days, the Winter Garden contains a collage of hardy specimens such as wintersweet, viburnum, witch hazel, cornelian cherry and aconite, whose various hues stand out against the evergreen backdrop.

For children there's the excellent indoor Bugs and Beetles play area, with plenty of vaguely educational bugs and flowers to climb about on.

TIP

» Take the Kew Explorer, a hop-on-hop-off mini land train that tours all the key sites in 40 minutes. Tickets are £2, child (under 17) £1, available on board. The Royal Botanical Gardens were given UNESCO World Heritage Site status in July 2003. Their magnificent glasshouses have been renovated and updated to make them more accessible to today's visitors.

Left *Giant lily pads up to 2m (6.5ft) across are grown annually from seed*
Below *The Palm House*

INFORMATION

Tourist information office

The Old Booking Hall, Windsor Royal Station, Thames Street, Windsor SL4 1PJ

01753 743900

HOW TO GET THERE

Windsor is 40km (25 miles) west of central London

District Line to Richmond (30 minutes from Embankment), then South West Trains to Windsor and Eton Riverside station

50 min from Waterloo to Windsor and Eton Riverside station or 25 min from Paddington to Slough, then 10 min from Slough to Windsor (▷ 62)

Daily Green Line services from Victoria Coach Station, London: 1 hour 10 min

M4 to junction 6 or M3 to junction 3, then A322/A332 (30 min)

Above *Windsor Castle's Henry VIII Gate*
Opposite *Banners of the Knights of the Garter hang in St. George's Chapel*

INTRODUCTION

Less than an hour from London are two neighbouring towns that offer a full day out: Windsor, with the largest castle in Europe, and Eton, with one of Britain's most famous public schools.

WHAT TO SEE

WINDSOR CASTLE

Windsor Castle is an unforgettable sight, towering above the town on a chalk cliff. It's the largest inhabited castle in the world and one of the principal residences of the sovereigns of England since the 12th century. Much of its present appearance dates from the 19th century, but the stone castle was built for Henry II in 1165, replacing William the Conqueror's original 11th-century fort.

There are several buildings to visit within the castle complex. St. George's Chapel is a masterpiece of Perpendicular Gothic architecture, begun in 1475 by Edward IV and completed in 1511. Queen Elizabeth the Queen Mother is buried here beside her husband, King George VI, and her daughter Princess Margaret. The monument in the northwest chapel to Princess Charlotte, who died in childbirth in 1817, shows her ascending to heaven with an angel carrying her stillborn child. The chapel's fan-vaulted ceiling is particularly beautiful, as are the elaborate 15th-century choir stalls covered in vignettes of animals, jesters, the Dance of Death and biblical stories, and surmounted by banners of the 26 Knights of the Garter, the highest order of knighthood, whose installation has taken place here since 1348. It was here that the Queen's youngest child, Edward, married Sophie Rhys-Jones in 1999, and the service of blessing for Prince Charles and Camilla Parker-Bowles was held in April 2005 after their wedding in the town's Guildhall.

The baroque State Apartments, restored after a devastating fire in 1992, are hung with works from the Royal Collection, one of the world's finest private art collections. Also on display is Queen Mary's Dolls' House, designed by Sir Edwin Lutyens for the Queen in 1924. The furnishings are designed at one-twelfth life-size, the plumbing and lighting really work, and eminent writers and artists contributed handwritten books and miniature paintings to the library.

Don't miss the Changing of the Guard at Windsor Castle: Apr–end Jul Mon–Sat 11am weather permitting; Aug–end Mar alternate days 11am (not Sun).

WINDSOR TOWN

After visiting the castle, it's worth exploring Windsor's many shops and public buildings. The Guildhall on the High Street was completed in 1689 by Sir Christopher Wren. Its Tuscan columns, on the ground floor, don't quite touch the ceiling; apparently the town council insisted on having them, but Wren left the gap at the top to make the point that they were structurally superfluous. Farther up the High Street pass the 19th-century parish church of St. John the Baptist and continue up Park Street to the Long Walk, a 5km-long (3-mile) avenue of elms in Windsor Great Park. Savill Garden (daily), 14ha (35 acres) of woodland within the park, is lovely in spring when the azaleas and camellias are in bloom.

ETON

Across the river from Windsor is Eton, its appealing main street fronted by Britain's best-known public school. Eton College was founded by Henry VI in 1440 for 70 King's Scholars, also known as Collegers, who lived in the college and were educated free, and a small number of 'Oppidans', who lived in the town of Eton and paid for their education.

Today Eton takes about 1,280 boys between the ages of 13 and 18, all of whom are boarders. You can see the school yard, the college chapel, the cloisters and the Museum of Eton Life (tel 01753 671177 for opening times) throughout the summer season. Princes William and Harry both went to Eton.

TIPS

» Ask your hotel about group tours to Windsor; many companies offer them daily and will pick you up at your hotel.

» You can catch a train to Windsor from Waterloo: Train tickets plus admission to Windsor Castle cost £18.80 for adults, £8.50 for children (5–15).

» In Windsor town centre, look for City Sightseeing Bus tours outside Windsor Castle. They run year-round (times vary, phone for details). Tickets can be booked online in advance (tel 01708 866 000, www.city-sightseeing.com).

» Call ahead before leaving London. Windsor Castle's State Apartments and Chapel sometimes close at short notice. St. George's Chapel is open only to worshippers on Sundays.

WHERE TO EAT

AURORA GARDEN HOTEL

www.auroragarden.co.uk

Water gardens set the scene for this conservatory restaurant, where you can eat such dishes as roast sweet peppers with feta cheese or pan-fried duck soaked in raspberry vinegar.

✉ Bolton Avenue, Windsor SL4 3JF ☎ 01753 868686 L from £15, D from £22, Wine from £13 Daily 12–2, 7–10

SIR CHRISTOPHER WREN'S HOTEL & SPA

www.sirchristopherwren.co.uk

Former home of the great architect, this art deco restaurant has views of the Thames. Old favourites with a modern twist include baked cod on feta cheese and chive mashed potatoes.

✉ Thames Street, Windsor SL4 1PX ☎ 01753 861354 L from £9.95, D from £29.50, Wine from £16.50 Daily 12.30–2.30, 6.30–10

PLACES TO VISIT

WINDSOR CASTLE

✉ Windsor SL4 1NJ ☎ 020 7766 7304 Mar–end Oct daily 9.45–5.15, Nov–end Feb 9.45–4.15 Adult £14.20, child under 17 £8 under 5 free

There are many organized tours in and around London and beyond. Choices range from escorted walking tours around the streets of the city to tailor-made tours in luxury chauffeur-driven limousines. River cruises, evening tours and specialist interest tours can all be found. Most tours are available in different languages and car or coach tours will pick you up from and take you back to your hotel.

For more organized tour options, see the Around Town section of the magazine *Time Out* or contact any tourist information office.

BICYCLE TOURS

See Cycling in London, ▷ 60.

BUS TOURS

BIG BUS COMPANY

www.bigbustours.com

Tours (lasting about two hours) of the central London sights in open-top buses with live commentary. Board on any signed stop on three routes: Green Park–St. James's Palace; Victoria Station–London Hilton; Marble Arch–Kensington Palace.

✉ 48 Buckingham Palace Road SW1W 0RN ☎ 020 7233 9533 Adult £25, child (5–15) £10, under 5s free, family £60. Tickets valid for 24 hours and interchangeable from route to route

THE ORIGINAL TOUR

www.theoriginaltour.com

Open-top buses run by a company founded during the Festival of Britain in 1951. Commentary in several languages. Board at any signed stop (there are over 90 of them to choose from).

✉ Jews Row SW18 1TB ☎ 020 8877 1722 Adult £22, child (5–15) £10, under 5s free; online discounts available

CANAL TRIPS

JASON'S TRIP

www.jasons.co.uk

Ninety-minute trips in beautifully painted canal boats with live commentary. From Little Venice past Regent's Park (▷ 218) and London Zoo (▷ 219) to Camden Lock.

✉ Jason's Wharf, Blomfield Road W9 2PD ☎ 020 7286 3428 Daily 12.30, 2.30 £6.50–£7.50 single/return, child (4–14) £5.50–£6.50, under 4s free Warwick Avenue 6, 46, 187

LONDON WATERBUS COMPANY

www.londonwaterbus.com

Travels the same route as Jason's Trip, but no live commentary. Also goes to London Zoo.

✉ West Yard, Camden Lock NW1 8AF ☎ 020 7482 2660 Daily, every hour between 10 and 5 Adult £6.50–£9.30, child (3–15) £5.20–£7.40, under 3s free Camden Town/Chalk Farm, Warwick Avenue 6, 46, 187

COACH TOURS

EVAN EVANS TOURS

www.evanevanstours.co.uk

A wide range of half-day and full-day tours.

✉ 258 Vauxhall Bridge Road SW1V 1BS ☎ 020 7950 1777

RIVER TRIPS

See The River Thames, ▷ 266–267.

TAILOR-MADE TOURS

TOUR GUIDES LTD

www.tourguides.co.uk

Blue Badge guides take you on a tour tailor-made to your specification, either within London or beyond. Walking, car and coach tours are available. Themed tours include antiques, literature and pubs.

✉ 57 Duke Street W1M 5DH ☎ 020 7495 5504 Half day in English £120, most other languages £139. Full day in English £190, other languages £215

TAXI TOUR

www.blacktaxitours.co.uk

Personalized tours in a black cab (maximum five people), with commentary from the cabbie. Tours usually last two hours, by day or by night. You can be picked up from and returned to your hotel.

✉ Black Taxi Tours of London ☎ 020 7935 9363 A two-hour guided tour around London by day between 8 and 6 costs £100 per taxi cab; by night the cost is £110 per taxi cab. Out-of-town trips are priced on request

WALKING TOURS

Walking tours take place throughout London daily. Typically, they start and finish at Underground stations—meet the guide outside the station designated. Normally, there's no need to book unless you are in a large group.

BLOOD AND TEARS WALK

www.shockinglondon.com

London's grim past, described by actor Declan McHugh. Tours depart from Barbican station. Call for times.

✉ 31 Dibdin House, Maida Vale, London W9 1QE ☎ 020 7625 5155 Adult £7, child (12–14) £5. Not suitable for children under 12

ORIGINAL LONDON WALKS

www.walks.com

Probably the best walking tour operators in London. Lots of interesting themed walks, with different options every day.

✉ PO Box 1708 NW6 4LW ☎ 020 7624 3978 Adult £7, child (under 15) free

BLUE BADGE GUIDES

The Blue Badge is the British national standard guiding qualification. Each Blue Badge guide is selected, trained and examined by the official British tourist boards. Companies with Blue Badge guides offer a wide range of languages (up to 40) and specialist knowledge, plus punctuality and reliability.

PRACTICALITIES

Practicalities gives you all the important practical information you will need during your visit, from money matters to emergency phone numbers.

LONDON

TEMPERATURE

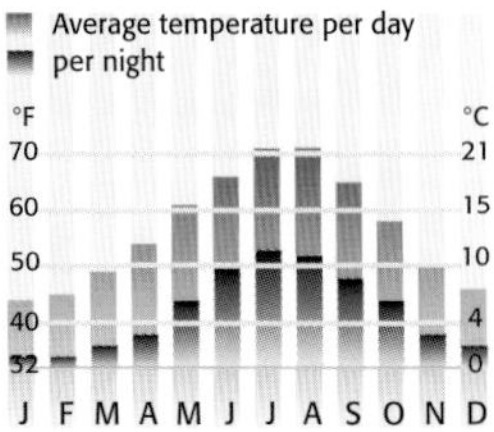

RAINFALL

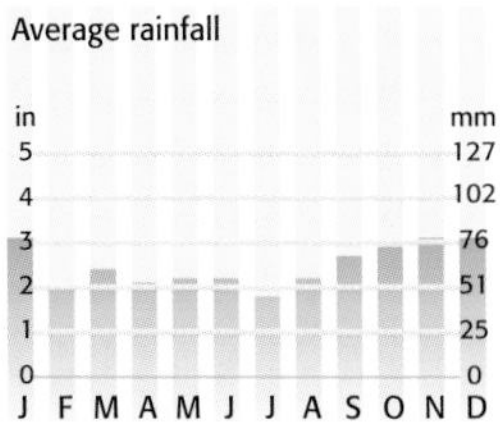

BEFORE YOU GO

CLIMATE AND WHEN TO GO

›› London's sprawl of heated buildings has created its own microclimate, so frost and lingering snow are very rare. The temperature seldom falls below freezing, although northerly winds can make it feel very chilly in the winter. On average, January remains the coldest month. The temperature in London is generally two degrees above that of the rest of Britain.

›› Be prepared for rain at any time of year. Officially, the wettest weeks are from late September to the end of November, but it can be just as wet in the middle of summer.

›› The period between June and August is the warmest and busiest (school holidays run from late July to early September). Spring and September are appreciably quieter, but the weather is less reliable. May and June have the bonus of long daylight hours (see table below).

›› The winter months can be a good time for visiting London, as sights are far less crowded and accommodation is often cheaper.

WEATHER REPORTS

›› Daily forecasts are given at the end of television and radio news shows. They are also available by phone, fax, text or on the internet. Telephone 09068 500401 for Greater London weather (calls cost 60p per minute from a BT landline), or fax 09065 300128 for South East (including London weather).

›› For forecasts texted to a mobile (cell) phone type wthr5 followed by a UK town or city. Send this message to 82222 (available on all networks except Virgin).

WHAT TO TAKE

You may find the following checklist useful, but if you forget or need to replace any items, there's every chance that you'll be able to find its equivalent in London.

DAYLIGHT HOURS	
January	8
February	9
March	11
April	13
May	15
June	17
July	16
August	15
September	13
October	11
November	10
December	8

›› A selection of clothing for a wide range of weather conditions. Rainwear is essential all year. Umbrellas can be more trouble than they're worth, especially on windy days; a lightweight waterproof jacket is a better option.

›› Addresses and phone numbers of emergency contacts.

›› Driver's licence (if you hold a licence or permit from Australia, Canada, Ireland, New Zealand or the USA, this will suffice) or International Driver's Licence (if your licence is not in English).

›› Photocopies of passport and travel insurance (or send scanned versions

TIME ZONES

Britain is on GMT (Greenwich Mean Time—also known as Universal Time or UTC) during winter. In summer (late March to late October) clocks go forward one hour to British Summer Time (BST). The world is divided into 24 time zones. The chart shows time differences from GMT.

City	Time difference	Time at 12 noon GMT
Amsterdam	+1	1pm
Auckland	+10	10pm
Berlin	+1	1pm
Brussels	+1	1pm
Chicago	-6	6am
Dublin	0	noon
Johannesburg	+2	2pm
Madrid	+1	1pm
Montréal	-6	6am
New York	-5	7am
Paris	+1	1pm
Perth, Australia	+8	8pm
Rome	+1	1pm
San Francisco	-8	4am
Sydney	+10	10pm
Tokyo	+9	9pm

WEATHER WEBSITES

ORGANIZATION	NOTES	WEBSITE
BBC	London, UK and world weather reports and forecasts, plus many related topics. Includes satellite imagery	www.bbc.co.uk/weather/
The Met Office (UK)	Clear government site with good specialist links	www.metoffice.gov.uk

of these to an e-mail account that you can access while you are away).

›› Credit cards (preferably more than one credit card), and/or travellers' cheques, and a small amount of cash in sterling.

›› Numbers of credit/debit cards, registration numbers of mobile (cell) phones, cameras and other expensive equipment (in case you need to report loss to the police). Keep these separately from the items.

›› Spare passport photos for Travelcards (▷ 48).

DOCUMENTS

PASSPORTS

›› Visitors from outside the UK must have a passport valid for at least six months from the date of entry into the country.

›› The United Kingdom (England, Wales, Scotland and Northern Ireland), the Channel Islands and the Isle of Man form a common travel area. Once you have entered any part of it through immigration control, you do not need further customs clearance to travel within it.

›› You must show photographic ID, such as a passport or driver's licence with a photo, for all internal flights.

VISAS

›› Before travelling you should double-check visa requirements: see www.ukvisas.gov.uk.

›› Citizens of countries in the European Economic Area (EEA)—the European Union (EU), Switzerland, Norway and Iceland—can enter the UK for purposes of holiday or work for any length of stay, without requiring a visa.

›› If you are a citizen of the United States, Australia, Canada or New Zealand, you do not require a visa for stays of up to six months. However, you must have enough money to support yourself without needing to work or receiving any money from public funds.

›› Those wishing to stay longer, and nationals of certain countries require a visa—check with the embassy or consulate in your own country.

›› You are usually allowed to enter and leave the UK as many times as you like while your visa is valid. On arrival in the UK, you must be able to produce documentation establishing your identity and nationality.

TRAVEL INSURANCE

›› Make sure you have adequate travel insurance. Some visitors (including citizens of EU countries, Australia and New Zealand) receive free or reduced-cost medical treatment under the National Health Service (▷ 278) with the relevant documentation, but travel insurance including medical expenses is still recommended. However, visitors from countries not included in this arrangement, such as the United States and Canada, must make provision for their own medical insurance.

›› An annual travel insurance policy may be the best value for those who make several trips away from home in any 12-month period. Be aware, however, that long trips abroad—typically stays longer than 30 or 45 days—may not be covered.

OTHER HEALTH DOCUMENTS

›› European Health Insurance Card for EU citizens (formerly the E111 form; ▷ 278).

CUSTOMS

Goods you buy in EU countries

If you bring into the UK large quantities of alcohol or tobacco, a Customs Officer is likely to ask about the purposes for which you hold the goods. This particularly applies if you have with you more than the amounts listed below:

- 3,200 cigarettes
- 400 cigarillos
- 200 cigars
- 3kg of smoking tobacco
- 110 litres of beer
- 10 litres of spirits
- 90 litres of wine (of which only 60 litres can be sparkling wine)
- 20 litres of fortified wine (such as port or sherry)

Bringing goods to the UK from outside the EU

You are entitled to the allowances shown below only if you travel with the goods and do not plan to sell them. For further information see the HM Customs and Excise website: www.hmce.gov.uk.

- 200 cigarettes; or
- 100 cigarillos; or
- 50 cigars; or
- 250g of tobacco
- 60cc/ml of perfume
- 250cc/ml of toilet water
- 4 litres of still table wine
- 1 litre of spirits or strong liqueurs over 22% by volume; or
- 2 litres of fortified wine, sparkling wine or other liqueurs
- 16 litres of beer
- £300 worth of all other goods including gifts and souvenirs

BRITISH EMBASSIES AND CONSULATES ABROAD

COUNTRY	ADDRESS	WEBSITE
Australia	High Commission, Commonwealth Avenue, Yarralumla, Canberra ACT 2600, tel 02 62706666	http://ukinaustralia.fco.gov.uk
Canada	High Commission, 80 Elgin Street, Ottowa 5K7, tel 613 237-1530	http://ukincanada.fco.gov.uk
Ireland	29 Merrion Road, Ballsbridge, Dublin 4, tel 01 2053700	http:/britishembassyinireland.fco.gov.uk
New Zealand	High Commission, 44 Hill Street, Wellington 1, tel 04 4734982	http://ukinnewzealand.fco.gov.uk
South Africa	High Commission, 255 Hill Street, Arcadia 0002, Pretoria, tel 12 421 7733	http://ukinsouthafrica.fco.gov.uk
US	3100 Massachusetts Avenue NW, Washington DC 20008, tel 202 588-6500	http://ukinusa.fco.gov.uk

MONEY

›› Britain is an expensive country to travel in, so it's a good idea to explore your options for carrying and changing money.

›› Expect to spend a minimum of about £40 per day excluding accommodation, if you're touring independently.

›› The best idea is to carry money in a range of forms—cash, at least one credit card, bank card/charge card/Maestro card and travellers' cheques. This gives you maximum flexibility.

CASH

›› Britain's currency is the pound sterling (£), which is divided into 100 pence (p).

›› Scotland has its own notes, which are legal tender throughout the UK, although some smaller shops may be reluctant to accept them.

›› There is no limit to the amount of cash you may import or export.

›› It is worth keeping a few 10p, 20p, 50p and £1 coins handy for pay-and-display parking machines and parking meters.

MAJOR BANKS

There are four main banks in the UK and they have branches all over London. All have foreign exchange facilities.

NAME	HEAD OFFICE ADDRESS	TELEPHONE
Barclays	54 Lombard Street EC3 P3AA	0800 400 100
Lloyds TSB	25 Gresham Street EC2V 7HN	020 7626 1500
NatWest	135 Bishopsgate EC2M 3UR	0870 240 1155
HSBC	8 Canada Square E14 5HQ	020 7991 8888

EVERYDAY ITEMS AND HOW MUCH THEY COST

Takeaway sandwich	£3
Bottle of water	£1
Cup of tea or coffee	£1.20–£2
Pint of beer	£2.50–£3.20
Glass of house wine	£3–£4
British national daily newspaper	40p–£1.90
20 cigarettes	£6
Ice cream	£1–£1.50
Litre of unleaded petrol	£1

CREDIT CARDS

›› Credit cards are widely accepted throughout London and Britain; Visa and MasterCard are the most popular, followed by American Express, Diners Club and JCB.

›› Credit cards can also be used for withdrawing currency at cashpoints (ATMs) at any bank displaying the appropriate sign.

›› If your credit cards or travellers' cheques are stolen or lost, call the issuer immediately, then report the loss to the police; you'll need a reference number for the insurance.

CASHPOINTS (ATMS)

›› Most bank branches have ATMs. Check with your bank if you are not sure whether you will be charged for using another bank's ATM.

›› LINK is the UK's only branded network of self-service cash machines. Use of LINK machines is free, except for credit, charge and store cards, for which you pay a cash advance fee.

›› You will be charged for using the convenience machines at certain private locations (such as fuel garages); fees are displayed, and are usually £1.25–£1.50.

TRAVELLERS' CHEQUES

›› These are the safest way to carry money, as you will be refunded in the event of loss usually within 24 hours (keep the counterfoil separate from the cheques themselves).

BANKS

» Most banks open Monday to Friday 9.30 to 4.30. Some branches also open on Saturday morning.
» It pays to shop around for the best exchange and commission rates on currency. You do not pay commission on sterling travellers' cheques, provided you cash them at a bank affiliated with the issuing bank.
» You need to present ID (usually a passport) when cashing travellers' cheques.

POST OFFICES

• Most post offices are open Monday–Friday 9–5.30 and Saturday 9–12.
• Apart from the main post offices offering full postal services, there are sub-post offices, often forming part of a newsagent.
» Many post offices offer commission-free bureaux de change services through an online ordering service available through www.postoffice.co.uk. Payment can be made in cash, or by cheque, banker's draft, Visa, MasterCard, Switch, Delta, Solo or Electron.

BUREAUX DE CHANGE

» These money-changing operations can be found at most major rail and Underground stations in central London, as well as at airports and at on-street locations, and are mostly open 8am to 10pm. Rates of exchange may be higher than at banks; it pays to shop around. Commission rates for currency and travellers' cheques should be clearly displayed.
» Beware of commission-free bureaux as they often offer very poor rates of exchange, and should generally be used only for changing small amounts.

LOST OR STOLEN CREDIT CARDS

American Express	01273 696933
Diners Club	01252 513500/0800 460800
MasterCard/Eurocard	0800 964767
Maestro/Solo	0113 277 8899
Visa/Connect	0800 895082

24-HOUR EXCHANGE SERVICES IN LONDON

Chequepoint

548 Oxford Street W1N 9HJ
Tel 020 7402 2159
Marble Arch Underground

71 Gloucester Road SW7 5BW
Tel 020 7373 9682
Gloucester Road Underground

2 Queensway W2 4RH
Tel 020 7229 0093
Queensway Underground

DISCOUNTS

» Reduced, or free fares, on buses, Underground services and trains are available for children under 16.
» Over 60s and 16- to 25-year-olds can purchase railcards for £25, giving a one-third reduction on off-peak national rail services (▷ 45).

THE EURO

» Britain has not yet committed itself to the euro currency, but it is possible to spend euros in Britain.
» One euro is made up of 100 cents. Euro notes come in denominations of 5, 10, 20, 50, 100, 200 and 500 euros. Coins come in denominations of 1 and 2 euros, and 1, 2, 5, 10, 20 and 50 cents.
» It is not always clear where you might be able to spend euros, but many major high-street chain stores accept them in some or all of their branches: for example the Body Shop, Clarks, Debenhams, Habitat, HMV, Marks and Spencer, Miss Selfridge, Topshop, Virgin, WH Smith and the bookstore Waterstone's.
» Some pubs owned by JD Wetherspoon, Scottish and Newcastle and Shepherd Neame take euros, as do some BP fuel stations.

TIPPING

Restaurants (where service is not included)	10%
Tour guides	£1–£2
Hairdressers	10%
Taxis	10%
Chambermaids	50p–£1 per day
Porters	50p–£1 per bag

» Train tickets on the Stansted Express, the Gatwick Express and Virgin trains can be paid for in euros.
» Outside London, in general the bigger the city, the more places will accept euros.

WIRING MONEY

» Having money wired from your home country can be expensive (agents charge fees for the service) and time-consuming.
» Money can be wired from bank to bank, which takes up to two working days, or to agents such as Travelex (tel 0870 010 0095, www.travelex.co.uk) and Western Union (tel 0800 833 833, www.westernunion.com).

VAT REFUNDS

▷ 290.

HEALTH

›› Britain's National Health Service (the NHS) was set up in 1948 to provide healthcare for the country's citizens based on need rather than the ability to pay. It is funded by the taxpayer and managed by a government department.

›› While NHS care for British citizens is free, private health care can also be bought from organizations such as BUPA.

›› Visitors from the EU are entitled to free or reduced-cost NHS treatment (see below), although health insurance is still advised for non-British citizens.

BEFORE YOU DEPART

›› Consult your doctor at least six to eight weeks before leaving.

›› Free or reduced-cost medical treatment is available through the NHS for visitors from EU countries, but you'll need to have a valid European Health Insurance Card (EHIC).

›› Several non-EU countries have reciprocal healthcare agreements with the United Kingdom (see below), although health insurance is still advised. In most cases a passport is sufficient identification for hospital treatment. Most countries, however, including the United States and Canada, do not have agreements with the UK, and for citizens of these countries a comprehensive travel insurance policy is required.

›› No inoculations are required to enter Britain. However, it is advisable to have an anti-tetanus booster. Check with your doctor whether you need immunization or health advice for: meningococcal meningitis; hepatitis B; diphtheria booster; or measles/MMR.

COUNTRIES WITH RECIPROCAL HEALTH AGREEMENTS WITH THE UNITED KINGDOM

Anguilla
Australia
Barbados
British Virgin Islands
Bulgaria
Channel Islands
Falkland Islands
Montserrat
New Zealand
Romania
Russia
St. Helena
Turks and Caicos Islands
Republics of the former USSR except Latvia, Lithuania and Estonia
Yugoslavia (that is, Serbia and Montenegro) and successor states (Croatia, Bosnia-Herzegovina and Macedonia)

WHAT TO TAKE WITH YOU

›› Vistors from the EU should bring a valid EHIC card and a photocopy of it, which should be kept separately and in a safe place.

›› Visitors from outside the European Union should bring their travel insurance policy and a photocopy.

HEALTHY FLYING

• Visitors to the UK from as far as the US, Australia or New Zealand may be concerned about the effect of long-haul flights on their health. The most widely publicized concern is deep vein thrombosis, or DVT. Misleadingly called 'economy class syndrome', DVT is the forming of a blood clot in the body's deep veins, particularly in the legs. The clot can move around the bloodstream and could be fatal.

• Those most at risk include the elderly, pregnant women and those using the contraceptive pill, smokers and the overweight. If you are at increased risk of DVT see your doctor before departing. Flying increases the likelihood of DVT because passengers are often seated in a cramped position for long periods of time and may become dehydrated.

To minimize risk:
Drink water (not alcohol)
Don't stay immobile for hours at a time
Stretch and exercise your legs periodically
Do wear elastic flight socks, which support veins and reduce the chances of a clot forming

Exercises

Ankle rotations
Lift feet off the floor. Draw a circle with the toes, moving one foot clockwise and the other counterclockwise

Calf stretches
Start with heel on the floor and point foot upward as high as you can. Then lift heel high, keeping ball of foot on the floor

Knee lifts
Lift leg with knee bent while contracting your thigh muscle. Then straighten leg pressing foot flat to the floor

Other health hazards for flyers are airborne diseases and bugs spread by the plane's air-conditioning system. These are largely unavoidable but if you have a serious medical condition seek advice from a doctor before flying.

» Visitors with existing medical conditions and allergies, for example to commonly used drugs, should wear a warning bracelet or tag.

IF YOU NEED TREATMENT

» If you are injured or in an accident, go immediately to a hospital casualty department (emergency room).

» Dial 999 for an ambulance if it is an emergency.

» If you are staying at a hotel or bed-and-breakfast, members of staff should be able to help you contact a doctor. Emergency telephone numbers are often on a noticeboard in a central area or in your room.

» Another option is to contact NHS Direct (tel 0845 4647 or www.nhsdirect.nhs.uk) and explain the problem. Free medical advice from a qualified nurse is available to everyone through this government-funded service. You do not have to give personal details.

» Non-urgent appointments can be made with any doctor listed in the Yellow Pages. There are also five NHS walk-in centres in central London, in Liverpool Street, Victoria, Soho, Canary Wharf and Whitechapel; these are open seven days a week and give fast access to treatment. Initial advice, such as if you need to go to hospital, will be given, but those visitors without a reciprocal arrangement with the UK, such as the United States and Canada, will be charged to speak to a nurse (approx. £25) or doctor (approx. £55) and for any prescription drugs required. You will be issued with a receipt to give to your insurance company.

» To find the nearest doctor, dentist or pharmacy, ask at your hotel, or search the website www.nhs.uk/servicedirectories.

» Major pharmacies and large supermarkets have a wide range of medicines that you can buy over the counter, although items such as antibiotics will require a prescription from a doctor.

» Pharmacists operate a roster system of out-of-hours opening times in many areas, with times of the duty pharmacist displayed in the shop window and in the local newspaper.

MAJOR PHARMACIES

NAME	TELEPHONE	WEBSITE
Alliance Pharmacy	020 8890 9333	www.alliancepharmacy.co.uk
Boots the Chemist	0800 917 2291	www.wellbeing.com
Lloyds Pharmacy	024 7643 2400	www.lloydspharmacy.com
Numark	0182 7841 200	www.numarkpharmacists.com
Superdrug	0800 096 1055	www.superdrug.com

WATER

» Tap water is safe to drink everywhere, but bottled water is readily available, though quite expensive in tourist hotspots.

SUMMER HAZARDS

» Between May and September the sun can be strong and a high-factor sunscreen of SPF 15 or above is recommended.

» Insect bites are irritating rather than dangerous, but it is advisable to take insect repellents in hot weather, especially if you are going near water.

DENTAL TREATMENT

» Non-British residents will have to pay for dental treatment as private patients.

» Dentists are listed in telephone directories or you can use the British Dental Association's online service at www.bda-findadentist.org.uk to find one.

OPTICIANS

» Bring your own prescription or a spare pair of spectacles in case of loss or breakage.

HOSPITALS WITH EMERGENCY DEPARTMENTS

NAME	ADDRESS	TELEPHONE
Charing Cross Hospital	Fulham Palace Road W6 8RF	020 8846 1234
Guy's Hospital	St. Thomas Street SE1 9RT	020 7188 7188
King's College Hospital	Denmark Hill SE5 9RS	020 3299 9000
Royal Free Hospital	Pond Street, Hampstead NW3 2QG	020 7794 0500
St. Thomas's Hospital	Lambeth Palace Road SE1 7EH	020 7188 7188
	Call 999 for an ambulance	

OPTICIANS

NAME	TELEPHONE	WEBSITE
Boots Opticians	0845 125 3752	www.bootsopticians.com
David Clulow (London)	020 8515 6700	www.davidclulow.com
Dollond & Aitchison	0121 697 2434	www.danda.co.uk
Specsavers	01481 236000	www.specsavers.co.uk
Vision Express	0115 986 5225	www.visionexpress.com

ALTERNATIVE MEDICAL TREATMENTS

A wide range of alternative treatments is available in the UK. These treatments are chargeable for visitors. The listings below are a starting point; local telephone directories will have more details.

NAME	TELEPHONE	WEBSITE
British Chiropractic Association	0118 950 5950	www.chiropractic-uk.co.uk enquiries@chiropractic-uk.co.uk
British Osteopathic Association	01582 488455	www.osteopathy.org enquiries@osteopathy.org
The Society of Homeopaths	0845 450 6611	www.homeopathy-soh.org info@homeopathy-soh.org

BASICS

ELECTRICITY

» Britain is on 240 volts AC, and plugs have three square pins. If you are bringing an electrical appliance from another country where the voltage is the same, a plug adaptor will work. If the voltage is different, as in the United States—110 volts—you may also need a converter, although items that use little power, such as laptops and iPod or mobile phone chargers, only need an adaptor.

» Small appliances such as razors can run on a 50-watt converter, while heating appliances, irons and hairdryers require a 1,600-watt converter. Combination converters cover both types. Always check the appliance manual first.

» Telephone sockets are also different and will require an adaptor.

LAUNDRY

» When you book your hotel or bed-and-breakfast, check whether there are laundry facilities.

» Telephone directories list launderettes and dry-cleaning companies.

» Some launderettes offer service washes, where the washing and drying is done for you (typical cost £5–£6 for a small bag), either within a day or with a 2- to 4-day turnaround.

» Dry cleaning is expensive, but widely available: A jacket or skirt individually cleaned might cost around £7. Some dry-cleaning companies also offer clothes-mending services or small repairs such as zipper replacement.

MEASUREMENTS

» Britain officially uses the metric system. Fuel is sold by the litre, and food in grams and kilograms. However, imperial measurements are still used widely in everyday speech (pounds, ounces and stones), and road distances and speed limits are in miles and miles per hour respectively.

• Beer in pubs is sold in pints (one pint is slightly less than 0.5 litres).

» Note that the British gallon (4.5460 litres) is larger than the US gallon (3.7854 litres).

PUBLIC TOILETS

» Generally these are well located, plentiful and free of charge in built-up areas. In some locations neat, self-cleaning stainless steel cubicles are available (usual cost 20p), and there is a small charge to use toilets at large rail stations. Some unpleasant facilities still survive, but most are modern and well maintained.

» All major road service stations and filling stations have free toilets. In rural areas toilets can be found at some roadside pull-ins and parking areas.

SMOKING

» Smoking is prohibited by a law introduced in July 2007 which extends to all public and work places, including hotels, restaurants and pubs. Some hotels have guest bedrooms available where smoking is allowed but this is at the discretion of the individual establishment.

» For a useful online guide to a smoke-free England look at www.ash.org.uk or www.smokefreeengland.co.uk

DOGS

» London is not an ideal place to bring dogs; few hotels accept them and the enforcement of bylaws is strict.

» There are no restrictions for taking dogs on London Underground, but all dogs must be carried on escalators.

» Dogs are accepted on buses at the discretion of the driver.

» Visit www.defra.gov.uk for information on bringing animals into the UK.

CHILDREN

» Some pubs and a small number of restaurants have a strict no-children policy or serve only those over a certain age. However, there are places to stay with excellent facilities for children, including babysitting services.

» Many tourist attractions offer reduced admission fees or are free for children, and most sell family tickets.

» In pubs, children must be accompanied by an adult (if they are allowed in at all). Children under 14 are not allowed in the bar area and it is illegal for anyone under 18 to purchase alcohol. Some restaurants and pubs provide high chairs, especially the larger chains.

» Most major department stores, shopping malls and public venues such as theatres have changing tables for babies, but these tend to be located in the women's toilet areas.

VISITORS WITH A DISABILITY

» Most tourist attractions and public places have facilities for visitors with disabilities, but it is always wise to check in advance in case your particular need is not catered for.

» Any special needs should be mentioned when you are booking accommodation, as many places may not be accessible to wheelchairs. The Holiday Care Service at Tourism for All (tel 08451 249971; www.holidaycare.org.uk) provides information on accommodation suitable for visitors with disabilities, classing hotels as Category 1—for independent wheelchair-users, Category 2—for wheelchair-users with a helper, and Category 3—for wheelchair-users who can take a few steps.

» The national organization for people with disabilities is RADAR (Royal Association for Disability and Rehabilitation), 12 City Forum, 250 City Road EC1V 8AF, tel 020 7250 3222, www.radar. org.uk.

» The best places for accessible public toilets for those with disabilities are in the major department stores, such as John Lewis and Selfridge's (Oxford Street), Harrods (Knightsbridge) and Peter Jones (Sloane Square).

» Artsline (tel 020 7388 2227, www.artsline.org.uk) has detailed information on arts, attractions and entertainment for those with disabilities.

›› The Royal National Institute for the Blind (tel 020 7388 1266, www.rnib.org.uk) publishes a hotel guide book.

›› For information on public transport services for visitors with disabilities, ▷ 64.

CAR RENTAL

›› Arranging a rental car through your travel agent before arriving saves money and allows you to find out in advance about deposits, drop-off charges, cancellation penalties and insurance costs. There are several established car rental companies in London. Large firms have offices around the city and at the main airports.

›› The majority of rental cars in London have manual rather than automatic transmission. Automatic cars are available but are usually more expensive.

Costs

›› You must have a driver's licence. An international driver's licence is not required unless your licence is in a language other than English.

›› Most rental firms require the driver to be at least 23 years old with at least 12 months' driving experience. If you are under 25 you will probably be charged a higher rate.

›› Rental rates usually include unlimited mileage. A cheaper option may be to opt for a limited mileage allowance, which makes an extra charge for additional mileage thereafter.

›› It is important to ensure that you have some form of personal insurance along with Collision Damage Waiver (CDW). Many companies also offer Damage Excess Reduction (DER) and Theft Protection, for an additional charge. You will also have to pay more for any additional drivers. Comprehensive insurance is advised.

›› Make sure you find out what equipment comes as standard (air-conditioning and automatic transmission are not always available) and check that the price quoted includes VAT (Value Added Tax), the sales tax levied on most goods and services.

›› Ask about optional extras such as roof racks and child seats before collecting the car.

›› If you rent from an airport, budget for about £45 per day for an economy car (such as a Ford Fiesta), £70 per day for a mid-range vehicle (such as a Ford Mondeo) and £90 or more for a premium car. Much better 'three days for two' and weekly rates are widely available. Town locations tend to be cheaper than airports, if often less convenient.

›› Most cars use unleaded fuel, except for a few that use diesel; make sure you know what's required before filling the tank.

›› When the car is returned, fuel should be topped up to the level shown when you first picked it up—otherwise you will be charged at the rental company's own tariff per litre, which is much higher than you would pay elsewhere.

CONVERSION CHART

FROM	TO	MULTIPLY BY
Inches	Centimetres	2.54
Centimetres	Inches	0.3937
Feet	Metres	0.3048
Metres	Feet	3.2810
Yards	Metres	0.9144
Metres	Yards	1.0940
Miles	Kilometres	1.6090
Kilometres	Miles	0.6214
Acres	Hectares	0.4047
Hectares	Acres	2.4710
Gallons	Litres	4.5460
Litres	Gallons	0.2200
Ounces	Grams	28.35
Grams	Ounces	0.0353
Pounds	Grams	453.6
Grams	Pounds	0.0022
Pounds	Kilograms	0.4536
Kilograms	Pounds	2.205
Tons	Tonnes	1.0160
Tonnes	Tons	0.9842

Before Driving Off

›› Although reputable companies operate new, well-serviced cars, make your own checks before accepting a car.

›› Check for minor bodywork damage—take a photo or alert staff—and tyre wear. Insist on a different vehicle if the tread is low or uneven or if there are cuts or bulges in any sidewalls.

›› Arrange for appropriate car seats if you have small children.

CAR RENTAL COMPANIES

NAME	DETAILS	WEBSITE
Alamo	Gatwick Airport, South Terminal, Lower Forecourt Road, tel 01293 567790 Heathrow Airport, Northern Perimeter Road, tel 020 8745 2800 Open daily 24 hours (airports); Mon 8–7, Sat 8–6, Sun 9–4 (central information office)	www.alamo.co.uk
Avis	Gatwick Airport, South Terminal, tel 0844 544 6001 Heathrow Airport, Northrop Road, tel 0870 157 8700 Open daily 24 hours (airports); 6am–midnight (central information office)	www.avis.co.uk
Europcar BCR	Gatwick Airport, International Arrivals, tel 0129 353 1062 Heathrow Airport, Northern Perimeter Road West, tel 020 8897 0811	www.europcar.com
Hertz	Gatwick Airport, International Arrivals Halls, tel 0870 846 0003 Heathrow Airport, Northern Perimeter Road West, tel 0870 846 0003 Open daily 24 hours	www.hertz.co.uk

FINDING HELP

PERSONAL SECURITY

Levels of violent crime remain relatively low, but there are hotspots to avoid in London. In most tourist areas, however, the main danger is petty theft.

» Be particularly wary of thieves on the London Underground, and in crowded public places.

» Avoid unlit urban areas at night, and carry bags close to you. If someone tries to grab your bag don't fight back; let go.

» If you are going out late, arrange a lift home with a friend or take a taxi, and use only reputable or licensed minicab firms, or black cabs.

» If you are driving alone, take a mobile phone.

» Lock the doors when the car is stationary, particularly at night.

» Don't pick up hitchhikers.

» Avoid empty carriages on trains and the Underground.

» Report unattended bags on public transport to a transport official. Never leave bags unattended.

LOST PROPERTY

» If you lose an item, contact the nearest police station and complete a lost property form. Give as much detail as possible, such as identifying marks, registration numbers and credit card numbers.

» www.lostandfound.co.uk and www.virtualbumblebee.co.uk are free-to-use lost and found services, where you can log a loss or search a database of lost and found items throughout the country.

» At airports, dedicated offices deal with lost property within terminal buildings, but you will need to contact the individual airline if you lose belongings on board the aircraft.

» In London, items found on buses and Underground trains and in taxis are forwarded to the Transport for London Lost Property Office, 200 Baker Street, London NW1 5RZ, tel 0845 330 9882. Open Monday–Friday 8.30–4. You may go in person to the office Monday–Friday 8.30–4. A small charge (from £3) is payable on collection.

LOST PASSPORT

» If you lose your passport, contact your embassy in the UK (see below). It will help if you have your passport number. Either carry a photocopy of the opening pages or e-mail the details to yourself at an account that you can access anywhere (such as www.hotmail.com).

SEEKING HELP

» Telephone 999 or 112 in an emergency. The operator will ask you which service you require. State where you are, the number of the phone you are using, what the problem is and where it occurred.

» If your police enquiry is not an emergency, contact the nearest police station. Call directory enquiries on 118 888.

» If you have non-urgent health concerns, contact NHS Direct on 0845 4647 or www.nhsdirect.nhs.uk, where trained medical staff listen to your problem, give advice and tell you where to find the nearest non-emergency doctor. This free service is available to all.

» Police officers who patrol the streets on foot will give directions and information if asked.

» The British Transport Police work on Britain's railways. Report any non-emergency crimes experienced while travelling on the railways on 0800 405040.

» If you are the victim of a crime, call Victim Support on 0845 303 0900 for support and advice.

ARREST, FINES AND THE LAW

» You cannot be arrested for minor offences such as speeding unless you compound this with another action, such as behaving violently or failing to give satisfactory proof of identity.

» If you are involved in a motoring incident you are obliged to give your name and address to the other parties involved.

» Police have the power to give on-the-spot fines for a few offences involving antisocial behaviour or wasting police time.

» You can be fined if you are found to be excessively drunk, or drunk and disorderly, in a public place, in licensed premises or on a highway.

» On-the-spot fixed penalty notices (traffic tickets) are also given out for speeding, driving in a bus lane, driving through a red light and other motoring offences.

EMERGENCY NUMBERS
Police, ambulance, fire services, coastguard and mountain rescue
999 or 112

EMBASSIES IN LONDON

COUNTRY	DETAILS	WEBSITE
Australian High Commission	Australia House, Strand WC2B 4LA, tel 020 7379 4334	www.australia.org.uk
Canadian High Commission	Macdonald House, 38 Grosvenor Street W1K 4AA, tel 020 7258 6600	www.unitedkingdom.gc.ca
New Zealand High Commission	Haymarket, Westminster SW1Y 4TQ, tel 020 7930 8422	www.nzembassy.com/uk
South African High Commission	South Africa House, Trafalgar Square WC2N 5DP, tel 020 7451 7299	www.southafricahouse.com
US Embassy	24 Grosvenor Square W1A 1AE, tel 020 7499 9000	www.usembassy.org.uk

COMMUNICATION

With technology rapidly changing the way we communicate, the humble postcard is in danger of looking old-fashioned. But however you want to keep in touch with friends and family, there is a multitude of generally swift, convenient and reliable options in Britain.

TELEPHONES

The main public telephone company, British Telecom (BT), operates more than 63,000 payphones throughout the UK.

Area Codes, Country Codes and Telephone Directories

» Most area codes are four- or five-digit numbers beginning with 01.

» For London the code is 020. Telephone directories (phone books) and *Yellow Pages* show the code in brackets for each telephone number.

» There is a full list of area codes and country codes in every phone book.

» When making a local call, omit the area code.

» When making an international call, dial the international code followed by the phone number minus the 0 of the area code.

Public Phones

» Phone booths are generally blue or red and are found at all major rail stations, Underground stations and on the streets throughout the city.

» You can use credit and debit cards to make calls from more than 63,000 BT payphones (£1.20 minimum charge; 20p per minute for all inland calls).

» Most payphones accept 10p, 20p, 50p and £1 coins; some also accept £2 coins. Only wholly unused coins are returned, so avoid using high denomination coins for short calls.

» Some establishments, such as hotels and pubs, have their own payphones, for which they set their own profit margin. These can be exorbitant and are recommended only in an emergency. Telephone calls made from hotel rooms will also be very expensive.

COUNTRY CODES FROM THE UK	
Australia	00 61
Belgium	00 32
Canada	00 1
France	00 33
Germany	00 49
Ireland	00 353
Italy	00 39
Netherlands	00 31
New Zealand	00 64
Spain	00 34
Sweden	00 46
USA	00 1

USING A MOBILE (CELL) PHONE

Britain has embraced mobile phone technology, although mobile phones are sometimes discouraged in some pubs and other public places (some rail carriages are dedicated quiet areas). There's a proliferation of mobile phone shops in almost every shopping area.

» Single band GSM (Global System for Mobile Communications) phones, which work on 900MHz freqency, can be used in more than 100 countries, but not in the US or Canada.

» Most mobile phones sold in the US work on 1900MHz and require an interchangeable sim card—this temporarily replaces your existing card, which slots into the phone and transfers it to the local network. You can purchase a sim card for between £10 and £20, and this will give you access to one of the main networks such as BT, Orange or Vodafone.

» Dual- (900 and 1900MHz) and tri-band phones can be used in most countries around the world without alteration.

» A pay-as-you-go option means you don't pay a subscription charge, but just pay for the calls you make. You can top up your account at supermarkets and other shops when necessary. You are usually given a choice of accounts, depending how much and when you are likely to make calls. A subscription-type account is more useful if you are staying in the country for a long period.

» It is also possible to use your own mobile phone and sim card, depending on what sort of phone you have.

» Note that there are still areas in London and around the country where you cannot get a mobile phone signal, and that these vary for each network.

» If you are coming from outside the UK, remember to pack a plug adaptor for the charger.

USEFUL TELEPHONE NUMBERS
Directory inquiries: competing services from several companies: try **118500** (BT) and **118111** (One.Tel)
International directory inquiries: competing services from several companies: try **118505** (BT) and **118211** (One.Tel)
International operator: **155**
Operator: **100**
Time: **123**

INTERNET ACCESS

» Multimedia web phones (blue boxes) are being installed by British Telecom in shopping areas, rail stations, airports and road service stations across the country. These enable users to surf the internet and send e-mails and text messages. Internet access costs £1 for up to 15 minutes, and 10p per 90 seconds thereafter. E-mails cost 20p and text 10p a message. Web phones may threaten the future of internet cafes

DIALLING CODE PREFIXES	
00	international codes
01	area codes
02	area codes
07	calls charged at mobile rates
080	free phone calls
084	special services (lower rate)
087	special services (higher rate)
09	calls charged at premium rates
For details of charges, call the operator on 100	
When calling Britain from abroad, dial +44 and omit the first 0 of the area code	

(charges typically £1–£2 per hour) in major cities and towns.

›› Additionally, some payphones allow you to send text messages and e-mail—look for the sign that indicates this.

›› Thousands of libraries have free internet access; for details go to www.peoplesnetwork.gov.uk.

›› In addition to internet cafes and web phones, BT has introduced hundreds of wireless hotspots in locations such as airports, hotels, service stations and bars. These hubs allow laptop- and pocket PC-users broadband access to the internet, using wireless technology known as WiFi. You need a laptop or pocket PC PDA running Microsoft Windows XP, 2000 or Microsoft Pocket PC Vista 2002, and a wireless LAN card. You need to be within a radius of 100m (330ft) of the hub.

›› Any WiFi approved card should work with BT Openzone, but this service is an expensive, if convenient, way of surfing the net.

USING A LAPTOP

›› If you are bringing your laptop from another country, remember to bring a plug adaptor for your charger (see Electricity, ▷ 280). A surge protector is also useful.

›› Wireless technology, such as Bluetooth, allows you to connect to the internet using a mobile phone; check beforehand what the charges will be. Dial tone frequencies vary from country to country, so set your modem to ignore dial tones.

POST

›› For all post office information, call Customer Services (tel 0845 7740 740).

›› Post boxes are painted bright red (except some in post offices) and are either set into walls or are stand-alone pillar boxes. Collection times are shown on each post box.

›› Stamps are available from newsagents, supermarkets and some other shops in addition to post offices. Look for the sign.

›› Generally, airmail is preferable for mail sent outside Europe; for bulky items surface mail is substantially cheaper, but typically takes around eight weeks outside Europe. Airmail to Europe takes around three days, and to the rest of the world from five days.

›› Large post offices have poste restante (mail holding) services. Mail addressed to the recipient and inscribed with the words Poste Restante will be kept at the specified post office until collected by the addressee, who will need to bring along a form of identification to collect it.

›› To send items within the UK for guaranteed next-day delivery, use special delivery. This service also enables you to insure the items in case of loss.

TELEPHONE PRICES	
Minimum charge	40p
All UK calls	40p for first 20 min, then 10p each 10 min thereafter
Calls to mobile phones	63p Mon–Fri 8–6, 38p per minute Mon–Fri after 6pm and before 8am, and 19p per minute all other times
Italy, US and Canada	75p per minute at all times
Belgium, France, Germany, Netherlands and Sweden	67p per minute at all times
Australia and New Zealand	£1 per minute at all times
Call Charges	These are lower after 6pm on weekdays and all day Saturday and Sunday. Local calls are cheaper than long-distance calls within Britain, and calls to mobile phones are generally more expensive than other calls.

POSTAGE RATES		
First class within UK	Up to 100g (3.5oz) (usually arrives next day, but not guaranteed)	39p
Second class within UK	Up to 100g (3.5oz) (usually two days)	30p
Airmail Rates		
Europe	Postcard and letter up to 20g (0.6oz)	56p
	Letter up to 40g (1.3oz)	81p
	Letter up to 100g (3.5oz)	£1.52
Rest of world	Postcard and letter up to 10g (0.3oz)	62p
	Letter up to 40g (1.3oz)	£1.35
	Letter up to 100g (3.5oz)	£2.80

OPENING TIMES AND TICKETS

ENTRANCE FEES

Most attractions have reduced entrance fees for children under 16, holders of student cards, those on unemployment benefit and those aged 60 and over. Family tickets, generally for two adults and two children, are also common.

HERITAGE ORGANIZATIONS

» National Trust (NT) membership is excellent value if you wish to visit more than two properties owned by the National Trust (there are 13 in London and many more within easy reach of the city).

» You can join at any NT property. Membership gives free admission to all properties. The NT Touring Pass (available to overseas visitors only) gives free entry to all NT properties for 7 or 14 days for one or two persons or a family. See www.nationaltrust.org.uk

» For further information contact the National Trust, PO Box 39, Warrington WA5 7WD, tel 0870 458 4000; fax 0870 609 0345, www.nationaltrust.org.uk

» English Heritage (EH), CADW in Wales and Historic Scotland (HS) in Scotland manage hundreds of historic properties, statues and monuments in Britain. EH membership gives free entry to all EH properties plus half-price admission to CADW and HS properties for one year, and free entry thereafter.

» You can join at any EH, CADW or HS staffed property: English Heritage, PO Box 569, Swindon SN2 2YR, tel 0870 333 1182, www.english-heritage.org.uk

DISCOUNT PASSES

» If you are planning extensive sightseeing, buy a discount card. The following are all available from the Britain and London Visitor Centre in Lower Regent Street (▷ 286), major tourist offices and airports.

London Pass

This gives free admission to over 56 attractions in and around London, free travel options and a pocket guide. Passes are for one, two, three or six days and cost £39 for a one-day adult pass (£46 inc. transport, zones 1–6) to £87 for six days (£129 inc. transport); www.londonpass.com

GREAT BRITISH HERITAGE PASS

Aimed at North American visitors, this pass allows free entry to over 580 historic properties and gardens. Passes for four, seven or fifteen days or one month. Passes range from £31 for a four-day adult pass to £80 for one month. See www.britishheritagepass.com

NATIONAL HOLIDAYS

Although banks and businesses close on public (bank) holidays, the trend in London is for tourist attractions and shops to remain open, except on 25 and 26 December and 1 January, when almost everything closes. If any of these days falls on a Saturday or Sunday, the next weekday is a holiday.

- New Year's Day (1 January)
- Good Friday
- Easter Monday
- First Monday in May
- Last Monday in May
- Last Monday in August
- Christmas Day (25 December)
- Boxing Day (26 December)

OPENING TIMES

Opening hours can vary so check in advance with individual sights.

Banks	Monday–Friday 9.30–4.30	Some large branches also open Saturday morning.
Doctors and Pharmacies	Most pharmacies open Monday–Saturday 9–5 or 5.30 Doctors' surgeries only Monday–Friday, typically 8.30–6.30 and on Saturday morning	Notices in the window and in local newspapers indicate extended-hour rosters of local pharmacies (usually for a few extra hours in the evening and for short periods on Sunday). Doctors and dentists are usually closed on Sunday.
Museums, Houses and Galleries	Many open Monday–Saturday 10–5, Sunday 12–5, but hours vary	Some do not admit visitors who arrive less than 30 minutes before closing time.
Post Offices	Monday–Friday 9–5.30, Saturday 9–12	
Pubs	Changes in licensing laws mean that pubs now negotiate their own individual opening hours	Most pubs, however, still maintain the traditional hours, which are from about 11–11. Some close between 3 and 6pm. In England and Wales pubs open on Sunday 12–10.30pm. Many stay open all afternoon, although food may not be available from 2/2.30pm until around 6.30–8.30pm.
Restaurants	No hard-and-fast opening hours, but typically around 12–2.30pm and 6–9pm	Takeaway restaurants stay open until around 11pm or later. Many places in the City are closed on Saturday and Sunday. or 6–11pm (slightly earlier on Sundays)
Shops	Usually open Monday–Saturday 9–5 or 5.30 but London shop hours vary (▷ 290)	Newsagents open on Sunday morning as well. Some corner shops and convenience stores open longer hours—8am–10pm or 11pm, seven days a week.
Supermarkets	Usually 8am–9pm or later and for six hours (usually 10–4) on Sunday	Some are open 24 hours.

TOURIST OFFICES

TOURIST INFORMATION CENTRES (TIC)

›› TICs are a useful source of brochures and information on places to stay, where to eat out, entertainment venues and local events in London. Many will also supply free street maps and sell guidebooks.

›› Most tourist information centres will book accommodation for you free of charge (the hotelier pays a commission); for bookings outside London, you may be charged a small fee (about £2.50) for this service.

›› After office hours, some tourist information centres display lists of accommodation in their office windows.

TOURIST INFORMATION CENTRES

LONDON AND AROUND

Britain and London Visitor Centre
1 Lower Regent Street SW1Y 4XT
www.visitlondon.com
No phone—visit the office in person.
Open Mon 9.30–6.30, Tue–Fri 9–6.30, Sat–Sun 10–4 (summer 10–5).
Visit London information line 0871 222 3118 open Mon–Fri 9–5.
This is the official London tourist office and website.

City Information Centre
St. Paul's Churchyard (opposite St. Paul's Cathedral) EC4M 8BX
Tel 020 7332 1456
Mon–Fri 8–6

Greenwich (Town) TIC
Pepys House
2 Cutty Sark Gardens
Greenwich SE10 9LW
Tel 0870 608 2000
Fax 020 8853 4607
Open daily 10–5

Kingston TIC
The Market House, Market Place
Kingston upon Thames, Surrey KT1 1JS
Tel 020 8547 5592
Fax 020 8547 5594
Open Mon–Sat 10–5, Sat 9–4

Richmond TIC
Old Town Hall
Whittaker Avenue
Richmond, Surrey TW9 1TP
Tel 020 8940 9125
Open Mon–Sat 10–5

Southwark TIC
Tate Modern, Level 2
Bankside SE1 9TG
Tel 020 7401 5266
Open Mon–Sun 10–6

Twickenham TIC
The Atrium, Civic Centre
York Street
Twickenham, Middlesex TW1 3BZ
Tel 020 8891 7738
Fax 020 8891 7990
Open Mon–Thu 9–5.15, Fri 9–5

Waterloo TIC
Arrivals Hall, Waterloo Station, SE1 7LT
Tel 020 7620 1550
Open daily 8.30am–10pm

OUTSIDE LONDON

Visit Britain
Thames Tower
Black's Road W6 9EL
Tel 020 8846 9000
www.visitbritain.com
The website has a search facility for tourist information centres across Britain, giving addresses, telephone numbers and opening hours.

Tourism South East England
40 Chamberlayne Road
Eastleigh, Hampshire SO50 5JH
Tel 02380 625400
www.visitsoutheastengland.com

South West England
Woodwater Park, Exeter, Devon EX2 5WT
Tel 01392 360050
www.visitsouthwest.co.uk

VISIT BRITAIN OFFICES OVERSEAS

Australia
15 Blue Street
N. Sydney
NSW 2000 Tel 02 9021 4400
Fax 02 9021 4499

Canada
Suite 120
5915 Airport Road
Mississauga
Ontario L4V 1T1 Tel 1 888 VISIT UK
Fax 0905 405 1835

New Zealand
151 Queen Street
Auckland Tel 0800 700 741
Fax 09 377 6965

South Africa
Lancaster Gate
Hyde Park Lane
Hyde Park
Sandton 2196
Tel 011 325 0343
Fax 011 325 0344

US
551 Fifth Avenue at 45th Street
New York
NY 10176-0799
Tel 1 800 462 2748
Fax 212 986 1188

Website for visitors to Britain:
www.visitbritain.com

MEDIA

Britain has a vibrant media culture, with some of the world's oldest newspapers, publicly funded TV channels, and the global media presence of the BBC (British Broadcasting Corporation).

TELEVISION

There are five main national terrestrial channels in Britain. There is no advertising on the BBC channels, which are funded by a licence fee from all owners of a TV.

›› **BBC1** focuses on soaps, lifestyle shows, children's TV, documentaries and drama.

›› **BBC2** specializes in cultural programmes, comedy and history.

›› **ITV 1** is the home of popular broadcasting, including soaps, quiz shows, children's programmes, reality TV, drama and films.

›› **Channel 4** broadcasts quality films, documentaries, comedy and quiz shows, science and natural history programmes.

›› **Channel 5** shows children's programmes, game shows, popular films, top US shows like *CSI* and reruns of soaps.

Cable and Digital

›› Although the number of homes with cable in Britain is rapidly increasing, there are few cable-specific channels. However, it is possible to get a greater variety of free channels via cable.

›› Digital satellite receivers allow viewers to receive an increasing number of free digital channels.

›› You have to pay a subscription to view sports and film channels.

›› Digital terrestrial television receivers can be purchased with one payment of around £40, allowing viewers to watch more channels than on normal terrestrial services.

›› Digital television offers many interactive services, such as shopping, e-mail and games.

›› Beginning in 2009, over a period of three years, terrestrial channels will be phased out throughout Britain, making digital the only option.

RADIO

›› Analogue FM and AM stations are now also available digitally.

›› Digital technology allows for more stations and choice while offering better sound quality with no interference.

›› Digital radio is free, but the radios themselves are quite expensive. It is also possible to listen to digital radio through digital television.

›› Information about current digital radio stations can be found at www.digitalradionow. com.

Radio Stations

The television licence funds the BBC's national and regional radio stations. There are also plenty of independent, commercial stations.

›› **Radio 1** A diverse selection of the latest music from mainstream dance, rock and pop to indie and R&B. There are regular national, international and entertainment news bulletins and every Sunday from 4 to 7pm the UK singles chart.
97–99 FM; www.bbc.co.uk/radio1

›› **Radio 2** New and old classic rock, pop, country, folk, reggae and soul interspersed with chat, regular news and travel bulletins and music documentaries.
88–91 FM; www.bbc.co.uk/radio2

›› **Radio 3** Classical and jazz to new and world music along with culture and drama. The BBC Proms, a classical music festival held every summer in the Royal Albert Hall, is broadcast live every summer.
90–93 FM; www.bbc.co.uk/radio3

›› **Radio 4** Topical and political news, comedy, art, drama and quiz shows, along with radio plays, interviews and documentaries. There are also in-depth news bulletins.
92–95 FM; www.bbc.co.uk/radio4

›› **Capital FM** bills itself as London's No. 1 hot music station and appeals to young, hip listeners.
95.8 FM; www.capitalfm.com

›› **Classic FM** is an independent station broadcasting classical music and music news.
100–102 FM; www.classicfm.com

›› **Absolute Radio** is a commercial radio station transmitting rock and new music along with sports and music news.
105.8 FM; www.absoluteradio.co.uk

NEWSPAPERS

›› National newspapers in Britain are divided into quality papers known as broadsheets (although only two are still in the large broadsheet format) and tabloids. Broadsheets focus on relatively objective news reporting while most tabloids cover sensational human-interest stories and celebrity gossip.

›› The Sunday newspapers are more expensive and bigger than their daily counterparts. The broadsheets have special sections on travel, property, finance, the arts and media, and contain supplements with listings, reviews and articles.

›› The streets and transport network are inundated with the free morning *Metro* and afternoon *The London Paper* and *London Lite*.

Evening Standard

›› Founded in 1827, the *Evening Standard* is the only paid-for evening newspaper that covers all of London. It also reports on international and regional news.

›› It also has city and entertainment news, sport reports, lifestyle and travel articles, and guides to London.

›› The first edition is on the streets at 11am, and on some days a week the paper is sold with a supplement.

International Newspapers

›› Newspapers from around the world, including foreign-language papers, can be purchased at airports and larger train stations.

›› The bookstore and newsagents WH Smith also stocks major international newspapers, including the *International Herald Tribune*.

MAGAZINES

›› *Time Out* is issued weekly and contains articles and features detailing what's on in London, from concerts and musicals to exhibitions and films, and with information and reviews on restaurants, pubs, shopping and accommodation.

BOOKS AND FILMS

London's vitality, variety, glamour and squalor have always provided rich pickings for writers and film-makers. Many have sung the city's praises; for some it's been a love-hate affair.

LITERATURE

Eminent historian Peter Ackroyd's biography of the great city, *London: The Biography* (Vintage, 2000), has been meticulously researched and presented and is essential reading for those wishing to understand the capital that defines the country. His latest book, *Thames: Sacred River* (Chatto & Windus 2007), explores the history of the river so central to London's existence.

The London Encyclopaedia, by Ben Weinreb and Christopher Hibbert (Macmillan, 1983), is a vast undertaking, and provides comprehensive information about London's buildings past and present.

Perhaps the most famous book about London is *The Diary of Samuel Pepys*, in which the observer, Pepys, recorded events in Britain from 1600 to 1669.

Jeremy Paxman's *The English: a Portrait of a People* (Penguin, 1999) makes delightful reading. A galloping overview of the English as a whole, the celebrated broadcaster's book covers topics such as their attitude to private property, and astutely perceives what defines the English character.

Several of Charles Dickens' novels were set in London—*Oliver Twist* (1837), *Bleak House* (1853) and *Little Dorrit* (1857). *Oliver Twist* tells the story of an orphan born into a workhouse who runs away to London, only to fall in with thieves. Dickens' social conscience is evident in this tale of hardship and reward.

William Blake (1757–1827), born in London, was another writer to express a keen awareness of cruelty and injustice, notably in his poem 'London', in *Songs of Experience*.

In 1887, Sir Arthur Conan Doyle first introduced his creation, Sherlock Holmes, perhaps the most famous fictional detective of all, in the novel *A Study in Scarlet*. Holmes lived at 221b Baker Street (▷ 219).

The amusing *Bridget Jones's Diary*, by Helen Fielding (Picador, 1997), defined a generation of 30-something single women living in London in the late 1990s. It and its sequel, *The Edge of Reason*, were made into hugely successful films.

Zadie Smith's *White Teeth* (Penguin, 2001) is the story of three generations of families—one white, one Indian and one mixed-race—living in north London in the 1990s.

Monica Ali has written sharply on a similar subject—multinational, multidenominational London, in her 2003 novel *Brick Lane* (Doubleday); the film appeared in 2007.

Nick Hornby's three highly successful novels, *Fever Pitch* (Cassell, 1992), *High Fidelity* (Cassell, 1995) and *About a Boy* (Cassell, 1998), are all set in London, in the varying worlds of football (Arsenal in particular), record shops and single mothers. All of them have been made into films.

FILMS

In the opening sequences of *The World Is Not Enough* (1999), James Bond hurtled from the MI6 building by Vauxhall Bridge, pursued by a beautiful assassin, and provided a fantastic high-speed river chase all the way to the Greenwich Dome.

Lock, Stock and Two Smoking Barrels (1998), directed by Guy Ritchie, is a pastiche of the old gangster movies.

Classic Ealing comedies such as *Passport to Pimlico* (1948), starring Stanley Holloway, were all made at Ealing Studios, founded in 1929 and the first British sound-film studios.

In 1998, playwright Tom Stoppard wrote the screenplay for *Shakespeare in Love*, with Joseph Fiennes as the eponymous hero and Gwyneth Paltrow as the lady with whom he falls in love, plus just about every other notable English and American actor at the time.

My Beautiful Launderette caused something of a stir in 1985 when Daniel Day-Lewis starred in this well-observed story of the relationship between two young gay men (one Asian) in the intolerant London of the time.

Other classic films that might transport you to your favourite part of London are *Alfie* (1966), which sees Michael Caine ducking and diving around town, *An American Werewolf in London* (1981), a comedy horror movie about a visiting American who gets bitten, and *A Fish Called Wanda* (1988), starring John Cleese, Jamie Lee Curtis and Michael Palin. More recent releases, with some great shots of London, are *Notes on Scandal* (2006), a sinister tale set around a London school starring Judi Dench and Cate Blanchett, and *Breaking and Entering* (2006), a London melodrama with Jude Law and Juliette Binoche.

GUIDEBOOKS

AA City Pack London
Pocket book and map.
London: A City Revealed
A visual tribute to London, with more than 350 large colour photographs.
Fodor's London
In-depth illustrated guide updated annually.
The AA Hotel Guide
The AA Restaurant Guide

MAPS

AA Street by Street Central London
Street by Street Z Maps

WEBSITES

A vast amount of information can be found online.

GENERAL TOURIST INFORMATION

www.visitbritain.com—the official website for the Britain and London Tourist Information Centre
www.southeastengland.com
www.fco.gov.uk—Foreign and Commonwealth Office
www.english-heritage.org.uk
www.nationaltrust.org.uk
www.hrp.org.uk—historic royal palaces
www.royal.gov.uk—royal residences
www.artsline.org.uk—information on arts and attractions for visitors with disabilities

ABOUT LONDON

www.visitlondon.com
www.londontown.com
www.netlondon.com—a directory covering sights, events and accommodation
www.londoneverything.co.uk—a portal to London websites
www.londonforfun.com—information on attractions and sights
www.travellondon.com
www.londonnet.co.uk
www.virtual-london.com
www.visiting-london.com
www.thelondonvisitor.com—a monthly guide to London
www.tripadvisor.com
www.gingerbeer.co.uk—the London lesbian and bisexual scene
www.royalparks.gov.uk

NEWS AND REVIEWS

www.bbc.co.uk/london
www.guardian.co.uk
www.timesonline.co.uk

THEATRE/MUSIC

www.londontheatre.co.uk
www.ticketmaster.co.uk—tickets
www.ambassadortickets.com—information on what's on, what's coming up and where to get tickets
www.reallyuseful.com—the Really Useful Theatre group
www.sbc.org.uk—the website for the South Bank Centre, including the Royal Festival Hall, Purcell Room and Queen Elizabeth Hall
www.royalalberthall.com
www.roh.org.uk—Royal Opera House

CINEMA

www.bfi.org.uk—British Film Institute
www.ugicinemas.co.uk
www.odeon.co.uk

TRAVEL

Airports

www.gatwickairport.com
www.heathrowairport.com
www.stanstedairport.com
www.london-luton.co.uk
www.londoncityairport.com

Bus/Coach

www.greenline.co.uk
www.nationalexpress.com
www.megabus.com

Rail

www.firstcapitalconnect.co.uk
www.heathrowexpress.co.uk
www.gatwickexpress.co.uk
www.stanstedexpress.co.uk
www.eurostar.com
www.thetrainline.com—book tickets and find out fares and journey times
www.nationalrail.co.uk—general information and train times

London Transport

www.tfl.gov.uk—official Transport for London website
www.dlr.co.uk—information on the Docklands Light Railway
www.thamesriverservice.co.uk

Car Rental

www.alamo.co.uk
www.avis.co.uk
www.europcar.com
www.hertz.co.uk

Car Breakdown

www.theaa.com
www.rac.co.uk

WEATHER REPORTS

www.bbc.co.uk/weather
www.metoffice.com
www.weathercall.co.uk

HEALTH

www.nhsdirect.nhs.uk
www.medicentre.co.uk—walk-in private doctor and health service

MAJOR SIGHTS

SIGHT	WEBSITE	PAGE
British Museum	www.britishmuseum.org	134
Buckingham Palace	www.royal.gov.uk	176
HMS *Belfast*	www.hmsbelfast.iwm.org.uk	72
Houses of Parliament	www.parliament.uk	179
Imperial War Museum	www.iwm.org.uk	74
Kensington Palace	www.hrp.org.uk	214
London Eye	www.ba-londoneye.com	75
Madame Tussauds	www.madame-tussauds.com	217
Museum of London	www.museumoflondon.org.uk	103
National Gallery	www.nationalgallery.org.uk	182
National Portrait Gallery	www.npg.org.uk	188
Natural History Museum	www.nhm.ac.uk	220
St. Paul's Cathedral	www.stpauls.co.uk	104
Science Museum	www.sciencemuseum.org.uk	222
Shakespeare's Globe	www.shakespeares-globe.org	78
Sir John Soane's Museum	www.soane.org	148
Somerset House	www.somerset-house.org.uk	150
Tate Britain/Modern	www.tate.org.uk	192/80
Tower Bridge	www.towerbridge.org.uk	111
Tower of London	www.hrp.org.uk	112
Victoria & Albert Museum	www.vam.ac.uk	224
Wallace Collection	www.wallacecollection.org	229
Westminster Abbey	www.westminster-abbey.org	194

SHOPPING

London offers shoppers a vast range, from smart department stores and speciality shops to market stalls and bargain basements. Many people come to London just to shop. Oxford Street and Regent Street can be crammed to bursting point in summer and during the Christmas shopping season—which starts in November. Particularly long queues can be expected at the most popular stores such as Hamleys, the world-famous toy shop, but there are quieter areas too.

Shops have adopted increasingly flexible opening hours and it is difficult to generalize. Late opening, until 9 or 10, is common in the busiest areas and many shops also open on Sundays at varying times.

SALE TIME

Twice a year, stores traditionally slash their prices in order to sell off the previous season's remaining stock. The best bargains are at the January sales, starting immediately after Christmas—sometimes before—and continuing well into February. Determined bargain-hunters camp out in the streets in advance to be first in line when the sales open at Harrods (▷ 233) or Selfridge's (▷ 234). Summer sales begin in June or July and last to the end of August. Nowadays mid-season reductions are also common.

Strict rules govern the way that sales operate in Britain, and the fact that you buy an item in a sale does not affect your statutory rights as a consumer. You are, for example, entitled to a full refund if the goods prove faulty—but you must retain your receipt as proof of purchase.

TAX-FREE SHOPPING

If you are visiting from a non-European Union country, you are exempt from Value Added Tax on certain goods that you take out of the country if you spend a minimum amount (VAT is a 17.5 per cent sales tax). This can amount to a hefty saving. Most leading stores have details of the tax-free shopping policy and can help with your claims.

PAYING

Most shops accept the major credit cards, but there are exceptions. Travellers' cheques may be accepted, but you will need to show your passport. Personal cheques must be drawn from a UK bank account. Street markets may not accept credit cards or cheques.

STREET SELLERS

With the exception of market traders, who pay to maintain regular spots at established markets, it's smart to beware of street sellers anywhere in London. The products they sell may not be what they're claimed to be.

MARKETS

Markets come in all shapes and sizes in London, from the stylish to the basic. For wonderful atmosphere, cheeky traders' patter and piled-high goods ranging from leather jackets to second-hand records, visit Petticoat Lane (▷ 120) near Liverpool Street or Brick Lane (▷ 120), both in the East End and reached from Liverpool Street or Aldgate East Underground station. At Camden Lock, reached from Camden Town Underground station, students and antique-hunters flock to the stalls of bric-a-brac and trendy clothes (daily 10–6). Berwick Street market (▷ 154) sells produce and an assortment of household goods.

SHOPPING AREAS

If you want department stores and brand-name shopping and can stand the crowds, head to the West End around Oxford Street, Regent Street and Bond Street. Covent Garden is full of quirky specialist shops and street entertainment, the King's Road in Chelsea has more avant-garde labels among the mainstream stores, while Knightsbridge has the most exclusive and expensive shopping.

Below *London's most famous shopping street is 2km (1.5 miles) of major brands' flagship stores, imposing department stores—and tacky souvenir outlets*

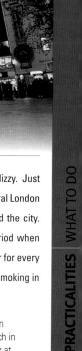

ENTERTAINMENT AND NIGHTLIFE

The range and variety of performing arts and entertainment in London is enough to make you dizzy. Just wandering through the West End gives an idea of what's on offer, but it's also worth looking beyond central London and scanning the pages of *Time Out*, the city's most comprehensive guide to what's on in and around the city. And if you've got the energy and the inclination you can party 24 hours a day in London. After a period when superclubs for the young and affluent ruled the scene, there's now a variety of venues and styles to cater for every taste, budget and age range. Note that almost all performance venues, other than clubs, do not permit smoking in the auditorium.

CINEMA

The choice of films in London is huge. In addition to the multiscreen chain complexes that show new release blockbusters (many on and around Leicester Square), there are independent repertory cinemas that screen a range of special-interest films and international fare with English subtitles. These include the Institute of Contemporary Arts (ICA), (▷ 178) at Carlton House Terrace and the National Film Theatre (▷ 79 and 87) on the South Bank, which has themed festivals and guest speakers.

CLASSICAL MUSIC, DANCE AND OPERA

A useful place to start is the Southbank Centre (▷ 79), which has a full schedule of dance (staged by the English National Ballet) and concerts, either in the Royal Festival Hall or the more intimate Queen Elizabeth Hall or Purcell Room (▷ 87). For conventional classical music and big names, check the Barbican (▷ 121), where the London Symphony Orchestra has its base. The Royal Opera House (▷ 158), Covent Garden, still has a reputation for high prices and stuffiness, despite its flashy new setting. Productions by the Royal Ballet Company, based here, cost less than opera performances. For opera sung in English, head for the London Coliseum (▷ 158), home of the English National Opera.

Between July and September the Proms season (BBC Henry Wood Promenade Concerts, ▷ 294–295) gets underway at the Royal Albert Hall (▷ 235), with lunchtime chamber concerts as well as evening perfor-mances. If you don't mind standing, it doesn't cost that much to get in.

Churches also host excellent recitals and concerts, particularly St. James's Piccadilly (▷ 199) and St. Martin-in-the-Fields (▷ 199).

CONTEMPORARY LIVE MUSIC

At one end of the spectrum, the live-music scene features massive stadium gigs. At the other, rock bands frequently perform in local pubs, and there's much in between—for example jazz at Ronnie Scott's (▷ 158) in Soho and at the Pizza on the Park (▷ 235), among other venues. Free live music is available in the Royal Festival Hall and sometimes in the National Theatre foyer at lunchtime.

For folk, world music, blues, rock 'n' roll, salsa and what-ever else, stray into outlying areas such as Camden, Kentish Town or Islington for lively pub-and-club scenes.

THEATRE

Much of the West End's Theatreland now seems obsessed with long-running musicals, and to get tickets to these you must book several months in advance. The National Theatre stages classic and experimental work on the South Bank—cross Waterloo Bridge to see the current schedule digitally displayed on the facade.

Above *Leicester Square is ringed by luxurious cinemas showing the latest movies*

Fringe theatre finds its place in pub rooms and other cramped or quirky venues, as well as in more conventional spaces such as The Gate in Notting Hill (⊳ 235), dedicated to staging work by new writers.

To book major theatrical and musical performances it's often easiest to use the internet. Visit www.ticketmaster.co.uk or www.keithprowse.com.

CLUBBING

London has a diverse choice of nightclubs so you need to do a bit of homework to find the club that's right for you. Look in listings magazines (such as *Time Out*), pick up flyers, talk to other clubbers in the trendy pre-club bars near your chosen nightspot. Once you've decided on where to go you must also check out what is happening on that particular night, as many clubs have different theme nights throughout the week. The good news is you can go clubbing most nights—even on Mondays and Tuesdays, you'll find places that are buzzing.

Queues usually start to form outside popular venues from around 11pm. Some clubs offer free admission early in the evening, relying on the price of drinks to make up the cost (and that often doesn't take long). Others also ratchet up their charges later at night. Theme nights, special events, guest bands and DJs are generally advertised at the club or online. Clubs with restaurants and/or shows sometimes offer special menu deals to keep you going.

Always check your chosen venue's dress code. Some are relaxed, some insist on 'smart' dress (definitions vary wildly), and some object to specific items of clothing such as jeans or trainers. Once there you will often have to pass muster with tough-looking doormen (bouncers). If they refuse to admit you, just accept it and walk away. They don't need to give a reason and there's no point arguing—they won't listen, you won't win, and it may lead to trouble. Just try your luck elsewhere. A sure way of invoking the bouncers' displeasure is to turn up drunk.

Once past the door, you may be frisked by security staff.

OTHER CLUB OPTIONS

For moderate sound volume, more space and a wider age range, head for clubs hosting salsa or other Latin sessions or a classic cabaret-and-dinner club—not all of these charge exorbitant prices, but many require smart dress (again, definitions vary). One of the best things about some of these places is that they offer dance lessons (often free) before the night starts properly. All you have to do is swallow a little pride and turn up early!

OLDER CLUBBERS

If techno, hip hop, electro and drum 'n' bass gives you a headache and you'd like to dance to some music that you might recognize, then look for nightspots offering mainstream, disco or 1970s and 80s music.

The official website www.visitlondon.com is a good source of ideas, but double-check with venues for events and times.

'ADULT'

You don't have to look far in Soho to find a fairly dubious assortment of peep shows and sex shows, where sharks await tourists. It's easy to wander into Soho by accident, but it is best to stay well away from these places.

COMEDY

Comedy clubs boomed in the 1980s, and there's still an impressive choice of revues, improvised shows and stand-up comedy to choose from, from open-mike novice spots to crowd-pulling big names such as Jack Dee and Lee Evans.

GETTING HOME

Before setting out, plan how you're going to get back. Night buses and some regular routes run all night (⊳ 53), but if the venue is out on a limb or too far from the bus stop it's best to ask about taxis (there's often a rank outside). Remember that Underground trains stop running at around midnight.

SPORTS AND ACTIVITIES

Sport is a passion for the British, despite their tendency to caricature themselves as good-humoured losers.

London is the setting for several iconic sporting venues, including historic Lord's Cricket Ground (⊳ 216), Wimbledon's All England Lawn Tennis Club (⊳ 263), where the world-famous championships are held every June–July (⊳ 294), and Wembley Stadium. The old Wembley Stadium, much-loved for its historical associations rather than its antiquated facilities, has now been replaced by a state-of-the-art arena. The new stadium (⊳ 17) was finally opened in March 2007. The iconic Twin Towers have been replaced by a massive arch 133m (440ft) high which can be seen from 21km (13 miles) away. There are no quibbles with the quality of the new facility but the location, in one of London's least pleasant suburbs and awkward to get to by all forms of transport, still riles many people, particularly in the provinces. Rugby's main London stadium, which hosts international contests, is at Twickenham (⊳ 259), in west London. There are countless other, small-scale venues, but the easiest way to catch a game of cricket, football or rugby is simply to turn up at a surburban municipal park or playing field and stand on the sidelines as local teams battle it out.

There's nothing more quintessentially English than watching a local game of cricket on a sunny Sunday afternoon. Kew Green is the perfect venue but there are lots of others around town which are free and open to everyone. By contrast, tickets for football matches in the Premiership (England's top flight) are particularly difficult to get hold of and very expensive (from £30 to £50), though they do attract the cream of world talent.

The football and rugby seasons run from late August to May; cricket is played between April and September.

Two of Britain's most famous horse-racing events take place close to London: the Epsom Derby in early to mid-June, and Ascot Week (▷ 294), in mid-June. The latter is attended by royalty, the rich and famous and anyone wanting to see and be seen, as well as crowds of punters there for the thrill of placing a bet—and is known as much for the women's outrageous hats as for the races themselves.

To book tickets for most major sporting events contact Ticketmaster (tel 0870 534 4444, www.ticketmaster.co.uk) or Keith Prowse (tel 0870 840 1111, www.keithprowse.com).

Innumerable sports centres have sprung up around the capital over the past 20 years. These range from expensive clubs, where you may be able to buy short-term membership to use gyms, saunas, swimming pools and squash courts, to municipal operations providing no-frills versions of the same kind of facilities at much lower prices.

If you want to be part of a real London institution, consider applying (well in advance) to join the thousands of participants in April's annual London Marathon, when everyone from top athletes to TV celebrities and charity collectors in chicken outfits pounds the course between Blackheath and The Mall (▷ 17 and 294). Contact Virgin London Marathon (tel 020 7902 0200, www.london-marathon.co.uk) or Sportstours International (tel 0161 703 8161, www.sportstoursinternational.co.uk) for details, though unless you are a serious club runner your chances are restricted.

London's greatest offerings for the active of all ages are its parks, greens and commons. Nothing beats walking, jogging, flying a kite or sailing a model boat at Hampstead Heath, Hyde Park, Battersea Park, Wimbledon Common or Clapham Common—each of which provides a little slice of countryside in the city.

HEALTH AND BEAUTY

The health and beauty industry is one of London's most rapidly growing sectors. There are scores of clinics and clubs throughout the capital offering every kind of treatment, from acupressure to zero balancing, cosseting you quite literally from head to toe. After a day's shopping or sightseeing amid the bustle, noise and traffic fumes of the metropolis, it's heaven to relax in a quiet space with a facial, a pedicure, a massage or some aromatherapy.

For most visitors these basic therapies and techniques will more than suffice, though if you seek more specialist treatment you will no doubt find it. The best source of information and advice on where to go is the *Time Out London's Health & Fitness guide*. All reputable clinics abide by local regulations, are fully insured and have qualified staff, so safety is never an issue.

Some venues are for members only, with monthly or annual charges which are prohibitive to most short-term visitors. Many more, however, take short-notice bookings and some are just walk-in, though it's always best to call first. Most clubs are open to both sexes, though one of the more recent trends is for men to start discovering their 'inner-self' via health and beauty treatments and a small number of men-only salons have opened.

CHILDREN'S LONDON

London is particularly well equipped with attractions and museums of all kinds that set out to capture young imaginations. There are children's areas and of course there's no lack of costumed ceremonial display to appeal to all ages.

Most fee-charging attractions have children's prices and discounted family tickets, though definitions of 'child' and 'family' vary considerably. Many places have free entry for children under five or six. Inevitably, the most crowded times are during school holidays—two weeks at Easter, from mid-July to the first week of September, two weeks at Christmas and week-long half-term breaks throughout the year. During those times, prices are often lower and opening hours longer.

One of the most useful sources of information on special events, shows and regular attractions alike is *Time Out's* annual *London for Children* magazine (available in bookshops). It's also worth checking the children's section of *Time Out* each week, and the website www.visitlondon.com also has an entertaining children's section.

FESTIVALS AND EVENTS

London has many festivals and traditions. Listed below, month by month, are the major events that take place annually. They are free unless stated otherwise.

JANUARY

NEW YEAR'S DAY PARADE

1 January
www.londonparade.co.uk
Up to 10,000 dancers, musicians and floats gather in Parliament Square at noon and parade up Whitehall, round Trafalgar Square and along Piccadilly.
✉ Parliament Square SW1A 0AA
☎ 020 8566 8586

JANUARY–FEBRUARY

CHINESE NEW YEAR

End January/early February
www.chinatown-online.co.uk
Chinese dragons snake their way around Chinatown (▷ 140) collecting money and gifts.
✉ Around Gerrard Street, Chinatown W1

MARCH–APRIL

OXFORD AND CAMBRIDGE BOAT RACE

March or April
www.theboatrace.org
Annual race held on the Thames, from Putney to Mortlake, between rowing eights from Oxford and Cambridge universities.
Ⓤ Putney Bridge, Hammersmith, Ravenscourt Park, Stamford Brook, Turnham Green 🚌 Central London–Putney 14, 22, 74; Putney Bridge 14, 220; Central London–Hammersmith 9, 10, 27, 211; Hammersmith Bridge 33, 72, 209, 283, 419; Hammersmith–Mortlake 209, 419; Chiswick Bridge 190; Hammersmith–Putney 200

APRIL

VIRGIN LONDON MARATHON

www.london-marathon.co.uk
More than 30,000 runners compete in one of the world's biggest road races (▷ 17).
☎ 020 7902 0200 Ⓤ Start: North Greenwich. Finish: Green Park, St. James's Park 🚌 Start: 188. Finish: 11, 12, 24, 159, 453

MAY

CHELSEA FLOWER SHOW

www.rhs.org.uk
Fabulous flower show at the Chelsea Royal Hospital, attended by the Queen and huge crowds.
✉ Royal Hospital, Royal Hospital Road SW3 4SR ☎ 020 7649 1885 ✋ £12–£35 Ⓤ Sloane Square 🚌 11, 137, 170

JUNE

DERBY DAY

First Saturday in June
www.epsomderby.co.uk
The premier flat race (a type of horse race) of the year, with a lively fairground atmosphere.
✉ Epsom Downs Racecourse, Epsom KT18 5LQ ☎ 01372 470047 ✋ £15–£35 🚆 Epsom Town Centre or Tattenham Corner, then take the shuttle bus

ROYAL ACADEMY SUMMER EXHIBITION

▷ 21.

TROOPING THE COLOUR

Second Saturday in June
On the Queen's official birthday the 'colour' (flag) of one of her seven Household regiments is carried for her inspection at a military ceremony on Horseguards Parade.
✉ Horse Guards Parade, Whitehall SW1A 2AX ☎ 020 7414 2479 Ⓤ Westminster, Charing Cross 🚌 11, 12, 24, 159

ROYAL ASCOT

Mid-June
www.ascot.co.uk
One of the world's most famous race meetings, dating back to 1711, and attended by the queen. There is a strict dress code, and usually there is as much attention paid to the ladies' often startling outfits as to the racing.
✉ High Street, Ascot SL5 7JX ☎ 0870 727 1234 ✋ £15–£35 🚆 Ascot

JUNE–JULY

CITY OF LONDON FESTIVAL

Late June to mid-July
www.colf.org
Dance, music, theatre, cinema and literary events, plus walks, across the City of London.
✉ Bishopsgate Hall, 230 Bishopsgate EC2M 4HW ☎ 020 7377 0540

WIMBLEDON LAWN TENNIS CHAMPIONSHIPS

Last week in June, first week in July
www.wimbledon.org
This the oldest major tennis championship in the world and the only one played on grass. In the early rounds, you can queue for tickets on the day, but the only way for members of the public to get tickets for the final four days is to enter a public ballot the autumn before.
✉ All England Lawn Tennis and Croquet Club, Church Road, Wimbledon SW19 5AE ☎ 020 8946 2244 Ⓤ Southfields 🚌 39, 93 🚆 Wimbledon

JULY

HAMPTON COURT PALACE FLOWER SHOW

Second week in July
www.rhs.org.uk
The world's largest annual flower show.
✉ Hampton Court Palace, East Molesey KT8 9AU ☎ 0870 906 3791 ✋ £15–£23, child (5–15) £5 🚌 111, 216, 411, R68 🚆 Hampton Court ⛴ From Westminster, Richmond, Kingston

BBC HENRY WOOD PROMENADE CONCERTS

Mid-July to mid-September
www.royalalberthall.com
The world-famous Proms feature an eclectic mix of music from world premieres and startling modern music to classical standbys. The

Last Night, also held in Hyde Park, draws huge crowds.

✉ Royal Albert Hall, Kensington Gore SW7 2AP ☎ 020 7589 8212 £5 (standing; on the door only)–£40. Proms in the Park £20 South Kensington 9, 10, 52, 70

LONDON PRIDE PARADE

Late July

www.prideinthepark.com

Themed floats and exotic costumes celebrate London's gay and lesbian community and end with a Pride in the Park event in Hyde Park.

✉ City Hall, The Queen's Walk SE1 2AA e-mail enquiries only to info@pridelondon.org Start: Embankment. End: Hyde Park Start: 9, 11, 13. End: 12, 73, 74

AUGUST

NOTTING HILL CARNIVAL

August bank holiday Sunday and Monday

www.mynottinghill.co.uk

More than a million people get together for this event—one of the biggest street parties in Europe. Fabulous costumes, steel drum, bands and mega sound systems.

✉ Notting Hill W10/W11 ☎ 020 8964 0544 Ladbroke Grove, Holland Park, Notting Hill Gate 23, 52, 94

SEPTEMBER

GREAT RIVER RACE

Early September; dates vary

www.greatriverrace.co.uk

Around 300 Cornish gigs, Chinese dragonboats with drummers, cutters, longboats and other craft compete to win the UK Traditional Boat Championship.

✉ On the River Thames from Ham House, Richmond, to Island Gardens, Greenwich ☎ 020 8398 9057 Start: Richmond. Finish: Tower Bridge Start: 190. Finish 42, 78, RV1

OCTOBER

PEARLY KINGS AND QUEENS HARVEST FESTIVAL

First Sunday in October

www.pearlysociety.co.uk

Victorian costermongers (market traders) elected their own 'royalty' to protect their trading interests. Today, the pearly kings and queens, who mostly devote their spare time to raising money for charity, gather in their elaborate outfits covered in mother-of-pearl buttons.

✉ St. Paul's Church, Bedford Street WC2E 9ED ☎ 020 7836 5221 Covent Garden, Leicester Square 24, 29, 176

OCTOBER–NOVEMBER

LONDON FILM FESTIVAL

Two weeks late October/early November

www.lff.org.uk

The UK's biggest film festival, centred on the National Film Theatre (▷ 87) and the Odeon West End.

✉ National Film Theatre, South Bank SE1 8XT ☎ 020 7633 0274

NOVEMBER

STATE OPENING OF PARLIAMENT

www.parliament.uk

The Queen arrives in a State coach attended by the Household Cavalry to reopen Parliament officially following its summer recess.

✉ House of Lords, Parliament Square, Westminster SW1A 0PW ☎ 020 7219 3107 Westminster 3, 11, 12, 24

LORD MAYOR'S SHOW

Second Saturday in November

www.lordmayorsshow.org

The newly elected Lord Mayor of London processes with about 140 floats to the Royal Courts of Justice, where the oath of allegiance is taken before the return journey. There are spectacular fireworks in the evening from a barge moored between Waterloo Bridge and Blackfriars Bridge.

✉ Streets between Mansion House and Royal Courts of Justice in the Strand ☎ 020 7332 1456, box office 0845 458 0654 Free along route; grandstand tickets £27 Procession: Mansion House, Temple; fireworks: Blackfriars, Embankment Procession: 11, 15, 23; fireworks: 1, 45, 100, 168, RV1

REMEMBRANCE SUNDAY PARADE

Sunday nearest 11 November

The Queen, the Prime Minister and other dignitaries lay wreaths to commemorate those who have died fighting in wars.

✉ Cenotaph, Whitehall SW1 Charing Cross 11, 12, 24, 159

NOVEMBER–DECEMBER

CHRISTMAS LIGHTS

Late November–early December

Celebrities are invited to switch on the Christmas lights decorating the most famous shopping streets, plus a huge Norwegian spruce in Trafalgar Square—an annual gift from Norway since 1947 to express the nation's gratitude for British support during World War II.

✉ Trafalgar Square, Oxford Street, Regent Street, Bond Street, Covent Garden Charing Cross, Leicester Square 24, 29, 176

DAILY CEREMONIES

CEREMONY OF THE KEYS

www.hrp.org.uk

Every evening at 9.53pm the ceremony of locking up the Tower begins. For free tickets, apply in writing to the Ceremony of the Keys Office, Tower of London (▷ 116) at least two months in advance.

✉ Tower of London EC3N 4AB ☎ 0870 756 7070 Nightly Tower Hill 15, 42, 78, 100, RV1

CHANGING OF THE GUARD

www.royal.gov.uk

Footguards in full dress uniform—red tunics and bearskin hats—can be seen changing shifts in a stirring display of pageantry at three locations in London. You will need to arrive early to get into position for a good view.

✉ Buckingham Palace SW1A 1AA, Horse Guards SW1A 2AX, Tower of London EC3N 4AB Buckingham Palace forecourt: May–Jul (and other dates) daily 11.30am (no ceremony in very wet weather). Horse Guards Arch: Mon–Sat 11am, Sun 10am. Tower Green, Tower of London: daily 11.30am Buckingham Palace: St. James's Park; Horse Guards: Charing Cross; Tower of London: Tower Hill Buckingham Palace: 11, 139, 211, C1; Horse Guards: 11, 12, 24, 159; Tower of London: 15, 25, RV1

EATING

Britain's reputation for food has undergone a radical change in the last few years, and now ranks with the best in the world. The public has become more discerning, chefs have higher profiles and the country now creates its own culinary trends. Top restaurants celebrate traditional British food, adding glamorous touches to such staples as bangers and mash, fish and chips or steak and kidney pie.

These are also standard dishes on most pub menus, along with adventurous offerings served in the new breed of 'gastropubs', which provide first-class meals as well as good beer.

Britain's colonial past adds to its culinary mix: curry is said to be the nation's favourite dish. London has exciting modern restaurants serving traditional Indian, Pakistani or Bangladeshi dishes, fusions of Indian and European cooking or the latest innovations from Mumbai. Thai food is currently enjoying a boom, and Middle Eastern and North African restaurants are particularly popular in the City.

Another long-standing British favourite is Italian food. As well as the home-grown pasta and pizza chains there are innumerable Italian-run restaurants and cafes—often the best bet for a decent cup of coffee and a snack.

London is at the hub of all this gastronomic innovation and you can find pretty well anything in its streets, from cutting-edge modern cuisine through to the Bangladeshi delights of Brick Lane. In some parts of the City basic cafes still sell pie and mash and jellied eels, the latter being something of an acquired taste, but worth trying as part of London's culinary heritage.

RESERVATIONS

In many restaurants, especially on quieter days, it's possible to walk in off the street and get a table, but if you have your heart set on dining in a particular place, it's always best to book a table in advance. Less formal establishments, especially pubs,

A QUICK GUIDE TO TRADITIONAL BRITISH FOOD

BREAKFAST

Traditional British breakfasts are filling, fatty and enormously comforting. A 'fry-up' is based on fried egg and bacon, usually accompanied by fried bread or toast, sausages, mushrooms, grilled tomatoes, baked beans and sometimes black pudding (made from barley, oats and pigs' blood).

In hotels a cooked breakfast will usually be preceded by orange juice and cereals, and followed by toast.

PIE AND MASH SHOPS

London's East End's eel, pie and mash shops are still a popular café option. Steak or steak and kidney pies are cooked in the back of the shop then served up with mashed potatoes.

Pie and mash shops also sell eel, either cooked or jellied. Cooked eels are served with mash and a thin green parsley sauce; jellied eels are cooked in large, white basins, then left to cool, so that the liquor sets, and served cold.

FISH

Another traditional London catch is whitebait, and these days very small quantities are actually caught in the River Thames. These tiny fish—the mixed fry of fish such as herring and sprat—are deep fried and eaten whole, crunchy. Whitebait dinners were customarily eaten in the Houses of Parliament at the end of the parliamentary season.

One of Britain's perennial favourites is fish and chips: white fish—usually cod or haddock—coated in batter then deep fried and served with chips, and, optionally, mushy peas.

DRINKS

Traditional British wine is usually made from fruit or even flowers such as elderflower, but there is a growing number of vineyards in southern England and occasionally a wine list might offer a native white wine. Cider, made from cider apples, remains a popular British drink, and is available in most pubs.

Traditional British ale (beer) is more strongly flavoured and less fizzy than lagers and European beers. There are hundreds of independent brewers in Britain, each one producing a distinctive style of beer. Local London brewers include Fuller's and Young's, who both produce traditional award-winning beers. Try Fuller's ESB or Young's Double Chocolate Stout.

AFTERNOON TEA

This great British institution remains popular and is widely available in hotels and tea rooms from about 2 or 3pm. There are many variations, but it always includes a pot of tea and something to eat. In the smartest hotels it's an impressive spread, including cucumber and other sandwiches, and cakes; cream teas include a scone (small, doughy bun) with cream, butter and jam.

Tea arrived in Britain in the 17th century. By the 19th century it was a very fashionable drink, with tea merchants creating special blends.

may tell you that they do not accept bookings but work on a 'first come, first served' basis. At the other end of the spectrum, many of the UK's top restaurants are booked up for weeks or even months in advance.

It's fairly common for a table booking to last only a couple of hours, after which time guests will be expected to move on to make way for the next sitting. Many restaurants stop serving food relatively early, compared with other—particularly Mediterranean—European countries. Don't expect to turn up at 10.30pm and be fed unless you've checked in advance.

DRESS CODE

In the past the British loved to dress for dinner and the more formal restaurants tended to have strict dress codes, especially where jackets and ties were concerned. These days things are far more flexible, though it's unwise to turn up at a pricey restaurant wearing jeans and a T-shirt.

SMOKING

It is illegal to smoke in any enclosed public space, including pubs, bars and restaurants. Smokers have to smoke outside.

LICENSING LAWS

Since November 2005 '24-hour drinking' laws have been in operation. In practice, most premises only open for a couple of extra hours more than the standard 11pm, and only on Thursday, Friday and Saturday nights. Children aged 16 to 18 can drink alcohol only if it accompanies a meal. Some restaurants—especially those not licensed to sell alcohol—operate a 'bring your own' system, in which case it's usual for diners to pay a small corkage fee.

VEGETARIAN MEALS

Most British restaurants offer meat-free dishes, and the choices are generally becoming greater and more imaginative. Some do not include a vegetarian option on the menu but are happy to prepare one on request. Thai, Vietnamese and Indian restaurants are usually good options.

CAFES, BRASSERIES AND BISTROS

These days the word 'cafe' refers to the stylish, urban, Continental-style establishments that bridge the gap between pubs, restaurants and coffee bars by selling hot drinks, snacks, wine and meals. Like brasseries and bistros, they often stay open all day—in fact it can be difficult to distinguish between the three. The 'greasy spoon' is a cheap-and-cheerful version of the cafe, usually serving simple traditional, calorie-filled British meals such as sausage and mash, fry-up breakfasts (served all day), tea, coffee and other hot drinks.

PUBS

You'll find Irish bars, sports bars, traditional street corner pubs and slick futuristic bars. Bare stone walls, open fires and wooden beams typify older establishments, often imitated in modern chains, though many London pubs feature trendy modern styling or themed decor.

One of the newest trends is the gastropub—a fusion of pub and restaurant that promises not only a place to drink, but also good-quality food. Pub menus have traditionally included bar snacks—lighter, cheaper meals such as sandwiches, baked potatoes with fillings and savoury dishes—but these days most also serve substantial meals.

MENU READER

SAVOURY DISHES

Bangers and mash:
Sausages and mashed potato usually served with onion gravy

Bubble and squeak:
Pre-cooked cabbage and potato fried up together

Cottage pie:
Minced beef (and vegetables) topped with mashed potato

Kedgeree:
Smoked haddock, eggs and rice with curry powder

Lancashire hotpot:
Casserole of lamb and vegetables topped with sliced potato

Scotch egg:
Hard-boiled egg covered with sausage meat; eaten cold, often as a snack

Shepherd's pie:
Minced lamb and vegetables topped with mashed potato and baked

Toad in the hole:
Sausages baked in batter

Welsh rarebit:
Thick cheese sauce spread on toast, then grilled

Yorkshire pudding:
Batter cooked in the juices of roast beef, its accompaniment.

PUDDINGS

Bakewell tart:
Almond-flavoured flan, with jam and a pastry base

Bread-and-butter pudding:
Slices of bread and butter baked with dried fruit, milk and eggs

Fruit crumble:
Stewed fruit with a topping of crumbled flour and butter, baked in the oven and served warm, with custard

Fruit fool:
Cooked soft fruit blended with cream or custard (served cold)

Spotted dick:
Hot pudding made with suet pastry and raisins

Summer pudding:
Cooked soft fruit in a shell of white bread; served cold with cream

Trifle:
Layers of sponge cake, fruit, jelly and custard, topped with whipped cream; served cold

STAYING

London has some of the best hotels in the world, but the cost of accommodation is high. You can expect to pay £150 a night for a reasonable room, and the rates begin to soar if you stay at one of the grand old hotels such as Claridge's, the Dorchester or the Savoy. Good value hotels and guest houses do exist, but these rooms are very much in demand and you must book in advance.

Many hotels will ask you to confirm your reservation and will charge a fee if you cancel at short notice or fail to turn up. You may lose your deposit and some hotels will charge the cost of the room to your credit card.

CHEAPER ACCOMMODATION

Consider alternatives to hotels, such as renting apartments or staying with a London family. The London Tourist Board has leaflets on these and other options.

Youth hostels run by the Youth Hostel Association (YHA) are a good option for visitors on a tight budget. You need to be a member of the association; either join in advance or in person at any hostel or online at www.yha.org.uk. Annual membership for British residents is £15.95, which includes children or young people under 18 travelling with you; under 26s pay £9.95). More adventurous types may like to try getting a free stay via www.couchsurfing.com.

HOTEL FACILITIES

The biggest problem with London hotels (after price) is noise, as many are on busy streets. Some have double glazing, but that can make rooms unbearably stuffy, especially since air-conditioning is not standard. If you value peace and quiet, look for hotels on side streets in residential areas; or request a room at the rear or higher up in the building. Most hotels also have rooms of different sizes, so always ask whether there is a choice. You will not necessarily automatically be allocated the best room available.

For facilities such as parking, 24-hour room service, gyms and swimming pools, expect to pay a high premium in central London.

TIPS

» Many hotels offer cheaper rates on Saturday and Sunday. Sometimes big chains offer weekend discounts. Some hotels also offer lower rates for stays of a week or more.

» Rates can be cheaper during February and March, and October and November.

» The higher the rate, the more chance there is of getting a significant discount. Go online to check out any special offers.

GUIDE TO ARCHITECTURAL PERIODS

ROMAN
London's growth as a city began when the invading Romans founded their base of Londinium, occupying roughly the same area as today's City. A well-preserved remnant of the thick stone wall built around the city after its sacking by Queen Boudicca in AD61 stands next to Tower Hill Underground station and Cooper's Row. The unearthed Temple of Mithras is now adjacent to the Bucklersbury House office block on Queen Victoria Street.

ANGLO-SAXON
Churches were built of stone and characterized by their simple arched windows with thick central supports. The first St. Paul's Cathedral was founded in AD604 and Edward the Confessor had Westminster Abbey (▷ 194–195) completed in 1066.

NORMAN
In the late 11th and 12th centuries the Norman conquerors brought new styles and craftsmen from Normandy. Massive fortified buildings and churches were thrown up in the wake of the Norman invasion, recognizable by their round arches, heavy masonry and decorated walls and doorways.
Examples: Westminster Hall, the oldest remaining part of the medieval Westminster Palace, erected in 1097 (but renovated in the 14th century).

The White Tower, at the heart of the Tower of London (▷ 112–117), built in 1078.

EARLY ENGLISH AND DECORATED
Architecture of the late 12th and 13th centuries became lighter, using pointed rather than rounded arches, especially in lancet windows. This period marked the move towards the long, vertical lines of the Gothic style and an increasing focus on window space. As windows became bigger, buttresses were added to transfer the outward thrust of the roof to the ground.
Examples: Southwark Cathedral's choir and retrochoir (▷ 79); Westminster Abbey.

PERPENDICULAR GOTHIC
Evolving from the Decorated style, simpler lines and more uniform tracery on windows and walls emerged during the late 14th and 15th centuries, with much use of fan-vaulting and four-centred arches. Designs used greater areas of glass.
Examples: Henry VII Chapel, Westminster Abbey.

TUDOR AND EARLY STUART
The late 15th and 16th centuries marked a shift from the Gothic to the Renaissance styles, with the emphasis on domestic architecture for the gentry. Brick and wood-panelling became popular.
Examples: Hampton Court Palace (above; ▷ 260–261); Shakespeare's Globe Theatre (▷ 78), Southwark—a reconstruction of the 16th-century original.

LATE STUART
The Palladian style, recalling the work of 16th-century Italian architect Andrea Palladio, reflected classical Roman influences in porticoes and restrained symmetrical façades. Classical styles merged in the 18th century with baroque ornamentation and rich detail.
Major Architects: Inigo Jones (1573–1652): designed the Queen's House (▷ 257), Greenwich, and Banqueting House (▷ 175). Brought the Palladian style into fashion, as well as the use of movable scenery and the proscenium arch.
Sir Christopher Wren (1632–1723): designed St. Paul's Cathedral

(▷ 104–109), Greenwich Hospital and many of the City churches following the Great Fire of 1666. Professor of Astronomy at London and Oxford.
Nicholas Hawksmoor (1661–1736): Wren's assistant, who favoured monumental classicism. Designed many churches, including St. George's Bloomsbury, St. Mary Woolnoth, Christchurch Spitalfields.
James Gibbs (1682–1754): Scottish architect who designed St. Martin-in-the-Fields (▷ 190) and St. Clement Danes (▷ 147).

GEORGIAN AND REGENCY

During the Georgian period architects turned back to the Palladian style, and in the late 18th and early 19th centuries Greek classical influences came to the fore, prompting an emphasis on simplicity and symmetry, especially in the new terraced town houses. The Regency period saw the introduction of floor-to-roof bow windows and wrought-ironwork in staircases and balconies.
Major Architects: Robert Adam (1728–92): designed Osterley House (▷ 262) and Syon House (▷ 262) and undertook decoration and furniture as well as exteriors.
William Kent (1684–1748): a Yorkshireman who advocated the return to Palladianism. Designed Chiswick House (▷ 255) and Kensington Palace (▷ 214–215).
John Nash (1752–1835): known for his Regency houses and responsible for Regent's Park (▷ 218) terraces.
Sir John Soane (1753–1837): favoured austere classical designs. Responsible for the Bank of England (▷ 101) and Dulwich Picture Gallery (▷ 255).
Sir William Chambers (1726–96): first treasurer of the Royal Academy; designed Somerset House (▷ 150–151).

VICTORIAN

Architecture of the period 1837–1901 called on a mish-mash of influences as new public buildings such as railway stations and municipal offices sprang up. These were notable for their neo-Gothic designs, romanticized medieval motifs, rich details and extensive use of steel, iron and glass. Examples: Houses of Parliament; Natural History Museum; Albert Memorial; St. Pancras Station; Tower Bridge.
Major Architects: Sir Charles Barry (1795–1860): designed the Houses of Parliament (▷ 179–180) after their destruction by fire in 1834.
Sir George Gilbert Scott (1811–78): designed St. Pancras Station; compelled to tone down his neo-Gothic design for the Foreign Office.
Augustus Welby Northmore Pugin (1812–52): led the neo-Gothic movement and worked with Barry on the Houses of Parliament, as well as designing several churches.
Alfred Waterhouse (1830–1905): designed the Natural History Museum (▷ 220–221) and many churches.
William Butterfield (1814–1900): leading exponent of the Gothic Revival. Used red brick and a wooden spire in All Saints' Church (▷ 133).
Sir Aston Webb (1849–1930): a president of the Royal Academy, who designed Admiralty Arch, the façade of Buckingham Palace's east front (▷ 176–177), and the Victoria & Albert Museum (▷ 224–228).

LATE VICTORIAN AND EDWARDIAN

In the late 19th century the Arts and Crafts movement was promoted by William Morris as a reaction against mass production, with the aim of making hand-made objects and fine art an integral part of daily life. Its influence extended to architecture as suburban brick houses, with terracotta panelling, balconies and large gardens. The organic motifs of art nouveau were popular until about 1914.
Examples: Red House, Bexleyheath; Holy Trinity Church, Chelsea.
Major Architects: Philip Webb (1831–1915): an exponent of simple domestic architecture who worked with Morris on the Red House.
Sir Edwin Lutyens (1869–1944): designed the Cenotaph in Whitehall (▷ 191), as well as many characterful country houses.
Sir Herbert Baker (1862–1946): worked with Lutyens. Best known in Britain for his controversial reconstruction of the Bank of England. Designed India House, on Aldwych, and South Africa House, overlooking Trafalgar Square, in Cape Dutch style.

INTER-WAR

Public and domestic buildings made full use of art deco's geometric lines, bold colours and exotic motifs, often using Egyptian themes, marking the huge public interest in archaeologist Howard Carter's discovery of the tomb of Tutankhamun. Traditional materials such as coloured tiles and stained glass were combined with modern chromium plating.
Examples: BBC Broadcasting House, Langham Place; Odeon Cinema, Islington; Hoover Building, Perivale; Daily Express Building, Fleet Street.
Major Architects: Berthold Lubetkin (1901–90): Russian architect who was prolific in the 1930s, designing the Gorilla House and Penguin Pool in London Zoo (▷ 219).

POST WORLD WAR II

After 1945 designs became increasingly stark and massive, using materials such as concrete, especially in the tower blocks of the 1960s and the rough, unfinished designs of Brutalism. In contrast, the high-tech style of the 1970s and 1980s exposed the inner workings of public buildings. Stainless steel and glass were popular materials.
Examples: National Theatre and South Bank Centre (▷ 79); Lloyds Building (▷ 118); Millennium Bridge (▷ 100).
Major Architects: Sir Richard Rogers (1933–): designed the Lloyds Building.
Sir Norman Foster (1935–): responsible for the Millennium Bridge (▷ 77) and the Swiss Re headquarters (The Gherkin, ▷ 21).

GLOSSARY FOR THE US VISITOR

anticlockwise .... counterclockwise
aubergine .... eggplant

bank holiday .... a public holiday, when all banks are closed (n307)
bill .... check (at restaurant)
biscuit .... cookie
bonnet .... hood (car)
boot .... trunk (car)
busker .... street musician

caravan .... house trailer or RV
car park .... parking lot
carriage .... car (on a train)
cashpoint .... ATM or cash machine
casualty .... emergency room (hospital department)
chemist .... pharmacy
chips .... french fries
coach .... long-distance bus
concessions .... reduced entrance fees or fares
coriander .... cilantro
courgette .... zucchini
crèche .... day care
crisps .... potato chips

directory enquiries .... directory assistance
dual carriageway. two-lane highway

en suite .... a bedroom with its own private bathroom; may also just refer to the bathroom

football .... soccer
full board .... a hotel tariff that includes all meals

garage .... gas station
garden .... yard (residential)
GP .... doctor

half board .... hotel tariff that includes breakfast and either lunch or dinner
high street .... main street
hire .... rent

inland .... within the UK

jelly .... Jello™
jumper, jersey .... sweater
junction .... intersection

layby .... pull-off
level crossing .... grade crossing
lorry .... truck
licensed .... a cafe or restaurant that has a licence to serve alcohol (beer and wine only unless it's 'fully' licensed)
lift .... elevator
listed building ..... protected building

mainline station .... a train station as opposed to an underground or subway station (although it may be served by the underground/subway)

nappy .... diaper
newsagent.. newsstand, newspaper shop
note .... paper money

off-licence .... liquor store

pants .... underpants (men's)
pavement .... sidewalk
petrol .... gas
phone box .... phone booth
plaster .... Band-Aid or bandage
post .... mail
public school .... private school
pudding .... dessert
purse .... change purse
pushchair .... stroller

quay .... wharf/pier

return ticket .... roundtrip ticket
rocket (salad leaves) .... arugula
roundabout .... traffic circle or rotary

self-catering .... accommodation including a kitchen
single ticket .... one-way ticket
solicitor .... lawyer
stalls .... orchestra seats (in theatre)
subway .... underpass
surgery .... doctor's office
swede .... American turnip

tailback, traffic jam .... stalled line of traffic
takeaway .... takeout
taxi rank .... taxi stand
terrace .... row houses
tights .... panty-hose
T-junction .... an intersection where one road meets another at right angles (making a T shape)
toilets .... restrooms
torch .... flashlight
trolley .... cart
trousers .... pants

vest .... undershirt

waistcoat .... vest
way out .... exit

zebra crossing .... crosswalk

BRITISH FLOOR NUMBERING

In Britain the first floor of a building is called the ground floor, and the floor above it is the first floor. So a British second floor is a US third floor, and so on. This is something to watch for in museums and galleries in particular.

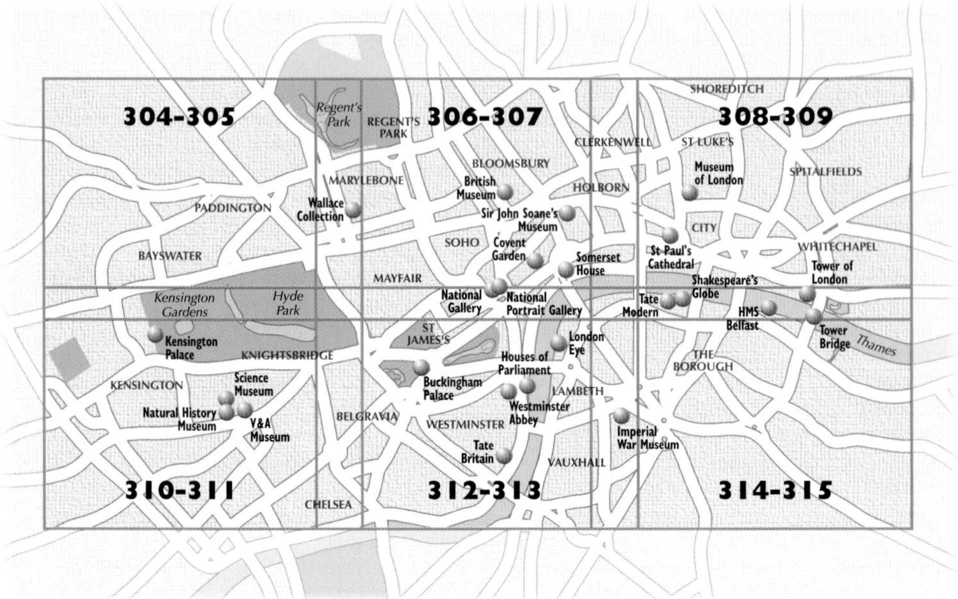

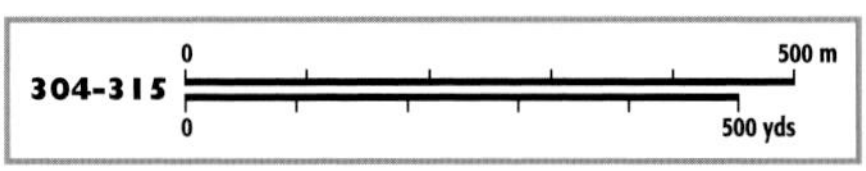

- Main through road
- Secondary road
- Other road
- Dual carriageway
- Road in tunnel
- Congestion Charging Zone
- Footpath
- Railway station
- Park or garden
- Building of interest
- Recommended sight
- Monument
- Tourist information centre
- Church
- Underground station
- Car parking
- Bus / Coach station

MAPS

Map references for the sights refer to the individual locator maps within the regional chapters. For example, Buckingham Palace has the reference ✚ 172 G6, indicating the locator map page number (172) and the grid square in which Buckingham Palace sits (G6). These same grid references can also be used to locate the sights in this section. For example, Buckingham Palace appears again in square G6 within the atlas, on page 312.

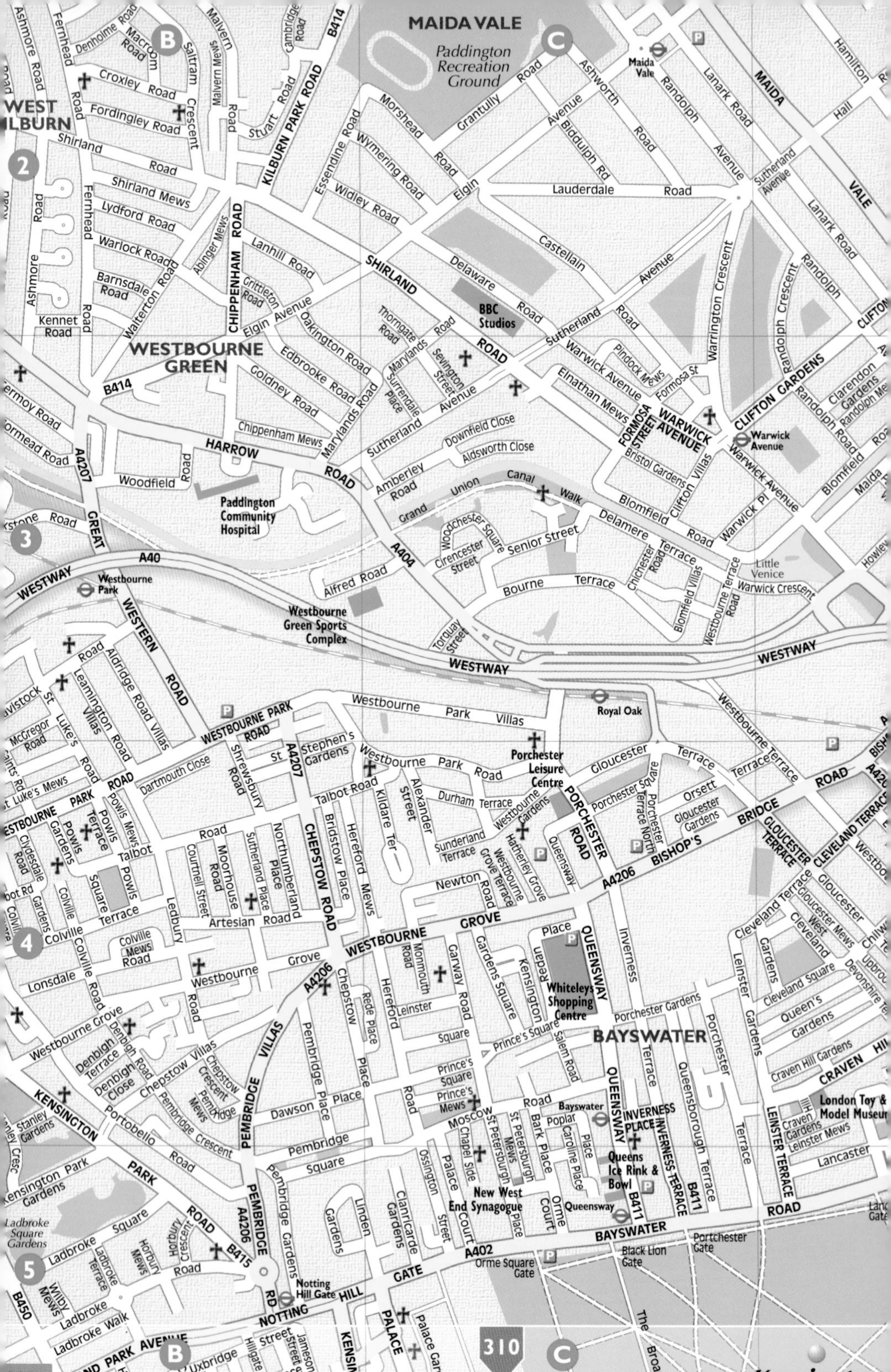
MAIDA VALE
Paddington Recreation Ground
WEST KILBURN
WESTBOURNE GREEN
BAYSWATER
B
C
2
3
4
5
Ashmore Road
Fernhead Road
Denholme Road
Macroom Road
Saltram Crescent
Malvern Road
Malvern Mews
Cambridge Road
B414
Croxley Road
Fordingley Road
Shirland Road
Shirland Mews
Lydford Road
Warlock Road
Barnsdale Road
Walterton Road
Kennet Road
Stuart Road
KILBURN PARK ROAD
Abinger Mews
CHIPPENHAM ROAD
Lanhill Road
Grittleton Road
Elgin Avenue
Oakington Road
Edbrooke Road
Goldney Road
Chippenham Mews
Essendine Road
Morshead Road
Wymering Road
Widley Road
Grantully Road
Elgin Avenue
Ashworth Road
Biddulph Rd
Randolph Avenue
Lanark Road
MAIDA VALE
Hamilton
Hall
Maida Vale
Sutherland Avenue
Lauderdale Road
Castellain Road
Delaware Road
BBC Studios
SHIRLAND ROAD
Thorngate Road
Marylands Road
Sevington Street
Surrendale Place
Sutherland Avenue
Warrington Crescent
Randolph Crescent
Randolph Road
Clarendon Gardens
CLIFTON GARDENS
Warwick Avenue
Pindock Mews
Formosa St
Elnathan Mews
FORMOSA STREET
WARWICK AVENUE
Bristol Gardens
Clifton Villas
Warwick Pl
Blomfield Road
Delamere Terrace
Elmfield
Maida
Downfield Close
Aldsworth Close
Amberley Road
Grand Union Canal Walk
Woodchester Square
Cirencester Street
Senior Street
Chichester Road
Bourne Terrace
Blomfield Villas
Westbourne Terrace Road
Little Venice
Warwick Crescent
Hermoy Road
Ormead Road
A4207
B414
HARROW ROAD
Woodfield Road
Paddington Community Hospital
Kilburn Road
GREAT
WESTERN ROAD
WESTWAY
A40
Westbourne Park
Alfred Road
A404
Westbourne Green Sports Complex
Torquay Street
WESTWAY
Royal Oak
Aldridge Road Villas
Leamington Road Villas
St Luke's Road
Tavistock
McGregor Road
St Luke's Mews
WESTBOURNE PARK ROAD
Westbourne Park Villas
Dartmouth Close
Shrewsbury Road
St Stephen's Gardens
A4207
Westbourne Park Road
Porchester Leisure Centre
Gloucester Terrace
Westbourne Terrace
Porchester Square
Porchester Terrace North
Orsett Terrace
Gloucester Gardens
Talbot Road
Kildare Ter
Alexander Street
Durham Terrace
Westbourne Gardens
PORCHESTER ROAD
BISHOP'S BRIDGE ROAD
A4206
GLOUCESTER TERRACE
CLEVELAND TERRACE
Powis Terrace
Powis Mews
Powis Gardens
Powis Square
Clydesdale Road
Colville Gardens
Colville Square
Talbot Road
Courtnell Street
Moorhouse Road
Sutherland Place
Northumberland Place
Bridstow Place
Hereford Mews
CHEPSTOW ROAD
Sunderland Terrace
Hatherley Grove
Westbourne Grove Terrace
Queensway
Newton Road
Ledbury
Artesian Road
Colville Mews
Colville Road
Lonsdale Road
Westbourne Grove
WESTBOURNE GROVE
Monmouth Road
Garway Road
Gardens Square
Kensington Gardens Square
QUEENSWAY
Whiteleys Shopping Centre
Inverness Terrace
Porchester Gardens
Cleveland Terrace
Cleveland Gardens
Cleveland Square
Gloucester Mews West
Devonshire Terrace
Queen's Gardens
Craven Hill Gardens
CRAVEN HILL
Westbourne Grove
Denbigh Terrace
Denbigh Road
Denbigh Close
Chepstow Villas
Chepstow Crescent
Pembridge Mews
Pembridge Crescent
PEMBRIDGE VILLAS
A4206
Chepstow Place
Rede Place
Pembridge Place
Hereford Road
Leinster Square
Prince's Square
Prince's Mews
Salem Road
Moscow Road
Bayswater
INVERNESS PLACE
INVERNESS TERRACE
Queensborough Terrace
Porchester Terrace
LEINSTER TERRACE
Leinster Gardens
London Toy & Model Museum
Craven Gardens
Leinster Mews
Lancaster
KENSINGTON PARK ROAD
Stanley Gardens
Portobello Road
Dawson Place
Pembridge Square
Pembridge Gardens
Ossington Street
Palace Court
Chapel Side
St Petersburgh Place
St Petersburgh Mews
Bark Place
Poplar Place
Caroline Place
Orme Court
Queens Ice Rink & Bowl
B411
Queensway
New West End Synagogue
Kensington Park Gardens
Ladbroke Square Gardens
Ladbroke Square
Ladbroke Terrace
Horbury Mews
Horbury Crescent
Ladbroke Road
B415
PEMBRIDGE RD
Linden Gardens
Clanricarde Gardens
BAYSWATER ROAD
A402
Orme Square Gate
Black Lion Gate
Porchester Gate
Lancaster Gate
Notting Hill Gate
NOTTING HILL GATE
Wilby Mews
Ladbroke Walk
B450
HOLLAND PARK AVENUE
Uxbridge Street
Hillgate Street
Jameson Street
Hillgate Place
KENSINGTON
PALACE GARDENS
Palace Gardens
310
The Broad Walk

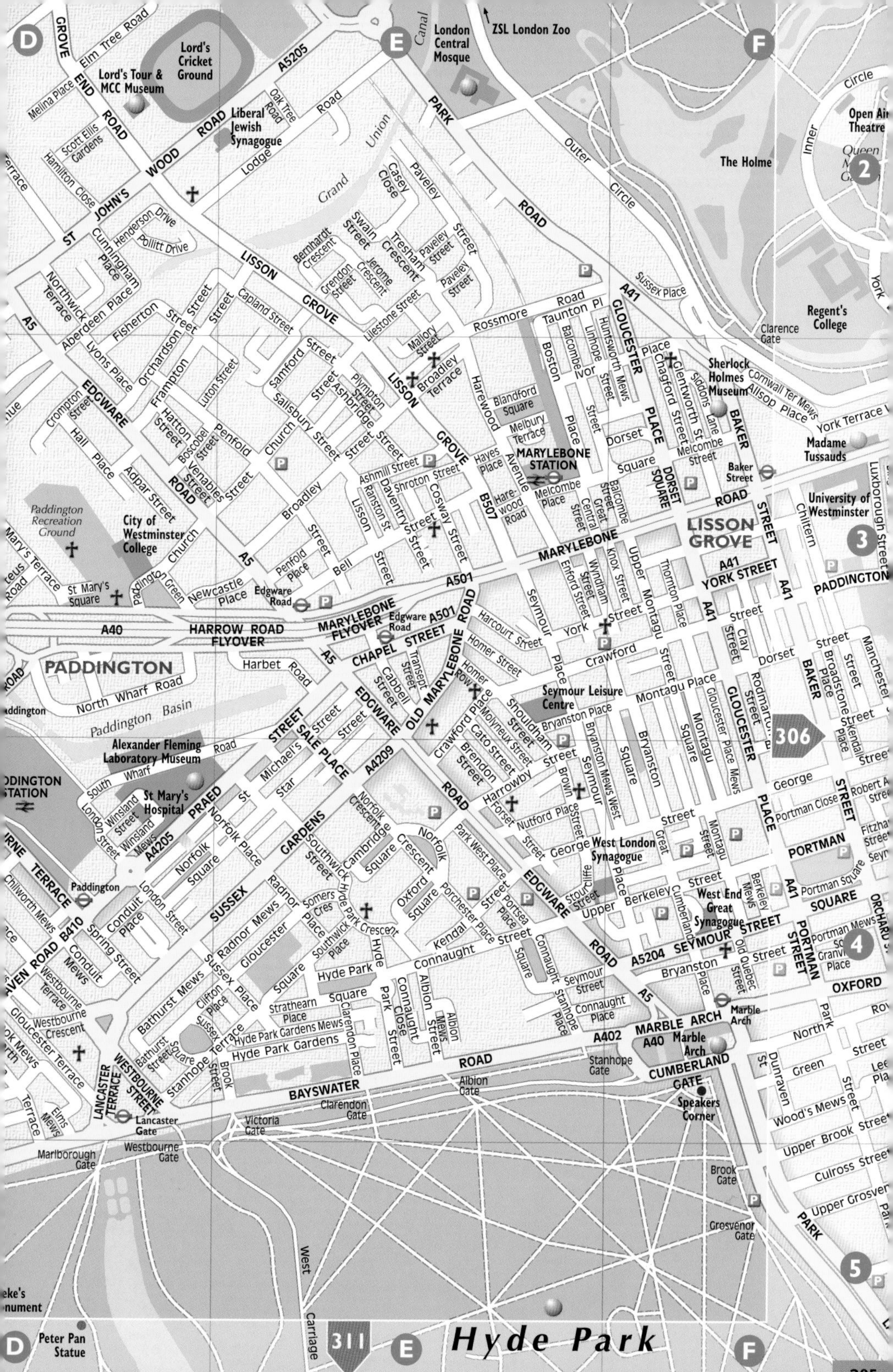

D
E
F
Lord's Cricket Ground
Lord's Tour & MCC Museum
Liberal Jewish Synagogue
London Central Mosque
ZSL London Zoo
The Holme
Open Air Theatre
Regent's College
Clarence Gate
Sherlock Holmes Museum
Madame Tussauds
University of Westminster
Baker Street
MARYLEBONE STATION
LISSON GROVE
Paddington Recreation Ground
City of Westminster College
Edgware Road
PADDINGTON
Paddington Basin
Alexander Fleming Laboratory Museum
St Mary's Hospital
PADDINGTON STATION
Paddington
Seymour Leisure Centre
West London Synagogue
West End Great Synagogue
Marble Arch
MARBLE ARCH
CUMBERLAND GATE
Speakers Corner
Stanhope Gate
Albion Gate
Clarendon Gate
Victoria Gate
Lancaster Gate
Westbourne Gate
Marlborough Gate
Brook Gate
Grosvenor Gate
Peter Pan Statue
West Carriage
Hyde Park
GROVE END ROAD
Elm Tree Road
ST JOHN'S WOOD ROAD
A5205
Lodge Road
Grand Union Canal
PARK ROAD
Outer Circle
Inner Circle
LISSON GROVE
Rossmore Road
GLOUCESTER PLACE
A41
BAKER STREET
MARYLEBONE ROAD
A501
EDGWARE ROAD
A5
A40
HARROW ROAD FLYOVER
MARYLEBONE FLYOVER
CHAPEL STREET
OLD MARYLEBONE ROAD
PRAED STREET
A4205
SALE PLACE
SUSSEX GARDENS
A4209
BAYSWATER ROAD
A402
A5204
SEYMOUR STREET
PORTMAN SQUARE
PORTMAN STREET
OXFORD
PARK
YORK STREET
PADDINGTON
Dorset Square
Blandford Square
Bryanston Square
Montagu Square
Connaught Square
Hyde Park Gardens
Norfolk Square
WESTBOURNE STREET
LANCASTER TERRACE
306
311
2
3
4
5

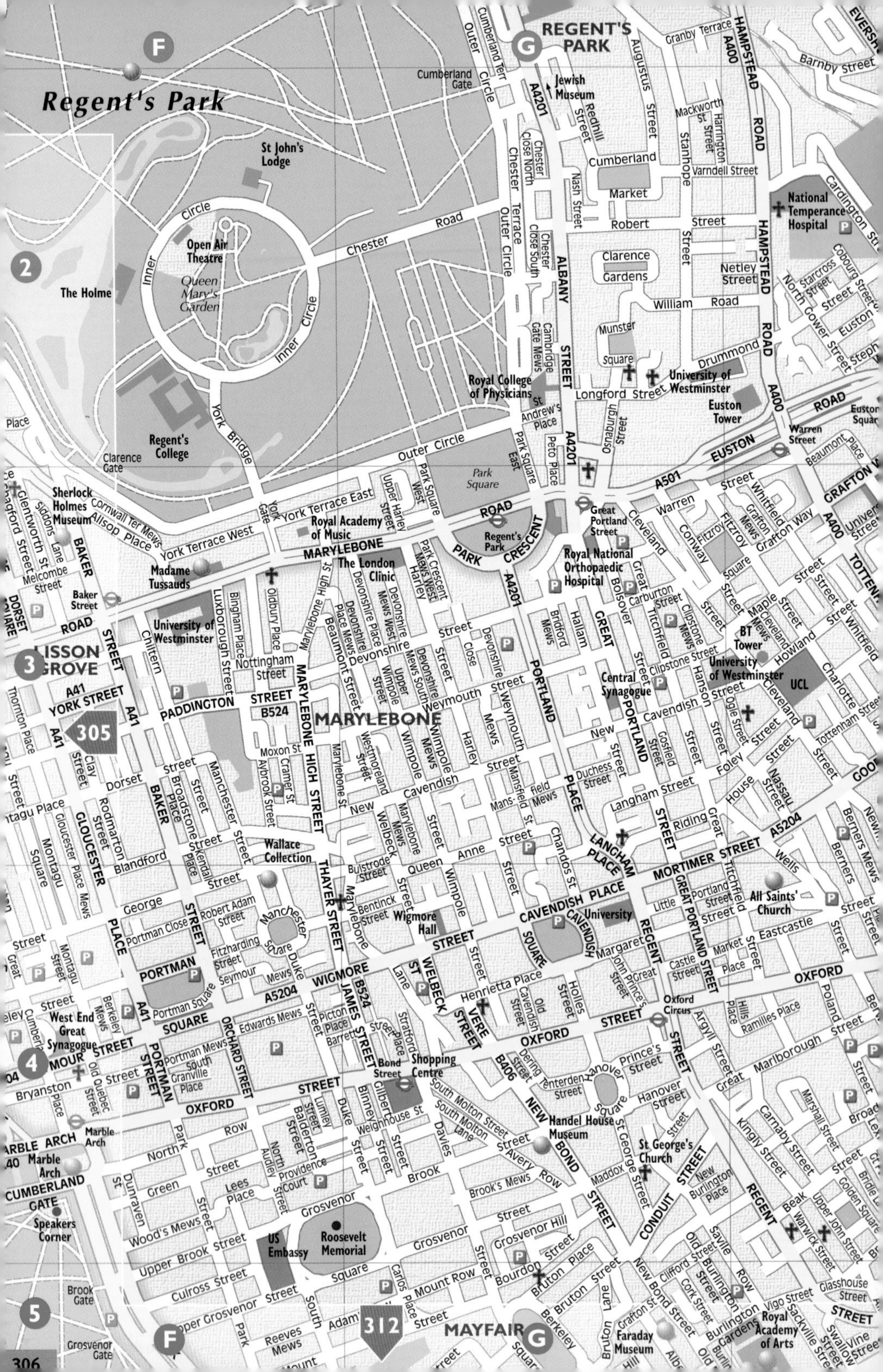
Regent's Park
REGENT'S PARK
St John's Lodge
Open Air Theatre
Queen Mary's Gardens
Inner Circle
Chester Road
The Holme
York Bridge
Regent's College
Clarence Gate
Outer Circle
Cumberland Gate
Cumberland Terr
Jewish Museum
A4201
Chester Terrace
Chester Close North
Chester Close South
Cambridge Gate Mews
Royal College of Physicians
St Andrew's Place
Park Square East
Park Square West
Park Square
Peto Place
ALBANY STREET
Redhill Street
Augustus Street
Granby Terrace
HAMPSTEAD ROAD
A400
Barnby Street
Mackworth St
Harrington Street
Stanhope Street
Varndell Street
Cumberland Market
Nash Street
Robert Street
Clarence Gardens
Netley Street
William Road
Munster Square
Drummond Street
University of Westminster
Longford Street
Osnaburgh Street
Euston Tower
National Temperance Hospital
Cardington Street
North Gower Street
Starcross Street
Coburg Street
Euston Street
EUSTON ROAD
A501
Warren Street
Euston Square
Beaumont Place
GRAFTON WAY
Sherlock Holmes Museum
Cornwall Ter Mews
Allsop Place
York Terrace West
York Terrace East
York Gate
Upper Harley Street
Royal Academy of Music
MARYLEBONE ROAD
The London Clinic
Park Crescent Mews West
PARK CRESCENT
Regent's Park
Great Portland Street
Royal National Orthopaedic Hospital
Madame Tussauds
Baker Street
BAKER STREET
Melcombe Street
Glentworth St
Siddons Lane
DORSET SQUARE
LISSON GROVE
University of Westminster
Chiltern Street
Luxborough Street
Bingham Place
Oldbury Place
Nottingham Street
Marylebone High St
Devonshire Place
Devonshire Place Mews
Devonshire Mews West
Devonshire Street
Beaumont Street
Harley Street
Devonshire Close
Weymouth Street
Bolsover Street
Carburton Street
Bridford Mews
Hallam Street
Great Titchfield Street
Clipstone Street
Clipstone Mews
Conway Street
Fitzroy Square
Fitzroy Street
Grafton Mews
Whitfield Street
Maple Street
Cleveland Mews
BT Tower
Howland Street
University of Westminster
UCL
Central Synagogue
Hanson Street
Cavendish Street
Ogle Street
Cleveland Street
Tottenham Street
Charlotte Street
A41
YORK STREET
305
PADDINGTON STREET
B524
MARYLEBONE
Thornton Place
Clay Street
Dorset Street
Moxon St
Cramer St
Aybrook Street
Broadstone Place
Manchester Street
Westmoreland Street
Wimpole Street
Wimpole Mews
Weymouth Mews
Harley Street
New Cavendish Street
Mansfield Street
Mansfield Mews
Duchess Street
PORTLAND PLACE
Gosfield Street
Foley Street
Langham Street
Riding House Street
Nassau Street
Great Portland Street
Montagu Place
Gloucester Place Mews
GLOUCESTER PLACE
Rodmarton Street
Montagu Square
Blandford Street
Kendall Place
Wallace Collection
THAYER STREET
Marylebone Lane
Bulstrode Street
Welbeck Street
Queen Anne Street
Chandos St
LANGHAM PLACE
MORTIMER STREET
A5204
Wells Street
Berners Street
Berners Mews
All Saints' Church
George Street
Robert Adam Street
Manchester Square
Bentinck Street
Wigmore Hall
CAVENDISH PLACE
University
CAVENDISH SQUARE
Little Portland Street
Eastcastle Street
Portman Close
Fitzharding Street
Seymour Mews
Duke Street
WIGMORE STREET
JAMES STREET
WELBECK STREET
Henrietta Place
Margaret Street
John Prince's Street
Great Castle Street
Market Place
PORTMAN SQUARE
Portman Square
Montagu Street
Great Cumberland
West End Great Synagogue
Berkeley Mews
SEYMOUR STREET
Edwards Mews
Picton Place
Barrett Street
Lane
Stratford Place
VERE STREET
Cavendish Street
Old Cavendish Street
Holles Street
Oxford Circus
Argyll Street
Hills Place
Ramillies Place
Poland Street
OXFORD STREET
Portman Mews South
Granville Place
ORCHARD STREET
PORTMAN STREET
Old Quebec Street
Bryanston Place
Bond Street
Shopping Centre
B406
Dering Street
Tenterden Street
Hanover Square
Prince's Street
Hanover Street
Great Marlborough Street
Marble Arch
MARBLE ARCH
North Row
Park Street
Lumley Street
Balderton Street
North Audley Street
Binney Street
Gilbert Street
Weighhouse St
South Molton Street
South Molton Lane
Davies Street
NEW BOND STREET
Handel House Museum
St George Street
St George's Church
Carnaby Street
Kingly Street
Marshall Street
Broad
CUMBERLAND GATE
Speakers Corner
Dunraven St
Green Street
Lees Place
Providence Court
Brook Street
Avery Row
Brook's Mews
Maddox Street
CONDUIT STREET
New Burlington Place
REGENT STREET
Beak Street
Upper John Street
Warwick Street
Golden Square
Wood's Mews
Grosvenor Square
US Embassy
Roosevelt Memorial
Grosvenor Street
Grosvenor Hill
Bourdon Street
Bruton Place
Bruton Street
Clifford Street
Old Burlington Street
Savile Row
Cork Street
Upper Brook Street
Culross Street
Carlos Place
Mount Row
Brook Gate
Upper Grosvenor Street
South Audley Street
Adam's Row
Reeves Mews
312
MAYFAIR
Berkeley Square
Bruton Lane
Grafton St
New Bond Street
Faraday Museum
Burlington Gardens
Vigo Street
Royal Academy of Arts
Sackville Street
Glasshouse Street
Swallow Street
Vine Street
Grosvenor Gate
F
G
2
3
4
5

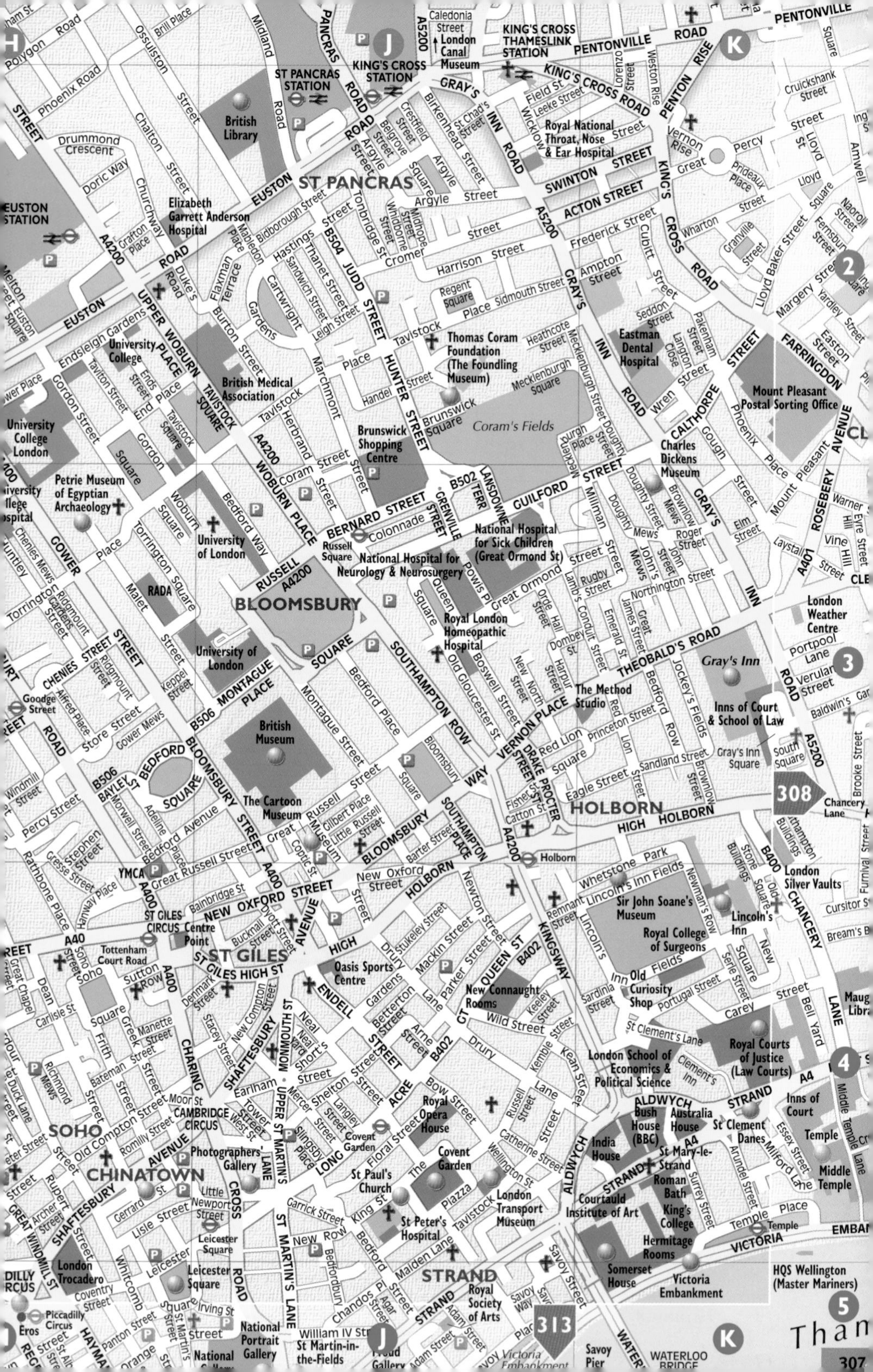
St Pancras Station
King's Cross Station
King's Cross Thameslink Station
British Library
London Canal Museum
Caledonia Street
Pentonville Road
Penton Rise
Gray's Inn Road
King's Cross Road
Royal National Throat, Nose & Ear Hospital
Swinton Street
Acton Street
St Pancras
Euston Road
Euston Station
Elizabeth Garrett Anderson Hospital
Pancras Road
Midland Road
Ossulston Street
Chalton Street
Polygon Road
Phoenix Road
Drummond Crescent
Doric Way
Churchway
Argyle Street
Argyle Square
Judd Street
B504
Hastings Street
Cartwright Gardens
Regent Square
Sidmouth Street
Harrison Street
Frederick Street
Ampton Street
Cubitt Street
Great Percy Street
Lloyd Baker Street
Margery Street
Farringdon Road
Mount Pleasant Postal Sorting Office
Eastman Dental Hospital
Calthorpe Street
Wren Street
Thomas Coram Foundation (The Foundling Museum)
Mecklenburgh Square
Coram's Fields
Brunswick Square
Brunswick Shopping Centre
Hunter Street
Tavistock Place
Handel Street
Marchmont Street
University College
University College London
Upper Woburn Place
Tavistock Square
British Medical Association
Gordon Square
Gordon Street
Endsleigh Gardens
Petrie Museum of Egyptian Archaeology
Gower Street
Woburn Place
A4200
University of London
Bedford Way
Bernard Street
Russell Square
Guilford Street
Lansdowne Terr
Grenville Street
B502
National Hospital for Sick Children (Great Ormond St)
National Hospital for Neurology & Neurosurgery
Charles Dickens Museum
Doughty Street
Rosebery Avenue
Bloomsbury
RADA
Malet Street
Torrington Square
Chenies Street
Goodge Street
Tottenham Court Road
Great Ormond Street
Queen Square
Royal London Homeopathic Hospital
Lamb's Conduit Street
Northington Street
Theobald's Road
Gray's Inn
London Weather Centre
Portpool Lane
Inns of Court & School of Law
Gray's Inn Square
South Square
Southampton Row
Montague Place
Bloomsbury Square
British Museum
The Cartoon Museum
Montague Street
Bedford Place
The Method Studio
Red Lion Square
Vernon Place
Procter Street
Holborn
High Holborn
Chancery Lane
308
London Silver Vaults
Bedford Square
Bloomsbury Street
Great Russell Street
YMCA
New Oxford Street
St Giles Circus
Centre Point
St Giles
St Giles High St
Sir John Soane's Museum
Lincoln's Inn Fields
Lincoln's Inn
Royal College of Surgeons
Kingsway
Oasis Sports Centre
New Connaught Rooms
Old Curiosity Shop
Royal Courts of Justice (Law Courts)
London School of Economics & Political Science
Shaftesbury Avenue
Charing Cross Road
Soho Square
Soho
Chinatown
Cambridge Circus
Photographers' Gallery
Endell Street
Long Acre
Royal Opera House
Covent Garden
Drury Lane
Aldwych
Bush House (BBC)
Australia House
India House
St Clement Danes
St Mary-le-Strand
Roman Bath
King's College
Courtauld Institute of Art
Somerset House
Hermitage Rooms
Strand
Temple
Inns of Court
Middle Temple
Victoria Embankment
HQS Wellington (Master Mariners)
London Transport Museum
St Paul's Church
St Peter's Hospital
Royal Society of Arts
313
London Trocadero
Leicester Square
Piccadilly Circus
Eros
National Portrait Gallery
St Martin-in-the-Fields
St Martin's Lane
Savoy Pier
Waterloo Bridge
Thames

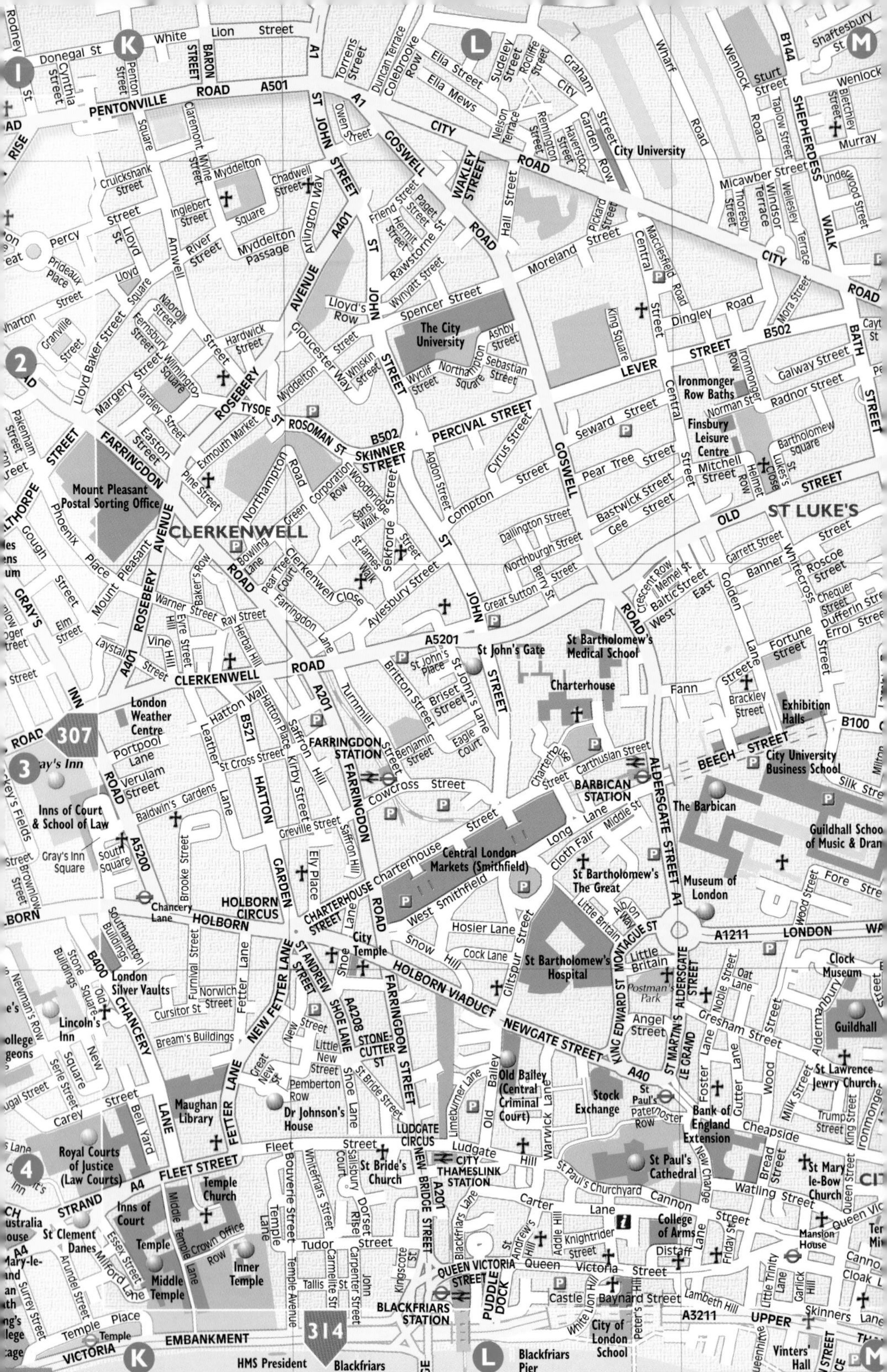

K
L
M
I
2
3
4
307
314
Rodney
Donegal St
White Lion Street
Cynthia Street
Penton Street
BARON STREET
PENTONVILLE ROAD A501
A1
Torrens Street
Duncan Terrace
Colebrooke Row
Elia Street
Elia Mews
Sudeley Street
Rocliffe Street
Graham
Wharf Road
Wenlock
Sturt Street
B144
Shaftesbury St
Wenlock
Bletchley Street
Murray
RISE
Claremont Square
Mylne Street
Myddelton Square
Chadwell Street
Owen St
ST JOHN STREET
GOSWELL
CITY ROAD
Nelson Terrace
Remington Street
Haverstock Street
City Garden Row
City University
Taplow Street
SHEPHERDESS WALK
Cruickshank Street
Inglebert Street
Arlington Way
Friend Street
Paget Street
Hermit Street
Rawstorne St
WAKLEY STREET
Hall Street
Pickard Street
Micawber Street
Thoresby Street
Windsor Terrace
Wellesley Terrace
Underwood Street
Percy Street
Lloyd Street
Amwell Street
River Street
Myddelton Passage
A401
AVENUE
Wynyatt Street
Moreland Street
Central Street
Macclesfield Road
CITY ROAD
Prideaux Place
Lloyd Square
Wharton Street
Granville Street
Naoroji Street
Fernsbury Street
Wilmington Square
Hardwick Street
Lloyd Baker Street
Margery Street
Yardley Street
Lloyd's Row
Gloucester Way
Whiskin Street
Spencer Street
The City University
Ashby Street
Sebastian Street
Northampton Square
Wyclif Street
King Square
Dingley Road
B502
BATH STREET
Mora Street
Galway Street
Radnor Street
LEVER STREET
Ironmonger Row
Ironmonger Row Baths
Norman St
Finsbury Leisure Centre
Bartholomew Square
Pakenham Street
Easton Street
ROSEBERY
TYSOE ST
Myddelton
ROSOMAN ST
B502
SKINNER STREET
PERCIVAL STREET
Seward Street
Cyrus Street
Pear Tree Street
Mitchell Street
Helmet Row
St Luke's Close
STREET
FARRINGDON
Mount Pleasant Postal Sorting Office
Exmouth Market
Pine Street
Northampton Road
Corporation Row
Woodbridge Street
Agdon Street
Compton
Bastwick Street
Gee Street
OLD STREET
ST LUKE'S
Phoenix Place
CLERKENWELL
AVENUE
Mount Pleasant
Bowling Lane
Pear Tree Court
Sans Walk
St James Walk
Sekforde Street
GOSWELL ROAD
Dallington Street
Northburgh Street
Garrett Street
Banner Street
Roscoe Street
Whitecross Street
Golden Lane
Gough Street
GRAY'S INN ROAD
Elm Street
ROSEBERY AVENUE
Baker's Row
Clerkenwell Close
Aylesbury Street
ST JOHN STREET
Great Sutton Street
Berry St
Crescent Row
Memel St
Baltic Street East
Baltic Street West
Chequer Street
Dufferin Street
Errol Street
Warner Street
Ray Street
Eyre Street Hill
Herbal Hill
Farringdon Lane
Vine Hill
Laystall Street
A401
CLERKENWELL ROAD
A5201
St John's Gate
St Bartholomew's Medical School
Fortune Street
Fann Street
Brackley Street
Exhibition Halls
B100
London Weather Centre
Hatton Wall
Hatton Place
A201
Turnmill Street
Britton Street
St John's Place
Briset Street
St John's Lane
Charterhouse
Eagle Court
Benjamin Street
Portpool Lane
Verulam Street
Leather Lane
B521
St Cross Street
HATTON GARDEN
Saffron Hill
Kirby Street
FARRINGDON STATION
FARRINGDON ROAD
Cowcross Street
Charterhouse Street
Carthusian Street
BARBICAN STATION
ALDERSGATE STREET A1
BEECH STREET
City University Business School
Silk Street
The Barbican
Gray's Inn
Inns of Court & School of Law
Baldwin's Gardens
Greville Street
Saffron Hill
Ely Place
Central London Markets (Smithfield)
Long Lane
Cloth Fair
Middle St
St Bartholomew's The Great
Guildhall School of Music & Drama
Gray's Inn Square
South Square
A5200
Brooke Street
Chancery Lane
HOLBORN CIRCUS
CHARTERHOUSE STREET
West Smithfield
Little Britain
Albion Way
Museum of London
Fore Street
Wood Street
HOLBORN
Southampton Buildings
Furnival Street
Fetter Lane
City Temple
Shoe Lane
Hosier Lane
Cock Lane
Giltspur Street
St Bartholomew's Hospital
MONTAGUE ST
A1211 LONDON WALL
Clock Museum
Stone Buildings
B400
London Silver Vaults
Norwich Street
NEW FETTER LANE
ST ANDREW STREET
HOLBORN VIADUCT
Snow Hill
Little Britain
Postman's Park
Noble Street
Oat Lane
Old Square
Lincoln's Inn
Cursitor St
Bream's Buildings
New Street
Little New Street
SHOE LANE
A4208
STONECUTTER ST
FARRINGDON STREET
NEWGATE STREET
KING EDWARD ST
Angel Street
ST MARTIN'S LE GRAND
Gresham Street
Aldermanbury
Guildhall
New Square
CHANCERY LANE
Great New Street
Pemberton Row
St Bride Street
Limeburner Lane
Old Bailey
Old Bailey (Central Criminal Court)
Warwick Lane
A40
Stock Exchange
St Paul's
Paternoster Row
Foster Lane
Gutter Lane
Milk Street
St Lawrence Jewry Church
Ironmonger
Serle Street
Carey Street
Bell Yard
Maughan Library
FETTER LANE
Dr Johnson's House
LUDGATE CIRCUS
Bank of England Extension
Cheapside
Trump Street
King Street
Royal Courts of Justice (Law Courts)
Fleet Street
Whitefriars Street
Salisbury Court
St Bride's Church
NEW BRIDGE STREET
Ludgate Hill
CITY THAMESLINK STATION
St Paul's Cathedral
New Change
Bread Street
St Mary le-Bow Church
Queen Street
A4
FLEET STREET
Temple Church
Bouverie Street
Dorset Rise
A201
Carter Lane
St Paul's Churchyard
Cannon Street
Watling Street
STRAND
Inns of Court
Middle Temple Lane
Temple Lane
College of Arms
Queen Victoria Street
Australia House
St Clement Danes
Essex Street
Crown Office Row
Tudor Street
Carmelite Str
Carpenter Street
John Street
Kingscote St
Blackfriars Lane
St Andrew's Hill
Addle Hill
Knightrider Street
Distaff Lane
Friday St
Mansion House
Little Trinity Lane
Garlick Hill
Cannon
Cloak Lane
A4
St Mary-le-Strand
Arundel Street
Milford Lane
Temple
Middle Temple
Inner Temple
Temple Avenue
Tallis St
QUEEN VICTORIA STREET
PUDDLE DOCK
Castle Baynard Street
White Lion Hill
Peter's Hill
Lambeth Hill
Surrey Street
King's College
Temple Place
Temple
EMBANKMENT
VICTORIA
BLACKFRIARS STATION
City of London School
A3211 UPPER
Queenhithe
Skinners Lane
Vintners' Hall
HMS President
HQS Wellington
Blackfriars Millennium Pier
Blackfriars Pier

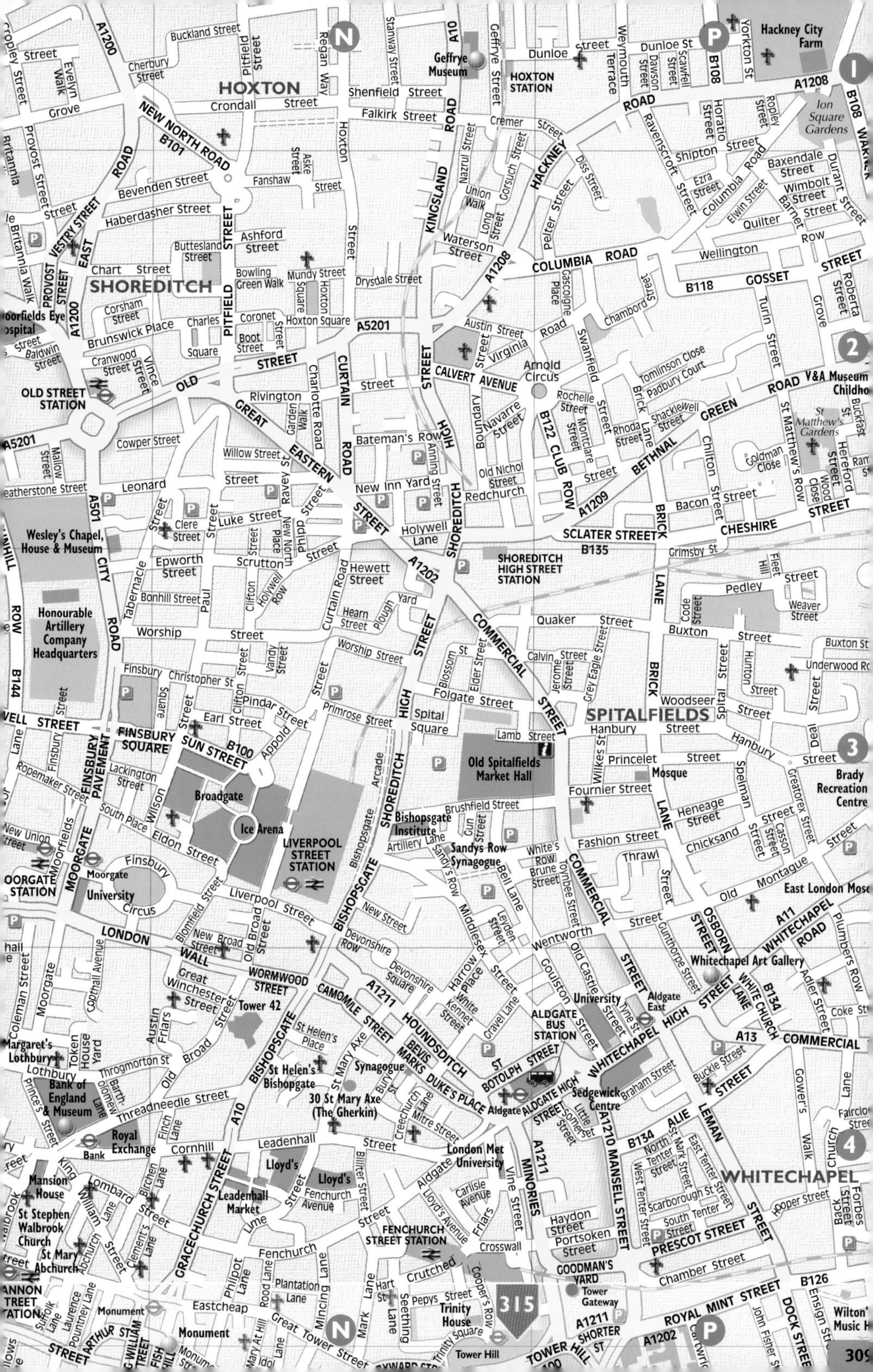
HOXTON
SHOREDITCH
SPITALFIELDS
WHITECHAPEL
Hackney City Farm
Ion Square Gardens
Geffrye Museum
HOXTON STATION
OLD STREET STATION
Moorfields Eye Hospital
Wesley's Chapel, House & Museum
Honourable Artillery Company Headquarters
SHOREDITCH HIGH STREET STATION
Arnold Circus
V&A Museum of Childhood
St Matthew's Gardens
Old Spitalfields Market Hall
Mosque
Brady Recreation Centre
Bishopsgate Institute
Sandys Row Synagogue
Broadgate
Ice Arena
LIVERPOOL STREET STATION
MOORGATE STATION
Moorgate University
Finsbury Circus
East London Mosque
Whitechapel Art Gallery
Aldgate East
ALDGATE BUS STATION
University
Sedgewick Centre
Tower 42
St Helen's Bishopsgate
Synagogue
30 St Mary Axe (The Gherkin)
Bank of England & Museum
Royal Exchange
Bank
Lloyd's
Leadenhall Market
London Met University
Aldgate
Mansion House
St Stephen Walbrook Church
St Mary Abchurch
CANNON STREET STATION
Monument
FENCHURCH STREET STATION
Trinity House
Tower Hill
Tower Gateway
Wilton's Music Hall
GOODMAN'S YARD
KINGSLAND ROAD
HACKNEY ROAD
NEW NORTH ROAD
CITY ROAD
OLD STREET
GREAT EASTERN STREET
CURTAIN ROAD
SHOREDITCH HIGH STREET
COLUMBIA ROAD
BETHNAL GREEN ROAD
COMMERCIAL STREET
BRICK LANE
BISHOPSGATE
LONDON WALL
MOORGATE
FINSBURY PAVEMENT
HOUNDSDITCH
WHITECHAPEL HIGH STREET
WHITECHAPEL ROAD
COMMERCIAL ROAD
LEMAN STREET
MANSELL STREET
MINORIES
GRACECHURCH STREET
ROYAL MINT STREET
PRESCOT STREET
DOCK STREET
OSBORN STREET
SCLATER STREET
CHESHIRE STREET
GOSSET STREET
CALVERT AVENUE
CAMOMILE STREET
WORMWOOD STREET
DUKE'S PLACE
BEVIS MARKS
ST BOTOLPH STREET
ALDGATE HIGH STREET
SUN STREET
FINSBURY SQUARE
A1200
A10
A1208
A5201
A501
A1202
A1209
A1211
A11
A13
A1210
B101
B100
B108
B118
B122
B134
B135
B144
B126
315

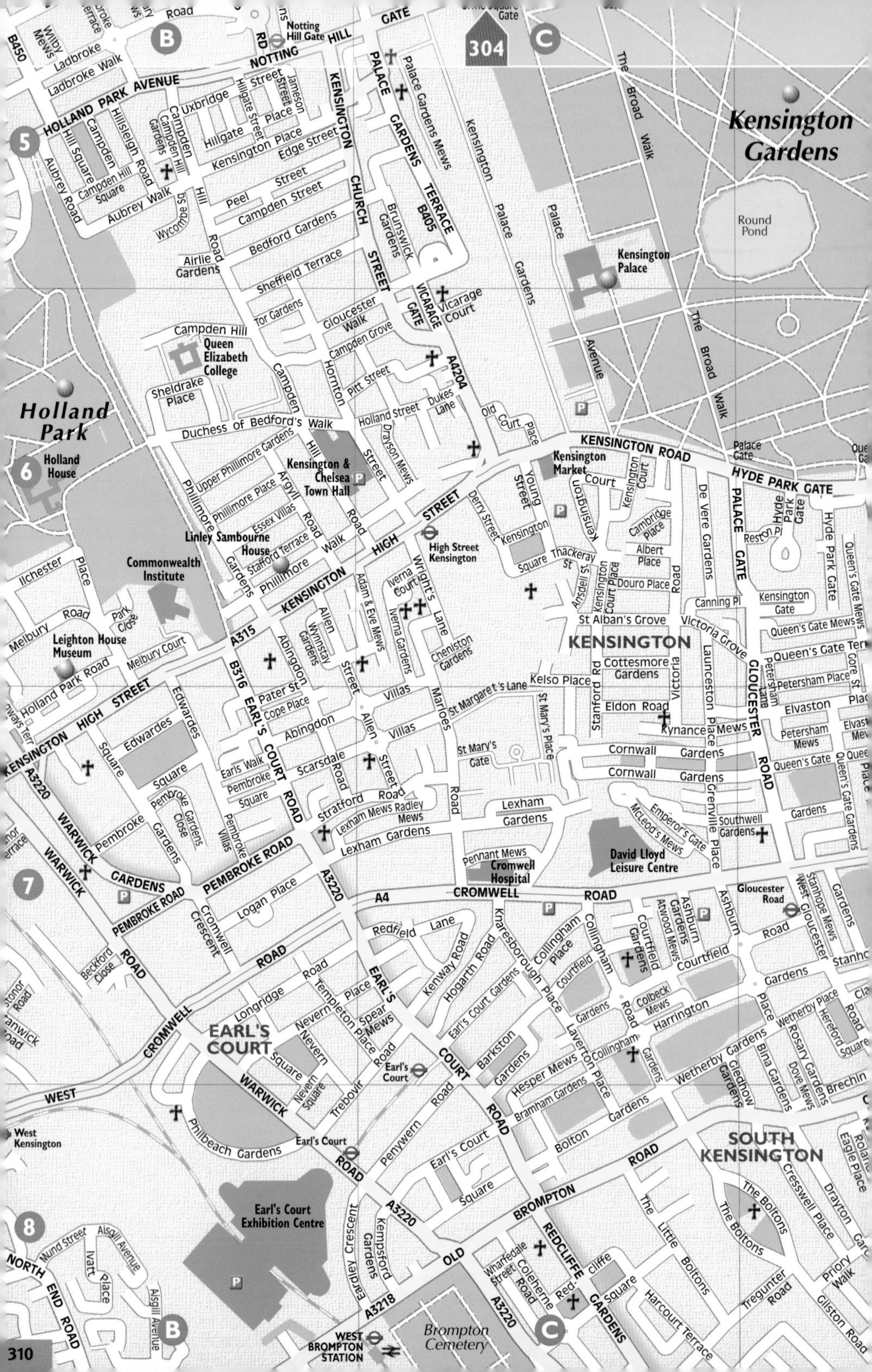

304
Kensington Gardens
Round Pond
The Broad Walk
Kensington Palace
Holland Park
Holland House
Notting Hill Gate
Notting Hill Gate
Kensington Church Street
Kensington Palace Gardens
Palace Gardens Terrace
Holland Park Avenue
Ladbroke Walk
Campden Hill Road
Campden Hill Square
Aubrey Walk
Aubrey Road
Peel Street
Campden Street
Bedford Gardens
Sheffield Terrace
Airlie Gardens
Tor Gardens
Gloucester Walk
Vicarage Gate
Vicarage Court
Queen Elizabeth College
Campden Hill
Sheldrake Place
Duchess of Bedford's Walk
Hornton Street
Holland Street
Kensington & Chelsea Town Hall
Phillimore Gardens
Phillimore Walk
Linley Sambourne House
Commonwealth Institute
Ilchester Place
Melbury Road
Melbury Court
Leighton House Museum
Holland Park Road
Kensington High Street
High Street Kensington
Kensington Road
Kensington Market
Hyde Park Gate
Palace Gate
De Vere Gardens
Kensington Square
Thackeray St
Young Street
Derry Street
Kensington Court
Kensington Court Place
St Alban's Grove
KENSINGTON
Victoria Grove
Launceston Place
Gloucester Road
Queen's Gate
Queen's Gate Mews
Queen's Gate Terrace
Cottesmore Gardens
Kelso Place
St Margaret's Lane
Eldon Road
Stanford Rd
Kynance Mews
Cornwall Gardens
Petersham Mews
Elvaston Place
Abingdon Road
Earl's Court Road
Pembroke Road
Pembroke Gardens
Edwardes Square
Scarsdale Villas
Allen Street
Marloes Road
Lexham Gardens
Stratford Road
St Mary's Gate
Emperor's Gate
McLeod's Mews
Grenville Place
Southwell Gardens
David Lloyd Leisure Centre
Cromwell Hospital
Pennant Mews
Cromwell Road
Cromwell Crescent
Warwick Gardens
Warwick Road
Logan Place
Beckford Close
Redfield Lane
Kenway Road
Hogarth Road
Knaresborough Place
Collingham Place
Collingham Road
Courtfield Gardens
Courtfield Road
Ashburn Gardens
Ashburn Place
Atwood Mews
Gloucester Road
Stanhope Gardens
Harrington Gardens
Wetherby Gardens
Wetherby Place
Hereford Square
Rosary Gardens
Bina Gardens
Dove Mews
Gledhow Gardens
Laverton Place
Hesper Mews
Barkston Gardens
Bramham Gardens
Earl's Court Gardens
EARL'S COURT
Earl's Court
Nevern Square
Nevern Place
Templeton Place
Trebovir Road
Spear Mews
Longridge Road
Philbeach Gardens
West Cromwell Road
West Kensington
Earl's Court Exhibition Centre
Penywern Road
Earl's Court Square
Bolton Gardens
Old Brompton Road
Redcliffe Gardens
Redcliffe Square
Coleherne Road
Wharfedale Street
Kempsford Gardens
Eardley Crescent
West Brompton Station
Brompton Cemetery
SOUTH KENSINGTON
The Boltons
The Little Boltons
Cresswell Place
Drayton Gardens
Tregunter Road
Harcourt Terrace
Gilston Road
Priory Walk
North End Road
Mund Street
Aisgill Avenue
Ivatt Place
A4
A315
A3220
A3218
A4204
B316
B405
B450

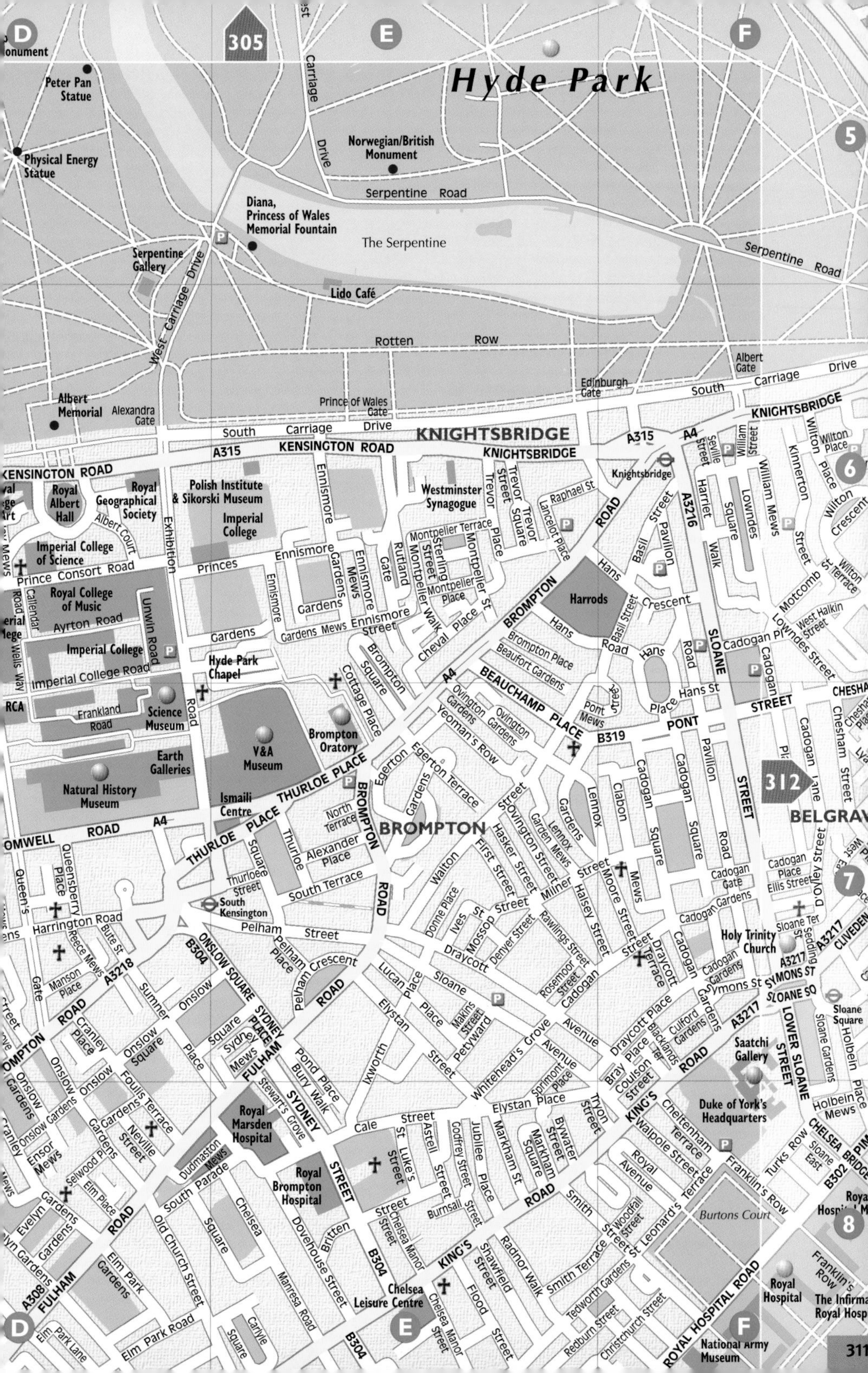
D
305
E
F
Hyde Park
5
6
7
8
Peter Pan Statue
Physical Energy Statue
Norwegian/British Monument
Serpentine Road
Diana, Princess of Wales Memorial Fountain
The Serpentine
Serpentine Gallery
West Carriage Drive
Carriage Drive
Lido Café
Rotten Row
Albert Gate
South Carriage Drive
Edinburgh Gate
Prince of Wales Gate
Albert Memorial
Alexandra Gate
KNIGHTSBRIDGE
A315
KENSINGTON ROAD
A4
Knightsbridge
Royal Albert Hall
Royal Geographical Society
Polish Institute & Sikorski Museum
Imperial College
Westminster Synagogue
Imperial College of Science
Prince Consort Road
Royal College of Music
Ayrton Road
Imperial College Road
Frankland Road
Science Museum
Earth Galleries
Natural History Museum
V&A Museum
Ismaili Centre
Hyde Park Chapel
Brompton Oratory
Harrods
Exhibition Road
Ennismore Gardens
Ennismore Mews
Ennismore Street
Princes Gardens
Montpelier Terrace
Montpelier Street
Montpelier Walk
Montpelier Place
Rutland Gate
Trevor Street
Trevor Square
Trevor Place
Raphael St
Lancelot Place
BROMPTON ROAD
Basil Street
Hans Crescent
Hans Road
Hans Place
Hans St
Pavilion Road
A3216
SLOANE STREET
Cadogan Pl
Lowndes Square
Lowndes Street
William Mews
Kinnerton Street
Wilton Place
Wilton Crescent
Motcomb St
West Halkin Street
BEAUCHAMP PLACE
Brompton Square
Cottage Place
Cheval Place
Brompton Place
Beaufort Gardens
Ovington Gardens
Yeoman's Row
Egerton Gardens
Egerton Terrace
Pont Street
B319
CHESHAM
Chesham Street
Cadogan Lane
312
BELGRAVIA
BROMPTON
THURLOE PLACE
Thurloe Square
Thurloe Street
Alexander Place
North Terrace
South Terrace
South Kensington
Pelham Street
Pelham Place
Pelham Crescent
CROMWELL ROAD
Queensberry Place
Harrington Road
Reece Mews
Bute St
Manson Place
A3218
B304
ONSLOW SQUARE
SYDNEY PLACE
FULHAM ROAD
Walton Street
Lennox Gardens
Lennox Garden Mews
Milner Street
Moore Street
Halsey Street
Cadogan Square
Clabon Mews
Cadogan Gate
Cadogan Gardens
Draycott Place
Draycott Terrace
Sloane Avenue
Elystan Place
Elystan Street
Whitehead's Grove
Holy Trinity Church
A3217
SLOANE SQ
Sloane Square
LOWER SLOANE STREET
Saatchi Gallery
Duke of York's Headquarters
KING'S ROAD
Royal Marsden Hospital
Royal Brompton Hospital
Chelsea Leisure Centre
Burtons Court
Royal Hospital
ROYAL HOSPITAL ROAD
National Army Museum
The Infirmary Royal Hospital
CHELSEA BRIDGE
Franklin's Row
Old Church Street
Elm Park Road
Elm Park Gardens
Manresa Road
Dovehouse Street
Oakley Street
Smith Street
Flood Street
A308

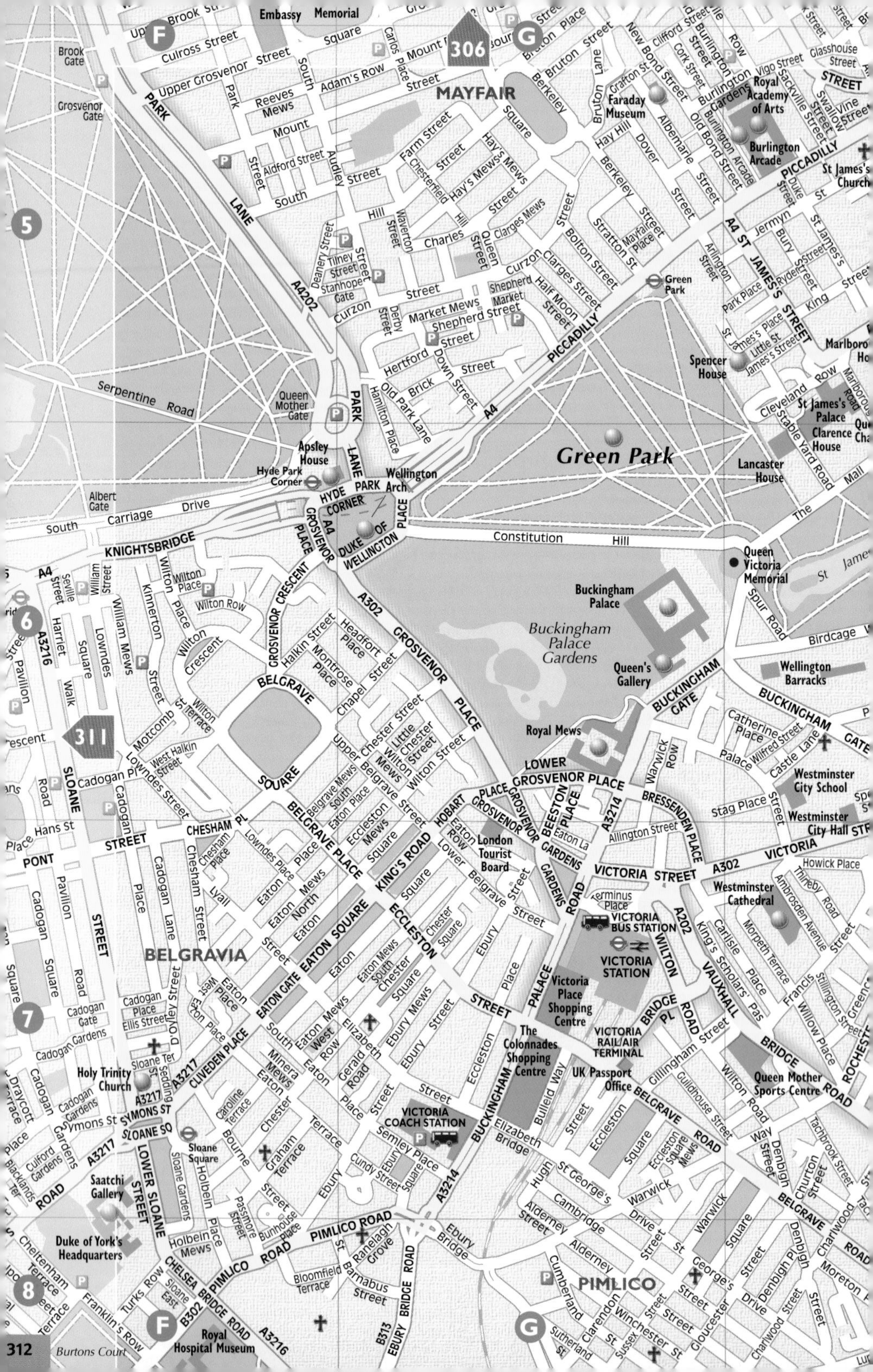

F
G
306
311
5
6
7
8
MAYFAIR
BELGRAVIA
PIMLICO
Green Park
Buckingham Palace Gardens
Buckingham Palace
Queen's Gallery
Royal Mews
Queen Victoria Memorial
Wellington Barracks
Westminster City School
Westminster City Hall
Westminster Cathedral
Queen Mother Sports Centre
Lancaster House
St James's Palace
Clarence House
Spencer House
Royal Academy of Arts
Burlington Arcade
Faraday Museum
St James's Church
Apsley House
Hyde Park Corner
Wellington Arch
Queen Mother Gate
Albert Gate
Brook Gate
Grosvenor Gate
Serpentine Road
South Carriage Drive
Constitution Hill
KNIGHTSBRIDGE
PICCADILLY
PARK LANE
HYDE PARK CORNER
DUKE OF WELLINGTON PLACE
GROSVENOR PLACE
GROSVENOR CRESCENT
BELGRAVE SQUARE
BELGRAVE PLACE
EATON SQUARE
EATON GATE
KING'S ROAD
ECCLESTON STREET
LOWER GROSVENOR PLACE
BUCKINGHAM GATE
BUCKINGHAM PALACE ROAD
VICTORIA STREET
VAUXHALL BRIDGE ROAD
WILTON ROAD
BELGRAVE ROAD
PIMLICO ROAD
CHELSEA BRIDGE ROAD
LOWER SLOANE STREET
SLOANE SQ
SLOANE STREET
PONT STREET
CHESHAM PL
CLIVEDEN PLACE
SYMONS ST
EBURY BRIDGE ROAD
London Tourist Board
VICTORIA BUS STATION
VICTORIA STATION
Victoria Place Shopping Centre
The Colonnades Shopping Centre
VICTORIA RAIL/AIR TERMINAL
UK Passport Office
VICTORIA COACH STATION
Holy Trinity Church
Saatchi Gallery
Duke of York's Headquarters
Royal Hospital Museum
Sloane Square
Green Park
Burtons Court

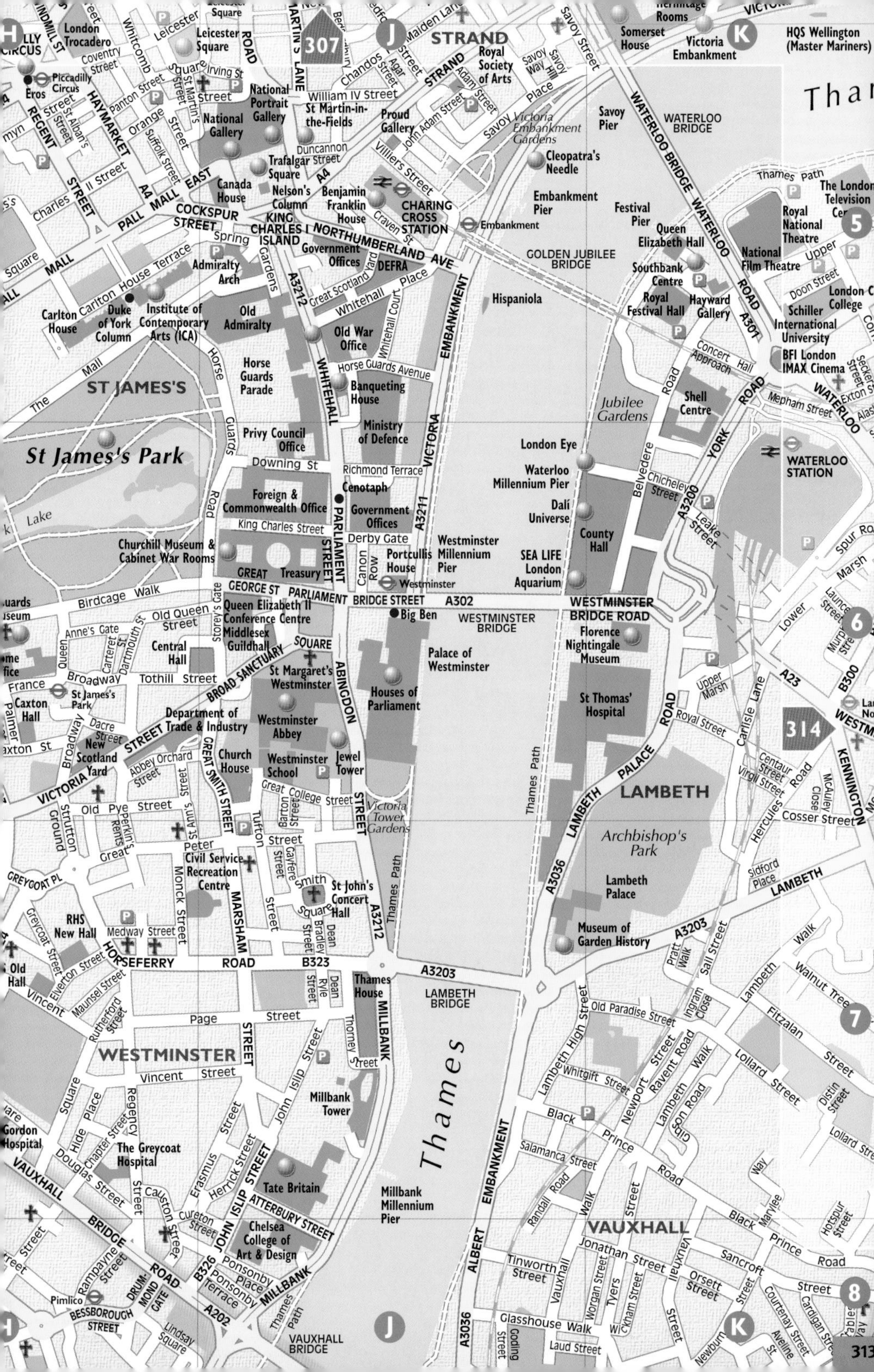

H
J
K
307
314
5
6
7
8
STRAND
Thames
London Trocadero
Leicester Square
Piccadilly Circus
Eros
Coventry Street
Whitcomb Street
Irving St
St Martin's Street
Panton Street
Orange Street
Suffolk Street
Haymarket
Regent Street
St Alban's Street
Jermyn Street
Charles II Street
Pall Mall East
Pall Mall
Cockspur Street
National Portrait Gallery
National Gallery
St Martin-in-the-Fields
William IV Street
Duncannon Street
Trafalgar Square
Canada House
Nelson's Column
Benjamin Franklin House
Proud Gallery
Chandos Place
Agar Street
Maiden Lane
Bedford Street
Adam Street
John Adam Street
Villiers Street
Craven St
Charing Cross Station
Royal Society of Arts
Savoy Way
Savoy Hill
Savoy Place
Savoy Street
Victoria Embankment Gardens
Somerset House
Hermitage Rooms
Victoria Embankment
HQS Wellington (Master Mariners)
Savoy Pier
Waterloo Bridge
Cleopatra's Needle
Embankment Pier
Embankment
Golden Jubilee Bridge
Festival Pier
Queen Elizabeth Hall
Southbank Centre
Royal Festival Hall
Hayward Gallery
National Film Theatre
Royal National Theatre
The London Television Centre
Thames Path
Upper Ground
Doon Street
London College
Schiller International University
BFI London IMAX Cinema
Concert Hall Approach
Waterloo Road
Mepham Street
Exton Street
Secker Street
Waterloo Station
Shell Centre
York Road
Jubilee Gardens
London Eye
Waterloo Millennium Pier
Dalí Universe
County Hall
SEA LIFE London Aquarium
Belvedere Road
Chicheley Street
Leake Street
Spur Road
Lower Marsh
Launcelot Street
Westminster Bridge Road
Florence Nightingale Museum
St Thomas' Hospital
Upper Marsh
Royal Street
Carlisle Lane
Lambeth Palace Road
Lambeth
Archbishop's Park
Lambeth Palace
Museum of Garden History
Centaur Street
Virgil Street
Hercules Road
McAulley Close
Cosser Street
Kennington Road
Sidford Place
Lambeth Road
Pratt Walk
Sail Street
Walnut Tree Walk
Fitzalan Street
Lollard Street
Distin Street
Old Paradise Street
Ingram Close
Lambeth High Street
Whitgift Street
Newport Street
Ravent Road
Lambeth Walk
Gibson Road
Black Prince Road
Salamanca Street
Randall Road
Vauxhall Walk
Vauxhall
Marylee Way
Hotspur Street
Tinworth Street
Jonathan Street
Sancroft Street
Orsett Street
Courtenay Street
Cardigan Street
Worgan Street
Tyers Street
Wickham Street
Vauxhall Street
Glasshouse Walk
Goding Street
Laud Street
Newburn Street
Aveline St
Tablet Way
Albert Embankment
A3036
A3203
Lambeth Bridge
Vauxhall Bridge
Thames Path
Millbank Millennium Pier
Admiralty Arch
Spring Gardens
King Charles I Island
Northumberland Ave
Government Offices
DEFRA
Great Scotland Yard
Whitehall Place
Whitehall Court
Carlton House Terrace
Carlton House
Duke of York Column
Institute of Contemporary Arts (ICA)
Old Admiralty
Old War Office
Horse Guards Avenue
Banqueting House
Horse Guards Parade
Horse Guards Road
Whitehall
The Mall
St James's
St James's Park
Lake
Privy Council Office
Ministry of Defence
Victoria Embankment
Hispaniola
Downing St
Richmond Terrace
Cenotaph
Foreign & Commonwealth Office
King Charles Street
Government Offices
Derby Gate
Churchill Museum & Cabinet War Rooms
Great George St
Treasury
Parliament Street
Canon Row
Portcullis House
Westminster
Westminster Millennium Pier
Birdcage Walk
Guards Museum
Queen Elizabeth II Conference Centre
Middlesex Guildhall
Bridge Street
Westminster Bridge
Big Ben
Palace of Westminster
Houses of Parliament
Old Queen Street
Queen Anne's Gate
Carteret St
Dartmouth St
Storey's Gate
Central Hall
Tothill Street
Broad Sanctuary
Parliament Square
St Margaret's Westminster
Westminster Abbey
Abingdon Street
Jewel Tower
Westminster School
Broadway
St James's Park
Caxton Hall
Petty France
Home Office
Palmer Street
Caxton St
Dacre Street
Department of Trade & Industry
New Scotland Yard
Victoria Street
Abbey Orchard Street
Great Smith Street
Church House
Great College Street
Barton Street
Victoria Tower Gardens
Strutton Ground
Old Pye Street
Perkin's Rents
Great Peter Street
St Ann's Street
Tufton Street
Civil Service Recreation Centre
Gayfere Street
Smith Square
St John's Concert Hall
Lord North Street
Monck Street
Marsham Street
Greycoat Pl
Greycoat Street
RHS New Hall
Old Hall
Medway Street
Horseferry Road
B323
A3212
Dean Bradley Street
Dean Ryle Street
Thames House
Millbank
Thorney Street
Elverton Street
Maunsel Street
Vincent Square
Rutherford Street
Page Street
Westminster
Marsham Street
John Islip Street
Millbank Tower
Vincent Street
Regency Street
Hide Place
Chapter Street
The Greycoat Hospital
Gordon Hospital
Douglas Street
Erasmus Street
Herrick Street
Caulston Street
Cureton Street
Tate Britain
Atterbury Street
Chelsea College of Art & Design
Vauxhall Bridge Road
Rampayne Street
Drummond Gate
Ponsonby Place
Ponsonby Terrace
B326
A202
Pimlico
Bessborough Street
Lindsay Square

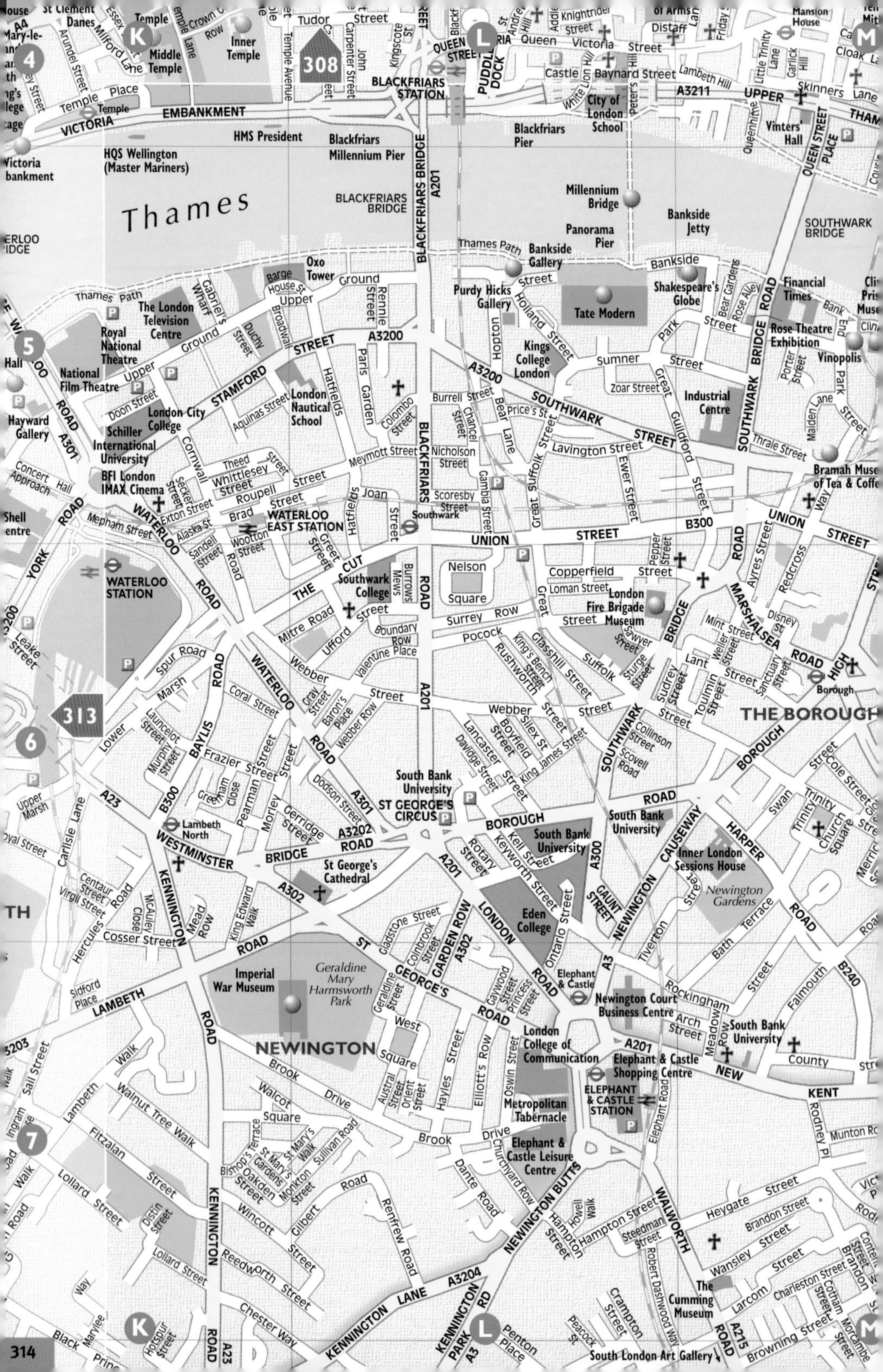
Thames
St Clement Danes
Temple
Middle Temple
Inner Temple
308
Tudor Street
Temple Avenue
Carpenter Street
John Street
Kingscote St
Temple Place
EMBANKMENT
VICTORIA
Victoria Embankment
BLACKFRIARS STATION
QUEEN VICTORIA STREET
PUDDLE DOCK
Castle Baynard Street
City of London School
Knightrider Street
Distaff Lane
Mansion House
Cloak Lane
Skinners Lane
UPPER THAMES
A3211
Vinters' Hall
QUEEN STREET PLACE
Lambeth Hill
White Lion Hill
Peter's Hill
Little Trinity Lane
Garlick Hill
Queenhithe
HMS President
HQS Wellington (Master Mariners)
Blackfriars Millennium Pier
BLACKFRIARS BRIDGE
A201
Blackfriars Pier
Millennium Bridge
Panorama Pier
Bankside Jetty
SOUTHWARK BRIDGE
WATERLOO BRIDGE
Thames Path
Bankside Gallery
Bankside
Tate Modern
Shakespeare's Globe
Financial Times
Bear Gardens
Rose Alley
Rose Theatre Exhibition
Vinopolis
Clink Prison Museum
Oxo Tower
Barge House St
Upper Ground
Gabriel's Wharf
Rennie Street
The London Television Centre
Royal National Theatre
National Film Theatre
Hayward Gallery
Duchy Street
Broadwall
STAMFORD STREET
A3200
London Nautical School
Paris Garden
Hatfields
Colombo Street
London City College
Schiller International University
Aquinas Street
Doon Street
BFI London IMAX Cinema
Cornwall Road
Theed Street
Whittlesey Street
Roupell Street
Meymott Street
Secker Street
Exton Street
Alaska St
Brad Street
WATERLOO EAST STATION
Wootton Street
Mepham Street
Concert Hall Approach
Shell Centre
YORK ROAD
WATERLOO ROAD
A301
WATERLOO STATION
Leake Street
Sandell Street
Greet Street
THE CUT
Southwark College
Burrows Mews
Joan Street
Southwark
BLACKFRIARS ROAD
Purdy Hicks Gallery
Holland Street
Hopton Street
Kings College London
Sumner Street
Park Street
Zoar Street
Great Guildford Street
Industrial Centre
SOUTHWARK STREET
Burrell Street
Chancel Street
Bear Lane
Price's St
Nicholson Street
Lavington Street
Ewer Street
Great Suffolk Street
Gambia Street
Scoresby Street
Thrale Street
Porter Street
Maiden Lane
Bramah Museum of Tea & Coffee
Redcross Way
UNION STREET
B300
Ayres Street
Nelson Square
Copperfield Street
Loman Street
Pepper Street
London Fire Brigade Museum
Surrey Row
Pocock Street
Mitre Road
Ufford Street
Boundary Row
Valentine Place
Webber Street
Spur Road
Marsh
BAYLIS ROAD
Coral Street
Gray Street
Baron's Place
Webber Row
King's Bench Street
Rushworth Street
Glasshill Street
Sawyer Street
Suffolk Street
Sturge Street
MARSHALSEA ROAD
Mint Street
Weller Street
Disney St
Lant Street
Sudrey Street
Toulmin Street
Sanctuary Street
Borough
HIGH
THE BOROUGH
313
Lower Marsh
Launcelot Street
Murphy Street
Frazier Street
Greenham Close
Pearman Street
Morley Street
Gerridge Street
Dodson Street
Boyfield Street
Silex St
King James Street
Lancaster Street
Davidge Street
Collinson Street
Scovell Road
SOUTHWARK BRIDGE ROAD
South Bank University
ST GEORGE'S CIRCUS
BOROUGH ROAD
Cole Street
Trinity Church Square
Swan Street
HARPER ROAD
Merrick Square
Upper Marsh
Carlisle Lane
Royal Street
Lambeth North
WESTMINSTER BRIDGE ROAD
A3202
A302
B300
Rotary Street
Keyworth Street
Kell Street
South Bank University
A300
GAUNT STREET
NEWINGTON CAUSEWAY
Inner London Sessions House
Newington Gardens
St George's Cathedral
Centaur Street
Virgil Street
Hercules Road
McAuley Close
KENNINGTON ROAD
Mead Row
King Edward Walk
Cosser Street
Gladstone Street
Colnbrook Street
GARDEN ROW
A302
LONDON ROAD
Eden College
Ontario Street
Tiverton Street
Bath Terrace
B240
Falmouth Road
Rockingham Street
Sidford Place
LAMBETH ROAD
Imperial War Museum
Geraldine Mary Harmsworth Park
ST GEORGE'S ROAD
Geraldine Street
West Square
Gaywood Street
Princess Street
Elephant & Castle
Newington Court Business Centre
Arch Street
Meadow Row
South Bank University
County Street
NEW KENT
NEWINGTON
London College of Communication
Elephant & Castle Shopping Centre
ELEPHANT & CASTLE STATION
Metropolitan Tabernacle
Elephant & Castle Leisure Centre
A3203
Sail Street
Ingram Close
Lambeth Walk
Walnut Tree Walk
Brook Drive
Walcot Square
Austral Street
Orient Street
Hayles Street
Elliott's Row
Oswin Street
Churchyard Row
Elephant Road
Rodney Pl
Munton Road
Bishop's Terrace
St Mary's Gardens
St Mary's Walk
Sullivan Road
Oakden Street
Monkton Street
Fitzalan Street
Lollard Street
Distin Street
Wincott Street
Gilbert Road
Renfrew Road
Dante Road
NEWINGTON BUTTS
Hampton Street
Howell Walk
Steedman Street
Robert Dashwood Way
WALWORTH ROAD
Heygate Street
Brandon Street
Wansley Street
The Cumming Museum
Larcom Street
Charleston Street
Brandon Street
Cotham Street
Content Street
Reedworth Street
Chester Way
KENNINGTON LANE
A3204
KENNINGTON PARK RD
A3
Penton Place
Peacock St
Crampton Street
A215
Browning Street
Morecambe Street
South London Art Gallery
Hotspur Street
Black Prince
Marylee Way
A23
A4
Mary-le-Strand
Arundel Street
Milford Lane
Essex Street
Crown Office Row
Temple Lane
4
5
6
7
K
L
M

St Stephen Walbrook Church
St Mary Abchurch
Cannon Street Station
Monument
Fenchurch Street Station
Fenchurch Street
Plantation Lane
Mincing Lane
Mark Lane
Hart St
Crutched Friars
Pepys Street
Seething Lane
Trinity House
Trinity Square
Tower Hill
Cooper's Row
309
Haydon Street
Portsoken Street
Goodman's Yard
Tower Gateway
South Tenter Street
Prescot Street
Chamber Street
Royal Mint Street
B126
Ensign Street
Wilton's Music Hall
Dock Street
Cartwright Street
John Fisher Street
A1202
Royal Mint Court
A1211
Shorter St
St George in the East
A1203
East Smithfield
Thomas More Street
Vaughan Way
Nesham St
London Commodity Exchange
St Katharine Docks
Mews Street
St Katharine's Way
Eastcheap
Great Tower Street
Byward Street
Philpot Lane
Rood Lane
St Mary At Hill
Idol Lane
Monument Street
Arthur St
King William Street
Fish Hill
Swan Lane
Lower Thames Street
Fishmonger's Hall
London Bridge Sports Centre
Custom House
All Hallows-by-the-Tower
Swan Lane Pier
London Bridge
Tower Stairs
Tower of London
A100
Tower Bridge Approach
St Katharine's Way
Thames Path
RNLI Lifeboat Station
Tower Millennium Pier
London Bridge City Pier
Golden Hinde
Montague Close
London Bridge Hospital
Tooley Street
HMS Belfast
Hay's Galleria
Duke Street Hill
Southwark Cathedral
Railway Approach
London Bridge Street
London Dungeon
London Bridge Station
Battle Bridge Lane
Southwark Crown Court
Tower Bridge
St Katharine Pier
Thames
A200
A3
Guy's Hospital
St Thomas Street
Britain at War Experience
A2205
Greater London Authority Headquarters (City Hall)
Potters Fields
Butler's Wharf Pier
Shad Thames
Horselydown Lane
Magdalen Street
Holyrood Street
Shand Street
Barnham Street
Queen Elizabeth Street
Gainsford Street
Curlew Street
Maguire Street
Design Museum
Weston Street
Mellor Street
Snowsfields
Crucifix Lane
London City Mission
Druid Street
Tower Bridge Road
Lafone Street
Three Oak Lane
Bermondsey Wall West
Providence Square
Jacob Street
Chambers Street
Mill Street
Wolseley Street
St Saviour's Dock
Newcomen Street
Crosby Row
Kirby Grove
Bermondsey Street
Fashion & Textile Museum
White's Grounds
Brunswick Court
Roper Lane
Guy Street
Porlock Street
Kipling Street
Leathermarket Gardens
Tyers Gate
A2198
Leathermarket Street
Tanner Street
Dockhead
George Row
John Felton Road
Sterry Street
Long Lane
Hankey Place
Staple Street
London Glass Blowing Workshop
Morocco St
Lamb Walk
City Walk
Druid Street
Sweeney Crescent
Jamaica Road
Scott Lidgett Crescent
Manciple Street
Tabard Garden
Tabard Street
Maltby Street
Millstream Road
Riley Road
Purbrook Street
B202
Abbey Street
Marine Street
Old Jamaica Road
Enid Street
Dover Street
Pardoner Street
Wild's Rents
Decima Street
Cluny Place
The Grange
Grange Walk
Neckinger
Frean Street
Thurland Road
Spurgeon Street
Law Street
Rothsay Street
Grange Walk
Fendall St
Bermondsey Town Hall
Spa Road
Burbage Close
Deverell Street
Potier Street
Alice Street
A2206
Grange Road
Grange Yard
Vauban Street
Dunlop Place
Rouel Road
Dockley Road
Lucey Road
Burge Street
Prioress Street
Tower Bridge Road
Webb Street
Swan Mead
Page's Walk
Crimscott Street
Bacon Grove
Bartholomew Street
New Kent Road
Aberdour Street
Leroy Street
Guinness Square
Alscot Road
Cadbury Way
Henley Drive
Yalding Road
Linsey Street
Macks Road
A2
Curtis Street
Willow Walk
Alscot Way
Searles Road
John Maurice Close
Henshaw Street
Chatham Street
Darwin Street
Mason Street
Townsend Street
Mandela Way
Setchell Road
Southwark Park Road
Longley Street
Hillery Close
Barlow Street
Crail Row
Comus Place
Congreve Street
Old Kent Road
Hendre Road
Dunton Road
Fort Road
Balaclava Road
Alma Grove
Reverdy Road
Catesby Street
Elsted Street
Tatum Street
Halpin Place
Beckway Street
Flint Street
Orb Street
Dean's Buildings
Tisdall Place
Exon Street
Freeman St
East Street
Marcia Road
Mandela Way
B203
Milton Close
Chaucer Drive
Lynton Road
Bushwood Dr
Simms Road
Esmeralda Road
Welsford Street
Monnow Road

MAPS | INDEX

MAPS INDEX

MAPS | INDEX

MAPS | INDEX

MAPS INDEX

A

B

C

D

E

PICTURES

The Automobile Association would like to thank the following photographers, companies and picture libraries for their assistance in the preparation of this book.

Abbreviations for the picture credits are as follows: (t) top;
(b) bottom;
(l) left;
(r) right;
(c) centre;
(AA) AA World Travel Library.

2 AA/S McBride;
3t V&A Images;
3c AA/J Tims;
3b AA/J Tims;
4 AA/R Victor;
5 AA/J Tims;
6 AA/N Setchfield;
8 AA/R Mort;
9 AA/M Jourdan;
10 AA/J Tims;
11 Courtesy of the Landmark Hotel, London;
12l Britain on View/photolibrary.com;
12r AA/M Jourdan;
13 AA/S Montgomery;
14 AA/J Tims;
15t AA/M Jourdan;
15b Rune Hellestad/Corbis;
16 RFU/R Cheyne;
17l AA/N Setchfield;
17r AA/J Tims;
18 Liz Allen;
19l AP/PA Photos;
19r AA/R Strange;
20 ANDY RAIN/epa/Corbis;
21t Image Source/Corbis;
21b Pictorial Press Ltd/Alamy;
22 AA/J Tims;
23t AA/N Setchfield;
23b Rolf Richardson/Alamy;
24l Edward Parker/Alamy;
24r Rob Judges London/Alamy;
25 Private Collection/Bridgeman Art Library, London;
26 AA/P Kenward;
27t AA/S&O Mathews;
27b AA/T Woodcock;
28 British Library, London, UK/©British Library Board. All Rights Reserved/The Bridgeman Art Library;
29l The Lions of London, Jackson, Peter (1922-2003)/Private Collection/ © Look and Learn/The Bridgeman Art Library;
29r Bettmann/Corbis;
30 AA/R Strange;
31t Mary Evans Picture Library;
31b AA/S&O Mathews;
32 AA/P Kenward;
33t AA;
33b Giffard Stock/Alamy;
34 Angelo Hornak/Alamy;
35t Mary Evans Picture Library;
35b Trinity Mirror/Mirrorpix/Alamy;
36 Mary Evans Picture Library;
37t AA/M Jourdan;
37b Mary Evans Picture Library;
38 Mary Evans Picture Library;
39l AA/J Tims;
39r Popperfoto/Getty Images;
40 AA/S Montgomery;
41 AA/J Tims;
42 Digitalvision;
45 AA/J Tims;
48 AA/B Smith;
49 AA/M Jourdan;
50 AA/J Tims;
51 AA/J Tims;
52 AA/S Montgomery;
53t AA/J Tims;
53b AA/N Setchfield;
56 Britain on View/photolibrary.com;
57 AA;
62 Tony French/Alamy;
63 Alvey & Towers Picture Library/ Alamy;
65 AA/C Sawyer;
66 AA/M Jourdan;
70 AA/N Setchfield;
72 AA/S McBride;
73 AA/S Montgomery;
74 AA/B Smith;
75 AA/M Moody;
76 AA/J Tims;
77 AA/M Trelawny;
78 AA/R Turpin;
79 AA/S Montgomery;
80 AA/S Montgomery;
81 AA/M Jourdan;
82 AA/M Jourdan;
84 AA/J Tims;
86 AA/M Jourdan;
87 AA/M Jourdan;
89 AA/N Setchfield;
90 Courtesy of the Oxo Tower Restaurant;
92 London Bridge Hotel;
93 London Bridge Hotel;
96 AA/W Voysey;
100 Anthony Hatley/Alamy;
101 Geffrye Museum;
102 Holmes Garden Photos/Alamy;
103 Britain on View/photolibrary.com;
104 AA/J Tims;
105 AA/S McBride;
106 AA/R Strange;
107 AA/B Smith;
109l AA/R Strange;
109r AA/P Baker;
110 AA/J Tims;
111 AA/J Tims;
112 AA/S Montgomery;
114 photolibrary.com;
115 Britain on View/photolibrary.com;
116l AA/M Trelawny;
116r AA/S Montgomery;
118 AA/R Turpin;
119 AA/P Kenward;
120 AA/R Turpin;
122 Courtesy of Lanes Restaurant and Bar;
125 Courtesy of the Chamberlain Hotel;
128 AA/J Tims;
132 AA/J Tims;
133 AA/J Tims;
134 Helmet, from the Sutton Hoo Ship Burial, *c.* AD625–30 (iron & gilt bronze), Anglo-Saxon (7th century)/ British Museum, London, UK/The Bridgeman Art Library;
136 AA/G Wrona;
137l AA/J Tims;
137r AA/J Tims;
139 AA;
140 AA/R Victor;

141 AA/J Tims;
142 AA/M Jourdan;
143l AA/J Tims;
143r AA/J Tims;
144 AA/J Tims;
145 AA/M Jourdan;
146 AA/J Tims;
147 Adrian Chinery/Alamy;
148 Martin Charles;
149l Martin Charles;
149r Martin Charles;
150 AA/M Jourdan;
151 AA/M Jourdan;
152 AA/S Montgomery;
153 AA/S Montgomery;
154 AA/J Tims;
159 AA/J Tims;
161 Courtesy of The Sanctuary, London;
162 Courtesy of L'Escargot;
166 Courtesy of One Aldwych;
170 AA/J Tims;
174 AA/J Tims;
175 AA/J Tims;
176 AA/J Tims;
177l AA/J Tims;
177r Derry Moore/The Royal Collection © 2010 Her Majesty Queen Elizabeth II;
178 AA/J McMillan;
179 AA/J Tims;
180l AA/J Tims;
180r AA/J Tims;
181 AA/T Woodcock;
182 AA/J Tims;
184 AA/R Strange;
185 *Sunflowers,* 1889 (oil on canvas) by Vincent van Gogh (1853–90)/ Private Collection/Photo © Christie's Images/The Bridgeman Art Library;
186 *The Beach at Trouville,* 1870 by Claude Monet (1840–1926) National Gallery, London UK/Bridgeman Art Library;
187 The National Gallery, London;
188 AA/J Tims;
189 AA/R Turpin;
190 AA/J Tims;
191l AA/J Tims;
191r AA/T Woodcock;
192 Tate. Bequeathed by Miss Isabel Constable as the gift of Maria Louisa, Isabel and Lionel Bicknell Constable 1888;
193 Britain on View/photolibrary.com;
194 AA/S Montgomery;
196 AA/S McBride;
197 AA/B Smith;
198 AA/J Tims;
200 L'Oranger;
202 The Halkin Hotel;
206 AA/S Montgomery;
210 AA/S Montgomery;
211 AA/S Montgomery;
213 AA/J Tims;
214 AA/P Kenward;
215l AA/J Tims;
215r AA/P Kenward;
216 AA/R Mort;
217 AA/J Tims;
218 AA/J Tims;
219 AA/S Montgomery;
220 AA/S Montgomery;
222 AA/J Tims;
224 Richard Waite;
225 V&A Images;
226 V&A Images;
227l Edina van der Wyck;
227r AA/N Setchfield;
229 AA/S Montgomery;
230 AA/J Tims;
232 AA/J Tims;
237 Babylon;
242 AA/J Tims;
248 Roman Baths & Pump Room;
252 Travelshots.com/Alamy;
254 AA/J Tims;
255 AA/S Montgomery;
256 AA/N Setchfield;
257t AA/N Setchfield;
257b Cutty Sark Trust ;
258 AA/R Strange;
260 AA/R Turpin;
261 AA/R Turpin;
262 AA/M Trelawny;
263 AA/T Woodcock;
264 AA/S&O Mathews;
266 AA/J Tims;
267 AA/N Setchfield;
268 AA/N Setchfield;
269l AA/R Mort
269r Patricia Spinelli/Alamy;
270 AA/R Strange;
271 AA/W Voysey/THE DEAN AND CANONS OF WINDSOR;
273 AA/S Montgomery;
276 AA/R Strange;
277 AA/S Montgomery;
278 AA/J Tims;
282 AA/M Jourdan;
284 Photodisc;
290 AA/P Kenward;
291 AA/P Wilson;
298 Strand Palace Hotel;
299 AA/P Baker;
303 Kevin Allen/Alamy

Every effort has been made to trace the copyright holders, and we apologise in advance for any accidental errors. We would be happy to apply any corrections in the following edition of this publication.

CREDITS

Managing editor
Sheila Hawkins

Project editor
Stephanie Smith

Design
Drew Jones, pentacorbig, Nick Otway

Cover design
Chie Ushio

Picture research
Sarah Hopper

Image retouching and repro
Sarah Montgomery, James Tims

Mapping
Maps produced by the Mapping Services Department of AA Publishing

Main contributors
Judith Bamber, Richard Cavendish, Nick Edwards, Colin Follet, Stephen Frost, Tim Locke, John Mabbett, Heather Morley, Michael Nation, Nia Williams

Updater
Nick Edwards

Indexer
Marie Lorimer

Production
Lorraine Taylor

See It London
ISBN 978-1-4000-04973
Fourth Edition

Published in the United States by Fodor's Travel and simultaneously in Canada by Random House of Canada Limited, Toronto.
Published in the United Kingdom by AA Publishing.
Fodor's is a registered trademark of Random House, Inc., and Fodor's See It is a trademark of Random House, Inc.
Fodor's Travel is a division of Random House, Inc.

Color separation by AA Digital Department
Printed and bound by Leo Paper Products, China
10 9 8 7 6 5 4 3 2 1

Special Sales: This book is available for special discounts for bulk purchases for sales promotions or premiums. Special editions, including personalized covers, excerpts of existing books, and corporate imprints, can be created in large quantities for special needs.
For more information, write to Special Markets/Premium Sales, 1745 Broadway, MD 6-2, New York, NY 10019
or e-mail specialmarkets@randomhouse.com
Important Note: Time inevitably brings changes, so always confirm prices, travel facts, and other perishable information when it matters. Although Fodor's cannot accept responsibility for errors, you can use this guide in the confidence that we have taken every care to ensure its accuracy.

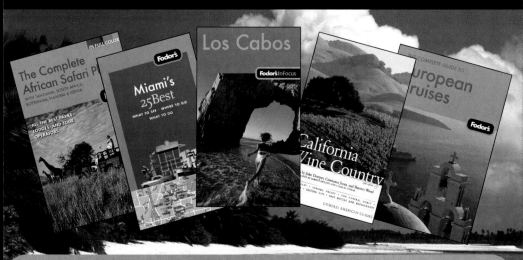

Dear Traveler,

From buying a plane ticket to booking a room and seeing the sights, a trip goes much more smoothly when you have a good travel guide. Dozens of writers, editors, designers, and cartographers have worked hard to make the book you hold in your hands a good one. Was it everything you expected? Were our descriptions accurate? Were our recommendations on target? And did you find our tips and practical advice helpful? Your ideas and experiences matter to us. If we have missed or misstated something, we'd love to hear about it. Fill out our survey at www.fodors.com/books/feedback/, or e-mail us at seeit@fodors.com. Or you can snail mail to the See It Editor at Fodor's, 1745 Broadway, New York, New York 10019. We'll look forward to hearing from you.

Tim Jarrell
Publisher